APPLYING ANTHROPOLOGY

An Introductory Reader

NINTH EDITION

Aaron Podolefsky
Central Missouri State University

Peter J. Brown
Emory University

Scott M. Lacy
Emory University

 Higher Education

Boston   Burr Ridge, IL   Dubuque, IA   New York   San Francisco   St. Louis
Bangkok   Bogotá   Caracas   Kuala Lumpur   Lisbon   London   Madrid   Mexico City
Milan   Montreal   New Delhi   Santiago   Seoul   Singapore   Sydney   Taipei   Toronto

The McGraw·Hill Companies

Higher Education

APPLYING ANTHROPOLOGY: AN INTRODUCTORY READER

Published by McGraw-Hill, a business unit of The McGraw-Hill Companies, Inc.,
1221 Avenue of the Americas, New York, NY, 10020. Copyright © 2009, 2007, 2003, 2001,
1999, 1997, 1994, 1992, 1989 by The McGraw-Hill Companies, Inc. All rights reserved. No
part of this publication may be reproduced or distributed in any form or by any means, or
stored in a database or retrieval system, without the prior written consent of The McGraw-
Hill Companies, Inc., including, but not limited to, in any network or other electronic storage
or transmission, or broadcast for distance learning.

Some ancillaries, including electronic and print components, may not be available to
customers outside the United States.

This book is printed on acid-free paper.

1 2 3 4 5 6 7 8 9 0 QPD/QPD 0 9 8

ISBN: 978-0-07-340535-3
MHID: 0-07-340535-3

Vice President and Editor in Chief: *Michael Ryan*
Publisher: *Frank Mortimer*
Sponsoring Editor: *Gina Boedeker*
Development Editor: *Larry Goldberg*
Editorial Coordinator: *Jordan Killam*
Executive Marketing Manager: *Leslie Oberhuber*
Production Editors: *Melissa Williams/Erika Jordan, Pine Tree Composition, Inc.*
Cover Designer: *Ashley Bedell*
Production Supervisor: *Louis Swaim*
Composition: *10/12 Palatino, by Laserwords Ltd.*
Printing: *45# New Era Matte Plus by Quebecor World, Inc.*

Library of Congress Cataloging-in-Publication Data

Applying anthropology : an introductory reader / [edited by] Aaron Podolefsky,
    Peter J. Brown, Scott M. Lacy—9th ed.
        p. cm.
    Includes bibliographical references and index.
    ISBN-13: 978-0-07-340535-3 (softcover : alk. paper)
    ISBN-10: 0-07-340535-3 (softcover : alk. paper)
    1. Applied anthropology.   2. Anthropology.   I. Podolefsky, Aaron.
    II. Brown, Peter J. III. Lacy, Scott M.
GN397.5.A67 2009
301—dc22   200867741

The Internet addresses listed in the text were accurate at the time of publication. The
inclusion of a Web site does not indicate an endorsement by the authors or McGraw-Hill, and
McGraw-Hill does not guarantee the accuracy of the information presented at these sites.

www.mhhe.com

There are things I couldn't have known when Peter and I began developing the ideas for this book during the late 1980s. I could not predict its growth and development nor how grateful I now am that the numerous editions have brought enlightenment to so many students over the years. In a similar way, my sons—young boys at the time—were also works in progress and at the start of their own lives. Looking back I reflect with great joy, pride, and satisfaction as I have watched these young boys blossom into men of character and wisdom.

This book is dedicated to my sons, Noah and Isaac, who have grown to be men since our first edition eighteen years ago.

—Aaron Podolefsky

Contents

PART I   *Biological Anthropology*   3

PART IV   *Cultural Anthropology*   *155*

CULTURE AND FIELDWORK

FAMILY & KINSHIP

GLOBALIZATION AND CULTURE CHANGE

Theme Finder for Chapters

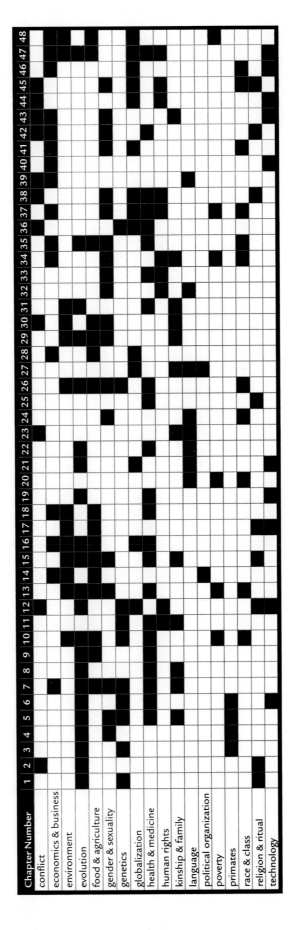

■ Denotes theme present in chapter

To the Student

An introductory course in any discipline is full of new terminology, concepts, and facts. Sometimes students forget that these new ideas and vocabulary are actually intellectual tools that can be put to work for analyzing and solving problems. In preparing this book, we have selected readings that will show you how anthropological concepts, discoveries, and methods can be applied in today's world.

The study of anthropology can help you view the world in a completely different way than you ever have before. You can come to appreciate the great diversity of human cultures and the interrelatedness of economic, sociopolitical, and religious systems. Anthropology can give you a broad perspective on humanity and help you understand other people's beliefs and customs. In doing so, it can help you become a better citizen in an increasingly global society. But your motivation need not be completely altruistic—there are many examples in this book of how cross-cultural awareness can improve performances in business, negotiations, and clinical medicine.

The fascinating side of anthropology seems obvious to most educated people, but there is also a lesser-known practical side of the discipline. The readings we have selected demonstrate that practical, applied side. Many of the articles depict anthropological ideas and research methods in action—as they are used to understand and solve practical problems. We have included articles on anthropologists working outside the academic setting to show how they are applying anthropology. We believe that the fundamental lessons of anthropology can be applied to many careers and all areas of human endeavor.

To benefit from the study of anthropology, you need to study effectively. Over the years, we have found that students often read assignments without planning, and this actually makes studying less efficient. Before you read a selection, spend a few moments skimming it to get an idea of what it is about, where it is going, and what you should look for. This kind of preliminary reading is a poor idea for mystery novels but is essential for academic assignments. Without this preparation, the article may become a hodgepodge of facts and figures; details may be meaningless because you have missed the big picture. By planning your reading, you can see how the details are relevant to the central themes of an article.

To help you plan your reading, at the beginning of each article we have included questions and a list of glossary terms. Looking at these questions in advance, you may gain an idea of what is to come and why the article is important. This will help make the time you spend reading more fruitful. Most of the questions highlight the central themes of the selection or draw your attention to interesting details. Some of the questions, however, do not have straightforward answers—they are food for thought and topics for debate. Some of the selections refer directly to current discussions of HIV, migration, obesity, gender diversity, and drug use. Our idea is to challenge you to think about how anthropology can be applied to your own life and education.

These articles have been selected with you, the student, in mind. We hope they convey our excitement about the anthropological adventure, and we trust that you will find them both enjoyable and thought-provoking.

"Applied anthropology" most often refers to a situation in which a client hires an anthropologist to do research that will help the client resolve a particular problem. Some applied anthropologists run their own research companies that bid and win research contracts from clients and funding agencies; other applied anthropologists work directly for corporations. Applied anthropologists write their reports specifically for their clients. A good place to find out about applied anthropology is at the society for applied anthropology's Web site, www.sfaa.net. There are many master's degree programs in this field. You may also run across the term "public anthropology" in your studies. This refers to anthropological research and writing that engages important public issues (like many of those addressed in this book) and whose audience is the lay educated public. As "public scholars," anthropologists want to communicate their perspective on contemporary issues and influence public opinion and policy. A good place to find out what is happening in public anthropology is through the Web site of the American Anthropological Association (www.aaanet.org) or the Public Anthropology Web site (www.publicanthropology.org).

If you are interested in reading more about applied anthropology, there are several excellent books available, such as *Applied Anthropology: A Practical Guide,* by Erve Chambers; *Applied Anthropology: An Introduction,* by John van Willigen; *Anthropological Praxis: Translating Knowledge into Action,* by Robert M. Wulff and Shirley J. Fiske; *Applied Anthropology in America,* by Elizabeth M. Eddy and William L. Partridge; and *Making Our Research Useful,* by John van Willigen, Barbara Rylko-Bauer, and Anne McElroy.

If you are interested in medical matters, you may want to consult *Understanding and Applying Medical Anthropology,* by Peter J. Brown, or *Anthropology and Public Health,* by Robert Hahn. You may also want to look at the journals *Human Organization* and *Practicing Anthropology,* both of which are published by the Society for Applied Anthropology. The National Association of Practicing Anthropologists (NAPA) also publishes interesting works on specific fields such as medical anthropology.

To the Instructor

Introductory anthropology has become an established part of the college curriculum, and through this course our profession communicates with a large and diverse undergraduate audience. Members of that audience differ in experience, academic concentration, and career aspirations. For those students considering anthropology as a major, we need to provide (among other things) a vision of the future, a view of anthropological work to be done in the public domain as well as within academia. For them, we need to provide some answers to the question, what can I do with a degree in anthropology? For students majoring in other areas, such as business, engineering, or psychology, we need to address the question, how can anthropological insights or research methods help me understand and solve human problems? If we can provide such a service, we increase the likelihood that students will find creative solutions to the professional problems that await them, and we brighten the future for our anthropology majors by underscoring the usefulness of an anthropological perspective in attempts to solve the practical problems of today's world.

Over the years we have found that many introductory texts do little more than include a chapter on applied anthropology at the end of the book. This suggests, at least to students, that most of anthropology has no relevance to their lives. Such treatment also implies that the application of anthropological knowledge is a tangent or afterthought—at best an additional subject area, such as kinship or politics.

We disagree. We believe that the applications of anthropology cut across and infuse all the discipline's subfields. This book is a collection of articles that provide examples of both basic and applied research in all four fields of anthropology.

One of our primary goals is to demonstrate some of the ways our discipline is used outside the academic arena. We want anthropology to be seen as a field that is intellectually compelling as well as relevant to the real world. Like the public at large, students seem well aware that the subject matter of anthropology is fascinating, but they seem unaware of both the fundamental questions of humanity addressed by anthropologists and the practical applications of the field. Increased public awareness of the practical contributions of anthropology is a goal that we share with many

in the profession. In fact, this is a major long-term goal of the American Anthropological Association.

Since we first started editing these readers in 1989, the general field of anthropology has changed in precisely this direction of emphasizing public relevance. "Public anthropology" refers to anthropological research and writing that engages important public issues (like many of those addressed in this book) and whose audience is the lay educated public. Our discipline has a long history in this regard, as in the work of Franz Boas on racial discrimination and Margaret Mead's famous articles in *Redbook* magazine. As "public scholars," anthropologists must communicate their perspective on contemporary issues and influence public opinion and policy. In this age of globalization and increased cultural intolerance often linked to religious fundamentalism, the basic messages of public anthropology are more important than ever. Being an effective public anthropologist is just being a great teacher in a larger classroom. A good place to find out what is happening in public anthropology is through the Web site of the American Anthropological Association (www.aaanet.org) or the Public Anthropology Web site (www.publicanthropology.org).

Although people distinguish between basic and applied research, much of anthropology falls into a gray area, having elements of both. Many selections in this book fall into that gray zone—they are brief ethnographic accounts that contain important implications for understanding and resolving problems. We could have included a large number of articles exemplifying strictly applied research—an evaluation report of agency performance, for example. Although this sort of research is fascinating and challenging to do, it is usually not exciting for students to read. We have selected articles that we believe are fascinating for students and convey the dual nature (basic/applied) of social science research. We think that it is not the scholarly writing style that is most important, but rather the content of the research as a way to get students to think and to challenge their own assumptions about the world.

Anthropological research is oriented by certain basic human values. These include being against ethnocentrism, racism, and ignorance. Anthropology is about understanding and appreciating human similarities and differences. Such an understanding can lead students to new attitudes—such as tolerance for cultural differences, commitment to human equality, stewardship of the environment, appreciation of the past, and personal dedication to the continued and honest pursuit of knowledge.

Any student who completes an introductory course in anthropology should learn that anthropological work, in its broadest sense, may include (or at least contribute to) international business, epidemiology, program evaluation, social impact studies, conflict resolution, organizational analysis, market research, and nutrition research, even though their introductory anthropology texts make no mention of those fields. The selections in this book should help students understand why anthropology is important in today's world and also make the course more memorable and meaningful.

FEATURES OF THIS EDITION

- To spark student discussion and thinking about controversial issues and issues of public policy, we have included selections dealing with contemporary topics like globalization, HIV/AIDS, racism, cell phones, gender diversity, migration, obesity, intelligent design, and the US military in Afghanistan and Iraq. These selections are clearly anthropological in perspective and approach. When students are able to relate the concepts and examples of anthropology to current debates, they recognize the value of their education.

- We chose readings that complement typical courses in introductory anthropology. The sequence of articles follows the organization of standard anthropology textbooks, grouped under headings with terms such as kinship, gender, marriage, and conflict, rather than headings based on areas of applied anthropology like medical anthropology or the anthropology of development. At the same time, we include headings such as globalization and health and medicine, reflecting growth and development in the anthropological discipline and purview. Had we meant this book as a reader on applied anthropology, our organization would have been different. Although this book could be used by students in upper-level courses on applied anthropology (as earlier editions have been), those students are not our intended audience. For this reason, we have not provided extensive discussion of the history or definition of applied anthropology.

- For students interested in pursuing applied anthropology on their own, there are a number of fine books. These include *Applied Anthropology: A Practical Guide*, by Erve Chambers; *Applied Anthropology: An Introduction*, by John van Willigen; *Anthropological Praxis: Translating Knowledge into Action*, by Robert M. Wulff and Shirley J. Fiske; *Applied Anthropology in America*, by Elizabeth M. Eddy and William L. Partridge; and *Making Our Research Useful*, by John van Willigen, Barbara Rylko-Bauer, and Anne McElroy. Students interested in medical matters may want to consult *Understanding and Applying Medical Anthropology*, by Peter J. Brown, or *Anthropology and Public Health* by Robert Hahn.

- To emphasize how anthropology can be put to work in different settings, we include examples of anthropologists whose careers involve applying anthropology outside the university setting.

- To help students better understand the subject matter, we include a number of pedagogical aids: introductions, a list of glossary terms, and guiding questions for each article; a world map that pinpoints the locations of places and peoples discussed in the articles; and, for easy reference, an extensive glossary and index.

- A *new feature* called **Theme Finder for Chapters**, which follows the table of contents, allows instructors and students to identify critical cross-chapter themes including environment, globalization, human rights, poverty, race and class, and technology.

NEW TO THIS EDITION

In this edition we have continued to juxtapose "classic" anthropological articles with features that highlight issues of this new millennium. One such juxtaposition is the continued issue of the central biological theory of evolution as opposed to creationism that has recently been reborn as "intelligent design." In the field of human paleontology, we have a new article that explores the continuing "big questions" of human evolution, in part because the corpus of fossil evidence has become so large that it is ever more complex for undergraduate students.

There are eleven new articles that refer to contemporary social issues and events, like health care inequalities, endemic poverty, and the current wars in the Middle East. The new selections also deal with hot-button issues like alternative forms of marriage and the teaching of evolution in high schools.

To better reflect the four-field approach of American Anthropology, we created a new linguistics anthropology section instead of including linguistics within the cultural anthropology section. The linguistic anthropology section includes a selection on the development of a rare sign language and a selection on how children and migration impact the evolution of language.

We have continued our previous commitment to the discussion of race as a salient topic for introductory anthropology. We added a new selection on race and American Archaeology, but we continued to place all other race articles within the cultural anthropology sections because race is a cultural construction, not a biological fact. In this regard, students need to understand that whiteness, as a cultural construction, brings with it certain privileges despite progress since the emergence of

the Civil Rights Movement. Racism, sexism, severe economic inequality, and intolerance for cultural differences are continuing problems of our society. Throughout this edition we have also emphasized globalization and its human dimensions.

ACKNOWLEDGMENTS

We thank the following reviewers of this edition for their helpful comments and suggestions: Sheela Athreya, Texas A&M University; Kathy Ann Betters, Genesee Community College; Helen Cho, Davidson College; Arthur Durband, Texas Tech University; Elizabeth Jones, University of North Carolina at Chapel Hill; Rachel Mason, University of Alaska Anchorage; and Joan T. Miller, San Diego State University.

Aaron Podolefsky
Peter J. Brown
Scott M. Lacy

INTRODUCTION

Understanding Humans and Human Problems

To the uninitiated, the term *anthropology* conjures up images of mummies' tombs, Indiana Jones, and treks through steaming jungles or over high alpine peaks. Anthropologists agree that their chosen field is exciting, that they have been places and seen things that few experience firsthand, and that they have been deeply and emotionally involved in understanding the human condition. At the same time, however, the vision of anthropology presented by Hollywood has probably done more to obscure the true nature of the profession than it has to enlighten the public about what we really do.

Providing an accurate image of anthropology and anthropological work is both simple and complex. Essentially, anthropology is the study of people, or more properly, of humankind. But, you may say, many disciplines study people: psychology, sociology, history, biology, medicine, and so on. True, but anthropology is different in that it seeks to integrate these separate and perhaps narrower views of humanity. To understand ourselves, we need to join these disparate views into a single framework, a process that begins with our biological and evolutionary roots, explores the development of culture through the prehistoric and historical periods, probes the uniquely human ability to develop culture through communication, and examines the diversity of recent and present-day cultures that inhabit the globe.

From this conception of the *holistic* and *comparative* study of humankind emerge what are termed the four fields of anthropology: biological (or physical) anthropology, archaeology, anthropological linguistics, and cultural anthropology. Some universities offer an introductory course that covers all four subfields. Other schools cover the subfields in two or three separate introductory courses. Each approach has its advantage. The former may more fully integrate the biocultural and historical dimensions of humanity; the latter allows students to explore each subfield in greater depth. This book introduces you to the four fields of anthropology and how they are used in today's world.

Another way to divide the discipline—in fact almost any discipline—is into *basic* and *applied* research. These categories are important in this reader because we would like students to appreciate both the basic and the applied sides of anthropology.

A survey of natural and social scientists and engineers conducted by the U.S. Census Bureau for the National Science Foundation used the following definitions of these fundamental concepts: *Basic research* is study directed toward gaining scientific knowledge primarily for its own sake. *Applied research* is study directed toward gaining scientific knowledge in an effort to meet a recognized need.

Anthropology is a discipline concerned primarily with basic research. It asks "big" questions concerning the origins of humankind, the roots of human nature, the development of civilization, and the functions of our major social institutions (such as marriage and religion). Nevertheless, anthropologists have put the methods and skills developed in basic research to use in solving human problems and fulfilling the needs of society. Anthropologists have, for example, worked with medical examiners in the identification of skeletal remains. They have also helped communities preserve their cultural heritage and businesses and government agencies understand the social impact of programs or development projects.

Although the application of anthropology has a long history, it has, until recent years, remained in the shadows of pure or basic research. The last twenty-five years have seen a change. Anthropologists have moved beyond their traditional roles in universities and museums and now work in a broad range of settings. They are employed in many government agencies, in the private sector, and in a variety of nonresearch capacities (such as administrators, evaluators, or policy analysts). Profiles of anthropologists in nonacademic careers (high-tech industry) can be found in this book.

In response to the growing opportunities for anthropologists outside academia and to the demands of students, an increasing number of master's degree and doctoral programs provide training specifically in the applications of anthropology. This is not to say that the classified ads list jobs titled "anthropologist." Rather, for those interested in anthropology, there are increasing opportunities to find careers that draw on anthropological training and skills. At the same time, studies have shown that there will be increasing job opportunities for anthropologists in universities and colleges during the next decade and beyond.

In this era of multiculturalism, there is increasing recognition that our society—indeed, our world—is a culturally diverse social mosaic. Living in a multicultural society presents real challenges stemming from chronic ethnocentrism and persistent social tension. But it also brings a cultural richness, even luxuriance, of diversity in art, food, language, values, and beliefs.

Applications of anthropology are found in all four fields and include the identification of skeletal remains (forensics); the study of size and fit for the design of clothing, furniture, or airplane cockpits (ergonomics); exploration of the patterns and causes of disease (epidemiology); evaluation of the effectiveness of programs (from Third World development to crime prevention); assessment of community needs; prediction of the social impact of change; analysis of organizations such as businesses and government agencies; market research; and research into health and nutrition—just to name a few. School administrators, engineers, doctors, business leaders, lawyers, medical researchers, and government officials now recognize that the knowledge, unique perspective, and research skills of anthropologists are applicable to practical problems—in the United States and elsewhere in the world.

As we explore anthropology, keep in mind the interplay between and interdependence of basic cultural research and the applications of anthropological knowledge and research methods to the solution of human problems.

PART I

Biological Anthropology

To understand ourselves, we must first understand the human animal. Fundamentally, humans are flesh-and-blood biological beings. Although we are qualitatively different from the other animals, anthropology nonetheless takes the position that we must begin our understanding of humanity by examining our biological heritage. *Biological anthropology* (also known as *physical anthropology*) has the goal of increasing the knowledge about our species, *Homo sapiens sapiens,* by examining the evolutionary roots of our biology and behavior. There are three primary ways in which this evolutionary story is studied: In *paleoanthropology,* anthropologists discover and analyze the fossil remains of our ancestors; in *primatology,* anthropologists examine the survival strategies, social organization, and behavior of the nonhuman primates; and in *human biology,* anthropologists explore variations in the physical characteristics of human populations, which represent genetic differences shaped by environmental conditions through the processes of evolution.

Anthropological research in all these areas, particularly human biology, can have important applications for understanding and solving today's human problems. Much of the applied work in biological anthropology is related to health problems. Through the study of genetics, anthropologists study hereditary predispositions to particular diseases like obesity or Tay-Sachs. Through the study of human anatomy, anthropologists study skeletal disorders, bone development, and the relationship between poor nutrition and health. Biological anthropologists also examine the physiological adaptations of humans to environmental stressors like extreme temperatures or high altitude. They also describe the variations in the human life cycle—childhood, puberty, reproduction, and aging. One of the major tools of biological anthropology is *anthropometry,* the measurement of the human body. Anthropometry is used in the design of clothing and furniture; it is also used to assess the health of a prehistoric population as well as to identify human remains after an accident or murder.

Although the ongoing research in paleoanthropology, for example, is *basic science*—the search for fundamental knowledge not necessarily related to solving specific problems—the detailed study of the fossil record can reveal much about human nature and about what Melvin Konner has called "biological constraints on the human spirit."

When we study ourselves, we need to remember that the human animal is the product of millions of years of evolutionary history. The genes that we inherit from our parents (and that we pass to our children) are exact duplicates of the genes of our ancestors passed down through countless generations. The biology of our own bodies (and that of all our fellow humans) represents thousands of centuries of natural selection in action, that is, interaction between people and the environment affecting patterns of survival and reproduction. Natural selection is no trivial concept. It signifies nothing less than the cumulative effects of the lives and deaths of our ancestors. The scientific study of our evolutionary heritage might therefore be motivated as much by a respect for our own unnamed ancestors as by our curiosity about what happened in the distant past. Yet in the United States today, the study of our own evolutionary history has been attacked, and many students are deprived of the opportunity to learn about the evolutionary heritage of all humanity.

Evolution is a central concept in all of anthropology because humans adapt through both biology and culture. *Culture*, the learned patterns of thought and behavior characteristic of a social group, is the primary reason for the amazing success of our species.

The story of human evolution is still unfolding. Important new fossils are discovered almost every year, and their interpretation is often the subject of vigorous scholarly debate. These debates are a normal part of the scientific enterprise. However, bones do not tell the whole story. To answer questions about the evolution of behavior, anthropologists sometimes make analogies with the behavior of nonhuman primates. The comparison of humans with nonhuman primates is important for both basic and applied research. Fundamental aspects of social organization, like the social alliances between "friends" in a baboon troop described by Barbara Smuts in Selection 4, can be understood only after thousands of hours of observation of the animals in their natural setting. Similarly, research on the sex lives of Bonobo chimpanzees may shed light on the nonreproductive functions of sex in human societies. Such research can help in understanding principles of social behavior and can serve as a model of the evolutionary past.

Primatological research may also have practical applications. For example, apes have been shown to have the ability to learn nonverbal human languages using symbols from American Sign Language or artificial languages (Yerkish). One spin-off of these discoveries is the development of new tools for enabling mentally and physically disabled people to communicate. Similarly, studies of peacemaking among primates may help in identifying fundamental keys for maintaining social relations.

Anthropologists have lived with and studied people whose economy is based on food foraging—a combination of hunting and gathering wild foods. Their culture might be thought of as the original human lifestyle. Only a few groups of people in today's world primarily hunt and collect their food, and they have been displaced to marginal environments. No doubt their lives have also been influenced by the farming groups who may live near them. Nevertheless, the study of hunters and gatherers can serve as a model or analogy for understanding the lives of prehistoric peoples. One mistake that anthropologists made in the past was to overemphasize the role of male-dominated hunting in early prehistory. Anthropologists now argue that women played a key role in the evolutionary story through food gathering, food sharing, and the creation of social cooperation.

Some of the lessons we learn from studying the culture and lifestyle of food foragers and other traditional societies may help us understand our own health. The diet of Paleolithic people, for example, might be considered an ideal diet for the prevention of certain diseases of civilization, like hypertension, diabetes, cardiovascular disease, and obesity, to name a few. Western medicine has borrowed many of the fundamental drugs in our modern pharmacopoeia from technologically simple peoples. In recent years, some anthropologists have begun to examine health and illness from a Darwinian perspective of the pathogen as well as the human host. This work is leading to the development of Darwinian medicine, as described by Elizabeth Whitaker in Selection 7.

A central concern of biological anthropology has been the description of (and explanation for) biological differences between ethnic groups. Some of the physical differences between groups are evolutionarily interesting, and some have important medical ramifications. The scientific study of these differences—of what was once called *race*—must be understood in the context of two basic facts: We are all members of a single human species, and all humans are unique individuals. Human variation may be described in terms of morphological characteristics (stature, skin color, and so on) or underlying genetic characteristics. Both techniques have led anthropologists to conclude that much of human biology is influenced by an environment that is in turn shaped by culture.

Applied biological anthropology is associated with a wide variety of career opportunities. Research techniques originally developed to describe and analyze long-buried human remains unearthed by the archaeologist or paleontologist, for example, can be used to identify remains from a disaster or crime. This application of anthropological knowledge is called *forensic anthropology* because it is used in courts of law.

Other biological anthropologists have worked in forensic settings by using genetic lab techniques to untangle legal questions of identity.

The relevance of biological anthropology to down-to-earth human problems is evident. Using knowledge of human morphology and human variation, physical anthropologists have, for example, worked in the field of human factors engineering, designing uniforms, aircraft seats, and other equipment. Biological anthropologists have also studied complex problems like malnutrition and child growth in Third World nations, the interaction of malnutrition and infection, and the effect of high-altitude living on work performance.

Biological anthropologists have discovered how particular patterns of breast-feeding result in natural four-year birth spacing in some societies like the food-foraging !Kung. They are also discovering that newer reproductive patterns may result in high rates of breast cancer. Moreover, biological anthropologists have helped untangle the phenomenon of sudden infant death syndrome (SIDS).

The contribution of anthropologists to understanding practical human problems extends beyond the collection of data on human biological variation. The research and discoveries of biological anthropology are being applied to the solution of those problems.

1

Teaching Theories
The Evolution-Creation Controversy

Robert Root-Bernstein and Donald L. McEachron

At the beginning of a book of readings on anthropology as a biosocial science, we can appropriately concern ourselves with defining science and scientific explanation. When asked, most people describe science by naming disciplines: "Oh, science, let's see, that's physics, chemistry, biology, and so on." However, science is more than a list of subjects or particular fields of study. Rather, it is a process for drawing conclusions. Stated differently, science is a particular way of knowing. We have, of course, many ways of knowing things. For example, one might see something in a dream and be convinced that it is true. One might be told some fact or theory by a teacher (such as what goes up must come down) and accept it based on the teacher's authority. In this case, the student has learned a scientific principle but has not participated in hypothesis testing or theory building.

In their work, scientists give special definitions to some common, everyday words. Words such as *validity, reliability, random, hypothesis,* and *theory* take on meanings that are precise and often significantly different from their everyday counterparts. These meanings can lead to serious misunderstandings as scientists try to communicate with the public.

In recent years, questions about the nature of science have been at the root of public debate over the teaching of human evolution in the public schools.

As anthropologists, we respect and value the belief systems of other people, and we recognize that many of the cultures of the world have their own beliefs about creation. Yet the only scientific model that can explain the fossil and genetic record is evolution.

As you read this selection, ask yourself the following questions:

- How is the term *theory* used differently by scientists and nonscientists?
- Why is it so important that scientific theories be testable and correctable?
- What does the phrase "scientific skepticism" mean to you?
- Who do you think should decide what is science and what is not?
- Why has the evolution versus creationism debate been such an emotional issue in some sectors of American society?

The following terms discussed in this selection are included in the Glossary at the back of the book:

contingent truths	*natural selection*
creationism	*religion*
evolution	*scientific theory*
hypothesis	

I̤n recent years, a controversy has developed in the United States over the teaching of evolutionism and creationism in the public schools. The controversy, while nominally a scientific one, also has philosophical, historical, religious, and legal implications as well. Since some twenty state legislatures or courts are presently

Root-Bernstein, Robert & McEachron, Donald L. "Teaching Theories: The Evolution-Creation Controversy." From The American Biology Teacher, October 1982. Reprinted with permission of the National Assoc. of Biology Teachers.

considering or have considered legislation and lawsuits concerning the controversy, we believe that it is in the best interest of the voting public to be informed of the issues.

We believe that there are four basic issues: (1) What is a scientific theory? (2) What is a religious belief? (3) Who has the right to decide these issues? (4) How do one's answers to the previous three questions affect one's view on whether evolutionism and creationism are scientific and should be taught in public schools?

Very briefly, a controversy has arisen between evolutionists and creationists because they disagree on all four basic issues. Evolutionists generally believe: (1) that evolutionism is a valid scientific theory, whereas creationism is not; (2) that evolutionism is not a religious belief, whereas creationism is; and (3) that the validity of a religious belief should be decided by religious believers. In consequence, evolutionists conclude (4) that since evolutionism is a valid scientific theory, it should be taught in the public schools; whereas, since creationism is not a scientific theory, it should not be taught as science in the public schools.

Creationists disagree completely. Creationists generally believe (1) that evolutionism is not a valid scientific theory, whereas creationism is; (2) that evolutionism is a dogmatic, secular religion, whereas "scientific creationism" is not; and (3) that the state (that is, either the legislature or the courts) has the right to decide whether any theory is scientifically valid or not. Thus, creationists argue (4) that the state has the right to decide that evolutionism must be censored as a dogmatic religious belief and equal time given to creationism as a valid scientific theory. Creationists argue that either both should be taught in the public schools, or neither.

Clearly, to decide between these two positions, one must understand what a scientific theory is and how it differs from a religious belief. It is our purpose to explore these issues in this essay.

WHAT IS A SCIENTIFIC THEORY?

Begin by considering the question, "What is a scientific theory?" There is nothing mysterious about the answer; a scientific theory is a simple, *testable,* and *correctable* explanation of *observable* phenomena that yields *new information* about nature in answer to a set of pre-existing problems. While this definition may sound complicated or imposing, in practice it is not. All of us use scientific theories in our daily thinking. Consider the following situation as an example.

You come home one evening, open the front door, and turn on the light switch. The lights do not come on. This is an *observation.* One compares this observation to memories of observations made under similar circumstances: every other time you've turned on the light switch, the lights have come on. One has an *anomaly*— that is, something that should work the same as always, but doesn't. Why do the lights not come on? This is your *problem.*

How do you resolve your problem? First, it occurs to you that something about the electrical system is different tonight. You consider possible differences: perhaps the light switch isn't working properly. You've invented an *hypothesis.* Can you *test* it? Sure. You jiggle the switch. Nothing happens. Your hypothesis is probably wrong. You reject it. But you still have your problem.

Can there be some other explanation? Yes. Maybe the fuse has burned out. Another hypothesis. Can it be tested? Easily. You go turn on the light switch in the next room and the lights in there go on. So your problem isn't the fuse. There must be some other explanation.

But wait a minute: you've made an *assumption* about the fuse that may not be correct! What if the two rooms are controlled by two different fuses? Then the fact that the lights work in the second room proves nothing at all about the first fuse. The manner in which you've tested your hypothesis about the fuse being burned out is not valid. If your *assumption* about both rooms being controlled by a single fuse is wrong, then the test is useless. Thus, one must be careful to test not only one's hypothesis, but the assumptions upon which it rests as well. This is a very important point to which we will return later.

Checking your fuses, you find that all are fine. So, still in the dark, you hypothesize that the bulb is burned out. You take out the bulb, put in a new one, throw the switch, and, lo and behold—light! So you conclude that your third hypothesis was correct. The reason the light would not go on was because it was burned out.

But wait! You've made another assumption, haven't you? You've assumed the light bulb is burned out, but have you tested the light bulb in another socket to see whether it really *is* burned out? If you are acting scientifically, you must not only test your hypothesis; you must also test your assumptions. So, you screw the light bulb into another socket and— much to your surprise—it lights! Your last hypothesis was wrong! And just think—if you hadn't bothered testing your assumption, you would never have known you were wrong. Indeed, you would have thrown away a perfectly good light bulb.

Now, how do you explain why the light bulb failed to light before? It wasn't burned out. The power was on. The fuse was fine. The switch works. Logically, there seems to be only one other likely explanation of all these observations: perhaps the light bulb wasn't screwed in properly. This is your new hypothesis.

As with any scientific hypothesis, you ask once again: Is it testable? But this time your answer is both yes and no. Yes, one may test the general hypothesis that an unscrewed light bulb won't light. That's easy to do: just loosen any light bulb in its socket and you can verify that it doesn't go on when you turn the switch. However, one cannot test the *particular* hypothesis that the cause of your problem tonight was a loose bulb; you've already removed the bulb from its socket. There is now no way to tell whether the bulb was loose or not. One concludes that it had to have been loose because one cannot think of any other *test hypothesis.*

Note that one accepts one's *particular* hypothesis only when *two* conditions are met: (1) that its corresponding *general* hypothesis is testable; and (2) when no other *testable* hypothesis is available to explain the problem. If one's explanation meets these criteria, then it is a scientific theory. But note also that one's theory is not actually *true*—it is only *probable.* It is only probable because there might be another testable hypothesis that might explain the collection of observations better; or there might be a test that demonstrates that one's theory is wrong. One might, for example, someday discover that one's lights go out sporadically because a mouse causes short circuits by gnawing on the wires in the wall. But, if you don't know you have a mouse then you are unlikely to think of this hypothesis and even less likely to test it by looking for the mouse. In consequence, theories are always tentative, even when tested and found correct. For, as you saw when you thought your problem was a burned-out bulb, it sometimes takes only one more simple test to reveal your error.

Now, we may draw several important conclusions about scientific theories from this example. Most important of these is the fact that scientific theories can never be proven absolutely. A mouse may always be hiding, unknown, in some wall waiting to be discovered, thereby disproving your loose-light-bulb theory. The same is true of *any* scientific theory. Science is not, therefore, truth—at best it is the unending *search* for truth. The conclusions reached by science are only *contingent* truths—truths contingent upon man's limited knowledge of himself and the world around him.[1]

Now, one may ask what good is a theory if it is not true? A theory is good because it is *useful* and it is *fruitful of new knowledge.* Scientific methods have explained more of the empirical world than any alternative approaches including religion. Science allows man to work in the universe as no other system of knowledge does. It allows one to do things that one could not otherwise do, and it allows one to learn things one would otherwise not learn. For example, Faraday's theory of electricity allowed him to invent the first electric motor. Pasteur's germ theory has allowed the control of innumerable diseases. The laws of thermodynamics allowed atomic power to be harnessed by mankind. The list could go on almost indefinitely. So, scientific theories are important because they give mankind knowledge of this world and the ability to act wisely in this world. In our case, it gave us knowledge of the electrical system and thus the ability to fix the light.

Man's ability to act usefully from the predictions of a theory, however, depend upon his ability to test the predictions made by the theory. The process of testing, as we saw with the light bulb, is more important than the theory itself. For even when the theory was wrong, the test yielded new information that was used to invent the next theory. Thus, right or wrong, a testable theory always yields new information about the problem it claims to resolve. This new information is *cumulative.* It adds up. First we tested the switch and found that it worked. So, we knew the problem was not the switch. Then we tested the fuse, and found that the fuse worked. So we knew the problem was not the fuse or the switch. Then we tested the light bub . . . and so on. The more we tested, the more we learned. And the more we learned, the fewer the possible explanations left to try. We knew more, and our ignorance was less. We were converging on the correct answer. All good scientific theories work this way. Thus, although scientific truths are always contingent ones, the method by which they are advanced and tested ensures their improvement.

In short, the power of scientific theories results from the fact that they are *correctable.* They may be tested. Whether the theory is right or wrong, these tests yield new information about the world. And, if the theory is wrong, then this new information can be used to invent a new and better theory. Thus, while scientific theories are never perfect, they become better and better with time. And, as theories become better, mankind knows more, can act more wisely, and can solve more problems.

CAN GOD BE USED IN A SCIENTIFIC THEORY?

One further explanation of our light problem remains to be discussed before considering whether evolutionism and creationism are scientific theories. One might explain the failure of the light by saying that "It was God's will." Indeed, it might have been. "God's will" cannot, however, be part of a *scientific* explanation.

Three reasons preclude the use of God, or other supernatural agencies, in scientific theories. First, scientific theories must be *bounded.* That is, they must apply only to a particular field of inquiry. A simple analogy can be made to sports. Each sport has its own rules that are valid only for that sport. And every sport is played within an area *bounded* by sidelines, goals, or a defined course. In this sense, science is the attempt to discover the rules by which nature plays its various "games" and the boundaries within which each different "game" is played. In our light bulb example, we concluded that a rule must exist that says: the light will not go on if the bulb is not screwed in properly. This is a *bounded* explanation that applies to all light bulbs, but which could not, for example, be used to explain other natural events such as a flood or a death. "God's will" is, on the other hand, an *unbounded* explanation. It can be used to explain the light problem, floods, deaths, and anything else imaginable. In consequence, "God's will" and other supernatural powers cannot be invoked in a scientific theory because they would make the theory *unbounded*. The rules of science would not apply, just as the rules of baseball do not apply to tennis.

Unbounded explanations have a second problem. They cannot be tested. As we stated above, all theories must be testable. Testability, in turn, is necessary if a theory is to be correctable. To be testable, and therefore correctable, a theory must state *how* an event occurs. Because God's actions are beyond man's knowledge, we cannot know *how* He works His will. The same is true of any supernatural explanation. Supernatural, by definition, means beyond man's comprehension. Since God's power is supernatural, He is capable of doing anything. Thus, there is no test imaginable that could disprove an hypothesis stating that an event occurred because of "God's will." In consequence, there would be no way to discover if one's hypothesis were wrong, and no way to correct one's error.

Untestable explanations present a third difficulty. They can neither be harnessed to useful ends nor to the discovery of new knowledge. Explaining the light bulb problem as "God's will," for example, does not enable us to correct the problem. On the contrary, it places the problem beyond our comprehension. By proposing that the light bulb failed to light because it was unscrewed, we could correct the problem immediately. Further, we would be able to recognize and solve that problem if it ever arose again. Thus, we have learned something new. We have acquired new knowledge. Invoking "God's will" does not yield the same sort of new and useful knowledge.

One must not conclude from the foregoing that science is anti-religious. On the contrary, scientific and religious explanations can be completely compatible. What the light bulb problem shows us is that scientific explanations are simply a very select subset of all possible explanations. Religious, or supernatural, explanations form another subset. Sometimes these two subsets overlap. Then, something may be "God's will" and also have a scientific explanation. In these cases, one should be able to explain *how* "God's will" was implemented. If one can do this, then science and religion are in harmony. If not, then they represent two irreconcilable views of the problem. On this point, Pope John Paul II recently quoted the following conclusion from the Vatican II Ecumenical Council: "research performed in a truly scientific manner can never be in contrast with faith because both profane and religious realities have their origin in the same God." Religious leaders of almost all religious denominations agree.

EVOLUTION: SCIENCE OR RELIGION?

Now, how does the light bulb example illuminate the question of whether evolution is a scientific explanation of nature? First of all, as in the light bulb example, one must have a *problem* to address. The problem evolutionists face is to explain *how* the living organisms that exist on the earth today developed through history, and *how* they achieved the forms and distributions characteristic of each species, alive or extinct. Many hypotheses have been proposed to resolve these problems during the 2,000 years of man's recorded history. Each has been found wanting. Perhaps the best known of these was Lamarck's idea that organisms could modify their structures by force of will. Lamarck's idea did not pass the test of observation and its assumptions were never verified. Thus, it, like our hypothesis concerning the fuses, was retired to scientific purgatory. Not until Darwin invented the concept of evolution by natural selection of the fittest organisms was an hypothesis suggested that explained all of the data accumulated during tests of previous hypotheses. It did so in a simple, harmonious, and verifiable way. Thus, if one looks at the history of science, one finds that Darwin's is neither the first nor the only theory to attempt to explain the history and development of life. It is the culmination of 2,000 years of theory building. In this, evolution is analogous to our loose-light-bulb hypothesis: it is the end product of a long chain of hypothesizing and testing. It is the best theory so far devised.

Darwin's basic hypothesis was that only the best-adapted organisms survive the competition for food, the ravages of disease, and the attacks of natural predators to reproduce themselves. The weeding out of weaker organisms creates a steady change in the adaptive characteristics of the individual organisms comprising each species. As the individual characteristics change, so does the profile of the whole species. Thus, evolution.

Is evolution a scientific theory? Just as with the light bulb example, the first question that must be asked about the Darwinian hypothesis is whether it is testable. In this case, as in the case of the loose-light-bulb hypothesis, one must answer both yes and no. Yes, the *general* mechanism of natural selection is testable because it is operating today. No, the specific application of natural selection to extinct species is not directly testable because they, like the light bulb in our analogy, have (metaphorically) already been taken out of the socket. Like the light bulb taken out of its socket, however, fossil remains provide enough information to disprove all hypotheses so far invented *other than* evolution by natural selection. Thus, just as in the light bulb example, one accepts evolution as a valid scientific theory for two reasons: (1) its corresponding *general* hypothesis is testable; and (2) no other *testable hypothesis* is available to explain the problem. It is, of course, always possible that a better theory will be invented in the future.

It was stated above that the general mechanism of natural selection is testable. Since many creationists have denied this conclusion, we present two examples here. Everyone knows that germs cause disease and that various insects, such as mosquitoes, can transmit diseases to man. Natural selection has been observed, occurring in both germs and insects. The selection process has even been controlled in the laboratory by means of antibiotics and pesticides. The invention of antibiotics has virtually allowed man to wipe out certain diseases. The few disease germs that have survived man's ingenuity, however, have developed into antibiotic-resistant strains which man can no longer easily control. The same thing has happened with insects sprayed repeatedly with insecticides. The hardiest have survived to reproduce new races of insects that are insecticide-resistant. Thus, in some areas of the world, diseases like yellow fever and malaria are once again becoming major health problems. Even in the United States, farmers are faced with crop-eating insects that are harder and harder to eliminate. Direct observation leaves no doubt that natural selection does occur. The fittest do survive, and they breed new populations of better-adapted individuals.

It is not sufficient to test just the hypothesis of natural selection. One must, as we pointed out repeatedly in our light bulb example, also test one's assumptions. Several assumptions underlie evolutionary theory. One assumption is that there is a mechanism for creating a spectrum of different individuals within a species so that natural selection can weed out the weakest. Another assumption is that some mechanism exists by which those individuals that survive can pass their adaptive traits on to future generations. And finally, evolution by natural selection assumes sufficient time for new species to be formed by the accumulation of adaptive traits. Each of these assumptions has been questioned, doubted, and tested. Each assumption is correct to the best of current scientific knowledge.

The primary mechanism for producing genetic variability in evolving organisms is mutation. Mutation theory has been given a firm experimental basis by numerous scientists including Nobel Laureates T. H. Morgan and J. H. Mueller. Geneticists, such as

Barbara McClintock, have evidence that rearrangements of whole genes and even chromosomes may also play a role in creating genetic variability.

The mechanism of genetic inheritance of mutations and rearrangements is also well understood. Despite early fears by nineteenth-century biologists that adaptive variations would blend out of existence like a drop of ink in a gallon of paint, Gregor Mendel and his successors established that inheritance is not blending—it is particulate. The ink spot does not blend into the paint in genetics. Rather, it stays separate and definable, like a water drop in oil. If the water-based ink is better adapted than the oil-based paint, then the ink will reproduce faster than the paint and so come to dominate the mixture. Thus, beneficial mutations, while rare, are not lost from the population. Mendel's "laws" and the population genetics of R. A. Fisher, J. B. S. Haldane, and their colleagues explain the rules by which such populations evolve. James Watson and Sir Francis Crick, two more Nobel Laureates, have explained the details of the inheritance process itself at the molecular level of DNA.

Finally, astronomers, physicists, and geologists have established that the earth is definitely old enough to make evolution by natural selection plausible. One hundred years ago, scientific opinion was just the opposite. Physicists such as Lord Kelvin calculated that the age of the earth was only a few million years—too short to allow evolution. Even Darwin was worried by his arguments. But Kelvin's calculation turned out to be incorrect, for it was based on a faulty hypothesis. Kelvin *assumed* that there was no internal source of energy heating the earth because he knew of none. In fact, his assumption was incorrect. In this case there was a metaphorical "mouse in the wall" called radioactivity. Kelvin did not know about radioactivity because it was discovered after he died. Once other physicists took the heating effects of radioactivity into account in new calculations, it became clear that the earth was billions, not millions, of years old. Astronomers measuring the age of the solar system and geologists dating rocks and fossils have reached the same conclusion. There has been sufficient time for evolution to have occurred.

In short, evolution by natural selection is a valid scientific theory because it and its underlying assumptions have been tested and validated by observation or experiment. Further, anyone who has walked through a modern research library or flipped through a general science magazine will not fail to realize the amount of new knowledge this theory has evoked. Much of this new knowledge has even been useful, especially in the production of new breeds of farm animals and hybrid crops. Evolution by natural selection has thus fulfilled the requirements of a scientific theory superbly. To what degree it may someday need to be modified by new discoveries, only the future will tell.

CREATIONISM: SCIENCE OR RELIGION?

Now, is "scientific creationism" also a scientific theory? "Scientific" creationists claim to be interested in solving the same problems that evolutionists address: how does one explain the forms of living organisms and their geological and geographical distribution? In place of evolution by natural selection, creationists postulate the existence of a supernatural "God," "Creator" or "Intelligence" who created the earth and all of the living organisms on it and in it. They claim that this supernatural agent produced the earth and its life within a period of thousands of years. The question we must address is whether or not the "creation explanation" is a scientific one. In other words, is it testable? Is it correctable? Have its assumptions been tested and verified? And is it fruitful of new or useful information concerning nature?

It is important to point out that our criteria for evaluating scientific theories are identical to those used by creationists such as Robert Kofahl, Kelly Segraves, Duane Gish, and Henry Morris in the course of this controversy. We are not, therefore, asking of "creation science" any more than the creationists ask of science itself.

Can "scientific" or "special" creationism be tested? Creationist scientists themselves admit that it cannot be. Gish, for example, writes in his book *Evolution? The Fossils Say No!* that

> . . . we do not know how God created, what processes He used, for God used processes which are not now operating anywhere in the natural universe. This is why we refer to divine creation as special creation. We cannot discover by scientific investigations anything about the creative processes used by God.

Instead, creationists maintain that the Creator used catastrophic or supernatural means to His end. The Noahic Flood is an example of such a supernatural catastrophe. But, Morris, Director of the Institute for Creation Research (ICR), has written in his book *Biblical Cosmology and Modern Science,* "the main trouble with catastrophist theories is that there is no way of subjecting them to empirical test." Thus, the scientific methods of hypothesis followed by testing, which were so useful in solving our light bulb problem, are totally useless for solving the problems addressed by creationists.

The second characteristic of a theory is that it is correctable. Once again, creationist scientists admit that the creation explanation fails to possess this characteristic. Morris, for example, lists 23 predictions from Genesis 1–11 in his book. His own conclusion is that all 23 predictions are contradicted by the past century of geological research. Does he therefore treat Genesis 1–11 as a scientific hypothesis in need of correction? No. On the contrary, Morris states that "no geological difficulties, *real or imagined,* can be allowed to take precedence over the clear statements and necessary inferences of Scriptures." In short, creationism is uncorrectable.

Indeed, another creationist scientist, John N. Moore of the ICR, has written in several pamphlets that the major advantage creationism has over evolution is that creationism is "the *only unchanging* explanation of origins." It is so unchanging that "scientific creationism" is essentially identical to the prescientific form of Biblical creationism espoused by Jews over 2,000 years ago. This makes creationism one of the oldest surviving explanations for anything. No doubt this intellectual stability is comforting in these times of rapid change, but is stability, in and of itself, necessarily good?

Think back a moment to our light bulb analogy. Would an unchanging, uncorrectable explanation of our problem have been an advantage to us there? Certainly not. Just imagine the depths of our ignorance had we stuck with our first light bulb hypothesis no matter what the evidence indicated. Instead of accumulating new knowledge through the testing of new hypotheses until we discovered that the light bulb was loose, we would still be standing at the light switch wondering what in Heaven's name could be wrong. After a while, no doubt, we would conclude that whatever it is, it is beyond our comprehension. Unfortunately, this is exactly what the creationists have concluded.

All creationist literature falls back, at some point, upon the assumption that a supernatural, omniscient, omnipotent God, Creator, or Intelligence must exist to direct the creative process. Some creationists make this assumption explicit. Others, especially those writing public school texts, do not. These others believe that if they leave God out of the text, then it will be "less religious" and "more scientific." Their belief is unfounded. As we have demonstrated with examples both from the light bulb analogy and from evolutionary theory, all assumptions must be tested whether they are stated explicitly or not. Failure to state an assumption simply makes the explanation less scientific because it is then harder to test it. In this case, whether one explicitly states that God is the Creator or one leaves the Creator unidentified, Someone or Something must cause Creation. These assumed causes (or mechanisms) have been identified and tested for evolution. They must also be identified and tested for creationism if it is to be considered scientific.

Unfortunately, creation scientists are on the horns of a scientific dilemma. If they leave the Creator out of their explanations, they provide no testable mechanism for creation. This form of the creation explanation is therefore unscientific. On the other horn, if they identify the Creator with God or other supernatural powers, then they are also being unscientific. As the great and pious astronomer Sir Isaac Newton said more than a century before Darwin was born, the use of any final cause such as God automatically takes the explanation out of the realm of science. Morris and A. E. Wilder-Smith of ICR and Kofahl and Segraves of the Creation Research Center (CRC) consistently and blatantly identify the Creator as a final cause in their textbooks. But, "God's will," as we discussed with regard to our light bulb analogy, cannot be used as a *scientific* explanation of anything.

Nonetheless, the "scientific creationists" attempt to do just that. Morris and Gish of ICR, Kofahl and Segraves of CRC, and the hundreds of members of the Creation Research Society have all stated that the Creator is the God of the Bible and that the Creation itself occurred exactly as described in Genesis. These same individuals also admit that, to use Morris' words from his textbook *Scientific Creationism,*

> . . . it is impossible to devise a scientific experiment to describe the creation process, or even to ascertain whether such a process can take place. The Creator does not create at the whim of a scientist.

So we come to the crux of the evolution-creation debate. Science depends upon observation, testing, and control. Religion depends upon faith in the existence of an unobservable, untestable, uncontrollable God. As scientists, we can turn off and on a light at will; we can create mutations and breed new varieties of plants and animals at will; we can observe the natural processes of evolution in fossils, fields, forests, and laboratories—at will. How different is creationism. No one can turn off or on the Creator at will. No one can cause Him to create new varieties of plants or animals at will. No one can observe any of the processes by which He creates. Creationism, because it depends upon the existence of such an unobservable, untestable, uncorrectable Creator can not be a scientific theory.

Indeed, the attempt to use a Creator as a scientific explanation only promotes *scientific* ignorance. Invoking "God's will" did not help us to understand or fix our light problem. Invoking "God's will" as the cause of Creation is no more enlightening. "God's will," because it is not testable or correctable, yields no new or useful knowledge concerning nature. Thus, creationism fails to possess the final characteristic required of all scientific theories: that it be fruitful of new scientific knowledge. Creationism is not *scientifically* fruitful.

There are two ways of demonstrating this. The first is to search the historical record since Darwin to determine whether creationism has been used in the formulation of any major scientific discovery. The history of science shows that it has not. On the contrary, almost all important discoveries made during the last century in biology and geology either stem from or add to our understanding of evolution.

This conclusion may be verified in a second manner. Reference to the numerous sources cited by the creationists themselves demonstrates that their conclusions are almost entirely dependent upon research carried out by evolutionists. Only in the rarest instances have the creationist scientists created any of their own data. This is a sorry state of affairs for an explanation that is hundreds and thousands of years older than evolutionary theory. Yet, it makes sense when you think about it. Science, as we pointed out initially, is based upon recognizing and answering new questions or problems. Creationists have no new problems. Accepting the Biblical account of Creation as the True Word of God, creationists can assert, as Kofahl and Segraves have done in their book *The Creation Explanation,* that "the Genesis record [already] provides the answers." For creationists, nothing more can be known; nothing more needs to be known.

CONCLUSION: SCIENCE AND RELIGION

In summary, we have argued that evolution qualifies as a valid scientific theory while creationism does not. We have also argued that evolutionary theory is not a religious explanation while creationism is. We do not conclude thereby that evolution is "true" and creationism "false," nor can the opposite conclusion be maintained. We conclude only that evolution and creationism are two totally different sorts of explanations of nature. They should not be confused.

It is also clear to us that evolution, as the best available scientific explanation of nature, deserves to be taught as a scientific theory in science classes. Creationism, since it is not a scientific theory, should not be taught as science in science classes. On the other hand, we have no objection to seeing creationism taught as a *religious* explanation of nature. Although religion is constitutionally banned from the public schools, perhaps some time could be made available for the teaching of creationism in its proper historical and philosophical context. Such an arrangement would teach students the differences between scientific and religious explanations that have been summarized here.

We believe that it is particularly important that students do learn the differences between scientific and religious beliefs. Indeed, we believe that it is the confusion between the two that has caused the present controversy. Despite the rhetoric used by the creationists, their view is not scientific, nor is science a religion. Yet "scientific creationists" have made both claims. Historically, this is nothing new. Fundamentalists have created the same confusion ever since Darwin first published *On the Origin of Species* in 1859. Harvey Cox, Professor of Divinity at the Harvard Divinity School, has recently written that

> . . . the notorious nineteenth century "Warfare Between Science and Religion" arose from mistaken notions of what religion and science are. Although there are still occasional border skirmishes, most theologians and scientists now recognize that religion overstepped its boundaries when—at least in the West—it tried to make geological and biological history into matters of revelation.

We can only regret that a small group of fundamentalists believe it necessary once again to overstep the boundaries differentiating science from religion. The result is needless confusion, confusion that could be eliminated by proper teaching of what science is, what religion is, and how they differ.

Science and religion, as Cox pointed out, need not be at war. They can be, as we pointed out initially, complementary. It is only when science poses as religion or religion as science that controversy erupts. Otherwise faith and reason are compatible. In fact, the English clergyman Charles Kingsley pointed this compatibility out to Darwin in a letter written in 1860. Kingsley wrote:

> I have gradually learnt to see that it is just as noble a conception of Deity to believe that He created animal forms capable of self-development into all forms needful . . . as to believe that He required a fresh act of intervention to supply the lacunae which He Himself made. I question whether the former be not the loftier thought.

Whether one agrees with Kingsley's view or not, it illustrates an important point. There are many possible conceptions of the relationship between science and religion. It does not seem appropriate to us that any group, such as the creationists, should attempt to legislate their particular view of this relationship into law. Our Constitution guarantees freedom of religious choice. We believe that an equal guarantee exists for all intellectual choices, including those involving science. Thus, just as the courts and legislatures may not judge the validity of various religious beliefs or impose one in preference to another, neither should courts and legislatures be involved in determining the validity of scientific ideas nor should they impose one in preference to another. Just as religious practice is left to the individual religious practitioner, so should scientific research be left to the individual scientist. To do otherwise infringes upon the rights of individuals to decide for themselves the relationship between scientific ideas and religious beliefs. To do otherwise is thus not only an abridgment of intellectual freedom, but of religious freedom as well.

It may strike some people as odd that we equate protection of religion with protection of science. There is good reason for the equation. Several governments in the past have usurped to themselves the control of science. They are not commendable examples to follow: Nazi Germany, Soviet Russia, and Communist Red China. Science, religion, and liberty suffered hand-in-hand in these countries. Let us not begin the journey down their road by harnessing science to legislatures and courts. On the other hand, let us learn from the evolutionism-creationism controversy that dogmatism, be it scientific or religious, is best left out of the classroom. Dogmatism teaches only narrow-mindedness at a time when it is clear that better understanding of the issues is what is needed. We must teach the best of man's knowledge to the best of our ability. But we must also teach how we can recognize it as best. And we must always remain humbly aware that we may be ignorant of something better. That is the lesson of science.

NOTE

1. The authors of this article used the term *man* to refer to humanity in general. This term is not used by modern anthropologists because, to many people, it reflects an unconscious sexist bias in language and rhetoric. At the time that this article was written, however, the generalized *man* was a common convention in writing. In the interest of historical accuracy we have not changed the wording in this article, but students should be aware that nonsexist terms (*humans, people, Homo sapiens,* and so on) are preferred.—The Editors.

REFERENCES

Barbour, I. 1966. *Issues in science and religion.* New York: Harper and Row.

Baum, R. M. 1982. Science confronts creationist assault. *Chemical and Engineering News* 12(26):19.

Beckner, M. 1968. *The biological way of thought.* Berkeley and Los Angeles: University of California Press.

Clark, H. W. 1968. *Fossils, flood and fire.* Escondido, Calif.: Outdoor Picture Press.

Colloms, B. 1975. *Charles Kingsley.* London: Constable; New York: Barnes and Noble.

Cox, H. 1981. Religion. In Villoldo, A., and Dychtwald, K. (eds.). *Millennium: Glimpses into the 21st century.* Los Angeles: J. P. Tarcher.

Eldredge, N. 1981. The elusive eureka. *Natural History* August 24–26.

Gillispie, C. C. 1959. *Genesis and geology.* New York: Harper and Row.

Gish, D. T. 1978. *Evolution? The fossils say no!* San Diego: Creation-Life Publishers.

_____. n.d. *Have you been brainwashed?* San Diego: Creation-Life Publishers.

_____. 1981. Letter to the editor. *Science Teacher* 48: 20.

Gould, S. J. 1982. On paleontology and prediction. *Discover* July 56–57.

Hardin, G. 1959. *Nature and man's fate.* New York: Holt, Rinehart and Winston.

Huxley, T. H. 1892. *Essays on controverted questions.* London and New York: Macmillan and Co.

Kofahl, R. E., and Segraves, K. L. 1975. *The creation explanation.* Wheaton, Ill.: Shaw.

Lammerts, W. (ed.) 1970. *Why not creation?* Phillipsburg, NJ Presbyterian and Reformed Publishing Co.

_____. 1971. *Scientific studies in special creation.* Phillipsburg, NJ Presbyterian and Reformed Publishing Co.

Lewin, R. 1982. Where is the science in creation science? *Science* 215: 142–146.

Moore, J. R. 1979. *The post-Darwinian controversies.* Cambridge and New York: Cambridge University Press.

Morris, H. M. 1975. *Introducing scientific creationism into the public schools.* San Diego: Institute for Creation Research.

_____. 1970. *Biblical cosmology and modern science.* Nutley, N.J.: Craig Press.

Overton, W. R. 1982. Creationism in schools: The decision in *McLean versus the Arkansas Board of Education* [Text of 5 January 1982 Judgment]. *Science* 215: 934–943.

Peacocke, A. R. 1979. *Creation and the world of science.* Oxford: The Clarendon Press.

Pupin, M. (ed.) 1969. *Science and religion.* Freeport, N.Y.: Books for Libraries Press.

Root-Bernstein, R. S. 1982. On defining a scientific theory: Creationism considered. In Montagu, A. (ed.) *Evolution and creationism.* Oxford: The University Press.

_____. 1982. Ignorance versus knowledge in the evolutionist creationist controversy. Paper presented June 22 at the symposium, "Evolutionists Confront Creationists," American Association for the Advancement of Science, Pacific Division, Santa Barbara, Calif.

Ruse, M. 1982. A philosopher at the monkey trial. *New Scientist* 317–319.

Skoog, G. 1980. The textbook battle over creationism. *Christian Century* 97: 974–976.

_____. 1982. We must not succumb to specious arguments for equal time. *Education Week* 1(18): 19.

Zimmerman, P. A. (ed.) 1970. *Rock strata and the Bible record.* St. Louis: Concordia Publishing House.

2

Re-reading Root-Bernstein and McEachron in Cobb County, Georgia

A Year Past and Present

Benjamin Z. Freed

The following selection is a recent update of the important issues raised in the first article by Root-Bernstein and McEachron. As a holistic science that looks at many different aspects of the human condition over time, anthropology incorporates different approaches to data collection and interpretation. Some areas of anthropology, such as biological and physical anthropology, primatology, and archaeology, generally adhere to the tenets of hypothetico-deductive science. In other words, anthropologists in these fields propose theories that can be tested using empirical data.

Insights into how living organisms function and how they change over time have been generated by a set of concepts and theories collectively known as evolutionary theory. Modern biology, from the understanding of cells to populations of animals, relies heavily on evolutionary theory for explanations about why living things are the way they are. As discussed in the following article, evolutionary theory provides an explanatory backdrop for understanding biological phenomena, much as any explanation of physical movement or a chemical reaction should be compatible with the laws of physics and chemistry.

Although it is almost universally accepted by the scientific community, some people (particularly fundamentalist groups) have seen evolutionary theory as incompatible with Christian beliefs. The past two decades have seen a resurgence of popular debate over evolutionary theory, especially as it is taught in high schools in the United States. There has been a push in some religiously conservative communities to have evolutionary theory removed from schools, or to have its teaching presented as mere theory rather than scientific fact. One alternative explanation of complex biological mechanisms has been proposed called "intelligent design."

In this selection, the author re-examines many of the principles in the first article. He looks at the religious underpinnings of creationist beliefs and then examines the supposedly "scientific" intelligent design theory. Using basic criteria for the evaluation of scientific theory, he concludes that intelligent design fails to qualify as hypothetico-deductive science. He then goes on to discuss how anthropology both suggests a need to understand the religious motivation for attacks on evolutionary theory and, at the same time, provides a strong impetus for anthropologists who work on evolution to defend the teaching of evolution on the basis of its scientific merit.

As you read this selection, ask yourself the following questions:

- Why did the Cobb County, Georgia, school board decide to put warning stickers inside every high school biology textbook that contained material on evolution?

- Why does the author, himself a biological anthropologist and a Cobb County resident, find the stickers objectionable?

- What does the author mean when he says that science is not monolithic?

- Why haven't the claims of intelligent design been tested and reviewed according to the usual rules and procedures of science?

- Are religion and science compatible? Is this even a reasonable question to ask? Why or why not?

The following terms discussed in this selection are included in the Glossary at the back of the book:

creationism	*intelligent design*
evolution	*natural selection*
hypothesis	*peer review*
hypothetico-deductive method	

This article was written especially for Applying Anthropology:
An Introductory Reader, 9/e.

In 1984 I took a graduate course on the history of biology. In preparation for that seminar I read Root-Bernstein & McEachron's (RBM) treatise on what is a scientific theory. Little did I realize that the article would later catch up to my everyday life some twenty years later.

I am now an anthropologist at Emory University, and I live in the suburban Atlanta, Georgia community of Cobb County—a place that has recently been in the news because of debates concerning the teaching of evolution in public schools. I not only must write about my results on lemur ecology, behavior, and evolution, but I must also transfer the information to the general public, especially within my community. In my case, I give guest lectures at schools, provide workshops for teachers, and talk with parents and students at coffee shops and PTA meetings. Moore and Kraemer (2005) have shown that teachers face many issues if and when they teach evolution. Many teachers have had to learn to come to terms with teaching evolution. Kyzer (2004) found that teachers with different beliefs, training, community involvement, and comfort were likely to teach evolutionary biology much differently, in terms of time and content. From these and other studies, I have seen that, without direct contact and further training from universities, teachers in my own community could have remained isolated, and would have been less likely to communicate the core principle in modern biology. Workshops and discussions provided teachers a convenient way to keep up with materials, to generate new lessons, and to address lingering questions. More importantly, by discussing biological anthropology with teachers, I gave them better ways of understanding how relevant evolutionary biology is to understanding our own biology. We continue to discuss primates, fossils, human variation, disease, health, and many other topics.

In the 1990s and early 2000s, anti-evolution proponents from Kansas, Ohio, Pennsylvania, and Georgia (Cobb County) brought their arguments to local school boards, state legislatures, and even the national political stage. For example, prior to 2002, Cobb public school students' exposure to evolutionary biology was limited. The subject had been excised from some lessons and books, and students whose classes and books did deal with the subject had the choice of opting out of those lessons. Three primary effects were observed by many of us at local universities: 1) relatively few students went on to major in the biological sciences; 2) students were at a disadvantage in intro-level college biology when asked to compete with other students who had received high school evolutionary biology instruction; and 3) students continued to misunderstand and underappreciate science, especially biology.

In 2002, the Cobb County school board approved a college-compatible biology textbook. Shortly afterwards, a creationist-led petition was announced and the board soon after began affixing in each biology textbook stickers that read: "This textbook contains material on evolution. Evolution is a theory, not a fact, regarding the origin of living things. This material should be approached with an open mind, studied carefully and critically considered." Likewise, similar moves were raised elsewhere under the banners of "critical consideration," "teach the controversy," "alternative scientific views," and "theory, not fact" legislation. Soon after the Cobb stickers, anti-evolution proponents in Dover, Pennsylvania required that "intelligent design" (ID) objections to evolution be raised before science lessons on evolutionary biology.

WHY WOULD A SCIENTIST, SUCH AS MYSELF, GET UPSET OVER A SUCH A STICKER?

Strictly speaking, the stickers confound student comprehension of evolution in several ways. First, evolution is fact AND scientific theory, overwhelmingly observed and discussed in the peer-reviewed, scientific literature. To those who claim that evolution has never been observed, I point to peer-reviewed research on Anolis lizards, tomatoes, and North American fossil primates, among numerous other topics. Secondly, evolution is not a hunch, a guess, or a theory, as the term is used in the common vernacular. To conflate scientific theory (as described by RBM) and the vernacular use of the term "theory" is to confound student comprehension of the strengths and limitations of the scientific method. Thirdly, evolution is NOT a scientific theory about origins of life. It is a well-substantiated scientific explanation for critical aspects of origins, such as its timing, but primarily evolution is about biological change over time. Fourthly, facts themselves are mutable; they are subject to re-evaluation as techniques and accuracy improve. Finally, the school board singled out evolution. No other scientific theories (e.g., gravity, germ theory, plate tectonics) needed to be approached with an open mind, studied carefully, and granted critical consideration. The board went out of its way to have students be wary of one scientific theory, the theory at the core of modern biology.

To be clear, the school board's stickers were completely at odds with RBM's article and the scientific literature. Twenty years after my initiation into anti-evolutionist arguments, here I was faced with a sticker and policy that showed no comprehension as to what is science, theory, and evolution, the very topics discussed in RBM. To me, as a scientist, the sticker was technically inaccurate, misleading, and confusing. It was typical of a new wave of anti-evolutionism.

DOES THIS VERSION OF ANTI-EVOLUTIONISM, INCLUDING ID, MEET THE STANDARD OF SCIENCE AS DEFINED IN RBM?

RBM's article was written during the early 1980s, when biologists, legal scholars, and historians dealt with the first legal wave of modern creationism. After a resounding series of legal decisions against this religious-based movement, a new wave of anti-evolution approaches emerged under the name "Intelligent Design" (ID). ID is a belief that a so-called irreducible complexity of living forms is too great to be explained by evolution. To this movement's proponents, only an "intelligence" (e.g., an omnipotent deity) could account for the origin and diversity of life. Strictly speaking, intelligent design can be traced to early nineteenth century theologian William Paley. Like 1980s creationism, ID represents a belief about a scientific issue rather than a scientific view of the same issue.

In recent years, biochemist Michael Behe, mathematician William Dembski, and other proponents of ID have called into question Darwinian natural selection's ability to explain origins and evolution of organisms. For instance, they point to developments in the field of molecular biology, which have shown cells to be much more complex than once suspected (Behe, 1996). At the cellular level, ID supporters suggest that a bacterium's flagellum, or propeller-like tail, could not have evolved independently of all the complex cellular structures which move the tail. They argue that, because all of these complex parts must 'fit' together to function, like the parts of a mousetrap, no one element could evolve independent of the others, and so they must be evidence for an intelligent designer. Other proponents of intelligent design point to mathematical models that suggest Darwinian selection might not be any better than random accumulations of changes, and is unlikely to explain complex living organisms.

Fortunately, evolutionary theory is up to these challenges. So-called irreducibly complex structures can evolve from non-irreducible complexity if a structure evolves with one function and is then co-opted for another. Moreover, a species does not evolve in a vacuum, but rather co-evolves alongside other species that are also evolving—a condition left unaccounted for by the mathematical models of evolution.

Biologists, such as Miller (1996, 1999, 2004) and Padian (2002), have shown serious scientific flaws with ID. Miller (2004) noted that the bacterial flagellum is not as irreducibly complex as people have been led to believe. ID is not considered science by anyone actually studying evolutionary biology (see discussions in Pennock, 2001; Larson, 2003; Scott, 2004) because it does not fulfill basic requirements of scientific endeavor. Many scientific theories have proven wrong in whole or part, but they are scientific nevertheless because they can be tested against empirical data. If one re-examines RBM, an ID proponent would have to relax at least two tenets of the scientific method: the need for testable and falsifiable hypotheses, and the reliance on above-nature forces. Evolution by natural selection is built on scientific evaluation of testable and falsifiable hypotheses of natural phenomena without the invocation of above-nature forces. ID fails on all of these criteria. For that reason, evolutionary theory has generated a wealth of research in which hypotheses are tested and confirmed, while ID has produced no such research programs or scholarship.

THEN WHY HAVE SO MANY PEOPLE TAKEN TO ID AND OTHER FORMS OF ANTI-EVOLUTION?

To many people ID is a satisfying rubric or explanation. The notion of an "intelligence" matches many religious viewpoints or world views of a single, omnipotent deity. Forrest and Gross (2004), for example, noted the religious ties between ID and creationism. As part of a long series of surveys of people's beliefs in pseudoscience, Eve (2004) and Harrold and Eve (1987) surveyed creationists, Wiccans, and university students, and found strong evidence that adherence to creationism was more strongly related to social beliefs, attitudes, and politics than to actual scientific literacy. Belief in creationism was more a matter of the ways that people use to judge "truth claims" about evidence of the ancient human past. In an ethnography of a creationist study group (which included scientists), Toumey (1994) found that these people were often well-read. What I personally have seen is that a person who is willing to suspend acceptance of scientific principles may choose to ignore overwhelming scientific evidence. Such a person may choose to believe spectacular and pseudoscientific claims that more closely match his or her own belief system (see recent discussions in Plavcan 2007).

I suspect what Eve found occurs in my community as well. Few people readily access the scientific literature. Many anti-evolutionists incorrectly, but readily equate evolution, natural selection, and Darwin. By doing so, Darwin has been made into a strawman, one that is viewed as being opposed to local religious beliefs. To many people, science is used to support religious beliefs. If it cannot do so, it must be viewed with great skepticism. Many of these people turn to internet accessible, readily available opinion, political, and religious pieces to confirm their views. Science is viewed as an opposing monolith that directly contradicts and opposes religious belief.

AS MANY IN MY COMMUNITY HAVE ASKED ME, HOW DOES SCIENCE CRITICIZE ITS THEORIES? OR IS SCIENCE A MONOLITH?

Science criticizes itself primarily through peer-review. In peer-review, a manuscript is sent to a journal's editor, who then solicits evaluations from independent scientists. These reviewers receive no payment for their time and effort. Each manuscript is checked for its authenticity, overall scientific merit, adherence to professional, ethical, and scientific guidelines, and accuracy in review of previous works. Based on the reviewers' comments, the editor decides whether or not to publish the article, and whether revisions or clarifications are required before publication. In this way, peer-review affords the reader the assurance that an article has fulfilled its overall scientific mission, and contributed to the overall understanding about a topic. If a scientist takes issue with an article, the scientist may write a response in the publication.

This is the level of scholarship that scientists have come to expect. I suspect that the public expects no less of science. Responsible? Yes. Tough? You bet. Manuscripts get rejected all the time. We revise and re-submit. Democratic? Not necessarily. Scientists don't vote in opinion polls or cast ballots about each item, but at least scientists have a way to "critically consider" material. If an ID follower wanted to write a scientific research article, the peer-review process would yield an evaluation of the article's scientific merits, ethics, and scholarship, just like any scientific manuscript. Science is no monolith.

To many of us in evolutionary biology and anthropology, ID followers have not only failed to show clear scientific merit in method, they have yet to show true scholarship. Reviewing the peer-reviewed scientific literature, one finds no research articles nor any evidence that ID is being used to explain biology. ID has not been shown to be a best-fit or useful scientific explanation for understanding nature. In Cobb, anti-evolution material that was not vetted by scientific peer-review was introduced to the public access television, and the local op-ed pages. Many people could not then understand why this material shouldn't be available for science classes. Padian & Gishlick (2002), however, have cited numerous flaws in the science and scholarship of this material. Rennie (2002) and Young and Edis (2004) have also discussed many of the most frequent claims (see more recent discussions in Petto and Godfrey

2007). Position statements against ID proponents' claims have also been brought forth by the American Institute of Biological Sciences, the American Association for the Advancement of Science, the National Science Teachers Association, and many other scientific organizations, including those from anthropology.

In Cobb, local parents sued the school board, seeing an unnecessary intrusion of religion into government. Scientists from the region's major colleges spoke up, submitted affidavits, in some cases testified, and worked with local parents, educators, and students to explain more about the scientific method. Initially, a district judge decision forced the school board to remove the stickers from the texts. Although the board appealed the decision, the case was sent back to the original judge. Before the case was re-tried (more than four years after the stickers went into the books), the board settled with the plaintiffs. In doing so, the board promised never again to interfere as it had with the teaching of evolution. Although the scientist in me wished the board had finally comprehended the scientific merits, the decision to settle may have had little to do with the actual science. The board had been through an arduous and costly legal process, lived through several protracted political battles with its superintendent and chair (unrelated to the sticker), and had just lost one sticker-supporting member in an election. The decision to settle also came after resounding legal decisions elsewhere, particularly in Dover, PA. Likewise, shortly after the settlement, the legal firm of the initial creationist petitioner was subsumed by the board's own legal firm. People on the board wanted to make a fresh start, devoid of divisive public issues.

Similar anti-evolution tactics and claims were repeated elsewhere, most notably in Dover, Pennsylvania. The school board tried to diminish evolution and to provide alternate scientific theory discussion for its science classrooms. Parents in the district sued the school board, arguing an unnecessary religious intrusion into biology lessons. Proponents of evolutionary biology and ID provided testimony before a federal judge. In December 2005 the judge ruled that the tactics, claims, and literature of anti-evolution proponents were not divorced from religious motives. In some cases, what was presented as an alternate scientific view was thinly-veiled creationism. The proposed alternative scientific views, including ID, were not science. The effect of the board's policy was to diminish evolutionary biology education, and to presuppose in students' minds that alternate scientific views exist. The overall effect of Dover has had a profound impact throughout the country. Although ID is not dead, the various forms of creationism are changing along with the times (see Scott 2007). Creationism is evolving.

On the bright side, both Cobb and Dover have forced educators at all levels to think more about what is science. In Cobb, scientists and educators have begun to interact more directly with the general public and with each other. The school district science administration has also formed a unique partnership with businesses and educators to improve science outreach, to establish greater links between teachers and college educators, and to foster greater student interest in science. Many of us are now re-reading and discussing philosophy of science papers. Perhaps most important, in the midst of the Cobb issue, scientists, teachers, and politicians were able to work together to strengthen the state's science standards. Evolution is now a firm part of the state's biology curriculum; student comprehension of it is tested. Teachers and students question me thoroughly whenever I see them. It's refreshing to go into a public biology classroom on an off day from my college duties.

In Cobb, it's not a question of whether or not students and teachers believe in evolution. Scientists don't *believe* in it; they *accept* this overarching scientific theory. The overall goal in education is to be sure that students and teachers comprehend it. Do they make proper sense of it? Does it relate to the world around them? People are starting to focus on these goals.

WHAT IS THE VIEW OF GENERAL ANTHROPOLOGY?

As a rule, anthropologists are trained to respect the fact that different groups of people possess vastly different worldviews. Indeed, the variation among different ways of seeing, understanding, and making sense of the world lies at the root of many anthropologists' curiosity about humanity and human experience. While anthropology teaches respect and appreciation for such diversity, it also teaches that respect does not equal agreement. A North American anthropologist, for instance, may be fascinated by the origin myths or healing rituals of aboriginal peoples in Australia, Central Africa, or the Amazonian rainforest. But he can be respectful of cultural differences and still insist on taking antimalarial drugs to prevent infection, or refuse to participate in a healing ceremony involving traditional surgery even if the host community is convinced that it would help.

As a biological anthropologist trained in the scientific method, I can appreciate the fact that some belief systems are rooted in stories about the nature and origins of life that are fundamentally distinct from—and even contradict—the basic tenets of scientific research

and scholarship. Anthropology does, however, help demonstrate that different systems of knowledge address different questions. Some knowledge systems, like religious traditions, address questions about the ultimate meaning and purpose of the human life and of the world as we know it. As RBM so clearly describe it, science is designed to address a different set of concerns. Rather than seeking answers to questions of ultimate meaning, science seeks explanations for how the natural world operates, and for how it has come to exist as we observe it today. Science uses tools, methods of gathering and evaluating knowledge, and methods for determining the validity, reliability, and relevance of such knowledge that differ markedly from those of the world's myriad religious systems. These tools, methods, and procedures are the very hallmarks of science, and they are what allow scientists across the globe to communicate and evaluate one another's work through a common language.

Religious beliefs, like those motivating the ID movement, often have profound meaning and significance for proponents. We must, nonetheless, keep in mind the fundamental distinction between forms of religious belief and scientifically validated forms of knowledge. While evolutionary biologists and biological anthropologists may be deeply frustrated by the challenges the ID movement poses for science education and scientific literacy in the United States, this frustration does not come from a sense of disrespect for ID advocates' religious beliefs. Rather it stems from an overriding commitment to the fact that different kinds of questions demand different kinds of information, different methods of evaluation, and different criteria for establishing what is "true." Ultimately, anthropology teaches that religion and science aim to define and establish different kinds of truth about humanity, human life, and the world we live in.

Looking back, the RBM article has helped me refocus and analyze science as it relates to my community and my students. For those of us who view science as a way of explaining many critical aspects of life, we find an overwhelming preponderance of peer-reviewed evidence for evolution. For anthropologists, evolution is the best-fit scientific explanation for the genetic and paleontological record, and it offers us much understanding about medicine, ecology, and ourselves. Scientists have thorough and responsible scholarly debates on many aspects about evolution, such as its mechanisms, effects, and pace. To many of us in science, evolution is a tremendous theory, one that holds power in explaining the available scientific evidence, and the vast data yet to be discovered. Theories are powerful and wonderful; they're not just hunches.

REFERENCES

Behe, M. 1996. *Darwin's Black Box.* New York, NY: The Free Press.

Eve, R. 2004. "Creationism, evolution, and a struggle for the means of cultural reproduction," American Anthropological Association meetings. Atlanta, GA, December, 19, 2004.

Forrest, B., and Gross, P. 2004. *Creationism's Trojan Horse: The Wedge of Intelligent Design.* Oxford University Press.

Harrold F. B. and Eve R. A. 1987. Patterns of creationist belief among college students. In *Cult archaeology and creationism: Understanding pseudoscientific beliefs about the past,* eds. Harrold, F. B., and Eve, R. A. Iowa City: University of Iowa Press. 6: 68–90.

Kyzer P. M. 2004. Three Southern high school biology teachers' perspectives on teaching evolution: Sociocultural influences. PhD thesis. University of Alabama. pp. 244

Larson, E. 2003. *Trial and error: The American controversy over creation and evolution.* 3rd ed. Oxford: Oxford University Press.

Miller, K. R. 1996. "A review of Darwin's Black Box," *Creation/Evolution* 16: 36–40.

Miller, K. R. 1999. *Finding Darwin's God.* Harper Collins.

Miller, K. R. 2004. The flagellum unspun: The collapse of irreducible complexity, In *Debating design: From Darwin to DNA,* eds. Dembski, W. and Ruse, M. 81–97. Cambridge University Press.

Moore, R. and Kraemer, K. 2005. The teaching of evolution and creationism in Minnesota. *Am. Biol. Teach.* 67: 457–466.

Padian, K. 2002. "Waiting for the watchmaker," *Science* 295: 2373–2374.

Padian, K., and Gishlick, A. 2002. "The talented Mr. Wells," *Quarterly Review of Biology* 77(1): 33–37.

Pennock, R. T. 2001. *Intelligent design creationism and its critics: Philosophical, theological, and scientific perspectives.* Cambridge University Press.

Petto, A. J., and, Godfrey, L. R. (eds.). 2007. *Scientists confront creationism: Intelligent design and beyond.* New York: WW Norton.

Plavcan, J. M. 2007. The invisible Bible: The logic of creation science. In *Scientists confront creationism: Intelligent design and beyond,* eds. Petto, A. J., and Godfrey, L. R., 361–380. New York: WW Norton.

Rennie, J. 2002. "15 answers to creationist nonsense," *Scientific American* 287(1): 78–85.

Scott, E. 2004. *Evolution vs. creationism: An introduction.* Greenwood Press.

Scott E. C. 2007. Creation science lite: "Intelligent Design" as the new anti-evolutionism. In *Scientists confront creationism: Intelligent design and beyond,* eds. Petto, A. J., and Godfrey, L. R., 59–109. New York: WW Norton.

Toumey, C. P. 1994. *God's own scientists: Creationists in a secular world.* New Brunswick, NJ: Rutgers University Press.

Young, M. and Edis, T. (eds.). 2004. *Why intelligent design fails: A scientific critique of the new creationism.* Rutgers University Press.

3

The Human Family Tree Has Become
a Bush with Many Branches

John Noble Wilford

Approximately three and a half million years ago, two human ancestors and a small child took a stroll through what is now northern Tanzania. Shortly after, a volcano named Sadiman erupted, spreading a layer of ash over the landscape. Then, when a light rain turned this ash into a cement-like substance, it preserved the footprints of these bipedal hominins leaving a fossil record of this prehistoric walk. Several million years later, Paleoanthropologist Andrew Hill stumbled upon these fossilized footprints while working with a group of researchers led by Meave Leakey.

Hill discovered the footprints in 1976, just two years after Donald Johanson unearthed the historic remains of Lucy, an *Australopithecus afarensis* whose partial skeleton represents one of the earliest hominins found in the known fossil record. After dating these fossil remains, the way we think of early human history was drastically changed; we revised our earliest estimates of when the human lineage diverged from the other apes.

Today, new discoveries continue to shed light on the history and timeline of our prehistoric ancestors. In this selection, John Noble Wilford explains how the ever-increasing fossil record, along with the development of molecular biology continue to reveal and push back the timeline of the divergence of humankind from our common ancestry with other apes.

As you read this selection, ask yourself the following questions:

- What is the primary difference between the work of paleoanthropologists and biologists in terms of their contributions to our understanding of our early hominid ancestors?

- How has our knowledge about our earliest human ancestors changed since the 1990s, and what evidence supports this new understanding?

- What does the author mean when he states that the human family tree is more like a bush with many branches?

- According to recent molecular research and the fossil record, how long ago did humans split from other primates? Why is it difficult to pinpoint the exact point of divergence of the human lineage from a common ape ancestor?

The following terms discussed in this selection are included in the Glossary at the back of the book:

African Eve *Australopithecus anamensis*
Homo floresiensis *morphology*

T ime was, fossils and a few stone artifacts were about the only means scientists had of tracing the lines of early human evolution. And gaps in such material evidence were frustratingly wide.

When molecular biologists joined the investigation some 30 years ago, their techniques of genetic analysis yielded striking insights. DNA studies pointed to a common maternal ancestor of all anatomically modern humans in Africa by at least 130,000 years. She inevitably became known as the African Eve.

Other genetic research plotted ancestral migration patterns and the extremely close DNA relationship between humans and chimpanzees, our nearest living relatives. Genetic clues also set the approximate time of the divergence of the human lineage from a common ancestor with apes: between six million and eight million years ago.

Fossil researchers were skeptical at first, a reaction colored perhaps by their dismay at finding scientific poachers on their turf. These paleoanthropologists contended that the biologists' "molecular clocks" were unreliable, and in some cases they were, though apparently not to a significant degree.

Now paleoanthropologists say they accept the biologists as allies triangulating the search for human origins from different angles. As much as anything, a rapid succession of fossil discoveries since the early 1990s has restored the confidence of paleoanthropologists in the relevance of their approach to the study of early hominids, those fossil ancestors and related species in human evolution.

The new finds have filled in some of the yawning gaps in the fossil record. They have doubled the record's time span from 3.5 million back almost to 7 million years ago and more than doubled the number of earliest known hominid species. The teeth and bone fragments suggest the form—the morphology—of these ancestors that lived presumably just this side of the human-ape split.

"The amount of discord between morphology and molecules is actually not that great anymore," said Frederick E. Grine, a paleoanthropologist at the State University of New York at Stony Brook.

With more abundant data, Dr. Grine said, scientists are, in a sense, fleshing out the genetic insights with increasingly earlier fossils. It takes the right bones to establish that a species walked upright, which is thought to be a defining trait of hominids after the split with the ape lineage.

"All biology can tell you is that my nearest relative is a chimpanzee and about when we had a common ancestor," he said. "But biology can't tell us what the common ancestor looked like, what shaped that evolutionary change or at what rate that change took place."

Although hominid species were much more apelike in their earliest forms, Tim D. White of the University of California, Berkeley, said: "We've come to appreciate that you cannot simply extrapolate from the modern chimp to get a picture of the last common ancestor. Humans and chimps have been changing down through time."

But Dr. White, one of the most experienced hominid hunters, credits the genetic data with giving paleoanthropologists a temporal framework for their research. Their eyes are always fixed on a time horizon for hominid origins, which now appears to be at least seven million years ago.

Ever since its discovery in 1973, the species *Australopithecus afarensis*, personified by the famous Lucy skeleton, has been the continental divide in the exploration of hominid evolution. Donald Johanson, the

Lucy discoverer, and Dr. White determined that the apelike individual lived 3.2 million years ago, walked upright and was probably a direct human ancestor. Other afarensis specimens and some evocative footprints showed the species existed for almost a million years, down to three million years ago.

In the 1990s, scientists finally crossed the Lucy divide. In Kenya, Meave G. Leakey of the celebrated fossil-hunting family came up with *Australopithecus anamensis*, which lived about four million years ago and appeared to be an afarensis precursor. Another discovery by Dr. Leakey challenged the prevailing view that the **family tree** had a more or less single trunk rising from ape roots to a pinnacle occupied by *Homo sapiens*. Yet here was evidence that the new species *Kenyanthropus platyops* co-existed with Lucy's afarensis kin.

The **family tree** now looks more like a **bush** with many branches. "Just because there's only one human species around now doesn't mean it was always that way," Dr. Grine said.

Few hominid fossils have turned up from the three-million- to two-million-year period, during which hominids began making stone tools. The first *Homo* species enter the fossil record sometime before two million years ago, and the transition to much larger brains began with *Homo erectus*, about 1.7 million years ago.

Other recent discoveries have pushed deeper in time, closer to the hominid origins predicted by molecular biologists.

Dr. White was involved in excavations in Ethiopia of many specimens that lived 4.4 million years ago and were more primitive and apelike than Lucy. The species was named *Ardipithecus ramidus*. Later, a related species from 5.2 million to 5.8 million years ago was classified *Ardipithecus kadabba*.

At that time, six years ago, C. Owen Lovejoy of Kent State University said, "We are indeed coming very close to that point in the fossil record where we simply will not be able to distinguish ancestral hominid from ancestral" chimpanzees, because, he said, "They were so anatomically similar."

Two even earlier specimens are even harder to interpret. One found in Kenya by a French team has been dated to six million years and named *Orrorin tugenensis*. The teeth and bone pieces are few, though the discoverers think a thigh fragment suggests that the individual was a biped—a walker on two legs.

Another French group then uncovered 6.7-million-year-old fossils in Chad. Named *Sahelanthropus tchadensis*, the sole specimen includes only a few teeth, a jawbone and a crushed cranium. Scientists said the head appeared to have perched atop a biped.

"These are clearly the earliest hominids we have," said Eric Delson, a human-origins scientist at the American Museum of Natural History. "But we still know rather little about any of these specimens. The farther back we go toward the divergence point, the more similar specimens will look on both sides of the split."

Other challenges arise from human evolution in more recent epochs. Just who were the "little people" found a few years ago in a cave on the island of Flores in Indonesia? The Australian and Indonesian discoverers concluded that one partial skeleton and other bones belonged to a now-extinct separate human species, *Homo floresiensis*, which lived as recently as 18,000 years ago.

The apparent diminutive stature and braincase of the species prompted howls of dispute. Critics contended that this was not a distinct species, but just another dwarf-size *Homo sapiens*, possibly with a brain disorder. Several prominent scientists, however, support the new-species designation.

The tempest over the Indonesian find is nothing new in a field known for controversy. Some scholars counsel patience, recalling that it was years after the discovery of the first Neanderthal skull, in 1856, before it was accepted as an ancient branch of the human family. Critics had at first dismissed the find as only the skull of a degenerate modern human or a Cossack who died in the Napoleonic wars.

Perhaps the analogy is not as encouraging as intended. Scientists to this day are arguing about Neanderthals, their exact relationship to us and the cause of their extinction 30,000 years ago, not long after the arrival in Europe of the sole surviving hominid that is so curious about its origins.

4

What Are Friends For?

Barbara Smuts

In tracing the evolution of humanity, anthropologists are concerned with both biological features and socio-cultural forms. Some people believe that a prerequisite for culture was the emergence of more permanent relationships between men and women and the formation of families. How this actually occurred in evolution has been the subject of controversy. The traditional view centered on dominant males who, as mighty hunters, put the proverbial meat on the table, selected females, and, through protection of the helpless females and their offspring, ensured the transmission of their genes to future generations. The conventional wisdom left little room for the role of women in human adaptation. This is no longer the case.

In recent years, much research has helped to revise and refine our understanding of ancestral lifeways. In this selection, Barbara Smuts examines sex and friendship among baboons. The implications for the origin of male–female relations and the role of female choice are fascinating.

As you read this selection, ask yourself the following questions:

- Why do some anthropologists study monkeys and apes to better understand human behavior?
- Why do females prefer some males over others?
- Who forms the core membership of a baboon troop?
- What criteria does the author use to determine friendship?
- Do the bonds between adult male baboons and infants arise from paternity or from a relationship with the infant's mother?
- In what three ways does this article challenge the conventional wisdom about the origin of the nuclear family?

The following terms discussed in this selection are included in the Glossary at the back of the book:

aggression	grooming
dominance	paternity
estrus	primatology

Virgil, a burly adult male olive baboon, closely followed Zizi, a middle-aged female easily distinguished by her grizzled coat and square muzzle. On her rump Zizi sported a bright pink swelling, indicating that she was sexually receptive and probably fertile. Virgil's extreme attentiveness to Zizi suggested to me—and all rival males in the troop—that he was her current and exclusive mate.

Zizi, however, apparently had something else in mind. She broke away from Virgil, moved rapidly through the troop, and presented her alluring sexual swelling to one male after another. Before Virgil caught up with her, she had managed to announce her receptive condition to several of his rivals. When Virgil tried to grab her, Zizi screamed and dashed into the bushes with Virgil in hot pursuit. I heard sounds of chasing and fighting coming from the thicket. Moments later Zizi emerged from the bushes with an older male named Cyclops. They remained together for several days, copulating often. In Cyclops's presence, Zizi no longer approached or even glanced at other males.

Primatologists describe Zizi and other olive baboons (*Papio cynocephalus anubis*) as promiscuous, meaning that both males and females usually mate with several members of the opposite sex within a short period of time. Promiscuous mating behavior characterizes many of the larger, more familiar primates, including chimpanzees, rhesus macaques, and gray langurs, as well as olive, yellow, and chacma baboons, the three subspecies of savanna baboon. In colloquial usage, promiscuity often connotes wanton and random sex, and several early studies of primates supported this

Smuts, Barbara. "What Are Friends For" from Natural History (Feb. 1987):36, 38–44. Copyright © Natural History Magazine, Inc. 2006. Reprinted with permission.

stereotype. However, after years of laboriously recording thousands of copulations under natural conditions, the Peeping Toms of primate fieldwork have shown that, even in promiscuous species, sexual pairings are far from random.

Some adult males, for example, typically copulate much more often than others. Primatologists have explained these differences in terms of competition: the most dominant males monopolize females and prevent lower-ranking rivals from mating. But exceptions are frequent. Among baboons, the exceptions often involve scruffy, older males who mate in full view of younger, more dominant rivals.

A clue to the reason for these puzzling exceptions emerged when primatologists began to question an implicit assumption of the dominance hypothesis—that females were merely passive objects of male competition. But what if females were active arbiters in this system? If females preferred some males over others and were able to express these preferences, then models of mating activity based on male dominance alone would be far too simple.

Once researchers recognized the possibility of female choice, evidence for it turned up in species after species. The story of Zizi, Virgil, and Cyclops is one of hundreds of examples of female primates rejecting the sexual advances of particular males and enthusiastically cooperating with others. But what is the basis for female choice? Why might they prefer some males over others?

This question guided my research on the Eburru Cliffs troop of olive baboons, named after one of their favorite sleeping sites, a sheer rocky outcrop rising several hundred feet above the floor of the Great Rift Valley, about 100 miles northwest of Nairobi, Kenya. The 120 members of Eburru Cliffs spent their days wandering through open grassland studded with occasional acacia thorn trees. Each night they retired to one of a dozen sets of cliffs that provided protection from nocturnal predators such as leopards.

Most previous studies of baboon sexuality had focused on females who, like Zizi, were at the peak of sexual receptivity. A female baboon does not mate when she is pregnant or lactating, a period of abstinence lasting about eighteen months. The female then goes into estrus, and for about two weeks out of every thirty-five-day cycle, she mates. Toward the end of this two-week period she may ovulate, but usually the female undergoes four or five estrous cycles before she conceives. During pregnancy, she once again resumes a chaste existence. As a result, the typical female baboon is sexually active for less than 10 percent of her adult life. I thought that by focusing on the other 90 percent, I might learn something new. In particular, I suspected that routine, day-to-day relationships between males and pregnant or lactating (nonestrous) females might provide clues to female mating preferences.

Nearly every day for sixteen months, I joined the Eburru Cliffs baboons at their sleeping cliffs at dawn and traveled several miles with them while they foraged for roots, seeds, grass, and occasionally, small prey items, such as baby gazelles or hares (see "Predatory Baboons of Kekopey," *Natural History*, March 1976). Like all savanna baboon troops, Eburru Cliffs functioned as a cohesive unit organized around a core of related females, all of whom were born in the troop. Unlike the females, male savanna baboons leave their natal troop to join another where they may remain for many years, so most of the Eburru Cliffs adult males were immigrants. Since membership in the troop remained relatively constant during the period of my study, I learned to identify each individual. I relied on differences in size, posture, gait, and especially facial features. To the practiced observer, baboons look as different from one another as human beings do.

As soon as I could recognize individuals, I noticed that particular females tended to turn up near particular males again and again. I came to think of these pairs as friends. Friendship among animals is not a well-documented phenomenon, so to convince skeptical colleagues that baboon friendship was real, I needed to develop objective criteria for distinguishing friendly pairs.

I began by investigating grooming, the amiable simian habit of picking through a companion's fur to remove dead skin and ectoparasites (see "Little Things That Tick Off Baboons," *Natural History*, February 1984). Baboons spend much more time grooming than is necessary for hygiene, and previous research had indicated that it is a good measure of social bonds. Although eighteen adult males lived in the troop, each nonestrous female performed most of her grooming with just one, two, or occasionally three males. For example, of Zizi's twenty-four grooming bouts with males, Cyclops accounted for thirteen, and a second male, Sherlock, accounted for all the rest. Different females tended to favor different males as grooming partners.

Another measure of social bonds was simply who was observed near whom. When foraging, traveling, or resting, each pregnant or lactating female spent a lot of time near a few males and associated with the others no more often than expected by chance. When I compared the identities of favorite grooming partners and frequent companions, they overlapped almost completely. This enabled me to develop a formal definition of friendship: any male that scored high on both grooming and proximity measures was considered a friend.

Virtually all baboons made friends; only one female and the three males who had most recently joined the troop lacked such companions. Out of more than 600 possible adult female–adult male pairs in the troop, however, only about one in ten qualified as friends; these really were special relationships.

Several factors seemed to influence which baboons paired up. In most cases, friends were unrelated to each other, since the male had immigrated from another troop. (Four friendships, however, involved a female and an adolescent son who had not yet emigrated. Unlike other friends, these related pairs never mated.) Older females tended to be friends with older males; younger females with younger males. I witnessed occasional May–December romances, usually involving older females and young adult males. Adolescent males and females were strongly rule-bound, and with the exception of mother–son pairs, they formed friendships only with one another.

Regardless of age or dominance rank, most females had just one or two male friends. But among males, the number of female friends varied greatly from none to eight. Although high-ranking males enjoyed priority of access to food and sometimes mates, dominant males did not have more female friends than low-ranking males. Instead it was the older males who had lived in the troop for many years who had the most friends. When a male had several female friends, the females were often closely related to one another. Since female baboons spend a lot of time near their kin, it is probably easier for a male to maintain bonds with several related females at once.

When collecting data, I focused on one nonestrous female at a time and kept track of her every movement toward or away from any male; similarly, I noted every male who moved toward or away from her. Whenever the female and a male moved close enough to exchange intimacies, I wrote down exactly what happened. When foraging together, friends tended to remain a few yards apart. Males more often wandered away from females than the reverse, and females, more often than males, closed the gap. The female behaved as if she wanted to keep the male within calling distance, in case she needed his protection. The male, however, was more likely to make approaches that brought them within actual touching distance. Often, he would plunk himself down right next to his friend and ask her to groom him by holding a pose with exaggerated stillness. The female sometimes responded by grooming, but more often, she exhibited the most reliable sign of true intimacy: she ignored her friend and simply continued whatever she was doing.

In sharp contrast, when a male who was not a friend moved close to a female, she dared not ignore him. She stopped whatever she was doing and held still, often glancing surreptitiously at the intruder. If he did not move away, she sometimes lifted her tail and presented her rump. When a female is not in estrus, this is a gesture of appeasement, not sexual enticement. Immediately after this respectful acknowledgement of his presence, the female would slip away. But such tense interactions with nonfriend males were rare, because females usually moved away before the males came too close.

These observations suggest that females were afraid of most of the males in their troop, which is not surprising: male baboons are twice the size of females, and their canines are longer and sharper than those of a lion. All Eburru Cliffs males directed both mild and severe aggression toward females. Mild aggression, which usually involved threats and chases but no body contact, occurred most often during feeding competition or when the male redirected aggression toward a female after losing a fight with another male. Females and juveniles showed aggression toward other females and juveniles in similar circumstances and occasionally inflicted superficial wounds. Severe aggression by males, which involved body contact and sometimes biting, was less common and also more puzzling, since there was no apparent cause.

An explanation for at least some of these attacks emerged one day when I was watching Pegasus, a young adult male, and his friend Cicily, sitting together in the middle of a small clearing. Cicily moved to the edge of the clearing to feed, and a higher-ranking female, Zora, suddenly attacked her. Pegasus stood up and looked as if he were about to intervene when both females disappeared into the bushes. He sat back down, and I remained with him. A full ten minutes later, Zora appeared at the edge of the clearing; this was the first time she had come into view since her attack on Cicily. Pegasus instantly pounced on Zora, repeatedly grabbed her neck in his mouth and lifted her off the ground, shook her whole body, and then dropped her. Zora screamed continuously and tried to escape. Each time, Pegasus caught her and continued his brutal attack. When he finally released her five minutes later she had a deep canine gash on the palm of her hand that made her limp for several days.

This attack was similar in form and intensity to those I had seen before and labeled "unprovoked." Certainly, had I come upon the scene after Zora's aggression toward Cicily, I would not have understood why Pegasus attacked Zora. This suggested that some, perhaps many, severe attacks by males actually represented punishment for actions that had occurred some time before.

Whatever the reasons for male attacks on females, they represent a serious threat. Records of fresh injuries indicated that Eburru Cliffs adult females received canine slash wounds from males at the rate of one for every female each year, and during my study, one female died of her injuries. Males probably pose an even greater threat to infants. Although only one infant was killed during my study, observers in Botswana and Tanzania have seen recent male immigrants kill several young infants.

Protection from male aggression, and from the less injurious but more frequent aggression of other females and juveniles, seems to be one of the main advantages of friendship for a female baboon. Seventy times I observed an adult male defend a female or her offspring against aggression by another troop member, not infrequently a high-ranking male. In all but six of these cases, the defender was a friend. Very few of these confrontations involved actual fighting; no male baboon, subordinate or dominant, is anxious to risk injury by the sharp canines of another.

Males are particularly solicitous guardians of their friends' youngest infants. If another male gets too close to an infant or if a juvenile female plays with it too roughly, the friend may intervene. Other troop members soon learn to be cautious when the mother's friend is nearby, and his presence provides the mother with a welcome respite from the annoying pokes and prods of curious females and juveniles obsessed with the new baby. Male baboons at Gombe Park in Tanzania and Amboseli Park in Kenya have also been seen rescuing infants from chimpanzees and lions. These several forms of male protection help to explain why females in Eburru Cliffs stuck closer to their friends in the first few months after giving birth than at any other time.

The male–infant relationship develops out of the male's friendship with the mother, but as the infant matures, this new bond takes on a life of its own. My co-worker Nancy Nicolson found that by about nine months of age, infants actively sought out their male friends when the mother was a few yards away, suggesting that the male may function as an alternative caregiver. This seemed to be especially true for infants undergoing unusually early or severe weaning. (Weaning is generally a gradual, prolonged process, but there is tremendous variation among mothers in the timing and intensity of weaning. See "Mother Baboons," *Natural History,* September 1980.) After being rejected by the mother, the crying infant often approached the male friend and sat huddled against him until its whimpers subsided. Two of the infants in Eburru Cliffs lost their mothers when they were still quite young. In each case, their bond with the mother's friend subsequently intensified, and—perhaps as a result—both infants survived.

A close bond with a male may also improve the infant's nutrition. Larger than all other troop members, adult males monopolize the best feeding sites. In general, the personal space surrounding a feeding male is inviolate, but he usually tolerates intrusions by the infants of his female friends, giving them access to choice feeding spots.

Although infants follow their male friends around rather than the reverse, the males seem genuinely attached to their tiny companions. During feeding, the male and infant express their pleasure in each other's company by sharing spirited, antiphonal grunting duets. If the infant whimpers in distress, the male friend is likely to cease feeding, look at the infant, and grunt softly, as if in sympathy, until the whimpers cease. When the male rests, the infants of his female friends may huddle behind him, one after the other, forming a "train," or, if feeling energetic, they may use his body as a trampoline.

When I returned to Eburru Cliffs four years after my initial study ended, several of the bonds formed between males and the infants of their female friends were still intact (in other cases, either the male or the infant or both had disappeared). When these bonds involved recently matured females, their long-time male associates showed no sexual interest in them, even though the females mated with other adult males. Mothers and sons, and usually maternal siblings, show similar sexual inhibitions in baboons and many other primate species.

The development of an intimate relationship between a male and the infant of his female friend raises an obvious question: Is the male the infant's father? To answer this question definitely we would need to conduct genetic analysis, which was not possible for these baboons. Instead, I estimated paternity probabilities from observations of the temporary (a few hours or days) exclusive mating relationships, or consortships, that estrous females form with a series of different males. These estimates were apt to be fairly accurate, since changes in the female's sexual swelling allow one to pinpoint the timing of conception to within a few days. Most females consorted with only two or three males during this period, and these males were termed likely fathers.

In about half the friendships, the male was indeed likely to be the father of his friend's most recent infant, but in the other half he was not—in fact, he had never been seen mating with the female. Interestingly, males who were friends with the mother but not likely fathers nearly always developed a relationship with her infant, while males who had mated with the female but were not her friend usually did not. Thus friendship with the mother, rather than paternity, seems to mediate the development of male–infant bonds. Recently, a similar pattern was documented for South American capuchin monkeys in a laboratory study in which paternity was determined genetically.

These results fly in the face of a prominent theory that claims males will invest in infants only when they are closely related. If males are not fostering the survival of their own genes by caring for the infant, then why do they do so? I suspected that the key was female choice. If females preferred to mate with males who had already demonstrated friendly behavior, then friendships with mothers and their infants might pay off in the future when the mothers were ready to mate again.

To find out if this was the case, I examined each male's sexual behavior with females he had befriended before they resumed estrus. In most cases, males consorted considerably more often with their friends than with other females. Baboon females typically mate with several different males, including both friends and nonfriends, but prior friendship increased a male's probability of mating with a female above what it would have been otherwise.

This increased probability seemed to reflect female preferences. Females occasionally overtly advertised their disdain for certain males and their desire for others. Zizi's behavior, described above, is a good example. Virgil was not one of her friends, but Cyclops was. Usually, however, females expressed preferences and aversions more subtly. For example, Delphi, a petite adolescent female, found herself pursued by Hector, a middle-aged adult male. She did not run away or refuse to mate with him, but whenever he wasn't watching, she looked around for her friend Homer, an adolescent male. When she succeeded in catching Homer's eye, she narrowed her eyes and flattened her ears against her skull, the friendliest face one baboon can send another. This told Homer she would rather be with him. Females expressed satisfaction with a current consort partner by staying close to him, initiating copulations, and not making advances toward other males. Baboons are very sensitive to such cues, as indicated by an experimental study in which rival hamadryas baboons rarely challenged a male–female pair if the female strongly preferred her current partner. Similarly, in Eburru Cliffs, males were less apt to challenge consorts involving a pair that shared a long-term friendship.

Even though females usually consorted with their friends, they also mated with other males, so it is not surprising that friendships were most vulnerable during periods of sexual activity. In a few cases, the female consorted with another male more often than with her friend, but the friendship survived nevertheless. One female, however, formed a strong sexual bond with a new male. This bond persisted after conception, replacing her previous friendship. My observations suggest that adolescent and young adult females tend to have shorter, less stable friendships than do older females. Some friendships, however, last a very long time. When I returned to Eburru Cliffs six years after my study began, five couples were still together. It is possible that friendships occasionally last for life (baboons probably live twenty to thirty years in the wild), but it will require longer studies, and some very patient scientists, to find out.

By increasing both the male's chances of mating in the future and the likelihood that a female's infant will survive, friendship contributes to the reproductive success of both partners. This clarifies the evolutionary basis of friendship-forming tendencies in baboons, but what does friendship mean to a baboon? To answer this question we need to view baboons as sentient beings with feelings and goals not unlike our own in similar circumstances. Consider, for example, the friendship between Thalia and Alexander.

The affair began one evening as Alex and Thalia sat about fifteen feet apart on the sleeping cliffs. It was like watching two novices in a singles bar. Alex stared at Thalia until she turned and almost caught him looking at her. He glanced away immediately, and then she stared at him until his head began to turn toward her. She suddenly became engrossed in grooming her toes. But as soon as Alex looked away, her gaze returned to him. They went on like this for more than fifteen minutes, always with split-second timing. Finally, Alex managed to catch Thalia looking at him. He made the friendly eyes-narrowed, ears-back face and smacked his lips together rhythmically. Thalia froze, and for a second she looked into his eyes. Alex approached, and Thalia, still nervous, groomed him. Soon she calmed down, and I found them still together on the cliffs the next morning. Looking back on this event months later, I realized that it marked the beginning of their friendship. Six years later, when I returned to Eburru Cliffs, they were still friends.

If flirtation forms an integral part of baboon friendship, so does jealousy. Overt displays of jealousy, such as chasing a friend away from a potential rival, occur occasionally, but like humans, baboons often express their emotions in more subtle ways. One evening a colleague and I climbed the cliffs and settled down near Sherlock, who was friends with Cybelle, a middle-aged female still foraging on the ground below the cliffs. I observed Cybelle while my colleague watched Sherlock, and we kept up a running commentary. As long as Cybelle was feeding or interacting with females, Sherlock was relaxed, but each time she approached another male, his body would stiffen, and he would stare intently at the scene below. When Cybelle presented politely to a male who had recently tried to befriend her, Sherlock even made threatening sounds under his breath. Cybelle was not in estrus at the time, indicating that male baboon jealousy extends beyond the sexual arena to include affiliative interactions between a female friend and other males.

Because baboon friendships are embedded in a network of friendly and antagonistic relationships, they inevitably lead to repercussions extending beyond the pair. For example, Virgil once provoked his weaker rival Cyclops into a fight by first attacking Cyclops's friend Phoebe. On another occasion, Sherlock chased Circe, Hector's best friend, just after Hector had chased Antigone, Sherlock's friend.

In another incident, the prime adult male Triton challenged Cyclops's possession of meat. Cyclops grew increasingly tense and seemed about to abandon the prey to the younger male. Then Cyclops's friend Phoebe appeared with her infant Phyllis. Phyllis wandered over to Cyclops. He immediately grabbed her, held her close, and threatened Triton away from the prey. Because any challenge to Cyclops now involved a threat to Phyllis as well, Triton risked being mobbed by Phoebe and her relatives and friends. For this reason, he backed down. Males frequently use the infants of their female friends as buffers in this way. Thus, friendship involves costs as well as benefits because it makes the participants vulnerable to social manipulation or redirected aggression by others.

Finally, as with humans, friendship seems to mean something different to each baboon. Several females in Eburru Cliffs had only one friend. They were devoted companions. Louise and Pandora, for example, groomed their friend Virgil and no other male. Then there was Leda, who, with five friends, spread herself more thinly than any other female. These contrasting patterns of friendship were associated with striking personality differences. Louise and Pandora were unobtrusive females who hung around quietly with Virgil and their close relatives. Leda seemed to be everywhere at once, playing with infants, fighting with juveniles, and making friends with males. Similar differences were apparent among the males. Some devoted a great deal of time and energy to cultivating friendships with females, while others focused more on challenging other males. Although we probably will never fully understand the basis of these individual differences, they contribute immeasurably to the richness and complexity of baboon society.

Male–female friendships may be widespread among primates. They have been reported for many other groups of savanna baboons, and they also occur in rhesus and Japanese macaques, capuchin monkeys, and perhaps in bonobos (pygmy chimpanzees). These relationships should give us pause when considering popular scenarios for the evolution of male–female relationships in humans. Most of these scenarios assume that, except for mating, males and females had little to do with one another until the development of a sexual division of labor, when, the story goes, females began to rely on males to provide meat in exchange for gathered food. This, it has been argued, set up new selection pressures favoring the development of long-term bonds between individual males and females, female sexual fidelity, and as paternity certainty increased, greater male investment in the offspring of these unions. In other words, once women began to gather and men to hunt, presto—we had the nuclear family.

This scenario may have more to do with cultural biases about women's economic dependence on men and idealized views of the nuclear family than with the actual behavior of our hominid ancestors. The nonhuman primate evidence challenges this story in at least three ways.

First, long-term bonds between the sexes can evolve in the absence of a sexual division of labor or food sharing. In our primate relatives, such relationships rest on exchanges of social, not economic, benefits.

Second, primate research shows that highly differentiated, emotionally intense male–female relationships can occur without sexual exclusivity. Ancestral men and women may have experienced intimate friendships long before they invented marriage and norms of sexual fidelity.

Third, among our closest primate relatives, males clearly provide mothers and infants with social benefits even when they are unlikely to be the fathers of those infants. In return, females provide a variety of benefits to the friendly males, including acceptance into the group and, at least in baboons, increased mating opportunities in the future. This suggests that efforts to reconstruct the evolution of hominid societies may have overemphasized what the female must supposedly do (restrict her mating to just one male) in order to obtain male parental investment.

Maybe it is time to pay more attention to what the male must do (provide benefits to females and young) in order to obtain female cooperation. Perhaps among our ancestors, as in baboons today, sex and friendship went hand in hand. As for marriage—well, that's another story.

5

Mothers and Others

Sarah Blaffer Hrdy

Ethnocentrism is everywhere; it affects our views of human nature. In North America and the West, we have grown up with beliefs about our species' emergence as mighty hunters. As such, there is a cultural self-image of "man the hunter" as master of nature. Similarly, we have cultural ideas of the original human society as characterized by the division of labor in two spheres of primordial importance: subsistence (bringing home the bacon) and breeding, nourishing, and nurturing (homemaking). Our imaginary view of our ancestors, shaped by our self-image, can result in depictions like *The Flintstones*. For example, we have assumed that women stayed at home by their campfires nurturing the young while men set off to hunt big game and make war on their neighbors— other bands of "primitive" hunters. We have typically assumed that prehistoric men hunted in groups, whereas women, despite cooperation in communal food gathering, individually nursed and otherwise nourished their children.

But is this Western-style nuclear family, with our traditional division of labor between mothers and fathers or between mothers and neighbors, the natural human adaptation that emerged from our biological heritage? Or does the evolutionary record, and observations of our closest biological kin, point in other directions?

Theories and observations of both nonhuman primates as well as hunter-gatherer societies may cast doubt on our long-held ideas about the past. This selection examines both biological and cultural mechanisms that engender *cooperation* in child rearing. The argument presented here emphasizes the importance of social cooperation in child rearing both for individuals and for society as a whole.

This is a new way of thinking about our "human nature." Thinking about humans and some other primates as "cooperative breeders" has fascinating implications for child rearing and gender roles, the critical importance of kin groups, and the practices and policies for our ever-expanding day-care system.

As you read this selection, ask yourself the following questions:

- In what ways do human infants and children differ from the young of nonhuman primates such as chimpanzees, gorillas, and orangutans?
- How do Western habits of child care in individual nuclear families differ from the practices of many other cultures? Do we put too much pressure on individual mothers to do everything as the so-called supermom?
- How does the belief in *partible paternity* affect cultural beliefs about sex and marriage and increased support for children?
- According to Hrdy, what are three ways that humans are motivated to protect and care for babies?
- How are hormones affected by nurturing, even in fathers and other males?
- What does this theory suggest about day-care policies? Extended families? Supermoms? Child abuse?

The following terms discussed in this selection are included in the Glossary at the back of the book:

gestation	Pleistocene
matrilineal	primate
parturient	sociobiology

Mother apes—chimpanzees, gorillas, orangutans, humans—dote on their babies. And why not? They give birth to an infant after a long gestation and, in

most cases, suckle it for years. With humans, however, the job of providing for a juvenile goes on and on. Unlike all other ape babies, ours mature slowly and reach independence late. A mother in a foraging society may give birth every four years or so, and her first few children remain dependent long after each new baby arrives; among nomadic foragers, grown-ups may provide food to children for eighteen or more years. To

"Mothers and Others" by Sarah Blaffer Hrdy from Co-operation, Empathy, and the Needs of Human Infants. Delivered as a Tanner Lecture on Human Values. Printed with permission of the Tanner Lectures on Human Values, a Corporation, University of Utah, Salt Lake City, Utah.

come up with the 10–13 million calories that anthropologists such as Hillard Kaplan calculate are needed to rear a young human to independence, a mother needs help.

So how did our prehuman and early human ancestresses living in the Pleistocene Epoch (from 1.6 million until roughly 10,000 years ago) manage to get those calories? And under what conditions would natural selection allow a female ape to produce babies so large and slow to develop that they are beyond her means to rear on her own?

The old answer was that fathers helped out by hunting. And so they do. But hunting is a risky occupation, and fathers may die or defect or take up with other females. And when they do, what then? New evidence from surviving traditional cultures suggests that mothers in the Pleistocene may have had a significant degree of help—from men who thought they just might have been the fathers, from grandmothers and great-aunts, from older children.

These helpers other than the mother, called allomothers by sociobiologists, do not just protect and provision youngsters. In groups such as the Efe and Aka Pygmies of central Africa, allomothers actually hold children and carry them about. In these tight-knit communities of communal foragers—within which men, women, and children still hunt with nets, much as humans are thought to have done tens of thousands of years ago—siblings, aunts, uncles, fathers, and grandmothers hold newborns on the first day of life. When University of New Mexico anthropologist Paula Ivey asked an Efe woman, "Who cares for babies?" the immediate answer was, "We all do!" By three weeks of age, the babies are in contact with allomothers 40 percent of the time. By eighteen weeks, infants actually spend more time with allomothers than with their gestational mothers. On average, Efe babies have fourteen different caretakers, most of whom are close kin. According to Washington State University anthropologist Barry Hewlett, Aka babies are within arm's reach of their fathers for more than half of every day.

Accustomed to celebrating the antiquity and naturalness of mother-centered models of child care, as well as the nuclear family in which the mother nurtures while the father provides, we Westerners tend to regard the practices of the Efe and the Aka as exotic. But to sociobiologists, whose stock in trade is comparisons across species, all this helping has a familiar ring. It's called cooperative breeding. During the past quarter century, as anthropologists and sociobiologists started to compare notes, one of the spectacular surprises has been how much allomaternal care goes on, not just within various human societies but among animals generally. Evidently, diverse organisms have converged on cooperative breeding for the best of evolutionary reasons.

A broad look at the most recent evidence has convinced me that cooperative breeding was the strategy that permitted our own ancestors to produce costly, slow-maturing infants at shorter intervals, to take advantage of new kinds of resources in habitats other than the mixed savanna-woodland of tropical Africa, and to spread more widely and swiftly than any primate had before. We already know that animal mothers who delegate some of the costs of infant care to others are thereby freed to produce more or larger young or to breed more frequently. Consider the case of silver-backed jackals. Patricia Moehlman, of the World Conservation Union, has shown that for every extra helper bringing back food, jackal parents rear one extra pup per litter. Cooperative breeding also helps various species expand into habitats in which they would normally not be able to rear any young at all. Florida scrub-jays, for example, breed in an exposed landscape where unrelenting predation from hawks and snakes usually precludes the fledging of young; survival in this habitat is possible only because older siblings help guard and feed the young. Such cooperative arrangements permit animals as different as naked mole rats (the social insects of the mammal world) and wolves to move into new habitats and sometimes to spread over vast areas.

What does it take to become a cooperative breeder? Obviously, this lifestyle is an option only for creatures capable of living in groups. It is facilitated when young but fully mature individuals (such as young Florida scrub-jays) do not or cannot immediately leave their natal group to breed on their own and instead remain among kin in their natal location. As with delayed maturation, delayed dispersal of young means that teenagers, "spinster" aunts, real and honorary uncles will be on hand to help their kin rear young. Flexibility is another criterion for cooperative breeders. Helpers must be ready to shift to breeding mode should the opportunity arise. In marmosets and tamarins—the little South American monkeys that are, besides us, the only full-fledged cooperative breeders among primates—a female has to be ready to be a helper this year and a mother the next. She may have one mate or several. In canids such as wolves or wild dogs, usually only the dominant, or alpha, male and female in a pack reproduce, but younger group members hunt with the mother and return to the den to regurgitate predigested meat into the mouths of her pups. In a fascinating instance of physiological flexibility, a subordinate female may actually undergo hormonal transformations similar to those of a real pregnancy: her belly swells, and she begins to manufacture milk and may help nurse the pups of the alpha pair. Vestiges of cooperative breeding crop up as well in domestic dogs, the distant descendants of wolves. After undergoing a pseudopregnancy, my neighbors'

Jack Russell terrier chased away the family's cat and adopted and suckled her kittens. To suckle the young of another species is hardly what Darwinians call an adaptive trait (because it does not contribute to the surrogate's own survival). But in the environment in which the dog family evolved, a female's tendency to respond when infants signaled their need—combined with her capacity for pseudopregnancy—would have increased the survival chances for large litters born to the dominant female.

According to the late W. D. Hamilton, evolutionary logic predicts that an animal with poor prospects of reproducing on his or her own should be predisposed to assist kin with better prospects so that at least some of their shared genes will be perpetuated. Among wolves, for example, both male and female helpers in the pack are likely to be genetically related to the alpha litter and to have good reasons for not trying to reproduce on their own: in a number of cooperatively breeding species (wild dogs, wolves, hyenas, dingoes, dwarf mongooses, marmosets), the helpers do try, but the dominant female is likely to bite their babies to death. The threat of coercion makes postponing ovulation the better part of valor, the least-bad option for females who must wait to breed until their circumstances improve, either through the death of a higher-ranking female or by finding a mate with an unoccupied territory.

One primate strategy is to line up extra fathers. Among common marmosets and several species of tamarins, females mate with several males, all of which help rear her young. As primatologist Charles T. Snowdon points out, in three of the four genera of Callitrichidae (*Callithrix, Saguinus,* and *Leontopithecus*), the more adult males the group has available to help, the more young survive. Among many of these species, females ovulate just after giving birth, perhaps encouraging males to stick around until after babies are born. (In cotton-top tamarins, males also undergo hormonal changes that prepare them to care for infants at the time of birth.) Among cooperative breeders of certain other species, such as wolves and jackals, pups born in the same litter can be sired by different fathers.

Human mothers, by contrast, don't ovulate again right after birth, nor do they produce offspring with more than one genetic father at a time. Ever inventive, though, humans solve the problem of enlisting help from several adult males by other means. In some cultures, mothers rely on a peculiar belief that anthropologists call partible paternity—the notion that a fetus is built up by contributions of semen from all the men with whom women have had sex in the ten months or so prior to giving birth. Among the Canela, a matrilineal tribe in Brazil studied for many years by William Crocker of the Smithsonian Institution,

publicly sanctioned intercourse between women and men other than their husbands—sometimes many men—takes place during villagewide ceremonies. What might lead to marital disaster elsewhere works among the Canela because the men believe in partible paternity. Across a broad swath of South America—from Paraguay up into Brazil, westward to Peru, and northward to Venezuela—mothers rely on this convenient folk wisdom to line up multiple honorary fathers to help them provision both themselves and their children. Over hundreds of generations, this belief has helped children thrive in a part of the world where food sources are unpredictable and where husbands are as likely as not to return from the hunt empty-handed.

The Bari people of Venezuela are among those who believe in shared paternity, and according to anthropologist Stephen Beckerman, Bari children with more than one father do especially well. In Beckerman's study of 822 children, 80 percent of those who had both a "primary" father (the man married to their mother) and a "secondary" father survived to age fifteen, compared with 64 percent survival for those with a primary father alone. Not surprisingly, as soon as a Bari woman suspects she is pregnant, she accepts sexual advances from the more successful fishermen or hunters in her group. Belief that fatherhood can be shared draws more men into the web of possible paternity, which effectively translates into more food and more protection.

But for human mothers, extra mates aren't the only source of effective help. Older children, too, play a significant role in family survival. University of Nebraska anthropologists Patricia Draper and Raymond Hames have just shown that among !Kung hunters and gatherers living in the Kalahari Desert, there is a significant correlation between how many children a parent successfully raises and how many older siblings were on hand to help during that person's own childhood.

Older matrilineal kin may be the most valuable helpers of all. University of Utah anthropologists Kristen Hawkes and James O'Connell and their UCLA colleague Nicholas Blurton Jones, who have demonstrated the important food-gathering role of older women among Hazda hunter-gatherers in Tanzania, delight in explaining that since human life spans may extend for a few decades after menopause, older women become available to care for—and to provide vital food for—children born to younger kin. Hawkes, O'Connell, and Blurton Jones further believe that dating from the earliest days of *Homo erectus,* the survival of weaned children during food shortages may have depended on tubers dug up by older kin.

At various times in human history, people have also relied on a range of customs, as well as on coercion, to line up allomaternal assistance—for example, by using slaves or hiring poor women as wet nurses. But all the helpers in the world are of no use if they're not motivated to protect, carry, or provision babies. For both humans and nonhumans, this motivation arises in three main ways: through the manipulation of information about kinship; through appealing signals coming from the babies themselves; and, at the heart of it all, from the endocrinological and neural processes that induce individuals to respond to infants' signals. Indeed, all primates and many other mammals eventually respond to infants in a nurturing way if exposed long enough to their signals. Trouble is, "long enough" can mean very different things in males and females, with their very different response thresholds.

For decades, animal behaviorists have been aware of the phenomenon known as priming. A mouse or rat encountering a strange pup is likely to respond by either ignoring the pup or eating it. But presented with pup after pup, rodents of either sex eventually become sensitized to the baby and start caring for it. Even a male may gather pups into a nest and lick or huddle over them. Although nurturing is not a routine part of a male's repertoire, when sufficiently primed he behaves as a mother would. Hormonal change is an obvious candidate for explaining this transformation. Consider the case of the cooperatively breeding Florida scrub-jays studied by Stephan Schoech, of the University of Memphis. Prolactin, a protein hormone that initiates the secretion of milk in female mammals, is also present in male mammals and in birds of both sexes. Schoech showed that levels of prolactin go up in a male and female jay as they build their nest and incubate eggs and that these levels reach a peak when they feed their young. Moreover, prolactin levels rise in the jays' nonbreeding helpers and are also at their highest when they assist in feeding nestlings.

As it happens, male, as well as immature and nonbreeding female, primates can respond to infants' signals, although quite different levels of exposure and stimulation are required to get them going. Twenty years ago, when elevated prolactin levels were first reported in common marmoset males (by Alan Dixson, for *Callithrix jacchus*), many scientists refused to believe it. Later, when the finding was confirmed, scientists assumed this effect would be found only in fathers. But based on work by Scott Nunes, Jeffrey Fite, Jeffrey French, Charles Snowdon, Lucille Roberts, and many others—work that deals with a variety of species of marmosets and tamarins—we now know that all sorts of hormonal changes are associated with increased nurturing in males. For example, in the tufted-eared marmosets studied by French and colleagues, testosterone levels in males went down as they engaged in caretaking after the birth of an infant. Testosterone levels

tended to be lowest in those with the most paternal experience.

The biggest surprise, however, has been that something similar goes on in males of our own species. Anne Storey and colleagues in Canada have reported that prolactin levels in men who were living with pregnant women went up toward the end of the pregnancy. But the most significant finding was a 30 percent drop in testosterone in men right after the birth. (Some endocrinologically literate wags have proposed that this drop in testosterone levels is due to sleep deprivation, but this would probably not explain the parallel testosterone drop in marmoset males housed with parturient females.) Hormonal changes during pregnancy and lactation are, of course, indisputably more pronounced in mothers than in the men consorting with them, and no one is suggesting that male consorts are equivalent to mothers. But both sexes are surprisingly susceptible to infant signals—explaining why fathers, adoptive parents, wet nurses, and day-care workers can become deeply involved with the infants they care for.

Genetic relatedness alone, in fact, is a surprisingly unreliable predictor of love. What matters are cues from infants and how these cues are processed emotionally. The capacity for becoming emotionally hooked—or primed—also explains how a fully engaged father who is in frequent contact with his infant can become more committed to the infant's well-being than a detached mother will.

But we can't forget the real protagonist of this story: the baby. From birth, newborns are powerfully motivated to stay close, to root—even to creep—in quest of nipples, which they instinctively suck on. These are the first innate behaviors that any of us engage in. But maintaining contact is harder for little humans to do than it is for other primates. One problem is that human mothers are not very hairy, so a human mother not only has to position the baby on her breast but also has to keep him there. She must be motivated to pick up her baby even *before* her milk comes in, bringing with it a host of hormonal transformations.

Within minutes of birth, human babies can cry and vocalize just as other primates do, but human newborns can also read facial expressions and make a few of their own. Even with blurry vision, they engage in eye-to-eye contact with the people around them. Newborn babies, when alert, can see about eighteen inches away. When people put their faces within range, babies may reward this attention by looking back or even imitating facial expressions. Orang and chimp babies, too, are strongly attached to and interested in their mothers' faces. But unlike humans, other ape mothers and infants do not get absorbed in gazing deeply into each other's eyes.

To the extent that psychiatrists and pediatricians have thought about this difference between us and the other apes, they tend to attribute it to human mental agility and our ability to use language. Interactions between mother and baby, including vocal play and babbling, have been interpreted as protoconversations: revving up the baby to learn to talk. Yet even babies who lack face-to-face stimulation—babies born blind, say—learn to talk. Furthermore, humans are not the only primates to engage in the continuous rhythmic streams of vocalization known as babbling. Interestingly, marmoset and tamarin babies also babble. It may be that the infants of cooperative breeders are specially equipped to communicate with caretakers. This is not to say that babbling is not an important part of learning to talk, only to question which came first—babbling so as to develop into a talker, or a predisposition to evolve into a talker because among cooperative breeders, babies that babble are better tended and more likely to survive.

If humans evolved as cooperative breeders, the degree of a human mother's commitment to her infant should be linked to how much social support she herself can expect. Mothers in cooperatively breeding primate species can afford to bear and rear such costly offspring as they do only if they have help on hand. Maternal abandonment and abuse are very rarely observed among primates in the wild. In fact, the only primate species in which mothers are anywhere near as likely to abandon infants at birth as mothers of our own species are the other cooperative breeders. A study of cotton-top tamarins at the New England Regional Primate Research Center showed a 12 percent chance of abandonment if mothers had older siblings on hand to help them rear twins, but a 57 percent chance when no help was available. Overburdened mothers abandoned infants within seventy-two hours after birth.

This new way of thinking about our species' history, with its implications for children, has made me concerned about the future. So far, most Western researchers studying infant development have presumed that living in a nuclear family with a fixed division of labor (mom nurturing, dad providing) is the normal human adaptation. Most contemporary research on children's psychosocial development is derived from John Bowlby's theories of attachment and has focused on such variables as how available and responsive the mother is, whether the father is present or absent, and whether the child is in the mother's care or in day care. Sure enough, studies done with this model in mind always show that children with less responsive mothers are at greater risk.

It is the baby, first and foremost, who senses how available and how committed its mother is. But I know of no studies that take into account the possibility that humans evolved as cooperative breeders and that a mother's responsiveness also happens to be a good indicator of her social supports. In terms of developmental outcomes, the most relevant factor might not be how securely or insecurely attached to the mother the baby is—the variable that developmental psychologists are trained to measure—but rather how secure the baby is in relation to *all* the people caring for him or her. Measuring attachment this way might help explain why even children whose relations with their mother suggest they are at extreme risk manage to do just fine because of the interventions of a committed father, an older sibling, or a there-when-you-need-her grandmother.

The most comprehensive study ever done on how nonmaternal care affects kids is compatible with both the hypothesis that humans evolved as cooperative breeders and the conventional hypothesis that human babies are adapted to be reared exclusively by mothers. Undertaken by the National Institute of Child Health and Human Development (NICHD) in 1991, the seven-year study included 1,364 children and their families (from diverse ethnic and economic backgrounds) and was conducted in ten different U.S. locations. This extraordinarily ambitious study was launched because statistics showed that 62 percent of U.S. mothers with children under age six were working outside the home and that the majority of them (willingly or unwillingly) were back at work within three to five months of giving birth. Because this was an entirely new social phenomenon, no one really knew what the NICHD's research would reveal.

The study's main finding was that both maternal and hired caretakers' sensitivity to infant needs was a better predictor of a child's subsequent development and behavior (such traits as social "compliance," respect for others, and self-control were measured) than was actual time spent apart from the mother. In other words, the crucial variable was not the continuous presence of the mother herself but rather how secure infants felt when cared for by someone else. People who had been convinced that babies need full-time care from mothers to develop normally were stunned by these results, while advocates of day care felt vindicated. But do these and other, similar findings mean that day care is not something we need to worry about anymore?

Not at all. We should keep worrying. The NICHD study showed only that day care was better than mother care if the mother was neglectful or abusive. But excluding such worst-case scenarios, the study showed no detectable ill effects from day care *only* when infants had a secure relationship with parents to begin with (which I take to mean that babies felt wanted) and *only* when the day care was of high quality. And in this study's context, "high quality" meant that the facility had a high ratio of caretakers to babies, that it had the same caretakers all the time, and that the caretakers were sensitive to infants' needs—in other words, that the day care staff acted like committed kin.

Bluntly put, this kind of day care is almost impossible to find. Where it exists at all, it's expensive. Waiting lists are long, even for cheap or inadequate care. The average rate of staff turnover in day care centers is 30 percent per year, primarily because these workers are paid barely the minimum wage (usually less, in fact, than parking-lot attendants). Furthermore, day care tends to be age-graded, so even at centers where staff members stay put, kids move annually to new teachers. This kind of day care is unlikely to foster trusting relationships.

What conclusion can we draw from all this? Instead of arguing over mother-care versus "other care," we need to make day care better. And this is where I think today's evolution-minded researchers have something to say. Impressed by just how variable child-rearing conditions can be in human societies, several anthropologists and psychologists (including Michael Lamb, Patricia Draper, Henry Harpending, and James Chisholm) have suggested that babies are up to more than just maintaining the relationship with their mothers. These researchers propose that babies actually monitor mothers to gain information about the world they have been born into. Babies ask, in effect, Is this world filled with people who are going to provide for me and help me survive? Can I count on them to care about me? If the answer to those questions is yes, they begin to sense that developing a conscience and a capacity for compassion would be a great idea. If the answer is no, they may then be asking, Can I not afford to count on others? Would I be better off just grabbing what I need, however I can? In this case, empathy, or thinking about others' needs, would be more of a hindrance than a help.

For a developing baby and child, the most practical way to behave might vary drastically, depending on whether the mother has kin who help, whether the father is around, whether foster parents are well-meaning or exploitative. These factors, however unconsciously perceived by the child, affect important developmental decisions. Being extremely self-centered or selfish, being oblivious to others or lacking in conscience—traits that psychologists and child-development theorists may view as pathological—are probably quite adaptive traits for an individual who is short on support from other group members.

If I am right that humans evolved as cooperative breeders, Pleistocene babies whose mothers lacked social support and were less than fully committed to infant care would have been unlikely to survive. But once people started to settle down—10,000 or 20,000 or perhaps 30,000 years ago—the picture changed. Ironically, survival chances for neglected children increased. As people lingered longer in one place, eliminated predators, built walled houses, stored food—not to mention inventing things such as rubber nipples and pasteurized milk—infant survival became decoupled from continuous contact with a caregiver.

Since the end of the Pleistocene, whether in preindustrial or industrialized environments, some children have been surviving levels of social neglect that previously would have meant certain death. Some children get very little attention, even in the most benign of contemporary homes. In the industrialized world, children routinely survive caretaking practices that an Efe or a !Kung mother would find appallingly negligent. In traditional societies, no decent mother leaves her baby alone at any time, and traditional mothers are shocked to learn that Western mothers leave infants unattended in a crib all night.

Without passing judgment, one may point out that only in the recent history of humankind could infants deprived of supportive human contact survive to reproduce themselves. Certainly there are a lot of humanitarian reasons to worry about this situation: one wants each baby, each child, to be lovingly cared for. From my evolutionary perspective, though, even more is at stake.

Even if we manage to survive what most people are worrying about—global warming, emergent diseases, rogue viruses, meteorites crashing into earth—will we still be human thousands of years down the line? By that I mean human in the way we currently define ourselves. The reason our species has managed to survive and proliferate to the extent that 6 billion people currently occupy the planet has to do with how readily we can learn to cooperate when we want to. And our capacity for empathy is one of the things that make us good at doing that.

At a rudimentary level, of course, all sorts of creatures are good at reading intentions and movements and anticipating what other animals are going to do. Predators from gopher snakes to lions have to be able to anticipate where their quarry will dart. Chimps and gorillas can figure out what another individual is likely to know or not know. But compared with that of humans this capacity to entertain the psychological perspective of other individuals is crude.

The capacity for empathy is uniquely well developed in our species, so much so that many people (including me) believe that along with language and symbolic thought, it is what makes us human. We are capable of compassion, of understanding other people's "fears and motives, their longings and griefs and vanities," as novelist Edmund White puts it. We spend time and energy worrying about people we have never even met, about babies left in dumpsters, about the existence of more than 12 million AIDS orphans in Africa.

Psychologists know that there is a heritable component to emotional capacity and that this affects the development of compassion among individuals. By fourteen months of age, identical twins (who share all genes) are more alike in how they react to an experimenter who pretends to painfully pinch her finger on a clipboard than are fraternal twins (who share only half their genes). But empathy also has a learned component, which has more to do with analytical skills. During the first years of life, within the context of early relationships with mothers and other committed caretakers, each individual learns to look at the world from someone else's perspective.

And this is why I get so worried. Just because humans have evolved to be smart enough to chronicle our species' histories, to speculate about its origins, and to figure out that we have about 30,000 genes in our genome is no reason to assume that evolution has come to a standstill. As gene frequencies change,

natural selection acts on the outcome: the expression of those genes. No one doubts, for instance, that fish benefit from being able to see. Yet species reared in total darkness—as are the small cave-dwelling characin of Mexico—fail to develop their visual capacity. Through evolutionary time, traits that are unexpressed are eventually lost. If populations of these fish are isolated in caves long enough, youngsters descended from those original populations will no longer be able to develop eyesight at all, even if reared in sunlight.

If human compassion develops under particular rearing conditions, and if an increasing proportion of the species survives to breeding age without developing compassion, it won't make any difference how useful this trait was among our ancestors. It will become like sight in cave-dwelling fish.

No doubt our descendants thousands of years from now (should our species survive) will still be bipedal, symbol-generating apes. Most likely they will be adept at using sophisticated technologies. But will they still be human in the way we, shaped by a long heritage of cooperative breeding, currently define ourselves?

6

Great Mysteries of Human Evolution

Carl Zimmer

Paleoanthropology—the discovery, description, and analysis of the fossil evidence of human evolution—is an important branch of biological anthropology. The methods of paleontology and skeletal biology are used to understand the distant biological prehistory of our hominid ancestors. The fossils of hominids are relatively hard to find compared to, for example, the fossils of other species like horses. In fact, paleontologists have traced the evolution of the modern horse throughout the Cenozoic era (the age of mammals) in great detail. Although it might be easier to study the evolution of other species, it seems "natural" that we are more interested in the prehistory of humans. Human evolution has been a subject surrounded by controversy—not only because of religious beliefs as seen in Selection 1, but also because there have been so many debates about the interpretation of the fossils. There has been an incredible increase in the number of hominid fossils found in recent years. These are facts—hard as stone—that provide clues for understanding the distant past. As in all areas of science, the more we discover, the more questions we can generate about the complexities of our biological history.

This selection considers some of the serious questions that continue to puzzle paleoanthropologists about our hominid origins. Despite the tremendous increase in the number of fossil hominids, the origins and evolutionary history of the human line are still unclear. These discoveries have shown that hominid evolution was a complicated process and not a unilinear stairway of species on their way to becoming modern *Homo sapiens*. We know about humans' upright posture; their large, modern brains; and their use of tools; but we do not necessarily understand why or how those adaptations arose. The author considers eight mysteries about what makes us human, and the paleoanthropological evidence that exists to answer those questions.

As you read this selection, ask yourself the following questions:

- Why do people like to think that human evolution is a grand story of linear progression rather than a complex history of multiple species?
- Why does the author think questions about human origins are important? Why are they so difficult to answer?
- How, and why, does the author think humans are so different from other primates?
- What arguments does the author offer to explain why *Homo sapiens* ultimately emerged as the sole remaining hominid species?

The following terms discussed in this selection are included in the Glossary at the back of the book:

> adaptations
> *Australopithecus afarensis*
> bipedal
> *FOXP2*
> *Homo erectus*
> *Homo ergaster*
> *Homo neanderthalensis* (Neaderthals)
> *Sahelanthropus tchadensis*

Everything you do has a history. You wake up each morning and get out of bed using an anatomy that allowed your ancestors to stand upright at least 4 million years ago. You go to the kitchen and eat cereal with a bowl and spoon that are part of a toolmaking tradition at least 2.5 million years old. As you munch your cereal, you page through the newspaper, which you can understand thanks to a brain capable of language, abstract thought, and prodigious memory—a brain that has been expanding for 2 million years.

Until a few decades ago, most of that evolutionary history was hidden from science's view. But these days hardly a month goes by without news of a significant discovery. Paleoanthropologists keep digging up new

Zimmer, Carl. "Great Mysteries of Human Evolution." Discover Magazine (Sept. 2003):34–43. Reprinted with permission of the author.

fossils of our ancestors, and some of those fossils have even yielded DNA fragments. Meanwhile, geneticists have compiled a veritable encyclopedia of evolution—the sequenced human genome—and within a few years they'll be able to compare it with the genome of one of our closest living relatives, the common chimpanzee. Still, what we don't know about our evolution vastly outweighs what we do know. Age-old questions defy a full accounting, and new discoveries introduce new questions. That's not unusual for any field of science, but the eight mysteries on the following pages are intimate ones, because understanding our origins is key to understanding ourselves.

WHO WAS THE FIRST HOMINID?

Time travel would make everything so much easier. Imagine that you could drop down by an African lake some 7 million years ago and watch the parade of aardvarks, antelopes, and elephants pass by until, sooner or later, you caught sight of a group of apes. They'd probably look something like chimpanzees—about the same height, with the same coat of hair—but their flat faces and the other odd proportions of their bodies would indicate that they belong to a different species. Perhaps they would turn your way and look you in the eye—a gaze from your most distant hominid ancestors, the first primates to split off from the other apes and begin the family that produced us. Such are the daydreams paleoanthropologists indulge in as they endure blazing heat, merciless sandstorms, and years of fruitless fieldwork.

If the earliest hominids were anything like chimps, bonobos, and other living apes, each species may have numbered in the hundreds of thousands, even millions. But few left fossils behind. Most of their bones were scavenged and scattered by hyenas or other animals, and what little remained rotted. When it comes to early hominids, paleoanthropologists have to make do with a few teeth or skull fragments.

Yet paleoanthropologists are learning a lot about our origins. Not long ago, the oldest known hominid was *Australopithecus afarensis,* a species that walked the savannas of East Africa around 3.6 million years ago and is best known from one well-preserved female skeleton found in Ethiopia in 1974 and nicknamed Lucy. In recent years, paleoanthropologists have found perhaps as many as five species that are older than *A. afarensis*—in some cases much older. Just last year, Michel Brunet of the University of Poitiers, in France, and his team of explorers announced that amid the sand dunes of the Sahara they had found a species between 6 million and 7 million years old: *Sahelanthropus tchadensis.*

These new fossils have thrown cherished orthodoxies into question. "We saw human evolution as a nice, straight line," says Leslie Aiello of University College London. Now some researchers are arguing that human evolution looked more like a bush, with lots of species branching off in different directions.

No new orthodoxy has gained enough strength yet to take over the old one. Instead, there's lots of debate. Some paleoanthropologists, for example, have declared *Sahelanthropus* to be on the line that led to gorillas, not humans. "That's crazy," replies Brunet, who points to small teeth and other key traits that link the creature with hominids rather than apes. But while Brunet is confident he has discovered the oldest known hominid, he doesn't think it's possible yet to make grand pronouncements about the shape of the hominid tree and its various branches. "You can't say that it's bushy," he says. "Maybe it is; we don't know. Our story has just doubled in time, and we're just beginning to understand it."

WHY DO WE WALK UPRIGHT?

For millions of years, the earliest hominids were a lot like other apes. They were short, had tiny brains compared with modern humans, and could not speak or fashion a spear. But there was a profound difference that set them apart: They could stand up and walk. Bipedalism was the first great transformation of our ancestors, coming long before the evolution of all the other things that make us uniquely human.

The answer to the question of how our ancestors evolved into bipeds seemed pretty clear for decades. "The long-standing idea was that we became bipedal because we moved out of the forest and onto the savanna, either because we had to look over tall grass or get to isolated stands of trees," says Craig Stanford, a primatologist at the University of Southern California's Jane Goodall Research Center.

But in recent years new evidence has thrown that scenario into doubt. "The time-honored idea that a weakling hominid left the safety of the forest for the dangerous savanna and had to live by its wits and stood upright is a nice story, but it's probably fiction," says Stanford. As researchers have looked closer at the older hominid sites, many have concluded that the areas were not savannas at all but a variety of lightly to densely wooded landscapes. Hominids may not have lived in savannas until 2 million to 2.5 million years ago—2.5 million to 3 million years after the earliest known hominids walked on two legs.

Now scientists are trying to figure out what evolutionary pressure led hominids to become bipedal in the forest. To answer that question, they have to figure out what upright walking evolved from. Fossils offer some clues, but opinion is divided over what the clues mean. Some paleoanthropologists studying Lucy's skeleton say she walked much as we do, for example, while others say she moved awkwardly on the ground and spent a lot of time in trees. Paleoanthropologists can say even less about the oldest hominids, because they've found hardly anything below the skull.

The best clues to our upright origins may come from living apes, although no one knows for sure how much chimpanzees have evolved from the last common ancestor they shared with us. Some primatologists are conducting lab studies of how modern apes knuckle-walk and clamber through trees to see which movements are most like human walking. Other researchers, like Craig Stanford, watch apes in the wild. "Chimpanzees may stand upright on a big limb of a fig tree and pluck figs just overhead," Stanford says. "And when they're on the ground, they'll stand up to pull down branches." He backs a hypothesis originally devised by Kevin Hunt of Indiana University: The earliest hominids may have become specialists in getting food by standing up for short spells, both in the trees or on the ground. It may not seem as heroic as striding out into the savanna, but then again, many great chapters in the book of evolution have been built from such modest changes.

WHY ARE OUR BRAINS SO BIG?

Our brains are not just big—they're grotesquely huge. A typical mammal our size would have a brain one-seventh as large as ours. And big brains are relatively new for hominids. From 7 million to 2 million years ago, our ancestors had brains about the size of a modern chimpanzee's. Hominid brains only began to increase 2 million years ago, and they continued to balloon, in fits and starts, until they neared their present size at least 160,000 years ago.

When it comes to explaining this explosion in brain size, scientists agree on one thing: It must have offered a powerful evolutionary advantage. "It costs you an awful lot in terms of energy," says Aiello. "You don't evolve large and expensive organs unless there's a reason."

But paleoanthropologists are divided about that reason. One possibility is that bigger brains gave hominids extra information-processing power they could use to make better tools. After all, stone tools unlocked new supplies of food, and so better tool users could support more offspring. Another possibility is that the driving force was hominid social life. Primates living in big groups tend to have bigger brains, possibly because there's an evolutionary advantage to keeping

track of other members of your group. And certainly the human brain has evolved into an awesome social computer, able to draw subtle clues about other people's thoughts from their faces in a fraction of a second.

On the other hand, big brains may have prompted humans to become more social. For one thing, big brains made children helpless. Hominid kids, then as now, needed years to develop large brains, during which time they depended on adults for high-energy foods. It's possible that the basic shape of the human family as a group of parents, siblings, and grandparents formed to feed the brains of their children.

WHEN DID WE FIRST USE TOOLS?

It is hard to imagine life without tools—finding food with our bare hands, eating it raw with our teeth, seeking a cave or a tree for shelter. In fact, our reliance on tools is reflected in our brains and bodies. The areas of our brains responsible for things like controlling our hands are enlarged compared with other primates. Our hands themselves are different, with proportionately longer thumbs and other anatomic changes that allow us to touch our fingertips and hold tools with more skill. The dawn of tool use was a crucial turning point in human history: It let our ancestors take control of their lives by finding food in places that were off-limits to their ancestors. But scientists still have hardly any clues to how that evolutionary transition took place.

The most reliable record of our technological history comes from the tools themselves. The oldest known hominid tools date back 2.5 million years, to a collection of chipped rocks in Ethiopia. They don't look like much, but with them hominids could butcher an elephant or crack open a wildebeest's bones and suck out the marrow. Mentally, they're also a big accomplishment: They require a brain capable of looking at an untouched rock and seeing a tool hiding within it.

In recent years, however, some hints have emerged that human technology may have roots reaching back millions of years further into the past. For one thing, chimpanzees and other apes have proved surprisingly gifted at making tools. In order to walk across thorn-covered ground, chimpanzees can fashion sandals out of leaves. In order to eat termites, they can strip sticks to create fishing tools. Unfortunately, a leaf-sandal doesn't leave a fossil. But some researchers believe that the hands of hominids may shed some light on the mystery of tools. For example, Lucy and her *A. afarensis* fellows lived a million years before the oldest tools. Despite having curved, chimplike fingers, this hominid also had an elongated thumb that could make contact with its fingertips. "There's nothing to say that these creatures couldn't make crude stone tools," says

Bernard Wood of George Washington University. It's possible that hominids had already become skilled with wood and other materials 3.5 million years ago, paving the way to mental breakthroughs for making stone tools.

As intriguing as this hypothesis may be, however, many researchers think there's not enough evidence to say anything definitive about the evolution of tool use. Tim White, a paleo-anthropologist at the University of California at Berkeley, says any speculations "would be strictly *X-Files*."

HOW DID WE GET MODERN MINDS?

Walking upright, growing a big brain, and even making tools are not enough to make an ape truly human. Consider *Homo ergaster*, a species that lived in Africa between 1.7 million and 600,000 years ago and probably gave rise to our own species. *H. ergaster* stood up to six feet tall, had a medium-size brain, and could survive even in arid grasslands thanks to an impressive kit of stone axes and other tools. Despite all that, this species' brain didn't work like ours. For hundreds of thousands of years, *H. ergaster* was content to use the same set of tools, with few modifications. Putting a stone axe on the end of a stick to make a spear would have allowed these hominids to become much better hunters, and yet this simple idea apparently never occurred to them. Such an idea seems simple only to our modern minds, which can see new possibilities in the world, discover hidden connections, and think and communicate with symbols.

Scientists don't yet know how that modern mind came into existence. The question is particularly hard to answer because they can't get into the brain of *H. ergaster* or any of our other ancestors. Instead, they have to infer what those ancient minds were like by looking at the things they made. The people who painted pictures of mammoths and woolly rhinos in French caves almost 32,000 years ago must have already had minds much like our own. Archaeologists have documented an explosion of expressions of the modern mind after roughly 50,000 years ago, in the form of jewelry, elaborate graves, bone-tipped spears, and other new kinds of tools. The bones of the people who made these things look like our own. They were members of *Homo sapiens*, complete with long, slender arms and legs, a flat face, a jutting chin, and a high forehead that fronted a big brain. But they were hardly the first people with our anatomy. *H. sapiens* fossils have been found in Africa from at least 160,000 years ago, and some experts argue that the earliest members of our species may have existed over 200,000 years ago.

Richard Klein, a paleoanthropologist at Stanford University, has offered a controversial theory: The modern mind is the result of a rapid genetic change. He puts the date of the change at around 50,000 years ago, pointing out that the rise of cultural artifacts comes after that date, as does the spread of modern humans from Africa. The evolution of the modern mind allowed humans to thrive as never before, Klein argues, and soon even a continent as huge as Africa could not contain their expanding population.

Many other paleoanthropologists beg to differ. Sally McBrearty, an archaeologist at the University of Connecticut, believes the evidence shows that the technology and artistic expression of modern humans emerged slowly over hundreds of thousands of years, as humans gradually moved into new habitats and increased their population. She points to a long list of tantalizing clues in Africa that predate Klein's 50,000-year milestone. Humans may have been grinding pigments 250,000 years ago, for example, and researchers have found barbed bone fishing hooks in Central Africa that they estimate are 90,000 years old. Last year scientists in South Africa discovered stones covered with geometrical cross-hatching dating back 77,000 years.

Klein dismisses the evidence for such slow-fuse change as paltry and misleading. "It's a little bit here, it's a little bit there. Most sites don't have anything like this at all, but when you get to 50,000 years ago, they all do. Then you get real art—not stuff you can argue about whether it shows some form of symbolism—and elaborate graves and houses and the rest of it."

A resolution to this debate may be waiting in Africa, at archaeological sites scattered across the continent. "We know what we'd like to find and where we ought to look for it," says McBrearty. "But are we going to have the money and the perseverance to mount the assault and come up with the goods?"

WHY DID WE OUTLIVE OUR RELATIVES?

Humans today are driving other species toward extinction at a disturbing pace—a quarter of all mammal species, for example, are officially listed as threatened. But the evidence from fossils suggests that this wave of extinctions has been rising for thousands of years. And there's a grim irony in the possibility that two of the first species to fall victim to us may have been our closest relatives.

Studies on human mitochondrial DNA indicate that all humans alive today can trace their ancestry back to members of *Homo sapiens* who lived in Africa roughly 150,000 years ago. At the time, there were two other hominid species. Members of *Homo neanderthalensis* (Neanderthals), who lived in Europe, have a reputation as lumbering brutes, but they had brains as big as or bigger than those of humans and awesome hunting skills that helped them survive cyclic ice ages for half a million years or more. In Asia, *Homo erectus* survived for about 1.5 million years. And yet not long after *H. sapiens* spread from Africa, both of these species vanished. Our close kinship with these hominids makes their disappearance all the more puzzling. "It's very difficult to get your head around the idea that there could be another species so closely related to us, but isn't us," says McBrearty.

It wasn't very long ago, geologically speaking, when our ancestors came face to face with these other species, and yet scientists still know little about the encounter. About *H. erectus,* all they can say is that the youngest *H. erectus* fossils, Indonesian skulls from perhaps 50,000 years ago, come from a time when our own species had already settled in Asia and moved on to Australia. "We don't know what the hell is going on there," says Klein. "We need more fossils with good dates. It'll come—within a decade we'll know something more about this." Neanderthals left behind more hints, although the picture is still far from clear. Scientists have isolated six fragments of Neanderthal DNA and have concluded that the Neanderthal did not interbreed much—if at all—with *H. sapiens.* Neanderthals appear to have clung to existence for 15,000 years after encountering our own species in Europe. But over time they became rarer and rarer, until they could be found only in isolated mountain valleys. And then they could be found nowhere at all.

Over the years, scientists have tried to explain the disappearance of Neanderthals and *H. erectus* with everything from warfare to exotic viruses that their *H. sapiens* relatives brought with them from Africa. But the cause of their demise could have been far more subtle. Even if our species had just a slight evolutionary edge over the other hominids, the effect could have been devastating, given enough time. It's possible, for example, that humans benefited from long-distance trade and better tools, allowing them to withstand droughts, ice ages, and other hard times better than their competitors. Our ancestors may have had just a few more children in each generation, and gradually they took over the best places for hunting and living. After a few hundred generations, they unwittingly squeezed their cousins out of existence.

"It may have been something as simple as modern humans having better clothing," says Leslie Aiello.

WHAT GENES MAKE US HUMAN?

In April 2003, geneticists finished sequencing the human genome, and now they're well on their way to decoding the genome of one of our closest relatives, the common chimpanzee. The sight of these two sequences placed side by side is astonishing. For thousands of positions at a stretch, their codes are identical.

Recently Morris Goodman, a biologist at the Wayne State University School of Medicine, and his colleagues analyzed the portions of DNA that are responsible for the structure of proteins. In this crucial part of the genome, humans and chimps were 99.4 percent identical. In other words, much of what makes us uniquely human may be found in just .6 percent of our genome.

That tiny fraction will be the focus of a huge amount of research in years to come. "There will be a gold mine of information," predicts Sean Carroll, a geneticist at the University of Wisconsin and an investigator with the Howard Hughes Medical Institute. As the differences between humans and chimps come to light, for instance, medicine will be revolutionized. Scientists hope to find the genetic differences that explain why chimpanzees don't get AIDS, Alzheimer's, and other diseases that plague humans.

Scientists will also be searching the two genomes for clues to how and why humans evolved traits that distinguish us from chimpanzees, including a bipedal body, a big brain, and language. A taste of things to come is the recent study of a gene called *FOXP2.* People who inherit mutant forms of *FOXP2* have trouble speaking and understanding grammar. Scientists have reconstructed the evolutionary history of the gene by comparing the subtle variations in *FOXP2* that different people carry. The researchers found that in the past 200,000 years, the gene underwent an intense burst of evolutionary selection. It's possible that changes to this gene may have helped prompt the transformation of simple apelike grunts into language.

But it would be a mistake to think that any single gene will tell us much about human nature, or even just the ability to talk. "We're just not going to have two or three speech genes and that's the end of the story," says Carroll. "It's going to be much more subtle than that."

The early evidence already suggests that perhaps several thousand human genes have undergone intense natural selection since our ancestors split with the chimp lineage. And those genes can only build a modern human being by co-operating with one another rather than working alone. This comes as no surprise to scientists who have studied the evolution of other animals. "We look for simple answers, but we almost always find a mess," says Carroll.

HAVE WE STOPPED EVOLVING?

It has been an amazing run: over 7 million years our lineage has evolved from diminutive apes to the planet's dominant species. We've evolved brains that are capable of things never achieved on our planet, and perhaps in the universe. Why shouldn't we continue evolving more powerful brains? It's easy to think that we'll just keep marching ahead, that in another million years we'll have gigantic brains like out of some episode of *Star Trek.* But scientists can't say where we're headed. It's even possible that we've reached an evolutionary dead end.

Consider the fact that the human brain hasn't expanded all that much in at least 160,000 years. You might think that if bigger brains meant more intelligence, natural selection would still be inflating them today. But big brains have their draw-backs. Like an expanding computer network, a growing brain needs more and more wiring to connect its processors together. The human brain may be reaching the edge of this computational limit. Big brains also make a lot of demands on the human body—particularly the bodies of pregnant women. A woman's birth canal has to be wide enough for a big-brained baby to get out. But there's a limit to how wide the female pelvis can become: If it became too wide, women would struggle to walk upright. That constraint may make it impossible for the human brain to get any bigger.

The only way to know the answer to this particular question, however, may be to wait for the future to become the past. "One of the reasons why people are fascinated with human evolution is because it's about where we came from and where we're going," says Aiello. "But we don't know where we're going. It's too much of a lottery."

7

Ancient Bodies, Modern Customs, and Our Health

Elizabeth D. Whitaker

Culture determines the way we have children and how we raise children. The American way of childbirth—with the woman in a hospital, lying on her back with her legs up in stirrups, connected to a fetal monitor, and numbed with an epidural anesthetic—is a cultural creation that has developed in recent history. Rarely do we question our cultural traditions, especially when there are experts and expert opinions. People in all cultures take comfort in the fact that they are doing things the "right way," that is, the way things are supposed to be as dictated by tradition. The comfort derived from our traditions is most evident in rituals, like weddings or funerals. But cultural traditions (and dependence on cultural experts) also play a major role in how people go about being parents. In the United States, mothers and fathers try to do the best they can for their children, often unaware how the larger cultural context shapes or limits the possibilities. Children, in turn, get not just their genes but also their ideas, beliefs, and values from their parents, thus perpetuating the culture. But people also have minds of their own, and there are more rational ways to choose one's child-rearing practices than to simply accept the opinions of "experts" and authorities. After all, it is also part of our culture to question authority!

Biological anthropologists believe that evolution has shaped our bodies and therefore strongly influences our health. In this selection, Elizabeth Whitaker reviews evidence from evolutionary medicine about the health implications of infant feeding and sleeping patterns. She demonstrates that American cultural ideas emphasizing the individual have detracted from the fact that mothers and their infants form a biological interacting pair during pregnancy and continuing in infancy. Patterns of breast-feeding in other cultures are undoubtedly linked to health issues such as birth spacing, allergies, and infant diarrhea and dehydration. It is less obvious, however, that the disappearance of evolutionary patterns of breast-feeding is also linked to the increasing incidence of breast cancer in countries like the United States. Finally, there is solid evidence that the cultural pattern of babies sleeping in their own cribs—by themselves, in a separate room, and often placed on their stomachs—is linked to the risk of sudden infant death syndrome.

As you read this selection, ask yourself the following questions:

- What benefits does breast-feeding have for the mother? What benefits does it have for the child?
- Why do people get fevers? Why do people take medicine to stop fevers?
- Does the U.S. socioeconomic system shape our patterns of breast-feeding and weaning?
- Is evolutionary medicine against progress?

The following terms discussed in this selection are included in the Glossary at the back of the book:

diseases of civilization	*ovulation*
evolutionary medicine	*SIDS*
food foragers	

Mothers and infants are physiologically interconnected from conception to the termination of breast-feeding. While this mutual biological relationship is obvious during pregnancy, to many people it is less clear in the period following birth. In Western society,

individuals are expected to be autonomous and independent, and this ideal extends to mothers and their babies. Individual autonomy is a core value in our economy, society, and family life: even to our understanding of health and disease. However, it is not a widely shared notion, as more *sociocentric* conceptions of personhood are very common in other cultures and have prevailed in other time periods. Until the

Industrial Revolution, Western society also recognized the dependence relationships among individuals and families, and this matched an agrarian social structure involving mutual responsibilities and obligations. Mothers and infants were considered interdependent and there was relatively little cultural intervention in or manipulation of gestation or lactation.

Until a century ago, medical experts followed Aristotle, Hippocrates, and Galen in saying that *not* to breast-feed was to have half a birth, because mother's milk came from the same blood which nourished the fetus. Today, in many cultures around the world, infants are not expected to be independent of their mothers for as long as they breast-feed—that is, for at least the first few years of life. These beliefs reflect an appreciation of the fact that breast-feeding represents a physiological process for both mothers and infants and is more than a simple question of nutrition.

Cultural interventions in the mother–infant relationship are bound to bring significant biological outcomes. Common infant feeding practices in Western societies, such as timed, widely spaced meals, early weaning, pacifier use, and isolated infant sleep with few or no nighttime feedings, are very new and rare in human history, and do not reflect "natural" needs or optimal behaviors, as is commonly presumed. They result in partial or short-term breast-feeding that is very different from the "traditional" or ancient pattern humans have known over evolutionary time. This pattern involves frequent, exclusive, and prolonged breast-feeding, and brings the greatest benefits to mothers and infants. These benefits include reduced risk of breast cancer and the Sudden Infant Death Syndrome (SIDS), diseases which share a common thread in their history: the decline in breast-feeding in the Western industrial societies. By examining them together, we will try to overcome the assumption of individual autonomy, which is so entrenched in Western culture that studies on breast-feeding commonly focus on either the mother or child, but not both.

OLD GENES, NEW LIFESTYLES

Beyond the level of personal experience, breast-feeding concerns both biological processes and cultural interpretation and manipulation. Biocultural anthropology examines such a topic by bringing together cross-cultural comparison and evolutionary considerations. This can mean, for example, comparing human physiology and behavior to those of other primates, such as chimpanzees and gorillas, with whom we share common ancestors and diverge genetically by less than 2%. It also involves looking at different strategies for making a living among human populations. In particular, anthropologists are interested in comparing hunter-gatherers, or foragers, to agricultural or industrial societies. We study modern-day foragers such as the !Kung San of Botswana or the Gainj of Papua New Guinea because their diet, exercise, and health patterns roughly represent those of humans for the vast majority of evolutionary history.

With a few exceptions, our genetic endowment has not changed since the first foraging groups began to practice settled agriculture and animal husbandry between 13,000 and 9,000 years ago (the *Neolithic Revolution*). From the start, the lifestyle change produced notable health consequences. Early agriculturists had shorter stature, greater nutritional stress, and higher infant mortality, especially at the age of weaning. Whereas foragers suffered annual seasonal food shortages, these were less severe than the famines that resulted when crops or livestock were lost. Although famines are rare now, especially in the wealthier countries, constant over-nutrition produces new health problems. At the same time, the diet in many impoverished countries remains scanter and less varied than the foraging diet.

In contrast to what we think of as proper nutrition, foragers subsist on a low-calorie diet made up exclusively of wild plant parts (roots, seeds, stalks, leaves, nuts, fruits) and game or fish. There are no dairy products (except mother's milk) or processed grains in their diet. Most of the food comes from plants, while meat is a less reliable but highly valued supply of concentrated protein, fat (though only one-seventh the amount in the meat of domesticated animals), and vitamins and minerals.

Foragers collect these foods over distances of 10 or more kilometers per day, often carried out in a pattern of one or two days of work for six to eight hours and one or two days of other activities. This averages out to more than 6½ kilometers per day. Women routinely carry up to 15 kilograms (almost 35 pounds) of food, a bundle which can reach half their body weight. They also carry children up to three or four years of age, adding up to another 15 kilograms. In addition to this physical activity, foragers move camp several times each year. Because they work outdoors and do not have climate control indoors, they are constantly exposed to the elements.

Unlike people in affluent societies, foragers do not experience any "natural" rise in blood pressure with age. They do not undergo hearing loss or become overweight as inevitable consequences of aging, nor does their body mass increase. They are not free of disorders including accidents and injuries, degenerative bone disease, complications of childbirth, and infectious disease, but the major health problems of the Western societies are very rare. These "diseases of civilization" or "chronic diseases" include heart disease, hypertension, strokes, and cancer, as well as emphysema, cirrhosis, diabetes, and obesity.

While we all share a genetic propensity for the chronic diseases, it is our lifestyle and environment which cause their wide expression today. Our biological characteristics are those of Stone Age humans practicing a hardy foraging lifestyle, making our bodies adept at storing fat against the likelihood of periodic food shortage. This helps to explain why overweight and obesity are so common wherever physical activity and exposure to the elements are minimal while food supplies are plentiful and steady.

Similarly, the perspective of evolutionary medicine helps us to understand cancer as the cost of the beneficial biological adaptation of tissue repair and regeneration through cell division. In all living things, the body's various ways of regulating and suppressing cell division become less effective in older age. However, over the past centuries, cancer rates have risen way beyond those which would result simply from the increase in the proportion of individuals living into old age. Beyond exposure to carcinogenic and viral agents, this can be explained in terms of changes in diet and lifestyle away from the foraging pattern. Our diet is scarce in protective micro-nutrients such as beta-carotene and selenium, but abundant in macro-nutrients such as fat, protein, and calories which, in themselves and in relation to body composition and size, promote cancer.

Compared to the chronic diseases, we have been adapting to infectious organisms for ages, and vice versa. In many cases, fever is an adaptive defense against infection. It raises the body's temperature and speeds up its metabolic processes, helping to eliminate viruses and bacteria. When ectothermic ("cold-blooded") animals are injected with virus, they seek out a hotter place, and are more likely to die from the infection if prevented from doing so. Recent studies have found that people who take antipyretics (drugs such as aspirin or acetaminophen, which suppress fever) are infectious longer and take longer to recover from colds, flu, and chicken pox.

Fever also promotes the sequestration of iron which takes place as a defense against many kinds of infection. The iron is bound more tightly to protein and hidden in the liver, reducing the amount that circulates in the blood. The resulting anemia is typically treated with iron supplements, but iron is a necessary mineral to many bacteria and their need for it is increased by fever. This pair of evolved defensive systems—increased heat and decreased iron—is therefore blocked by human interventions such as iron supplements and antipyretics. On the other hand, some pathogens actually reproduce better or become more toxic in the presence of fever and reduced iron, which

would be expected since their rapid reproductive rates and short lives give them an evolutionary advantage. What this suggests is that an evolutionary perspective is needed to better target and treat symptoms appropriately, just as it contributes to our analysis of lactation and the health outcomes of variations in its practice.

MOTHERS AND INFANTS

When breast-feeding patterns are compared across mammals (from *mamma*, Latin for "breast"), non-human primates, and humans, "on-demand" or baby-fed feeding emerges as the evolutionary norm for our species. Many aspects of the ancestral pattern are shared by non-Western societies today and were common in Western populations until a few generations ago. A relationship of interdependence and mutuality is expressed in parent–infant co-sleeping and exclusive, unrestricted breast-feeding well beyond the first year.

The ancestral pattern involves frequent feedings (from several times an hour to once every hour or two) all day and night with no limit on their duration; no supplementary foods before six months and low to moderate use of pre-chewed foods or very ripe fruits thereafter; and complete weaning at 2½ to 4 years, when the child is able to walk long distances on its own. Mother's milk remains the principal food until 15 to 18 months, after which it continues to be a significant source of nutrition. When these conditions prevail, infants are more likely to survive, pregnancy is prevented for 2 to 3 years or more, and births are spaced 3 to 5 years apart. In all but one family of primates, lactation implies *anovulation* (lack of ovulation). In our closest relatives, births are spaced as far as 5 (in chimpanzees) to 8 (in orangutans) years apart.

In foraging societies such as the !Kung, the mother carries her child in a sling against her body, providing constant physical contact and access to the breast. Infants hardly ever cry, and are not expected to cry. Their signs of distress bring an immediate response from their mother or another relative, but never with any kind of pacifier other than the breast. Infants are constantly cuddled and kissed all over the body, including the genitals. Parents are bewildered to hear that Western infants cry and are left alone in a crib, swaddled perhaps, to do so for long periods without being held or allowed to suckle. They do not share the idea that infants and children need to be denied what they want or they will grow up spoiled or dependent. Indeed, the opposition between independence and dependence has relatively little meaning in these societies.

Milk production and release are regulated by pituitary hormones secreted in response to nipple stimulation, the emptying of the breast, and psychological factors. Prolactin is released in response to suckling, stimulating the synthesis of milk in the lacteal cells within a couple of hours. Oxytocin is also released in response to nipple stimulation, and immediately causes the cells around the milk-producing bulbs and ducts to contract and secrete milk. This pathway can be affected by psychological factors in positive and negative ways. A thought, emotion, or sound or sight of an infant can cause the release of oxytocin. Contrariwise, fear and other stressful emotions lead to the secretion of epinephrine, which impedes the circulation of oxytocin to breast tissue by constricting the blood vessels around it.

After the surge following nipple stimulation, prolactin levels drop off quickly, reaching baseline levels within two hours. Consequently, to maintain continuous milk production it is necessary to breast-feed at short intervals and keep prolactin levels high. Especially in the early months, more frequent feedings result in greater milk production. Milk that is not secreted but left in the breast has an independent dampening effect on production through both a substance in the milk and the mechanical pressure it exerts on the surrounding cells. This kind of control over milk production seems to apply in a preponderant way after the first two or three months, against a diminishing but still important background of hormonal regulation. Moreover, more frequent feedings and complete removal of milk lead to higher average fat and calorie content. Infants fed without restrictions are able to vary feed frequencies and the degree of breast-emptying and thereby regulate their nutrition very closely. They tend to be satiated and satisfied after feedings.

High prolactin levels inhibit ovulation, so that infrequent feedings and reduced time at the breast lead to less effective suppression of fertility. In addition, other hormones involved in the menstrual cycle are affected by frequent breast-feeding, interfering with normal follicle growth, ovulation (should an egg mature), development of the endometrium, and implantation of a fertilized ovum. As women space feedings at wider intervals, introduce supplementary foods, and reduce nighttime feeding, the contraceptive effect of breast-feeding weakens and ovulation and menstruation resume.

The composition of human milk also indicates that it is made to be given frequently. Unlike other mammals such as rabbits or tree shrews, who keep their young in nests and leave them all day or even longer, primates carry their babies and thereby provide them with transportation and temperature regulation, for which their milk is less fatty. Primate infants are born less mature and grow more slowly, explaining why protein is relatively scarce in the milk. Continuous

breast-feeding and physical contact also protect the infant from predators, as well as illness. Contact with others is reduced, while exposure to the same diseases leads to the production of immunological substances, which are then transmitted in the mother's milk.

In recent years, there has been wide publication of the wonderful properties of breast-milk, from nutritional components to immunological factors, sedative substances to anti-allergenic properties. These benefits make breast-fed infants better able to resist and overcome infections, including those of the gastrointestinal and respiratory tract (which includes the middle ear). Breast-feeding promotes optimal growth and development of the body's systems, such as the cardiovascular, immune, nervous, and gastrointestinal systems. It also protects breast-fed infants from protein malnutrition, even in areas of the world in which it is common. This is because the quality of milk is remarkably constant across mothers, regardless of their diet or nutritional status.

The uniform quality of mother's milk, even in conditions of stress, brings up two points. It implies that we should focus upon infant demand and suckling behavior when there are problems in breast-feeding, but the tendency is instead to search for maternal causes. Secondly, by focusing on the benefits of breast-feeding in terms of the useful properties of the milk, we may fail to acknowledge the impacts of breast-feeding on the mother. Mothers who are overworked and poorly nourished may become depleted, their lives shortened by repeated cycles of gestation and lactation.

On the other hand, assuming good conditions, breast-feeding has many positive effects on mothers. It helps the uterus to return to its normal size and shape after childbirth, hastens weight loss and moderates digestion, metabolism, blood circulation, and sensations of well-being. It favors bone consolidation, preventing osteoporosis and hip and other fractures in later life, and reduces the risk of women's reproductive cancers. In order to appreciate these benefits, we must go beyond looking at breast-milk as a mere product manufactured for the advantage of the child.

Whereas in foraging and agricultural societies mothers and their fetuses or infants are considered inseparable, even when physically divided after childbirth, in Western society they are considered independent even during gestation. In evolutionary biology, this is an appropriate concept since the interests of the child and the mother may conflict: for example, the fetus of humans and all placental animals taps into the mother's blood circulation, injecting fetal hormones into it and drawing nutrients from the mother's organs if they are not available through her diet. Yet, the biological concept of individuality simultaneously presumes physiological interdependence. The cultural concept of the autonomous individual denies it. After childbirth, the separation between mother and child is complete, and the physiological interrelationship in breast-feeding is obscured by a focus on the infant's nutritional and psychological independence. This has notable health outcomes for both mothers and infants, some of which we will now examine in light of an evolutionary perspective.

BREAST CANCER

Until the nineteenth century, European medical philosophers observed that well-off women who lived in cities were much more susceptible to breast cancer than women who lived in the countryside. They attributed this difference to the abandonment of breast-feeding, which, they noted, caused numerous other maladies and grave health effects. Even today, not only is breast cancer more common in affluent societies, but within them it is more frequent among the wealthier classes.

The decline in breast-feeding has been part of a broad change in reproductive and child-rearing patterns since the Industrial Revolution. Urban women were the first to undergo the *secular trend* of earlier maturation and greater achieved stature. They experienced earlier puberty, delayed marriage and first birth, fewer pregnancies, and reduced or forsaken breast-feeding. Over time, these patterns diffused through the entire population.

Many of the things we consider "natural" are therefore more like aberrations or deviations from what evolution has produced. To illustrate, a typical woman of a foraging or pre-industrial society reaches puberty and her first menstrual period *(menarche)* at the age of 16 to 18. She becomes pregnant within three or four years, breast-feeds for three or four years, and has a subsequent child four or five years after the first. This sequence repeats itself between four and six times before she reaches menopause at around the age of 45. As a result, she has about 150 ovulations in her lifetime, taking account of non-ovulatory cycles at the near and far end of her reproductive years. Periodic nutritional and exercise stress reduce the number of ovulations even more. Because only half of her children survive long enough to reproduce, population grows very slowly, as was the case until historical times. Lactation has represented humankind's main method of birth control for most of our existence.

In contrast, Western women enjoy a stable food supply, including foods concentrated in fat, protein, and calories, and experience very little stress from exercise and exposure. Over the past centuries, this has caused them, and men, to reach higher stature and lower age at puberty. Girls arrive at menarche at the age of 12 or 13, while menopause is delayed to 50 or 55 years. Significantly, the first birth is postponed for 13 or 14 years, to the age of 25 or 26, and the average number of births is reduced to two or three. The average Western woman breast-feeds for a few months, if at all. Because she spaces feedings at long intervals and supplements with other foods, breast-feeding does not inhibit ovulation for long. As a result, population growth was very rapid in Europe for several centuries (and in many developing countries today) not only because mortality rates were falling but also because women did not have a long interval of infertility associated with lactation.

If she does not take oral contraceptives, the average woman will ovulate around 450 times over her lifetime. Ovulation will rarely be suppressed due to physiological constraints associated with nutritional or exercise stress. This amounts to three or four times as many ovulations over the life-span, and some scholars have suggested that the proportion may be as high as nine times.

The differences in reproductive patterns between women in foraging as opposed to affluent societies match some of the currently known risk factors for women's reproductive cancers (breast, endometrium, ovary), including age at menarche and menopause, *parity* (number of births), and breast-feeding. Differences in diet and physical activity, as well as body composition, also agree with identified non-reproductive risk factors such as fat intake and percent body fat. Together with other factors, they give Western women, especially below the age of 60, at least 20 times the risk of reproductive cancer. The risk for breast cancer may be more than 100 times higher. In nonhuman primates, these cancers are extremely rare.

For all three cancers, earlier age at menarche and later age at menopause increase risk, while greater parity reduces risk. Like these factors, breast-feeding is protective against ovarian cancer because it inhibits ovulation. This reduces the monthly mechanical injury to the ovarian epithelium and the release of hormones by the follicle, which are considered the main elements in the etiology of ovarian cancer. For breast cancer, lactation and earlier first birth are also protective factors.

The breast's susceptibility to carcinogenesis is directly related to the rate of epithelial cell proliferation. Consequently, the lengthening of the period between menarche and first birth widens the window of time in which undifferentiated structures destined to become secretory glands are vulnerable to carcinogenic agents and therefore the initiation of tumors. In breast tissue, cell proliferation is promoted by exposure to estrogen, apparently in concert with progesterone, and cell division rates are highest during the first five years after menarche. With pregnancy and lactation, these structures differentiate and develop, devoting themselves less ardently to cell proliferation. Their cell cycle is longer, and they are more resistant to chemical carcinogens. Subsequent pregnancies may also be protective because they increase the proportion of fully differentiated secretory lobules, until in advanced age pregnancy increases risk by favoring the expansion of initiated tumors.

While the age at first pregnancy seems to be of primary importance and may even modulate the protective effect of breast-feeding and later pregnancies, breast-feeding in itself provides protection against breast cancer in step with the number of children breast-fed and the cumulative duration of breast-feeding. The reason some studies have found no effect or a weak one is that they were based upon the experiences of Western women, who do not generally conform to the ancient pattern of breast-feeding at close intervals for at least a year. Short periods of breast-feeding may in fact provide very little protection.

At the level of the breast fluid, there are lower levels of a potential carcinogen, cholesterol-epoxide, as well as cholesterol, in breast-feeding women, a reduction that persists for two years after childbirth or lactation. Estrogen levels are also lower, protecting the breast tissue directly as opposed to systemically through variations in blood estrogen levels. Breast-feeding also affects the turnover rate of substances in the breast fluid, so that prolonged breast-feeding reduces exposure of the breast epithelial tissue to potential exogenous carcinogens.

Exercise, high consumption of dietary fiber, and low fat consumption and percent body fat are all protective against breast and other cancers. High dietary levels of fat and protein (especially from animal sources) and total calories are associated with higher levels of breast cancer across populations and within subpopulations of single countries. Animal studies have shown that dietary protein promotes tumor development while restriction of protein intake inhibits tumor growth. The enzymes in adipose tissue convert precursor adrenal hormones into active estrogens. Dietary fat raises serum estrogen levels and promotes tumor development and may also play a role in originating tumors. In contrast to Western women, women in foraging societies have low serum estrogen levels.

Western women's skinfold thickness (a measure of the proportion of body fat) is almost twice that of pre-agricultural women. Compared to college athletes, women who are not athletic in college (and less active in adolescence and somewhat less active after college) have two to five times the rates of breast, uterine, and ovarian cancer. Women in affluent societies consume

40% or more of their calories in the form of fat, against 20 to 25% among pre-agricultural women, but only 20 as opposed to 100 grams of fiber per day. Dietary fiber is protective because it reduces free estrogen levels in the blood. It helps to prevent bowel dysfunction, which has been associated with breast cancer, and the severe constipation which can lead to the migration of mutagenic substances from the gastrointestinal tract to the breast fluid.

The protective effect of breast-feeding goes beyond the current generation to the next one, for early nutritional influences seem to have an important effect on later susceptibility to cancer. Breast-feeding contributes to the development and regulation of the immune system, which plays a central role in suppressing the initiation and growth of tumors. It prevents over-consumption of fat, protein, and calories. This influences body size and composition, the baseline against which nutrition works throughout life. That is, breast-feeding prevents the accelerated growth of muscles and fat stores associated with breast cancer risk factors: faster growth rates, earlier menarche, and greater achieved stature and size. Women who have been breast-fed themselves are less likely to develop breast cancer.

We have seen that breast-feeding benefits both the mother and child with respect to prevention of breast cancer. In the mother, breast-feeding according to the ancient pattern influences systemic hormone levels and the micro-environment of the breast tissue, reducing exposure to exogenous and endogenous carcinogens. In the child, breast-milk provides an appropriate balance of nutrients that prevents over-nutrition, rapid growth, and early maturation. This circular interaction of factors expresses and can be predicted by the concept of the mother-infant dyad as a biological interacting pair.

SUDDEN INFANT DEATH SYNDROME

From a global perspective, Western society's expectation that infants should sleep alone for long hours away from their parents stands out as anomalous, even if it fits well in its cultural context. One unfortunate consequence is that the diffusion of lone infant sleep over the past several generations may be related to the rise in the frequency of infant death from the Sudden Infant Death Syndrome (SIDS).

The meaning of reproduction and child-rearing changed with the emergence of industrial society and its predominance of small, simple families (couples plus children). In this kind of society, the crib symbolizes the child's place and is usually placed in a separate room. By contrast, in rural pre-industrial Europe and in a survey of over 90 contemporary non-Western societies, infants invariably slept in the same bed or room as their parents. SIDS does not appear to exist in these societies, nor is it found among non-human primates or other mammals. In many Western societies, SIDS is the major cause of infant death, though rates are very low among sub-populations in which there is co-sleeping and nocturnal breast-feeding. Peak mortality is between the ages of two and four months, with 90% of all deaths occurring before the age of six months.

While there seem to be many intrinsic and secondary factors that affect infants in different ways to bring about SIDS events, one common factor is that SIDS usually happens during sleep. While breast-feeding in itself reduces risk, it is the frequent, intensive, prolonged breast-feeding implying mother–infant co-sleeping that may provide the best environment for avoiding the disease.

Co-sleeping infants lie on their backs or sides with their heads turned toward the breast and feed through the night, often without waking their mothers. Even newborns and very young infants are able to attach to the breast on their own, provided it is within reach. In non-industrialized societies, it is rare for infants younger than one year to sleep long hours with only a few arousals or feedings. They do not increase the length of their longest sleep episode within the first few months, nor do they stop feeding at night, as parents in Western societies expect.

These same patterns are observed in sleep laboratories, where mothers report waking up and feeding their child many times fewer than the number recorded on the monitors. They and their infants move through the various stages of sleep in synchrony, shifting between them more frequently and spending less time in the deep sleep which makes arousal more difficult. If in the laboratory the breast-feeding mother spends the night in a separate room from her child, on average she breast-feeds less than half as often. She also tends to put the child on its stomach when leaving it to sleep alone. Notably, breast-feeding mothers who routinely sleep in a separate room from their infants actually sleep for a shorter amount of time during the night, even though they feed their infants less often and for a shorter overall time period than mothers who co-sleep.

One factor common to a majority of cases is that the infant had been placed on its stomach to sleep: the opposite of the position used by infants who sleep with their mothers and breast-feed throughout the night. This may be due to suffocation because the child is unable to move out of pockets of its own carbon dioxide in puffy mattresses or bean bag cushions. It also may be the result of developmental changes related to a shift in the position of the larynx (windpipe) which takes place at four to six months.

At birth, the larynx is in contact with the back of the palate, allowing air inhaled by the nostrils to go by its own route to the lungs. It then begins to descend in the throat to a position below the back of the tongue, so that the two openings leading to the lungs and stomach lie side by side (which is why food sometimes "goes down the wrong tube"). During this shift, problems can occur if breathing through the nose (which infants greatly prefer) is impeded by a cold or other factor. Breathing through the mouth can be blocked by the uvula (the fleshy structure hanging over the back of the tongue) if it enters the descending larynx, especially if the child is lying at the wrong angle. Huge reductions in SIDS rates have taken place over the past decade in many European countries and the United Kingdom since the initiation of campaigns against the face-down position, and the U.S. is also beginning to show rapid improvement in SIDS rates.

There is more to the story than sleep position, which itself inculpates the crib since co-sleeping is associated with the safer position. More directly, the crib implies isolated, prolonged, deep sleep. Like adults, infants are able to fall into deep sleep, but they are less equipped to arouse themselves out of it. All people have temporary lapses in breathing during the night, but their brains generally respond to them appropriately. Infants are different, for they are born at a much earlier stage of neurological development than other primates, even our closest relatives.

During sleep, infants may need frequent arousals to allow them to emerge from episodes of apnea or cardiorespiratory crisis. External stimuli and parental monitoring from co-sleeping and breast-feeding give them practice at doing so, and keep them from spending long periods of time in deep stages of sleep. SIDS deaths peak at the same age at which the amount of deep sleep relative to REM sleep increases dramatically, at two to three months. Moreover, at this time infants begin to exercise more voluntary control of breathing, as parents notice in their more expressive cries. This is a step toward the speech breathing they will use later, but may complicate breathing in the short term.

The rhythm of sound and silence in the mother's breathing gives the infant auditory stimulation, while contact with her body provides tactile stimulation. The carbon dioxide which her breathing releases into the air they share induces the infant to breathe. Frequent waking for breast-feeding is a behavior common to primates and prevents hypoglycemia, which has been implicated in some SIDS deaths. Human milk also provides immunological protection against several infectious organisms (and preparations of them given as immunizations) considered responsible for some deaths. This protection is especially needed after two months, when inherited maternal antibodies become scarce but the infant's own immune system is not yet developed. Breast-feeding and constant physical contact prevent overheating and the exhausting crying spells which seem to be factors in the disease. In addition, the infant is sensitive to other aspects of its microenvironment, including temperature, humidity, and odors.

While many experts and parents advise against or avoid co-sleeping because they fear suffocating the infant, in fact this risk is very low, especially where people sleep on hard bedding or the floor. Modern bedding is dangerous because of the conformation of bed frames and the use of soft mattresses and heavy coverings. Yet, these factors are at least as relevant to cribs as parents' beds. On the other hand, some parents should not sleep with their infants, such as those who go to bed affected by drugs or alcohol. Cigarette smoke in the sleeping room could cancel the benefit of co-sleeping.

While isolated infant sleep may be consistent with parents' desires and the primacy of the conjugal bond and other Western values, it is a new behavioral norm in human history and does not represent a "natural" need. It is neither in the infant's best interest nor in conformity with behavioral patterns and biological conditions established long before our time. By contrast, parent–infant co-sleeping matches evolutionary considerations such as the need for temperature regulation, frequent nutrition, and protection from predators and disease. There may be some wisdom to the popular term, "crib death," or "cot death," for it points to the crib and the Western concept of infant independence as major factors in the disease.

SOCIAL AND CULTURAL INTERVENTION

We have seen that mothers and infants are physiologically bound together from conception to weaning, not just conception to birth. The Western ideal of the autonomous individual, even the neonate, is not shared by other societies today or by those of the past. The biocultural model shows that evolution has favored frequent, exclusive, and prolonged breast-feeding in humans. This entails constant physical contact, parent–infant co-sleeping, and nighttime breast-feeding. It leads to postpartum infertility and protects against SIDS and breast and other reproductive system cancers. Breast-feeding, therefore, has significant health outcomes, beyond the usual benefits of breast-milk, which have been popularized in recent years.

Unfortunately, the health benefits of breast-feeding, especially for mothers, are generally overshadowed by assertions regarding the supposed convenience of bottle feeding and the nutritional adequacy of artificial milk. Even the promotion of breast-feeding on the basis of the milk's value to infants does not always induce women to breast-feed, since there is little if any mention of a benefit to them. To the contrary, there are many disincentives to breast-feeding, such as beliefs that it causes the breasts to sag and makes it difficult to lose weight, or that it makes the husband feel jealous and left out. The lack of familiarity with breast-feeding which has resulted from a couple of generations of preference for the bottle also discourages it. Many people have never seen a woman breast-feed, and would prefer not to.

The degree to which our culture has come to favor intervention in the fundamental relationship between nurslings and mothers is evident in the nearly universal use of pacifiers. This has been promoted by the notion, sanctioned by professional medicine, that infants need to suckle, and better a scientifically designed object than the thumb or finger (the nipple is not even among the choices). However, in evolutionary perspective, a pacifier is completely unnecessary since infants who are breast-fed according to the ancient pattern are allowed to suckle to their heart's content. Not surprisingly, pacifier use has been found to reduce the duration of breast-feeding.

The birthing process is focused upon the infant, while the mother is considered and often treated as an impediment to the physician's efforts to extract the child. Afterward, the medical care of the two is split between obstetricians and pediatricians, reflecting the conceptual splitting of the mother–infant relationship at birth. There is little or no breast-feeding (in the United States, only one half of all infants begin life feeding at the breast). Weaning takes place within a few months and almost always within the first year, and the mother resumes her menstrual cycle within a few months. Mothers are strongly encouraged to put their children on feeding schedules and eliminate nighttime feeding as quickly as possible, and to teach them to get to sleep and stay asleep on their own, in their own bed and room. Instead of being carried and cuddled throughout the day and night, infants are left in cribs, strollers, and playpens and are touched relatively rarely. They are expected to cry and left to do so, sometimes for hours. Often, the door to their room is closed at nap time and during the night.

On a social-structural level, cultural interference in breast-feeding seems to be more common in societies which are based upon vertical inheritance and the simple family structure, than societies in which families are wide and inheritance is lateral. In the former, the institution of marriage is emphasized over kin relationships. Women's sexual and conjugal duties take precedence over their role as kinswomen and mothers, while children are considered heirs rather than links in a kinship network. These conditions can make breast-feeding seem to interfere with sexuality, and pit the husband against the child in competition over the woman's sexualized breast.

Notably, our culture describes breasts as "secondary *sexual* characteristics," highlighting a tendency to regard them as objects of display rather than functional organs. In medieval to modern Europe, the post-partum taboo against sex during lactation was circumvented among the elite classes by wet-nursing, so that women could be available to their husbands instead of breast-feeding. This was subsequently replaced by formula feeding and practiced by a much wider segment of the population.

The rise of the modern nation-state over the past two centuries meanwhile has brought an expansion of the authority of medical experts. Beginning with early industrialization, the state and its emerging medical system sought to shape public morality and oppose traditional authority by reaching into the private, intimate world of the family. As a result, reproduction and child-rearing became medicalized well before professional medicine had much legitimate knowledge or expertise in these areas. As multiple families broke up due to socioeconomic changes, families became more dependent upon outside experts in areas which had previously been handled by older relatives or other authorities such as midwives and clerics.

By now, it is rare for anyone to question the authority of the medical community in questions such as birth control or infant feeding. This phenomenon has emerged hand-in-hand with the notion of the autonomous individual. By considering fetuses and infants as beings independent of their mothers, Western society has allowed and welcomed experts into the life of the dyad and granted them predominant authority in decisions regarding the care and upbringing of the young. Mothers are not encouraged to think of themselves as competent or knowledgeable enough to breast-feed without expert intervention and surveillance. This is reinforced by the regimen of ever-more numerous obstetric and pediatric examinations before and after childbirth, and the literature directed at mothers by the medical and pharmaceutical communities.

In contrast to agricultural and foraging societies, in ours breast-feeding does not easily fit into women's work or social lives. Few professions allow women much flexibility in time scheduling, and there is a deep, underlying expectation that the new mother will immediately be independent from her child. Many working women are forced to pump their milk in bathrooms, often in secrecy. Women who do not work

outside the home are targeted by formula manufacturers, who capitalize on cultural values such as work and efficiency by suggesting that formula feeding with an increasingly complex array of products demonstrates a woman's capability in scientific mothering.

Firms that sell formula, pacifiers, and other infant care products distribute samples and coupons through hospitals and physicians' offices, lending their products a medical stamp of approval that appeals to many parents. Often, they are able to "hook" babies even before they leave the hospital because the staff supplements the mother's milk with formula or sugar water, and the infant comes to prefer the easier flow of the bottle.

Thus, even when breast-feeding is promoted and women feel committed to it, social and cultural obstacles can make it difficult. A biocultural understanding of breast-feeding as an evolved, two-way process could help to make conditions more favorable. It would highlight the fact that women are normally able to breast-feed without medical approval, surveillance, and intervention and reduce the public's receptiveness to industrially produced formula and baby foods. Most importantly, the biocultural perspective would foster an appreciation of the intricate mechanisms linking mothers and infants together in a dynamic system of nutrition that benefits them both.

SUGGESTED READING

Cohen, Mark Nathan. 1989. *Health and the Rise of Civilization.* New Haven: Yale University Press.

Daly, S. E. J., and P. E. Hartmann. 1995. Infant Demand and Milk Supply. *Journal of Human Lactation* 11(1): 21–37.

Dettwyler, Katherine. 1995. A Time to Wean. In *Breast-feeding: Biocultural Perspectives,* eds. Patricia Stuart-Macadam and Katherine Dettwyler. New York: Aldine de Gruyter.

Eaton, S. Boyd, Melvin Konner, and Marjorie Shostak. 1988. *The Paleolithic Prescription.* New York: Harper and Row.

Eaton, S. Boyd, et al. 1994. Women's Reproductive Cancers in Evolutionary Perspective. *The Quarterly Review of Biology* 69(3): 353–367.

Ellison, Peter. 1995. Breast-feeding, Fertility, and Maternal Condition. In *Breast-feeding: Biocultural Perspectives,* eds. Patricia Stuart-Macadam and Katherine Dettwyler. New York: Aldine de Gruyter.

Ewald, Paul W. 1994. *Evolution of Infectious Disease.* New York: Oxford University Press.

Konner, Melvin, and Marjorie Shostak. 1987. Timing and Management of Birth among the !Kung. *Cultural Anthropology* 2(1): 11–28.

Konner, Melvin, and Carol Worthman. 1980. Nursing Frequency, Gonadal Function, and Birth Spacing among !Kung Hunter-Gatherers. *Science* 207: 788–791.

Maher, Vanessa (ed.). 1992. *The Anthropology of Breast-feeding.* Oxford: Berg.

McKenna, James. 1986. An Anthropological Perspective on the Sudden Infant Death Syndrome (SIDS): The Role of Parental Breathing Cues and Speech Breathing Adaptations. *Medical Anthropology* 10(1): 9–53.

McKenna, James, and Sarah Mosko. 1990. Evolution and the Sudden Infant Death Syndrome (SIDS). Part 3: Infant Arousal and Parent–Infant Co-Sleeping. *Human Nature* 1(3): 291–330.

Micozzi, Marc. 1995. Breast Cancer, Reproductive Biology, and Breast-feeding. In *Breast-feeding: Biocultural Perspectives,* eds. Patricia Stuart-Macadam and Katherine Dettwyler. New York: Aldine de Gruyter.

Nesse, Randolph M., and George C. Williams. 1994. *Why We Get Sick: The New Science of Darwinian Medicine.* New York: Random House.

Riordan, Jan, and Kathleen Auerbach. 1993. *Breast-feeding and Human Lactation.* Boston: Jones and Bartlett.

Scheper-Hughes, Nancy, and Margaret Lock. 1987. The Mindful Body: A Prolegomenon to Future Work in Medical Anthropology. *Medical Anthropology Quarterly* 1(1): 6–41.

Stuart-Macadam, Patricia. 1995. Breast-feeding in Prehistory. In *Breast-feeding: Biocultural Perspectives,* eds. Patricia Stuart-Macadam and Katherine Dettwyler. New York: Aldine de Gruyter.

Williams, George C., and Randolph M. Nesse. 1991. The Dawn of Darwinian Medicine. *The Quarterly Review of Biology* 66(1): 1–22.

Wood, James W. et al. 1985. Lactation and Birth Spacing in Highland New Guinea. *Journal of Biosocial Sciences, Supplement* 9: 159–173.

Woolridge, Michael W. 1995. Baby-Controlled Breast-feeding. In *Breast-feeding: Biocultural Perspectives,* eds. Patricia Stuart-Macadam and Katherin Dettwyler. New York: Aldine de Gruyter.

8

Slumber's Unexplored Landscape

Bruce Bower

Why might our sleep be shaped by culture? All people need to sleep, but our expectations of what is normal sleep and how we go about arranging sleep are dictated by our cultural background. Therefore, our need for sleep may be a biological universal, but there are significant variations in the way that our need for sleep is satisfied. Similarly, culture shapes the way that our need for food is satisfied—what and when we eat and which foods we most enjoy. Of course, we can learn to enjoy and desire new foods. In fact, expanding our palates through cultural learning can be a delicious experience. From another perspective, we might consider pain as a way that culture shapes biology. All people experience pain, but there are cultural rules about the way in which we communicate our discomfort. For example, some societies may have gender-specific rules about the expression of pain ("boys don't cry") that become internalized so that adult men seek health care less frequently than women and children and consequently die at earlier ages.

Human biologists do not completely understand what the neurophysiological and psychological functions of dreams might be. In this selection, we see that nearly all scientific sleep research is conducted in artificial laboratory settings and based on the particular patterns of sleep found in Western culture. In this way, medical definitions of insomnia are based upon cultural assumptions of what "normal" sleep patterns are.

In traditional societies, sleep is often communal and in contexts that are noisy. People in these societies see the North American pattern of putting babies in their own cribs in their own rooms as strange and barbaric. Cross-cultural comparison based on direct observations of people in the field is the hallmark of research in cultural anthropology. In this selection we find that people in traditional societies sleep in eye-opening ways.

As you read this selection, ask yourself the following questions:

- Many students find that their sleeping patterns change when they go to college. What are the ways that your social and cultural contexts determine your sleep?
- Does the two-phase sleep pattern described at the end of this selection make sense to you?
- When we sleep, we dream. Does culture affect the content of our dreams? Why are dreams more discussed in some other societies?
- What is the value of cross-cultural anthropological research in sleep research?

The following terms discussed in this selection are included in the Glossary at the back of the book:

communal	rapid eye movement (REM)
cross-cultural	séance

$\mathbf{A}$h, the sweet simplicity of sleep. You tramp into your bedroom with sagging eyelids and stifle a yawn. After disrobing, you douse the lights and climb into bed. Maybe a little reading or television massages the nerves, loosening them up for slumber's velvet fingers. In a while, you nod off. Suddenly, an alarm clock's shrill blast breaks up the dozefest as the sun pokes

over the horizon. You feel a bit drowsy but shake it off and face the new day. Images of a dream dissolve like sugar in the morning's first cup of coffee.

There's a surprising twist, however, at the heart of this familiar ritual. It simply doesn't apply to people currently living outside of the modern Western world—or even to inhabitants of Western Europe as recently as 200 years ago.

In such contexts, and probably throughout human evolution, solitary shut-eye organized around a regular bedtime and a single bout of sleep proves about as common as stock car racing or teleconferencing. Surprisingly, anthropologists have rarely scrutinized the

Bower, Bruce. "Slumber's Unexplored Landscape." *SCIENCE NEWS* 156 (Sept. 25, 1999):205–207. Copyright 1999 by Science Services, Inc. Reproduced with permission of Science Service, Inc. in the format Textbook via Copyright Clearance Center.

sleep patterns and practices of different cultures, much less those of different classes and ethnic groups in the United States.

An initial attempt to draw back the veils of sleep in hunter-gatherer groups and other traditional societies has uncovered a wide variety of sleep customs, reports anthropologist Carol M. Worthman of Emory University in Atlanta. None of these snooze styles, however, looks anything like what modern Western folk take for granted.

This finding raises profound questions for the burgeoning discipline of sleep research, Worthman says. Over the past 50 years, scientists have avidly delved into slumber's biology. Early research identified periods of rapid-eye-movement (REM) sleep, during which intense dreams often occur. Current efforts pursue genes involved in wakefulness and sleeping (SN: 8/14/99, p. 100). Researchers have also taken strides toward treating insomnia and other sleep disturbances.

While investigators readily concede that they don't yet know why people sleep and dream, they assume that they at least know how people should sleep: alone or with a partner for a solid chunk of the night. Sleep studies therefore take place in laboratories where individuals catch winks while hooked up to a bevy of brain and body monitors.

However, the distinctive sleep styles of non-Western groups may mold sleep's biology in ways undreamed of in sleep labs, Worthman suggests. They may influence factors ranging from sleep-related genes to the brain's electrical output during various sleep phases.

"It's time for scientists to get out into natural sleep environments," Worthman remarks. "It's embarrassing that anthropologists haven't done this, and the lack of such work is impeding sleep research."

A seemingly innocent question awakened Worthman to her discipline's ignorance of how people sleep. In 1994, she had a conversation with pediatrician Ronald E. Dahl of the University of Pittsburgh School of Medicine, who studies the effects of mood disorders on sleep. He asked the Emory scientist to tell him what anthropologists know about the history and prehistory of sleep. "[My] bald, if somewhat overstated, answer was 'zero,'" she says.

Sleep scarcely figures in the literature on either cross-cultural differences or human evolution, Worthman realized. Investigators generally relegate slumber to the sidelines, treating it as a biological given with little potential for variation from one place to another, she holds.

A few researchers have bucked this trend. For instance, anthropologist James J. McKenna of the

University of Notre Dame in Indiana has reported that babies in many countries outside the United States sleep next to or in the same room as their parents. Contact with a parent's body helps regulate an infant's breathing and other physiological functions, he asserts, perhaps lowering the risk for sudden infant death syndrome (SN:12/4/93, p. 380).

McKenna's work should have roused investigators of traditional societies out of their sleep-related torpor, Worthman says. Yet, even seasoned field-workers have tended to ignore sleep—at least in their published works—while describing food production, sexual practices, and other facets of daily life.

So, Worthman contacted seven researchers who she knew had intimate knowledge of one or more traditional societies, including nomadic foragers, herders, and village-based farmers. Among these far-flung populations, none of the investigators, by their own admission, had systematically studied how people sleep. After plumbing what the researchers had absorbed about nighttime activities, Worthman has assembled a preliminary picture of sleep practices in 10 non-Western populations.

Worthman's findings rip the covers off any lingering suspicions that people everywhere sleep pretty much alike. Far from the wallpapered confines of middle-class bedrooms, sleep typically unfolds in shared spaces that feature constant background noise emanating from other sleepers, various domestic animals, fires maintained for warmth and protection from predators, and other people's nearby night-time activities.

Groups in Worthman's analysis include Ache foragers in Paraguay, !Kung hunter-gatherers in Africa, Swat Pathan herders in Pakistan, and Balinese farmers in Indonesia. For all these groups and six others, communal sleep equals safe sleep, because sleepers can count on there being someone else up or easily awakened at all hours of the night to warn others of a threat or emergency.

Adult sleepers in traditional societies recline on skins, mats, wooden platforms, the ground, or just about anything except a thick, springy mattress. Pillows or head supports are rare, and people doze in whatever they happen to be wearing. Virtually no one, including children, keeps a regular bedtime. Individuals tend to slip in and out of slumber several times during the night. In these unplugged worlds, darkness greatly limits activity and determines the time allotted to sleep. Folks there frequently complain of getting too much sleep, not too little.

Many rituals occur at night and exploit the need to sleep. For instance, initiation rites often force participants to cope with sleep deprivation. In other ceremonies, individuals enter somnolent, or near-sleep, states in order to magnify an occasion's psychological impact and to induce spiritual visions.

Consider the communal sleep of the Gebusi, New Guinea, rainforest dwellers, who grow fruit in small gardens and occasionally hunt wild pigs. Women, girls, and babies crowd into a narrow section of a community longhouse to sleep on mats. Men and boys retreat to an adjacent, more spacious longhouse area, where they sleep on wooden platforms.

Gebusi females retire at dark for about 10 hours of rest and sleep. In contrast, the men stay up later and frequently conduct rituals. About once a month, everyone attends an all-night dance and feast, catching up on sleep the next day.

Each week or two, Gebusi men go to séances led by a "spirit medium," at which they try to keep spirits awake throughout the night. Participants attempt to slip in and out of a near-sleep state as the medium, who's usually adept at operating in this half-conscious condition, sings about the spirit world and other matters.

As in most of the other studied societies, the Gebusi express concerns about exposure to ghosts, evil spirits, and witchcraft during sleep. They consider deep sleep risky, since a sleeper's spirit may wander off too far and fail to return. The Gebusi view group slumber as a way to lessen the danger of spirit loss, which they view as especially likely while a person dreams.

Whether or not one believes that sleeping puts a person's spirit at risk, slumber appears to have crucial effects on body and mind. A culture's sleeping style serves as a growing child's training ground for managing biologically based systems of attention and alertness, Worthman contends. Balinese farmers provide a striking example of this sleep-related tutoring.

Balinese infants are carried and held continuously by caregivers so that they learn to fall asleep even in hectic and noisy situations. This grooms them to exhibit what the Balinese call "fear sleep" later in life, Worthman says. Children and adults enter fear sleep by suddenly slumping over in a deep slumber when they or family members confront intense anxiety or an unexpected fright. They are literally scared into sleep.

Infants in middle-class American homes, who usually sleep alone, may not learn to ground their sleeping and waking cycles in a flow of sensations that include bodily contact, smells, and background noises, Worthman proposes. In fact, babies forced to bounce back and forth between the sensory overload of the waking world and the sensory barrenness of dark, quiet bedrooms may often find it difficult to relax, fall asleep, wake up, or concentrate, she theorizes.

Only cross-cultural studies of children's sleep and behavior can clarify such issues, Worthman says.

She described her findings and their implications in June at the annual meeting of the Associated Professional Sleep Societies in Orlando, Fla.

Sleep researchers at the meeting expressed considerable excitement about the potential for cross-cultural studies. "Worthman is doing innovative and important work," comments neuroscientist Robert A. Stickgold of the Massachusetts Mental Health Center in Boston. "It's awakening us to the many different ways in which people organize sleep."

Stickgold has developed snug-fitting, electrode-studded caps that people can wear in their own beds to measure brain activity linked to REM and other sleep stages. Worthman plans to take these "nightcaps," which hook up to mobile recorders, into the field to study sleep biology in traditional societies.

"I've been hoping anthropologists would examine sleep cross-culturally for the past 20 years," remarks psychologist Mary A. Carskadon of the Brown University School of Medicine in Providence, R.I.

Carskadon has directed studies that indicate that the body's so-called biological clock gets pushed back during adolescence. Teenagers may require more sleep than adults and may have a natural tendency to go to sleep later and wake up later than at other ages, she says.

A related study, directed by neuroscientist Louis J. Ptáček of the University of Utah in Salt Lake City, finds that a specific gene yanks the biological clock forward in some adults. People who have this gene tend to fall asleep by 8:30 P.M. and to awaken before 5:30 A.M., the researchers report in the September *Nature Medicine*.

In modern Western cultures, teens' backward shift in sleep timing is considered a nuisance or a sign of rebellion, while extreme early birds get diagnosed as sleep disordered. In traditional settings, however, highly variable sleep schedules among individuals and age groups prove invaluable, since they allow for someone to be awake or easily roused at all times should danger arise, Worthman holds.

If sleeping patterns in traditional societies remain little known, those of prehistoric humans are a total mystery. Still, in settings that roughly mimic ancient nighttime conditions, sleep undergoes an intriguing shift, says psychiatrist Thomas A. Wehr of the National Institute of Mental Health (NIMH) in Bethesda, Md.

When prohibited from using artificial light from dusk until dawn, people who formerly slumbered in solid blocks of time begin to sleep in two periods separated by an hour or two of quiet rest and reflection.

Wehr and his coworkers asked 15 healthy adults to rest and sleep in darkness for 14 hours (6 P.M. to 8 A.M.) each night for several weeks. Volunteers slept for 11 hours each of the first few nights, apparently to catch up on their sleep. They then settled into a pattern of lying awake for a couple of hours before falling asleep for 3 to 5 hours in the evening. An hour or so of quiet wakefulness ensued, followed by about 4 more hours of sleep in the early morning.

Many mammals sleep in two major bouts during the night or day, Wehr says. Animals from rodents to giraffes and the experimental human sleepers secrete elevated amounts of the hormone prolactin when they rest quietly, even if they are not asleep. Prolactin may promote a state of calmness that accompanies sleep, the NIMH scientist suggests.

Participants in Wehr's study usually awoke out of REM sleep to end their first slumber session. During REM sleep, the brain becomes about as active as it is when wide awake. One function of this sleep phase may be to set the stage for waking up, Wehr holds.

If prehistoric people slept in two nightly periods, then regularly awakening out of REM sleep may have allowed them to reflect on and remember their dreams in a semiconscious state that's generally unavailable to modern sleepers. Sleep compressed into a single stint may thus encourage modern humans to lose touch with dreams, myths, and fantasies, Wehr argues.

These results, first reported in 1993, also raise the possibility that people who wake up once or twice each night don't necessarily suffer from insomnia. "A natural human sleep pattern may reassert itself in an unwelcome world and get labeled as a disorder," Wehr says.

The two-phase sleep pattern observed by Wehr corresponds remarkably closely to the way in which most Western Europeans slept between 500 to 200 years ago, according to historian A. Roger Ekirch of Virginia Polytechnic Institute and State University in Blacksburg. While doing research for a book on nighttime behaviors during that era, Ekirch came across several hundred references to what he identifies as "segmented sleep."

From country farms and villages to city apartments, early modern Europeans usually sank each evening into what they called a "first sleep," which lasted for several hours. Shortly after midnight, they awoke and spent 1 or 2 hours in a "watching period." A "second," or "morning," sleep followed.

The watching period presented many opportunities, Ekirch notes. People coming out of their first sleep often stayed in bed to pray, converse with a bedfellow, contemplate the day's events or the meaning of a dream, or simply let their minds wander in a semiconscious state of contentment that was prized at the time.

A sixteenth-century physician wrote that many laborers dozed off exhausted at the start of each night. Sexual intercourse with their wives typically occurred in the watching period, after a recuperative first sleep.

These days, Western societies treat sleep more as an unavoidable stretch of downtime than as a prelude to sex or a time for inner reflection. Only intensive investigations across cultures and classes will illuminate the lushness of sleep's landscape, Worthman predicts.

Adds Wehr, "We're going to have to reconceptualize what it means to sleep normally."

9

Ancient Genes and Modern Health

S. Boyd Eaton and Melvin Konner

The best available evidence about prehistory is that early humans were scavengers and gatherers of wild plants, not mighty hunters. This idea might at first seem far removed from the daily worries of people in complex societies like the United States. What do the food-getting methods of prehistoric people have to do with us and our world?

Two points are relevant here. First, anthropologists believe that food-getting and food-producing systems have been important factors in historical change, as we will see in Selection 13, "The Worst Mistake in the History of the Human Race." Second, a major problem confronting Western society has been the rise in particular chronic illnesses—sometimes called the diseases of civilization—that ultimately kill most Americans. In this article, S. Boyd Eaton and Melvin Konner demonstrate how information from paleoanthropology and the study of contemporary hunters and gatherers can shed new light on the origins of some present-day health problems.

As you read this selection, ask yourself the following questions:

- What is the difference between biological and cultural evolution?

- Do biological culture and cultural evolution advance at the same rate? If not, what sorts of things might happen as cultural changes occur faster than biological changes?
- What was the diet of our Paleolithic ancestors?
- What sort of nutritional changes accompanied the development of agriculture?
- What sorts of illnesses are found in the West but not among hunter-gatherers?
- In addition to diet, what other lifestyle differences are related to chronic illness in the Western world?

The following terms discussed in this selection are included in the Glossary at the back of the book:

agricultural development	*foraging*
Cro-Magnon	*hunter-gatherers*
cultural evolution	*Paleolithic*
dental anthropology	*paleontology*
epidemiology	*prehistoric*

For the past ten years we have been investigating the proposition that the major chronic illnesses which afflict humans living in affluent industrialized Western nations are promoted by a mismatch between our genetic constitution and a variety of lifestyle factors which have bioenvironmental relevance. The diseases include atherosclerosis with its sequels of heart attacks, strokes, and peripheral vascular disease; adult-onset diabetes; many important forms of cancer; hypertension (high blood pressure); emphysema; and obesity. The main lifestyle variables are diet, exercise patterns and exposure to abusive substances—chiefly

Eaton, S. Boyd & Melvin Konner. "Ancient Genes and Modern Health." Courtesy of the Leakey Foundation.

alcohol and tobacco. We have taken the basic position that the genetic constitution of humanity, which controls our physiology, biochemistry, and metabolism, has not been altered in any fundamental way since *Homo sapiens sapiens* first became widespread. In contrast, cultural evolution during the relatively brief period since the appearance of agriculture has been breathtakingly rapid, so that genes selected over the preceding geologic eras must now function in a foreign and, in many ways, hostile Atomic Age milieu.

In order to better understand our current lifestyle/genetic discord and to appreciate what steps might be taken to eliminate its harmful etiologic consequences, we needed to determine, as best we could, the actual constituents of our ancestral lifestyle. For most people speculation about our Stone Age ancestors exerts a strong fascination: How did they live, what did they look like, how did they differ from us and how were they similar? For us, the effort to characterize their nutritional practices and the exercise patterns necessitated by their daily activities has been exciting as well as scientifically rewarding. The bulk of our understanding has come from the fields of paleontology, anthropology, epidemiology, and nutritional science.

Paleontology is the study of fossil remains. For example, the stature of Paleolithic humans can be estimated from the length of femora (thigh bones) according to a formula which relates total height to femoral length; it is not necessary to have all the bony components of a skeleton to make this determination. Such studies have shown that humans living in the eastern Mediterranean area 30,000 years ago were probably tall; males averaged 177.1 cm (5' 9¾") and females 166.5 cm (5' 5½"), whereas in 1960 Americans averaged 174.2 cm (5' 8½") and 163.4 cm (5' 4½"), respectively.

Skeletal height and pelvic depth both probably reflect nutritional factors, especially protein intake. With the advent of agriculture, animal protein intake decreased markedly so that average stature for both men and women ultimately declined by over 10 centimeters. The same phenomenon, a decrease in the animal protein content of the diet around the time that agriculture first appeared, is also documented by analysis of strontium/calcium ratios in bony remains. Strontium reaches the skeletons of living animals mainly through ingestion of plant foods so that herbivores have higher strontium levels in their bones than do carnivores. Studies of strontium/calcium ratios in the bones of humans who lived just before and during the changeover to agriculture confirm that the consumption of meat declined relative to that of vegetable foods around this period.

Skeletons also indicate muscularity; the prominence of muscular insertion sites and the area of articular surfaces both vary directly with the forces exerted by the muscles acting on them. Analyses of these features show that average preagricultural humans were apparently generally stronger than those who lived thereafter, including us today. Because of their hardness, teeth are very well represented in paleontological material. It is a telling comment about our current consumption of sugar (which approaches 125 lbs per person per year in the United States) that only about 2 percent of teeth from the Late Paleolithic period exhibit dental caries whereas some recent European populations have had more than 70 percent of their teeth so affected.

Anthropology is a broad discipline which includes the study of recent hunter-gatherers whose lives can be considered to mirror those of our remote ancestors in many ways. Of course, there are important differences: Such people have been increasingly forced from the most environmentally desirable areas into desert, arctic, or jungle habitats where the food quest must be far more difficult than it was for Paleolithic hunter-gatherers who exploited the most abundant and fruitful regions then available without competition from encroaching civilization. On the other hand, the technology of recent foragers is more advanced than that available to those living 25,000 years ago; an excellent example is the bow and arrow, perhaps developed no earlier than 10 to 15 thousand years ago. Nevertheless, study of recent hunter-gatherers does provide a kind of window into the Stone Age world; the nutrition, physical attributes, and health of individuals who have such parallel lives must be reasonably similar despite the millennia which separate them in time.

Anthropologists have studied over 50 hunter-gatherer societies sufficiently well to justify nutritional generalizations about them. When data from these groups are analyzed statistically, the average values all center around a subsistence pattern of 35 percent meat and 65 percent vegetable foods (by weight). There is, of course, considerable variation; arctic peoples may eat up to 90 percent animal products, whereas arid desert dwellers may obtain only 15 percent of their diet from such sources. Nevertheless, these data allow us to reasonably conclude that Paleolithic humans had a roughly similar range of subsistence patterns.

Epidemiology is the study of disease patterns. When a pathologic condition, such as lung cancer, is common in a specified population, for example, cigarette smokers, and uncommon in another specified group, such as nonsmokers, differences between the two groups may bear on the etiology of the disease condition under scrutiny. Information derived from various epidemiologic investigations can be used to help estimate what sorts of diseases might have afflicted Paleolithic humans and which ones must have been uncommon. For example, in today's world, people who consume a minimal amount of saturated fat tend to have little coronary heart disease and a relatively low incidence of cancer involving the breast, uterus, prostate, and colon. If we could be confident that the Stone Age diet contained little saturated fat we could rationally assume that individuals living then had a lower incidence of heart disease and cancers related to fat intake than do persons living in affluent, industrialized Western nations today. Similar arguments might be made concerning hypertension (as related to dietary sodium, potassium, and calcium) and, of course, lung cancer and emphysema (cigarettes). A tempting assumption is that, since illnesses of this sort tend to become manifest in older persons, Paleolithic humans (whose life expectancy was less than ours) would not have had the opportunity to develop them, no matter what their lifestyle. However, epidemiologists and pathologists have shown that young people in the Western world commonly have developing, asymptomatic forms of these illnesses, but hunter-gatherer youths do not. Furthermore, those members of technologically primitive cultures who survive to the age of 60 or more remain relatively free from these disorders, unlike their "civilized" counterparts.

Nutritional science furthers evaluation of Paleolithic life by providing analyses of the foods such people were likely to have eaten. An understanding of their overall nutrition is impossible without knowing that, although they ate more red meat than we do now, they nevertheless consumed much less saturated fat since wild game has less than a fifth the fat found in the domesticated animals currently bred and raised for meat production. Similarly, nutrition analyses of the wild, uncultivated fruits, vegetables, and nuts eaten by recent hunter-gatherers allow us to estimate the average nutritional values of the plant foods our ancestors ate. To this end we have been able to accumulate nutritional data characterizing 43 different wild animals ranging from kangaroos to wart hogs and 153 different wild vegetable foods—mainly roots, beans, nuts, tubers, and fruit but including items as diverse as truffles and seed pods. The search for this information has been challenging but entertaining; how else would one learn that bison meat contains only 40 mg of cholesterol per 100 grams of tissue or that the Australian green plum has the world's highest known vitamin C content (3150 mg per 100 grams)!

When information from these disparate scientific disciplines is correlated and coordinated, what is the picture that emerges? What was the diet of our ancestors; what are other important ways in which their lifestyle differs from ours; and do these differences have any relationship to the chronic illnesses from which we suffer, but from which recent hunter-gatherers seem immune?

To address the most straightforward, but certainly not unimportant, issues first, it is clear that our Stone Age ancestors were rarely if ever exposed to tobacco and alcohol. The manufacture of barley beer can be dated as early as 7000 years ago, but there is no convincing evidence for consumption of alcohol before this time, and recent technologically primitive groups have not been found to manufacture alcoholic beverages. Similarly, there is no indication that tobacco was available in Eurasia prior to the voyages of discovery only 500 years ago. But Late Paleolithic peoples were probably not altogether free from abusive substances; several recent hunter-gatherer groups have used some form of consciousness-altering drugs for ceremonial purposes and it seems likely that similar agents may have been available in the Late Stone Age although their use could hardly have been as prevalent as is currently the case.

The physical demands of life in the Late Paleolithic period insured that our ancestors, both men and women, were strong, fit, lean, and muscular. Their bones prove that they were robust—they resemble those of today's superior athletes. Furthermore, hunter-gatherers studied in the last 150 years have been trim and athletic in their appearance.

Modern nutritionists generally feel that items from four basic food groups—meat and fish; vegetables, nuts, and fruits; milk and milk products; and breads and cereals—are necessary for a balanced diet. But during the Paleolithic period older children and adults derived all their nutrients from the first two groups: wild game and vegetables, fruits, and nuts. Except for very young children, who were weaned much later than they are today, no one had any dairy foods at all and they apparently made comparatively little use of grain. Their only "refined" carbohydrate was honey, available only seasonally and obtained painfully. They seem to have eaten little seafood until fairly late in prehistory, though this assumption is questionable since the ancient sea level was much lower (because of water locked up in the extensive glaciers of that period), and the sites of Paleolithic seacoast dwellers are now under water.

After weaning, Paleolithic humans drank water, but the beverages we now consume generally deliver an appreciable caloric load as they quench our thirst. Mundane as it is, this example illustrates a pervasive pattern—caloric concentration. Since our meat is fattier, it contains more calories per unit weight (typically two to three times as many) than does wild game. Furthermore, the plant foods we eat are commonly refined and adulterated so that their basic caloric load is multiplied: french fries have more than twice and potato chips over five times the calories present in an equal weight of baked potato. Pumpkin pie has ten times the calories found in the same weight of pumpkin served alone.

The salt added to our foods as a seasoning and as a preservative insures that we now consume an average of six times the daily sodium intake of Paleolithic humans. In a similar vein, the process of refining carbohydrate foods provides us with quantities of sugar and white flour far in excess of what was available to our ancestors while reducing our complex carbohydrate (starch) and dietary fiber intake much below the levels they consumed. Not only do we eat twice the fat eaten by Stone Agers, its nature is different. Structural fat is a necessary constituent of cellular membranous structures; this type of fat is predominantly polyunsaturated in nature and was the major fat consumed by our remote ancestors. Conversely, depot or storage fat is the main type found in the adipose tissue stores of domesticated animals; this variety of fat is largely saturated and is very prominent in today's diets. Like game available now, the wild animals eaten 25,000 years ago had minimal depot fat; accordingly humans then ate considerably more polyunsaturated than saturated fat—but the reverse occurs in twentieth century affluent Western nations.

To summarize, these observations indicate that the Cro-Magnons and similar Late Paleolithic peoples consumed nearly three times the amount of protein we do, about a sixth of the sodium, more potassium, more calcium (which is very interesting in view of the prevalence of osteoporosis in today's society), and considerably more vitamin C (though not the amounts megavitamin enthusiasts would recommend). They ate about the same amount of carbohydrate that we do; however, it was predominantly in the form of starch and other complex carbohydrates, providing a good deal more dietary fiber than we have in our diet. For them refined carbohydrate and simple sugar, from honey and fruit, were available only seasonally and in limited amounts. They ate only half the fat we consume in twentieth century America and their fat was more polyunsaturated than saturated in nature.

Certain aspects of our ancestors' physical fitness bear further emphasis: Their "exercise program" was lifelong, it developed both endurance and strength, it applied to men and women alike, and the activities which comprised their "workouts" varied predictably with seasonal changes. Today's fitness enthusiasts might well ponder these Paleolithic training guidelines. Pre-agricultural humans were more like decathlon athletes than either marathoners or power lifters; our genes appear to have been programmed for the synergism which results when endurance and strength occur together. A lifelong program was unavoidable for them; for us it requires strategic planning. Really long-term training in just one exercise mode is almost impossible to maintain; overtraining, boredom, and burn-out tend to overcome even the most intense dedication. Paleolithic men and women were spared these phenomena because the activities of each season differed from those of the next. The Russians have perhaps unconsciously recreated these circumstances in a training approach they call "periodization." This system employs planned daily, weekly, and quarterly variation in the mode, volume, and intensity of exercise so that training remains fresh and invigorating, not dull and endlessly repetitive. Perhaps this recapitulation of our ancestral pattern partially explains the success their athletes have experienced in international competition.

What about the proposition we advanced at the beginning of this article: Do the diseases of civilization result from the mismatch between our genes and our current lifestyle? The evidence is strong that such a connection exists. In important respects the lifestyle of Paleolithic humans, that for which our genes have been selected, parallels recommendations made by the American Cancer Society, the American Heart Association, the American Diabetes Association and the Senate Select Committee on Nutrition. Furthermore, recent hunter-gatherers have been essentially free from the chronic illnesses which kill most Americans.

Anthropology, paleontology, medicine, epidemiology and nutrition can be likened to the facets of a prism, each providing a different view of the same subject. Our subject is the health and disease of persons living in affluent, industrialized Western society and when views provided by diverse scientific disciplines converge, the resulting implications acquire profound significance. There is nothing especially distinctive about human hunter-gatherers in biochemical and physiological terms. What they ate and how they lived fall well within the broad mammalian spectrum. During the past 10,000 years, however, humans have exceeded the bounds. Many of the lifestyle factors we now take for granted (particularly sedentary living, alcohol, tobacco and our high salt, high saturated fat, high refined carbohydrate diet) are unique in free-living vertebrate experience. They constitute a deviation so extreme that our bodies have responded by developing forms of illness not otherwise seen in nature. These are the diseases of civilization.

10

The Tall and the Short of It

Barry Bogin

An important area of biological anthropology is the description and explanation of human biological diversity among people living today. When we look around, it is easy to see diversity in people's outward appearance (their phenotype) that results from differences in genetic inheritance (genotype) as well as their interaction with the environment, particularly during critical times in child growth and development. There was a time in the not-too-distant past when scientists thought that differences in groups' outward physical characteristics were completely inherited, fixed, and unchangeable. They also thought that such traits could be placed into biologically meaningful categories or races. Today it is clear that both of these ideas are wrong, even if they persist in people's folk biology.

Biological anthropologists do research on child growth and development—that is, measuring and explaining patterns of growth through the life cycle. Measurement of human biology—in stature, weight, fat folds, and so forth—is called anthropometry. In pediatrics, an individual baby's growth is plotted along a standardized growth curve; failure to grow is an indication that something is wrong. But is this to say that being short is a sign of unhealthiness? To what extent are anthropometric measurements a reflection of our genes, and to what extent do our body size and shape reflect environmental conditions? The most important environmental condition is nutrition—whether a child is getting enough food and the right kinds of food. If a child lives in poverty, his or her adult phenotype and overall health will be affected.

This topic was explored by the father of American anthropology, Franz Boas, who compared immigrant populations and their children raised in the United States during the 1920s. He documented a rapid increase in all anthropometric measurements, including stature and cranial measurement, for the U.S.-raised offspring, even though the genetic composition was identical. These people experienced a change in environment, particularly in child nutrition. Boas used this data to argue against the notion of fixed races based on phenotypic characteristics.

In this selection, Barry Bogin describes what is known about human plasticity—the change in phenotypic characteristics of a group over time. He raises hypotheses about why Americans used to be the tallest population in the world but are now behind the Dutch in height. These discoveries in biological anthropology have implications for public policy.

As you read this selection, ask yourself the following questions:

- Because biological anthropologists used aggregate data to talk about changes in average stature of a population, is it possible to extend these observations to the individual level?

- Is it correct to think of poverty as part of the environment? To what extent do humans create their own environment?

- Does access to food and social stimulation affect brain development? What does this mean in regard to the genetic potential and the actual achievements of children growing up in poverty?

- Why might Americans be one of the fattest populations of the world? What cultural factors might cause such biological changes?

The following terms discussed in this selection are included in the Glossary at the back of the book:

adaptation   plasticity
anthropometry   stature
lactose intolerance

Bogin, Barry. "The Tall and the Short of It." Discover Magazine
(Feb. 1998):40–44. Reprinted with permission of the author.

As a biological anthropologist, I have just one word of advice for you: plasticity. *Plasticity* refers to the ability of many organisms, including humans, to alter themselves—their behavior or even their biology—in response to changes in the environment. We tend to think that our bodies get locked into their final form by our genes, but in fact we alter our bodies as the conditions surrounding us shift, particularly as we grow during childhood. Plasticity is as much a product of evolution's fine-tuning as any particular gene, and it makes just as much evolutionary good sense. Rather than being able to adapt to a single environment, we can, thanks to plasticity, change our bodies to cope with a wide range of environments. Combined with the genes we inherit from our parents, plasticity accounts for what we are and what we can become.

Anthropologists began to think about human plasticity around the turn of the century, but the concept was first clearly defined in 1969 by Gabriel Lasker, a biological anthropologist at Wayne State University in Detroit. At that time scientists tended to consider only those adaptations that were built into the genetic makeup of a person and passed on automatically to the next generation. A classic example of this is the ability of adults in some human societies to drink milk. As children, we all produce an enzyme called lactase, which we need to break down the sugar lactose in our mother's milk. In many of us, however, the lactase gene slows down dramatically as we approach adolescence—probably as the result of another gene that regulates its activity. When that regulating gene turns down the production of lactase, we can no longer digest milk.

Lactose intolerance—which causes intestinal gas and diarrhea—affects between 70 and 90 percent of African Americans, Native Americans, Asians, and people who come from around the Mediterranean. But others, such as people of central and western European descent and the Fulani of West Africa, typically have no problem drinking milk as adults. That's because they are descended from societies with long histories of raising goats and cattle. Among these people there was a clear benefit to being able to drink milk, so natural selection gradually changed the regulation of their lactase gene, keeping it functioning throughout life.

That kind of adaptation takes many centuries to become established, but Lasker pointed out that there are two other kinds of adaptation in humans that need far less time to kick in. If people have to face a cold winter with little or no heat, for example, their metabolic rates rise over the course of a few weeks and they produce more body heat. When summer returns, the rates sink again.

Lasker's other mode of adaptation concerned the irreversible, lifelong modification of people as they develop—that is, their plasticity. Because we humans take so many years to grow to adulthood, and because we live in so many different environments, from forests to cities and from deserts to the Arctic, we are among the world's most variable species in our physical form and behavior. Indeed, we are one of the most plastic of all species.

One of the most obvious manifestations of human malleability is our great range of height, and it is a subject I've made a special study of for the last 25 years. Consider these statistics: in 1850 Americans were the tallest people in the world, with American men averaging 5'6". Almost 150 years later, American men now average 5'8", but we have fallen in the standings and are now only the third tallest people in the world. In first place are the Dutch. Back in 1850 they averaged only 5'4"—the shortest men in Europe—but today they are a towering 5'10". (In these two groups, and just about everywhere else, women average about five inches less than men at all times.)

So what happened? Did all the short Dutch sail over to the United States? Did the Dutch back in Europe get an infusion of "tall genes"? Neither. In both America and the Netherlands life got better, but more so for the Dutch, and height increased as a result. We know this is true thanks in part to studies on how height is determined. It's the product of plasticity in our childhood and in our mothers' childhood as well. If a girl is undernourished and suffers poor health, the growth of her body, including her reproductive system, is usually reduced. With a shortage of raw materials, she can't build more cells to construct a bigger body; at the same time, she has to invest what materials she can get into repairing already existing cells and tissues from the damage caused by disease. Her shorter stature as an adult is the result of a compromise her body makes while growing up.

Such a woman can pass on her short stature to her child, but genes have nothing to do with it for either of them. If she becomes pregnant, her small reproductive system probably won't be able to supply a normal level of nutrients and oxygen to her fetus. This harsh environment reprograms the fetus to grow more slowly than it would if the woman was healthier, so she is more likely to give birth to a smaller baby. Low-birth-weight babies (weighing less than 5.5 pounds) tend to continue their prenatal program of slow growth through childhood. By the time they are teenagers, they are usually significantly shorter than people of normal birth weight. Some particularly striking evidence of this reprogramming comes from studies on monozygotic twins, which develop from a single fertilized egg cell and are therefore identical genetically. But in certain cases, monozygotic twins end up being nourished by unequal portions of the placenta. The twin with the smaller fraction of the placenta is often born with low birth weight, while the other one is normal. Follow-up studies show that this difference between the twins can last throughout their lives.

As such research suggests, we can use the average height of any group of people as a barometer of the health of their society. After the turn of the century both the United States and the Netherlands began to protect the health of their citizens by purifying drinking water, installing sewer systems, regulating the safety of food, and, most important, providing better health care and diets to children. The children responded to their changed environment by growing taller. But the differences in Dutch and American societies determined their differing heights today. The Dutch decided to provide public health benefits to all the public, including the poor. In the United States, meanwhile, improved health is enjoyed most by those who can afford it. The poor often lack adequate housing, sanitation, and health care. The difference in our two societies can be seen at birth: in 1990 only 4 percent of Dutch babies were born at low birth weight, compared with 7 percent in the United States. For white Americans the rate was 5.7 percent, and for black Americans the rate was a whopping 13.3 percent. The disparity between rich and poor in the United States carries through to adulthood: poor Americans are shorter than the better-off by about one inch. Thus, despite great affluence in the United States, our average height has fallen to third place.

People are often surprised when I tell them the Dutch are the tallest people in the world. Aren't they shrimps compared with the famously tall Tutsi (or "Watusi," as you probably first encountered them) of Central Africa? Actually, the supposed great height of the Tutsi is one of the most durable myths from the age of European exploration. Careful investigation reveals that today's Tutsi men average 5'7" and that they have maintained that average for more than 100 years. That means that back in the 1800s, when puny European men first met the Tutsi, the Europeans suffered strained necks from looking up all the time. The two-to-three-inch difference in average height back then could easily have turned into fantastic stories of African giants by European adventurers and writers.

The Tutsi could be as tall or taller than the Dutch if equally good health care and diets were available in Rwanda and Burundi, where the Tutsi live. But poverty rules the lives of most African people, punctuated by warfare, which makes the conditions for growth during childhood even worse. And indeed, it turns out that the Tutsi and other Africans who migrate to Western Europe or North America at young ages end up taller than Africans remaining in Africa.

At the other end of the height spectrum, Pygmies tell a similar story. The shortest people in the world today are the Mbuti, the Efe, and other Pygmy peoples of Central Africa. Their average stature is about 4'9" for adult men and 4'6" for women. Part of the reason Pygmies are short is indeed genetic: some evidently lack the genes for producing the growth-promoting hormones that course through other people's bodies, while others are genetically incapable of using these hormones to trigger the cascade of reactions that lead to growth. But another important reason for their small size is environmental. Pygmies living as hunter-gatherers in the forests of Central African countries appear to be undernourished, which further limits their growth. Pygmies who live on farms and ranches outside the forest are better fed than their hunter-gatherer relatives and are taller as well. Both genes and nutrition thus account for the size of Pygmies.

Peoples in other parts of the world have also been labeled pygmies, such as some groups in Southeast Asia and the Maya of Guatemala. Well-meaning explorers and scientists have often claimed that they are genetically short, but here we encounter another myth of height. A group of extremely short people in New Guinea, for example, turned out to eat a diet deficient in iodine and other essential nutrients. When they were supplied with cheap mineral and vitamin supplements, their supposedly genetic short stature vanished in their children, who grew to a more normal height.

Another way for these so-called pygmies to stop being pygmies is to immigrate to the United States. In my own research, I study the growth of two groups of Mayan children. One group lives in their homeland of Guatemala, and the other is a group of refugees living in the United States. The Maya in Guatemala live in the village of San Pedro, which has no safe source of drinking water. Most of the water is contaminated with fertilizers and pesticides used on nearby agricultural fields. Until recently, when a deep well was dug, the townspeople depended on an unreliable supply of water from rain-swollen streams. Most homes still lack running water and have only pit toilets. The parents of the Mayan children work mostly at clothing factories and are paid only a few dollars a day.

I began working with the schoolchildren in this village in 1979, and my research shows that most of them eat only 80 percent of the food they need. Other research shows that almost 30 percent of the girls and 20 percent of the boys are deficient in iodine, that most of the children suffer from intestinal parasites, and that many have persistent ear and eye infections. As a consequence, their health is poor and their height reflects it: they average about three inches shorter than better-fed Guatemalan children.

The Mayan refugees I work with in the United States live in Los Angeles and in the rural agricultural community of Indiantown in central Florida. Although the adults work mostly in minimum-wage jobs, the children in these communities are generally better off than their counterparts in Guatemala. Most Maya arrived in the 1980s as refugees escaping a civil war as well as a political system that threatened them and their children. In the United States they found security and started new lives, and before long their children began growing faster and bigger. My data show that the average increase in height among the first generation of these immigrants was 2.2 inches, which means that these so-called pygmies have undergone one of the largest single-generation increases in height ever recorded. When people such as my own grandparents migrated from the poverty of rural life in Eastern Europe to the cities of the United States just after World War I, the increase in height of the next generation was only about one inch.

One reason for the rapid increase in stature is that in the United States the Maya have access to treated drinking water and to a reliable supply of food. Especially critical are school breakfast and lunch programs for children from low-income families, as well as public assistance programs such as the federal Women, Infants, and Children (WIC) program and food stamps. That these programs improve health and growth is no secret. What is surprising is how fast they work. Mayan mothers in the United States tell me that even their babies are bigger and healthier than the babies they raised in Guatemala, and hospital statistics bear them out. These women must be enjoying a level of health so improved from that of their lives in Guatemala that their babies are growing faster in the womb. Of course, plasticity means that such changes are dependent on external conditions, and unfortunately the rising height—and health—of the Maya is in danger from political forces that are attempting to cut funding for food stamps and the WIC program. If that funding is cut, the negative impact on the lives of poor Americans, including the Mayan refugees, will be as dramatic as were the former positive effects.

Height is only the most obvious example of plasticity's power; there are others to be found everywhere you look. The Andes-dwelling Quechua people of Peru are well adapted to their high-altitude homes. Their large, barrel-shaped chests house big lungs that inspire huge amounts of air with each breath, and they manage to survive on the lower pressure of oxygen they breathe with an unusually high level of red blood cells. Yet these secrets of mountain living are not hereditary. Instead the bodies of young Quechua adapt as they grow in their particular environment, just as those of European children do when they live at high altitudes.

Plasticity may also have a hand in determining our risks for developing a number of diseases. For example, scientists have long been searching for a cause for Parkinson's disease. Because Parkinson's tends to run in families, it is natural to think there is a genetic cause. But while a genetic mutation linked to some types of Parkinson's disease was reported in mid-1997, the gene accounts for only a fraction of people with the disease. Many more people with Parkinson's do not have the gene, and not all people with the mutated gene develop the disease.

Ralph Garruto, a medical researcher and biological anthropologist at the National Institutes of Health, is investigating the role of the environment and human plasticity not only in Parkinson's but in Lou Gehrig's disease as well. Garruto and his team traveled to the islands of Guam and New Guinea, where rates of both diseases are 50 to 100 times higher than in the United States. Among the native Chamorro people of Guam these diseases kill one person out of every five over the age of 25. The scientists found that both diseases are linked to a shortage of calcium in the diet. This shortage sets off a cascade of events that result in the digestive system's absorbing too much of the aluminum present in the diet. The aluminum wreaks havoc on various parts of the body, including the brain, where it destroys neurons and eventually causes paralysis and death.

The most amazing discovery made by Garruto's team is that up to 70 percent of the people they studied in Guam had some brain damage, but only 20 percent progressed all the way to Parkinson's or Lou Gehrig's disease. Genes and plasticity seem to be working hand in hand to produce these lower-than-expected rates of disease. There is a certain amount of genetic variation in the ability that all people have in coping with calcium shortages—some can function better than others. But thanks to plasticity, it's also possible for people's bodies to gradually develop ways to protect themselves against aluminum poisoning. Some people develop biochemical barriers to the aluminum they eat, while others develop ways to prevent the aluminum from reaching the brain.

An appreciation of plasticity may temper some of our fears about these diseases and even offer some hope. For if Parkinson's and Lou Gehrig's diseases can be prevented among the Chamorro by plasticity, then maybe medical researchers can figure out a way to produce the same sort of plastic changes in you and me. Maybe Lou Gehrig's disease and Parkinson's disease—as well as many others, including some cancers—aren't our genetic doom but a product of our development, just like variations in human height. And maybe their danger will in time prove as illusory as the notion that the Tutsi are giants, or the Maya pygmies—or Americans still the tallest of the tall.

11

Identifying Victims after a Disaster

Dick Gould

Popular television shows like *CSI, Law and Order,* and *Bones* provide drama-hungry viewers with glimpses of the kinds of questions and answers that real-life forensic scientists face every day. What can the physical evidence—the clothes, artifacts, bones, hair, blood, and other traces—tell us about the life and death of the victim? Some biological anthropologists trained in skeletal biology and some archaeologists work in the area of forensic investigation—that is, science used for legal purposes.

The methods and tools of skeletal biologists and archaeologists have proven critical in the wake of both natural and humanly created disasters. Besides working in areas of war crimes such as Bosnia and Guatemala, forensic anthropologists have helped identify the bodies of victims killed in both the collapse of the World Trade Center on September 11, 2001, and the Hurricane Katrina disaster that swept through New Orleans in 2005.

This selection explores the traditional role forensics has played in the work of archaeologists, whose conclusions must withstand challenges in what the author calls the "court of history." It also sheds light on the increasing importance of forensic anthropology's methods and analyses within contemporary courts of law. Not only are archaeologists and forensic anthropologists able to help solve both historical and contemporary mysteries, but they can also provide an important humanitarian function: to help the families of deceased individuals put their loved ones' remains to rest once and for all. Identifying victims after a disaster may seem like ghastly work, but its purpose is very humane.

As you read this selection, ask yourself the following questions:

- What are the primary goals of forensic anthropology, and what are its primary research methods?

- What does the author mean when he describes himself as "an archaeologist pretending to be a forensic anthropologist"?

- How would you describe the historical relationship between archaeology and forensic science, and how is that relationship changing?

- What does the author mean by a "forensically controlled environment"?

- How, and why, has the demand for forensic anthropologists changed in response to the Family Assistance Act of 1996, the destruction of the World Trade Center on September 11, 2001, and Hurricane Katrina in 2005?

The following terms discussed in this selection are included in the Glossary at the back of the book:

forensic anthropology
osteology

After Hurricane Katrina struck the Gulf coast I was deployed to the area for 17 days by the national Disaster Mortuary Operations Team (DMORT). The first week I volunteered identifying victims in Gulfport, Mississippi. The remaining time I assisted recovering human remains from hospitals, nursing homes, and

schools in New Orleans and St. Bernard Parish. In New Orleans we recovered 48 victims at Memorial Hospital, mainly elders.

Many responders to the disaster, such as myself, are still coming up for air. At the same time, the aftermath of Katrina—both the long recovery process and our analyses of the event—has only just begun. And while it is too soon to come to any conclusions about the role of anthropology in responding to the hurricane, one thing is obvious: anthropologists will continue to become an increasingly important part of major disaster recovery operations.

DISASTER ANTHROPOLOGY

Anthropologists join funeral directors, medical examiners, coroners, pathologists, medical records technicians and transcribers, finger print specialists, forensic odontologists, dental assistants, x-ray technicians, mental health specialists, computer professionals, administrative support staff, and security and investigative personnel in volunteering with DMORT. As part of its national response to disasters plan, the Federal Emergency Management Administration calls on DMORT to identify victims and provide assistance to families. Since 1996 when Congress passed the Family Assistance Act, this humanitarian role of forensics and DMORT has continued to become central to the work of identifying victims of disasters. The Family Assistance Act was passed in response to families who had lost loved ones in airline incidents. These families testified they had received inadequate treatment, often left wondering the fate of those they lost. The act requires all public and private entities operating in the United States to have a plan to assist families, in part by providing them with the information to help them grieve, in the event of a disaster.

Many DMORT volunteers have years of experience in rapidly responding to disasters. Gina Hart, a forensic anthropologist from the New Jersey State Medical Examiner's Office, was a well of expertise in Gulfport, drawing from her past work for the UN in identifying victims of ethnic violence and human rights abuses in Bosnia. Forensic work is based on a powerful method: comparing pre- and post-mortem data to identify a person. The resulting information not only assists families, but it constitutes evidence that can later be used in a court case. In Gulfport we had our challenges, largely because like in Bosnia and other areas torn by disaster, there was little ante-mortem data available to us. Dental records were destroyed by the storm, or perhaps never even existed.

Before the processing of human remains can begin, or the forensic work, the remains must first be recovered from the field. It is in this role that the importance of archaeology is emerging. I often joke that I am an archaeologist pretending to be a forensic anthropologist. There is some truth to this. Yet, the need for archaeologists in recovering field remains and helping to carefully record the scene where remains are found cannot be ignored. An archaeologist's questions about the linking of material remains to a carefully documented field site can only strengthen the work of accurately and rapidly identifying remains. As insurance claims are processed and the question is asked—was it the storm, flood, or something else that killed this person—carefully recorded details of the scene are vital, along with the careful treatment of the recovered remains.

STANDARDS OF EVIDENCE

All forensic investigations share similar standards of evidence. They all assume that evidence recovered at a crime or disaster scene must be documented and maintained under control from the point of collection to the courtroom or to the medical examiner's office in an unbroken evidentiary chain. This is usually referred to as the "chain of custody" (or "chain of evidence"). Evidence collected in this way for medical and legal purposes must be able to withstand challenges in the court of law, which may be very different from a scholarly context or what can be called the "court of history."

Although forensic anthropology is a profession of long standing, the role of forensic anthropologists has been expanding dramatically since the World Trade Center disaster in 2001. Since Sept. 11, not only have queries about forensics as a profession increased, but the scope of anthropological investigations and recoveries has shifted into the realm of humanitarianism—especially at mass-fatality disaster scenes. Prior to Sept. 11 the focus of forensics was largely in terms of investigation, or providing evidence for courts of law, rather than its humanitarian role in assisting grieving families.

Forensic anthropology, or the "CSI model" after the popular television program, has been applied, for example, for decades to standard crime-scene investigations, often involving the FBI or Bureau of Alcohol, Tobacco, Firearms and Explosives.

Human rights archaeologists have played a major role in investigating the fate of "disappeared" individuals in places like Argentina or Guatemala or assisting the UN to identify victims of genocide in places like Rwanda or Bosnia. Primarily these efforts have aimed to provide evidence of atrocities for tribunals of leaders who ordered mass killings.

Since the mid-1980s, U.S.-government-sponsored teams involving trained archaeologists and anthropologists have ventured into remote areas, especially in Asia and the Pacific. The teams deployed by the U.S. Army Joint POW/MIA Accounting Command locate, document, and recover the remains of U.S. military personnel who were missing in action during past conflicts. Once identified, these remains and personal effects are repatriated to their families whenever possible.

Forensic science, of course, has proved valuable in the more traditional archaeological arena of human history and prehistory, where issues such as ancient cannibalism among Indians of the American Southwest and the events surrounding the Battle of the Little Bighorn have been studied in detail. Human osteology has always been an essential part of research and teaching in the evolution of human origins and in biocultural anthropology, and it shares many of the same principles with forensic anthropology. Indeed, focusing on empirical evidence in both the courts of history—where anthropological and archaeological theory provide frameworks for interpretation—and law—where evidence must be tightly linked to claims of guilt or innocence—can only strengthen the general standards of archaeology and anthropology in all realms.

BALANCING ACT

The aftermath of the World Trade Center disaster was perhaps the most painful period in the history of New York City. To say that it was a "life-changing experience" now seems trite, but it was. Forensic anthropologists volunteering with DMORT conducted round-the-clock operations near the Office of the Chief Medical Examiner (OCME) to identify victims. This was a daunting task. There were extraordinary amounts of fragmented and commingled human remains.

It was also apparent that large amounts of fragmented human remains were scattered over wide areas of lower Manhattan beyond Ground Zero, and much of this was lost during the city cleanup. There was clearly a need for trained field teams of archaeologists to work in these areas to recover remains, personal effects, office documents, and other materials in a forensically controlled manner. This did not happen, however, until a trial recovery excavation a few months later under an invitation from the OCME demonstrated that such recoveries were possible. This volunteer team of field archaeologists, Providence Police, and other members of the Rhode Island community, known as Forensic Archaeology Recovery (FAR), continues to train regularly and to deploy as needed. Arguably, so much vital evidence was lost outside Ground Zero that the number of WTC victims identified so far from human remains stands at just under 60%. For archaeologists and forensic anthropologists, the World Trade Center was one of the first "wake-up" calls that there was a need to strengthen the field recovery remains as a first step in identifying victims.

A year after this trial effort, a terrible fire destroyed "The Station" nightclub in West Warwick, Rhode Island, killing 100 people and leaving over twice as many horribly burned or injured. Although small compared with the WTC, the aftermath was similar in its effects. Rhode Island is a small community, and many people who have lived here for a while had close ties with the fire victims. Once again, DMORT assisted the local authorities—in this case the State Medical Examiner's Office—with the result that all of the fire victims were identified within three days. This was my first deployment with DMORT, and as a learning experience it was like drinking from a fire hose. Then FAR was called to "The Station" site by the Rhode Island State Fire Marshal's Office and performed forensic recoveries there for the next 11 days, finally closing the site.

In this case, FAR's primary task was to recover personal effects and enter them in custody to go to the Medical Examiner's lab for eventual repatriation to the victims' families. Another equally important task, however, was to "clean up" the site. The Fire Marshal explained that after the police lines and fences come down after a major fire, people swarm over the site collecting everything they can find—including human remains. It may be hard to imagine, but it happens. We agreed that we would not let it happen in this case, and by the end of the operation nothing of that nature was left there for people to collect. This was a service to our community that we had never envisioned beforehand, but it demonstrated the value of controlled forensic archaeology at a disaster scene in a way that had major, positive effects within our community.

The experiences of major disasters in the scope of Sept. 11, "The Station" nightclub fire, and Hurricane Katrina have shown us that disaster anthropology is as much a humanitarian mission as it is an exercise of anthropologists' professional and academic skills. Those of us who participate in this work train like maniacs to prepare for the very thing we dread most, but when it happens we would not want to be anywhere else.

PART II

Archaeology

To be human is to have a cultural heritage. Although we are born into a social group, we must, through the processes of growing up, learn to become members of our society. In the context of the family, children learn not simply how to talk and how to "behave" but, more important, how to think and what to think. In other words, we learn the fundamental ideas, beliefs, and values of our society—assumptions about life and reality that are seldom questioned, at least by most people.

Anthropologists have studied and described the lifestyles and beliefs of hundreds of different societies throughout the modern world. The striking diversity of the cultures of humankind, each of which deserves to be understood in its own context, is one of the most important lessons of anthropology.

Anthropologists believe that despite this diversity, all cultures have some basic features in common. All cultures can be divided into three interdependent parts: (1) a material economy and technology; (2) a system of social organization; and (3) a system of beliefs and values. These components fit together; for example, the belief system may reinforce the social order and therefore help keep the economy running smoothly. A change in one cultural system, such as the economy, will result in changes in the other two systems. Culture is the primary mechanism by which humans adapt and survive in their environment. Cultural systems are always changing, and anthropologists are particularly interested in how and why cultures change. The major goal of the subfield of archaeology is the documentation and explanation of patterns of cultural change, or cultural evolution.

Every society has a unique cultural history—a story about how things got to be the way they are. However, written documents are available for only a tiny fraction of the time since the beginning of cultural history, and writing itself was used by only a minority of the world's cultures. Archaeology is a tool that allows us to overcome the temporal shallowness and the uneven cultural distribution of written historical documentation. Archaeology provides a key to understanding the chronologies of different prehistoric cultures; it is a scholarly method of uncovering and analyzing the material remains of people long dead. Archaeology is both a method and a body of knowledge about the prehistoric past. Of course, archaeology can also be applied to the historic past, not only to supplement the historic record but also to focus attention on the daily lives of people.

Most people have a general idea about what archaeologists do, but the popular caricature of the archaeologist as Indiana Jones is wrong. Indeed, archaeology may involve discovery, dirt, and even adventure, but most archaeological work requires careful and painstaking scholarship. When he or she digs, the archaeologist is not looking for valuable ancient artifacts as if they were pirate treasure. Artifacts taken out of context—that is, without knowing their relationship with other artifacts and nonartifactual remains at a particular depth and location—have little or no scholarly value. The isolated artifact is only a piece of a large and complex puzzle. The questions that the archaeologist asks are closely related to anthropological theory: How did cultures change and why did they change? The goal of the archaeologist is to establish a chronology of cultural change and to describe the lifeways of past societies. In doing this, the archaeologist preserves and interprets the cultural heritage—of ourselves and others—that was once buried in the ground.

The process of scientific archaeology has three parts: excavation, analysis, and interpretation. The methods must be very exact because the excavation of a particular place cannot be repeated. After locating an archaeological site, the modern archaeologist uses precise techniques to uncover, record, and preserve all possible information in a precise area. Excavation is followed by descriptive analysis of the artifacts in the laboratory; this analysis emphasizes the patterning of artifacts at different stratigraphic levels in the site. Sophisticated laboratory techniques developed in other sciences are now being applied to this archaeological analysis, such as reconstructing prehistoric ecological settings with pollen analysis or diagnosing a disease like schistosomiasis from an ancient burial.

The things archaeologists analyze are often the discarded "garbage" of prehistoric peoples. Artifacts might give clues to the economy and technology of a society or to its social organization or belief system. Most of the garbage, the material culture unearthed, is representative of the economic and technological spheres. The function of such artifacts is often better understood by drawing analogies to primitive societies studied by cultural anthropologists. Finally, the archaeologist interprets and explains what has been found and writes up these findings in the form of a report. Archaelogical analysis and interpretation are best when it comes to the economic system and least certain for artifacts as reflections of belief systems.

The methods developed for the study of prehistoric artifacts can be applied to our own society as well, with interesting results. In Selection 18, for example, Timothy Jones uses archaeological methods to investigate the problem of food loss.

Archaeology, like the other subdisciplines of anthropology, has both basic and applied dimensions. By establishing chronologies of cultural change in prehistoric societies, archaeologists add an important dimension of time depth to our understanding of the human story. For anthropology, this prehistoric information is critical for testing cultural evolutionary hypotheses about the patterns and direction of change. When we look at cultural history from this evolutionary standpoint, two "events" of the past seem particularly important: the domestication of plants and animals (that is, the beginning of farming) and the development of state societies characterized by urban centers and social stratification. These might be considered as two of the most important events in human history (see Selections 13 and 16).

The cultural evolutionary perspective shows a general pattern in cultural history, namely, the change from simple, small-scale organizations based on food foraging to large and complex ones based on agriculture and institutionalized inequality. When archaeologists examine a particular culture and how it changed over time, however, they often find that a traditional culture was clearly adapted to a particular local environment. Yet the archaeological record has many "cultural experiments" that failed—that is, cultures that flourished and then disappeared. These extinct societies and cultures, understood through the archaeological method, can be important lessons—warnings, really—for our contemporary world and our future.

One example would be the prehistoric southwestern United States, where the Anasazi culture reached a zenith in the fifteenth century; the monumental stone architecture of this culture was as impressive as the stone cathedrals of medieval Europe. Within a few years, however, magnificent cities were abandoned. Although many theories exist for this decline, most archaeologists believe that the Anasazi agricultural system, which depended on the concentrated use of irrigation systems, was poorly suited to the climate. The concentrated cultural system was not resistant to drought, and the civilization collapsed for lack of water.

The fact that these sophisticated cultures died out should make us pause and think about the directions of change in our own culture. The archaeological record contains other examples of how people have changed the face of the earth, often with unexpected negative consequences for the economy or the health of the people. We do not always recognize that our relationship with the environment is fragile and that ecological change is difficult to reverse. The economy and consumption patterns of contemporary American society have created a garbage crisis with few clear solutions.

In the United States, public policy protects our prehistoric and historic cultural resources, which include unexcavated archaeological sites. Before a large construction project, like a new road or building, is begun, the area must be surveyed for possible archaeological sites. If major sites are discovered, they must be excavated before the construction continues (sometimes to the consternation of builders). As a consequence, "contract archaeology" provides many jobs today.

Salvage archaeology is only one aspect of the protection and management of our prehistoric and historic cultural resources. Archaeological sites do indeed need to be protected, particularly from the many untrained archaeological "pot hunters" who destroy the context of prehistoric sites in their search for artifacts as treasure. These pot hunters rob us of the possibility of learning more about prehistoric societies; more

important, in the United States, these criminals have shown reckless disrespect for the cultural heritage of Native American peoples. Trained archaeologists, on the other hand, work for the preservation of prehistoric artifacts and information from excavated sites that often exist in conjunction with educational institutions like museums and parks.

In summary, archaeology is an integral part of anthropology and contributes both a method and a wealth of information about the cultures and processes of cultural change in the past. The discoveries of archaeological sites and their excavation can lead to more detailed understanding of cultural history; this is a good example of basic research. Equally important, the discoveries of archaeology can have lessons for practical problems in today's world—problems like disease and landfill overfill—as well as aid in the invention of new and appropriate technologies.

12

Battle of the Bones

Robson Bonnichsen and Alan L. Schneider

The first selection in this group of archaeological papers, like the first selection in the section on biological anthropology, addresses a controversial topic that pits the values of scientific research against, in this case, the religious values of some Native American groups. However, even this characterization oversimplifies the range of issues involved in the controversy. The flashpoint is the desire of some anthropologists to study the skeletal remains of some of the first people to set foot on the North or South American continents and the desire of some Native Americans to rebury these remains without permitting scientific inquiry.

The authors contrast various Native Americans' theories of their origins with scientific theories of the migration of peoples in the New World. They argue that only scientific theories are built on evidence, which can be overturned or adjusted as new evidence is unearthed. Therefore, the authors contend, the repatriation of bones before there is sufficient time to examine the evidence is not acceptable because scientific understanding is necessary. Although it might sound ironic, these anthropological archaeologists believe that, with all due respect for Native American religious beliefs, tradition should not cause us to abandon science. The complications, of course, revolve around the fact that not all Native Americans share the same beliefs about the sacredness of bones, and it is sometimes difficult to know which Native American group should receive and rebury skeletal remains. A crime in north Georgia in February of 2002 involved a crematory operator who did not incinerate the bodies that were entrusted to him, but rather hid the bodies willy-nilly on the property. If we want to understand the strong reaction of Native Americans to the skeleton repatriation issue, it might be worthwhile to remember the public outrage and grief that surrounded the crematory scandal.

In the "battle of the bones," it is clear that people of goodwill on both sides of this controversy may seem intractably at odds. As you will see, even scientists differ with regard to this issue. We are once again faced with dilemmas involving the nature of science and scientific investigation, the rights of individuals to hold and act on particular belief systems, the rights of other individuals to know the facts as they can best be understood, and the role of public policy in finding common ground between strongly held positions.

How do we or will we know the history and prehistory of America? From where did our nation's first inhabitants come, and when did they arrive? How important is the answer to this question when it brings people with different belief systems into direct conflict? The answers to these questions are not easy, and we suspect that readers will come away from this selection with quite differing point of views.

As you read this selection, ask yourself the following questions:

- How do nonscientific, traditional origin stories differ from those proposed by scientists?

- Do you feel Native American origin theories and scientifically based origin theories are equally legitimate? What criteria might be used for determining legitimacy?

- Is it possible that the inhabitants who met Columbus when he landed in the New World were not descendants of the earliest Americans?

- How do you feel about the legal battle over the study of these skeletal remains? Make separate lists of the arguments for one side and for the other.

The following terms discussed in this selection are included in the Glossary at the back of the book:

Clovis point	*radiocarbon dating*
DNA	*repatriate*
mitochondrial DNA	*Solutrean*

Bonnichsen, Robson & Alan L. Schneider, "Battle of the Bones."
This article is reprinted by permission of the New York Academy
of Sciences from THE SCIENCES (July/Aug. 2000):40–46.

Some Crow traditionalists believe that the world, the animals and all humans were created by a wise and powerful being named Old Man Coyote. The Brule Sioux have a different tradition: after a great flood, the only survivor was a beautiful girl, who was rescued by an eagle. She married the eagle, and their children became the Sioux people. Where did the native people of the Americas really come from? When did they first appear in those lands, and how? Just as the Judeo-Christian tradition teaches that human beings originated when God created Adam and Eve in the Garden of Eden, so every Native American tribe has at least one creation story.

Archaeologists, meanwhile, take a different view of how people first appeared in the Americas. Although they are sharply divided about the details, they are convinced by the archaeological record that the original peoples of the Americas migrated there from elsewhere. Where they came from and when they arrived are questions that remain to be resolved. Some answers, however, are beginning to emerge, and they indicate a process that was far more complicated than was ever imagined.

In one sense, both scientific theories about human origins and nonscientific traditions about the genesis of a particular tribe have something in common. All people and all cultures strive to understand the world and their place in it. Origin stories—whether traditional accounts or scientific theories—help satisfy those yearnings. They describe how and when people came to be on the earth, and they explain how people survived and prospered in their surroundings. But there are key differences as well. Scientific origin theories are subject to reevaluation as new evidence emerges: indeed, in the past several years the prevailing scientific view about the origins of the first Americans has shifted dramatically. Nonscientific origin theories, by contrast, derive from supernatural or mystical revelation; they tolerate neither doubt nor revision, and must be accepted on faith.

Until recently, archaeologists were able to pin only a few firm dates on the ancient human remains that had been discovered in the Americas. Part of the reason was that the existing dating technology required that large samples—sometimes an entire bone—be destroyed, and so the process was infrequently applied. But in the past decade several new analytical methods have emerged: DNA typing of ancient biological material, comparative skull measurements and accelerator mass spectrometry, a radiocarbon-dating technique that requires only minuscule amounts of bone. Those new techniques have made it possible to accurately determine the ages of skeletal remains, as well as to classify the various human ethnic groups far more precisely than ever before. Moreover, in recent years a few very ancient and well-preserved new skeletons have been unearthed. Those discoveries, combined with the new analyses, have led archaeologists to some startling conclusions—including the possibility that modern-day Native Americans are not descended from the earliest people who colonized the Americas.

Thus the past few years have been an exciting time in the field of Paleo-American prehistory (also known as First Americans studies). And yet, ironically, the period has also been one of disappointment and uncertainty, as government and museum officials are being asked to curtail and even prohibit archaeological research. The reason for the political ferment is that Native American origin theories, which had long been relegated to the realm of personal religious beliefs, are suddenly being thrust into the domain of public policy. That clash between science and religion has commanded the attention of the media, and a surge of new books and articles about the first Americans has been released in recent months. The subject is of more than topical interest: the outcome of the debate could determine the course of American archaeology for decades to come.

The shifts in public policy stem largely from a ten-year-old federal law, the Native American Graves Protection and Repatriation Act (NAGPRA). Bolstered by that law, some Native American activists are demanding possession of all prehistoric human remains found on federal or tribal lands in the United States and a halt to all study of those remains. In most cases, their intent is to rebury the ancient bones. Native American activists maintain that they already know where they come from, and see no need for further inquiry. They say their oral traditions report that their ancestors have lived in the Americas since the beginning of time. To them, the bones and skulls of ancient people are family members to be put to rest with dignity. Not all Native Americans share those views; many want to learn more about American prehistory and support the scientific study of all relevant remains, artifacts and associated information. Unfortunately, though, many government decision makers seem disposed to side with the anti-science advocates, assigning more legitimacy to Native American religious traditions than to scientific investigation and discourse.

Kennewick Man, a 9,200-year-old skeleton that was discovered on federal land in eastern Washington State on July 28, 1996, has become an important test case. Four weeks after it was found, preliminary radiocarbon-dating results were released, indicating that the skeleton was among the oldest ever unearthed in North America. Within a few days, however, federal officials decided to give the remains to a coalition of five local tribes—despite the fact that the bones had received only a preliminary examination. To forestall what would have been a tragic loss for science, one of us (Bonnichsen) and seven other experts in Paleo-American studies filed a federal lawsuit in Portland, Oregon, to prevent transfer of the skeleton. (The other author, Schneider, is an attorney in the case.) We requested, successfully, that the skeleton be kept in federal custody until our lawsuit was resolved. Today the bones remain in limbo as the dispute drags on.

Native American beliefs about the past and the dead certainly deserve respect, but they should not be allowed to dictate government policy on the investigation and interpretation of early American prehistory. If a choice must be made among competing theories of human origins, primacy should be given to theories based on the scientific method. Only scientific theories are built on empirical evidence; only scientific theories can be adjusted or overturned. True, influential scientists have sometimes been able to temporarily smother scholarly debate on views they opposed. But as recent developments in First Americans studies demonstrate, science is an inherently flexible, self-correcting endeavor. Even long-accepted scientific views can be challenged, and truth eventually wins out.

Ever since Thomas Jefferson began collecting Native American artifacts and displaying them in his foyer, many theories have been proposed to explain how people first came to North and South America. The most widely accepted was the Clovis-first theory, named for the elegant, fluted spear points found in association with the remains of mammoths, bison, and other animals near Clovis, New Mexico, in 1932. In subsequent years many similar stone spearheads were found throughout the Great Plains, and eventually in much of the United States and Central and South America. By the late 1960s radiocarbon dating had confirmed that the Clovis artifacts were between 10,800 and 11,500 years old.

In the 1960s and early 1970s the ecologist Paul S. Martin and the geoarchaelogist C. Vance Haynes Jr., both of the University of Arizona in Tucson, together with James E. Mossiman of the National Institutes of Health in Bethesda, Maryland, began to develop a dramatic theory about how the Americas were settled. They hypothesized that about 11,500 years ago, at the end of the most recent Ice Age, a single band of mammoth hunters from Siberia crossed the Bering land bridge into Alaska, and from there began spreading across North America. According to the theory of Martin and his colleagues, there were no people in the New World, as the Americas are sometimes called, until that time. The new arrivals and their descendants

prospered and, in just a few centuries, purportedly settled two continents.

The Clovis-first model gained enormous scientific prominence—in fact, to question it was to risk virtual professional suicide. Implicit in the theory is the premise that a single biological population, with a single culture and language, spawned the enormously diverse array of peoples—with their widely divergent cultures and languages—who were living in the New World at the time of European contact. Now, however, thanks to the new archaeological finds and analytical advances, the Clovis-first model has been refuted.

In 1977 Thomas D. Dillehay—an anthropologist at the University of Kentucky in Lexington and the author of one of the books under review, *The Settlement of the Americas*—began excavations at the Monte Verde site in southern Chile. Dillehay's work showed Monte Verde to be at least 12,500 years old, and he was widely criticized for challenging the validity of the Clovis-first theory [see "The Battle of Monte Verde," by Thomas D. Dillehay, January/February 1997]. Dillehay, however, did not back down, and three years ago a special team of archaeologists, including avowed skeptics, inspected Monte Verde. The result was vindication: the experts confirmed that Monte Verde was a legitimate pre-Clovis site. Acceptance of Dillehay's site broke a logjam in First Americans studies. Other sites—and there were many—that had been in limbo because they seemed to predate Clovis could now be acknowledged, too.

Some of those potential pre-Clovis sites include several in southeastern Wisconsin, where the archaeologist David F. Overstreet of Marquette University in Milwaukee has found 12,250-year-old stone tools and mammoth bones with cut marks. And at the Meadowcroft Rockshelter near Pittsburgh, Pennsylvania, the archaeologist James M. Adovasio of Mercyhurst College in Erie, Pennsylvania, has discovered tapered points and bladelike flakes dated to between 12,000 and 16,000 years ago. Similar artifacts have been excavated at the Cactus Hill site near Richmond, Virginia; investigators have dated that site to between 12,000 and 17,000 years old. And in the oldest archaeological deposits at Monte Verde, Dillehay himself has uncovered flaked stone tools that are apparently about 33,000 years old.

In *The Settlement of the Americas*, Dillehay provides a well organized synthesis of early Paleo-American archaeological findings. But the book falters in an important way. Dillehay is reluctant to recognize human presence in the Americas prior to 15,000 to 20,000 years ago, despite the older artifacts found at his own site. Although Dillehay assures the reader that his research at Monte Verde is sound, he will not accept the 33,000-year-old radiocarbon dates associated with the stone tools, he writes, until additional artifacts of such antiquity are confirmed at other sites. We find it disappointing the Dillehay, who has done so much to push back the date for the peopling of the Americas, is hesitant to confront the implications of his own data for early human presence in the New World.

In *Bones, Boats, and Bison,* E. James Dixon does for North America what Dillehay did for South America, providing a useful, up-to-date overview of the complex and scattered archaeological literature. Dixon is even more conservative than Dillehay: he favors the idea that the first Americans arrived only about 13,500 years ago. Around that time, he theorizes, people from the Pacific Rim of Asia traveled in small boats to North and South America and settled on the western shores of both continents. But like Dillehay, Dixon is resolute that the Americas were inhabited long before the Clovis artifacts were deposited.

Not only has the idea that the Americas were devoid of people until 11,500 years ago been disproved, but a second important tenet of the Clovis-first theory has also crumbled: the assertion that the Americas were colonized only once. The latest research shows that the New World probably underwent multiple colonizations: instead of originating in a small area of northeast Siberia, as predicted by the Clovis-first model, the first Americans probably came from many parts of Eurasia.

Perhaps the nail in the coffin for the Clovis-first theory is that no Clovis-style artifacts have ever been retrieved from archaeological sites in Siberia. Furthermore, the variety of the artifacts discovered in the rain forests, deserts, and coastal areas of South America indicate that early New World people were not members of one homogeneous clan of big-game hunters, as the Clovis-first theory proposed. Depending on their environments, some survived by hunting small game, some by fishing, and some by general foraging. As a result, investigators have concluded that, rather than signaling a distinct migration, the Clovis spear points that appear in the archaeological record beginning around 11,500 years ago may simply be the evidence of a technological innovation that took place at that time within groups of people who already lived in the Americas.

The idea that the Americas were settled more than once and by different groups of people is supported by evidence from ancient skeletons that have been examined with new techniques, such as the study of the DNA in the mitochondria of cells. Mitochondrial DNA is a more stable source of information about genetic lineages than is the DNA in the nucleus of a cell because, rather than representing a melding of maternal and paternal genes, mitochondrial DNA is almost always passed on by the mother alone.

The molecular anthropologist Theodore Schurr of the Southwest Foundation for Biomedical Research in San Antonio, Texas, and other investigators have identified five distinct mitochondrial lineages, or haplogroups, as they are called, in modern Native Americans. Four of the haplogroups—A, B, C, and D—are also found in varying frequencies in different Asian populations, which suggests that early immigrants to the Americas may have come from more than one region of Asia. The fifth haplogroup, known as X, is much rarer than the other four haplogroups, and its origin is not clear. It occurs among certain European populations but is absent in contemporary Asian populations, which suggests that it may record another discrete migration to the Americas, possibly from western Eurasia.

In fact, there is growing speculation that Europeans may have traveled to the Americas thousands of years before Columbus and the Vikings made their westward forays. The archaeologists Dennis J. Stanford of the Smithsonian Institution in Washington, D.C., and Bruce A. Bradley of Primitive Tech Enterprises, Inc., in Cortex, Colorado, have noted distinct similarities between the stone tools of the Clovis people and the ones made in France and Spain by members of the Solutrean culture, which flourished between 16,500 and 21,000 years ago. (The theory, only recently proposed, is highly controversial and has yet to be explored in depth.)

The advent of the personal computer has enabled Paleo-American investigators to apply powerful statistical techniques to multiple sets of data. As a result, teams of physical anthropologists have been able to perform comparative analyses of skeletal remains from Asia, North America, and South America, based on extensive measurements of skulls, limb bones, and teeth, and on dates derived from accelerator mass spectrometry.

The work has yielded some tantalizing results that corroborate much of the DNA evidence. For example, the physical anthropologist C. Loring Brace and his research team from the University of Michigan in Ann Arbor have concluded that the modern native peoples of North America are the descendants of at least four different colonizing populations from two different parts of Asia. Furthermore, Brace argues, those populations probably arrived in the New World at different times and by various routes.

Likewise, the physical anthropologists D. Gentry Steele of Texas A&M University in College Station, Douglas Owsley of the Smithsonian Institution, Richard L. Jantz of the University of Tennessee in Knoxville, and Walter Neves of the University of São Paulo in Brazil have compiled and analyzed measurements from the earliest known North and South American skeletons. Their research has demonstrated that early New World skulls are quite distinct from the skulls of modern Native Americans. Many of the early skulls display relatively narrow faces, long crania, and oval-shaped eye sockets—characteristics that are more typical of skulls from the Pacific Islands and southern Asia than they are of skulls from modern Native Americans.

The reasons for the difference between early and later New World skulls have yet to be fully explained. The discrepancies may be the result of gradual evolutionary changes that took place over time. On the other hand, the differences may indicate that the early skeletons are unrelated to those of modern Native Americans.

Thus a radical new idea has emerged: The people who inhabited the Americas when Columbus arrived—the tribes referred to today as Native Americans—may not be descended from the earliest Americans. There is no reason to assume that the first immigrants to the Americas took hold and prospered. Perhaps some of the early colonizing groups died out before later groups arrived. Or it may be that later colonizing groups replaced earlier groups as a result of warfare, the introduction of new diseases, or higher birth or survival rates. If so, the question then becomes not which tribe does Kennewick Man belong to, but whether the skeleton belongs to any existing tribe at all.

Two new books—*Riddle of the Bones,* by the freelance writer Roger Downey, and *Skull Wars,* by David Hurst Thomas, an anthropologist at the American Museum of Natural History in New York City—present the Native American perspective on the argument. We must concede up front that we are far from impartial reviewers. Both of those books discuss the lawsuit that we initiated, and both seem to support the position of our adversaries: that tribal permission is needed before the Kennewick skeleton can be studied.

Downey attempts to relate the Kennewick Man controversy to the more fundamental question of the peopling of the Americas, but his analysis lacks depth and understanding. He presents a misleading view of the scientists involved in the lawsuit, often resorting to simplistic characterizations and innuendos to attack their motives and research goals. Moreover, he implies that science is not a credible method for explaining the past. From Downey's perspective, Native American origin theories are as legitimate as the scientific ones; in his view, both are only theories, and it is impossible to choose between them.

In *Skull Wars* Thomas attempts to provide the historical context that led to the passage of NAGPRA. He describes, for instance, the so-called skull science of

the nineteenth century, which was pioneered by the American physician Samuel George Morton. Morton asserted that the variation in skull size among various ethnic groups proved the intellectual superiority of people of white European stock. Thomas writes that Morton's ideas led to a disregard for the right of Native Americans, and provided a justification for the looting and robbing of Native American graves.

Thomas's treatment of the past, however, is selective and largely one-sided. He seems to delight in pointing out the failings and racial biases of early investigators, as if to convince the reader that modern science is fatally tainted by past wrongdoing. Meanwhile, he pays little attention to investigators who championed the cause of Native Americans, dedicating their lives to the preservation of knowledge about those vanishing cultures.

Thomas argues that traditional Native American views about the past should be accommodated in decisions concerning the investigation and interpretation of American prehistory. He makes no attempt, however, to explain how belief systems that reject the need for research and critical analysis can provide a workable basis for scientific programs or for setting public policy. Given Thomas's scholarly stature and professional credentials, his failure to address the fundamental differences that separate supernatural origin theories from scientific explanations may confuse both the public and scientists who are not familiar with the subject.

Downey's outlook—that scientific ideas about the settling of the Americas are only theories, and thus no more reliable than any other account—evokes a familiar precedent. Fundamentalist Christians, who maintain that people were created by the God of the Bible, often assert that evolution deserves little respect because it is only a theory. Indeed, the controversy about the first Americans is similar to the dispute about whether children should be taught evolution or creationism in public schools. In both cases, what is at stake is the role of religion in public institutions. One debate threatens educational standards; the other, the future of American archaeology.

Until a decade ago, government intervention in archaeology was limited to the protection and preservation of archaeological sites and resources. Knowledge of American prehistory was considered the common heritage of all Americans, and investigators were free to explore new theories, regardless of their perspectives or research objectives. But now, even though biological knowledge of the earliest humans in the Americas is amazingly thin—fewer than ten relatively complete, securely dated skeletons more than 8,000 years old have been unearthed in North America—government decision makers are bowing to tribal demands for the control of ancient human skeletal remains and artifacts.

For example, the 10,600-year-old Buhl Woman, discovered in Idaho in 1989, was turned over by Idaho state officials to the Shoshone-Bannock tribes, even though scientific evidence indicates that the Shoshone-Bannock have resided in the area for less than 2,000 years. Before its reburial the Buhl skeleton was examined by only one physical anthropologist. Likewise, just a few years later, the 7,800-year-old Hourglass Cave skeleton from Colorado was reburied after limited study. Recently a 7,800-year-old human skull known as Pelican Rapids Woman, along with the 8,700-year-old so-called Browns Valley Man, both from Minnesota, were repatriated to a coalition of Sioux tribes and subsequently reburied in South Dakota.

In addition, the study of key archaeological materials and sites is becoming increasingly difficult. In deference to tribal religious beliefs, the government prohibited independent scientists from studying the Kennewick Man discovery site, then buried the site under 600 tons of rock and fill. Genetic analysis of a 9,400-year-old skeleton that was discovered in Nevada, known as the Spirit Cave Mummy, has yet to be allowed because of objections from the Paiute. And several years ago, a team led by one of us (Bonnichsen) was prevented from conducting DNA tests on ancient human hair from the Mammoth Meadow site in Montana, because several tribes claimed possession of the hair [see "Roots," by Robson Bonnichsen and Alan L. Schneider, May/June 1995].

Those decisions by the government to hand over key archaeological evidence and to restrict scientific work are dictated by misguided public policy. Congress did not anticipate that NAGPRA would be applied to very early human remains that might have no direct relation to modern Native Americans. The purpose of NAGPRA was to reunite Native American skeletal remains, funerary items, and ceremonial objects with living members of the culture that had produced them. Yet in many cases the tribes invoking NAGPRA to block scientific study have no known cultural or biological connection with the remains or artifacts in question.

Traditional stories about supernatural origins may provide a workable structure for ordering human affairs when all the people affected share the same belief system. They do not, however, provide a satisfactory mechanism for setting government policy in a pluralistic, multicultural society such as the United States. If Native American origin theories are accepted as a basis for determining the ownership and study of archaeological resources uncovered on public land, a dangerous precedent will have been set. What will stop the government from incorporating other religious beliefs into its policies?

Scientific theories often offend one or more segments of society because the conclusions of science may differ from those expected by people seeking spiritual answers. Such conflicts are to be expected. But when the government attempts to mediate disputes of that kind, it inevitably ends up censoring the open dissemination of information and ideas. In the quest to understand the history of our species, we need more information, not less. Respect for Native Americans should not cause us to abandon science in favor of politically expedient compromises.

13

The Worst Mistake in the History of the Human Race

Jared Diamond

What we eat and how we eat are important both nutritionally and culturally. This selection suggests that how we get what we eat—through gathering and hunting versus agriculture, for example—has dramatic consequences. This seems pretty obvious. We all imagine what a struggle it must have been before the development of agriculture. We think of our ancestors spending their days searching for roots and berries to eat or, out at the crack of dawn, hunting wild animals. In fact, this was not quite the case. Nevertheless, isn't it really better simply to go to the refrigerator, open the door, and reach for a container of milk to pour into a bowl of flaked grain for your regular morning meal? What could be simpler and more nutritious?

There are many things that we seldom question; the truth seems so evident and the answers obvious. One such sacred cow is the tremendous prosperity brought about by the agricultural revolution. This selection is a thought-provoking introduction to the connection between culture and agriculture. The transition from food foraging to farming (what archaeologists call the Neolithic revolution) may have been the worst mistake in human history or its most important event. You be the judge. But for better or worse, this cultural evolution has occurred, and the world will never be the same again.

As you read this selection, ask yourself the following questions:

- What is the fundamental difference between the progressivist view and the revisionist interpretation?
- How did the development of agriculture affect people's health?
- What three reasons explain the changes brought about by the development of agriculture?
- How did the development of agriculture affect social equality, including gender equality?

The following terms discussed in this selection are included in the Glossary at the back of the book:

agricultural development
civilization
domestication of plants and animals
hunter-gatherers
Neolithic
paleontology
paleopathology
social stratification

To science we owe dramatic changes in our smug self-image. Astronomy taught us that our earth isn't the center of the universe but merely one of billions of heavenly bodies. From biology we learned that we weren't specially created by God but evolved along with millions of other species. Now archaeology is demolishing another sacred belief: that human history over the past million years has been a long tale of progress. In particular, recent discoveries suggest that the adoption of agriculture, supposedly our most decisive step toward a better life, was in many ways a catastrophe from which we have never recovered. With agriculture came the gross social and sexual inequality, the disease and despotism, that curse our existence.

At first, the evidence against this revisionist interpretation will strike twentieth-century Americans as irrefutable. We're better off in almost every respect than the people of the Middle Ages, who in turn had it easier than cavemen, who in turn were better off than apes. Just count our advantages. We enjoy the most abundant and varied foods, the best tools and material goods, some of the longest and healthiest lives, in history. Most of us are safe from starvation and predators. We get our energy from oil and machines, not

Diamond, Jared. "The Worst Mistake in the History of the Human Race." Discover Magazine. (May 1987):64–66. Reprinted with permission of the author.

from our sweat. What neo-Luddite among us would trade his life for that of a medieval peasant, a caveman, or an ape?

For most of our history we supported ourselves by hunting and gathering: we hunted wild animals and foraged for wild plants. It's a life that philosophers have traditionally regarded as nasty, brutish, and short. Since no food is grown and little is stored, there is (in this view) no respite from the struggle that starts anew each day to find wild foods and avoid starving. Our escape from this misery was facilitated only 10,000 years ago, when in different parts of the world people began to domesticate plants and animals. The agricultural revolution gradually spread until today it's nearly universal, and few tribes of hunter-gatherers survive.

From the progressivist perspective on which I was brought up, to ask "Why did almost all our hunter-gatherer ancestors adopt agriculture?" is silly. Of course they adopted it because agriculture is an efficient way to get more food for less work. Planted crops yield far more tons per acre than roots and berries. Just imagine a band of savages, exhausted from searching for nuts or chasing wild animals, suddenly gazing for the first time at a fruit-laden orchard or a pasture full of sheep. How many milliseconds do you think it would take them to appreciate the advantages of agriculture?

The progressivist party line sometimes even goes so far as to credit agriculture with the remarkable flowering of art that has taken place over the past few thousand years. Since crops can be stored, and since it takes less time to pick food from a garden than to find it in the wild, agriculture gave us free time that hunter-gatherers never had. Thus it was agriculture that enabled us to build the Parthenon and compose the B-minor Mass.

While the case for the progressivist view seems overwhelming, it's hard to prove. How do you show that the lives of people 10,000 years ago got better when they abandoned hunting and gathering for farming? Until recently, archaeologists had to resort to indirect tests, whose results (surprisingly) failed to support the progressivist view. Here's one example of an indirect test: Are twentieth-century hunter-gatherers really worse off than farmers? Scattered throughout the world, several dozen groups of so-called primitive people, like the Kalahari Bushmen, continue to support themselves that way. It turns out that these people have plenty of leisure time, sleep a good deal, and work less hard than their farming neighbors. For instance, the average time devoted each week to obtaining food is only 12 to 19 hours for one group of Bushmen, 14 hours or less for the Hadza nomads of Tanzania. One Bushman, when asked why he hadn't emulated neighboring tribes by adopting agriculture, replied,

"Why should we, when there are so many mongongo nuts in the world?"

While farmers concentrate on high-carbohydrate crops like rice and potatoes, the mix of wild plants and animals in the diets of surviving hunter-gatherers provides more protein and a better balance of other nutrients. In one study, the Bushmen's average daily food intake (during a month when food was plentiful) was 2,140 calories and 93 grams of protein, considerably greater than the recommended daily allowance for people of their size. It's almost inconceivable that Bushmen, who eat 75 or so wild plants, could die of starvation the way hundreds of thousands of Irish farmers and their families did during the potato famine of the 1840s.

So the lives of at least the surviving hunter-gatherers aren't nasty and brutish, even though farmers have pushed them into some of the world's worst real estate. But modern hunter-gatherer societies that have rubbed shoulders with farming societies for thousands of years don't tell us about conditions before the agricultural revolution. The progressivist view is really making a claim about the distant past: that the lives of primitive people improved when they switched from gathering to farming. Archaeologists can date that switch by distinguishing remains of wild plants and animals from those of domesticated ones in prehistoric garbage dumps.

How can one deduce the health of the prehistoric garbage makers, and thereby directly test the progressivist view? That question has become answerable only in recent years, in part through the newly emerging techniques of paleopathology, the study of signs of disease in the remains of ancient peoples.

In some lucky situations, the paleopathologist has almost as much material to study as a pathologist today. For example, archaeologists in the Chilean deserts found well preserved mummies whose medical conditions at time of death could be determined by autopsy. And feces of long-dead Indians who lived in dry caves in Nevada remain sufficiently well preserved to be examined for hookworm and other parasites.

Usually the only human remains available for study are skeletons, but they permit a surprising number of deductions. To begin with, a skeleton reveals its owner's sex, weight, and approximate age. In the few cases where there are many skeletons, one can construct mortality tables like the ones life insurance companies use to calculate expected life span and risk of death at any given age. Paleopathologists can also calculate growth rates by measuring bones of people of different ages, examining teeth for enamel defects (signs of childhood malnutrition), and recognizing scars left on bones by anemia, tuberculosis, leprosy, and other diseases.

One straightforward example of what paleopathologists have learned from skeletons concerns historical changes in height. Skeletons from Greece and Turkey show that the average height of hunter-gatherers toward the end of the ice ages was a generous 5'9" for men, 5'5" for women. With the adoption of agriculture, height crashed, and by 3000 B.C. had reached a low of only 5'3" for men, 5' for women. By classical times heights were very slowly on the rise again, but modern Greeks and Turks have still not regained the average height of their distant ancestors.

Another example of paleopathology at work is the study of Indian skeletons from burial mounds in the Illinois and Ohio river valleys. At Dickson Mounds, located near the confluence of the Spoon and Illinois Rivers, archaeologists have excavated some 800 skeletons that paint a picture of the health changes that occurred when a hunter-gatherer culture gave way to intensive maize farming around A.D. 1150. Studies by George Armelagos and his colleagues then at the University of Massachusetts show these early farmers paid a price for their new-found livelihood. Compared to the hunter-gatherers who preceded them, the farmers had a nearly 50 percent increase in enamel defects indicative of malnutrition, a fourfold increase in iron-deficiency anemia (evidenced by a bone condition called porotic hyperostosis), a threefold rise in bone lesions reflecting infectious disease in general, and an increase in degenerative conditions of the spine, probably reflecting a lot of hard physical labor. "Life expectancy at birth in the pre-agricultural community was about twenty-six years," says Armelagos, "but in the post-agricultural community it was nineteen years. So these episodes of nutritional stress and infectious disease were seriously affecting their ability to survive."

The evidence suggests that the Indians at Dickson Mounds, like many other primitive peoples, took up farming not by choice but from necessity in order to feed their constantly growing numbers. "I don't think most hunter-gatherers farmed until they had to, and when they switched to farming they traded quality for quantity," says Mark Cohen of the State University of New York at Plattsburgh, co-editor, with Armelagos, of one of the seminal books in the field, *Paleopathology at the Origins of Agriculture.* "When I first started making that argument ten years ago, not many people agreed with me. Now it's become a respectable, albeit controversial, side of the debate."

There are at least three sets of reasons to explain the findings that agriculture was bad for health. First, hunter-gatherers enjoyed a varied diet, while early farmers obtained most of their food from one or a few starchy crops. The farmers gained cheap calories at the cost of poor nutrition. (Today just three high-carbohydrate plants—wheat, rice, and corn—provide the bulk of the calories consumed by the human species, yet each one is deficient in certain vitamins or amino acids essential to life.) Second, because of dependence on a limited number of crops, farmers ran the risk of starvation if one crop failed. Finally, the mere fact that agriculture encouraged people to clump together in crowded societies, many of which then carried on trade with other crowded societies, led to the spread of parasites and infectious disease. (Some archaeologists think it was crowding, rather than agriculture, that promoted disease, but this is a chicken-and-egg argument, because crowding encourages agriculture and vice versa.) Epidemics couldn't take hold when populations were scattered in small bands that constantly shifted camp. Tuberculosis and diarrheal disease had to await the rise of farming, measles and bubonic plague the appearance of large cities.

Besides malnutrition, starvation, and epidemic diseases, farming helped bring another curse upon humanity: deep class divisions. Hunter-gatherers have little or no stored food, and no concentrated food sources, like an orchard or a herd of cows: they live off the wild plants and animals they obtain each day. Therefore, there can be no kings, no class of social parasites who grow fat on food seized from others. Only in farming populations could a healthy, non-producing elite set itself above the disease-ridden masses. Skeletons from Greek tombs at Mycenae c. 1500 B.C. suggest that royals enjoyed a better diet than commoners, since the royal skeletons were two or three inches taller and had better teeth (on the average, one instead of six cavities or missing teeth). Among Chilean mummies from c. A.D. 1000, the élite were distinguished not only by ornaments and gold hair clips but also by a fourfold lower rate of bone lesions caused by disease.

Similar contrasts in nutrition and health persist on a global scale today. To people in rich countries like the U.S., it sounds ridiculous to extol the virtues of hunting and gathering. But Americans are an élite, dependent on oil and minerals that must often be imported from countries with poorer health and nutrition. If one could choose between being a peasant farmer in Ethiopia or a Bushman gatherer in the Kalahari, which do you think would be the better choice?

Farming may have encouraged inequality between the sexes, as well. Freed from the need to transport their babies during a nomadic existence, and under pressure to produce more hands to till the fields, farming women tended to have more frequent pregnancies than their hunter-gatherer counterparts—with consequent drains on their health. Among the Chilean mummies, for example, more women than men had bone lesions from infectious disease.

Women in agricultural societies were sometimes made beasts of burden. In New Guinea farming communities today I often see women staggering under loads of vegetables and firewood while the men walk empty-handed. Once while on a field trip there studying birds, I offered to pay some villagers to carry supplies from an airstrip to my mountain camp. The heaviest item was a 110-pound bag of rice, which I lashed to a pole and assigned to a team of four men to shoulder together. When I eventually caught up with the villagers, the men were carrying light loads, while one small woman weighing less than the bag of rice was bent under it, supporting its weight by a cord across her temples.

As for the claim that agriculture encouraged the flowering of art by providing us with leisure time, modern hunter-gatherers have at least as much free time as do farmers. The whole emphasis on leisure time as a critical factor seems to me misguided. Gorillas have had ample free time to build their own Parthenon, had they wanted to. While post-agricultural technological advances did make new art forms possible and preservation of art easier, great paintings and sculptures were already being produced by hunter-gatherers 15,000 years ago, and were still being produced as recently as the last century by such hunter-gatherers as some Eskimos and the Indians of the Pacific Northwest.

Thus with the advent of agriculture an élite became better off, but most people became worse off. Instead of swallowing the progressivist party line that we chose agriculture because it was good for us, we must ask how we got trapped by it despite its pitfalls.

One answer boils down to the adage "Might makes right." Farming could support many more people than hunting, albeit with a poorer quality of life. (Population densities of hunter-gatherers are rarely over one person per ten square miles, while farmers average 100 times that.) Partly, this is because a field planted entirely in edible crops lets one feed far more mouths than a forest with scattered edible plants. Partly, too, it's because nomadic hunter-gatherers have to keep their children spaced at four-year intervals by infanticide and other means, since a mother must carry her toddler until it's old enough to keep up with the

adults. Because farm women don't have that burden, they can and often do bear a child every two years.

As population densities of hunter-gatherers slowly rose at the end of the ice ages, bands had to choose between feeding more mouths by taking the first steps toward agriculture, or else finding ways to limit growth. Some bands chose the former solution, unable to anticipate the evils of farming, and seduced by the transient abundance they enjoyed until population growth caught up with increased food production. Such bands outbred and then drove off or killed the bands that chose to remain hunter-gatherers, because a hundred malnourished farmers can still outfight one healthy hunter. It's not that hunter-gatherers abandoned their life style, but that those sensible enough not to abandon it were forced out of all areas except the ones farmers didn't want.

At this point it's instructive to recall the common complaint that archaeology is a luxury, concerned with the remote past, and offering no lessons for the present. Archaeologists studying the rise of farming have reconstructed a crucial stage at which we made the worst mistake in human history. Forced to choose between limiting population or trying to increase food production, we chose the latter and ended up with starvation, warfare, and tyranny.

Hunter-gatherers practiced the most successful and longest-lasting life style in human history. In contrast, we're still struggling with the mess into which agriculture has tumbled us, and it's unclear whether we can solve it. Suppose that an archaeologist who had visited us from outer space were trying to explain human history to his fellow spacelings. He might illustrate the results of his digs by a 24-hour clock on which one hour represents 100,000 years of real past time. If the history of the human race began at midnight, then we would now be almost at the end of our first day. We lived as hunter-gatherers for nearly the whole of that day, from midnight through dawn, noon, and sunset. Finally, at 11:54 p.m., we adopted agriculture. As our second midnight approaches, will the plight of famine-stricken peasants gradually spread to engulf us all? Or will we somehow achieve those seductive blessings that we imagine behind agriculture's glittering façade, and that have so far eluded us?

14

Uncovering America's Pyramid Builders

Karen Wright

Travelers who pass through Collinsville, Illinois may know this Midwestern city as the "Horseradish Capital of the World" or as the home of a water tower in the shape of the world's largest ketchup bottle, but these superlatives are not what put this city on the list of United Nations World Heritage Sites. An earthen mound within city limits once served as the foundation of a 5,000 square foot temple bigger than any of the Egyptian pyramids at Giza. This mound, now known as Monks Mound, sat at the center of a thriving civilization that disappeared approximately 700 years ago.

The Cahokian civilization that built Monks Mound established their early city at the confluence of the Mississippi, Missouri, and Illinois rivers, creating an urban center that was a hub for regional trade. Many mysteries remain about Cohokia and its downfall, largely because this civilization did not use a written language and they used building materials that do not leave an enduring archaeological record. In this selection, Karen Wright presents conflicting interpretations about the size, nature, and collapse of what may have been the largest prehistoric settlement north of Mexico.

As you read this selection, ask yourself the following questions:

- How do the mounds of Cahokia and the civilization that built them compare with Pharaonic Egypt and the Great Pyramids of Giza?
- Why did migrants come to Cahokia in such great numbers?
- What factors may have contributed to the downfall of Cahokia?
- How and when were the Cahokian mounds re-discovered?
- How were Cahokia and Monks Mound named?

The following terms discussed in this selection are included in the Glossary at the back of the book:

chiefdom   *matriarchal*
United Nations World Heritage Site   *woodhenge*

Wchen U.S. 40 reaches Collinsville, Illinois, the land is flat and open. Seedy storefronts line the highway: a pawnshop, a discount carpet warehouse, a taco joint, a bar. Only the Indian Mound Motel gives any hint that the road bisects something more than underdeveloped farmland. This is the Cahokia Mounds State Historic Site, a United Nations World Heritage Site on a par with the Great Wall of China, the Egyptian pyramids, and the Taj Mahal. The 4,000-acre complex preserves the remnants of the largest prehistoric settlement north of Mexico, a walled city that flourished on the floodplain of the Mississippi River 10 centuries ago. Covering an area more than five miles square, Cahokia dwarfs the ancient pueblos of New Mexico's Chaco Canyon and every other ruin left by the storied Anasazi of the American Southwest. Yet despite its size and importance, archaeologists still don't understand how this vast, lost culture began, how it ended, and what went on in between.

A thousand years ago, no one could have missed Cahokia—a complex, sophisticated society with an urban center, satellite villages, and as many as 50,000 people in all. Thatched-roof houses lined the central plazas. Merchants swapped copper, mica, and seashells from as far away as the Great Lakes and the Gulf of Mexico. Thousands of cooking fires burned night and day. And between A.D. 1000 and 1300, Cahokians built more than 120 earthen mounds as landmarks, tombs, and ceremonial platforms. The largest of these monuments, now called Monks Mound, still dominates the site. It is a flat-topped pyramid of dirt that covers more than 14 acres and once supported a 5,000-square-foot temple. Monks

Mound is bigger than any of the three great pyramids at Giza outside Cairo. "This is the third or fourth biggest pyramid in the world, in terms of volume," says archaeologist Tim Pauketat of the University of Illinois at Urbana-Champaign. It towers 100 feet over a 40-acre plaza that was surrounded by lesser mounds and a two-mile-long stockade. The monument was the crowning achievement of a mound-building culture that began thousands of years earlier and was never duplicated on this continent.

Why Cahokia crumbled and its people vanished is unknown. Malnutrition, overcrowding, a dwindling resource base, the raids of jealous trade partners—any or all of these reasons may have contributed to the city's demise. No one knows whether the populace cleared out all at once or dispersed gradually, but by A.D. 1300 Cahokia was a ghost town. By the time Europeans arrived in the Mississippi bottomland, the region was only sparsely settled, and none of the native residents could recount what had happened there centuries before. So far, archaeologists have uncovered no evidence of invasion, rampant disease, overpopulation, deforestation, or any of the other hallmarks of the decline and fall of civilization. Cahokia abounds in artifacts, but archaeologists have not yet made sense of them in a meaningful way. "It actually becomes quite scary," says John Kelly of Washington University in St. Louis. "After a while you begin to realize that you're dealing with rituals that had a great deal of meaning 800 years ago and that you're kind of clueless."

Intellectual frustration is not the only reason for Cahokia's obscurity. Pauketat complains that the region is geographically challenged. It has the look and feel of a place "like Buffalo, except warmer," he says. Cahokia doesn't exactly lure others away from more exotic digs in Turkey, Mexico, or Peru, he says. "That's the problem with this site." Another reason for its lack of popularity is the ordinary, perishable building materials used by the residents. "Cahokians are discounted because they built with dirt—dirt and wood, things they valued," says Pauketat. "I get tired of hearing people say, 'We have civilization and you guys don't.'"

Meanwhile, developers see Cahokia as ripe for expansion; strip malls and subdivisions threaten on every side. "It's developing faster than we can survey," Pauketat says. "We don't know what we're losing out there." Although a good portion of the central city is now protected, archaeologists are discovering related sites throughout a six-county region on both sides of the nearby Mississippi—an area 3,600 miles square. Indeed, digs are under way in such unlikely places as a railroad yard eight miles west in East St. Louis, where a new bridge is scheduled. "If you want to find out the archaeology of an area," says Brad Koldehoff of the Illinois Department of Transportation's archaeology team, "build a road through it."

One morning last September, a warm red sun rose behind Monks Mound, inching above the level terrace where a tribal palace once stood, burning the mist off the flat green expanses of former plazas. To the west of the mound, in a circle more than 400 feet in diameter, several dozen cedar posts rise to the height of telephone poles. The woodhenge, as the structure is known, is a reconstruction of a series of circles found in the 1960s and '70s when excavations to build a mammoth clover-leaf joining three interstate highways unearthed the remains of several hundred houses and dozens of post pits. (The findings persuaded the Federal Highway Administration to relocate the cloverleaf a few miles north.)

At the autumnal equinox, the rising sun aligns exactly with one post when viewed from the center of the circle, just as it does at the spring equinox and the solstices. William Iseminger, assistant site manager for the Cahokia Mounds State Historic Society, takes these alignments as evidence that the posts may have functioned as a kind of calendar, marking the turn of the seasons. Other woodhenges may have been part of lesser mounds, but, says Iseminger, they are nearly impossible to find because the post pits are so far apart, and wood rarely survives centuries underground.

Many archaeologists point to the size and ambition of structures like the woodhenge as evidence of Cahokia's sophistication. The construction of Monks Mound, for example, used between 15 billion and 20 billion pounds of soil, which were lugged to the site in woven baskets that held 50 to 60 pounds of dirt each. Grading and draining the 40-acre plaza in front of it meant moving just as much earth. The stockade walls consumed 20,000 trees. Subsidiary mounds in the city "grid" seem to be placed according to a rational design. These accomplishments imply organized feats of labor and planning enacted by a central authority.

In many excavations, the number of artifacts and the amount of refuse indicate the population spiked sharply around A.D. 1100, jumping from hundreds to perhaps tens of thousands of people. Large homes and mounds appeared where villages of small houses had existed just a generation before. In the mid-1990s, excavations by Pauketat, Kelly, and others showed that the hills east of Cahokia were far more populous than anyone had suspected. A wooded rise among farmhouses in the city of O'Fallon marks the site of an ancient acropolis that probably served more than 500 people. At a site south of O'Fallon, Pauketat found remnants of 80 houses, three temples, clay pots, hoe blades, ax heads, and carved redstone statues. On a tree-lined street in Lebanon, a flagpole is planted in the center of a former platform mound marking another temple center.

Based on these findings, Pauketat estimates that as many as 50,000 people may have lived in Cahokia's greater metropolitan area at the settlement's peak. They seem to have appeared as if from nowhere. "Cahokia had to be created by large-scale migration from other places," says Tom Emerson, director of the state transportation department's archaeological program. "Nobody can breed that fast."

Why did migrants come to Cahokia? Past theories suggested that the dual forces of nature and commerce drove the city's rapid growth. The fertile bottomland was ripe for cultivation by farmers skilled in raising corn, squash, and sunflowers. The nearby confluence of the Illinois, Missouri, and Mississippi rivers could have put Cahokia at the nexus of trade networks that spanned much of the continent. But American Indians had been building modest mounds in the Mississippi River valley since 3500 B.C.; they'd been growing corn with much the same tools for hundreds of years, and the rivers and flood-plains had been there for thousands. Economic and geographic felicities alone cannot account for the sudden concentration of people in the area at a particular moment.

Pauketat has come to believe that charismatic leaders created a dynamic social movement with Cahokia at the epicenter, luring inhabitants of far-flung communities away from their home-steads to the fast urban action. Pauketat resists the term *cult*, but it evokes the phenomenon he envisions. "There were certainly individuals who were movers and shakers, but they weren't consciously, deliberately exploiting people," he asserts.

"Cahokia is a political construct," Emerson adds. "It's not due to some massive change in subsistence, it's not archaeological, it's not technological. It's the kind of place that results from changes in how you conduct yourself socially and politically. What happened at Cahokia is politics, probably in the guise of religion."

Not all scholars see a burgeoning statehood in Cahokia's remains. Anthropologist George Milner of Pennsylvania State University believes there were at most 8,000 people at Cahokia, and he calculates that with even half that population one person per household working just a few weeks a year could have built Monks Mound. The construction would have proceeded at a desultory pace, he concedes; it may have required hundreds of years to complete. Only if the woodhenges and mounds were rapidly constructed would they require full-time laborers or engineers. And he is skeptical that the ecology of the region, abundant as it was, could have supported a community as vast as that supposed by Pauketat and others.

The trump card for Milner and other minimalists is the fact that, unlike the ancient Mesopotamians, Maya, Egyptians, and Chinese, Cahokians never developed a written counterpart to their spoken language. Writing is generally considered a prerequisite for the kind of record keeping typical of organized governments. (The names "Cahokia" and "Monks Mound" were applied long after the fact: Cahokia was the name of an Illini tribe that occupied the area in the 1600s, and Monks Mound was named for French Trappists who settled on one of its terraces in the 1800s.)

But champions of an advanced Cahokian civilization would rather make their case with numbers than with language anyway. Even Milner admits that if Cahokia was as populous or expansive as some claim, it would have exerted statelike control over its citizens. To support his theory, Pauketat is looking for evidence that the settlements outside of Cahokia follow a planned pattern—a support network of communities allied with the power center, perhaps communicating with the capital using runners and smoke signals. He found traces of buildings at the intersection of Routes 159 and 64, now home to a Toys 'R' Us and a Ramada Inn, and he believes they may have faced Cahokia, a six-hour walk away. That orientation would bolster his contention that the outlying villages were all part of one big polity.

Early in his career at the state department of transportation, Tom Emerson found an eight-inch statuette at the site of a temple two or three miles from Cahokia. Five pounds of distinctive redstone called flint clay had been carved into a kneeling female figure sinking a hoe into the back of a serpent. The serpent's tail climbs up the woman's back, bearing squash and gourds like a vine. The images echo familiar pre-Columbian themes of reproductive and agricultural fertility. As similar figures were discovered in the Cahokian environs, a pattern emerged. Around A.D. 1100, Emerson says, the elite of Cahokia seem to have co-opted or codified the fertility symbol, raising it to an unprecedented stature that became a kind of brand identity for the budding metropolis. "They're taking a symbolism that exists across the entire hemisphere and selectively emphasizing parts of it to their own benefit," Emerson says.

Some archaeologists have taken the emphasis on the bucolic feminine as a sign that Cahokian society was peaceful, egalitarian, and possibly matriarchal. There is, in fact, no evidence that the city was ever invaded, and no indication of bellicose tendencies other than the robust stockade surrounding the city center. But Emerson warns against this interpretation.

For one thing, he says, war wasn't necessary, because it would have been clear from the city's size alone that it could mount raiding parties with more members than the total of men, women, and children in any of the surrounding villages. "Nobody could stand against Cahokia. I don't know that they had to do much actual conflict. It was mostly intimidation."

Cahokia's downfall has been blamed on a variety of culprits. A corn-based, protein-poor diet might have sent urban dwellers west in search of buffalo. A centuries-long cold spell could have crippled the region's agricultural productivity. Deforestation of the uplands would have choked downstream water supplies with silt and exacerbated flooding. Or the cause could have been those same intangibles invoked by latter-day theorists to describe Cahokia's rise: a shift in belief systems or the balance of power. Certainly the sprawling pacts that Cahokian chiefs may have forged with nearby villages would have challenged any lasting centralization of power.

"The typical life history of a chiefdom is that it comes together, it has its heyday, and it falls apart, all within a couple of generations," says Emerson. "The interesting thing about Cahokia is that it managed to hang together. The fact that it didn't go on forever isn't unusual at all."

One of Cahokia's chiefs appears to be buried in Mound 72, which lies a half mile south of Monks Mound. It is a modest hillock by comparison, but the site holds far grimmer implications about Cahokian society. During excavations there in the late 1960s, Melvin Fowler of the University of Wisconsin at Milwaukee uncovered the remains of more than 250 people. One middle-aged male had been laid on a shelf of 20,000 seashell beads arranged in the shape of a bird. Near him were the bones of six other people, a cache of more than 800 flint arrowheads, a rolled-up sheet of copper, and several bushels of unprocessed mica—all seemingly placed in tribute to the Beaded Birdman.

In other parts of the mound, skeletons of more than 100 young women clearly indicate human sacrifice, and another grouping of four men with no hands or heads denotes the same. Another 40 bodies seemed to have been tossed into a grave hap-hazardly. Other mass burials in Mound 72 show varying degrees of respect and carelessness—and seem to reflect some sort of social hierarchy as yet undeciphered. Human sacrifice, for example, can be a sign of a coercive society or of a cultlike mentality. "Mound 72 is an ancient text with its own set of Rosetta stones and is slow to give up its secrets," Fowler wrote in *Cahokia*, a book he coauthored with Biloine Whiting Young.

The cause of Cahokia's demise is no more certain, but at least one expert links it to the Toltec civilization of south-central Mexico some 1,400 miles away. Although no Mexican artifacts have ever been found at Cahokia, similarities in the monumental and ornamental styles are conspicuous—and far from accidental, according to anthropologist Stephen Lekson of the University of Colorado at Boulder. Lekson and anthropologist Peter Peregrine of Lawrence University in Wisconsin believe that the mound cultures of the American East, the pueblo cultures of the American Southwest, and the pyramid cultures of the Mexican highlands were not only familiar but possibly even integrated with one another. There's plenty of evidence for such an exchange at Chaco Canyon, where copper bells, macaw feathers, pyrite mirrors, and other Mexican goods turn up. But Chaco was a wannabe compared with Cahokia—much smaller, far less populous, and without a centuries-long tradition preceding its development. Cahokia, with its central location, entrenched culture, and extensive trade network, didn't need Mexican trinkets to bolster its stature, Lekson says. "If someone from Cahokia showed up in any major town in Mexico, he'd be taken seriously," says Lekson. "But if someone from Chaco wandered in, they'd ask him if he had an appointment."

The Toltec, Chaco, and Cahokian societies all collapsed at very nearly the same moment, and Lekson believes that that, too, is no accident. Events in Mexico may have rippled up the Gulf Coast to the Mississippi and thence to Cahokia. "I'm not saying that Mexico is pulling everybody's strings," says Lekson. "But [the cultures] are more alike than not, and it's interesting to ask why."

Interesting as it might be, a continental perspective doesn't yield an explanation, because no one's sure what caused the Toltec regime to fall, either. It may be that if scientists ever determine why Cahokia fell, they may be able to help explain what happened elsewhere in the Americas. At present it's still anyone's guess. "We are telling stories that will fall apart in the future," says Pauketat. "But we can't ignore the evidence, either. You could make the mistake of saying this is a coercive society, based on Mound 72. Or you could look at the outlying villages and say, 'This is a peaceful community.' They must have *wanted* to build Cahokia. The truth may be somewhere in between. We don't really know what happened here."

15

New Women of the Ice Age

Heather Pringle

Anthropology is primarily a comparative study. We compare the human experience across cultures (as in the last selection) and across diverse periods of time. This selection asks a question about early European ancestors from the Paleolithic age, specifically a period of cold temperatures and glaciation. The central question regards gender roles and the interpretation of a certain type of artifact—the so-called Venus figurines. What can these sculptures tell us about the position of women in prehistoric societies?

Gender is not biology. It is a social construction, a cultural agreement about who men and women are and how they should behave. Cross-cultural comparison of gender shows that gender ideologies are correlated to other aspects of society, particularly the economy.

Archaeologists interpret the meaning and function of cultural artifacts in the context of ecology. They do this, in large part, by making ethnographic analogies with societies that have been studied by ethnographers. Archaeologists try to reconstruct the economy and the social system; finally, they interpret clues about the belief system. The problem is that such interpretations may be wrong. The archaeologists may be influenced by their own cultural biases, or they may be dealing with a sociocultural system that is extinct—and was never described by ethnographers. For example, the ethnographic record does not provide evidence of a truly matriarchal society (where political authority is controlled by women). On the other hand, there are certainly many cases of matrilineal societies (where kinship and descent are traced exclusively through the female line) with matrilocal postmarriage residence rules (the new couple lives with the bride's mother). While these societies afford women a great deal of influence and covert political power, they are not matriarchal. This does not mean, however, that matriarchal societies never existed in the past; rather, they may have become extinct.

The status of women in a society depends in large measure on their role in the economy. The reinterpretation of the Paleolithic past centers on new views of the role of women in the food-foraging economy. Historically, archaeological anthropologists first described a division of labor in which men hunted for meat and women gathered plants. This view has been rejected for three reasons: (1) it underemphasizes the importance of gathered foods in the diet; (2) in food-foraging societies women occasionally hunt small game and men gather; and (3) there is evidence to suggest that meat was obtained by scavenging from the kill-sites of carnivores rather than by hunting.

Discovering how gender systems worked in the past requires anthropologists to rethink their interpretations and to reanalyze previously excavated artifacts. This selection provides an excellent case study of that process.

As you read this selection, ask yourself the following questions:

- Was the interpretation of the Venus figurines wrong? If so, why did people believe it for such a long time?
- How might the anthropologist's own cultural notions about gender affect the interpretation of the prehistoric past?
- In what way might archaeological interpretations of Venus figurines have been different in the 1950s than today? Why?
- Would hunting with nets have been different in regard to gender and cooperation?
- How might anthropological analysis of the Venus figurines force us to reinterpret the meaning of art?
- How might the concept of "man the hunter" have shaped our cultural notions of male gender?

The following terms discussed in this selection are included in the Glossary at the back of the book:

hearth	*radiocarbon dating*
lithic	*shaman*

Pringle, Heather. "New Women of the Ice Age." Discover Magazine (April 1998):162–170. Reprinted with permission of the author.

The Black Venus of Dolní Věstonice, a small, splintered figurine sensuously fashioned from clay, is an envoy from a forgotten world. It is all soft curves, with breasts like giant pillows beneath a masked face. At nearly 26,000 years old, it ranks among the oldest known portrayals of women, and to generations of researchers, it has served as a powerful—if enigmatic—clue to the sexual politics of the Ice Age.

Excavators unearthed the Black Venus near the Czech village of Dolní Věstonice in 1924, on a hillside among charred, fractured mammoth bones and stone tools. (Despite its nickname, the Black Venus is actually reddish—it owes its name to the ash that covered it when it was found.) Since the mid-nineteenth century, researchers had discovered more than a dozen similar statuettes in caves and open-air sites from France to Russia. All were cradled in layers of earth littered with stone and bone weaponry, ivory jewelry, and the remains of extinct Ice Age animals. All were depicted naked or nearly so. Collectively, they came to be known as Venus figurines, after another ancient bare-breasted statue, the Venus de Milo. Guided at least in part by prevailing sexual stereotypes, experts interpreted the meaning of the figurines freely. The Ice Age camps that spawned this art, they concluded, were once the domain of hardworking male hunters and secluded, pampered women who spent their days in idleness like the harem slaves so popular in nineteenth-century art.

Over the next six decades, Czech archeologists expanded the excavations at Dolní Věstonice, painstakingly combing the site square meter by square meter. By the 1990s they had unearthed thousands of bone, stone, and clay artifacts and had wrested 19 radiocarbon dates from wood charcoal that sprinkled camp floors. And they had shaded and refined their portrait of Ice Age life. Between 29,000 and 25,000 years ago, they concluded, wandering bands had passed the cold months of the year repeatedly at Dolní Věstonice. Armed with short-range spears, the men appeared to have been specialists in hunting tusk-wielding mammoths and other big game, hauling home great mountains of meat to feed their dependent mates and children. At night men feasted on mammoth steaks, fed their fires with mammoth bone, and fueled their sexual fantasies with tiny figurines of women carved from mammoth ivory and fired from clay. It was the ultimate man's world.

Or was it? Over the past few months, a small team of American archeologists has raised some serious doubts. Amassing critical and previously overlooked evidence from Dolní Věstonice and the neighboring site of Pavlov, Olga Soffer, James Adovasio, and David Hyland now propose that human survival there had little to do with manly men hurling spears at big-game animals. Instead, observes Soffer, one of the world's leading authorities on Ice Age hunters and gatherers and an archeologist at the University of Illinois in Champaign-Urbana, it depended largely on women, plants, and a technique of hunting previously invisible in the archeological evidence—net hunting. "This is not the image we've always had of Upper Paleolithic macho guys out killing animals up close and personal," Soffer explains. "Net hunting is communal, and it involves the labor of children and women. And this has lots of implications."

Many of these implications make her conservative colleagues cringe because they raise serious questions about the focus of previous studies. European archeologists have long concentrated on analyzing broken stone tools and butchered big-game bones, the most plentiful and best preserved relics of the Upper Paleolithic era (which stretched from 40,000 to 12,000 years ago). From these analyses, researchers have developed theories about how these societies once hunted and gathered food. Most researchers ruled out the possibility of women hunters for biological reasons. Adult females, they reasoned, had to devote themselves to breast-feeding and tending infants. "Human babies have always been immature and dependent," says Soffer. "If women are the people who are always involved with biological reproduction and the rearing of the young, then that is going to constrain their behavior. They have to provision that child. For fathers, provisioning is optional."

To test theories about Upper Paleolithic life, researchers looked to ethnography, the scientific description of modern and historical cultural groups. While the lives of modern hunters do not exactly duplicate those of ancient hunters, they supply valuable clues to universal human behavior. "Modern ethnography cannot be used to clone the past," says Soffer. "But people have always had to solve problems. Nature and social relationships present problems to people. We use ethnography to look for theoretical insights into human behavior, test them with ethnography, and if they work, assume that they represent a universal feature of human behavior."

But when researchers began turning to ethnographic descriptions of hunting societies, they unknowingly relied on a very incomplete literature. Assuming that women in surviving hunting societies were homebodies who simply tended hearths and suckled children, most early male anthropologists spent their time with male informants. Their published ethnographies brim with descriptions of males making spears and harpoons and heaving these weapons at reindeer, walruses, and whales. Seldom do they mention the activities of women. Ethnography, it seemed, supported theories of ancient male big-game hunters. "When they talked about primitive man, it was always 'he,'" says Soffer. "The 'she' was missing."

Recent anthropological research has revealed just how much Soffer's colleagues overlooked. By observing women in the few remaining hunter-gatherer societies and by combing historical accounts of tribal groups more thoroughly, anthropologists have come to realize how critical the female half of the population has always been to survival. Women and children have set snares, laid spring traps, sighted game and participated in animal drives and surrounds—forms of hunting that endangered neither young mothers nor their offspring. They dug starchy roots and collected other plant carbohydrates essential to survival. They even hunted, on occasion, with the projectile points traditionally deemed men's weapons. "I found references to Inuit women carrying bows and arrows, especially the blunt arrows that were used for hunting birds," says Linda Owen, an archeologist at the University of Tübingen in Germany.

The revelations triggered a volley of new research. In North America, Soffer and her team have found tantalizing evidence of the hunting gear often favored by women in historical societies. In Europe, archeobotanists are analyzing Upper Paleolithic hearths for evidence of plant remains probably gathered by women and children, while lithics specialists are poring over stone tools to detect new clues to their uses. And the results are gradually reshaping our understanding of Ice Age society. The famous Venus figurines, say archeologists of the new school, were never intended as male pornography: instead they may have played a key part in Upper Paleolithic rituals that centered on women. And such findings, pointing toward a more important role for Paleolithic women than had previously been assumed, are giving many researchers pause.

Like many of her colleagues, Soffer clearly relishes the emerging picture of Upper Paleolithic life. "I think life back then was a hell of a lot more egalitarian than it was with your later peasant societies," she says. "Of course the Paleolithic women were pulling their own weight." After sifting through Ice Age research for nearly two decades, Soffer brings a new critical approach to the notion—flattering to so many of her male colleagues—of mighty male mammoth hunters. "Very few archeologists are hunters," she notes, so it never occurred to most of them to look into the mechanics of hunting dangerous tusked animals. They just accepted the ideas they'd inherited from past work.

But the details of hunting bothered Soffer. Before the fifth century B.C., no tribal hunters in Asia or Africa had ever dared make their living from slaying elephants; the great beasts were simply too menacing. With the advent of the Iron Age in Africa, the situation changed. New weapons allowed Africans to hunt elephants and trade their ivory with Greeks and Romans. A decade ago, keen to understand how prehistoric bands had slaughtered similar mammoths, Soffer began studying Upper Paleolithic sites on the Russian and Eastern European plains. To her surprise, the famous mammoth bone beds were strewn with cumbersome body parts, such as 220-pound skulls, that sensible hunters would generally abandon. Moreover, the bones exhibited widely differing degrees of weathering, as if they had sat on the ground for varying lengths of time. To Soffer, it looked suspiciously as if Upper Paleolithic hunters had simply camped next to places where the pachyderms had perished naturally—such as water holes or salt licks—and mined the bones for raw materials.

Soffer began analyzing data researchers had gathered describing the sex and age ratios of mammoths excavated from four Upper Paleolithic sites. She found many juveniles, a smaller number of adult females, and hardly any males. The distribution mirrored the death pattern other researchers had observed at African water holes, where the weakest animals perished closest to the water and the strongest farther off. "Imagine the worst time of year in Africa, which is the drought season," explains Soffer. "There is no water, and elephants need an enormous amount. The ones in the worst shape—your weakest, your infirm, your young—are going to be tethered to that water before they die. They are in such horrendous shape, they don't have any extra energy to go anywhere. The ones in better shape would wander off slight distances and then keel over farther away. You've got basket cases and you've got ones that can walk 20 feet."

To Soffer, the implications of this study were clear. Upper Paleolithic bands had pitched their camps next to critical resources such as ancient salt licks or water holes. There the men spent more time scavenging bones and ivory from mammoth carcasses than they did risking life and limb by attacking 6,600-pound pachyderms with short-range spears. "If one of these Upper Paleolithic guys killed a mammoth, and occasionally they did," concedes Soffer dryly, "they probably didn't stop talking about it for ten years."

But if Upper Paleolithic families weren't often tucking into mammoth steaks, what were they hunting and how? Soffer found the first unlikely clue in 1991, while sifting through hundreds of tiny clay fragments recovered from the Upper Paleolithic site of Pavlov, which lies just a short walk from Dolní Věstonice. Under a magnifying lens, Soffer noticed something strange on a few of the fragments: a series of parallel lines impressed on their surfaces. What could have left such a regular pattern? Puzzled, Soffer photographed the pieces, all of which had been unearthed from a zone sprinkled with wood charcoal that was radiocarbon-dated at between 27,000 and 25,000 years ago.

When she returned home, Soffer had the film developed. And one night on an impulse, she put on a slide show for a visiting colleague, Jim Adovasio. "We'd run out of cable films," she jokes. Staring at the images projected on Soffer's refrigerator, Adovasio, an archeologist at Mercyhurst College in Pennsylvania and an expert on ancient fiber technology, immediately recognized the impressions of plant fibers. On a few, he could actually discern a pattern of interlacing fibers—weaving.

Without a doubt, he said, he and Soffer were gazing at textiles or basketry. They were the oldest—by nearly 7,000 years—ever found. Just how these pieces of weaving got impressed in clay, he couldn't say. "It may be that a lot of these [materials] were lying around on clay floors," he notes. "When the houses burned, the walked-in images were subsequently left in the clay floors."

Soffer and Adovasio quickly made arrangements to fly back to the Czech Republic. At the Dolní Věstonice branch of the Institute of Archeology, Soffer sorted through nearly 8,400 fired clay pieces, weeding out the rejects. Adovasio made positive clay casts of 90. Back in Pennsylvania, he and his Mercyhurst colleague David Hyland peered at the casts under a zoom stereomicroscope, measuring warps and wefts. Forty-three revealed impressions of basketry and textiles. Some of the latter were as finely woven as a modern linen tablecloth. But as Hyland stared at four of the samples, he noted something potentially more fascinating: impressions of cordage bearing weaver's knots, a technique that joins two lengths of cord and that is commonly used for making nets of secure mesh. It looked like a tiny shred of a net bag, or perhaps a hunting net. Fascinated, Soffer expanded the study. She spent six weeks at the Moravian Museum in Brno, sifting through the remainder of the collections from Dolní Věstonice. Last fall, Adovasio spied the telltale impressions of Ice Age mesh on one of the new casts.

The mesh, measuring two inches across, is far too delicate for hunting deer or other large prey. But hunters at Dolní Věstonice could have set nets of this size to capture hefty Ice Age hares, each carrying some six pounds of meat, and other furbearers such as arctic fox and red fox. As it turns out, the bones of hares and foxes litter camp floors at Dolní Věstonice and Pavlov. Indeed, this small game accounts for 46 percent of the individual animals recovered at Pavlov. Soffer, moreover, doesn't rule out the possibility

of turning up bits of even larger nets. Accomplished weavers in North America once knotted mesh with which they captured 1,000-pound elk and 300-pound bighorn sheep. "In fact, when game officials have to move sheep out west, it's by nets," she adds. "You throw nets on them and they just lie down. It's a very safe way of hunting."

In many historical societies, she observes, women played a key part in net hunting since the technique did not call for brute strength nor did it place young mothers in physical peril. Among Australian aborigines, for example, women as well as men knotted the mesh, laboring for as much as two or three years on a fine net. Among Native American groups, they helped lay out their handiwork on poles across a valley floor. Then the entire camp joined forces as beaters. Fanning out across the valley, men, women, and children alike shouted and screamed, flushing out game and driving it in the direction of the net. "Everybody and their mother could participate," says Soffer. "Some people were beating, others were screaming or holding the net. And once you got the net on these animals, they were immobilized. You didn't need brute force. You could club them, hit them any old way."

People seldom returned home empty-handed. Researchers living among the net-hunting Mbuti in the forests of Congo report that they capture game every time they lay out their woven traps, scooping up 50 percent of the animals encountered. "Nets are a far more valued item in their panoply of food-producing things than bows and arrows are," says Adovasio. So lethal are these traps that the Mbuti generally rack up more meat than they can consume, trading the surplus with neighbors. Other net hunters traditionally smoked or dried their catch and stored it for leaner times. Or they polished it off immediately in large ceremonial feasts. The hunters of Dolní Věstonice and Pavlov, says Soffer, probably feasted during ancient rituals. Archeologists unearthed no evidence of food storage pits at either site. But there is much evidence of ceremony. At Dolní Věstonice, for example, many clay figurines appear to have been ritually destroyed in secluded parts of the site.

Soffer doubts that the inhabitants of Dolní Věstonice and Pavlov were the only net makers in Ice Age Europe. Camps stretching from Germany to Russia are littered with a notable abundance of small-game bones, from hares to birds like ptarmigan. And at least some of their inhabitants whittled bone tools that look much like the awls and net spacers favored by historical net makers. Such findings, agree Soffer and Adovasio, reveal just how shaky the most widely accepted reconstructions of Upper Paleolithic life are. "These terribly stilted interpretations," says Adovasio, "with men hunting big animals all the time and the poor females waiting at home for these guys to bring home the bacon—what crap."

In her home outside Munich, Linda Owen finds other faults with this traditional image. Owen, an American born and raised, specializes in the microscopic analysis of stone tools. In her years of work, she often noticed that many of the tools made by hunters who roamed Europe near the end of the Upper Paleolithic era, some 18,000 to 12,000 years ago, resembled pounding stones and other gear for harvesting and processing plants. Were women and children gathering and storing wild plant foods?

Most of her colleagues saw little value in pursuing the question. Indeed, some German archeologists contended that 90 percent of the human diet during the Upper Paleolithic era came from meat. But as Owen began reading nutritional studies, she saw that heavy meat consumption would spell death. To stoke the body's cellular engines, human beings require energy from protein, fat, or carbohydrates. Of these, protein is the least efficient. To burn it, the body must boost its metabolic rate by 10 percent, straining the liver's ability to absorb oxygen. Unlike carnivorous animals, whose digestive and metabolic systems are well adapted to a meat-only diet, humans who consume more than half their calories as lean meat will die from protein poisoning. In Upper Paleolithic times, hunters undoubtedly tried to round out their diets with fat from wild game. But in winter, spring, and early summer, the meat would have been very lean. So how did humans survive?

Owen began sifting for clues through anthropological and historical accounts from subarctic and arctic North America. These environments, she reasoned, are similar to that of Ice Age Europe and pose similar challenges to their inhabitants. Even in the far north, Inuit societies harvested berries for winter storage and gathered other plants for medicines and for fibers. To see if any of the flora that thrived in Upper Paleolithic Europe could be put to similar uses, Owen drew up a list of plants economically important to people living in cold-climate regions of North America and Europe and compared it with a list of species that botanists had identified from pollen trapped in Ice Age sediment cores from southern Germany. Nearly 70 plants were found on both lists. "I came up with just a fantastic list of plants that were available at that time. Among others, there were a number of reeds that are used by the Eskimo and subarctic people in North America for making baskets. There are a lot of plants with edible leaves and stems, and things that were used as drugs and dyes. So the plants were there."

The chief plant collectors in historical societies were undoubtedly women. "It was typically women's work," says Owen. "I did find several comments that the men on hunting expeditions would gather berries or plants for their own meals, but they did not participate in the plant-gathering expeditions. They might go along, but they would be hunting or fishing."

Were Upper Paleolithic women gathering plants? The archeological literature was mostly silent on the subject. Few archeobotanists, Owen found, had ever looked for plant seeds and shreds in Upper Paleolithic camps. Most were convinced such efforts would be futile in sites so ancient. At University College London, however, Owen reached a determined young archeobotanist, Sarah Mason, who had analyzed a small sample of charcoal-like remains from a 26,390-year-old hearth at Dolní Věstonice.

The sample held more than charcoal. Examining it with a scanning electron microscope, Mason and her colleagues found fragments of fleshy plant taproots with distinctive secretory cavities—trademarks of the daisy and aster family, which boasts several species with edible roots. In all likelihood, women at Dolní Věstonice had dug the roots and cooked them into starchy meals. And they had very likely simmered other plant foods too. Mason and her colleagues detected a strange pulverized substance in the charred sample. It looked as if the women had either ground plants into flour and then boiled the results to make gruel or pounded vegetable material into a mush for their babies. Either way, says Soffer, the results are telling. "They're stuffing carbohydrates."

Owen is pursuing the research further. "If you do look," she says, "you can find things." At her urging, colleagues at the University of Tübingen are now analyzing Paleolithic hearths for botanical remains as they unearth them. Already they have turned up more plants, including berries, all clearly preserved after thousands of years. In light of these findings, Owen suggests that it was women, not men, who brought home most of the calories to Upper Paleolithic families. Indeed, she estimates that if Ice Age females collected plants, bird eggs, shellfish, and edible insects, and if they hunted or trapped small game and participated in the hunting of large game—as northern women did in historical times—they most likely contributed 70 percent of the consumed calories.

Moreover, some women may have enjoyed even greater power, judging from the most contentious relics of Ice Age life: the famous Venus figurines. Excavators have recovered more than 100 of the small statuettes, which were crafted between 29,000 and 23,000 years ago from such enduring materials as bone, stone, antler, ivory, and fired clay. The figurines share a strange blend of abstraction and realism. They bear prominent breasts, for example, but lack nipples. Their bodies are often minutely detailed down to the swaying lines of their backbones and the tiny rolls of flesh—fat folds—beneath their shoulder blades, but they often lack eyes, mouths, and any facial expression. For years researchers viewed them as a male art form. Early anthropologists, after all, had observed only male hunters carving stone, ivory, and other hard materials. Females were thought to lack the necessary strength. Moreover, reasoned experts, only men would take such loving interest in a woman's body. Struck by the voluptuousness of the small stone, ivory, and clay bodies, some researchers suggested they were Ice Age erotica, intended to be touched and fondled by their male makers. The idea still lingers. In the 1980s, for example, the well-known American paleontologist Dale Guthrie wrote a scholarly article comparing the postures of the figurines with the provocative poses of *Playboy* centerfolds.

But most experts now dismiss such contentions. Owen's careful scouring of ethnographic sources, for example, revealed that women in arctic and subarctic societies did indeed work stone and ivory on occasion. And there is little reason to suggest the figurines figured as male erotica. The Black Venus, for example, seems to have belonged to a secret world of ceremony and ritual far removed from everyday sexual life.

The evidence, says Soffer, lies in the raw material from which the Black Venus is made. Clay objects sometimes break or explode when fired, a process called thermal-shock fracturing. Studies conducted by Pamela Vandiver of the Smithsonian Institution have demonstrated that the Black Venus and other human and animal figurines recovered from Dolní Věstonice— as well as nearly 2,000 fired ceramic pellets that litter the site—were made from a local clay that is resistant to thermal-shock fracturing. But many of the figurines, including the celebrated Black Venus, bear the distinctive jagged branching splinters created by thermal shock. Intriguingly, the fired clay pellets do not.

Curious, Vandiver decided to replicate the ancient firing process. Her analysis of the small Dolní Věstonice kilns revealed that they had been fired to temperatures around 1450 degrees Fahrenheit—similar to those of an ordinary hearth. So Vandiver set about making figurines of local soil and firing them in a similar earthen kiln, which a local archeological crew had built nearby. To produce thermal shock, she had to place objects larger than half an inch on the hottest part of the fire; moreover, the pieces had to be so wet they barely held their shape.

To Vandiver and Soffer, the experiment—which was repeated several times back at the Smithsonian Institution—suggests that thermal shock was no accident. "Stuff can explode naturally in the kiln," says Soffer, "or you can make it explode. Which was going

on at Dolní Věstonice? We toyed with both ideas. Either we're dealing with the most inept potters, people with two left hands, or they are doing it on purpose. And we reject the idea that they were totally inept, because other materials didn't explode. So what are the odds that this would happen only with a very particular category of objects?"

These exploding figurines could well have played a role in rituals, an idea supported by the location of the kilns. They are situated far away from the dwellings, as ritual buildings often are. Although the nature of the ceremonies is not clear, Soffer speculates that they might have served as divination rites for discerning what the future held. "Some stuff is going to explode. Some stuff is not going to explode. It's evocative, like picking petals off a daisy. She loves me, she loves me not."

Moreover, ritualists at Dolní Věstonice could have read significance into the fracturing patterns of the figurines. Many historical cultures, for example, attempted to read the future by a related method called scapulimancy. In North America, Cree ceremonialists often placed the shoulder blade, or scapula, of a desired animal in the center of a lodge. During the ceremonies, cracks began splintering the bone: a few of these fractures leaked droplets of fat. To Cree hunters, this was a sign that they would find game if they journeyed in the directions indicated by the cracks.

Venus figurines from other sites also seem to have been cloaked in ceremony. "They were not just something made to look pretty," says Margherita Mussi, an archeologist at the University of Rome-La Sapienza who studies Upper Paleolithic figurines. Mussi notes that several small statuettes from the Grimaldi Cave carvings of southern Italy, one of the largest troves of Ice Age figurines ever found in Western Europe, were carved from rare materials, which the artists obtained with great difficulty, sometimes through trade or distant travel. The statuettes were laboriously whittled and polished, then rubbed with ocher, a pigment that appears to have had ceremonial significance, suggesting that they could have been reserved for special events like rituals.

The nature of these rites is still unclear. But Mussi is convinced that women took part, and some archeologists believe they stood at the center. One of the clearest clues, says Mussi, lies in a recently rediscovered Grimaldi figurine known as Beauty and the Beast. This greenish yellow serpentine sculpture portrays two arched bodies facing away from each other and joined at the head, shoulders, and lower extremities. One body is that of a Venus figurine. The other is a strange creature that combines the triangular head of a reptile, the pinched waist of a wasp, tiny arms, and horns. "It is clearly not a creature of this world," says Mussi.

The pairing of woman and supernatural beast, adds Mussi, is highly significant. "I believe that these women were related to the capacity of communicating with a different world," she says. "I think they were believed to be the gateway to a different dimension." Possessing powers that far surpassed others in their communities, such women may have formed part of a spiritual elite, rather like the shamans of ancient Siberia. As intermediaries between the real and spirit worlds, Siberian shamans were said to be able to cure illnesses and intercede on behalf of others for hunting success. It is possible that Upper Paleolithic women performed similar services for their followers.

Although the full range of their activities is unlikely ever to be known for certain, there is good reason to believe that Ice Age women played a host of powerful roles—from plant collectors and weavers to hunters and spiritual leaders. And the research that suggests those roles is rapidly changing our mental images of the past. For Soffer and others, these are exciting times. "The data do speak for themselves," she says finally. "They answer the questions we have. But if we don't envision the questions, we're not going to see the data."

16

Disease and Death
at Dr. Dickson's Mounds

Alan H. Goodman and George J. Armelagos

In a popular book, *The Third Wave*, Alvin Toffler identified three major "transformations" of global consequence. The first of these was the agricultural revolution, the second was the industrial revolution, and the third is the present-day technological revolution. The impacts of these events and processes are far-reaching and generally assumed to be quite positive. However, it is possible that there have been subtle, but exceedingly important, unintended consequences that have gone undetected. One of the best ways to raise awareness of these problems is to reexamine history. Of course, the agricultural revolution, which some anthropologists think may have been the most important event in human history, occurred during the prehistoric period. No written records were left, and it is therefore up to archaeologists to provide insights into the changes the agricultural revolution brought.

We do not need to go to the Near East, Asia, or Mesoamerica to study the transformation from hunting and gathering to agriculture. You can find it right in your own backyard. In this selection, Alan Goodman and George Armelagos examine the health consequences of the rise of agriculture. The paleopathological study of bones can be an important supplement to traditional archaeological description and analysis. Like the conclusions of Eaton and Konner on Paleolithic diet (Selection 9), cultural evolution does not always mean progress.

As you read this selection, ask yourself the following questions:

- What happened to the population density around Dickson's Mounds during the first fifty years of agriculture?
- What social changes seem to accompany the rise of agriculture?
- What three factors made possible the tracing of changing health patterns from preagricultural to postagricultural subsistence patterns?
- Did agriculture lead to a better diet and improved health conditions?
- Why did prehistoric people become farmers?

The following terms discussed in this selection are included in the Glossary at the back of the book:

dental anthropology   population pressure
Mississippian tradition   sickle-cell anemia
paleopathology

Clustered in west-central Illinois, atop a bluff near the confluence of the Illinois and Spoon rivers, are twelve to thirteen poorly defined earthen mounds. The mounds, which overlap each other to some extent, cover a crescent-shaped area of about an acre. Since at least the middle of the nineteenth century, local residents have known that prehistoric Native Americans built these mounds to bury their dead. But it was not until the late 1920s that Don Dickson, a chiropractor, undertook the first systematic excavation of the mounds located on farmland owned by his father. Barely into his thirties at the time, Dickson became so involved in the venture that he never returned to his chiropractic practice. Apparently, he was intrigued by the novel undertaking of unearthing skeletons and trying to diagnose the maladies of long-dead individuals. Later on, he became more concerned with the patterns of disease and death in this extinct group in order to understand how these people lived and why they often died at an early age.

The "Dickson Mounds" (the site also includes two early, unmounded burial grounds) quickly attracted the attention of professional anthropologists. In the early

1930s, a team of University of Chicago archeologists exposed about 200 of the estimated 3,000 burials and identified a number of settlement sites in a 100-square-mile area. A second phase of excavation at Dickson began in the 1960s under the direction of Alan Harn, an archeologist working for the state of Illinois, whose crew excavated many of the local living sites and more than 800 additional burials. The archeological research revealed that these prehistoric people had taken part in an important transition, from hunting and gathering to an agricultural way of life.

About A.D. 950, hunter-gatherers lived along the Illinois River valley area near Dickson, subsisting on a wide range of local plants and animals, including grasses and seeds, fruits and berries, roots and tubers, vines, herbs, large and small mammals, migratory waterfowl and riverine birds, and fish. The moderate climate, copious water supply, and rich soil made this a bountiful and attractive area for hunter-gatherers. Groups occupied campsites that consisted of a few small structures, and the debris scattered around these sites suggests seasonal use. The population density was low, perhaps on the order of two to three persons per square mile. Then, about 1050, broken hoes and other agricultural tools, as well as maize, began to form part of village refuse, evidence of the introduction of maize agriculture. At the same time, the population grew. By 1200 the population density may have increased by a factor of ten, to about twenty-five persons per square mile. Living sites became larger and more permanent. The largest settlement in the area, Larson, was a residential and ceremonial center where some 1,000 inhabitants lived, many behind a palisaded wall.

Trade also flourished. Dickson became part of what archeologists call the Mississippian tradition, a network of maize-growing, mound-building societies that spread throughout most of the eastern United States. More and more, items used at the village sites or deposited as grave offerings were not of local origin. Some, such as marine shell necklaces, came from as far away as the Gulf of Mexico and Florida, one thousand miles to the south. Everyday objects such as spoons and jars were received from peoples of the eastern plains and the western prairies, while luxury items of ceremonial or decorative value arrived in trade from the south, probably coming upriver to Dickson through Cahokia, a Mississippian center some 110 miles away. Cahokia is a massive site that includes some 120 mounds within a six-square-mile area. As many as 30,000 persons lived at Cahokia and in the surrounding villages.

What we know about Dickson might have ended at this point, but continues because the skeletal remains that Harn excavated have been used to evaluate how the health of these prehistoric people fared following the adoption of agriculture and other changes in their life style. Interest in this issue stems from the writings of the eminent British archeologist V. Gordon Childe (1892–1957), who believed that the development of agriculture prompted the first great revolution in human technology, ushering in fundamental changes in economy, social organization, and ideology. Archeologists continue to debate the causes of agricultural revolutions. For example, some believe that in various regions of the world, increased population pressure, leading to food shortages and declining health, spurred the switch to agricultural food production. Others believe population increase was one of the consequences of agricultural revolutions. More important to us are the effects of an agricultural revolution on the health of people who lived at the time of such change.

Three circumstances have made it possible to test the effects agriculture had upon health at Dickson. First, Harn and those working with him valued the potential information to be gained from skeletons and therefore paid close attention to their excavation. Ultimately, the skeletal remains were sent to the University of Massachusetts at Amherst for analysis by George Armelagos and many of his graduate students (this is how we became involved). Second, the recovered remains include both individuals who lived before the development of maize agriculture (Late Woodland, or pre-Mississippian) and after (Mississippian). The two groups of individuals could be distinguished according to the mounds they were buried in, their placement within each mound, and their burial position (in earlier burials the bodies tend to be in a flexed or semiflexed position; in later burials they tend to be extended). The third enabling condition was provided by Janice Cohen, one of Armelagos's graduate students. Her analysis of highly heritable dental traits showed that although Dickson was in contact with persons from outside the central Illinois River valley area during the period of rapid cultural change, outside groups did not replace or significantly merge with the local groups. It is therefore possible to follow the health over time of a single population that, for all intents and purposes, was genetically stable.

As a doctoral student working under Armelagos in the early 1970s, John Lallo, now at Cleveland State University, set out to test whether health at Dickson improved, got worse, or remained the same with the advent of agriculture and its accompanying changes. Lallo argued that intensification of maize agriculture most likely resulted in a poorer diet. Although a common assumption is that the adoption of agriculture should have provided a prehistoric people with a better diet, there are good reasons to predict just the opposite. Heavy reliance on a single crop may lead to nutritional problems. Maize, for example, is deficient in lysine, an essential amino acid. Furthermore, agricultural societies that subsist on a few foodstuffs are more vulnerable to famines brought about by drought and other disasters. Finally, increased population density, a more sedentary life style, and greater trade, all of which are associated with agriculture, provide conditions for the spread and maintenance of infectious diseases.

The skeletons of individuals who lived before and after the introduction of maize agriculture were examined for a number of different health indicators, in order to provide a balanced picture of the pattern of stress, disease, and death that affected the Dickson population. The indicators that proved most sensitive to health differences were: bone lesions (scars) due to infection, nutritional deficiencies, trauma, and degenerative conditions; long bone growth; dental developmental defects; and age at death. To avoid unconscious bias, we and the other researchers involved measured these seven traits without knowing in advance which skeletons came from each of the two cultural periods.

Persistent bacterial infection leaves its mark on the outer, or periosteal, layer of bone. Tibias (shinbones) are the most frequently affected bones because they have relatively poor circulation and therefore tend to accumulate bacteria. Toxins produced by bacteria kill some of the bone cells; as new bone is produced, the periosteal bone becomes roughened and layered. Lallo and his co-workers found that following the introduction of agriculture there was a threefold increase in the percentage of individuals with such lesions. Eighty-four percent of the Mississippian tibias had these "periosteal reactions," as compared with only 26 percent of pre-Mississippian tibias. The lesions also tended to be more severe and to show up in younger individuals in the Mississippian population.

A second type of lesion, more easily seen in the thinner bones of the body (such as those of the skull), is a sign of anemia. In response to anemia, the body steps up its production of red blood cells, which are formed in the bone marrow. To accomplish this the marrow must expand at the expense of the outer layer of bone. In severe cases, this expansion may cause the outer layer of bone to disappear, exposing the porous, sieve-like inner bone. This lesion, called porotic hyperostosis, can occur with any kind of anemia. In the Dickson Mounds populations, the lesions are not severe, are restricted to the eye sockets and crania, and occur mainly in children and young adult females. This pattern suggests anemia resulting from a nutritional deficiency, specifically an iron deficiency. (A hereditary anemia, such as sickle-cell anemia, would have been more severe in its manifestation and would have affected all ages and both sexes in the population.)

There is a significant increase in the frequency of porotic hyperostosis during the Mississippian period. Half the Mississippian infants and children had porotic hyperostosis, twice the rate found for pre-Mississippian infants and children. Individuals with both periosteal reactions and porotic hyperostosis tend to have suffered more severely from each condition. This may be evidence of a deadly synergism of malnutrition and infection, like that often reported among contemporary populations.

Traumatic lesions were measured by diagnosis of healed fractures of the long bones of the legs and arms. Adult males had the highest frequency of such fractures. Approximately one out of three Mississippian males had at least one fracture, twice the frequency of their predecessors. These fractures often occurred at the midshaft of the ulna and radius, the bones of the lower arm. Fractures at this location are called parry fractures because they are typically the result of efforts to ward off a blow.

The frequency of degenerative pathologies, including arthritic conditions found on joints and the contacting surfaces of the vertebral column, also increased through time. One or more degenerative conditions were diagnosed in 40 percent of pre-Mississippian adults but in more than 70 percent of Mississippian adults.

In addition to the studies of the changing pattern of disease and trauma, we, along with Lallo and Jerome Rose, now at the University of Arkansas, assessed differences in skeletal growth and developmental timing. Skeletal growth and development are susceptible to a wide variety of stressful conditions and therefore reflect overall health. We found that in comparison to pre-Mississippians of the same age, Mississippian children between the ages of five and ten had significantly shorter and narrower tibias and femurs (the major long bones of the legs). This difference may be explained by a decreased rate of growth before the age of five. The Mississippians apparently were able to catch up in growth after age ten, however, since adult Mississippians are only slightly smaller than pre-Mississippians.

A more detailed exploration of developmental changes came from studying defects in enamel, the hard white coating of the crowns of teeth. Ameloblasts, the enamel-forming cells, secrete enamel matrix in ringlike fashion, starting at the biting surface and ending at the bottom of the crown. A deficiency in enamel thickness, called a hypoplasia, may result if the individual suffers a systemic physiological stress during enamel formation. Since the timing of enamel secretion is well known and relatively stable, the position of such a lesion on a tooth corresponds to an individual's age at the time of stress.

We examined the permanent teeth—teeth that form between birth and age seven. For skeletons with nearly complete sets of permanent teeth, 55 percent of pre-Mississippians had hypoplasias, while among Mississippians the figure rose to 80 percent. In both groups, hypoplasias were most frequently laid down between the ages of one and one-half and four. However, the hypoplasias in the Mississippian group peak at age two and one-half, approximately one-half year earlier than the pre-Mississippian peak. The peak is also more pronounced. This pattern of defects may indicate both an earlier age at weaning and the use of cereal products as weanling foods.

The repeated occurrence of hypoplasias within individuals revealed an annual cycle of stress. Most likely there was a seasonal food shortage. This seems to have worsened in the period just before the population becomes completely "Mississippianized," suggesting that it provided a rationale for intensifying agriculture.

All the above six indicators point toward a decrease in health associated with cultural change at Dickson. However, they are not meaningful apart from an analysis of the pattern of death in these populations. Healthy-looking skeletons, for example, may be the remains of young individuals who died outright because their bodies were too weak to cope in the face of disease, injury, and other forms of stress. Conversely, skeletons that show wear and tear may be those of individuals who survived during stressful times and lived to a ripe old age.

At Dickson, however, the trend is unambiguous. Individuals whose skeletons showed more signs of stress and disease (for example, enamel hypoplasias) also lived shorter lives, on average, than individuals with fewer such indications. For the population as a whole, life expectancy at birth decreased from twenty-six years in the pre-Mississippian to nineteen years in the Mississippian. The contrast in mortality is especially pronounced during the infant and childhood years. For example, 22 percent of Mississippians died during their first year as compared to 13 percent of the pre-Mississippians. Even for those who passed through the dangerous early years of childhood, there is a differential life expectancy. At fifteen years of age, pre-Mississippians could expect to live for an average of twenty-three more years, while Mississippians could expect to live for only eighteen more years.

What caused this decline in health? A number of possibilities have been proposed. Lallo and others have emphasized the effect of agriculture on diet. Most of the health trends may be explained by a decline in diet quality. These include the trends in growth, development, mortality, and nutritional disease, all four of which have obvious links to nutrition. The same explanation may be offered for the increase in infectious diseases, since increased susceptibility may be due to poor nutrition. Furthermore, a population subject to considerable infectious disease would be likely to suffer from other conditions, including increased rates of anemia and mortality and decreased growth rates.

The link between diet and infectious disease is bolstered by an analysis of trace elements from tibial bone cores. Robert Gilbert found that the Mississippian bones contain less zinc, an element that is limited in maize. Building on this research, Wadia Bahou, now a physician in Ann Arbor, Michigan, showed that the skeletons with the lowest levels of zinc had the highest frequency of infectious lesions. This is strong evidence that a diet of maize was relied on to a point where health was affected.

The population increase associated with the changeover to agriculture probably also contributed to the decline in health. We do not believe that the population ever threatened to exceed the carrying capacity of the bountiful Dickson area (and there are no signs of the environmental degradation one would expect to find if resources were overexploited). However, increased population density and sedentariness, coupled with intensification of contact with outsiders, create opportunities for the spread of infectious disease. George Milner of the University of Kentucky, while still a graduate student at Northwestern University, argued this point in comparing Dickson with the Kane Mounds populations. Kane is located near Cahokia, the major center south of Dickson. Despite Kane's proximity to this large center, its population density was much lower than at Larson, the major agricultural village of the Dickson population. Of the two, Kane had the lower rate of infectious diseases.

While the "agricultural hypothesis," including the effects of population pressure, offers an explanation for much of the health data, it doesn't automatically account for the two remaining measures: degenerative and traumatic pathologies. Poor nutrition and infectious disease may make people more susceptible to degenerative disease. However, the arthritic conditions found in the Dickson skeletons, involving movable joints, were probably caused by strenuous physical activity. The link, then, is not with the consumption of an agricultural diet but, if anything, with the physically taxing work of agricultural production. An explanation for the increase in traumatic injuries is harder to imagine. Possibly, the increased population density caused social tension and strife to arise within communities, but why should this have happened?

A curious fact makes us think that explanations based only on agricultural intensification and population increase are missing an important contributing factor. Recent archeological research at Dickson suggests that hunting and gathering remained productive enterprises and were never completely abandoned. Many of the local Mississippian sites have a great concentration of animal bones and projectile points used for hunting. A balanced diet apparently was available. The health and trace element data, however, suggest that the Mississippian diet was deficient. There is a disparity between what was available and what was eaten.

At present our search for an explanation for this paradox centers on the relationship between Dickson and the Cahokia population. The builders of the Dickson Mounds received many items of symbolic worth from the Cahokia region, such as copper-covered ear spools and marine shell necklaces. Much of the health data would be explained if Dickson had been trading perishable foodstuffs for these luxury items. In particular, the diversion of meat or fish to Cahokia would explain the apparent discrepancy between diet and resources.

To have a food surplus to trade, individuals from the Dickson area may have intensified their agricultural production while continuing to hunt and gather. The increase in degenerative conditions could have resulted from such a heavy workload. The system may also have put social strain on the community, leading to internal strife. And the accumulation of wealth in terms of ceremonial or other luxury items may have necessitated protection from outside groups. This would explain why the Larson site was palisaded. Both internal and external strain may have led to the increase in traumatic pathologies.

To test the validity of this scenario, we are hoping to gather additional evidence, concentrating on an analysis of trade. The flow of perishable goods such as meat is hard to trace, but we can study the sets of animal bones found at Cahokia and at Dickson village and butchering sites. The distribution of animal bones at the archeological sites can then be compared with

examples of bone distributions in areas where trading has been ethnographically recorded. Further evidence is provided by data such as Milner's, which showed that health at Kane—a community that shared in Cahokia's power—was better than at Dickson.

The trading of needed food for items of symbolic value, to the point where health is threatened, may not seem to make sense from an objective outsider's perspective. But it is a situation that has been observed in historic and modern times. An indigenous group learns that it can trade something it has access to (sugar cane, alpacas, turtles) for something it greatly admires but can only obtain from outside groups (metal products, radios, alcohol). The group's members do not perceive that the long-term health and economic results of such trade are usually unfavorable. Nor are all such arrangements a result of voluntary agreement. The pattern of health observed at Dickson is seen in most situations where there is a decline in access to, and control over, resources. For example, lower classes in stratified societies live shorter lives and suffer more from nearly all major diseases.

Agriculture is not invariably associated with declining health. A recent volume edited by Mark N. Cohen and George J. Armelagos, *Paleopathology and the Origins of Agriculture,* analyzed health changes in twenty-three regions of the world where agriculture developed. In many of these regions there was a clear, concurrent decline in health, while in others there was little or no change or slight improvements in health. Perhaps a decline is more likely to occur when agriculture is intensified in the hinterland of a political system. Groups living far away from the centers of trade and power are apt to be at a disadvantage. They may send the best fruits of their labors to market and receive little in return. And during times of economic hardship or political turmoil, they may be the ones to suffer the most, as resources are concentrated on maintaining the central parts of the system.

17

The Secrets of Ancient Tiwanaku
Are Benefiting Today's Bolivia

Baird Straughan

Archaeologists work to understand how prehistoric people lived and why their cultures changed. The artifacts they uncover and the site features they explore are often mysteries requiring interpretation. How is an archaeological discovery a clue about how prehistoric cultures worked? Archaeologists are most often motivated by genuine curiosity about the past. Many students of anthropology wonder if there is any practical usefulness that can come from archaeological curiosity and discovery. This case study is the result of an archaeological investigation that produced real practical solutions to current agricultural and socioeconomic problems in a poor country—Bolivia.

The archaeologists, Alan Kolata and Oswaldo Rivera, did not start their investigations with the goal of solving the problems of the local Aymara people. Rather, they wanted to understand an archaeological mystery—the expansion and eventual collapse of the prehistoric civilization of Tiwanaku, located 12,500 feet above sea level on the shores of Lake Titicaca. This civilization produced impressive monumental structures (like Dickson's Mounds described in Selection 16) for an urban area with a population as large as 50,000 people. Because this is an area with very poor agriculture today, the obvious question to the archaeologists was how this large population was fed. In answering this question, they "discovered" a very old solution that was practiced by the ancestors of the local Indians.

Serendipity can be a very important aspect of discovery. Over and over, there are cases in which researchers make important discoveries that were only marginally related to the topics that they intended to study. In the case of Tiwanaku, researchers discovered ways to apply knowledge to improve the human condition even when their purpose in doing the research was to advance basic knowledge. The archaeologists recognized the practical use of their discovery, and

they worked with local farmers to demonstrate that practical use. Ultimately, they significantly improved agricultural production in the area, and they consequently decreased local malnutrition.

This selection describes fascinating archaeological research that involves important basic research into a pre-Inca civilization and a practical application of anthropological knowledge. Like the case of Easter Island, the civilization at Tiwanaku ultimately collapsed. If the archaeologists can determine why that happened, there may be practical payoffs as well.

As you read this selection, ask yourself the following questions:

- How might the archaeologists have known the meaning of the ridges and depressions on the boggy lands near Tiwanaku?

- Why did most of the local people not wish to try the new agricultural methods suggested by the archaeologists?

- What was the population of Tiwanaku in its heyday? Was much effort put into religious structures? Did it have a class system? How long did this city survive?

- How have the new farming methods affected nutritional levels?

- What forces might have brought this civilization to an end?

The following terms discussed in this selection are included in the Glossary at the back of the book:

agrarian   excavation
arable land   mound
carrying capacity

Straughan, Baird. "The Secrets of Ancient Tiwanaku Are Benefiting Today's Bolivia." Smithsonian Magazine 21 (1991), no. 11:38–43, 46–47. Reprinted with author's permission.

In 1987, Roberto Cruz didn't know his ancestors had built a civilization that lasted for nearly a thousand years. If you had told him their capital had been the nearby town of Tiwanaku, or that new research indicates they exercised control over a vast territory from Peru to Argentina, from the Pacific to the eastern slope of the Andes, he probably wouldn't have cared.

Cruz, an Aymara Indian living at 12,500 feet near the southern shores of Lake Titicaca in Bolivia, had enough trouble just surviving. His lands on the lake's floodplain, the Pampa Koani, were useless. Frosts there killed the crops, and boggy conditions rotted potatoes in the ground. His small fields on the hillside were exhausted, and he had no time to think about "the grandfathers," as he calls them.

That was before they reached out from the centuries and touched his life. They reached him through two outsiders whom Cruz met one day in 1987 walking across the pampa, over the strange pattern of parallel ridges and depressions that stretches for miles across the floodplain. He knew that they had been working for years among the ancient ruins nearby. But the two men told him some things he found hard to believe: that a thousand years ago his boggy lands had been fertile; that the ridges and depressions were the remains of a system of raised planting surfaces separated by canals; that if he redug the canals, the raised fields would produce again.

Cruz called together his neighbors. Could this be true? No, the Aymara concluded, the strangers probably just wanted to steal the land. No, they would continue farming the hillsides, where they had been as long as anybody could remember. The frosts were milder there. But Cruz was curious. He told the two they could redig the canals on his lowland fields.

His neighbors were incensed. They called him to a meeting, and when he wouldn't go willingly, they trapped him, gathered the villagers and castigated him. Outsiders were bad luck, digging up "virgin earth that had never seen the light of the sun." That disturbed the weather. It was why the region was suffering a severe drought. Thanks to Cruz, they said, the whole town would starve. They threatened banishment.

Cruz wouldn't back down. He planted a crop on the raised platforms between the canals and watched his potato plants grow taller than he'd ever seen. Then, just before harvest, came his worst fear—frost. That whole night the villagers stood watch in their fields, Cruz with them. By early morning 90 percent of the crop on the hillsides was lost. Cruz walked down toward his fields on the pampa, knowing he'd made a terrible mistake. He could feel the coldest air flowing downhill to gather on the floodplain, where it would

kill everything. The community had been right. The strangers had tricked him.

But when Cruz arrived at his land he saw with surprise that a mist had formed over it, a low white cloud that covered his fields "like a blanket." It lasted until the first rays of the morning sun, then vanished. Cruz walked out onto the platforms and was amazed to find his plants virtually undamaged.

Shortly thereafter he took in a record harvest. Today the edge of the Pampa Koani near Cruz's home is lined with raised fields dug by his neighbors. Cruz is a respected member of the community again.

He still thinks back to that one particularly bitter frost, and how his crop was miraculously saved. In fact, he now knows that what he saw rising from his fields that freezing night was the genius of Tiwanaku, a powerful state built by some of the greatest hydrologists the world had ever known.

The altiplano gets a great deal of heat from the sun during the day, but at night that heat escapes from the soil. Because the canals, which make up about 30 percent of the surface area, retain heat, they remain at least tepid and create a large temperature gradient. Water begins to evaporate and produces a fine mist that covers the fields, creating an artificial microclimate. In addition to the fog blanket, water drawn up into the soil platform by capillary action conducts heat to the plants' root systems.

One of the outsiders Roberto Cruz met on the pampa in 1987 was Alan Kolata, who is a professor of archaeology and anthropology at the University of Chicago. He had come to Tiwanaku in 1978 through "a bit of serendipity," as he puts it. Given the opportunity to collaborate on a new archaeological project in Bolivia shortly after receiving his doctorate from Harvard, he flew to La Paz and was met by Oswaldo Rivera, a rising archaeologist from Bolivia's National Institute of Archaeology. Robert West, chairman of the board of Tesoro Petroleum Company of San Antonio, was setting up the Tiwanaku Archaeological Foundation to explore the ruins of the pre-Inca civilization on the altiplano bordering Lake Titicaca. Kolata and Rivera were to be in charge of it. "Dr. West has generously supported the project—and our work—with research funds ever since," Kolata says.

He began by surveying the Akapana Pyramid, Tiwanaku's most sacred temple. For the next four years the two archaeologists concentrated on excavation, finding fragments of Tiwanaku pottery and other artifacts among the ruins of the ancient city or on the nearby Pampa Koani.

A pattern of ridges and depressions on the floodplain intrigued them. They knew that similar

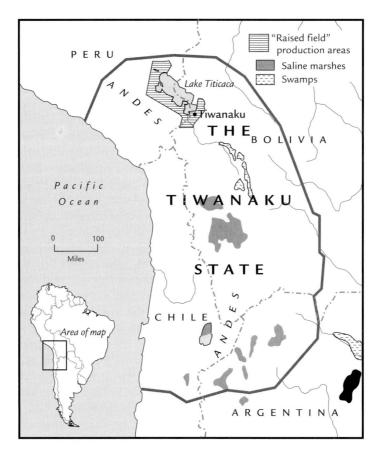

Tiwanaku map shows areas of historic raised fields; so far only a few of these have been reconstructed.
Straughan, Baird. "The Secrets of Ancient Tiwanaku Are Benefiting Today's Bolivia." Smithsonian Magazine 21 (1991), no. 11:38–43, 46–47. Reprinted with author's permission.

copography had been reconstructed into raised fields and irrigation canals in Maya and Aztec jungle areas of Central America. Could it be done here?

Soon after beginning their collaboration, Kolata and Rivera identified 40 square miles that were the remains of raised fields separated by interconnected irrigation canals linked to the Katari River. They were beginning to suspect that Tiwanaku had been a far larger civilization than had been thought, one that would have needed excess crop yields to sustain conquests, crafts, a complex social hierarchy. But Western agronomists consider the altiplano at best marginal land, beset as it is by frequent frosts and exhausted soils.

Could the ancient Tiwanakans have succeeded where modern mechanized agriculture has failed? Would these fields have produced enough to sustain such a civilization? Kolata and Rivera decided there was only one way to find out: rehabilitate a field and plant a crop. A similar project, led by a colleague, Clark Erickson of the University of Pennsylvania, was beginning across the lake in Peru.

In 1981, long before they met Cruz, they approached the community of Lacaya. Their presentation was well received. But as did the people of Cruz's village of Chokara several years later, the Lacayans soon blamed Kolata and Rivera for the severe drought. On one occasion campesinos stoned the two. "We were lucky to escape," Kolata recalls. It was not until 1987 that the reclamation project was back on track, first with Cruz and then at Lacaya. "We received major funding from the Inter-American Foundation. We put a lot of people to work and reintroduced the concept."

In April 1988, as Cruz was confounding his neighbors with his success, the first crop in the Lacaya fields yielded 90 metric tons of potatoes per hectare (about 2.5 acres); some were the size of grapefruit. It was seven times the average altiplano yield. There were also good crops of quinoa (a local grain), barley, oats, and vegetables such as lettuce and onions. Based on these yields, Kolata estimates that the Pampa Koani alone could have fed half a million people.

The new technique yielded another dividend: algae and aquatic plants began to grow, and with them, colonies of nitrogen-fixing bacteria. In several months a thick ooze formed at the bottom of the canals. When the harvest was in, the campesinos drained the canals and shoveled excellent organic fertilizer onto their fields.

There has been a complete turnabout in the reception the archaeologists receive. Kolata is now a welcome figure on the southern shores of Lake Titicaca. Clad in jeans and cowboy boots, his lanky 6-foot-2-inch frame towers above the Aymara, short people with broad torsos that house lungs big enough to cope with the thin air. Despite his appearance, he is completely at home among the campesinos in the fields or supervising the careful work of uncovering the secrets of the once glorious city called, according to legend, Taypi Kala, "The Stone in the Center."

A traveler who reached Tiwanaku, or Taypi Kala, at its height, around the seventh century A.D., would have come over the surrounding hills and been dazzled by the shining city, aglow with sunlight reflecting from gold-covered sculptural bas-reliefs on the walls of three major temples, all of them facing the rising sun.

A city of 50,000, it was situated on an ancient lake terrace that rose a few feet above a plain. Its ceremonial core, containing temples and the brightly painted palaces of the upper class, occupied almost a square mile, with the commoners sprinkled about the remaining three square miles. Of the major temples, the Akapana and Puma Punku were religious sites; Kolata believes the Kalasasaya to have been the seat of Tiwanaku's rulers. He also believes the state was basically a two-class society, an elite composed of the ruling class, its court and lesser nobility, with the rest being commoners. The discovery of bits of worked gold, obsidian and lapis lazuli in the royal sewer, and metalsmith's and lapidary's tools in the palace, indicates that the royal families may have been skilled craftsmen who fashioned the symbols of their own power.

The traveler might have been most likely to see the royalty on festival days. Sculpture and pottery show them emerging from their doorways, costumed as condors or pumas, or as highly stylized deities with enormous headdresses and capes. From the men's belts hung sacrificial knives and the trophy heads of their victims.

Human sacrifice was apparently a part of the celebrations. During these rituals, some archaeologists believe, the priests were under the influence of powerful hallucinogenic drugs, probably derivatives of cacti and other plants.

As in most ancient agrarian civilizations, the emperor-priest was responsible for propitiating the gods and assuring their blessing of the harvest.

Guaranteeing an abundant crop isn't easy under the harsh conditions of the altiplano, but Tiwanaku's rulers apparently managed it for about 800 years. Clearly, they provided their subjects with a better diet than most Bolivians have today. The commoners subsisted on quinoa, potatoes, and fish. Royalty and the nobility dined on llama and corn, the latter a luxury probably imported from colonies or trading partners at lower altitudes. The upper class had regular access to coca leaves from the high valleys of the Amazon, possibly ocean fish from the Pacific coast of Chile, and peppers from southern Peru.

Gold-hungry Spaniards, who arrived in Tiwanaku in the sixteenth century, found the remains of a culture that had endured from around A.D. 200 to 1000. It had left no written records and was barely remembered by the peasant farmers, who believed that the gigantic stones of the ruins "existed before the sun shone in the heavens." Monuments had already suffered pillage for centuries, but nothing compared to that visited upon them by the conquistadores. Precious metal ornaments were stripped, statues defaced, tombs looted. The invaders rooted to the bottom of the Akapana, destroying a large part of it and heaping debris on the rest. Much of the stone they threw aside was later used to construct railroad bridges or buildings in nearby La Paz.

When American archaeologist E. George Squier came to the barren valley, inhabited by a few thousand impoverished farmers, in the 1860s, he described the Akapana as "a great rectangular mound of earth, originally terraced." Around it, partially buried, were the scattered remains of other large edifices.

Squier could see that the original temples had been stupendous constructions, made of blocks ranging up to 160 tons, probably transported from quarries across Lake Titicaca and then precision-fitted together. But he could find no evidence of the society that built them: no remains of domestic dwellings, no evidence of a substantial population base, no conceivable source of sustenance for a major civilization. He concluded, "Tiahuanuco may have been a sacred spot or shrine . . . but I can hardly believe that it was the seat of a dominion." Such reasoning was implicit in the work that followed.

It was a Bolivian archaeologist, Carlos Ponce, who in the 1950s began to provide evidence that Tiwanaku had been a great capital. Alan Kolata's painstaking work reinforces the premise that it was the center of a powerful state, and his conclusions are now receiving careful scrutiny.

David Browman, of Washington University in St. Louis, believes Tiwanaku was "the dominant member of a religious and trading federation." Browman goes on to say that the guerrilla activities of the terrorist group Sendero Luminoso are making it impossible to work in central and northern Peru, where many of his colleagues always believed the most important civilizations were located. "Now, there is a lot of research being done in southern Peru and Bolivia and northern Chile and Argentina, the areas that came under Tiwanaku's influence. There will be real changes in our vision of Tiwanaku quite soon."

Many of the new discoveries will come from Alan Kolata's excavations. Kolata, his colleagues and students work closely with crews of Aymara, whom they have trained in the precise discipline of excavating and recovering artifacts. The Aymara speak fondly of *"el Doctor,"* who not only pays their wages but also drinks beer with them and sponsors their soccer teams.

The work force, consisting of Aymara excavators and about a dozen graduate students from the United States and Bolivia, is doing broad horizontal excavation, going down level by level over large areas to diagram domestic life in Tiwanaku.

RECOVERING TIWANAKU'S DAILY LIFE

Kolata belongs to the school of archaeology that finds the daily life of ancient peoples as fascinating as their monuments. Through advanced scientific techniques, he and his colleagues have been able to draw conclusions about Tiwanaku's social organization, and even about the diet of the average citizen. Graduate student Michael Marchbanks, back in his laboratory at the University of Wisconsin, is examining tiny samples of clay from the cooking pots and, through chemical tests, determining what foods the Tiwanakans ate. A team of limnologists is analyzing core sediment from Lake Titicaca, which contains layers of runoff from Tiwanaku's raised fields, to document past agricultural activity. Hydrologist Charles Ortloff is building computer models of Tiwanaku's water systems to see why they worked so well.

Kolata has not finished his interpretation of the results of all the combined research, to be published as a monograph by the Smithsonian Institution Press. But even the brief sketch he can give now is impressive.

On a walk around the temple complex, Kolata talks with respect of the Aymara, and with unreserved wonder at the achievements of their ancestors, "for instance, the drainage system of the Akapana." He points to the largest of Tiwanaku's structures, a 50-foot truncated pyramid with seven terraced levels, now emerging from the debris heaped upon it by the Spaniards. On the top, priests' residences surrounded a huge sunken court with a pool that collected tremendous amounts of water during the rainy season. The water flowed down inside the Akapana, gushed out onto the first terrace, flowed back into the temple, then out onto the next terrace and so on until it coursed from the bottom into a gigantic

moat surrounding the ceremonial core. "The running water would have set up an acoustic effect, a roaring sound from within the structure," Kolata says. "It's pure virtuosity." And the moat would have made the ceremonial core a symbolic island, in obeisance to the sacred Island of the Sun in nearby Lake Titicaca.

The Akapana was designed to mimic the Quimsachata, a sacred mountain range with spouting and retreating torrents of rain and springwater, representing a life-giving cycle, flowing, evaporating, and falling again as rain.

Kolata seems particularly intrigued by the royal sewer of the central city. Channels beneath the palace floors merge into a massive rectangular conduit built of sandstone blocks a yard square, held together with copper clamps—a technique used in ancient Greece and Rome but heretofore unknown in the Americas. The sewer was buried nine feet deep in impermeable red clay. "It functioned for around 500 years," he explains. "It maintains a 3-percent grade all the way down to the river, a half-mile away."

Alan Kolata sets out over the ancient lake terrace on which the city was built. Underfoot, the ground is littered with pottery sherds, "virtually all from Tiwanaku." Here, the researchers are coming up with some of their biggest finds—the remains of Tiwanaku's domestic structures, precisely what Squier and other archaeologists thought were lacking. Kolata's excavations have uncovered the foundations of what were tightly spaced adobe houses, layer upon layer throughout generations. Most of last season's work was in these residential areas, but what is thought to be part of the city's external wall came to light, as well as the remains of what seems to have been a ceramics factory.

So massive an agricultural system as Tiwanaku's would have had to be organized on a regional scale and would have required the support of a powerful, centralized state. One evidence of the existence of such a state is the large mounds in the center of the fields. Ashlar architectural remains, decorated pottery and indications of a varied diet point to them as homes for local overseers who monitored field production. These mounds were connected to one another, to the villages and cities, and to smaller mounds by a network of causeways. The small mounds, mere bulges at the ends of raised fields, supported simple adobe huts that were seasonal homes for the *kamani,* or field guardians, who protected ripening crops from predators.

It had been necessary to divert the river about a mile to the north of the center of the pampa to open up the land for raised-field production. To control flooding, the river was secured by a huge berm, or levee. Kolata and his colleagues estimate that excavation, diversion, and construction were a gigantic public works project of at least one million man-days' labor.

A LEGACY FROM "THE GRANDFATHERS"

Harvests such as those now being reaped on Tiwanaku's ancestral fields give hope for the future. About 1,200 campesinos are using raised fields. Oswaldo Rivera, who is now director of the National Institute of Archaeology, has requests for assistance from another 50 villages eager to apply the same principle. Some units of the Bolivian Army have begun a Plan Verde (Green Plan), teaching conscripts the raised-field technology. And the Bolivian government is looking for $40 million to spread the technique throughout the country. Large-scale development projects have a bad record in Bolivia, but if the government is successful in this one it would be in a better position to confront the country's burgeoning problems.

U.S. Ambassador Robert Gelbard, an enthusiastic supporter of and fundraiser for the project, urges that it be expanded as quickly as possible. "We are finding that nutritional levels have improved dramatically in these areas," he explains, "and not just because of the potato harvest. There are fish in the canals, the ducks lay eggs—protein levels have gone up considerably."

The potential benefits for Bolivia are tremendous. Chronic malnutrition afflicts nearly half of all Bolivian children, and the country must import food even though most of its citizens work in agriculture. Large numbers of farmers are abandoning their exhausted land on the altiplano and migrating to the Amazon basin, where they can grow coca or clear new farms in the rain forest by the slash-and-burn method.

Meanwhile, archaeological support is coming from another direction. The Getty Conservation Institute of Los Angeles is working with Bolivia's National Institute of Archaeology to devise plans for protection of ancient Tiwanaku's ruins from both environmental hazards and increased tourism.

Kolata ponders the most perplexing question still hanging over Tiwanaku: why it ended. "It was so good for so long, why did it collapse? We know that by A.D. 1000 the fields were no longer functional."

He has a possible answer. Ice cores from glaciers in southern Peru and sediment cores from Lake Titicaca indicate that sometime around the millennium the area suffered a severe drought lasting for decades. Rivers and underground springs watering the raised beds would have dried up, disrupting agricultural production. It is unlikely the Tiwanakans had enough provisions to withstand so prolonged a catastrophe. Starvation would have been widespread and most likely have led to the collapse of the government and its highly organized agricultural system. At present, this is just Kolata's hypothesis. But in the absence of historical records, paleoclimatological data may be the best evidence we have.

In any case, after A.D. 1000, Andean peoples moved to the hillsides, where they practiced the kind of terrace agriculture we associate with the later Inca civilization. The raised fields were abandoned and eventually forgotten. But luckily for the inhabitants of the Bolivian altiplano, Kolata and Rivera are now resurrecting them.

"The good thing about the system," according to Kolata, "is that it functions almost anywhere there's a secure source of water." As to the archaeologists' role, he says simply, "We're only giving back to the Aymara what their ancestors developed thousands of years ago."

18

"Clean Your Plate. There Are People Starving in Africa!"

The Application of Archaeology and Ethnography to America's Food Loss Issues

Timothy W. Jones

Excess food waste is a serious problem, particularly in the global context of widespread hunger, population growth, and dwindling environmental resources. As the author of this selection points out, millions of tons of edible food, worth more than $100 billion, are thrown out annually in the United States alone.

What causes this tremendous amount of waste? How do "normal" business practices, purchasing patterns, and eating habits contribute to this major problem? Moreover, how can a garbologist—an archaeologist specializing in the study of garbage—help explain the scope and nature of the problem or assist in finding solutions?

Understanding patterns of food use and food waste is no simple task. Researchers cannot obtain reliable information just by asking the people who grow, sell, or purchase and consume food. Many people simply do not know exactly how much food they waste, and others may be willing to answer questions but only offer the answers they think a researcher wants to hear. Moreover, food wastage, which the author of this selection calls "food loss," may be called by a different name, or it may be so ingrained in everyday business or household practices as to go unnoticed.

Although archaeology developed primarily as a means of studying the past, this article shows how its research methods can serve as important tools for understanding the problems of the present and, importantly, for developing solutions that can help bring about a better—and, in this case, a less wasteful—future.

As you read this selection, ask yourself the following questions:

- Why does America waste so much food?
- Why might behavioral data collected using interviews, questionnaires, or observation be inaccurate? How can archaeological research methods be used to gain a more accurate picture of what people actually do?
- Why might farmers choose to "walk by" a crop rather than harvest it?
- Why, according to this selection, is the commercial apple industry more efficient than most other forms of commercial agriculture?
- What is "shrinkage" in the retail food industry, and how might it be reduced?
- How did the author use archaeological methods to help understand the discrepancy between Americans' food purchasing behaviors and their food consumption patterns?

The following terms discussed in this selection are included in the Glossary at the back of the book:

> *food loss*
> *material culture*
> *waste behavior*

D id your mother ever talk to you about starving people in Africa in an effort to get you to eat all of your

Jones, Timothy W. "'Clean Your Plate. There Are People Starving in Africa!' The Application of Archaeology and Ethnography to America's Food Loss Issues." Reprinted with permission of the author.

food? If she did, it did not make much sense that the food could not be sent to starving people around the world. A recent study of food flows and losses in the American food system shows that food losses are having a negative economic, environmental, and social impact in the United States. The facts may encourage you to tell your children, "Don't waste your food. It hurts the American economy and the environment!"

Over the past two decades, archaeologists have started to study problems and issues in contemporary societies by applying archaeological theory, method, and techniques. Archaeology is unique in the social sciences in that its subject matter is material culture and the human-constructed world. Contemporary archaeology provides a window to human behavior as expressed in the manufacture, use, discard, and recycling of materials and in the physical transformation of the natural landscape. Archaeology seeks explanations for social and cultural variability in the ways in which people interact with material culture. It complements those social sciences that focus on perception, attitude, and belief by providing an independent measure of individual and social action.

You might ask, "Why do we have to do archaeological studies in contemporary society? Why don't we just ask people what they do and measure material use in that way?" Considerable research has shown that information about behavior derived from the study of modern materials can provide different information from that derived from interviews, questionnaires, and observation (Binford 1977; Dobyns and Rathje 1985; Harrison and Ritenbaugh 1987; Hughes and Ho 1987; Johnstone 1986; Jones 1995; McGuire 1985; Rathje 1977, 1984, 1985a,b; Rathje et al. 1987). Further research has shown that archaeologically measured behavior is different from reported behavior—particularly repetitive everyday behavior such as food consumption. People also report far wider varieties and types of behavior than are actually measured archaeologically since their perceptions and realities are more likely to influence their reported behavior than their actual behavior (Jones et al. 1994; Jones 1995).

FOOD LOSS

Food loss constitutes a significant portion of the solid waste stream, amounting to 12–15 percent of the waste that ends up in landfills (Environmental Protection Agency 2002, Rathje et al. 1992). The first studies on U.S. retail and service food loss estimated annual losses totalling nearly 80 billion pounds (Kantor et al. 1997), representing a loss of over $40 billion. Despite the significant implications of this degree of food loss, a comprehensive study had never been conducted. Instead, studies relied on compilations of existing information, much of which did not include empirical measures like those used in contemporary archaeology. To gain a better understanding of food loss, I conducted a study titled, "Food Loss from the Farm to the Landfill" for the United States Department of Agriculture (Jones 2003; Jones et al. 2002a, 2002b, 2003a, 2003b).

The study collected food data from three separate sectors: (1) commercial farms (fresh vegetable, apple, and citrus), (2) retail food establishments (restaurants, fast foods, grocery, convenience stores), and (3) private households. Research methods include, first, quantifying food produced or purchased using receipts, accounting data, and interviews with management and workers; second, direct observation of food production, handling, and use; and third, measurements of the food deposited in refuse. The results provide surprising insights into sources of inefficiency in the American food system and the economic, environmental, and social effects of these efficiencies.

FOOD LOSSES IN AMERICAN FARMING

If one looks across the nation's expansive fields of mechanized modern farms, it is difficult to imagine a more efficient food production system. But inefficiencies in farming and fresh-food processing keep more than 12 percent of America's agricultural bounty from reaching American tables. The cost to the farming and fresh-food-processing sector may be as much as $20 billion annually (Jones 2003).

Our study of farming food loss covered three core areas: the Salinas and inland valleys in California, the nation's primary center for growing and processing fresh vegetables; apple country in Washington and Oregon; and Florida's orange growing region. Each region experienced losses for different reasons.

The majority of the nation's fresh lettuce, cauliflower, broccoli, and carrots are grown in the Salinas Valley and some locations further inland. Most losses are due either to "walk-by's," when farmers decide not to harvest a crop, or to the production of "higher value" products, like salad mixes or broccoli crowns. A farmer's decision to walk by a ready crop is based on a whole host of factors, most focusing on profit. For instance, inconsistencies in predicting market prices often lead farmers to turn under marginally profitable crops rather than "take the risk" of a loss.

Prepared fresh vegetables offer convenience for consumers and higher profits for producers. But mechanized and rapid-hand preparation create more waste and make vegetables deteriorate more quickly. A head of lettuce will last for days in the refrigerator whereas a bag of lettuce is already on its way to becoming compost.

The focus on ever-higher profits comes out of the vegetable industry's gambling-style culture. By attempting to get the most money out of their crops, commercial growers keep playing in order to "hit" those years when prices soar and they bring in a "full house." They also complain about price fluctuations without much consideration for the ways in which their own practices accentuate those fluctuations.

The Florida orange industry has been besieged by cheap foreign frozen juice, catastrophic freezes and hurricanes, land-value pressures from the Florida housing boom, the dot-com crash, and soft consumer demand. During my fieldwork, I watched as one of the largest and most innovative orange processors and distributors declared bankruptcy, and I drank in local bars with industry employees who had been laid off for the first time in four generations. These difficult conditions have led to losses in the industry as high as 29 percent. Nearly half of these losses are due to a lack of interest in even harvesting the crops.

The apple orchards dotting the foothills of the Cascade Mountains, in contrast, represent an industry with a refreshing presentation of progress and innovation. Apple growers continue some very old and basic farming concepts. For them, it's all about respect for the land, a desire to feed fellow humans, a reverence for life and the life cycle, and the ability to make a decent living in a spectacular location. My interviews would often come to a halt as participants stopped to watch an eagle skirting the mountains or a deer nibbling fruit at the edge of an orchard. One participant commented, "I've seen those mountains every day for more than 80 years and every time I see them they take my breath away."

Losses in the Washington/Oregon apple industry appear high at about 12 percent. But apples are grown and harvested only seven or eight months of the year and stored the rest. For decades, the apple industry's goal has been to become a stable, sustainable, and profitable business in contrast to the race after short-term market fluctuations that characterizes much of today's farming.

To accomplish this degree of sustainability, growers work together to maximize orchard and harvest use and yields. In cooperation with one another, they determine the number of acres under cultivation based on demand, remove diseased and old trees, finance the development of higher-yielding varieties, and finance the development of more efficient storage mechanisms. They also cull apples that fail fresh standards to produce other products such as applesauce, apple juice, and sliced apples for canning and dehydration.

FOOD LOSS IN THE RETAIL FOOD INDUSTRY

Food retailers work hard to satisfy the American demand for prepared and instant foods, yet many are unaware of the profits they lose through food loss. Each year, at least 35 million tons of edible food worth nearly $30 billion are thrown away from the nation's restaurants (both traditional and fast food), convenience stores, and supermarkets (Jones et al. 2002b, 2003c).

You can never stop all food loss. Fallible humans and the machines that transport, handle, and prepare food aren't perfect. But losses could potentially be cut in half, thereby adding nearly $15 billion in profits to retail food companies. Just how much food is lost and why varies by sector and even within sectors. Nearly every retail food sector in the study included at least one company that understood the importance of food loss. These firms provided an opportunity to evaluate just how efficient their sector could be. On average, losses at small mom-and-pop restaurants, convenience stores, and fast-food restaurants were about one-tenth the losses of their large, corporate brethren.

Losses were proportionally highest at convenience stores, where they amounted to about 25 percent. "Instant" food is one culprit. An important market niche for convenience stores is ready-to-eat sandwiches, hot dogs, pizza, fried chicken, and nachos. If not purchased within a limited time, such "instant foods" quickly end up in the garbage.

The other reason for such high loss is a lack of management and training. Store workers generally don't know how long they can safely leave prepared food out for sale, nor are they skilled at predicting potential demand. They often throw food out when it is still good and prepare more food than necessary before lunch, for special events, and at other peak demand periods.

One exception was a locally owned, four-store chain that made significant profits from lunch and special event rushes. Their employees were well paid and, at the time of the study, most had been with the company for more than a decade. Given their experience, they were consistently able to predict demand, often selling more than 500 sandwiches in less than two hours. The four or five sandwiches that weren't sold were consumed by the employees as a well-deserved lunch break.

Losses in fast-food establishments are two to three times higher than they calculate, at about 10 percent, on average. The miscalculation comes from faulty inventory practices and from what is called "shrinkage." Inventory information is only as good as the accuracy of the counts upon which they are based, and shrinkage is a measure of unaccounted inventory. Retail businesses often believe their shrinkage is due to theft. Based on what we observed in our study, however, much of that assumed theft is probably loss. There also are losses that are not measured in the inventory system. While our study cannot explain why the inventory system does not account for all food (since we did not have access to those systems), we are certain first, that food loss occurs, and second, that companies are not aware of the extent of the loss.

We were surprised to find loss rates as high as 20 to 40 percent in medium-sized fast-food restaurant chains (those with a few stores in one city or state).

These extraordinarily high loss rates resulted in large part from the near absence of training and experienced management. Typically, one manager ran three to five stores. Employees with only a few months of experience trained new workers.

Another factor leading to increased food loss is that many companies treat food the same way factories ship auto parts, using "just-in-time" delivery systems. Such systems have allowed companies to redesign stores with less frozen and cold storage capacity. If managers misjudge consumer demand and their freezers are still full, they will check with other stores or consider returning deliveries to the warehouse. If that doesn't work, however, managers have no choice but to throw food away. Just-in-time delivery systems need considerable adjustments in order to reduce food loss.

While food loss in restaurants is relatively low at 3 to 4 percent, it still could be reduced. The greatest losses in large restaurant chains come from miscalculations in demand and advance preparation of too much food, particularly for salad and self-serve bars. The absence of food loss training and education, a notable characteristic of the entire retail food industry, was also a factor.

Supermarkets exhibited surprisingly little loss, at less than 1 percent. With their trash bins overflowing with food, they may appear to waste a lot. In fact, they handle massive quantities of food, particularly highly perishable fruit and vegetables, and what you see out back is only a fraction of what came into the store. Supermarket chains took on the issue of food loss years ago when their profit margins declined from intense competition in a soft economy. Unable to raise prices, they concentrated on efficiency, with positive effect. Supermarket chains are still struggling, but many exist today because they acted to reduce food loss. It's a lesson that other retailers would do well to learn as a way of increasing their bottom line.

FOOD LOSS IN THE HOUSEHOLD

Americans perceive food to be cheap and plentiful. While food in the United States is, indeed, plentiful, whether it is also cheap is an arguable point. According to the Bureau of Labor Statistics Consumer Expenditure, the typical household spent 11 percent of its expenditures on food in 2002 (Bureau of Labor Statistics 2002). Even this information may not be accurate since the data is derived from quarterly interviews and weekly diary surveys. Previous studies have shown that survey data on food use may be highly inaccurate. The Food Loss Study shows that much inaccuracy in food reporting is grounded in the fact that Americans are simply unaware of, or inattentive to, their actual food use patterns.

American households allow 14 percent of the food they purchase to end up in their garbage. This costs a household of four nearly $600 a year and deprives the American economy of $43 billion annually. Americans are unaware of the myriad ways in which they lose food. In fact, when most households are asked about how much food they lose, responses are usually "none" or "very little." During household interviews, it was not unusual to see household members throwing leftover food in the trash while simultaneously stating that they do not waste food (Jones et al. 2002a, 2003a, 2003b).

Nearly a fourth of fruits and vegetables, 13 percent of meat, and 16 percent of grains that Americans buy are trashed because they have "gone bad." Since many households do not know when a food has "gone bad," they throw leftovers out at the end of a meal. Food storage through freezing and airtight containers has become a withering American art.

Americans also tend to misjudge their future food use by basing it on their *perceptions* of how they should eat rather than how they *actually* eat. Americans typically purchase many more fruits and vegetables than they will eat. Basing their purchases' practices on the assumption that they live a healthy lifestyle, they tend to buy lots of nutritious fruits and vegetables expecting to consume them throughout the week. Many Americans, however, come home from a long workday exhausted and shove a frozen dinner into the microwave so they can eat before going to bed. By the time Saturday comes around and they have the time and energy to cook, the vegetables in the refrigerator have turned to mush.

Another interesting finding was that 14 percent of household food loss consists of packaged edible food, or foods that had not been taken out of their original packaging and had not yet expired. Much of this food loss is due to misjudgment in American food purchasing behavior. People purchase new products and never get around to using them since we tend to be creatures of habit. People also purchase more product than they will use in order to "save money" on large quantity purchases. Every so often, Americans clean out their cupboards and throw out these perfectly good foods. This was one of the household food loss patterns that showed potential for efficiently recovering food for America's food banks.

THE COST OF FOOD LOSS

Food loss in America is a major problem that costs Americans more than $100 billion annually. Annual retail sector losses amount to at least 35 million tons worth, nearly $30 billion (almost $20 billion in fast food alone), while losses in the farming industry reach $20 billion and in private households more than

$40 billion. These calculations do not include losses in food processing and wholesaling, two areas not included in our study.

Food loss represents a significant drain on the American economy, particularly since more than half of these losses could be stopped easily and economically. The result would increase profits in fast-food and convenience store companies by at least 5 percent, save farms and fresh fruit and vegetable processors billions, and potentially add another $200 to $300 per year to the budget of each American household. Reducing these losses would also yield other benefits, including more jobs, energy savings, and less environmental degradation.

So, too, would they reduce the amount of food that ends up in landfills. Current estimates suggest that food constitutes 12–15 percent of the garbage that ends up in landfills (Environmental Protection Agency 2002, Rathje et al. 1992). It is a major contributor to landfill methane, an ozone depleting gas, which accounts for at least a third of human-produced emissions in the United States (Intergovernmental Panel on Climate Change 1992). Landfill costs are expensive and do not end when a landfill "closes," since closed landfills cost millions of dollars annually to monitor and maintain. Future landfill costs are problematic since someday they will represent a major cleanup and recovery. Entombed in these landfills, the largest human structures ever built, are massive quantities of hazardous materials (Wilson et al. 1994, Wilson and Rathje 1990).

It takes land, fertilizer, water, soil nutrients, pesticides, herbicides, fuel, and labor to produce our food. The waste of precious energy resources (fertilizer, many pesticides and herbicides, diesel, and gasoline are produced from oil) is staggering, and the current level of waste is not sustainable from either a resource efficiency perspective or an economic perspective. Reducing food loss would take us a long way toward a sustainable food growing capacity.

REFERENCES

Adams, M. 2005. Obesity follows western culture's influence around the world. *Grocery Warning*, February 8.

Binford, L. 1977. *For Theory Building in Archaeology*. New York: Academic Press.

Bureau of Labor Statistics. 2002. *Consumer Expenditure Survey*. United States Department of Labor.

———. 2004. *Occupational Outlook Handbook*. United States Department of Labor.

Cheng, V. 2005. Many immigrants fall prey to America's obesity epidemic. *Scripps Howard News Service*, February 1.

Dobyns, S., and W. Rathje. 1985. Where's the beef? II: A second comparison of respondent reports and refuse records. *Proceedings of the American Meat Institute Research Conference* 1984: 48–68.

Doutrich, D. 2004. Education and practice: Dynamic partners for improving cultural competence in public health. *Family Community Health* 27(4): 298–307.

Environmental Protection Agency. 2002. *Municipal solid waste in the United States: 2000 facts and figures*, Office of Solid Waste, Environmental Protection Agency.

Gordon-Larsen, P., L. S. Adair, M. C. Nelson, and B. M. Popkin. 2004. Five-year obesity incidence in the transition period between adolescence and adulthood: The National Longitudinal Study of Adolescent Health. *American Journal of Clinical Nutrition* 80: 569–575.

Harris, M. J., F. Mitchell, and S. Schester. 1984. *The Homefront: America During World War II*. New York: G. P. Putnam's Sons.

Harrison, G., and C. Ritenbaugh. 1987. Multiple sources of variation in food consumption data. In *The NFCS Report/Refuse Study, Volume 1*, ed. S. Dobyns and W. L. Rathje, 45–58. A report to the Consumer Nutrition Division, USDA.

Hughes, W., and E. Ho. 1987. The Food Loss Project: Methodologies for estimating household food losses. In *The NFCS Report/Refuse Study, Volume 1*, ed. S. Dobyns and W. L. Rathje, 45–58. A report to the Consumer Nutrition Division, USDA.

Intergovernmental Panel on Climate Change. 1992. *Climate Change 1992: The Supplementary Report to the IPCC Scientific Assessment*. Report prepared for Intergovernmental Panel on Climate Change by Working Group 1. (J. T. Houghton, B. A. Callander, and S. K. Varney, eds). World Meteorological Organization and the United Nation Environment Program.

Johnstone, B. 1986. *Alternative approaches to nutritional assessment for studies of diet and disease: An anthropological perspective*. Ph.D. diss. Department of Anthropology, University of Arizona, Tucson.

Jones, T. 1995. *Archaeology as Archaeology*, Ph.D. Dissertation, Department of Anthropology, University of Arizona, Tucson, Arizona.

———. 2003. *USDA food losses in the fresh vegetable, apple and citrus farming industries*. Report to the United States Department of Agriculture, Economic Research Services.

Jones, T., S. Dahlen, K. Cisco, B. McKee, and A. Bockhorst. 2002a. *Household refuse food loss: The USDA Food Loss Study*. Bureau of Applied Research in Anthropology, University of Arizona. Report to the Economic Research Service, United States Department of Agriculture.

Jones, T., S. Dahlen, K. Cisco, A. Bockhorst, and B. McKee. 2002b. *Commercial Refuse Food Loss*. Bureau of Applied Research in Anthropology, University of Arizona. Report to the Economic Research Service, United States Department of Agriculture.

Jones, T., A. Bockhorst, B. McKee, and A. Ndiaye. 2003a. *Household food loss perceptions: Results of the household interviews, The USDA Food Loss Study*. Bureau of Applied Research in Anthropology, University of Arizona. Report to the Economic Research Service, United States Department of Agriculture.

Jones, T., A. Bockhorst, B. McKee, and A. Ndiaye. 2003b. *Percentage of food loss in the household, The USD A Food Loss Study.* Bureau of Applied Research in Anthropology, University of Arizona. Report to the Economic Research Service, United States Department of Agriculture.

Jones, T., S. Dahlen, K. Cisco, A. Bockhorst, and B. McKee. 2003c. *Commercial interview results and food loss percentages.* Bureau of Applied Research in Anthropology, University of Arizona. Report to the Economic Research Service, United States Department of Agriculture.

Jones, T., C. Steelink, and J. Sierka. 1994. An analysis of the causes of tooth decay in children in Tucson, Arizona. *Fluoride* 27(4).

Kantor, L., K. Lipton, A. Manchester, and V. Oliveira. 1997. Estimating and addressing America's food losses. *Food Review* 20: 3–11.

McGuire, R. 1985. Recycling. *American Behavioral Scientist* 28(1): 93–114.

Penny, G., L. Adair, and B. Popkin. 2003. The relationship of ethnicity, socioeconomic factors and overweight in U.S. adolescents. *Obesity Research* 11(1): 121–129.

Pool, R. 2001. *Fat: Fighting the Obesity Epidemic.* Oxford University Press.

Rathje, W. 1977. In praise of archaeology, Le Project du Garbage. In *Historic Archaeology and the Importance of Material Things,* ed. L. G. Ferguson, 36–42. Society for Historical Archaeology.

_____. 1984. The garbage decade. *American Behavioral Scientist* 28(1): 9–29.

_____. 1985a. Meat fat madness. *Livestock Industry Forum Proceedings, 1985,* pp. 14–15. Livestock Industry Institute, Kansas City.

_____. 1985b. The NFCS syndromes: Building a theory of the difference between respondent reports and material realities. In *The NFCS Report/Refuse Study, Vol. I,* ed. S. Dobyns and W. L. Rathje, Appendix A, 28–44. A report to the Consumer Nutrition Division.

Rathje, W., and E. Ho. 1987. Meat fat madness: Conflicting patterns of meat fat consumption and their public health implications. *Journal of the American Dietetic Association* 87: 1357–1362.

Rathje, W., D. Wilson, and W. Hughes. 1987. *A characterization of hazardous household wastes in Marin County, California.* A report to the Association of Bay Area Governments. The Garbage Project, Bureau of Applied Research in Anthropology, Department of Anthropology, University of Arizona, Tucson.

Rathje, W., D. Wilson, W. Hughes, M. Tani, and T. Jones. 1992. The archaeology of contemporary landfills. *American Antiquity* 57(3): 437.

Ware, Caroline F. 1942. *The consumer goes to war: A guide to victory on the home front.* New York: Funk and Wagnalls Company.

Wilson, D., and W. Rathje. 1990. Modern middens. *Natural History* 90(5): 54–57.

Wilson, D., W. Rathje, and M. Tani. 1994. *Characterization and assessment of household hazardous wastes in municipal solid wastes.* Final report to the Water Quality Engineering Program, National Science Foundation, Washington, D.C.

19

Dawn of a New Stone Age in Eye Surgery

Payson D. Sheets

So far, we have looked at studies in which archaeologists set out to study a particular phenomenon, whether it be ancient health at Dr. Dickson's mounds or Tucson's garbage. Scientific work most often proceeds in this fashion. Yet sometimes, right in the midst of doing basic research, a new idea, an insight, emerges. The combination of luck and intellectual curiosity has led to impressive discoveries and inventions; this is one source of culture change.

A more common way in which material culture has changed is through borrowing, or diffusion. Many features of our American way of life—including food, clothes, and medicine—were borrowed from other societies. Even in the area of technology, we may still learn from the past and from people in simpler societies if we are alert for new and innovative uses.

In this selection, archaeologist Payson Sheets describes the discovery of some extremely important uses for microlith blades made by ancient stone technology.

As you read this selection, ask yourself the following questions:

- What are the two methods for making stone blades?
- How does the sharpness of obsidian blades compare with the sharpness of quartzite, razor blades, and surgical scalpels?
- What are some of the advantages of the use of an obsidian blade for surgery?
- Why was this discovery more likely to be made by archaeologists than by surgeons or medical instrument manufacturing companies?

The following terms discussed in this selection are included in the Glossary at the back of the book:

artifact	*knapper*
blade	*microlith*
excavation	*technology*

Occasionally, archaeological findings can be applied to today's world and improve modern life. Archaeologists have rediscovered prehistoric crops and agricultural technologies that are no longer used but have considerable value for contemporary society. Ancient remedies, too, have been found that can help cure illnesses. This is an account of the rediscovery of an ancient technology for making stone tools that died out centuries ago but has an unexpectedly important potential for improving modern medical treatment.

Beginning in 1969, as a young graduate student, I participated in the Chalchuapa Archaeological Project

on the edge of the Maya area in El Salvador. Beyond supervising several project excavations, I was responsible for the analysis of the ancient stone tools—composed mostly of obsidian (volcanic glass)—as part of my doctoral dissertation. In my work I discovered that most previous studies classified stone tools by their shape. I did likewise, but I also wanted to contribute something different, so I kept looking for a new angle from which to analyze the Chalchuapa stone artifacts.

In 1970 I excavated a workshop at Chalchuapa where I recovered the remains of ancient obsidian tool manufacture. From the workshop debris I figured out the various techniques, and their sequence, that had been used by the ancient Maya knappers to make chipped stone tools. I also identified errors made during this process and how the ancient craftsmen corrected them. These data provided the new angle I was looking for—an analysis based on the ancient tool-making technology. The reconstruction of past behavior, within the structure of the obsidian tool industry, was the first step in developing modern surgical blades based on an ancient technology.

The following year I attended Don Crabtree's training program in lithic technology so that I could learn how to make stone tools. I learned to duplicate the ancient Maya technology including how to make tools and cores by percussion (striking the stone with strong blows to detach flakes) and long, thin obsidian blades by pressure (slowly increasing force applied to a core to detach flakes). Don suggested that the replicas of the ancient blades would be excellent surgical tools and that I should experiment with the technology to see if I could make scalpels that would be acceptable to surgeons. But I was unable to follow up these suggestions; after writing my dissertation, earning my Ph.D., and finding a teaching position at the University of Colorado, I embarked on a new research project in the Zapotitán basin of El Salvador. But by 1979 the guerrilla warfare in El Salvador made the area too dangerous to continue research, so I then had the time to explore the possibility of adapting obsidian blades for modern surgical use.

Meanwhile, Don had gone ahead and provided a dramatic demonstration of the obsidian blade's utility in surgery. Since he had undergone two thoracic operations in 1975, he had made obsidian blades for his surgeon to use. The operations were very successful, and his surgeon liked the obsidian blades for their ease in cutting and the improved healing of the incisions.

But before obsidian scalpels could find wide use in surgery, a series of problems had to be resolved. The first problem was to determine how sharp the obsidian blades were and how they compared with the various scalpels already used by surgeons. The answers came from examining the edges of obsidian blades, other kinds of stone (chert and quartzite), razor blades, and surgical scalpels under the tremendous magnification of a scanning electron microscope (SEM).

The results showed that the dullest edge belonged to a percussion flake made of chert. The quartzite flake was much sharper, having an edge 9.5 times sharper than the chert flake. I had expected the stainless steel surgical scalpel to be sharper than the razor blade, but the results were the opposite. The scalpel was only 1.5 times sharper than the quartzite flake. The razor blade, a standard Gillette stainless steel double-edged blade, was 2.1 times sharper than the surgical scalpel. This was a surprise to me, but not to surgeons, who often use razor blades for operations by adapting them with "blade breakers," small devices that snap razor blades into segments for surgical use.

Most significantly, the obsidian blade was far sharper than any of these edges. Depending on the

edge being measured, the obsidian was *100 to 500 times sharper* than the razor blade and thus was 210 to 1050 times sharper than the modern surgical scalpel!

By 1980 I was ready to see if there was any application in modern surgery for such sharp cutting edges. After calling several prominent eye surgeons, I reached Dr. Firmon Hardenbergh of Boulder, Colorado. The more I described the astounding sharpness of the obsidian edge, the more interested he became. He decided to use one of these blades for eye surgery. The results were quite successful, for the sharper edge did less damage to the tissue and the cleaner incision facilitated healing. And, very importantly, there was less resistance to the blade, so the eye moved far less, allowing the surgeon to make a more accurate incision.

Since that time obsidian blades have been used in other kinds of operations. Healing was usually faster, scarring was reduced (sometimes dramatically so), and often the pain during recovery was reduced or almost eliminated. Once the full research and development program for eye surgery is completed, Dr. Hardenbergh and I plan to modify the blades for use in general surgery and in specialized applications such as plastic surgery and neurosurgery.

We needed to compare the use of obsidian and steel scalpels. We did this by experimental cutting of muscle tissue with both kinds of blades and then examining the incisions with the SEM. The differences were dramatic. The metal blades tore and translocated large amounts of tissue, leaving the ragged edges of the incision littered with displaced chunks of flesh. The obsidian cut was strikingly crisp and clean.

We have improved the blades greatly from their early form in 1980; they are now more uniform in shape and are fitted with well-formed plastic handles. But they still must be made by hand, replicating the ancient Maya technology. The next step will be to engineer a transformation from a traditional handicraft to a modern manufacturing system. Because shapes of cores vary, each blade has to be individually planned and detached, and each blade varies in length and shape. This technology is not adequate for manufacturing large numbers of standardized surgical scalpels.

Part of the manufacturing problem has been solved by designing a metal mold into which we pour molten glass, producing uniformly shaped cores. This process also eliminates the impurities and structural imperfections present in natural obsidian, and it allows us to vary the glass chemistry to maximize desirable properties such as color and edge toughness. We have also designed a machine to detach the blades from the core, and this device is being tested and refined. These improvements in manufacturing have resulted in more consistent blades, but more work needs to be done to fully automate the process and produce precisely uniform obsidian surgical scalpels every time.

Once the blades are in production and are readily available to surgeons, they will have the advantage over even the sharpest scalpel presently used, the diamond blade. Based on present tests, our obsidian blades are just as sharp as diamond blades—in fact they are up to three times sharper. But diamond blades are extremely expensive, costing several thousand dollars apiece, and they are tiny, with only 3 mm of cutting edge. Obsidian scalpels will cost the surgeon only a few dollars each, and the blades can be as long as needed. Fortunately, the ancient Maya have shown us the way not only to sharper and cheaper scalpels, but to surgical instruments that have very real benefits for the patient in reducing trauma, scarring, and pain. In these ways the past has provided a very real improvement to the present.

20

The Challenge of Race to American Historical Archaeology

Charles E. Orser Jr.

Cultural and biological anthropologists play central roles in debates about race and racism, but archaeology has its own relevance as a subfield of anthropology which contributes to our understanding of how race shapes society (and vice versa).

While many archaeologists study ancient cultures and the early history of humankind, historical archaeologists apply their methods to learn about more recent societies and people. By uncovering the material remains of southern plantations, for example, we can better understand the daily lives and cultures of African slaves—people who are often marginalized through generalizations and insidious caricatures found within written documents from early U.S. history. Nonetheless, transcending historical constructions of race is not as simple as one may think.

Some historical archaeologists working in the United States, for example, conceal the dynamic construction of race when they analyze artifacts by identifying specific characteristics as indicative of whiteness or blackness. Other archaeologists, however, have shown that racially specific artifacts are buried in the imagination, not the soil. Archaeologist Vernon Baker analyzed ceramics excavated from the homesite of a freed slave who spent most of her life in Massachusetts; Baker undertook his study with the intention of revealing distinctly. African American ceramic characteristics, but found he could not determine whether the artifacts signified poverty or ethnicity.

While historical archaeology in the United States may sometimes misinterpret race by confusing it with ethnicity and class, this selection explores how archaeology can be applied to increase our understanding of race as a social construction. More specifically, it demonstrates how material dimensions of racial categorization reveal the dynamic nature of racial identity and class distinctions.

As you read this selection, ask yourself the following questions:

- What is the difference between race and ethnicity?
- Why are "knickknacks" and "kitsch" poor ethnic markers for African Americans in the archaeological record?
- Why do historical archaeologists have difficulties determining whether some artifacts reveal ethnic, racial, or class distinctions?
- How has historical archaeology interpreted material culture to determine racial and ethnic boundaries?
- What can historical archaeology contribute to our understanding of race?

The following terms discussed in this selection are included in the Glossary at the back of the book:

African survivals   *debt peonage*
ethnic markers   *historical archaeology*
material culture

Issues of race and racism, though never absent from the realities of American life, are once again assuming a prominent place in our collective anthropological

Orser, Charles, Jr. "The Challenge of Race to American Historical Archaeology" from AMERICAN ANTHROPOLOGIST 100 (1998), no. 3:61–668. Reprinted by permission of Wiley-Blackwell Publishing.

consciousness. This development is not completely surprising, since Americans, goaded by the writings of popsociologists and the comments of television's political pundits, tend to see every issue through a racial lens (Fischer et al. 1996:171). Scholars foregrounding race do not restrict themselves to any particular period of history, and reinterpretations of both the past and the present are well underway.

The pedigree of American anthropologists in the study of race is well documented, and it is only right that cultural and biological anthropologists should take center stage in the debates about race and racism that will surely emerge across the globe. But in light of the widespread interest that will undoubtedly be generated, we may well ask where archaeologists fit into the discussion. What is the role of these anthropologists in the work of examining race and racism? Will archaeologists be able to increase knowledge about the material dimensions of racism and to determine how material inequality has been attached to racial categorizations? When thinking about such questions in terms of the future, we may justifiably suppose that historical archaeologists will assume a prominent position in the intellectual enterprise of illuminating the material dimensions of American race and racism.

My purpose in this essay is to explore issues of race and racism in the archaeology of modern America, defined here as post-Columbian in time (see Orser 1996). Although American historical archaeologists should be in the forefront of the study of race and racism, with only a few exceptions their interest to date has been minimal. Overwhelmingly, the interest of American historical archaeologists has focused on issues of ethnicity rather than of race. This trend is showing signs of changing in line with current anthropological thinking, but historical archaeologists in America still have major strides to make before their research will become relevant to a wide range of scholars, including even their anthropological colleagues.

HISTORICAL ARCHAEOLOGISTS AND ETHNICITY

Archaeologists' interest in past cultural entities stretches back to the nineteenth century, when pioneering prehistorians struggled to identify archaeological "cultures" in the silent refuse from the past (Shennan 1989). In the course of their research, these early practitioners learned that to make meaningful statements about past cultures they had to be able to distinguish them with material culture. The act of segregating the remains of different peoples seems relatively simple. It follows logically that peoples with different traditions will create and use things that look appreciably different from the things made and used by peoples from other traditions. Thus, the presence of red pots at one site may be used to identify men and women from one culture, whereas the discovery of white pots at another site may identify a second, distinctive culture. As is the case with most archaeological research, however, reality often imposes on even the best model, and prehistorians have regularly been bedeviled by cultural

identification. Childe's (1926:200) observation of over seventy years ago is thus still pertinent today: "The path of the prehistorian who wishes to draw ethnographical conclusions from archaeological data is often beset with pitfalls." The wisdom of Childe's comment is intimately understood by every archaeologist who has ever attempted to identify a discrete group of people with recourse only to their material remains.

The problems of cultural identification that torment prehistorians also exist in historical archaeology. With the benefit of supplemental textual information, however, historical archaeologists have a somewhat easier time understanding what kinds of socially defined groups can be expected to have inhabited certain sites. Put most stereotypically, Asian immigrants can be assumed to have lived in Chinatowns, Welsh men and women in mining camps, and men and women of African descent on slave plantations. Having acquired such basic knowledge from textual sources, historical archaeologists have generally framed their studies in terms of ethnicity, beginning with the idea of using material objects to identify past social groups.

Studies assigning ethnic affiliation through material culture began in historical archaeology with the search for "ethnic markers," or specific artifacts that could be associated with certain peoples, or "ethnic peoplehoods." At sites associated with African Americans, for example, such research began with a search for African survivals in the archaeological deposits at southern plantations. The logic here was straightforward. African slaves in the Americas brought their cultural knowledge with them from Africa. When they made or refashioned physical things for their use, they invariably did so in ways that were consistent with their cultural knowledge. Archaeologists excavating slave cabins at plantation sites, then, should be able to locate these objects and to distinguish them as signs of African cultural survival in the New World. Once this kind of research became standard practice, it was not long before archaeologists expanded the search for ethnic markers to other peoples. Archaeologists who associated colonoware pottery with African Americans soon expanded this understanding to link smoking pipes embossed with harps to Irish immigrants, and opium pipes with transplanted Asians.

Many historical archaeologists today recognize this kind of archaeological stereotyping as reifying perceived artifact associations, while investing artifacts with a static ethnicity by assuming that only an Irishman could smoke from a pipe marked "Erin Go Bragh." This kind of rudimentary interpretation has not entirely left the field, but some historical archaeologists have adopted much more sophisticated efforts to envision artifacts as symbols of group identity that, rather than being static containers of ethnicity, are free to be manipulated by conscious human actors (Praetzellis et al. 1987). Within this more theoretically mature framework, some archaeologists have begun to see artifacts as tools for manipulating the social order while also creating and promoting a sense of people-hood (Praetzellis 1991; Staski 1993). Historical archaeologists who have stepped beyond the search for ethnic markers have begun with studies of assimilation and ethnic boundary maintenance, as well as investigations of ethnic pride, in which they have attempted to demonstrate the contribution of various nonelite groups to the multicultural history of the United States (Kelly and Kelly 1980; McGuire 1982:161–162; Staski 1990).

Numerous historical archaeologists have been drawn to the study of ethnicity, but fewer have shown an overt interest in the archaeological examination of race. Most historical archaeologists seemingly have been willing to accept the widely held, albeit nonanthropological, understanding that associates race with ethnicity. This facile understanding of race has made it possible for historical archaeologists to downplay or to sidestep racism as a means of creating and upholding the social inequalities that characterize American society. The failure of American historical archaeologists to address race and racism in any substantive way has served to maintain the field's tacit political conservatism, a stance consistent with the traditional use of historical archaeology to examine sites associated with places and personages important in the dominant national ideology. Race perception, though a major contributor to American social inequality, is largely absent from historical archaeological practice (but see comments in Orser and Fagan 1995:213–219).

HISTORICAL ARCHAEOLOGISTS AND RACE

Not every historical archaeologist, however, has entirely ignored race in American history. Examining sites associated with planters, overseers, and slaves at Cannon's Point Plantation in Georgia, John Otto (1980) made one of the earliest attempts to study race as an imposed condition. Otto argued that race was a fixed legal status that created a divide between "free white" planters and overseers, and "unfree black" slaves. Based on this caste model, Otto attempted to identify artifacts and artifact classes that had been distributed or acquired because of this categorization. In a way, Otto's use of race was just another way of looking at ethnicity, but he at least inserted the word race into the archaeological lexicon and made it a topic of serious archaeological investigation. Although his study is flawed in several serious and well-known respects

(Orser 1988a), the ambiguous results of his analysis demonstrated the complexities inherent in the static investigation of an extremely fluid social designation. Such simplistic analyses, though pioneering when first conducted, have been largely though not entirely abandoned for more sophisticated studies.

In an important statement on the importance of a historical archaeology of race, David Babson (1990) argued that by insisting on the study of ethnic groups as timeless, immutable social artifacts, historical archaeologists have missed important opportunities. Also, by reifying ethnic identity through association with specific artifacts or artifact classes, American historical archaeologists have ignored the ways in which racist beliefs have defined identity in relations of power. Babson argued that because racist ideology structures how people treat one another, racism should leave identifiable traces in archaeological deposits. To illustrate his point, Babson explored the material and spatial effects of racism at a slave plantation in South Carolina. The antebellum southern plantation is one category of site where we may expect racism to be readily apparent and therefore abundantly visible in archaeological deposits (also see Babson 1987). In a more recent though theoretically similar study, Robert Fitts (1996) demonstrated how racist beliefs were expressed in a segregationist use of space in the early plantations of Rhode Island.

In another study of plantation society, Terrence Epperson (1990b) argued that historical archaeologists must maintain a dual focus in their studies of race and racism. This dual perspective, modeled on W. E. B. Du Bois's (1961:16–17) concept of "double-consciousness," allows historical archaeologists—examining race in a racist society—to work toward two goals: the "valorization of the African American culture of resistance and the denaturalization of essentialist racial categories" (Epperson 1990b:36). This approach allows historical archaeologists to realize that racism "embodies contradictory tendencies of exclusion and incorporation, simultaneously providing a means of oppression and a locus of resistance" (Epperson 1990a:341).

These kinds of studies demonstrate the challenges faced by historical archaeologists when they attempt to examine race and racism. Race is a highly mutable, often situationally defined designation, and archaeologists do not know precisely how to study it using material culture. As if the changing nature of racial perception as expressed in material culture is not slippery enough, racism is inexorably intertwined with capitalism, another major topic of historical archaeological research. The presence of incipient and eventually full-blown capitalism in the New World after 1492 defines American historical archaeology, both in terms of its subject and its contemporary practice. Today, it is as impossible to conceptualize the post-Columbian world without global commercialism as it is to imagine historical archaeology without capitalism (Handsman 1985; Leone 1995; Orser 1988b, 1996).

The appearance of market forces in a capitalist world has practical significance for historical archaeologists. The vast majority of objects used by post-Columbian Americans were not made by them. Thus, with increasing frequency as we move closer to our own time, men and women were called upon to select the things they wished to use from an often broad, but still finite assemblage of products. These acts of selection, and the assignment of meaning to the decisions made, are exceedingly complex issues, even in observable market situations. Faced with myriad possibilities to account for artifact presence at an archaeological site, historical archaeologists seeking distinctions between "ethnic markers," economic markers of class, and visible symbols of racial designation usually provide only tentative interpretations. The problems inherent in this kind of study were exemplified in historical archaeology several years ago.

In 1943, Adelaide and Ripley Bullen (1945) excavated a homesite in Andover, Massachusetts, that was once inhabited by a freed slave named Lucy Foster. Foster died in 1845 at the age of 88 as an impoverished freedwoman who had been on the poor rolls beginning in 1812, the year her mistress died. Several years after the Bullens' excavation, Vernon Baker (1978, 1980) analyzed the excavated ceramics in an effort to illuminate "patterns of material culture distinctive of Afro-American behavior" (Baker 1980:29), or in other words, to determine which ceramics were indicative of African American ethnicity. In the end, Baker could not decide whether his findings reflected poverty or ethnicity, a central problem for historical archaeology that is still unresolved almost twenty years later (e.g., Yamin 1997). The major reason for the inability of historical archaeologists to decide whether the artifacts they excavate relate to past ethnic, racial, or class designations derives from the simple reality that these typological threads are never really separate in American life.

Without doubt, understanding the material relationships between and among reified categories of ethnicity, race, and class presents perhaps the greatest challenge to contemporary American historical archaeology. The way in which archaeologists respond to this challenge will establish the relevance of their discipline within both anthropology and within the broader transdisciplinary investigation of human life. Although historical archaeologists have yet to take this challenge seriously, one recent analysis stands out by offering one direction for future research.

In a sophisticated study, Paul Mullins (1996) provides a thought-provoking exposition on African America and the consumer culture of the United States between 1850 and 1930. Mullins argues that material consumption presented African American consumers with a Janus face. On one hand, consumption provided a mechanism for African Americans to cement and to improve their places in American society, but on the other, it offered a way for racists to subordinate them by imposing on them a sentence of material inferiority. Living in a country dedicated above all to capitalism, African Americans, with the rise of all-pervasive mass consumption, were confronted with a way to enter public spheres of consumption that were once closed to them.

We may well suppose that the movement of African Americans toward full-scale American consumerism undoubtedly took many material forms, but Mullins's (1996:528–533) exploration of the African American acquisition of bric-a-brac is particularly instructive. Although we may be inclined to view knickknacks as insignificant kitsch, in truth they were symbolically charged representations of American abundance, nationalism, and racial purity. In some sense they were tiny pieces of Americana that could sit in the parlors of European Americans, and being rich with meaning, could express their owner's affluence and belonging, even though the objects themselves were not expensively priced. With Emancipation, however, the ownership of knickknacks became contested. For example, some mid-nineteenth-century commentators argued that commissaries were indispensable institutions on the reorganized plantations of the American South because without them, once-enslaved African Americans would waste their money on cheap bric-a-brac. Thus, paternalistic non–African Americans saw an almost-frantic need to create capitalistic institutions that would ostensibly assist freed African Americans during their initiation to full membership in the marketplace. In reality, however, these institutions were intended to control African American buying habits even down to the smallest objects. Commissaries were significant creations because many African American tenant farmers, living in debt peonage on the same estates they inhabited as slaves, could only purchase what was available onsite. Even when tenants were issued money rather than the all-too-common commissary tickets, racism and terrorism kept many of them from visiting nearby towns to obtain the wider variety of goods available on the open market. Thus, when knickknacks began to appear in African American homes in the late-nineteenth century, they were especially meaningful because they served to distance their owners from the racial and class caricatures that were pervasive in racist America. Rather than having them represent simply a resistance to racist attitudes, African Americans recontextualized the knickknacks. What was important about them was not "what they were made to be, but what they have become" (Thomas 1991:4).

The meaning of knickknacks was further complicated when non–African American employers gave them as gifts to African American domestic servants. As Mullins (1996:532–533) observed, this seemingly simple act of gift-giving was highly significant. The ownership of such items could represent for African Americans a symbolic redefinition of their material world by allowing the ownership and display of objects once reserved strictly for others. Conversely, however, the knickknacks held a far different meaning for the non–African American gift givers. For them, the act of giving was a symbolic way of reproducing the social relations of dominance that pervaded American society. In offering something they perceived to be inexpensive, non–African Americans reasserted their power as dominant elites. Their recontextualization of the artifacts was really quite different from that which may have occurred among African Americans.

Mullins's insightful analysis reveals the always-close and ever-complicated relationship between race and acquisition in a capitalist environment. His analysis shows that historical archaeologists would be ill advised to use the presence of knickknacks as ethnic markers for African Americans. When found in archaeological deposits, brightly painted porcelain statuettes of a regal-looking George Washington or of quaintly dressed peasant girls do more than simply reify our already stereotypic understanding of the relationship between artifact ownership and past social standing. As Mullins (1996:533) observes, "Material goods and consumer space harbored a legion of possibilities which played on affluence, democratization, and nationalism and lurked within a rich range of accessible objects and flexible symbols." Clearly, when we begin to analyze even the most commonplace artifacts in terms of race and class, we enter a fluid world where meanings, being temporally and even situationally mutable, defy easy interpretation.

HISTORICAL ARCHAEOLOGY, RACE, AND POVERTY

In Mullins's analysis we see the glaring complexities inherent in analyzing race in American historical archaeology. Much of the interpretive challenge centers on the complex relationship between racism and consumerism. This relationship was succinctly expressed

by boxer Larry Holmes when he said, "I was black once, when I was poor" (Oates 1987:62). The problem with race, from a purely archaeological standpoint, is that it is not ethnicity. As a result, even if the search for archaeological "racial markers" was desirable as an end in itself, it would be appreciably more difficult than the search for "ethnic markers." On a practical level, though, the search for racial markers would be no more satisfying than the search for ethnic markers. Nonetheless, historical archaeologists still maintain a strong interest in examining archaeological deposits in terms of reified social entities, even in cases where the authors claim to do just the opposite (see Cook et al. 1996:58).

At present, the few historical archaeologists who are interested in questions of race confine themselves to African Americans. For historical archaeologists, it is as if race attaches only to men and women of color. But even a brief consideration of the Irish illustrates the flawed nature of this conclusion and suggests the immature state of race research in historical archaeology.

For the sake of convenience, we may consider the Irish to be an ethno-nationalistically defined people from an identifiable politico-geographical unit, an island in the North Atlantic (GAP 1987:24–25; Rose 1974:13). Given the American propensity for creating "us" and "them" categories around perceived racial categories, we may be willing today to consider the Irish as members of the White Race. The racialization of the Irish, however, was a much more contested process that took many years to be resolved. In short, the Irish were not always "white."

Recorded history shows that the colonizing English considered the native Irish to be a barbaric and inferior people. In 1366, English overlords passed the Statutes of Kilkenny as a way to legislate enforced acculturation. The native Irish were commanded to use the English language, to ride their horses with saddles in the English manner, to use English naming practices, and to wear English clothing (Bartlett 1993:239).

With the rise of large-scale enslavement in the New World many years later, it was not long before English observers began to compare the still-despised Irish with African American slaves. For example, in 1749, Anglican bishop and philosopher George Berkeley wrote that "The negroes in our Plantations have a saying— 'If negro was not negro, Irishman would be negro' " (Berkeley 1871:439). Just over one hundred years later, the staunchly anti-Catholic clergyman Charles Kingsley stated that he was "haunted by the human chimpanzees" he saw around Sligo. For him, "to see white chimpanzees is dreadful; if they were black, one would not feel it so much, but their skins, except where tanned by exposure, are as white as ours" (Gibbons 1991:96). Two years later, the English satirical magazine *Punch* referred to the Irish as "A creature manifestly between the Gorilla and the Negro," and as late as 1885, British anthropologist John Beddoe referred to the Irish as "Africanoid" (Foster 1993:184; Young 1995:72). Not surprisingly, such attitudes were also expressed visually, and it was common during the eighteenth and nineteenth centuries for English artists to portray the Irish with apelike features (Curtis 1971). Racism thus became a common element of English-Irish interaction, as the English strove to establish the Irish as the Other, comparable to the many Others their country's explorers and colonists encountered around the globe (Doan 1997; Lebow 1976; Waters 1995).

When Irish immigrants began to flood the streets of America in the early-nineteenth century, it was not at all clear that they were members of the so-called White Race (Ignatiev 1995:41). Since Congress decreed in 1790 that only "whites" could be naturalized citizens, Irish immigrants found that they had to fight for the national privilege of being perceived as white. The American White Race was an invention, and since the days of the Puritans, the American power elite consciously worked to build a homogeneous Americanized state based on their perception of whiteness (Allen 1994; Carlson 1987). Before Emancipation, foremen and labor-gang bosses often used Irish laborers instead of slaves for the most dangerous jobs because the Irish, as poor freemen, were wholly expendable (Ignatiev 1995:109). As a people, the Irish did not move into the ranks of "white" America until they repudiated the rights of those deemed nonwhite. The stereotypic character of the evil Irish overseer on the southern slave plantation is a literary device intended to show this accommodation. Tara, mythic America's most famous plantation, was named for a venerated site in Ireland, and its owners had the time-honored Irish name of O'Hara (Mitchell 1936).

To summarize, the Irish in America had to struggle to attain the racial designation that put them in the nation's highest racial category. To accomplish this act of wholesale racial advance, they had to overcome years of discrimination to create a place for themselves in the American scheme of whiteness. Some Irish immigrants even climbed to the highest echelons of the American elite, with their names becoming synonymous with wealth, power, and the American Dream (Birmingham 1973; Greeley 1981). Nonetheless, the movement of the Irish into the ranks of White America has yet to interest American historical archaeologists. The Irish in America are still perceived

monolithically as an ethnic group inhabiting the sphere of whiteness, and their place in White America is taken for granted.

RACE IN THE FUTURE OF HISTORICAL ARCHAEOLOGY

If the present corpus of scholarship is any guide, the way in which Americans address issues of race and racism will undoubtedly be many and varied over the next several years. There is danger, of course, in the notion that the most serious discussions will be restricted to the realm of scholastic inquiry and will not reach a wider audience (Cole 1995). The problem of intellectual isolation is particularly acute for archaeology, since the only times the field is regularly mentioned outside the profession is when the popular media designates a new discovery as especially spectacular, or when pseudo-scientists have made some new outlandish claim.

The possible courses of action for the development of serious, concerted research in the historical archaeology of race are infinite, and we may well hope and expect that the approaches taken by archaeologists will be varied. I believe, however, that the examination of the material side of race and racism provides archaeologists with a rare opportunity to use their discipline's unique transdisciplinary insights and methods to promote greater understanding far beyond archaeology. In a nation like the United States—where the national ideology is wholly given over to capitalist accumulation and conspicuous consumption—the role of historical archaeologists may be easily expanded beyond the narrow halls of a few universities and the conference rooms of cultural resource management firms. At a time when political conservatives are using race in a wrongheaded and divisive manner—the effusive excitement over *The Bell Curve* (Herrnstein and Murray 1994) being one clear example—historical archaeologists are afforded the opportunity to show the historic origins and manifestations of racial categorization and the relationship of such pigeonholing to social and material inequality.

In an important essay, Jesse L. Jackson Jr. (1997) argues that it is not enough to talk about race in America without taking action on employment. To discuss one without the other is to engage in what Jackson calls "race entertainment." Racial justice is not synonymous with economic justice, but the two are clearly linked. As Jackson (1997:24) notes, "In a nation with the economic and technological ability to provide every American with a decent life, it is a scandal that there should be so much social misery."

Will race ever become an important subject in historical archaeology, or will historical archaeologists only engage in "race entertainment," forever examining race as if it were ethnicity? This question cannot be answered now, but to become true partners in the expanding anthropological discourse on race in America, historical archaeologists must seek to illustrate the effects of racism on African Americans and other peoples, developing at the same time a historical archaeology of whiteness. Baker (1978:113) inadvertently made this suggestion when he stated that to interpret the meaning of the ceramics at Lucy Foster's homesite, historical archaeologists must also conduct research on sites inhabited by poor whites. Most historical archaeologists now accept "whiteness as an unassailable fact of nature" rather than as a social construct (Epperson 1997:10). This tendency is adequately demonstrated by examining how historical archaeologists have examined, or not examined, the Irish in America.

Because the appellations of whiteness and nonwhiteness contain deep-seated notions of social inequality, studies of domination and resistance should constitute a major focus of research in historical archaeology (Paynter and McGuire 1991). Through this sustained research activity, historical archaeologists will be able to denaturalize the condition of whiteness, and to demonstrate the material dimensions of using whiteness as a source of racial domination even in cases, such as with the Irish, where racism may initially appear absent (Harrison 1995:63).

Recently, Robert Paynter (1997) proposed that historical archaeologists must understand the complexities inherent in examining social inequality in historic America. Three questions he posed as worthy of future study in historical archaeology are particularly relevant here:

> Under what conditions do stratified societies mark and hide social cleavages with material culture? How, during the age of capital, did wage labor, mass consumption, and white supremacy produce distinctive and shifting identities? And, how did local communities redefine identities among these global shifts in race, class, and gender relations? [Paynter 1997:11]

Providing answers to such questions as these will not only make historical archaeology more relevant to anthropological inquiry, it will also raise the profile and societal relevance of the field. Whether large numbers of historical archaeologists ever move to the examination of the material dimensions of racial categorization is simply a matter of what historical archaeologists wish their field to be.

NOTE

Acknowledgments. I would like to thank Terry Epperson, Pedro Funari, and Paul Mullins for reading and providing their comments on this paper. My ideas about race and racism in historical archaeology have taken shape during discussions with these thoughtful scholars and with David Babson over the past few years. I would also like to thank Robert Paynter and the two anonymous reviewers for their thoughtful comments and suggestions. In addition, I wish to acknowledge the support and encouragement of Janice L. Orser. Needless to say, none of these individuals should be held in any way responsible for my statements and opinions.

REFERENCES

Allen, Theodore W. 1994. The Invention of the White Race. London: Verso.

Babson, David W. 1987. The Tanner Road Settlement: The Archaeology of Racism on Limerick Plantation. Master's thesis, University of South Carolina, Columbia.

_____. 1990. The Archaeology of Racism and Ethnicity on Southern Plantations. In *Historical Archaeology on Southern Plantations and Farms*, ed. Charles E. Orser Jr., Special issue. *Historical Archaeology* 24(4): 20–28.

Baker, Vernon G. 1978. Historical Archaeology at Black Lucy's Garden, Andover, Massachusetts: Ceramics from the Site of a Nineteenth Century Afro-American. Andover, MA: Phillips Academy.

_____. 1980. Archaeological Visibility of Afro-American Culture: An Example from Black Lucy's Garden, Andover, Massachusetts. In *Archaeological Perspectives on Ethnicity in America: Afro-American and Asian American Culture History*, ed. Robert L. Schuyler, 29–37. Farmingdale, NY: Baywood.

Bartlett, Robert. 1993. The Making of Europe: Conquest, Colonization, and Cultural Change, 950–1350. Princeton, NJ: Princeton University Press.

Berkeley, George. 1871. The Works of George Berkeley, D. D. A. C. Fraser, ed. Oxford: Clarendon.

Birmingham, Stephen. 1973. *Real Lace: America's Irish Rich.* New York: Harper and Row.

Bullen, Adelaide K., and Ripley P. Bullen. 1945. Black Lucy's Garden. *Bulletin of the Massachusetts Archaeological Society* 6(2): 17–28.

Carlson, Robert A. 1987. *The Americanization Syndrome: A Quest for Conformity.* London: Croom Helm.

Childe, V. Gordon. 1926. *The Aryans: A Study of Indo-European Origins.* London: Kegan Paul.

Cole, Johnnetta B. 1995. Human Rights and the Rights of Anthropologists. *American Anthropologist* 97: 445–456.

Cook, Lauren J., Rebecca Yamin, and John P. McCarthy. 1996. Shopping as Meaningful Action: Toward a Redefinition of Consumption in Historical Archaeology. *Historical Archaeology* 39(4): 50–65.

Curtis, L. Perry, Jr. 1971. *Apes and Angels: The Irishman in Victorian Caricature*. Washington, DC: Smithsonian Institution Press.

Doan, James E. 1997. "An Island in the Virginian Sea": Native Americans and the Irish in English Discourse, 1585–1640. *New Hibernia Review* 1: 79–99.

Du Bois, W. E. B. 1961. *The Souls of Black Folk*. New York: Dodd and Mead.

Epperson, Terrence W. 1990a. "To Fix a Perpetual Brand": The Social Construction of Race in Virginia, 1675–1750. Ph.D. dissertation, Department of Anthropology, Temple University, Philadelphia.

_____. 1990b. Race and the Disciplines of the Plantation. In *Historical Archaeology on Southern Plantations and Farms*, ed. Charles E. Orser Jr., *Historical Archaeology* 24(4): 29–36.

_____. 1997. Whiteness in Early Virginia. *Race Traitor* 7: 9–20.

Fischer, Claude S., Michael Hout, Martín Sánchez Jankowski, Samuel R. Lucas, Ann Swidler, and Kim Voss. 1996. *Inequality by Design: Cracking the Bell Curve Myth*. Princeton, NJ: Princeton University Press.

Fitts, Robert K. 1996. The Landscapes of Northern Bondage. *Historical Archaeology* 30(2): 54–73.

Foster, Roy F. 1993. *Paddy and Mr. Punch: Connections in Irish and English History*. London: Allen Lane.

GAP (Group for the Advancement of Psychiatry). 1987. *Us and Them: The Psychology of Ethnonationalism*. New York: Brunner/Mazel.

Gibbons, Luke. 1991. Race against Time: Racial Discourse and Irish History. *Oxford Literary Review* 13: 95–113.

Greeley, Andrew M. 1981. *The Irish Americans: The Rise to Money and Power*. New York: Harper and Row.

Handsman, Russell G. 1985. Thinking about a Historical Archaeology of Alienation and Class Struggle. Paper presented at the annual meeting of the Society for Historical Archaeology, Boston, January.

Harrison, Faye V. 1995. The Persistent Power of "Race" in the Cultural and Political Economy of Racism. *Annual Review of Anthropology* 24: 47–74.

Hermstein. Richard J., and Charles Murray. 1994. *The Bell Curve: Intelligence and Class Structure in American Life*. New York: The Free Press.

Ignatiev, Noel. 1995. *How the Irish Became White*. New York: Routledge.

Jackson, Jesse L., Jr. 1997. Why Race Dialogue Stutters. *The Nation* 264(12): 22–24.

Kelly, Marsha C. S., and Roger E. Kelly. 1980. Approaches to Ethnic Identification in Historical Archaeology. In *Archaeological Perspectives on Ethnicity in America:*

Afro-American and Asian American Culture History, ed. Robert L. Schuyler, 133–143. Farmingdale, NY: Baywood.

Lebow, Richard Ned. 1976. White Britain and Black Ireland: The Influence of Stereotypes on Colonical Policy. Philadelphia: Institute for the Study of Human Issues.

Leone, Mark P. 1995. A Historical Archaeology of Capitalism. *American Anthropologist* 97: 251–268.

McGuire, Randall H. 1982. The Study of Ethnicity in Historical Archaeology. *Journal of Anthropological Archaeology* 1: 159–178.

Mitchell, Margaret. 1936. *Gone with the Wind*. New York: Macmillan.

Mullins, Paul R. 1996. The Contradiction of Consumption: An Archaeology of African America and Consumer Culture, 1850–1930. Ph.D. dissertation, Department of Anthropology, University of Massachusetts, Amherst.

Oates, Joyce Carol. 1987. *On Boxing*. Garden City, NY: Dolphin Doubleday.

Orser, Charles E., Jr. 1988a. The Archaeological Analysis of Plantation Society: Replacing Status and Caste with Economics and Power. *American Antiquity* 53: 735–751.

_____. 1988b. Toward a Theory of Power for Historical Archaeology: Plantations and Property. In *The Recovery of Meaning: Historical Archaeology in the Eastern United States*, eds. Mark P. Leone and Parker B. Potter Jr., 313–343. Washington, DC: Smithsonian Institution Press.

_____. 1996. *A Historical Archaeology of the Modern World*. New York: Plenum.

Orser, Charles E., Jr., and Brian M. Fagan. 1995. *Historical Archaeology*. New York: HarperCollins.

Otto, John Solomon. 1980. Race and Class on Antebellum Plantations. In *Archaeological Perspectives on Ethnicity in America: Afro-American and Asian American Culture History*, ed. Robert L. Schuyler, 3–13. Farmingdale, NY: Baywood.

Paynter, Robert. 1997. Du Boisian Perspectives on Identities and Material Culture. *Anthropology Newsletter* 38(5): 11.

Paynter, Robert, and Randall H. McGuire. 1991. The Archaeology of Inequality: Material Culture, Domination, and Resistance. In *The Archaeology of Inequality*, eds. Randall H. McGuire and Robert Paynter, 1–27. Oxford: Blackwell.

Praetzellis, Adrian Charles. 1991. The Archaeology of a Victorian City: Sacramento, California. Ph.D. dissertation, Department of Anthropology, University of California, Berkeley.

Praetzellis, Adrian, Mary Praetzellis, and Marley Brown III. 1987. Artifacts as Symbols of Identity: An Example from Sacramento's Gold Rush Era Chinese Community. In *Living in Cities: Current Research in Urban Archaeology. Society for Historical Archaeology Special Publication Series,*

No. 5. ed. Edward Staski, 38–47. Tucson, AZ: Society for Historical Archaeology.

Rose, Peter I. 1974. *They and We: Racial and Ethnic Relations in the United States.* New York: Random House.

Shennan, Stephen. 1989. Introduction: Archaeological Approaches to Cultural Identity. In *Archaeological Approaches to Cultural Identity,* ed. Stephen Shennan, 1–32. London: Unwin Hyman.

Staski, Edward. 1990. Studies of Ethnicity in North American Historical Archaeology. *North American Archaeologist* 11: 121–145.

———. 1993. The Overseas Chinese in El Paso: Changing Goals, Changing Realities. In *Hidden Heritage: Historical Archaeology of the Overseas Chinese,* ed. Priscilla Wegars, 125–149. Amityville, NY: Baywood.

Thomas, Nicholas. 1991. *Entangled Objects: Exchange, Material Culture, and Colonialism in the Pacific.* Cambridge, MA: Harvard University Press.

Waters, Hazel. 1995. The Great Famine and the Rise of Anti-Irish Racism. *Race and Class* 37: 95–108.

Yamin, Rebecca. 1997. New York's Mythic Slums: Digging Lower Manhattan's Infamous Five Points. *Archaeology* 50(2): 44–53.

Young, Robert J. C. 1995. *Colonial Desire: Hybridity in Theory, Culture, and Race.* London: Routledge.

PART III

Linguistic Anthropology

Language, whether spoken, written, or non-verbal, allows anthropologists to connect and better understand the human condition across time, space, and cultures. Early in the history of American Anthropology, anthropologists like John Wesley Powell and Franz Boas embraced linguistics as a critical subfield of the discipline. Powell collected and compared vocabularies from American Indian languages as part of an effort to racially classify North American Indian Nations. Because Boas did not believe that culture and language were biologically determined, he disagreed with Powell's approach. Instead, Boas trained his students to use linguistic anthropology to facilitate fieldwork; in his view, language was a window into culture. Regardless of their contrasting theoretical positions regarding the nature of language, Powell and Boas considered linguistics a critical component of anthropology. European anthropologists like Bronislaw Malinowski and E. E. Evans-Pritchard also valued language research as a component of cultural anthropology, but only in the U.S. academy did anthropologists incorporate linguistics as an actual subfield of anthropology.

At the dawn of the twentieth century, the transformation of Anthropology from an armchair pastime to a scientific, academic discipline coincided with the rapid extinction of cultural traditions and languages. When undocumented or poorly documented languages go extinct, humanity loses the specialized knowledge, histories, and worldviews embedded in these languages. In order to preserve and document "disappearing" cultures, early linguistic anthropologists focused primarily on documenting the vocabularies and grammars of endangered cultural traditions. Nevertheless, of an estimated 7,000 languages spoken in the world today, linguists predict that approximately half of these languages will become extinct in the twenty-first century. Contemporary anthropologists continue to document endangered languages, but the field of linguistic anthropology has grown considerably as researchers have developed new approaches to study language scientifically to explore what it means to be human.

Today, linguistic anthropologists typically divide their subfield into three specializations: Historical Linguistics, Descriptive Linguistics, and Sociocultural Linguistics. Historical linguistics includes research on extinct languages as well as the evolution and migration of languages. In Selection 21, Bhattacharjee explains how computer modeling helps linguists see the influence of children and migration on the evolution of language throughout the history of humankind. Because language is not confined to speech and the written word, descriptive linguistics also studies the development of specialized sign languages to learn about the evolution of language (Selection 22).

Linguistic anthropologists who specialize in descriptive linguistics specialize in unraveling a language. Many anthropologists study descriptive linguistics so they can quickly learn an unwritten or lesser-known language in the field. Descriptive linguistics researchers study words (morphology), sentences (syntax), and meaning (semantics), as well as the physical qualities (phonetics) and structure (phonology) of speech. Sociocultural linguists, on the other hand, examine the relationship between language and sociocultural systems. For example, a focus on speech behavior and miscommunication between males and females (Selection 24), can tell an anthropological fieldworker a great deal about a society in which he or she studies and their cultural values.

In sum, linguistic anthropology is a multidisciplinary and scientific study of human language. Linguists apply their skills as teachers and researchers in universities, but you will also find them working in government agencies, professional consulting firms, the corporate setting, and more recently in the high-tech sector (to design and improve internet search engines, speech recognition, computer language modeling, the development of artificial intelligence, and computer mediated communication). Ultimately, the linguistic anthropologist uses her or his unique methodological toolkit to do what cultural anthropologists, biological anthropologists, and archaeologists do; they develop and test hypotheses to examine the complex diversity and universals of the human experience across time and space.

21

From Heofonum to Heavens

Yudhijit Bhattacharjee

New Technology is one of the many ways new words enter our daily vocabulary. Before 2001 the terms "iPod" and "podcast" did not exist, but now these are ubiquitous words used every day on college campuses throughout the United States. New words like "podcast" and "email" may seem like benign additions to our language, but not everyone is ambivalent to this technology-inspired linguistic evolution.

In 2008, for example, linguists from the Ministry of Culture in France banned the word "podcast" along with over 500 other words like "wi-fi" and "supermodel." Because these non-French words have crept into daily French vocabularies, the Ministry of Culture seeks to prevent these linguistic intrusions by offering alternative terms such as "courriel" instead of "email." Linguistic nationalism and transformation is not unique to France; it was not long ago that the U.S. Congress legislated that french fries in the Capitol Hill cafeteria would be called "freedom fries."

Languages evolve to fit the needs and lives of the people who use them. In this selection, Bhattacharjee explains how computer modeling helps linguists see the influence of children and migration on linguistic transformation throughout the history of humankind.

As you read this selection, ask yourself the following questions:

- Why do anthropologists study the evolution of words and grammar?
- Why do languages change, and why do linguists view language change as a paradox?
- What role do children play in linguistic evolution?
- How do non-native speakers transform a language?
- How does population growth impact the evolution of a language?

The following terms discussed in this selection are included in the Glossary at the back of the book:

computational linguistics	*creole*
sociolinguistics	*verb-second structure*

If a modern-day priest were to chance upon an eleventh century manuscript of *The Lord's Prayer* in English, he would need the Lord's help to decipher its meaning. Much of the text would be gobbledygook to him, apart from a few words that might have a recognizable ring, such as heofonum (heavens) and yfele (evil). And even after a word-for-word translation, the priest would be left with the puzzling grammatical structure of sentences like "Our daily bread give us today."

Although researchers generally think of languages as having evolved slowly over many millennia, language change occurring over time spans of a few centuries

has confounded scholars since medieval times. After trying to read a 600-year-old document, the first known printer of English works, William Caxton, lamented in 1490, "And certainly it was written in such a way that it was more like German than English. I could not recover it or make it understandable" (translated from Old English).

The comparative analysis of such texts is the closest that researchers can get to tracing the evolutionary path of a language. By studying the evolution of words and grammar over the past 1200 years of recorded history, linguists hope to understand the general principles underlying the development of languages. "Since we can assume that language and language change have operated in the same way for the past 50,000 years, modern language change can offer insights into earlier changes that led to the diversification of languages,"

Bhattacharjee, Yudhijit. "From Heofonum to Heavens." SCIENCE 303 (2004), no. 5662:1326–1328. Reprinted with permission from the American Association for the Advancement of Science (AAAS).

says Anthony Kroch, a linguist at the University of Pennsylvania in Philadelphia.

Since the mid-nineteenth century, that hope has driven scholars to document a variety of grammatical, morphological, and phonological changes in French, English, and other languages. In the past three decades, more and more theoretical and historical linguists have turned their attention to analyzing these changes, and sociolinguists have explored the social and historical forces at work. Now researchers in the growing field of computational linguistics are using computer models of speech communities to explore how such changes spread through a population and how language changes emerge in multilingual populations.

The simulations are infusing precision into the study of a phenomenon once thought to be the exclusive domain of humanistic inquiry. "Computational modeling of language change is in its infancy, but it is already helping us to reason more clearly about the factors underlying the process," says Ian Roberts, a linguist at the University of Cambridge, U.K.

VOICE OF THE VIKINGS

Linguists view language change as something of a paradox. Because children learn the language of their parents faithfully enough to be able to communicate with them, there seems no reason for language to change at all. But historical texts show that change is common, although the trajectory and rate of change may be unique for any given language. In the tenth century, to consider a classic example, English had an object-verb grammar like that used today in Modern German, requiring sentence constructions such as "Hans must the horse tame." By 1400 C.E., the English were using the familiar verb-object grammar of "Hans must tame the horse." French underwent a similar change before the sixteenth century, whereas German retained its basic grammar.

To find out why such changes happen, researchers explore the historical circumstances surrounding them. In the past few years, based on a comparative analysis of religious texts from northern and southern England, Kroch and his colleagues at the University of Pennsylvania have suggested that northern English was transformed during the eleventh and twelveth century as Viking conquerors married native Anglo-Saxon women, who spoke Old English. The resulting bilingual households became crucibles for linguistic change. For example, whereas Old English had distinct verb endings to mark differences in person, number, and tense, the speakers of what is now called Early Middle English began using simpler verbs—perhaps because the Scandinavians had difficulties keeping track of all the verb forms—and settled on a simplified system closer to what we use today.

In the absence of invasions and other external influences, languages can remain stable for long periods. Japanese and Icelandic, for instance, have hardly changed since 800 C.E. But researchers point out that isolation does not guarantee the status quo; grammatical shifts can also be triggered by internal forces such as minor changes in the way a language is spoken.

French is a case in point. In the sixteenth century, the language changed from a system in which the verb always had to be in second place (known as a verb-second structure) to one in which the verb (V) could be in any position as long as it came after the subject (S) and before the object (O); Modern French and Modern English both have this SVO structure. For example, "Lors oirent ils venir un escoiz de tonnere" (Then heard they come a clap of thunder) became "Lors ils oirent venir un escoiz de tonnere" (Then they heard come a clap of thunder). Roberts, who documented the transition by comparing a representative text from each century between the thirteenth and the seventeenth, believes that the change arose because speakers of Middle French reduced the emphasis on subject pronouns—"they" in this example—to the point where children learning the language barely heard the pronouns. Roberts inferred this decline in phonetic stress from usage changes in the written language. For example, subject pronouns were earlier used with modifiers, such as "I only," but later they did not carry such modifiers. The result of this reduced emphasis, says Roberts, "was that for sentences beginning with a subject pronoun, the verb sounded like the first word of the sentence to the listener." That ambiguity dealt a fatal blow to the verb-second rule, paving the way for the emergence of an SVO grammar.

JOHN THE BOOK BUYS

But a new grammatical feature cannot emerge overnight. For a variant such as an innovative construction by a single speaker or a novel form of syntax produced by a new adult learner to become part of the language, it must get picked up by other speakers and be transmitted to the next generation. Historical texts show that it can take centuries for a change to sweep through the entire community.

David Lightfoot, a linguist at Georgetown University in Washington, D.C., says the key to understanding large-scale linguistic transformation lies in the link between the diffusion of novel forms through one generation and large grammatical shifts occurring across generations—changes he calls "catastrophic." And this link, according to him and many others, is language acquisition. Children may simply carry forward a variant that arose in the preceding generation. But more significantly, says Lightfoot, children may themselves serve as agents of change "by reinterpreting a grammatical rule because of exposure to a variant during their learning experience." As adults, they may end up using a somewhat different grammatical system from that of their parents. Repeated over generations, this can lead to a dramatic makeover in the language.

Computational linguists such as Partha Niyogi of the University of Chicago have built computer models to understand the dynamics of such evolution. Their goal is to map out the relationship between learning by the individual and language change in the population, which Niyogi calls the "main plot in the story of language change."

In one of the first attempts to unravel that plot's outline, Niyogi and Robert Berwick, a computer scientist at the Massachusetts Institute of Technology, came up with a class of models simulating the transmission of language across generations. They started out by considering a virtual population with two types of adult speakers. The first type uses one set of grammatical rules—say, one that, like English, mandates a verb-object order for all constructions, generating sentences such as "John buys the book," and "I know that John buys the book." The rest of the speakers use a different grammar, for example one similar to German, in which the first verb goes in the second position but the second verb goes after the object. The speakers of the second grammar produce some sentences exactly like speakers of the first—"John buys the book"—but they also produce other kinds of sentences such as "I know that John the book buys." The researchers spelled out a learning algorithm for children in this population, providing each learner with logical steps for acquiring grammatical rules from linguistic encounters with adults.

Following the linguistic behavior of this virtual community over generations led Niyogi and Berwick to a startling conclusion. They found that contrary to expectation, the population does not inevitably converge on the grammar spoken by the majority, nor on the simpler of the two grammars. Instead, the winning grammar is the one with fewer grammatically ambiguous sentences like "John buys the book," which, although simple, might be analyzed as belonging to either grammatical type. In other words, if minority speakers consistently produce a smaller proportion of grammatically ambiguous sentences as compared to the majority, the population will over time shift completely to the minority grammar.

Niyogi, who first presented the work at the International Conference on the Evolution of Language at Harvard in April 2002 and has published it in his book, says the finding makes it possible to imagine how a grammatical variant spoken by a handful of individuals might replace an entrenched grammar. It's conceivable for the variant to pose no threat to the established grammar for many generations, he says, until the proportion of grammatically ambiguous sentences produced by speakers of the variant drops below the corresponding proportion for the dominant grammar. "For instance, sociocultural factors might change the content of conversations among minority, English-type speakers in a way that they stop using single-clause sentences like 'John buys the book,' " says Niyogi. That would make their speech more complex—but less grammatically ambiguous. Then learners would hear a higher proportion of the multiple-clause, uniquely English constructions in English speech than they would hear uniquely German constructions in German speech. This would make them more likely to infer the English grammatical system from what they heard, even though their overall exposure to German and even uniquely German constructions would be greater. Suddenly, the mainstream German grammar would become unstable and the English grammar would begin to take over.

"That a little good info should be able to trump a lot of bad [ambiguous] info makes sense," says Norbert Hornstein, a linguist at the University of Maryland, College Park, who sees the mechanism of change suggested by Niyogi as "a good fit with our understanding of language acquisition." He says it provides a possible explanation for how small local changes—for instance, a simplification of the verb system by mixed households in thirteenth century northern England—may have spread through the entire population. Confirming this account of change would require testing computational models with real-world data such as the proportion of specific syntactical forms in historical texts, assuming written language to be a faithful impression of speech. Niyogi admits that the task could take years.

In a broader sense, however, researchers have already validated the computational approach by matching the outlines of models to real-world situations. For example, University of Cambridge linguist Ted Briscoe modeled the birth of a creole, a linguistic patois that arises from prolonged contact between two or more groups. He specifically considered Hawaiian English, which developed between 1860 and 1930 through contact between Europeans, native Hawaiians, and laborers shipped in from China, Portugal, and other countries. Briscoe's simulation started out with a small but diverse group of speakers and factored in the periodic influx of adult immigrants. He found that a population with the right mix of children and new adult learners converged on an SVO grammar after two generations. That matches empirical studies showing that many features of Hawaiian Creole, including an SVO word order, did not stabilize until the second generation of learners.

Salikoko Mufwene, a sociolinguist at the University of Chicago, says that a detailed picture of mechanisms of language change could emerge if computational researchers succeed in modeling very specific contexts. For instance, he says, modeling spoken exchanges on a homestead of eight Europeans and two African slaves could help illuminate the linguistic evolution of the larger community. "The two Africans in this example are likely to be so well immersed that after a few months they would be speaking a second language variety of the European language. Say one of the Africans is a woman and bears a child with one of the white colonists. The child is likely to speak like the father because the father's language happens to be dominant at the homestead. Growing up, this child will serve as a model for children of new slaves," explains Mufwene. "Nonnative speakers will exert only a marginal influence on the emergent language of the community," in this case the native European variety.

But if the population increases significantly through a large influx of new slaves, he says, the dynamics of interaction change, and more adult nonnative speakers of the European language serve as models. Children now have a greater likelihood of acquiring some of the features spoken by adult nonnatives and transmitting them to future learners; over time, a new variety of the European language will emerge.

Detailed modeling along these lines, Mufwene says, could unveil the significance of factors that researchers may have missed, such as the pattern of population growth and the pace of demographic shifts. "Even without real-world number crunching," he says, "the exercise would suggest what questions we should be asking and what kinds of evidence we should be looking for."

REFERENCES

Niyogi, P. 2006. *The Computational Nature of Language Learning and Evolution.* MIT Press.

22

Village of the Deaf

In a Bedouin Town, a Language Is Born

Margalit Fox

Sign language, like any language, differs from place to place. In 1924 when athletes from Belgium, Czechoslovakia, France, Great Britain, Holland, and Poland gathered at the first World Games for the Deaf, they had to develop a new language to communicate with each other. Their impromptu system of hand signs became the foundation of a global sign language called International Sign.

Despite the existence of International Sign, deaf people and others throughout the world have developed unique sign languages to fit the uniqueness of their lived experiences. In recent years, for example, deaf and non-deaf poets have adapted sign languages to share their worldviews in ways that words and speech alone cannot. Pioneering sign language poets like Clayton Valli have helped the hearing world understand that signing, like speech, has rhymes, rhythm, and meter.

Humans communicate to connect and understand each other. This desire to connect is no different in the deaf community, even in remote locations where deaf people may not have opportunities to learn established sign languages. This selection describes the evolution of Al-Sayyid Bedouin Sign Language, a language created in a remote Israeli village where an inherited form of deafness has created an incidence of deafness approximately forty times that of the general population. Linguistic anthropologists "discovered" this island of the deaf in the late 1990s and have collaborated with the local population to learn more about the evolution of language.

As you read this selection, ask yourself the following questions:

- In what ways is Al-Sayyid an "island of the deaf?"
- What is the difference between first and second generation users of Al-Sayyid Bedouin Sign Language?
- How do Al-Sayyid Bedouin Sign Language, American Sign Language, and British Sign Language differ?
- In what ways is Al-Sayyid an "island of the deaf?"
- How does Bedouin Sign Language grammar differ from the verb-second grammar discussed in Bhattarcharjee's chapter "From Heofonum to Heavens?"

The following terms discussed in this selection are included in the Glossary at the back of the book:

Babel	*Bedouin*
homesigns	*language instinct*

On this summer evening, the house is alive with people. In the main room, the owner of the house, a stocky man in a plaid shirt, has set a long plastic banquet table on the earthen floor, with a dozen plastic patio chairs around it. Children materialize with platters of nuts, sunflower seeds, and miniature fruit. At the head of the table, the owner is joined by a group of men in their thirties and forties. Down one side of the table is a row of boys, from toddlers to teenagers. At the foot of the table sits a knot of six visitors: four linguistics scholars, a video camera operator, and me.

The man and his family are Bedouins, and the house is at the edge of their village, Al-Sayyid. Though they live in the desert, the Bedouins of Al-Sayyid are not nomads. Their people have inhabited this village, tucked into an obscure corner of what is now Israel, miles from the nearest town, for nearly 200 years. They are rooted, even middle class. Men and boys are

Fox, Margalit. "Village of the Deaf: In a Bedouin Town, a Language is Born." Discover Magazine (July 2007):66–69 from Talking Hands: What Sign Language Reveals About the Mind by Fox. (Simon & Schuster, 2007). Reprinted with permissiom of the author.

bareheaded and dressed in Western clothing, mostly T-shirts and jeans. They own automobiles, computers, and VCRs. But there is something even more remarkable about the Al-Sayyid Bedouins—an unusual language, never documented until now.

The house is a Babel tonight. Around the table, six languages are flowing. There are snatches of English, mostly for my benefit. There is Hebrew: two of the linguists are from an Israeli university, and many men in Al-Sayyid speak Hebrew as well. There is a great deal of Arabic, the language of the home for Bedouins throughout the Middle East. But in the illuminated room, it is the other languages that catch the eye. They are signed languages, the languages of the deaf. As night engulfs the desert and the cameraman's lights throw up huge, signing shadows, it looks as though language itself has become animate, as conversations play out in silhouette on the whitewashed walls.

There are three signed languages going. There is American Sign Language, used by one of the visitors, a deaf linguist from California. There is Israeli Sign Language (ISL), the language of the deaf in that country, whose structure the two Israeli scholars have devoted years to analyzing. And there is a third language, the one the linguists have journeyed here to see: Al-Sayyid Bedouin Sign Language (ABSL), which is spoken in this village and nowhere else in the world.

In Al-Sayyid, the four linguists have encountered a veritable island of the deaf. In this isolated traditional community, where marriage to outsiders is rare, a form of inherited deafness has been passed down from one generation to the next for the last 70 years. Of the 3,500 residents of the village today, nearly 150 are deaf, an incidence forty times that of the general population. As a result, an indigenous signed language has sprung up, evolving among the deaf villagers as a means of communication. But what is so striking about the sign language of Al-Sayyid is that many hearing villagers can also speak it. It permeates every aspect of community life, used between parents and children, husbands and wives, from sibling to sibling and neighbor to neighbor.

The team plans to observe the language, to record it, and to produce an illustrated dictionary, the first-ever documentary record of the villagers' signed communication system. But the linguists are after something even larger. Because Al-Sayyid Bedouin Sign Language has arisen entirely on its own, it offers a living demonstration of the "language instinct," man's inborn capacity to create language from thin air. If the linguists can decode this language—if they can isolate the formal elements that make Al-Sayyid Bedouin Sign Language a language—they will be in possession of compelling new evidence in the search for the ingredients essential to all language. And in so doing, they

will have helped illuminate one of the most fundamental aspects of what it means to be human.

When Wendy Sandler, a linguist at the University of Haifa, first heard about Al-Sayyid in the late 1990s, she knew at once that she had to investigate. Over the next few years, she and Irit Meir, a colleague at Haifa, made cautious forays into Al-Sayyid, setting in motion the diplomacy that is a critical part of linguistic fieldwork: explaining their intentions, hosting a day of activities at the village school, over time earning the trust of a number of the villagers.

Their work has a sense of urgency. Although the sign language of Al-Sayyid arose in a linguistic vacuum, the social realities of modern life, even in a remote desert community, make it impossible for it to remain that way. Over the years, many of Al-Sayyid's deaf children have been bused to special classes for the deaf in nearby towns, where they are taught all day in spoken language—Hebrew or Arabic—accompanied by signs from Israeli Sign Language, a language utterly different from their own. In just one generation, when the older Bedouin signers die, the unique signed language of the village, at least in its present form, may be significantly altered.

Omar, the owner of the home in which we gathered for the first recording session, greeted us in Hebrew. Although he is hearing, Omar has deaf siblings and knows the village sign language. Carol Padden, a linguist from the University of California, San Diego, who is deaf, starts to sign to him, using gestures international enough that they can be readily understood. Omar replies expansively in Al-Sayyid Bedouin Sign: the seeds of a simple contact pidgin have been sown. When signers of different languages come together, communication is achieved partly through the use of the most transparent gestures possible, partly through a shared understanding of the particular devices that signed languages use to convey meaning. (Just such a contact language, called International Sign Pidgin, has developed over the years at places like sign-linguistics meetings, where deaf people from many countries converge.)

The sign language of a particular country is rarely contingent on the spoken language that surrounds it. American and British Sign Languages are mutually unintelligible. A deaf American will have an easier time understanding a deaf Frenchman: ASL is historically descended from French Sign Language. Even the manual alphabet used by deaf signers can differ from one country to another. The letters of the American manual alphabet are signed using one hand; those of the British manual alphabet are made with two hands.

In her lab's mission statement, Wendy sums up how studying sign languages can illuminate how the mind works: "It usually comes as a surprise to the layman to learn that nobody sat down and invented the sign languages of the deaf. These languages arise spontaneously, wherever deaf people have an opportunity to congregate. That shows that they are the natural product of the human brain, just like spoken languages. But because these languages exist in a different physical modality, researchers believe that they offer a unique window into the kind of mental system that all human language belongs to."

Linguists have long believed that the ideal language to analyze would be one in its infancy. They even dream of the following experiment: simply grab a couple of babies, lock them in a room for a few years and record the utterances they produce. The scenario came to be known as the Forbidden Experiment.

It's been tried. The historian Herodotus, writing in the fifth century B.C., told of the Egyptian pharaoh Psammetichus, who, in an attempt to discover what the oldest civilization was, took two infants from their mothers and dispatched them to an isolated hut under the care of a mute shepherd. Eventually, one of the babies uttered the word *bekos*, which turned out to be the Phrygian word for "bread," bringing the experiment to a happy conclusion.

But near the end of the twentieth century, linguists began to realize that their sought-after virgin language existed in the sign language of the deaf. Signed languages spring from the same mental machinery that spoken languages do, but they are linguistic saplings.

The conditions that create an Al-Sayyid—a place where hundreds of people are habitual signers—are extremely particular. First, you need a gene for a form of inherited deafness. Second, you need huge families to pass the gene along, yielding an unusually large deaf population in a short span of time. Of Al-Sayyid's 3,500 residents, about one in 25 is deaf—4 percent of the population. For deafness, a rate of 4 percent is a staggering figure: in the United States, the incidence of deafness in the general population is about one in 1,000. The presence of so many deaf signers in their midst also encourages widespread signing among the hearing. This helps keep the indigenous signed language alive for the village as a whole.

Wendy and her colleagues aren't claiming that Al-Sayyid Bedouin Sign Language (ABSL) mirrors the evolutionary development of language in *Homo sapiens*. Rather, as Wendy explained, "we're able to see, given the fully developed human brain, what happens when it has to make a language out of nothing."

The first deaf children were born in Al-Sayyid 70 years ago, about ten of them in a single generation. By the time of our visit, only one member of the first deaf generation was still alive, an elderly woman too infirm to be interviewed. Today, the 150 or so deaf people of Al-Sayyid include the second generation, men and women in their thirties and forties; and the third generation, their children.

When they were small, the first-generation signers had developed systems of gestures, called homesigns, to communicate with their families. With so many homesigners in close proximity, a functional pidgin could develop quickly. And in just one generation, the children of these signers, like children of pidgin speakers everywhere, took their parents' signed pidgin and gave it grammar, spontaneously transforming it into the signed language of Al-Sayyid.

Over time, the language developed complexity. "People can talk about things that are not in the here-and-now," says Wendy. "They can talk about the traditional folklore of the tribe and say, 'People used to do it this way and now they don't,' They're able to transmit a lot of information—and things that are quite abstract." For example, "A signer told us about the traditional method of making babies immune to scorpion bites. It takes a high degree of sophistication about their culture, and it also takes a high degree of abstraction to be able to convey it."

Another villager, Anwar, is a particularly fine signer. On the linguists' previous visit, they recorded him telling a story nearly half an hour long, of how he was lost in Egypt for several years as a child. When Anwar was about eight, he somehow found his way onto a bus bound for Egypt. Because he couldn't communicate with anyone, he had no idea where he was supposed to be going, or where to get off. He left the bus somewhere in Egypt, where he knew no one. He was taken in by a local family and lived with them for three years. One day, someone from Al-Sayyid passed through and heard the story of the mysterious deaf boy. He recognized Anwar and brought him home. Anwar recounted this for the linguists entirely in the village sign language.

In all human languages, the task of showing who did what to whom is one of the principal functions of grammar. Many languages do this through verb agreement. But as a young, relatively bare language, ABSL displayed little of the elaborate verb agreement—made by altering the path of a verb's movement through space—that is the hallmark of established sign languages. Yet in the sentences they signed every day, the people of Al-Sayyid conveyed, clearly and without ambiguity, who did what to whom. Identifying the way in which they did so was the team's first important discovery.

In most spoken languages, there is a trade-off between verb agreement and rigid word order when it comes to expressing who did what to whom. And rigid word order the sign language of Al-Sayyid had with a vengeance. The second-generation signers of ABSL, the team discovered, routinely rely on word order to encode the who-did-what-to-whom of discourse. As the linguists wrote in their first major paper on the village, "In the space of one generation from its inception, systematic grammatical structure has emerged in the language."

As the team analyzed sentence after sentence of ABSL, they saw signers use the same word order again and again: subject-object-verb, or SOV. In some sentences, subject or object might be absent (as in MONEY COLLECT, "I saved money," which has no overt subject). But in almost all of them, the verb appeared at the very end of the sentence or clause.

It was noteworthy that this very young language already had word order of any kind, especially given that ABSL, like any signed language, could just as easily do without it. This was truly astonishing: the emerging language of Al-Sayyid makes vigorous use of word order even though it doesn't have to.

As long as the grant money holds out, and as long as the people of Al-Sayyid will have them, the linguists will come back to the village at least twice a year. It is too soon to tell whether the village sign language in the pure, isolated form will endure much beyond this generation. The signing of the deaf children, Al-Sayyid's third generation, is already permeated with ISL. Most parents in Al-Sayyid believe that for their deaf children to make their way in Israeli society, they will need to know the national signed language, and no one disputes their point. "We don't know how the language will change, and for us, that's where the drama is," Wendy wrote me in an e-mail message a few years after our trip. "And that's why we have to keep studying it very carefully across the generations."

23

"To Give up on Words"
Silence in Western Apache Culture

Keith H. Basso

Can you imagine working on a four-person cattle crew for several days without being introduced to or speaking with one of the other members, whom you did not know? For the Apache, this is a normal occurrence; they do not feel obligated to introduce strangers to one another. Instead, the Apache believe that when the time is right, the strangers will begin speaking to one another.

Would you find it uncomfortable to go on a date and sit in silence for an hour because you had only recently met your companion? What would you think if after returning home from several months' absence your parents and relatives didn't speak to you for several days? Although these situations seem unusual to us, they are considered appropriate among the Apache. Although it seems natural to us that when people first meet introductions are in order and that when friends and relatives reunite greetings and catching up will immediately follow, this is not the case for all cultures.

In this selection Keith Basso shows how, among the Apache, certain situations call for silence rather than communication and how silence makes sense within its cultural context.

As you read this selection, ask yourself the following questions:

- What are some of the ways silence is used in European American communication, and how are they different from those in Apache culture?
- How are the meaning and function of silence affected by the social and cultural context?
- What is the critical factor in an Apache's decision to speak or keep silent?
- How do Apaches interact upon meeting a stranger, courting, welcoming children home, "getting cussed out," and being with people who are sad?
- Despite the variety of situations in which Apaches are silent, what is the underlying determinant?

The following terms discussed in this selection are included in the Glossary at the back of the book:

hypothesis	*socialization*
informant	*sociolinguistics*
kinship	*status*

It is not the case that a man who is silent says nothing.
—Anonymous

I[1]

Anyone who has read about American Indians has probably encountered statements which impute to them a strong predilection for keeping silent or, as one writer has put it, "a fierce reluctance to speak except when

Basso, Keith H. "'To Give up on Words': Silence in Western Apache Culture." Southwestern Journal of Anthropology 26 (Autumn 1970), no. 3:213–230. Reprinted with permission of the Journal of Anthropological Research and the author.

absolutely necessary." In the popular literature, where this characterization is particularly widespread, it is commonly portrayed as the outgrowth of such dubious causes as "instinctive dignity," "an impoverished language," or, perhaps worst of all, the Indians' "lack of personal warmth." Although statements of this sort are plainly erroneous and dangerously misleading, it is noteworthy that professional anthropologists have made few attempts to correct them. Traditionally, ethnographers and linguists have paid little attention to cultural interpretations given to silence or, equally important, to the types of social contexts in which it regularly occurs.

This study investigates certain aspects of silence in the culture of the Western Apache of east-central Arizona. After considering some of the theoretical issues involved, I will briefly describe a number of situations—recurrent in Western Apache society—in which one or more of the participants typically refrain from speech for lengthy periods of time.[2] This is accompanied by a discussion of how such acts of silence are interpreted and why they are encouraged and deemed appropriate. I conclude by advancing an hypothesis that accounts for the reasons that the Western Apache refrain from speaking when they do, and I suggest that, with proper testing, this hypothesis may be shown to have relevance to silence behavior in other cultures.

II

A basic finding of sociolinguistics is that, although both language and language usage are structured, it is the latter which responds most sensitively to extralinguistic influences (Hymes 1962, 1964; Ervin-Tripp 1964, 1967; Gumperz 1964; Slobin 1967). Accordingly, a number of recent studies have addressed themselves to the problem of how factors in the social environment of speech events delimit the range and condition the selection of message forms (cf. Brown and Gilman 1960; Conklin 1959; Ervin-Tripp 1964, 1967; Frake 1964; Friedrich 1966; Gumperz 1961, 1964; Martin 1964). These studies may be viewed as taking the now familiar position that verbal communication is fundamentally a decision-making process in which, initially, a speaker, having elected to speak, selects from among a repertoire of available codes that which is most appropriately suited to the situation at hand. Once a code has been selected, the speaker picks a suitable channel of transmission and then, finally, makes a choice from a set of referentially equivalent expressions within the code. The intelligibility of the expression he chooses will, of course, be subject to grammatical constraints. But its acceptability will not. Rules for the selection of linguistic alternates operate on features of the social environment and are commensurate with rules governing the conduct of face-to-face interaction. As such, they are properly conceptualized as lying outside the structure of language itself.

It follows from this that for a stranger to communicate appropriately with the members of an unfamiliar society it is not enough that he learn to formulate messages intelligibly. Something else is needed: a knowledge of what kinds of codes, channels, and expressions to use in what kinds of situations and to what kinds of people—as Hymes (1964) has termed it, an "ethnography of communication."

There is considerable evidence to suggest that extralinguistic factors influence not only the use of speech but its actual occurrence as well. In our own culture, for example, remarks such as "Don't you know when to keep quiet?" "Don't talk until you're introduced," and "Remember now, no talking in church" all point to the fact that an individual's decision to speak may be directly contingent upon the character of his surroundings. Few of us would maintain that "silence is golden" for all people at all times. But we feel that silence is a virtue for some people some of the time, and we encourage children on the road to cultural competence to act accordingly.

Although the form of silence is always the same, the function of a specific act of silence—that is, its interpretation by and effect upon other people—will vary according to the social context in which it occurs. For example, if I choose to keep silent in the chambers of a Justice of the Supreme Court, my action is likely to be interpreted as a sign of politeness or respect. On the other hand, if I refrain from speaking to an established friend or colleague, I am apt to be accused of rudeness or harboring a grudge. In one instance, my behavior is judged by others to be "correct" or "fitting;" in the other, it is criticized as being "out of line."

The point, I think, is fairly obvious. For a stranger entering an alien society, a knowledge of when *not* to speak may be as basic to the production of culturally acceptable behavior as a knowledge of what to say. It stands to reason, then, that an adequate ethnography of communication should not confine itself exclusively to the analysis of choice within verbal repertoires. It should also, as Hymes (1962, 1964) has suggested, specify those conditions under which the members of the society regularly decide to refrain from verbal behavior altogether.

III

The research on which this paper is based was conducted over a period of sixteen months (1964–1969) in the Western Apache settlement of Cibecue, which is located near the center of the Fort Apache Indian Reservation in east-central Arizona. Cibecue's 800 residents participate in an unstable economy that combines subsistence agriculture, cattle-raising, sporadic wage-earning, and Government subsidies in the form of welfare checks and social security benefits. Unemployment is a serious problem, and substandard living conditions are widespread.

Although Reservation life has precipitated far-reaching changes in the composition and geographical distribution of Western Apache social groups, consanguineal kinship—real and imputed—remains the single most powerful force in the establishment and regulation of interpersonal relationships (Kaut 1957; Basso 1970). The focus of domestic activity is the individual "camp," or *gowąą*. This term labels both the occupants and the location of a single dwelling or, as is more apt to be the case, several dwellings built within a few feet of each other. The majority of *gową́ą́* in Cibecue are occupied by nuclear families. The next largest residential unit is the *gotáá* (camp cluster), which is a group of spatially localized *gową́ą́*, each having at least one adult member who is related by ties of matrilineal kinship to persons living in all the others. An intricate system of exogamous clans serves to extend kinship relationships beyond the *gową́ą́* and *gottáá* and facilitates concerted action in projects, most notably the presentation of ceremonials, requiring large amounts of manpower. Despite the presence in Cibecue of a variety of Anglo missionaries and a dwindling number of medicine men, diagnostic and curing rituals, as well as the girls' puberty ceremonial, continue to be performed with regularity (Basso 1966, 1970). Witchcraft persists in undiluted form (Basso 1969).

IV

Of the many broad categories of events, or scenes, that comprise the daily round of Western Apache life, I shall deal here only with those that are coterminous with what Goffman (1961, 1964) has termed "focused gatherings" or "encounters." The concept *situation*, in keeping with established usage, will refer inclusively to the location of such a gathering, its physical setting, its point in time, the standing behavior patterns that accompany it, and the social attributes of the persons involved (Hymes 1962, 1964; Ervin-Tripp 1964, 1967).

In what follows, however, I will be mainly concerned with the roles and statuses of participants. The reason for this is that the critical factor in the Apache's decision to speak or keep silent seems always to be the nature of his relationships to other people. To be sure, other features of the situation are significant, but apparently only to the extent that they influence the perception of status and role.[3] What this implies, of course, is that roles and statuses are not fixed attributes. Although they may be depicted as such in a static model (and often with good reason), they are appraised and acted upon in particular social contexts and, as a result, subject to redefinition and variation.[4] With this in mind, let us now turn our attention to the Western Apache and the types of situations in which, as one of my informants put it, "it is right to give up on words."

V

1. "Meeting strangers" (*nda dòhwą́ą́ iɬtséeda*). The term, *nda*, labels categories at two levels of contrast. At the most general level, it designates any person—Apache or non-Apache—who, prior to an initial meeting, has never been seen and therefore cannot be identified. In addition, the term is used to refer to Apaches who,

though previously seen and known by some external criteria such as clan affiliation or personal name, have never been engaged in face-to-face interaction. The latter category, which is more restricted than the first, typically includes individuals who live on the adjacent San Carlos Reservation, in Fort Apache settlements geographically removed from Cibecue, and those who fall into the category *kii dòhandáágo* (non-kinsmen). In all cases, "strangers" are separated by social distance. And in all cases it is considered appropriate, when encountering them for the first time, to refrain from speaking.

The type of situation described as "meeting strangers" (*nda dòhwą́ą́ iɬtséeda*) can take place in any number of different physical settings. However, it occurs most frequently in the context of events such as fairs and rodeos, which, owing to the large number of people in attendance, offer unusual opportunities for chance encounters. In large gatherings, the lack of verbal communication between strangers is apt to go unnoticed, but in smaller groups it becomes quite conspicuous. The following incident, involving two strangers who found themselves part of a four-man round-up crew, serves as a good example. My informant, who was also a member of the crew, recalled the following episode:

> One time, I was with A, B, and X down at Gleason Flat, working cattle. That man, X, was from East Fork [a community nearly 40 miles from Cibecue] where B's wife was from. But he didn't know A, never knew him before, I guess. First day, I worked with X. At night, when we camped, we talked with B, but X and A didn't say anything to each other. Same way, second day. Same way, third. Then, at night on fourth day, we were sitting by the fire. Still, X and A didn't talk. Then A said, "Well, I know there is a stranger to me here, but I've been watching him and I know he is all right." After that, X and A talked a lot. . . . Those two men didn't know each other, so they took it easy at first.

As this incident suggests, the Western Apache do not feel compelled to "introduce" persons who are unknown to each other. Eventually, it is assumed, strangers will begin to speak. However, this is a decision that is properly left to the individuals involved, and no attempt is made to hasten it. Outside help in the form of introductions or other verbal routines is viewed as presumptuous and unnecessary.

Strangers who are quick to launch into conversation are frequently eyed with undisguised suspicion. A typical reaction to such individuals is that they "want something," that is, their willingness to violate convention is attributed to some urgent need which is likely to result in requests for money, labor, or transportation. Another common reaction to talkative strangers is that they are drunk.

If the stranger is an Anglo, it is usually assumed that he "wants to teach us something" (i.e., give orders or instructions) or that he "wants to make friends in a hurry." The latter response is especially revealing, since Western Apaches are extremely reluctant to be hurried into friendships—with Anglos or each other. Their verbal reticence with strangers is directly related to the conviction that the establishment of social relationships is a serious matter that calls for caution, careful judgment, and plenty of time.

2. "Courting" (lʼgoláá). During the initial stages of courtship, young men and women go without speaking for conspicuous lengths of time. Courting may occur in a wide variety of settings—practically anywhere, in fact—and at virtually any time of the day or night, but it is most readily observable at large public gatherings such as ceremonials, wakes, and rodeos. At these events, "sweethearts" (zééde) may stand or sit (sometimes holding hands) for as long as an hour without exchanging a word. I am told by adult informants that the young people's reluctance to speak may become even more pronounced in situations where they find themselves alone.

Apaches who have just begun to court attribute their silence to "intense shyness" (ʼisté) and a feeling of acute "self-consciousness" (dàyééź) which, they claim, stems from their lack of familiarity with one another. More specifically, they complain of "not knowing what to do" in each other's presence and of the fear that whatever they say, no matter how well thought out in advance, will sound "dumb" or "stupid."[5]

One informant, a youth 17 years old, commented as follows:

It's hard to talk with your sweetheart at first. She doesn't know you and won't know what to say. It's the same way towards her. You don't know how to talk yet . . . so you get very bashful. That makes it sometimes so you don't say anything. So you just go around together and don't talk. At first, it's better that way. Then, after a while, when you know each other, you aren't shy anymore and can talk good.

The Western Apache draw an equation between the ease and frequency with which a young couple talks and how well they know each other. Thus, it is expected that after several months of steady companionship sweethearts will start to have lengthy conversations. Earlier in their relationship, however, protracted discussions may be openly discouraged. This is especially true for girls, who are informed by their mothers and older sisters that silence in courtship is a sign of modesty and that an eagerness to speak betrays previous experience with men. In extreme cases, they add, it may be interpreted as a willingness to engage in sexual relations. Said one woman, aged 32:

This way I have talked to my daughter. "Take it easy when boys come around this camp and want you to go somewhere with them. When they talk to you, just listen at first. Maybe you won't know what to say. So don't talk about just anything. If you talk with those boys right away, then they will know you know all about them. They will think you've been with many boys before, and they will start talking about that."

3. "Children, coming home" (čogoše nakáii). The Western Apache lexeme iltá ʼnatsáá (reunion) is used to describe encounters between an individual who has returned home after a long absence and his relatives and friends. The most common type of reunion, čogoše nakáii (children, coming home), involves boarding school students and their parents. It occurs in late May or early in June, and its setting is usually a trading post or school, where parents congregate to await the arrival of buses bringing the children home. As the latter disembark and locate their parents in the crowd, one anticipates a flurry of verbal greetings. Typically, however, there are few or none at all. Indeed, it is not unusual for parents and child to go without speaking for as long as 15 minutes.

When the silence is broken, it is almost always the child who breaks it. His parents listen attentively to everything he says but speak hardly at all themselves. This pattern persists even after the family has reached the privacy of its camp, and two or three days may pass before the child's parents seek to engage him in sustained conversation.

According to my informants, the silence of Western Apache parents at (and after) reunions with their children is ultimately predicated on the possibility that the latter have been adversely affected by their experiences away from home. Uppermost is the fear that, as a result of protracted exposure to Anglo attitudes and values, the children have come to view their parents as ignorant, old-fashioned, and no longer deserving of respect. One of my most thoughtful and articulate informants commented on the problem as follows:

You just can't tell about those children after they've been with White men for a long time. They get their minds turned around sometimes . . . they forget where they come from and get ashamed when they come home because their parents and relatives are poor. They forget how to act with these Apaches and get mad easy. They walk around all night and get into fights. They don't stay at home.

At school, some of them learn to want to be White men, so they come back and try to act that way. But we are still Apaches! So we don't know them anymore, and it is like we never knew them. It is hard to talk to them when they are like that.

Apache parents openly admit that, initially, children who have been away to school seem distant and unfamiliar. They have grown older, of course, and their physical appearance may have changed. But more fundamental is the concern that they have acquired new ideas and expectations which will alter their behavior in unpredictable ways. No matter how pressing this concern may be, however, it is considered inappropriate to directly interrogate a child after his arrival home. Instead, parents anticipate that within a short time he will begin to divulge information about himself that will enable them to determine in what ways, if any, his views and attitudes have changed. This, the Apache say, is why children do practically all the talking in the hours following a reunion, and their parents remain unusually silent.

Said one man, the father of two children who had recently returned from boarding school in Utah:

> Yes, it's right that we didn't talk much to them when they came back, my wife and me. They were away for a long time, and we didn't know how they would like it, being home. So we waited. Right away, they started to tell stories about what they did. Pretty soon we could tell they liked it, being back. That made us feel good. So it was easy to talk to them again. It was like they were before they went away.

4. "Getting cussed out" (*š`łditéé*). This lexeme is used to describe any situation in which one individual, angered and enraged, shouts insults and criticism at another. Although the object of such invective is in most cases the person or persons who provoked it, this is not always the case, because an Apache who is truly beside himself with rage is likely to vent his feelings on anyone whom he sees or who happens to be within range of his voice. Consequently, "getting cussed out" may involve large numbers of people who are totally innocent of the charges being hurled against them. But whether they are innocent or not, their response to the situation is the same. They refrain from speech.

Like the types of situations we have discussed thus far, "getting cussed out" can occur in a wide variety of physical settings: at ceremonial dancegrounds and trading posts, inside and outside wickiups and houses, on food-gathering expeditions and shopping trips—in short, wherever and whenever individuals lose control of their tempers and lash out verbally at persons nearby.

Although "getting cussed out" is basically free of setting self-imposed restrictions, the Western Apache fear it most at gatherings where alcohol is being consumed. My informants observed that especially at "drinking parties" (*dá'idłą́ą́*), where there is much rough joking and ostensibly mock criticism, it is easy for well-intentioned remarks to be misconstrued as insults. Provoked in this way, persons who are intoxicated may become hostile and launch into explosive tirades, often with no warning at all.

The silence of Apaches who are "getting cussed out" is consistently explained in reference to the belief that individuals who are "enraged" (*haškéé*) are also irrational or "crazy" (*b`né'id̦̦*). In this condition, it is said, they "forget who they are" and become oblivious to what they say or do. Concomitantly, they lose all concern for the consequences of their actions on other people. In a word, they are dangerous. Said one informant:

> When people get mad they get crazy. Then they start yelling and saying bad things. Some say they are going to kill somebody for what he has done. Some keep it up that way for a long time, maybe walk from camp to camp, real angry, yelling, crazy like that. They keep it up for a long time, some do.
>
> People like that don't know what they are saying, so you can't tell about them. When you see someone like that, just walk away. If he yells at you, let him say whatever he wants to. Let him say anything. Maybe he doesn't mean it. But he doesn't know that. He will be crazy, and he could try to kill you.

Another Apache said:

> When someone gets mad at you and starts yelling, then just don't do anything to make him get worse. Don't try to quiet him down because he won't know why you're doing it. If you try to do that, he may just get worse and try to hurt you.

As the last of these statements implies, the Western Apache operate on the assumption that enraged persons—because they are temporarily "crazy"—are difficult to reason with. Indeed, there is a widely held belief that attempts at mollification will serve to intensify anger, thus increasing the chances of physical violence. The appropriate strategy when "getting cussed out" is to do nothing, to avoid any action that will attract attention to oneself. Since speaking accomplishes just the opposite, the use of silence is strongly advised.

5. "Being with people who are sad" (*nde dòbiłgòzóóda bigą́ą́*). Although the Western Apache phrase that labels this situation has no precise equivalent in English, it refers quite specifically to gatherings in which an individual finds himself in the company of someone whose spouse or kinsman has recently died. Distinct from wakes and burials, which follow immediately after a death, "being with people who are sad" is most likely to occur several weeks later. At this time, close relatives of the deceased emerge from a period of intense mourning (during which they rarely venture beyond the limits of their camps) and start to resume their normal activities within the community.

To persons anxious to convey their sympathies, this is interpreted as a sign that visitors will be welcomed and, if possible, provided with food and drink. To those less solicitous, it means that unplanned encounters with the bereaved must be anticipated and prepared for.

"Being with people who are sad" can occur on a foot-path, in a camp, at church, or in a trading post; but whatever the setting—and regardless of whether it is the result of a planned visit or an accidental meeting—the situation is marked by a minimum of speech. Queried about this, my informants volunteered three types of explanations. The first is that persons "who are sad" are so burdened with "intense grief" (*dółgozóóda*) that speaking requires of them an unusual amount of physical effort. It is courteous and considerate, therefore, not to attempt to engage them in conversation.

A second native explanation is that in situations of this sort verbal communication is basically unnecessary. Everyone is familiar with what has happened, and talking about it, even for the purpose of conveying solace and sympathy, would only reinforce and augment the sadness felt by those who were close to the deceased. Again, for reasons of courtesy, this is something to be avoided.

The third explanation is rooted in the belief that "intense grief," like intense rage, produces changes in the personality of the individual who experiences it. As evidence for this, the Western Apache cite numerous instances in which the emotional strain of dealing with death, coupled with an overwhelming sense of irrevocable personal loss, has caused persons who were formerly mild and even-tempered to become abusive, hostile, and physically violent.

That old woman, X, who lives across Cibecue Creek, one time her first husband died. After that she cried all the time, for a long time. Then, I guess she got mean because everyone said she drank a lot and got into fights. Even with her close relatives, she did like that for a long time. She was too sad for her husband. That's what made her like that; it made her lose her mind.

My father was like that when his wife died. He just stayed home all the time and wouldn't go anywhere. He didn't talk to any of his relatives or children. He just said, "I'm hungry. Cook for me." That's all. He stayed that way for a long time. His mind was not with us. He was still with his wife.

My uncle died in 1911. His wife sure went crazy right after that. Two days after they buried the body, we went over there and stayed with those people who had been left alone. My aunt got mad at us. She said, "Why do you come back over here? You can't bring my husband back. I can take care of myself and those others in my camp, so why don't you go home." She sure was mad that time, too sad for someone who died. She

didn't know what she was saying because in about one week she came to our camp and said, "My relatives, I'm all right now. When you came to help me, I had too much sadness and my mind was no good. I said bad words to you. But now I am all right and I know what I am doing."

As these statements indicate, the Western Apache assume that a person suffering from "intense grief" is likely to be disturbed and unstable. Even though he may appear outwardly composed, they say, there is always the possibility that he is emotionally upset and therefore unusually prone to volatile outbursts. Apaches acknowledge that such an individual might welcome conversation in the context of "being with people who are sad," but, on the other hand, they fear it might prove incendiary. Under these conditions, which resemble those in Situation No. 4, it is considered both expedient and appropriate to keep silent.

6. "Being with someone for whom they sing" (*ndeb`dád`stááha bigą́ą́*). The last type of situation to be described is restricted to a small number of physical locations and is more directly influenced by temporal factors than any of the situations we have discussed so far. "Being with someone for whom they sing" takes place only in the context of "curing ceremonials" (*gòjitáł*). These events begin early at night and come to a close shortly before dawn the following day. In the late fall and throughout the winter, curing ceremonials are held inside the patient's wickiup or house. In the spring and summer, they are located outside, at some open place near the patient's camp or at specially designated dance grounds where group rituals of all kinds are regularly performed.

Prior to the start of a curing ceremonial, all persons in attendance may feel free to talk with the patient; indeed, because he is so much a focus of concern, it is expected that friends and relatives will seek him out to offer encouragement and support. Conversation breaks off, however, when the patient is informed that the ceremonial is about to begin, and it ceases entirely when the presiding medicine man commences to chant. From this point on, until the completion of the final chant next morning, it is inappropriate for anyone except the medicine man (and, if he has them, his aides) to speak to the patient.[6]

In order to appreciate the explanation Apaches give for this prescription, we must briefly discuss the concept of "supernatural power" (*diyí*) and describe some of the effects it is believed to have on persons at whom it is directed. Elsewhere (Basso 1969:30) I have defined "power" as follows:

The term *diyí* refers to one or all of a set of abstract and invisible forces which are said to derive from certain classes of animals, plants, minerals, meteorological phenomena, and mythological figures within the Western Apache universe. Any of the various powers may be acquired by man and, if properly handled, used for a variety of purposes.

A power that has been antagonized by disrespectful behavior towards its source may retaliate by causing the offender to become sick. "Power-caused illnesses" (*kásitį̃ kiy´bił*) are properly treated with curing ceremonials in which one or more medicine men, using chants and various items of ritual paraphernalia, attempt to neutralize the sickness-causing power with powers of their own.

Roughly two-thirds of my informants assert that a medicine man's power actually enters the body of the patient; others maintain that it simply closes in and envelops him. In any case, all agree that the patient is brought into intimate contact with a potent supernatural force which elevates him to a condition labeled *gòdiyò'* (sacred, holy).

The term *gòdiyò'* may also be translated as "potentially harmful" and, in this sense, is regularly used to describe classes of objects (including all sources of power) that are associated with taboos. In keeping with the semantics of *gòdiyò'*, the Western Apache explain that, besides making patients holy, power makes them potentially harmful. And it is this transformation, they explain, that is basically responsible for the cessation of verbal communication during curing ceremonials. Said one informant:

> When they start singing for someone like that, he sort of goes away with what the medicine man is working with (i.e., power). Sometimes people they sing for don't know you, even after it (the curing ceremonial) is over. They get holy, and you shouldn't try to talk to them when they are like that . . . it's best to leave them alone.

Another informant made similar comments:

> When they sing for someone, what happens is like this: that man they sing for doesn't know why he is sick or which way to go. So the medicine man has to show him and work on him. That is when he gets holy, and that makes him go off somewhere in his mind, so you should stay away from him.

Because Apaches undergoing ceremonial treatment are perceived as having been changed by power into something different from their normal selves, they are regarded with caution and apprehension. Their newly acquired status places them in close proximity to the supernatural and, as such, carries with it a very real element of danger and uncertainty. These conditions combine to make "being with someone for whom they sing" a situation in which speech is considered disrespectful and, if not exactly harmful, at least potentially hazardous.

VI

Although the types of situations described above differ from one another in obvious ways, I will argue in what follows that the underlying determinants of silence are in each case basically the same. Specifically, I will attempt to defend the hypothesis that keeping silent in Western Apache culture is associated with social situations in which participants perceive their relationships *vis-à-vis* one another to be ambiguous and/or unpredictable.

Let us begin with the observation that, in all the situations we have described, *silence is defined as appropriate with respect to a specific individual or individuals*. In other words, the use of speech is not directly curtailed by the setting of a situation nor by the physical activities that accompany it but, rather, by the perceived social and psychological attributes of at least one focal participant.

It may also be observed that, in each type of situation, *the status of the focal participant is marked by ambiguity*—either because he is unfamiliar to other participants in the situation or because, owing to some recent event, a status he formerly held has been changed or is in a process of transition.

Thus, in Situation No. 1, persons who earlier considered themselves "strangers" move towards some other relationship, perhaps "friend" (*š`dikéé*), perhaps "enemy" (*š`kédnd´*). In Situation No. 2, young people who have relatively limited exposure to one another attempt to adjust to the new and intimate status of "sweetheart." These two situations are similar in that the focal participants have little or no prior knowledge of each other. Their social identities are not as yet clearly defined, and their expectations, lacking the foundation of previous experience, are poorly developed.

Situation No. 3 is somewhat different. Although the participants—parents and their children—are well known to each other, their relationship has been seriously interrupted by the latter's prolonged absence from home. This, combined with the possibility that recent experiences at school have altered the children's attitudes, introduces a definite element of unfamiliarity and doubt. Situation No. 3 is not characterized by the absence of role expectations but by the participants' perception that those already in existence may be outmoded and in need of revision.

Status ambiguity is present in Situation No. 4 because a focal participant is enraged and, as a result, considered "crazy." Until he returns to a more rational condition, others in the situation have no way of predicting how he will behave. Situation No. 5 is similar in that the personality of a focal participant is seen to have undergone a marked shift which makes his actions more difficult to anticipate. In both situations, the status of focal participants is uncertain because of real or imagined changes in their psychological makeup.

In Situation No. 6, a focal participant is ritually transformed from an essentially neutral state to one which is contextually defined as "potentially harmful." Ambiguity and apprehension accompany this transition, and, as in Situations No. 4 and 5, established patterns of interaction must be waived until the focal participant reverts to a less threatening condition.

This discussion points up a third feature characteristic of all situations: *the ambiguous status of focal participants is accompanied either by the absence or suspension of established role expectations.* In every instance, nonfocal participants (i.e., those who refrain from speech) are either uncertain of how the focal participant will behave towards them or, conversely, how they should behave towards him. Stated in the simplest way possible, their roles become blurred with the result that established expectations—if they exist—lose their relevance as guidelines for social action and must be temporarily discarded or abruptly modified.

We are now in a position to expand upon our initial hypothesis and make it more explicit.

1. In Western Apache culture, the absence of verbal communication is associated with social situations in which the status of local participants is ambiguous.

2. Under these conditions, fixed role expectations lose their applicability and the illusion of predictability in social interaction is lost.

3. To sum up and reiterate: keeping silent among the Western Apache is a response to uncertainty and unpredictability in social relations.

VII

The question remains to what extent the foregoing hypothesis helps to account for silence behavior in other cultures. Unfortunately, it is impossible at the present time to provide anything approaching a conclusive answer. Standard ethnographies contain very little information about the circumstances under which verbal communication is discouraged, and it is only within the past few years that problems of this sort have engaged the attention of sociolinguists. The result is that adequate cross-cultural data are almost completely lacking.

As a first step towards the elimination of this deficiency, an attempt is now being made to investigate the occurrence and interpretation of silence in other Indian societies of the American Southwest. Our findings at this early stage, though neither fully representative nor

sufficiently comprehensive, are extremely suggestive. By way of illustration, I quote below from portions of a preliminary report prepared by Priscilla Mowrer (1970), herself a Navajo, who inquired into the situational features of Navajo silence behavior in the vicinity of Tuba City on the Navajo Reservation in east-central Arizona.

I. *Silence and Courting:* Navajo youngsters of opposite sexes just getting to know one another say nothing, except to sit close together and maybe hold hands. . . . In public, they may try not to let on that they are interested in each other, but in private it is another matter. If the girl is at a gathering where the boy is also present, she may go off by herself. Falling in step, the boy will generally follow. They may just walk around or find some place to sit down. But, at first, they will not say anything to each other.

II. *Silence and Long Absent Relatives:* When a male or female relative returns home after being gone for six months or more, he (or she) is first greeted with a handshake. If the returnee is male, the female greeter may embrace him and cry—the male, meanwhile, will remain dry-eyed and silent.

III. *Silence and Anger:* The Navajo tend to remain silent when being shouted at by a drunk or angered individual because that particular individual is considered temporarily insane. To speak to such an individual, the Navajo believe, just tends to make the situation worse. . . . People remain silent because they believe that the individual is not himself, that he may have been witched, and is not responsible for the change in his behavior.

IV. *Silent Mourning:* Navajos speak very little when mourning the death of a relative. . . . The Navajo mourn and cry together in pairs. Men will embrace one another and cry together. Women, however, will hold one another's hands and cry together.

V. *Silence and the Ceremonial Patient:* The Navajo consider it wrong to talk to a person being sung over. The only people who talk to the patient are the medicine man and a female relative (or male relative if the patient is male) who is in charge of food preparation. The only time the patient speaks openly is when the medicine man asks her (or him) to pray along with him.

These observations suggest that striking similarities may exist between the types of social contexts in which Navajos and Western Apaches refrain from speech. If this impression is confirmed by further research, it will lend obvious cross-cultural support to the hypothesis advanced above. But regardless of the final outcome, the situational determinants of silence seem eminently deserving of further study. For as we become better informed about the types of contextual variables that mitigate against the use of verbal codes, we should also learn more about those variables that encourage and promote them.

NOTES

1. At different times during the period extending from 1964–1969 the research on which this paper is based was supported by U. S. P. H. S. Grant MH-12691-01, a grant from the American Philosophical Society, and funds from the Doris Duke Oral History Project at the Arizona State Museum. I am pleased to acknowledge this support. I would also like to express my gratitude to the following scholars for commenting upon an earlier draft: Y. R. Chao, Harold C. Conklin, Roy G. D'Andrade, Charles O. Frake, Paul Friedrich, John Gumperz, Kenneth Hale, Harry Hoijer, Dell Hymes, Stanley Newman, David M. Schneider, Joel Sherzer, and Paul Turner. Although the final version gained much from their criticisms and suggestions, responsibility for its present form and content rests solely with the author. A preliminary version of this paper was presented to the Annual Meeting of the American Anthropological Association in New Orleans, Louisiana, November 1969. A modified version of this paper is scheduled to appear in *Studies in Apachean Culture and Ethnology* (ed. by Keith H. Basso and Morris Opler), Tucson: University of Arizona Press, 1970.

2. The situations described in this paper are not the only ones in which the Western Apache refrain from speech. There is a second set—not considered here because my data are incomplete—in which silence appears to occur as a gesture of respect, usually to persons in positions of authority. A third set, very poorly understood, involves ritual specialists who claim they must keep silent at certain points during the preparation of ceremonial paraphernalia.

3. Recent work in the sociology of interaction, most notably by Goffman (1963) and Garfinkel (1967), has led to the suggestion that social relationships are everywhere the major determinants of verbal behavior. In this case, as Gumperz (1967) makes clear, it becomes methodologically unsound to treat the various components of communicative events as independent variables. Gumperz (1967) has presented a hierarchical model, sensitive to dependency, in which components are seen as stages in the communication process. Each stage serves as the input for the next. The basic stage, i.e., the initial input, is "social identities or statuses." For further details see Slobin 1967:131–134.

4. I would like to stress that the emphasis placed on social relations is fully in keeping with the Western Apache interpretation of their own behavior. When my informants were asked to explain why they or someone else was silent on a particular occasion, they invariably did so in terms of *who* was present at the time.

5. Among the Western Apache, rules of exogamy discourage courtships between members of the same clan (*kii àɫhánigo*) and so-called "related" clans (*kii*), with the result that sweethearts are almost always "non-matrilineal kinsmen" (*dòhwàkˋda*). Compared to "matrilineal kinsmen" (*kii*), such individuals have fewer opportunities during childhood to establish close personal relationships and thus, when courtship begins, have relatively little knowledge of each other. It is not surprising, therefore, that their behavior is similar to that accorded strangers.

6. I have witnessed over 75 curing ceremonials since 1961 and have seen this rule violated only 6 times. On 4 occasions, drunks were at fault. In the other 2 cases, the patient fell asleep and had to be awakened.

REFERENCES

Basso, Keith H. 1966. *The Gift of Changing Woman.* Bureau of American Ethnology, Bulletin 196.

_____. 1969. *Western Apache Witchcraft.* Anthropological Papers of the University of Arizona, no. 15.

_____. 1970. *The Cibecue Apache.* New York: Holt, Rinehart and Winston, Inc.

Brown, R. W., and Albert Gilman. 1960. The Pronouns of Power and Solidarity. In *Style and Language,* ed. T. Sebeok, 253–276. Cambridge: The Technology Press of Massachusetts Institute of Technology.

Conklin, Harold C. 1959. Linguistic Play in Its Cultural Context. *Language* 35: 631–636.

Ervin-Tripp, Susan. 1964. An Analysis of the Interaction of Language, Topic and Listener. In *The Ethnography of Communication,* ed. J. J. Gumperz and D. Hymes, 86–102. *American Anthropologist,* Special Publication, vol. 66, no. 6, part 2.

_____. 1967. *Sociolinguistics.* Language-Behavior Research Laboratory, Working Paper no. 3. Berkeley: University of California.

Frake, Charles O. 1964. How to Ask for a Drink in Subanun. In *The Ethnography of Communication,* ed. J. J. Gumperz and D. Hymes, 127–132. *American Anthropologist,* Special Publication, vol. 66, no. 6, part 2.

Friedrich, P. 1966. Structural Implications of Russia Pronominal Usage. In *Sociolinguistics,* ed. W. Bright, 214–253. The Hague: Mouton.

Garfinkel, H. 1967. *Studies in Ethnomethodology.* Englewood Cliffs, N.J.: Prentice-Hall, Inc.

Goffman, E. 1961. *Encounters: Two Studies in the Sociology of Interaction.* Indianapolis: The Bobbs-Merrill Co., Inc.

_____. 1963. *Behavior in Public Places.* Glencoe, Ill.: Free Press.

_____. 1964. The Neglected Situation. In *The Ethnography of Communication,* ed. J. J. Gumperz and D. Hymes, 133–136. *American Anthropologist,* Special Publication, vol. 66, no. 6, part 2.

Gumperz, John J. 1961. Speech Variation and the Study of Indian Civilization. *American Anthropologist* 63: 976–988.

_____. 1964. Linguistic and Social Interaction in Two Communities. In *The Ethnography of Communication,* ed. J. J. Gumperz and D. Hymes, 137–153. *American Anthropologist,* Special Publication, vol. 66, no. 6, part 2.

_____. 1967. The Social Setting of Linguistic Behavior. In *A Field Manual for Cross-Cultural Study of the Acquisition of*

Communicative Competence (Second Draft), ed. D. I. Slobin, 129–134. Berkeley: University of California.

Hymes, Dell. 1962. The Ethnography of Speaking. In *Anthropology and Human Behavior*, ed. T. Gladwin and W. C. Sturtevant, 13–53. Washington, D. C.: The Anthropological Society of Washington.

_____. 1964. Introduction: Toward Ethnographies of Communication. In *The Ethnography of Communication*, ed, J. J. Gumperz and D. Hymes, 1–34. *American Anthropologist*, Special Publication, vol. 66, no. 6, part 2.

Kaut, Charles R. 1957. *The Western Apache Clan System: Its Origins and Development.* University of New Mexico Publications in Anthropology, no. 9.

Martin, Samuel. 1964. Speech Levels in Japan and Korea. In *Language in Culture and Society,* ed. D. Hymes, 407–415. New York: Harper & Row.

Mowrer, Priscilla. 1970. Notes on Navajo Silence Behavior. MS, University of Arizona.

Slobin, Dan I. (ed.). 1967. *A Field Manual for Cross-Cultural Study of the Acquisition of Communicative Competence (Second Draft).* Berkeley: University of California.

24

A Cultural Approach
to Male-Female Miscommunication

Daniel N. Maltz and Ruth A. Borker

Of the 60,000 or so words in the English language, the typical educated adult uses about 2,000. Five hundred of these words alone can convey over 14,000 meanings. But even with all these alternatives, this is not the central problem of miscommunication in North America. Rather, interethnic and cross-sex conversations are the central problem, because the participants possess different subcultural rules for speaking.

Conversation is a negotiated activity. Within a given culture, conversations rely on unspoken understandings about tone of voice, visual cues, silence, minimal responses (such as "mm hmm"), and a variety of other subtle conventions. A cultural approach to male-female conversation highlights unconscious meanings that can lead members of one group to misinterpret the intent of others. Evidence suggests, for example, that women use the response "mm hmm" to indicate they are listening, whereas men use the same response to indicate they are agreeing. Thus, a man who does not provide such cues may indicate to a female conversation partner that he is not listening, whereas a woman may appear to keep changing her mind when giving the same cue. This and similar insights are found throughout this selection and indicate the need for paying attention to communication across cultural and subcultural boundaries.

As you read this selection, ask yourself the following questions:

- What are some of the differences in the ways men and women talk to each other that have been noted in earlier research?

- How do differences between men and women in conversational style reflect differences in power in the larger society?

- If men and women exist in different linguistic subcultures, how and when were these subcultures learned? How does the world of girls differ from the world of boys?

- What kinds of miscommunications occur in cross-sex conversation?

- Can you think of situations that have occurred in your own life that can be better understood after reading this cultural analysis of cross-sex conversation?

The following terms discussed in this selection are included in the Glossary at the back of the book:

gender   *social networks*
metalinguistics   *sociolinguistics*
sex roles   *subculture*

INTRODUCTION

This chapter presents what we believe to be a useful new framework for examining differences in the speaking patterns of American men and women. It is based not on new data, but on a reexamination of a wide variety of material already available in the schol-

Maltz, Daniel N. & Ruth A. Borker. "A Cultural Approach to Male-Female Miscommunication." From Language and Identity, pp. 196–216, John Gumperz, ed. © 1982 Cambridge University Press. Reprinted with permission of Cambridge University Press.

arly literature. Our starting problem is the nature of the different roles of male and female speakers in informal cross-sex conversations in American English. Our attempts to think about this problem have taken us to preliminary examination of a wide variety of fields often on or beyond the margins of our present competencies: children's speech, children's play, styles and patterns of friendship, conversational turn-taking, discourse analysis, and interethnic communication. The research which most influenced the development of our present model includes John Gumperz's work on problems in interethnic communication (1982) and

Marjorie Goodwin's study of the linguistic aspects of play among black children in Philadelphia (1978, 1980a, 1980b).

Our major argument is that the general approach recently developed for the study of difficulties in cross-ethnic communication can be applied to cross-sex communication as well. We prefer to think of the difficulties in both cross-sex and cross-ethnic communication as two examples of the same larger phenomenon: cultural difference and miscommunication.

THE PROBLEM OF CROSS-SEX CONVERSATION

Study after study has shown that when men and women attempt to interact as equals in friendly cross-sex conversations they do not play the same role in interaction, even when there is no apparent element of flirting. We hope to explore some of these differences, examine the explanations that have been offered, and provide an alternative explanation for them.

The primary data on cross-sex conversations come from two general sources: social psychology studies from the 1950s such as Soskin and John's (1963) research on two young married couples and Strodbeck and Mann's (1956) research on jury deliberations, and more recent sociolinguistic studies from the University of California at Santa Barbara and the University of Pennsylvania by Candace West (Zimmerman and West 1975; West and Zimmerman 1977; West 1979), Pamela Fishman (1978), and Lynette Hirschman (1973).

WOMEN'S FEATURES

Several striking differences in male and female contributions to cross-sex conversation have been noticed in these studies.

First, women display a greater tendency to ask questions. Fishman (1978:400) comments that "at times I felt that all women did was ask questions," and Hirschman (1973:10) notes that "several of the female-male conversations fell into a question-answer pattern with the females asking the males questions."

Fishman (1978:408) sees this question-asking tendency as an example of a second, more general characteristic of women's speech, doing more of the routine "shitwork" involved in maintaining routine social interaction, doing more to facilitate the flow of conversation (Hirschman 1973:3). Women are more likely than men to make utterances that demand or encourage responses from their fellow speakers and are therefore, in Fishman's words, "more actively engaged in insuring interaction than the men" (1978:404). In the earlier social psychology studies, these features have been

coded under the general category of "positive reactions" including solidarity, tension release, and agreeing (Strodbeck and Mann 1956).

Third, women show a greater tendency to make use of positive minimal responses, especially "mm hmm" (Hirschman 1973:8), and are more likely to insert "such comments throughout streams of talk rather than [simply] at the end" (Fishman 1978:402).

Fourth, women are more likely to adopt a strategy of "silent protest" after they have been interrupted or have received a delayed minimal response (Zimmerman and West 1975; West and Zimmerman 1977:524).

Fifth, women show a greater tendency to use the pronouns "you" and "we," which explicitly acknowledge the existence of the other speaker (Hirschman 1973:6).

MEN'S FEATURES

Contrasting contributions to cross-sex conversations have been observed and described for men.

First, men are more likely to interrupt the speech of their conversational partners, that is, to interrupt the speech of women (Zimmerman and West 1975; West and Zimmerman 1977; West 1979).

Second, they are more likely to challenge or dispute their partners' utterances (Hirschman 1973:11).

Third, they are more likely to ignore the comments of the other speaker, that is, to offer no response or acknowledgment at all (Hirschman 1973:11), to respond slowly in what has been described as a "delayed minimal response" (Zimmerman and West 1975:118), or to respond unenthusiastically (Fishman 1978).

Fourth, men use more mechanisms for controlling the topic of conversation, including both topic development and the introduction of new topics, than do women (Zimmerman and West 1975).

Finally, men make more direct declarations of fact or opinion than do women (Fishman 1978:402), including suggestions, opinions, and "statements of orientation" as Strodbeck and Mann (1956) describe them, or "statements of focus and directives" as they are described by Soskin and John (1963).

EXPLANATIONS OFFERED

Most explanations for these features have focused on differences in the social power or in the personalities of men and women. One variant of the social power argument, presented by West (Zimmerman and West 1975; West and Zimmerman 1977), is that men's dominance in conversation parallels their dominance in society. Men enjoy power in society and also in conversation. The two levels are seen as part of a single social-political system. West sees interruptions and topic control as male displays of power—a power based in the larger social order but reinforced and expressed in face-to-face interaction with women. A second variant of this argument, stated by Fishman (1978), is that while the differential power of men and women is crucial, the specific mechanism through which it enters conversation is sex-role definition. Sex roles serve to obscure the issue of power for participants, but the fact is, Fishman argues, that norms of appropriate behavior for women and men serve to give power and interactional control to men while keeping it from women. To be socially acceptable as women, women cannot exert control and must actually support men in their control. In this casting of the social power argument, men are not necessarily seen to be consciously flaunting power, but simply reaping the rewards given them by the social system. In both variants, the link between macro and micro levels of social life is seen as direct and unproblematic, and the focus of explanation is the general social order.

Sex roles have also been central in psychological explanations. The primary advocate of the psychological position has been Robin Lakoff (1975). Basically, Lakoff asserts that, having been taught to speak and act like "ladies," women become as unassertive and insecure as they have been made to sound. The impossible task of trying to be both women and adults, which Lakoff sees as culturally incompatible, saps women of confidence and strength. As a result, they come to produce the speech they do, not just because it is how women are supposed to speak, but because it fits with the personalities they develop as a consequence of sex-role requirements.

The problem with these explanations is that they do not provide a means of explaining why these specific features appear as opposed to any number of others, nor do they allow us to differentiate between various types of male-female interaction. They do not really tell us why and how these specific interactional phenomena are linked to the general fact that men dominate within our social system.

AN ALTERNATIVE EXPLANATION: SOCIOLINGUISTIC SUBCULTURES

Our approach to cross-sex communication patterns is somewhat different from those that have been previously proposed. We place the stress not on psychological differences or power differentials, although these may make some contribution, but rather on a notion of cultural differences between men and women in their conceptions of friendly conversation, their rules for engaging in it, and, probably most important, their rules for interpreting it. We argue that American men and women come from different sociolinguistic subcultures, having learned to do different things with words in a conversation, so that when they attempt to carry on conversations with one another, even if both parties are attempting to treat one another as equals, cultural miscommunication results.

The idea of distinct male and female subcultures is not a new one for anthropology. It has been persuasively argued again and again for those parts of the world such as the Middle East and southern Europe in which men and women spend most of their lives spatially and interactionally segregated. The strongest case for sociolinguistic subcultures has been made by Susan Harding from her research in rural Spain (1975).

The major premise on which Harding builds her argument is that speech is a means for dealing with social and psychological situations. When men and women have different experiences and operate in different social contexts, they tend to develop different genres of speech and different skills for doing things with words. In the Spanish village in which she worked, the sexual division of labor was strong, with men involved in agricultural tasks and public politics while women were involved in a series of networks of personal relations with their children, their husbands, and their female neighbors. While men developed their verbal skills in economic negotiations and public political argument, women became more verbally adept at a quite different mode of interactional manipulation with words: gossip, social analysis, subtle information gathering through a carefully developed technique of verbal prying, and a kind of second-guessing the thoughts of others (commonly known as "women's intuition") through a skillful monitoring of the speech of others. The different social needs of men and women, she argues, have led them to sexually differentiated communicative cultures, with each sex learning a different set of skills for manipulating words effectively.

The question that Harding does not ask, however, is, if men and women possess different subcultural rules for speaking, what happens if and when they try to interact with each other? It is here that we turn to the research on interethnic miscommunication.

INTERETHNIC COMMUNICATION

Recent research (Gumperz 1977, 1978a, 1978b, 1979; Gumperz and Tannen 1978) has shown that systematic problems develop in communication when speakers of different speech cultures interact and that these problems are the result of differences in systems of conversational inference and the cues for signalling speech acts and speaker's intent. Conversation is a negotiated activity. It progresses in large part because of shared assumptions about what is going on.

Examining interactions between English-English and Indian-English speakers in Britain (Gumperz 1977, 1978a, 1979; Gumperz et al. 1977), Gumperz found that differences in cues resulted in systematic miscommunication over whether a question was being asked, whether an argument was being made, whether a person was being rude or polite, whether a speaker was relinquishing the floor or interrupting, whether and what a speaker was emphasizing, whether interactants were angry, concerned, or indifferent. Rather than being seen as problems in communication, the frustrating encounters that resulted were usually chalked up as personality clashes or interpreted in the light of racial stereotypes which tended to exacerbate already bad relations.

To take a simple case, Gumperz (1977) reports that Indian women working at a cafeteria, when offering food, used a falling intonation, e.g., "grạvy," which to them indicated a question, something like "do you want gravy?" Both Indian and English workers saw a question as an appropriate polite form, but to English-English speakers a falling intonation signalled not a question, which for them is signalled by a rising intonation such as "grạvy," but a declarative statement, which was both inappropriate and extremely rude.

A major advantage of Gumperz's framework is that it does not assume that problems are the result of bad faith, but rather sees them as the result of individuals wrongly interpreting cues according to their own rules.

THE INTERPRETATION OF MINIMAL RESPONSES

How might Gumperz's approach to the study of conflicting rules for interpreting conversation be applied to the communication between men and women? A simple example will illustrate our basic approach: the case of positive minimal responses. Minimal responses such as nods and comments like "yes" and "mm hmm" are common features of conversational interaction. Our claim, based on our attempts to understand personal experience, is that these minimal responses have significantly different meanings for men and women, leading to occasionally serious miscommunication.

We hypothesize that for women a minimal response of this type means simply something like "I'm

listening to you; please continue," and that for men it has a somewhat stronger meaning such as "I agree with you" or at least "I follow your argument so far." The fact that women use these responses more often than men is in part simply that women are listening more often than men are agreeing.

But our hypothesis explains more than simple differential frequency of usage. Different rules can lead to repeated misunderstandings. Imagine a male speaker who is receiving repeated nods or "mm hmm"s from the woman he is speaking to. She is merely indicating that she is listening, but he thinks she is agreeing with everything he says. Now imagine a female speaker who is receiving only occasional nods and "mm hmm"s from the man she is speaking to. He is indicating that he doesn't always agree; she thinks he isn't always listening.

What is appealing about this short example is that it seems to explain two of the most common complaints in male-female interaction: (1) men who think that women are always agreeing with them and then conclude that it's impossible to tell what a woman really thinks, and (2) women who get upset with men who never seem to be listening. What we think we have here are two separate rules for conversational maintenance which come into conflict and cause massive miscommunication.

SOURCES OF DIFFERENT CULTURES

A probable objection that many people will have to our discussion so far is that American men and women interact with one another far too often to possess different subcultures. What we need to explain is how it is that men and women can come to possess different cultural assumptions about friendly conversation.

Our explanation is really quite simple. It is based on the idea that by the time we have become adults we possess a wide variety of rules for interacting in different situations. Different sets of these rules were learned at different times and in different contexts. We have rules for dealing with people in dominant or subordinate social positions, rules which we first learned as young children interacting with our parents and teachers. We have rules for flirting and other sexual encounters which we probably started learning at or near adolescence. We have rules for dealing with service personnel and bureaucrats, rules we began learning when we first ventured into the public domain. Finally, we have rules for friendly interaction, for carrying on friendly conversation. What is striking about these last rules is that they were learned not from adults but from peers, and that they were learned during precisely that time period, approximately age 5 to 15, when boys and girls interact socially primarily with members of their own sex.

The idea that girls and boys in contemporary America learn different ways of speaking by the age of five or earlier has been postulated by Robin Lakoff (1975), demonstrated by Andrea Meditch (1975), and more fully explored by Adelaide Haas (1979). Haas's research on school-age children shows the early appearance of important male-female differences in patterns of language use, including a male tendency toward direct requests and information giving and a female tendency toward compliance (1979:107).

But the process of acquiring gender-specific speech and behavior patterns by school-age children is more complex than the simple copying of adult "genderlects" by preschoolers. Psychologists Brooks-Gunn and Matthews (1979) have labelled this process the "consolidation of sex roles;" we call it learning of gender-specific "cultures."

Among school-age children, patterns of friendly social interaction are learned not so much from adults as from members of one's peer group, and a major feature of most middle-childhood peer groups is homogeneity; "they are either all-boy or all-girl" (Brooks-Gunn and Matthews 1979). Members of each sex are learning self-consciously to differentiate their behavior from that of the other sex and to exaggerate these differences. The process can be profitably compared to accent divergence in which members of two groups that wish to become clearly distinguished from one another socially acquire increasingly divergent ways of speaking.[1]

Because they learn these gender-specific cultures from their age-mates, children tend to develop stereotypes and extreme versions of adult behavior patterns. For a boy learning to behave in a masculine way, for example, Ruth Hartley (1959, quoted in Brooks-Gunn and Matthews 1979:203) argues that:

> both the information and the practice he gets are distorted. Since his peers have no better sources of information than he has, all they can do is pool the impressions and anxieties they derived from their early training. Thus, the picture they draw is oversimplified and overemphasized. It is a picture drawn in black and white, with little or no modulation and it is incomplete, including a few of the many elements that go to make up the role of the mature male.

What we hope to argue is that boys and girls learn to use language in different ways because of the very different social contexts in which they learn how to carry on friendly conversation. Almost anyone who remembers being a child, has worked with school-age children, or has had an opportunity to observe school-age children can vouch for the fact that groups of girls and groups of boys interact and play in different ways. Systematic observations of children's play have tended to confirm these well-known differences in the ways girls and boys learn to interact with their friends.

In a major study of sex differences in the play of school-age children, for example, sociologist Janet Lever (1976) observed the following six differences between the play of boys and that of girls: (1) girls more often play indoors; (2) boys tend to play in larger groups; (3) boys' play groups tend to include a wider age range of participants; (4) girls play in predominantly male games more often than vice versa; (5) boys more often play competitive games, and (6) girls' games tend to last a shorter period of time than boys' games.

It is by examining these differences in the social organization of play and the accompanying differences in the patterns of social interaction they entail, we argue, that we can learn about the sources of male-female differences in patterns of language use. And it is these same patterns, learned in childhood and carried over into adulthood as the bases for patterns of single-sex friendship relations, we contend, that are potential sources of miscommunication in cross-sex interaction.

THE WORLD OF GIRLS

Our own experience and studies such as Goodwin's (1980b) of black children and Lever's (1976, 1978) of white children suggest a complex of features of girls' play and the speech within it. Girls play in small groups, most often in pairs (Lever 1976; Eder and Hallinan 1978; Brooks-Gunn and Matthews 1979), and their play groups tend to be remarkably homogeneous in terms of age. Their play is often in private or semi-private settings that require participants be invited in. Play is cooperative and activities are usually organized in noncompetitive ways (Lever 1976; Goodwin 1980b). Differentiation between girls is not made in terms of power, but relative closeness. Friendship is seen by girls as involving intimacy, equality, mutual commitment, and loyalty. The idea of "best friend" is central for girls. Relationships between girls are to some extent in opposition to one another, and new relationships are often formed at the expense of old ones. As Brooks-Gunn and Matthews (1979:280) observe, "friendships tend to be exclusive, with a few girls being exceptionally close to one another. Because of this breakups tend to be highly emotional," and Goodwin (1980a:172) notes that "the non-hierarchical framework of the girls provides a fertile ground for rather intricate processes of alliance formation between equals against some other party."

There is a basic contradiction in the structure of girls' social relationships. Friends are supposed to be equal and everyone is supposed to get along, but in fact they don't always. Conflict must be resolved, but a girl cannot assert social power or superiority as an individual to resolve it. Lever (1976), studying fifth-graders, found that girls simply could not deal with quarrels and that when conflict arose they made no attempt to settle it; the group just broke up. What girls learn to do with speech is cope with the contradiction created by an ideology of equality and cooperation and a social reality that includes differences and conflict. As they grow up they learn increasingly subtle ways of balancing the conflicting pressures created by a female social world and a female friendship ideology.

Basically girls learn to do three things with words: (1) to create and maintain relationships of closeness and equality, (2) to criticize others in acceptable ways, and (3) to interpret accurately the speech of other girls.

To a large extent friendships among girls are formed through talk. Girls need to learn to give support, to recognize the speech rights of others, to let others speak, and to acknowledge what they say in order to establish and maintain relationships of equality and closeness. In activities they need to learn to create cooperation through speech. Goodwin (1980a) found that inclusive forms such as "let's," "we gonna," "we could," and "we gotta" predominated in task-oriented activities. Furthermore, she found that most girls in the group she studied made suggestions and that the other girls usually agreed to them. But girls also learn to exchange information and confidences to create and maintain relationships of closeness. The exchange of personal thoughts not only expresses closeness but mutual commitment as well. Brooks-Gunn and Matthews (1979:280) note of adolescent girls:

> much time is spent talking, reflecting, and sharing intimate thought. Loyalty is of central concern to the 12- to 14-year-old girl, presumably because, if innermost secrets are shared, the friend may have "dangerous knowledge" at her disposal.

Friendships are not only formed through particular types of talk, but are ended through talk as well. As Lever (1976:4) says of "best friends," "sharing secrets binds the union together, and 'telling' the secrets to outsiders is symbolic of the 'break-up.'"

Secondly, girls learn to criticize and argue with other girls without seeming overly aggressive, without being perceived as either "bossy" or "mean," terms girls use to evaluate one another's speech and actions. Bossiness, ordering others around, is not legitimate because it denies equality. Goodwin (1980a) points out

that girls talked very negatively about the use of commands to equals, seeing it as appropriate only in role play or in unequal relationships such as those with younger siblings. Girls learn to direct things without seeming bossy, or they learn not to direct. While disputes are common, girls learn to phrase their arguments in terms of group needs and situational requirements rather than personal power or desire (Goodwin 1980a). Meanness is used by girls to describe nonlegitimate acts of exclusion, turning on someone, or withholding friendship. Excluding is a frequent occurrence (Eder and Hallinan 1978), but girls learn over time to discourage or even drive away other girls in ways that don't seem to be just personal whim. Cutting someone is justified in terms of the target's failure to meet group norms and a girl often rejects another using speech that is seemingly supportive on the surface. Conflict and criticism are risky in the world of girls because they can both rebound against the critic and can threaten social relationships. Girls learn to hide the source of criticism; they present it as coming from someone else or make it indirectly through a third party (Goodwin 1980a, 1980b).

Finally, girls must learn to decipher the degree of closeness being offered by other girls, to recognize what is being withheld, and to recognize criticism. Girls who don't actually read these cues run the risk of public censure or ridicule (Goodwin 1980a). Since the currency of closeness is the exchange of secrets which can be used against a girl, she must learn to read the intent and loyalty of others and to do so continuously, given the system of shifting alliances and indirect expressions of conflict. Girls must become increasingly sophisticated in reading the motives of others, in determining when closeness is real, when conventional, and when false, and to respond appropriately. They must learn who to confide in, what to confide, and who not to approach. Given the indirect expression of conflict, girls must learn to read relationships and situations sensitively. Learning to get things right is a fundamental skill for social success, if not just social survival.

THE WORLD OF BOYS

Boys play in larger, more hierarchically organized groups than do girls. Relative status in this ever-fluctuating hierarchy is the main thing that boys learn to manipulate in their interactions with their peers. Nondominant boys are rarely excluded from play but are made to feel the inferiority of their status positions in no uncertain terms. And since hierarchies fluctuate over time and over situation, every boy gets his chance to be victimized and must learn to take it. The social world of boys is one of posturing and counterposturing. In this world, speech is used in three major ways: (1) to assert one's position of dominance, (2) to attract and maintain an audience, and (3) to assert oneself when other speakers have the floor.

The use of speech for the expression of dominance is the most straightforward and probably the best-documented sociolinguistic pattern in boys' peer groups. Even ethological studies of human dominance patterns have made extensive use of various speech behaviors as indices of dominance. Richard Savin-Williams (1976), for example, in his study of dominance patterns among boys in a summer camp uses the following speech interactions as measures of dominance: (1) giving of verbal commands or orders, such as "Get up," "Give it to me," or "You go over there;" (2) name calling and other forms of verbal ridicule, such as "You're a dolt;" (3) verbal threats or boasts of authority, such as "If you don't shut up, I'm gonna come over and bust your teeth in;" (4) refusals to obey orders; and (5) winning a verbal argument as in the sequence: "I was here first"/"Tough," or in more elaborate forms of verbal duelling such as the "dozens."[2]

The same patterns of verbally asserting one's dominance and challenging the dominance claims of others form the central element in Goodwin's (1980a) observations of boys' play in Philadelphia. What is easy to forget in thinking about this use of words as weapons, however, is that the most successful boy in such interaction is not the one who is most aggressive and uses the most power-wielding forms of speech, but the boy who uses these forms most successfully. The simple use of assertiveness and aggression in boys' play is the sign not of a leader but of a bully. The skillful speaker in a boys' group is considerably more likeable and better liked by his peers than is a simple bully. Social success among boys is based on knowing both how and when to use words to express power as well as knowing when not to use them. A successful leader will use speech to put challengers in their place and to remind followers periodically of their nondominant position, but will not browbeat unnecessarily and will therefore gain the respect rather than the fear of less dominant boys.

A second sociolinguistic aspect of friendly interaction between boys is using words to gain and maintain an audience. Storytelling, joke telling, and other narrative performance events are common features of the social interaction of boys. But actual transcripts of such storytelling events collected by Harvey Sacks (Sacks 1974; Jefferson 1978) and Goodwin (1980a), as opposed to stories told directly to interviewers, reveal a suggestive feature of storytelling activities among boys: audience behavior is not overtly supportive. The storyteller is frequently faced with mockery, challenges, and side

comments on his story. A major sociolinguistic skill which a boy must apparently learn in interacting with his peers is to ride out this series of challenges, maintain his audience, and successfully get to the end of his story. In Sacks's account (1974) of some teenage boys involved in the telling of a dirty joke, for example, the narrator is challenged for his taste in jokes (an implication that he doesn't know a dirty joke from a non-dirty one) and for the potential ambiguity of his opening line "Three brothers married three sisters," not, as Sacks seems to imply, because audience members are really confused, but just to hassle the speaker. Through catches,[3] put-downs, the building of suspense, or other interest-grabbing devices, the speaker learns to control his audience. He also learns to continue when he gets no encouragement whatever, pausing slightly at various points for possible audience response but going on if there is nothing but silence.

A final sociolinguistic skill which boys must learn from interacting with other boys is how to act as audience members in the types of storytelling situations just discussed. As audience member as well as storyteller, a boy must learn to assert himself and his opinions. Boys seem to respond to the storytelling of other boys not so much with questions on deeper implications or with minimal-response encouragement as with side comments and challenges. These are not meant primarily to interrupt, to change topic, or to change the direction of the narrative itself, but to assert the identity of the individual audience member.

WOMEN'S SPEECH

The structures and strategies in women's conversation show a marked continuity with the talk of girls. The key logic suggested by Kalčik's (1975) study of women's rap groups, Hirschman's (1973) study of students and Abrahams's (1975) work on black women is that women's conversation is interactional. In friendly talk, women are negotiating and expressing a relationship, one that should be in the form of support and closeness, but which may also involve criticism and distance. Women orient themselves to the person they are talking to and expect such orientation in return. As interaction, conversation requires participation from those involved and back-and-forth movement between participants. Getting the floor is not seen as particularly problematic; that should come about automatically. What is problematic is getting people engaged and keeping them engaged—maintaining the conversation and the interaction.

This conception of conversation leads to a number of characteristic speech strategies and gives a particular dynamic to women's talk. First, women tend to use personal and inclusive pronouns, such as "you" and "we" (Hirschman 1973). Second, women give off and look for signs of engagement such as nods and minimal response (Kalčik 1975; Hirschman 1973). Third, women give more extended signs of interest and attention, such as interjecting comments or questions during a speaker's discourse. These sometimes take the form of interruptions. In fact, both Hirschman (1973) and Kalčik (1975) found that interruptions were extremely common, despite women's concern with politeness and decorum (Kalčik 1975). Kalčik (1975) comments that women often asked permission to speak but were concerned that each speaker be allowed to finish and that all present got a chance to speak. These interruptions were clearly not seen as attempts to grab the floor but as calls for elaboration and development, and were taken as signs of support and interest. Fourth, women at the beginning of their utterances explicitly acknowledge and respond to what has been said by others. Fifth, women attempt to link their utterance to the one preceding it by building on the previous utterance or talking about something parallel or related to it. Kalčik (1975) talks about strategies of tying together, filling in, and serializing as signs of women's desire to create continuity in conversation, and Hirschman (1973) describes elaboration as a key dynamic of women's talk.

While the idiom of much of women's friendly talk is that of support, the elements of criticism, competition, and conflict do occur in it. But as with girls, these tend to take forms that fit the friendship idiom. Abrahams (1975) points out that while "talking smart" is clearly one way women talk to women as well as to men, between women it tends to take a more playful form, to be more indirect and metaphoric in its phrasing and less prolonged than similar talk between men. Smartness, as he points out, puts distance in a relationship (Abrahams 1975). The target of criticism, whether present or not, is made out to be the one violating group norms and values (Abrahams 1975). Overt competitiveness is also disguised. As Kalčik (1975) points out, some stories that build on preceding ones are attempts to cap the original speaker, but they tend to have a form similar to supportive ones. It is the intent more than the form that differs. Intent is a central element in the concept of "bitchiness," one of women's terms for evaluating their talk, and it relates to this contradiction between form and intent, whether putting negative messages in overtly positive forms or acting supportive face to face while not being so elsewhere.

These strategies and the interactional orientation of women's talk give their conversation a particular dynamic. While there is often an unfinished quality to particular utterances (Kalčik 1975), there is a progressive development to the overall conversation. The conversation grows out of the interaction of its participants, rather than being directed by a single individual or series of individuals. In her very stimulating discussion, Kalčik (1975) argues that this is true as well for many of the narratives women tell in conversation. She shows how narrative "kernels" serve as conversational resources for individual women and the group as a whole. How and if a "kernel story" is developed by the narrator and/or audience on a particular occasion is a function of the conversational context from which it emerges (Kalčik 1975:8), and it takes very different forms at different tellings. Not only is the dynamic of women's conversation one of elaboration and continuity, but the idiom of support can give it a distinctive tone as well. Hannerz (1969:96), for example, contrasts the "tone of relaxed sweetness, sometimes bordering on the saccharine," that characterizes approving talk between women, to the heated argument found among men. Kalčik (1975:6) even goes so far as to suggest that there is an "underlying esthetic or organizing principle" of "harmony" being expressed in women's friendly talk.

MEN'S SPEECH

The speaking patterns of men, and of women for that matter, vary greatly from one North American subculture to another. As Gerry Philipsen (1975:13) summarizes it, "talk is not everywhere valued equally; nor is it anywhere valued equally in all social contexts." There are striking cultural variations between subcultures in whether men consider certain modes of speech appropriate for dealing with women, children, authority figures, or strangers; there are differences in performance rules for storytelling and joke telling; there are differences in the context of men's speech; and there are differences in the rules for distinguishing aggressive joking from true aggression.

But more surprising than these differences are the apparent similarities across subcultures in the patterns of friendly interaction between men and the resemblances between these patterns and those observed for boys. Research reports on the speaking patterns of men among urban blacks (Abrahams 1976; Hannerz 1969), rural Newfoundlanders (Faris 1966; Bauman 1972), and urban blue-collar whites (Philipsen 1975; LeMasters 1975) point again and again to the same three features: storytelling, arguing and verbal posturing.

Narratives such as jokes and stories are highly valued, especially when they are well performed for an audience. In Newfoundland, for example, Faris (1966:242) comments that "the reason 'news' is rarely passed between two men meeting in the road—it is simply not to one's advantage to relay information to such a small audience." Loud and aggressive argument is a second common feature of male-male speech. Such arguments, which may include shouting, wagering, name-calling, and verbal threats (Faris 1966:245), are often, as Hannerz (1969:86) describes them, "debates over minor questions of little direct import to anyone," enjoyed for their own sake and not taken as signs of real conflict. Practical jokes, challenges, put-downs, insults, and other forms of verbal aggression are a third feature of men's speech, accepted as normal among friends. LeMasters (1975:140), for example, describes life in a working-class tavern in the Midwest as follows:

> It seems clear that status at the Oasis is related to the ability to "dish it out" in the rapid-fire exchange called "joshing": you have to have a quick retort, and preferably one that puts you "one up" on your opponent. People who can't compete in the game lose status.

Thus challenges rather than statements of support are a typical way for men to respond to the speech of other men.

WHAT IS HAPPENING IN CROSS-SEX CONVERSATION

What we are suggesting is that women and men have different cultural rules for friendly conversation and that these rules come into conflict when women and men attempt to talk to each other as friends and equals in casual conversation. We can think of at least five areas, in addition to that of minimal responses already discussed, in which men and women probably possess different conversational rules, so that miscommunication is likely to occur in cross-sex interaction.

1. There are two interpretations of the meaning of questions. Women seem to see questions as a part of conversational maintenance, while men seem to view them primarily as requests for information.

2. There are two conventions for beginning an utterance and linking it to the preceding utterance. Women's rules seem to call for an explicit acknowledgment of what has been said and making a connection to it. Men seem to have no such rule and in fact some male strategies call for ignoring the preceding comments.

3. There are different interpretations of displays of verbal aggressiveness. Women seem to interpret overt aggressiveness as personally directed,

negative, and disruptive. Men seem to view it as one conventional organizing structure for conversational flow.

4. There are two understandings of topic flow and topic shift. The literature on storytelling in particular seems to indicate that men operate with a system in which topic is fairly narrowly defined and adhered to until finished and in which shifts between topics are abrupt, while women have a system in which topic is developed progressively and shifts gradually. These two systems imply very different rules for and interpretations of side comments, with major potential for miscommunication.

5. There appear to be two different attitudes towards problem sharing and advice giving. Women tend to discuss problems with one another, sharing experiences and offering reassurances. Men, in contrast, tend to hear women, and other men, who present them with problems as making explicit requests for solutions. They respond by giving advice, by acting as experts, lecturing to their audiences.[4]

CONCLUSIONS

Our purpose in this paper has been to present a framework for thinking about and tying together a number of strands in the analysis of differences between male and female conversational styles. We hope to prove the intellectual value of this framework by demonstrating its ability to do two things: to serve as a model both of and for sociolinguistic research.

As a model *of* past research findings, the power of our approach lies in its ability to suggest new explanations of previous findings on cross-sex communication while linking these findings to a wide range of other fields, including the study of language acquisition, of play, of friendship, of storytelling, of cross-cultural miscommunication, and of discourse analysis. Differences in the social interaction patterns of boys and girls appear to be widely known but rarely utilized in examinations of sociolinguistic acquisition or in explanations of observed gender differences in patterns of adult speech. Our proposed framework should serve to link together these and other known facts in new ways.

As a model *for* future research, we hope our framework will be even more promising. It suggests to us a number of potential research problems which remain to be investigated. Sociolinguistic studies of school-age children, especially studies of the use of speech in informal peer interaction, appear to be much rarer than studies of young children, although such studies may be of greater relevance for the understanding of adult patterns, particularly those related to gender. Our framework also suggests the need for many more studies of single-sex conversations among adults, trying to make more explicit some of the differences in conversational rules suggested by present research. Finally, the argument we have been making suggests a number of specific problems that appear to be highly promising lines for future research:

1. A study of the sociolinguistic socialization of "tomboys" to see how they combine male and female patterns of speech and interaction;

2. An examination of the conversational patterns of lesbians and gay men to see how these relate to the sex-related patterns of the dominant culture;

3. An examination of the conversational patterns of the elderly to see to what extent speech differences persist after power differences have become insignificant;

4. A study of children's cultural concepts for talking about speech and the ways these shape the acquisition of speech styles (for example, how does the concept of "bossiness" define a form of behavior which little girls must learn to recognize, then censure, and finally avoid?);

5. An examination of "assertiveness training" programs for women to see whether they are really teaching women the speaking skills that politically skillful men learn in boyhood or are merely teaching women how to act like bossy little girls or bullying little boys and not feel guilty about it.

We conclude this paper by reemphasizing three of the major ways in which we feel that an anthropological perspective on culture and social organization can prove useful for further research on differences between men's and women's speech.

First, an anthropological approach to culture and cultural rules forces us to reexamine the way we interpret what is going on in conversations. The rules for interpreting conversations are, after all, culturally determined. There may be more than one way of understanding what is happening in a particular conversation and we must be careful about the rules we use for interpreting cross-sex conversations, in which the two participants may not fully share their rules of conversational inference.

Second, a concern with the relation between cultural rules and their social contexts leads us to think seriously about differences in different kinds of talk,

ways of categorizing interactional situations, and ways in which conversational patterns may function as strategies for dealing with specific aspects of one's social world. Different types of interaction lead to different ways of speaking. The rules for friendly conversation between equals are different from those for service encounters, for flirting, for teaching, or for polite formal interaction. And even within the apparently uniform domain of friendly interaction, we argue that there are systematic differences between men and women in the way friendship is defined and thus in the conversational strategies that result.

Third and finally, our analysis suggests a different way of thinking about the connection between the gender-related behavior of children and that of adults. Most discussions of sex-role socialization have been based on the premise that gender differences are greatest for adults and that these adult differences are learned gradually throughout childhood. Our analysis, on the other hand, would suggest that at least some aspects of behavior are most strongly gender-differentiated during childhood and that adult patterns of friendly interaction, for example, involve learning to overcome at least partially some of the gender-specific cultural patterns typical of childhood.

NOTES

1. The analogy between the sociolinguistic processes of dialect divergence and genderlect divergence was pointed out to us by Ron Macaulay.

2. In the strict sense of the term, "dozens" refers to a culturally specific form of stylized argument through the exchange of insults that has been extensively documented by a variety of students of American black culture and is most frequently practiced by boys in their teens and pre-teens. Recently folklorist Simon Bronner (1978) has made a convincing case for the existence of a highly similar but independently derived form of insult exchange known as "ranking," "mocks," or "cutting" among white American adolescents. What we find striking and worthy of note is the tendency for both black and white versions of the dozens to be practiced primarily by boys.

3. "Catches" are a form of verbal play in which the main speaker ends up tricking a member of his or her audience into a vulnerable or ridiculous position. In an article on the folklore of black children in South Philadelphia, Roger Abrahams (1963) distinguishes between catches which are purely verbal and tricks in which the second player is forced into a position of being not only verbally but also physically abused, as in the following example of a catch which is also a trick:

   A. Adam and Eve and Pinch-Me-Tight
      Went up the hill to spend the night.

Adam and Eve came down the hill.
Who was left?

B: Pinch-Me-Tight

[A pinches B]

What is significant about both catches and tricks is that they allow for the expression of playful aggression and that they produce a temporary hierarchical relation between a winner and loser, but invite the loser to attempt to get revenge by responding with a counter-trick.

4. We thank Kitty Julien for first pointing out to us the tendency of male friends to give advice to women who are not necessarily seeking it and Niyi Akinnaso for pointing out that the sex difference among Yoruba speakers in Nigeria in the way people respond verbally to the problems of others is similar to that among English speakers in the U.S.

REFERENCES

Abrahams, R. D. 1963. The "Catch" in negro Philadelphia. *Keystone Folklore Quarterly* 8(3): 107–116.

Abrahams, R. D. 1975. Negotiating respect: Patterns of presentation among black women. In *Women in Folklore*, ed. C. R. Farrat, Austin: University of Texas Press.

Abrahams, R. D. 1976. *Talking Black*. Rowley, Mass.: Newbury House.

Bauman, R. 1972. The La Have Island General Store: Sociability and verbal art in a Nova Scotia community. *Journal of American Folklore* 85: 330–343.

Bronner, S. J. 1978. A Re-examining of white dozens. *Western Folklore* 37(2): 118–128.

Brooks-Gunn, J. and Matthews, W. S. 1979. *He and She: How Children Develop Their Sex-Role Identity*. Englewood Cliffs, NJ: Prentice Hall.

Eder, D. and Hallinan, M. T. 1978. Sex differences in children's friendships. *American Sociological Review* 43: 237–250.

Faris, J. C. 1966. The dynamics of verbal exchange: A Newfoundland example. *Anthropologica* (Ottawa) 8(2): 235–248.

Fishman, P. M. 1978. Interaction: The work women do. *Social Problems* 25(4): 397–406.

Goodwin, M. 1978. Conversational practices in a peer group of urban black children. Doctoral dissertation. University of Pennsylvania, Philadelphia.

Goodwin, M. 1980a. Directive-response speech sequences in girls' and boys' task activities. In *Women and Language in Literature and Society*, eds. S. McConnell-Ginet, R. Borker, and N. Furman. New York: Praeger.

Goodwin, M. 1980b. He-said-she-said: Formal cultural procedures for the construction of a gossip dispute activity. *American Ethnologist* 7(4): 674–695.

Gumperz, J. J. 1977. Sociocultural knowledge in conversational inference. In *Linguistics and Anthropology*, ed. M. Saville-Troike. Washington, DC: Georgetown University Press (Georgetown University Round Table on Languages and Linguistics), 1977.

Gumperz, J. J. 1978a. The conversational analysis of interethnic communication. In *Interethnic Communication*, ed. E. Lamar Ross. Athens, Ga.: University of Georgia Press.

Gumperz, J. J. 1978b. Dialect and conversational inference in urban communication. *Language in Society* 7(3): 393–409.

Gumperz, J. J. 1979. The sociolinguistic basis of speech act theory. In *Speech Act Ten Years After*, eds. J. Boyd and S. Fertara. Milan: Versus.

Gumperz, J. J. 1982. *Discourse Strategies*. Cambridge: Cambridge University Press.

Gumperz, J. J., Agrawal, A., and Aulakh, G. 1977. Prosody, paralinguistics and contextualization in Indian English. Language Behavior Research Laboratory, typescript. University of California, Berkeley.

Gumperz, J. J. and Tannen, D. 1978. Individual and social differences in language use. In *Individual Differences in Language Ability and Language Behavior*, eds. W. Wang and C. Fillmore. New York: Academic Press.

Haas, A. 1979. The acquisition of genederlect. In Language, Sex and Gender: Does La Différence Make a Difference? eds. J. Orasnu, M. Slater, and L. Adler. *Annals of the New York Academy of Sciences* 327: 101–113.

Hannerz, U. 1969. *Soulside*. New York: Columbia University Press.

Harding, S. 1975. Women and words in a Spanish village. In *Towards an Anthropology of Women*, ed. R. Reiter. New York: Monthly Review Press.

Hirschman, L. 1973. Female–male differences in conversational interaction. Paper presented at Linguistic Society of America, San Diego.

Jefferson, G. 1978. Sequential aspects of storytelling in conversation. In *Studies in the Organization of Conversation Interaction*, ed. J. Schenker. New York: Academic Press.

Kalčik, S. 1975. ". . . Like Anne's gynecologist or the time I was almost raped": Personal narratives in women's rap groups. In *Women and Folklore*, ed. C. R. Farrar. Austin: University of Texas Press.

Lakoff, R. 1975. *Language and Women's Place*. New York: Harper and Row.

LeMasters, E. E. 1975. *Blue Collar Aristocrats: Life-Styles at a Working-Class Tavern*. Madison: University of Wisconsin Press.

Lever, J. 1976. Sex differences in the games children play. *Social Problems* 23: 478–483.

Lever, J. 1978. Sex differences in the complexity of children's play and games. *American Sociological Review* 43: 471–483.

Meditch, A. 1975. The development of sex-specific speech patterns in young children. *Anthropological Linguistics* 17: 421–433.

Philipsen, G. 1975. Speaking "like a man" in Teamsterville: Cultural patterns of role enactment in an urban neighborhood. *Quarterly Journal of Speech* 61: 13–22.

Sacks, H. 1974. An analysis of the course of a joke's telling in conversation. In *Explorations in the Ethnography of Speaking*, eds. R. Bauman and J. Scherzer. Cambridge: Cambridge University Press.

Savin-Williams, R. C. 1976. The ethological study of dominance formation and maintenance in a group of human adolescents. *Child Development* 47: 972–979.

Soskin, W. F. and John, V. P. 1963. The study of spontaneous talk. In *The Stream of Behavior,* ed. R. G. Barker. New York: Appleton-Century-Croft.

Strodbeck, F. L. and Mann, R. D. 1956. Sex role differentiation in jury deliberations. *Sociometry* 19: 3–11.

West, C. 1979. Against our will: Male interruptions of females in cross-sex conversation. In *Language, Sex and Gender: Does La Différence Make a Difference?* eds. J. Oranzanu, M. Slater and L. Adler. *Annals of the New York Academy of Sciences* 327: 81–100.

West, C. and Zimmerman, D. H. 1977. Women's place in everyday talk: Reflections on parent–child interaction. *Social Problems* 24(5): 521–529.

Zimmerman, D. H. and West, C. 1975. Sex roles, interruptions, and silences in conversation. In *Language and Sex: Differences and Dominance,* eds. B. Thorne and N. Henley. Rowley, Mass.: Newbury House.

PART IV

Cultural Anthropology

Cultural anthropology is concerned with the description and analysis of people's lives and traditions. In the past, cultural anthropologists almost always did research in far-off "exotic" societies, but today we have expanded our research interests to include our own society. Cultural anthropology can add much to both the basic and the applied scientific understanding of human behaviors and beliefs. The study and interpretation of other societies—of their traditions, history, and view of the world—is inherently interesting and important because it documents the diversity of human lifestyles. The anthropological approach to understanding other societies also has practical value for addressing contemporary human problems and needs.

The concept of *culture* is central to anthropology. It refers to the patterns of economy, social organization, and belief that are learned and shared by members of a social group. Culture is traditional knowledge that is passed down from one generation to the next. Although generally stable over time, culture is flexible and fluid, changing through borrowing or invention. The influential American anthropologist Franz Boas championed the concept of culture for understanding human diversity; culture, Boas argued, is distinct from biological race or language. Anthropologists believe that all cultural lifestyles have intrinsic value and validity. Other societies deserve to be studied and understood without being prejudged using our own narrow (and sometimes intolerant) beliefs and values. This universal tendency to prejudge based on the supposed superiority of one's own group, called *ethnocentrism*, is something everyone should avoid.

Culture is the crowning achievement of human evolution. To understand ourselves is to appreciate cultural diversity. Dependence on culture as our primary mechanism of survival sets humans apart from other members of the animal kingdom. This dependence is responsible for the tremendous evolutionary success of our species, which has grown in population (sometimes to the point of overpopulation) and can inhabit nearly every niche on the planet.

The paradox of culture is that as we humans learn to accept our own cultural beliefs and values, we unconsciously learn to reject those of other peoples. At birth, we are capable of absorbing any culture and language. We are predisposed to cultural learning, but we are not programmed to adopt a particular culture. As we grow, our parents, our schools, and our society teach us what is right and wrong, good and evil, acceptable and unacceptable. At the subconscious level, we learn the symbolic meanings of behavior and through them interpret the meanings of actions. Beliefs, values, and symbols must be understood within the context of a particular culture. This is the principle of *cultural relativity*. At the same time, culture supplies us with the cognitive models or tools—software programs, if you will—that allow us to perceive or construct a particular version of reality. Culture permeates our thinking and our expectations; this is the principle of *cultural construction*.

The anthropological approach to the study of human behavior and belief has two essential characteristics: a holistic approach and a comparative framework. A *holistic approach* means that anthropologists see a particular part of culture—for example, politics, the economy, or religion—in relation to the larger social system. Individuals are viewed not in isolation but as part of an intricate web of social relationships. Although an anthropological study may have a particular focus, the holistic approach means that the broader cultural context is always considered important because the different parts of a cultural system are interrelated. When, for example, the economy or the technology changes, other aspects of the culture will change as well.

A *comparative framework* means that explanations or generalizations are achieved through cross-cultural research. Questions about humanity cannot be based on information from a single society or a single type of society—such as the industrial societies of the United States and Europe. Such a limited framework is simply too narrow for understanding the big picture that basic anthropological research seeks. By studying others, we can better understand ourselves. If other cultures are a mirror in which we see ourselves, then anthropology is a mirror for humankind.

The broad generalizations about culture and society that we have been talking about are based on detailed knowledge of the world's cultures. To gain this knowledge, anthropologists go to the people. Often accompanied by spouses and children, we pack our bags and travel to far-off lands—to the highlands of New Guinea, the frozen arctic, the savannas of Africa, or the jungles of South America. Increasingly, anthropologists are bringing their research methods and comparative, holistic perspective into the cities and suburbs of

America, the American schoolroom, and the corporate jungle. This research adventure has become the hallmark of cultural anthropology.

The research methods used by the cultural anthropologist are distinctive because they depend, to a large extent, on the firsthand experiences and interpretations of the field researcher. Cultural anthropologists conduct research in natural settings rather than in laboratories or over the telephone. This method for studying another society is often called *participant observation, ethnography,* or *qualitative methods*. The goal of describing, understanding, and explaining another culture is a large task. It is most often accomplished by living in the society for an extended period, by talking with people, and, as much as possible, by experiencing their lives.

The fieldwork experience usually involves a kind of culture shock in which the researcher questions his or her own assumptions about the world. In this way, fieldwork is often a rewarding period of personal growth. In their work, anthropologists expect to find that other people's behavior, even when it seems bizarre when seen from the outside, makes sense when viewed from the people's own point of view. That is why anthropological research often means letting people speak for themselves. While doing research, the anthropologist often thinks of herself or himself as a child—as being ignorant or uninformed and needing to be taught by the people being studied. This approach often involves in-depth interviewing with a few key informants and then interpreting (and writing about) that other culture for the researcher's own society. The ethnographic method, pioneered and developed in anthropology, is now being used in a range of applied areas, including marketing, management research, and school evaluation.

The applications of cultural anthropology are diverse. Internationally, anthropologists are involved in programs of technical assistance and economic aid to Third World nations. These programs address needs in such areas as agriculture and rural development; health, nutrition, and family planning; education; housing and community organizing; transportation and communication; and energy. Anthropologists do many of the same things domestically as well. They evaluate public education, study agricultural extension programs, administer projects, analyze policy (such as U.S. refugee resettlement programs), and research crime and crime prevention, for example.

In the private sector, cultural anthropologists can add a fresh perspective to market research (see Selection 39). Moreover they analyze office and industrial organization and culture and create language and cultural training workshops for businesspeople and others who are going overseas. These workshops reduce the likelihood of cross-cultural misunderstanding and the problems of culture shock for the employee and his or her family.

Applied anthropological work can be divided into three categories. In the first group, applied research and basic research look very much alike, except that the goal of applied research is more directly linked with a particular problem or need. For example, in Selection 43, Aaron Podolefsky studies the causes of the re-emergence of tribal warfare in New Guinea. Such a study provides planners and policymakers with important insights for understanding the problem. This knowledge can then be used in the design and implementation of programs that may help bring an end to warfare in the region.

In the second category, anthropologists may work as researchers for a government agency, a corporation, or an interest group on a specific task defined by the client.

In the third category, anthropologists work as consultants to business and industry or to government agencies that need in-depth cultural knowledge to solve or prevent a problem. Anthropologists often act as cultural brokers, mediating and translating between groups who are miscommunicating not because of their words but because of cultural meanings.

A great deal of anthropological work remains to be done, although this seems to be a well-kept secret. People have a far easier time focusing on the individual as the level of analysis. When divorce, drug abuse, or suicide affects small numbers of people, we may look to the individual and to psychology for answers. When divorce rates climb to 50 percent of all marriages and the suicide rate increases tenfold, however, we must look beyond the individual to forces that affect society at large. Because we are so immersed in our own culture, we have difficulty seeing it as a powerful force that guides—even controls—our behavior.

25

Body Ritual among the Nacirema

Horace Miner

Generations of anthropologists have traveled the globe, reaching to the far corners of the five continents to discover and describe the many ways of humankind. Anthropologists have gathered a diverse collection of exotic customs, from the mundane to the bizarre. Understanding and appreciating other societies requires us to be culturally relative. But people tend to judge others by their own cultural values in a way that is *ethnocentric.* This is because people take their cultural beliefs and behaviors for granted; they seem so natural that they are seldom questioned. Among the most interesting social customs on record are the rituals of the Nacirema. By viewing Nacirema behaviors as *rituals,* we gain insight into their culture and into the meaning of the concept of *culture.* We also gain insight into the problem of ethnocentrism.

Ritual is a cultural phenomenon. Ritual can be found in all societies. It can be defined as a set of acts that follow a sequence established by tradition.

Throughout the world, ritual reflects the fundamental cultural beliefs and values of a society by giving order to important activities and particular life crises like death and birth. Every day, however, mundane rituals are performed unconsciously. In fact, most Nacirema people do these things without being aware of their underlying symbolic meanings. Pay particular attention to the quotation at the end of the selection.

As you read this selection, ask yourself the following questions:

- How do the Nacirema feel about the human body?

- Do you think that the charms and magical potions used by the Nacirema really work?

- Can you list those aspects of social life in which magic plays an important role?

- What is your opinion of the importance of body ritual, and if you went to live among the Nacirema, would you tell them of your opinion?

- Viewed from the perspective of living among the Nacirema, their behaviors sometimes appear bizarre. Do you think the Nacirema themselves feel this way?

The following terms discussed in this selection are included in the Glossary at the back of the book:

clan   ethnocentrism

culture   ritual

The anthropologist has become so familiar with the diversity of ways in which different peoples behave in similar situations that he is not apt to be surprised by even the most exotic customs. In fact, if all of the logically possible combinations of behavior have not been found somewhere in the world, he is apt to suspect that they must be present in some yet undescribed tribe. This point has, in fact, been expressed with respect to clan organization by Murdock (1949:71). In this light, the magical beliefs and practices of the Nacirema present such unusual aspects that it seems desirable to describe them as an example of the extremes to which human behavior can go.

Professor Linton first brought the ritual of the Nacirema to the attention of anthropologists twenty years ago (1936:326), but the culture of this people is still very poorly understood. They are a North American group living in the territory between the Canadian Cree, the Yaqui and Tarahumare of Mexico, and the Carib and Arawak of the Antilles. Little is known of their origin, although tradition states that they came from the east. According to Nacirema mythology, their nation was originated by a culture hero, Notgnihsaw, who is otherwise known for two great feats of strength—the throwing of a piece of wampum across the river Pa-To-Mac and the chopping down of a cherry tree in which the Spirit of Truth resided.

From Anthropologist 58, no. 3 (1956) Courtesy of the American Anthropological Association.

Nacirema culture is characterized by a highly developed market economy which has evolved in a rich natural habitat. While much of the people's time is devoted to economic pursuits, a large part of the fruits of these labors and a considerable portion of the day are spent in ritual activity. The focus of this activity is the human body, the appearance and health of which loom as a dominant concern in the ethos of the people. While such a concern is certainly not unusual, its ceremonial aspects and associated philosophy are unique.

The fundamental belief underlying the whole system appears to be that the human body is ugly and that its natural tendency is to debility and disease. Incarcerated in such a body, man's only hope is to avert these characteristics through the use of the powerful influences of ritual and ceremony. Every household has one or more shrines devoted to this purpose. The more powerful individuals in the society have several shrines in their houses and, in fact, the opulence of a house is often referred to in terms of the number of such ritual centers it possesses. Most houses are of wattle and daub construction, but the shrine rooms of the more wealthy are walled with stone. Poorer families imitate the rich by applying pottery plaques to their shrine walls.

While each family has at least one such shrine, the rituals associated with it are not family ceremonies but are private and secret. The rites are normally only discussed with children, and then only during the period when they are being initiated into these mysteries. I was able, however, to establish sufficient rapport with the natives to examine these shrines and to have the rituals described to me.

The focal point of the shrine is a box or chest which is built into the wall. In this chest are kept the many charms and magical potions without which no native believes he could live. These preparations are secured from a variety of specialized practitioners. The most powerful of these are the medicine men, whose assistance must be rewarded with substantial gifts. However, the medicine men do not provide the curative potions for their clients, but decide what the ingredients should be and then write them down in an ancient and secret language. This writing is understood only by the medicine men and by the herbalists who, for another gift, provide the required charm.

The author of this article used the term *man* to refer to humanity in general. This term is not used by modern anthropologists because, to many people, it reflects an unconscious sexist bias in language and rhetoric. At the time that this article was written, however, the generalized *man* was a common convention in writing. In the interest of historical accuracy we have not changed the wording in this article, but students should be aware that nonsexist terms (*humans, people, Homo sapiens,* and so on) are preferred.—The Editors.

The charm is not disposed of after it has served its purpose, but is placed in the charm-box of the household shrine. As these magical materials are specific for certain ills, and the real or imagined maladies of the people are many, the charm-box is usually full to overflowing. The magical packets are so numerous that people forget what their purposes were and fear to use them again. While the natives are very vague on this point, we can only assume that the idea in retaining all the old magical materials is that their presence in the charm-box, before which the body rituals are conducted, will in some way protect the worshipper.

Beneath the charm-box is a small font. Each day every member of the family, in succession, enters the shrine room, bows his head before the charm-box, mingles different sorts of holy water in the font, and proceeds with a brief rite of ablution. The holy waters are secured from the Water Temple of the community, where the priests conduct elaborate ceremonies to make the liquid ritually pure.

In the hierarchy of magical practitioners, and below the medicine men in prestige, are specialists whose designation is best translated "holy-mouth-men." The Nacirema have an almost pathological horror of and fascination with the mouth, the condition of which is believed to have a supernatural influence on all social relationships. Were it not for the rituals of the mouth, they believe that their teeth would fall out, their gums bleed, their jaws shrink, their friends desert them, and their lovers reject them. They also believe that a strong relationship exists between oral and moral characteristics. For example, there is a ritual ablution of the mouth for children which is supposed to improve their moral fiber.

The daily body ritual performed by everyone includes a mouth-rite. Despite the fact that these people are so punctilious about care of the mouth, this rite involves a practice which strikes the uninitiated stranger as revolting. It was reported to me that the ritual consists of inserting a small bundle of hog hairs into the mouth, along with certain magical powders, and then moving the bundle in a highly formalized series of gestures.

In addition to the private mouth-rite, the people seek out a holy-mouth-man once or twice a year. These practitioners have an impressive set of paraphernalia, consisting of a variety of augers, awls, probes, and prods. The use of these objects in the exorcism of the evils of the mouth involves almost unbelievable ritual torture of the client. The holy-mouth-man opens the client's mouth, and using the above mentioned tools, enlarges any holes which decay may have created in the teeth. Magical materials are put into these holes. If there are no naturally occurring holes in the teeth, large sections of one or more teeth are gouged out so that the supernatural substance can be applied. In the client's view, the purpose of these ministrations is to arrest decay and to draw friends. The extremely sacred and traditional character of the rite is evident in the fact that the natives return to the holy-mouth-men year after year, despite the fact that their teeth continue to decay.

It is to be hoped that, when a thorough study of the Nacirema is made, there will be careful inquiry into the personality structure of these people. One has to but watch the gleam in the eye of a holy-mouth-man as he jabs an awl into an exposed nerve, to suspect that a certain amount of sadism is involved. If this can be established, a very interesting pattern emerges, for most of the population shows definite masochistic tendencies. It was to these that Professor Linton referred in discussing a distinctive part of the daily body ritual which is performed only by men. This part of the rite involves scraping and lacerating the surface of the face with a sharp instrument. Special women's rites are performed only four times during each lunar month, but what they lack in frequency is made up in barbarity. As part of this ceremony, women bake their heads in small ovens for about an hour. The theoretically interesting point is that what seems to be a preponderantly masochistic people have developed sadistic specialists.

The medicine men have an imposing temple, or *latipso*, in every community of any size. The more elaborate ceremonies required to treat very sick patients can only be performed at this temple. These ceremonies involve not only the thaumaturge but a permanent group of vestal maidens who move sedately about the temple chambers in distinctive costume and headdress.

The *latipso* ceremonies are so harsh that it is phenomenal that a fair proportion of the really sick natives who enter the temple ever recover. Small children whose indoctrination is still incomplete have been known to resist attempts to take them to the temple because "that is where you go to die." Despite this fact, sick adults are not only willing but eager to undergo the protracted ritual purification, if they can afford to do so. No matter how ill the supplicant or how grave the emergency, the guardians of many temples will not admit a client if he cannot give a rich gift to the custodian. Even after one has gained admission and survived the ceremonies, the guardians will not permit the neophyte to leave until he makes still another gift.

The supplicant entering the temple is first stripped of all his or her clothes. In everyday life the Nacirema avoids exposure of his body and its natural functions. Bathing and excretory acts are performed only in the secrecy of the household shrine, where they are ritualized as part of the body-rites. Psychological shock results from the fact that body secrecy is suddenly lost upon entry into the *latipso*. A man, whose own wife has

never seen him in an excretory act, suddenly finds himself naked and assisted by a vestal maiden while he performs his natural functions into a sacred vessel. This sort of ceremonial treatment is necessitated by the fact that the excreta are used by a diviner to ascertain the course and nature of the client's sickness. Female clients, on the other hand, find their naked bodies are subjected to the scrutiny, manipulation and prodding of the medicine men.

Few supplicants in the temple are well enough to do anything but lie on their hard beds. The daily ceremonies, like the rites of the holy-mouth-men, involve discomfort and torture. With ritual precision, the vestals awaken their miserable charges each dawn and roll them about on their beds of pain while performing ablutions, in the formal movements of which the maidens are highly trained. At other times they insert magic wands in the supplicant's mouth or force him to eat substances which are supposed to be healing. From time to time the medicine men come to their clients and jab magically treated needles into their flesh. The fact that these temple ceremonies may not cure, and may even kill the neophyte, in no way decreases the people's faith in the medicine men.

There remains one other kind of practitioner, known as a "listener." This witch-doctor has the power to exorcise the devils that lodge in the heads of people who have been bewitched. The Nacirema believe that parents bewitch their own children. Mothers are particularly suspected of putting a curse on children while teaching them the secret body rituals. The countermagic of the witch-doctor is unusual in its lack of ritual. The patient simply tells the "listener" all his troubles and fears, beginning with the earliest difficulties he can remember. The memory displayed by the Nacirema in these exorcism sessions is truly remarkable. It is not uncommon for the patient to bemoan the rejection he felt upon being weaned as a babe, and a few individuals even see their troubles going back to the traumatic effects of their own birth.

In conclusion, mention must be made of certain practices which have their base in native esthetics but which depend upon the pervasive aversion to the natural body and its functions. There are ritual fasts to make fat people thin and ceremonial feasts to make thin people fat. Still other rites are used to make women's breasts larger if they are small, and smaller if they are large. General dissatisfaction with breast shape is symbolized in the fact that the ideal form is virtually outside the range of human variation. A few women afflicted with almost inhuman hypermammary development are so idolized that they make a handsome living by simply going from village to village and permitting the natives to stare at them for a fee.

Reference has already been made to the fact that excretory functions are ritualized, routinized, and relegated to secrecy. Natural reproductive functions are similarly distorted. Intercourse is taboo as a topic and scheduled as an act. Efforts are made to avoid pregnancy by the use of magical materials or by limiting intercourse to certain phases of the moon. Conception is actually very infrequent. When pregnant, women dress so as to hide their condition. Parturition takes place in secret, without friends or relatives to assist, and the majority of women do not nurse their infants.

Our review of the ritual life of the Nacirema has certainly shown them to be a magic-ridden people. It is hard to understand how they have managed to exist so long under the burdens which they have imposed upon themselves. But even such exotic customs as these take on real meaning when they are viewed with the insight provided by Malinowski when he wrote (1948:70):

> Looking from far and above, from our high places of safety in the developed civilization, it is easy to see all the crudity and irrelevance of magic. But without its power and guidance early man could not have mastered his practical difficulties as he has done, nor could man have advanced to the higher stages of civilization.

REFERENCES

Linton, Ralph. 1936. *The Study of Man.* New York: D. Appleton-Century Co.

Malinowski, Bronislaw. 1948. *Magic, Science, and Religion.* Glencoe, IL: The Free Press.

Murdock, George P. 1949. *Social Structure.* New York: The Macmillan Co.

Diamond, Jared. "Race Without Color." *Discover Maga-* (Nov. 1994):82–89. Reprinted with permission of the author.

But we now ignore that eyes tell us around the Earth,

26

Race without Color

Jared Diamond

Looking at the title of this selection, you should ask yourself two questions. First, what is a reading about race doing in a cultural anthropology book? After all, it would seem that race is obviously a biological question. Second, what could the author possibly mean by "race without color?" Doesn't that sound like an oxymoron?

An important aspect of anthropological thinking is examining ideas, beliefs, and values within their own cultural context. Our own cultural ideas and concepts, including scientific ones, are grist for the anthropological mill because they are best understood within a larger cultural framework. Sometimes cultural anthropologists focus on a single cultural concept and take it apart, demonstrating its historical roots and its relation to other social beliefs. In postmodern parlance, this kind of intensive analysis can be called "deconstructing" a concept.

In this selection, a well-known natural scientist "deconstructs" the biological concept of race. Although the term *race* seems to have some use in the description of population variation in birds and in creating a taxonomy, the concept doesn't work very well for understanding human variation. In fact, from a biological standpoint, the concept of race based on skin color is scientifically useless. As the reading demonstrates, there are a lot of different ways to categorize human biological diversity, but these variations are independent from one another so that there is more variation within racial categories than between them. By deconstructing race, we see that it is a cultural category, not a biological one.

On the other hand, race is indeed an important historical and political concept—as a cultural construction that functions as a folk-biological rationalization for enforcing social inequalities. We decided to include this reading within this cultural anthropology book to emphasize the fact that race is a cultural invention. Race is not useful for understanding human biological diversity; it is essentially meaningless, like an oxymoron.

As you read this selection, ask yourself the following questions:

- Why does skin color seem to be such an obvious and commonsensical way to make distinctions among people?
- How might it be acceptable to use the concept of race for talking about birds, but not humans?
- What does it mean that taxonomists are "lumpers" and "splitters?"
- How is our understanding of most biological variations—like resistance to malaria or adults' ability to digest milk—not aided by the concept of race?
- If racial classifications are cultural constructions, what does the author think is the purpose of these arbitrary classifications?

The following terms discussed in this selection are included in the Glossary at the back of the book:

lactose intolerance	sickle-cell anemia
race	species

Basing race on body chemistry makes no more sense than basing race on appearance—but at least you get to move the membership around.

Science often violates simple common sense. Our [eyes tell] us that the Earth is flat, that the sun revolves [around us] and that we humans are not animals. [But we put aside the] evidence of our senses. We have learned that our planet is in fact round and revolves around the sun, and that humans are slightly modified chimpanzees. The reality of human races is another commonsense "truth" destined to follow the flat Earth into oblivion. The commonsense view of races goes somewhat as follows. All native Swedes differ from all native Nigerians in appearance: there is no Swede whom you would mistake for a Nigerian, and vice versa. Swedes have lighter skin than Nigerians do. They also generally have blond or light brown hair, while Nigerians have very dark hair. Nigerians usually have more tightly coiled hair than Swedes do, dark eyes as opposed to eyes that are blue or gray, and fuller lips and broader noses.

In addition, other Europeans look much more like Swedes than like Nigerians, while other peoples of sub-Saharan Africa—except perhaps the Khoisan peoples of southern Africa—look much more like Nigerians than like Swedes. Yes, skin color does get darker in Europe toward the Mediterranean, but it is still lighter than the skin of sub-Saharan Africans. In Europe, very dark or curly hair becomes more common outside Scandinavia, but European hair is still not as tightly coiled as in Africa. Since it's easy then to distinguish almost any native European from any native sub-Saharan African, we recognize Europeans and sub-Saharan Africans as distinct races, which we name for their skin colors: whites and blacks, respectively.

What could be more objective?

As it turns out, this seemingly unassailable reasoning is not objective. There are many different, equally valid procedures for defining races, and those different procedures yield very different classifications. One such procedure would group Italians and Greeks with most African blacks. It would classify Xhosas—the South African "black" group to which President Nelson Mandela belongs—with Swedes rather than Nigerians. Another equally valid procedure would place Swedes with Fulani (a Nigerian "black" group) and not with Italians who would again be grouped with most other African blacks. Still another procedure would keep Swedes and Italians separate from all African blacks but would throw the Swedes and Italians into the same race as New Guineans and American Indians. Faced with such differing classifications, many anthropologists today conclude that one cannot recognize any human races at all.

If we were just arguing about races of nonhuman animals, essentially the same uncertainties of classification would arise. But the debates would remain polite and would never attract attention outside the halls of academia. Classification of humans is different "only" in that it shapes our views of other peoples, fosters our subconscious differentiation between "us" and "them," and is invoked to justify political and socioeconomic discrimination. On this basis, many anthropologists therefore argue that even if one *could* classify humans into races, one should not.

To understand how such uncertainties in classification arise let's steer clear of humans for a moment and instead focus on warblers and lions, about which we can easily remain dispassionate. Biologists begin by classifying living creatures into species. A species is a group of populations whose individual members would, if given the opportunity, interbreed with

individuals of other populations of that group. But they would not interbreed with individuals of other species that are similarly defined. Thus all human populations, no matter how different they look belong to the same species because they do interbreed and have interbred whenever they have encountered each other. Gorillas and humans, however, belong to two different species because—to the best of our knowledge—they have never interbred despite their coexisting in close proximity for millions of years.

We know that different populations classified together in the human species are visibly different. The same proves true for most other animal and plant species as well, whenever biologists look carefully. For example, consider one of the most familiar species of bird in North America, the yellow-rumped warbler. Breeding males of eastern and western North America can be distinguished at a glance by their throat color, white in the east, yellow in the west. Hence they are classified into two different races, or subspecies (alternative words with identical meanings), termed the myrtle and Audubon races, respectively. The white-throated eastern birds differ from the yellow-throated western birds in other characteristics as well, such as in voice and habitat preference. But where the two races meet, in western Canada, white-throated birds do indeed interbreed with yellow-throated birds. That's why we consider myrtle warblers and Audubon warblers as races of the same species rather than different species.

Racial classification of these birds is easy. Throat color, voice, and habitat preference all vary geographically in yellow-rumped warblers, but the variation of those three traits is "concordant"—that is, voice differences or habitat differences lead to the same racial classification as differences in throat color because the same populations that differ in throat color also differ in voice and habitat.

Racial classification of many other species, though, presents problems of concordance. For instance, a Pacific island bird species called the golden whistler varies from one island to the next. Some populations consist of big birds, some of small birds; some have black-winged males, others green-winged males; some have yellow-breasted females, others gray-breasted females; many other characteristics vary as well. But, unfortunately for humans like me who study these birds, those characteristics don't vary concordantly. Islands with green-winged males can have either yellow-breasted or gray-breasted females, and green-winged males are big on some islands but small on other islands. As a result if you classified golden whistlers into races based on single traits, you would set entirely different classifications depending on which trait you chose.

Classification of these birds also presents problems of "hierarchy." Some of the golden whistler races recognized by ornithologists are wildly different from all the other races, but some are very similar to one another. They can therefore be grouped into a hierarchy of distinctness. You start by establishing the most distinct population as a race separate from all other populations. You then separate the most distinct of the remaining populations. You continue by grouping similar populations, and separating distinct populations or groups of populations as races or groups of races. The problem is that the extent to which you continue the racial classification is arbitrary, and it's a decision about which taxonomists disagree passionately. Some taxonomists, the "splitters," like to recognize many different races, partly for the egotistical motive of getting credit for having named a race. Other taxonomists, the "lumpers," prefer to recognize few races. Which type of taxonomist you are is a matter of personal preference.

How does that variability of traits by which we classify races come about in the first place? Some traits vary because of natural selection: that is, one form of the trait is advantageous for survival in one area, another form in a different area. For example, northern hares and weasels develop white fur in the winter, but southern ones retain brown fur year-round. The white winter fur is selected in the north for camouflage against the snow, while any animal unfortunate enough to turn white in the snowless southern states would stand out from afar against the brown ground and would be picked off by predators.

Other traits vary geographically because of sexual selection, meaning that those traits serve as arbitrary signals by which individuals of one sex attract mates of the opposite sex while intimidating rivals. Adult male lions, for instance, have a mane, but lionesses and young males don't. The adult male's mane signals to lionesses that he is sexually mature, and signals to young male rivals that he is a dangerous and experienced adversary. The length and color of a lion's mane vary among populations, being shorter and blacker in Indian lions than in African lions. Indian lions and lionesses evidently find short black manes sexy or intimidating; African lions don't.

Finally, some geographically variable traits have no known effect on survival and are invisible to rivals and to prospective sex partners. They merely reflect mutations that happened to arise and spread in one area. They could equally well have arisen and spread elsewhere—they just didn't.

RACE BY RESISTANCE

Traditionally we divide ourselves into races by the twin criteria of geographic location and visible physical characteris- tics. *But we could make an equally reasonable and arbitrary division by the presence or absence of a gene, such as the sickle-cell gene, that confers resistance to malaria. By this reckoning, we'd place Yemenites, Greeks, New Guineans, Thai, and Dinkas in one "race," Norwegians and several black African peoples in another.*

Nothing that I've said about geographic variation in animals is likely to get me branded a racist. We don't attribute higher IQ or social status to black-winged whistlers than to green-winged whistlers. But now let's consider geographic variation in humans. We'll start with invisible traits, about which it's easy to remain dispassionate.

Many geographically variable human traits evolved by natural selection to adapt humans to particular climates or environments—just as the winter color of a hare or weasel did. Good examples are the mutations that people in tropical parts of the Old World evolved to help them survive malaria, the leading infectious disease of the old-world tropics. One such mutation is the sickle-cell gene, so-called because the red blood cells of people with that mutation tend to assume a sickle shape. People bearing the gene are more resistant to malaria than people without it. Not surprisingly, the gene is absent from northern Europe, where malaria is nonexistent, but it's common in tropical Africa, where malaria is widespread. Up to 40 percent of Africans in such areas carry the sickle-cell gene. It's also common in the malaria-ridden Arabian Peninsula and southern India, and rare or absent in the southernmost parts of South Africa, among the Xhosas who live mostly beyond the tropical geographic range of malaria.

The geographic range of human malaria is much wider than the range of the sickle-cell gene. As it happens, other antimalarial genes take over the protective function of the sickle-cell gene in malarial Southeast Asia and New Guinea and in Italy, Greece, and other warm parts of the Mediterranean basin. Thus human races, if defined by antimalarial genes, would be very different from human races as traditionally defined by traits such as skin color. As classified by antimalarial genes (or their absence), Swedes are grouped with Xhosas but not with Italians or Greeks. Most other peoples usually viewed as African blacks are grouped with Arabia's "whites" and are kept separate from the "black" Xhosas.

RACE BY DIGESTION

We could define a race by any geographically variable trait—for example, the retention in adulthood of the enzyme lactase, which allows us to digest milk. Using this as our divisive criterion, we can place northern and central

Europeans with Arabians and such West African peoples as the Fulani; in a "lactase-negative race," we can group most other African blacks with east Asians, American Indians, southern Europeans, and Australian aborigines.

Antimalarial genes exemplify the many features of our body chemistry that vary geographically under the influence of natural selection. Another such feature is the enzyme lactase, which enables us to digest the milk-sugar lactose. Infant humans, like infants of almost all other mammal species, possess lactase and drink milk. Until about 6,000 years ago most humans, like all other mammal species, lost the lactase enzyme on reaching the age of weaning. The obvious reason is that it was unnecessary—no human or other mammal drank milk as an adult. Beginning around 4000 B.C., however, fresh milk obtained from domestic mammals became a major food for adults of a few human populations. Natural selection caused individuals in these populations to retain lactase into adulthood. Among such peoples are northern and central Europeans, Arabians, north Indians, and several milk-drinking black African peoples, such as the Fulani of West Africa. Adult lactase is much less common in southern European populations and in most other African black populations, as well as in all populations of east Asians, aboriginal Australians, and American Indians.

Once again races defined by body chemistry don't match races defined by skin color. Swedes belong with Fulani in the "lactase-positive race," while most African "blacks," Japanese, and American Indians belong in the "lactase-negative race."

Not all the effects of natural selection are as invisible as lactase and sickle cells. Environmental pressures have also produced more noticeable differences among peoples, particularly in body shapes. Among the tallest and most long-limbed peoples in the world are the Nilotic peoples, such as the Dinkas, who live in the hot, dry areas of East Africa. At the opposite extreme in body shape are the Inuit, or Eskimo, who have compact bodies and relatively short arms and legs. The reasons have to do with heat loss. The greater the surface area of a warm body, the more body heat that's lost, since heat loss is directly proportional to surface area. For people of a given weight, a long-limbed, tall shape maximizes surface area, while a compact, short-limbed shape minimizes it. Dinkas and Inuit have opposite problems of heat balance: the former usually need desperately to get rid of body heat, while the latter need desperately to conserve it. Thus natural selection molded their body shapes oppositely, based on their contrasting climates.

(In modern times, such considerations of body shape have become important to athletic performance as well as to heat loss. Tall basketball players, for example,

have an obvious advantage over short ones, and slender, long-limbed tall players have an advantage over stout, short-limbed tall players. In the United States, it's a familiar observation that African Americans are disproportionately represented among professional basketball players. Of course, a contributing reason has to do with their lack of socioeconomic opportunities. But part of the reason probably has to do with the prevalent body shapes of some black African groups as well. However, this example also illustrates the dangers in facile racial stereotyping. One can't make the sweeping generalization that "whites can't jump," or that "blacks' anatomy makes them better basketball players." Only certain African peoples are notably tall and long-limbed; even those exceptional peoples are tall and long-limbed only on the average and vary individually.)

Other visible traits that vary geographically among humans evolved by means of sexual selection. We all know that we find some individuals of the opposite sex more attractive than other individuals. We also know that in sizing up sex appeal, we pay more attention to certain parts of a prospective sex partner's body than to other parts. Men tend to be inordinately interested in women's breasts and much less concerned with women's toenails. Women, in turn, tend to be turned on by the shape of a man's buttocks or the details of a man's beard and body hair, if any, but not by the size of his feet.

But all those determinants of sex appeal vary geographically. Khoisan and Andaman Island women tend to have much larger buttocks than most other women. Nipple color and breast shape and size also vary geographically among women. European men are rather hairy by world standards, while Southeast Asian men tend to have very sparse beards and body hair.

What's the function of these traits that differ so markedly between men and women? They certainly don't aid survival: it's not the case that orange nipples help Khoisan women escape lions, while darker nipples help European women survive cold winters. Instead, these varying traits play a crucial role in sexual selection. Women with very large buttocks are a turn-on, or at least acceptable, to Khoisan and Andaman men but look freakish to many men from other parts of the world. Bearded and hairy men readily find mates in Europe but fare worse in Southeast Asia. The geographic variation of these traits, however, is as arbitrary as the geographic variation in the color of a lion's mane.

RACE BY FINGERPRINTS

Probably the most trivial division of humans we could manage would be based on fingerprint patterns. As it turns out, the prevalance of certain basic features varies predictably

| (a) Arches | (b) Loops | (c) Whorls |

Diamond, Jared. "Race Without Color." Discover Magazine (Nov. 1994):82–89. Reprinted with permission of the author.

among peoples: in the "Loops" race we could group together most Europeans, black Africans, and east Asians. Among the "Whorls" we could place Mongolians and Australian aborigines. Finally, in an "Arches" race, we could group Khoisans and some central Europeans.

There is a third possible explanation for the function of geographically variable human traits, besides survival or sexual selection—namely, no function at all. A good example is provided by fingerprints, whose complex pattern of arches, loops, and whorls is determined genetically. Fingerprints also vary geographically: for example, Europeans' fingerprints tend to have many loops, while aboriginal Australians' fingerprints tend to have many whorls.

If we classify human populations by their fingerprints, most Europeans and black Africans would sort out together in one race, Jews and some Indonesians in another, and aboriginal Australians in still another. But those geographic variations in fingerprint patterns possess no known function whatsoever. They play no role in survival: whorls aren't especially suitable for grabbing kangaroos, nor do loops help bar mitzvah candidates hold on to the pointer for the Torah. They also play no role in sexual selection: while you've undoubtedly noticed whether your mate is bearded or has brown nipples, you surely haven't the faintest idea whether his or her fingerprints have more loops than whorls. Instead it's purely a matter of chance that whorls became common in aboriginal Australians, and loops among Jews. Our rhesus factor blood groups and numerous other human traits fall into the same category of genetic characteristics whose geographic variation serves no function.

RACE BY GENES

One method that seems to offer a way out of arbitrariness is to classify people's degree of genetic distinctness. By this standard the Khoisans of southern Africa would be in a race by themselves. African blacks would form several other distinct races. All the rest of the world's peoples—Norwegians, Navajo, Greeks, Japanese, Australian aborigines, and so on— would, despite their greatly differing external appearance, belong to a single race.

You've probably been wondering when I was going to get back to skin color, eye color, and hair color and form. After all, those are the traits by which all of us members of the lay public, as well as traditional anthropologists, classify races. Does geographic variation in those traits function in survival, in sexual selection, or in nothing?

The usual view is that skin color varies geographically to enhance survival. Supposedly, people in sunny, tropical climates around the world have generally dark skin, which is supposedly analogous to the temporary skin darkening of European whites in the summer. The supposed function of dark skin in sunny climates is for protection against skin cancer. Variations in eye color and hair form and color are also supposed to enhance survival under particular conditions, though no one has ever proposed a plausible hypothesis for how those variations might actually enhance survival.

Alas, the evidence for natural selection of skin color dissolves under scrutiny. Among tropical peoples, anthropologists love to stress the dark skins of African blacks, people of the southern Indian peninsula, and New Guineans and love to forget the pale skins of Amazonian Indians and Southeast Asians living at the same latitudes. To wriggle out of those paradoxes, anthropologists then plead the excuse that Amazonian Indians and Southeast Asians may not have been living in their present locations long enough to evolve dark skins. However, the ancestors of fair-skinned Swedes arrived even more recently in Scandinavia, and aboriginal Tasmanians were black-skinned despite their ancestors' having lived for at least the last 10,000 years at the latitude of Vladivostok.

Besides, when one takes into account cloud cover, peoples of equatorial West Africa and the New Guinea mountains actually receive no more ultraviolet radiation or hours of sunshine each year than do the Swiss. Compared with infectious diseases and other selective agents, skin cancer has been utterly trivial as a cause of death in human history, even for modern white settlers in the tropics. This objection is so obvious to believers in natural selection of skin color that they have proposed at least seven other supposed survival functions of skin color, without reaching agreement. Those other supposed functions include protection against rickets, frostbite, folic acid deficiency, beryllium poisoning, overheating, and overcooling. The diversity of these contradictory theories makes clear how far we are from understanding the survival value (if any) of skin color.

It wouldn't surprise me if dark skins do eventually prove to offer some advantage in tropical climates, but I expect the advantage to turn out to be a slight one that is easily overridden. But there's an overwhelming importance to skin, eye, and hair color that is obvious to all of us—sexual selection. Before we can reach a condition of intimacy permitting us to assess the beauty of a prospective sex partner's hidden physical attractions, we first have to pass muster for skin, eyes, and hair.

We all know how those highly visible "beauty traits" guide our choice of sex partners. Even the briefest personal ad in a newspaper mentions the advertiser's skin color, and the color of skin that he or she seeks in a partner. Skin color, of course, is also of overwhelming importance in our social prejudices. If you're a black African American trying to raise your children in white U.S. society, rickets and overheating are the least of the problems that might be solved by your skin color. Eye color and hair form and color, while not so overwhelmingly important as skin color, also play an obvious role in our sexual and social preferences. Just ask yourself why hair dyes, hair curlers, and hair straighteners enjoy such wide sales. You can bet that it's not to improve our chances of surviving grizzly bear attacks and other risks endemic to the North American continent.

Nearly 125 years ago Charles Darwin himself, the discoverer of natural selection, dismissed its role as an explanation of geographic variation in human beauty traits. Everything that we have learned since then only reinforces Darwin's view.

We can now return to our original questions: Are human racial classifications that are based on different traits concordant with one another? What is the hierarchical relation among recognized races? What is the function of racially variable traits? What, really, are the traditional human races?

Regarding concordance, we *could* have classified races based on any number of geographically variable traits. The resulting classifications would not be at all concordant. Depending on whether we classified ourselves by antimalarial genes, lactase, fingerprints, or skin color, we could place Swedes in the same race as either Xhosas, Fulani, the Ainu of Japan, or Italians.

Regarding hierarchy, traditional classifications that emphasize skin color face unresolvable ambiguities. Anthropology textbooks often recognize five major races: "whites," "African blacks," "Mongoloids," "aboriginal Australians," and "Khoisans," each in turn divided into various numbers of sub-races. But there is no agreement on the number and delineation of the subraces, or even of the major races. Are all five of the major races equally distinctive? Are Nigerians really less different from Xhosas than aboriginal Australians are from both? Should we recognize 3 or 15 sub-races of Mongoloids? These questions have remained unresolved because skin color and other traditional racial criteria are difficult to formulate mathematically.

A method that could in principle overcome these problems is to base racial classification on a combination of as many geographically variable genes as possible. Within the past decade, some biologists have shown renewed interest in developing a hierarchical classification of human populations—hierarchical not in the sense that it identifies superior and inferior races but in the sense of grouping and separating populations based on mathematical measures of genetic distinctness. While the biologists still haven't reached agreement, some of their studies suggest that human genetic diversity may be greatest in Africa. If so, the primary races of humanity may consist of several African races, plus one race to encompass all peoples of all other continents. Swedes, New Guineans, Japanese, and Navajo would then belong to the same primary race; the Khoisans of southern Africa would constitute another primary race by themselves; and African "blacks" and Pygmies would be divided among several other primary races.

As regards the function of all those traits that are useful for classifying human races, some serve to enhance survival, some to enhance sexual selection, while some serve no function at all. The traits we traditionally use are ones subject to sexual selection, which is not really surprising. These traits are not only visible at a distance but also highly variable; that's why they became the ones used throughout recorded history to make quick judgments about people. Racial classification didn't come from science but from the body's signals for differentiating attractive from unattractive sex partners, and for differentiating friend from foe.

Such snap judgments didn't threaten our existence back when people were armed only with spears and surrounded by others who looked mostly like themselves. In the modern world, though, we are armed with guns and plutonium, and we live our lives surrounded by people who are much more varied in appearance. The last thing we need now is to continue codifying all those different appearances into an arbitrary system of racial classification.

27

Shakespeare in the Bush

Laura Bohannan

Communication is an essential characteristic of human social life. Through language we socialize our children and pass down cultural values from generation to generation. Communication forms and defines relations among individuals as well as among groups. Because communication is so natural, we seldom ask a critical question: When we speak, does the listener understand?

At a minimum, communication involves a sender, a receiver, and a shared code for exchanging information. When an individual or a group sends a message, the sender anticipates that those who receive the message will interpret and understand the message in the way the sender intended. Miscommunication is, of course, an unfortunately common phenomenon that can lead to fistfights, divorces, and wars.

What most of us do not appreciate is the degree to which culture affects our interpretation of messages. As Laura Bohannan tells the tale of *Hamlet,* we gradually discover how particular behaviors or events can have very different meanings in different places. What is interesting is that the miscommunication of interpretational differences is not a result of poor language or translation abilities. Miscommunication is not a result of speaking too quickly or not loudly enough. It reflects cultural differences.

As you read this selection, ask yourself the following questions:

- What were the author's original beliefs about the universality of the classics—such as *Hamlet*?
- How did the Tiv elders react to the marriage of Hamlet's mother to his uncle? How was this different from Hamlet's own emotional reaction?
- Why do the Tiv believe that a chief should have more than one wife?
- As the author tells the story, consider how the elders interpret various actions to fit Tiv culture and in so doing redefine the central meaning of the play.

The following terms discussed in this selection are included in the Glossary at the back of the book:

age grade	levirate
agnatic	polygyny
chiefdom	socialization
cultural relativism	

Just before I left Oxford for the Tiv in West Africa, conversation turned to the season at Stratford. "You Americans," said a friend, "often have difficulty with Shakespeare. He was, after all, a very English poet, and one can easily misinterpret the universal by misunderstanding the particular."

I protested that human nature is pretty much the same the whole world over; at least the general plot and motivation of the greater tragedies would always be clear—everywhere—although some details of custom might have to be explained and difficulties of translation might produce other slight changes. To end an argument we could not conclude, my friend gave me a copy of *Hamlet* to study in the African bush: it would, he hoped, lift my mind above its primitive surroundings, and possibly I might, by prolonged meditation, achieve the grace of correct interpretation.

It was my second field trip to that African tribe, and I thought myself ready to live in one of its remote sections—an area difficult to cross even on foot. I eventually settled on the hillock of a very knowledgeable old man, the head of a homestead of some hundred and forty people, all of whom were either his close relatives or their wives and children. Like the other elders of the vicinity, the old man spent most of his time performing ceremonies seldom seen these days in the more accessible parts of the tribe. I was delighted. Soon there would be three months of enforced isolation and leisure, between the harvest that takes place just before the rising of the

Bohannan, Laura. "Shakespeare in the Bush." Reprinted from Natural History (Aug/Sept. 1966.) Copyright © Natural History Magazine, Inc. 2006.

swamps and the clearing of new farms when the water goes down. Then, I thought, they would have even more time to perform ceremonies and explain them to me.

I was quite mistaken. Most of the ceremonies demanded the presence of elders from several homesteads. As the swamps rose, the old men found it too difficult to walk from one homestead to the next, and the ceremonies gradually ceased. As the swamps rose even higher, all activities but one came to an end. The women brewed beer from maize and millet. Men, women, and children sat on their hillocks and drank it.

People began to drink at dawn. By midmorning the whole homestead was singing, dancing, and drumming. When it rained, people had to sit inside their huts: there they drank and sang or they drank and told stories. In any case, by noon or before, I either had to join the party or retire to my own hut and my books. "One does not discuss serious matters when there is beer. Come, drink with us." Since I lacked their capacity for the thick native beer, I spent more and more time with *Hamlet*. Before the end of the second month, grace descended on me. I was quite sure that *Hamlet* had only one possible interpretation, and that one universally obvious.

Early every morning in the hope of having some serious talk before the beer party, I used to call on the old man at his reception hut—a circle of posts supporting a thatched roof above a low mud wall to keep out wind and rain. One day I crawled through the low doorway and found most of the men of the homestead sitting huddled in their ragged clothes on stools, low plank beds, and reclining chairs, warming themselves against the chill of the rain around a smoky fire. In the center were three pots of beer. The party had started.

The old man greeted me cordially. "Sit down and drink." I accepted a large calabash full of beer, poured some into a small drinking gourd, and tossed it down. Then I poured some more into the same gourd for the man second in seniority to my host before I handed my calabash over to a young man for further distribution. Important people shouldn't ladle beer themselves.

"It is better like this," the old man said, looking at me approvingly and plucking at the thatch that had caught in my hair. "You should sit and drink with us more often. Your servants tell me that when you are not with us, you sit inside your hut looking at a paper."

The old man was acquainted with four kinds of "papers:" tax receipts, bride price receipts, court fee receipts, and letters. The messenger who brought him letters from the chief used them mainly as a badge of office, for he always knew what was in them and told the old man. Personal letters for the few who had relatives in the government or mission stations were kept until someone went to a large market where there was a letter writer and reader. Since my arrival, letters were

brought to me to be read. A few men also brought me bride price receipts, privately, with requests to change the figures to a higher sum. I found moral arguments were of no avail, since in-laws are fair game, and the technical hazards of forgery difficult to explain to an illiterate people. I did not wish them to think me silly enough to look at any such papers for days on end, and I hastily explained that my "paper" was one of the "things of long ago" of my country.

"Ah," said the old man. "Tell us."

I protested that I was not a storyteller. Storytelling is a skilled art among them; their standards are high and the audiences critical—and vocal in their criticism. I protested in vain. This morning they wanted to hear a story while they drank. They threatened to tell me no more stories until I told them one of mine. Finally, the old man promised that no one would criticize my style "for we know you are struggling with our language." "But," put in one of the elders, "you must explain what we do not understand, as we do when we tell you our stories." Realizing that here was my chance to prove Hamlet universally intelligible, I agreed.

The old man handed me some more beer to help me on with my storytelling. Men filled their long wooden pipes and knocked coals from the fire to place in the pipe bowls; then, puffing contentedly, they sat back to listen. I began in the proper style, "Not yesterday, not yesterday, but long ago, a thing occurred. One night three men were keeping watch outside the homestead of the great chief, when suddenly they saw the former chief approach them."

"Why was he no longer their chief?"

"He was dead," I explained. "That is why they were troubled and afraid when they saw him."

"Impossible," began one of the elders, handing his pipe on to his neighbor, who interrupted, "Of course it wasn't the dead chief. It was an omen sent by a witch. Go on."

Slightly shaken, I continued. "One of these three was a man who knew things"—the closest translation for scholar, but unfortunately it also meant witch. The second elder looked triumphantly at the first. "So he spoke to the dead chief saying, 'Tell us what we must do so you may rest in your grave,' but the dead chief did not answer. He vanished, and they could see him no more. Then the man who knew things—his name was Horatio—said this event was the affair of the dead chief's son, Hamlet."

There was a general shaking of heads round the circle. "Had the dead chief no living brothers? Or was this son the chief?"

"No," I replied. "That is, he had one living brother who became the chief when the elder brother died."

The old men muttered: such omens were matters for chiefs and elders, not for youngsters; no good could come of going behind a chief's back; clearly Horatio was not a man who knew things.

"Yes, he was," I insisted, shooing a chicken away from my beer. "In our country the son is next to the father. The dead chief's younger brother had become the great chief. He had also married his elder brother's widow only about a month after the funeral."

"He did well," the old man beamed and announced to the others, "I told you that if we knew more about Europeans, we would find they really were very like us. In our country also," he added to me, "the younger brother marries the elder brother's widow and becomes the father of his children. Now, if your uncle, who married your widowed mother, is your father's full brother, then he will be a real father to you. Did Hamlet's father and uncle have one mother?"

His question barely penetrated my mind; I was too upset and thrown off balance by having one of the most important elements of *Hamlet* knocked straight out of the picture. Rather uncertainly I said that I thought they had the same mother, but I wasn't sure—the story didn't say. The old man told me severely that these genealogical details made all the difference and that when I got home I must ask the elders about it. He shouted out the door to one of his younger wives to bring his goatskin bag.

Determined to save what I could of the mother motif, I took a deep breath and began again. "The son Hamlet was very sad because his mother had married again so quickly. There was no need for her to do so, and it is our custom for a widow not to go to her next husband until she has mourned for two years."

"Two years is too long," objected the wife, who had appeared with the old man's battered goatskin bag. "Who will hoe your farms for you while you have no husband?"

"Hamlet," I retorted without thinking, "was old enough to hoe his mother's farms himself. There was no need for her to remarry." No one looked convinced. I gave up. "His mother and the great chief told Hamlet not to be sad, for the great chief himself would be a father to Hamlet. Furthermore, Hamlet would be the next chief: therefore he must stay to learn the things of a chief. Hamlet agreed to remain, and all the rest went off to drink beer."

While I paused, perplexed at how to render Hamlet's disgusted soliloquy to an audience convinced that Claudius and Gertrude had behaved in the best possible manner, one of the younger men asked me who had married the other wives of the dead chief.

"He had no other wives," I told him.

"But a chief must have many wives! How else can he brew beer and prepare food for all his guests?"

I said firmly that in our country even chiefs had only one wife, that they had servants to do their work, and that they paid them from tax money.

It was better, they returned, for a chief to have many wives and sons who would help him hoe his farms and feed his people; then everyone loved the chief who gave much and took nothing—taxes were a bad thing.

I agreed with the last comment, but for the rest fell back on their favorite way of fobbing off my questions: "That is the way it is done, so that is how we do it."

I decided to skip the soliloquy. Even if Claudius was here thought quite right to marry his brother's widow, there remained the poison motif, and I knew they would disapprove of fratricide. More hopefully I resumed, "That night Hamlet kept watch with the three who had seen his dead father. The dead chief again appeared, and although the others were afraid, Hamlet followed his dead father off to one side. When they were alone, Hamlet's dead father spoke."

"Omens can't talk!" The old man was emphatic.

"Hamlet's dead father wasn't an omen. Seeing him might have been an omen, but he was not." My audience looked as confused as I sounded. "It was Hamlet's dead father. It was a thing we call a 'ghost.' " I had to use the English word, for unlike many of the neighboring tribes, these people didn't believe in the survival after death of any individuating part of the personality.

"What is a 'ghost'? An omen?"

"No, a 'ghost' is someone who is dead but who walks around and can talk, and people can hear him and see him but not touch him."

They objected. "One can touch zombis."

"No, no! It was not a dead body the witches had animated to sacrifice and eat. No one else made Hamlet's dead father walk. He did it himself."

"Dead men can't walk," protested my audience as one man.

I was quite willing to compromise. "A 'ghost' is the dead man's shadow."

But again they objected. "Dead men cast no shadows."

"They do in my country," I snapped.

The old man quelled the babble of disbelief that arose immediately and told me with that insincere, but courteous, agreement one extends to the fancies of the young, ignorant, and superstitious, "No doubt in your country the dead can also walk without being zombis." From the depths of his bag he produced a withered fragment of kola nut, bit off one end to show it wasn't poisoned, and handed me the rest as a peace offering.

"Anyhow," I resumed, "Hamlet's dead father said that his own brother, the one who became chief, had poisoned him. He wanted Hamlet to avenge him. Hamlet believed this in his heart, for he did not like his father's brother." I took another swallow of beer.

"In the country of the great chief, living in the same homestead, for it was a very large one, was an important elder who was often with the chief to advise and help him. His name was Polonius. Hamlet was courting his daughter, but her father and her brother . . . (I cast hastily about for some tribal analogy) warned her not to let Hamlet visit her when she was alone on her farm, for he would be a great chief and so could not marry her."

"Why not?" asked the wife, who had settled down on the edge of the old man's chair. He frowned at her for asking stupid questions and growled, "They lived in the same homestead."

"That was not the reason," I informed them. "Polonius was a stranger who lived in the homestead because he helped the chief, not because he was a relative."

"Then why couldn't Hamlet marry her?"

"He could have," I explained, "but Polonius didn't think he would. After all, Hamlet was a man of great importance who ought to marry a chief's daughter, for in his country a man could have only one wife. Polonius was afraid that if Hamlet made love to his daughter, then no one else would give a high price for her."

"That might be true," remarked one of the shrewder elders, "but a chief's son would give his mistress's father enough presents and patronage to more than make up the difference. Polonius sounds like a fool to me."

"Many people think he was," I agreed. "Meanwhile Polonius sent his son Laertes off to Paris to learn the things of that country, for it was the homestead of a very great chief indeed. Because he was afraid that Laertes might waste a lot of money on beer and women and gambling, or get into trouble by fighting, he sent one of his servants to Paris secretly, to spy out what Laertes was doing. One day Hamlet came upon Polonius's daughter Ophelia. He behaved so oddly he frightened her. Indeed"—I was fumbling for words to express the dubious quality of Hamlet's madness—"the chief and many others had also noticed that when Hamlet talked one could understand the words but not what they meant. Many people thought that he had become mad." My audience suddenly became more attentive. "The great chief wanted to know what was wrong with Hamlet, so he sent for two of Hamlet's age mates (school friends would have taken long explanation) to talk to Hamlet and find out what troubled his heart. Hamlet, seeing that they had been bribed by the chief to betray him, told them nothing. Polonius, however, insisted that Hamlet was mad because he had been forbidden to see Ophelia, whom he loved."

"Why," inquired a bewildered voice, "should anyone bewitch Hamlet on that account?"

"Bewitch him?"

"Yes, only witchcraft can make anyone mad, unless, of course, one sees the beings that lurk in the forest."

I stopped being a storyteller, took out my notebook and demanded to be told more about these two causes of madness. Even while they spoke and I jotted notes, I tried to calculate the effect of this new factor on the plot. Hamlet had not been exposed to the beings that lurk in the forest. Only his relatives in the male line could bewitch him. Barring relatives not mentioned by Shakespeare, it had to be Claudius who was attempting to harm him. And, of course, it was.

For the moment I staved off questions by saying that the great chief also refused to believe that Hamlet was mad for the love of Ophelia and nothing else. "He was sure that something much more important was troubling Hamlet's heart."

"Now Hamlet's age mates," I continued, "had brought with them a famous storyteller. Hamlet decided to have this man tell the chief and all his homestead a story about a man who had poisoned his brother because he desired his brother's wife and wished to be chief himself. Hamlet was sure the great chief could not hear the story without making a sign if he was indeed guilty, and then he would discover whether his dead father had told him the truth."

The old man interrupted, with deep cunning, "Why should a father lie to his son?" he asked.

I hedged: "Hamlet wasn't sure that it really was his dead father." It was impossible to say anything, in that language, about devil-inspired visions.

"You mean," he said, "it actually was an omen, and he knew witches sometimes send false ones. Hamlet was a fool not to go to one skilled in reading omens and divining the truth in the first place. A man-who-sees-the-truth could have told him how his father died, if he really had been poisoned, and if there was witchcraft in it; then Hamlet could have called the elders to settle the matter."

The shrewd elder ventured to disagree. "Because his father's brother was a great chief, one-who-sees-the-truth might therefore have been afraid to tell it. I think it was for that reason that a friend of Hamlet's father—a witch and an elder—sent an omen so his friend's son would know. Was the omen true?"

"Yes," I said, abandoning ghosts and the devil; a witch-sent omen it would have to be. "It was true, for when the storyteller was telling his tale before all the homestead, the great chief rose in fear. Afraid that Hamlet knew his secret, he planned to have him killed."

The stage set of the next bit presented some difficulties of translation. I began cautiously. "The great chief told Hamlet's mother to find out from her son what he knew. But because a woman's children are always first in her heart, he had the important elder

Polonius hide behind a cloth that hung against the wall of Hamlet's mother's sleeping hut. Hamlet started to scold his mother for what she had done."

There was a shocked murmur from everyone. A man should never scold his mother.

"She called out in fear, and Polonius moved behind the cloth. Shouting, 'A rat!' Hamlet took his machete and slashed through the cloth." I paused for dramatic effect. "He had killed Polonius!"

The old men looked at each other in supreme disgust. "That Polonius truly was a fool and a man who knew nothing! What child would not know enough to shout, 'It's me!'" With a pang, I remembered that these people are ardent hunters, always armed with bow, arrow, and machete; at the first rustle in the grass an arrow is aimed and ready, and the hunter shouts "Game!" If no human voice answers immediately, the arrow speeds on its way. Like a good hunter Hamlet had shouted, "A rat!"

I rushed in to save Polonius's reputation. "Polonius did speak. Hamlet heard him. But he thought it was the chief and wished to kill him to avenge his father. He had meant to kill him earlier that evening . . ." I broke down, unable to describe to these pagans, who had no belief in individual afterlife, the difference between dying at one's prayers and dying "unhousell'd, disappointed, unaneled."

This time I had shocked my audience seriously. "For a man to raise his hand against his father's brother and the one who has become his father—that is a terrible thing. The elders ought to let such a man be bewitched."

I nibbled at my kola nut in some perplexity, then pointed out that after all the man had killed Hamlet's father.

"No," pronounced the old man, speaking less to me than to the young men sitting behind the elders. "If your father's brother has killed your father, you must appeal to your father's age mates; *they* may avenge him. No man may use violence against his senior relatives." Another thought struck him. "But if his father's brother had indeed been wicked enough to bewitch Hamlet and make him mad that would be a good story indeed, for it would be his fault that Hamlet, being mad, no longer had any sense and thus was ready to kill his father's brother."

There was a murmur of applause. *Hamlet* was again a good story to them, but it no longer seemed quite the same story to me. As I thought over the coming complications of plot and motive, I lost courage and decided to skim over dangerous ground quickly.

"The great chief," I went on, "was not sorry that Hamlet had killed Polonius. It gave him a reason to send Hamlet away, with his two treacherous age mates, with letters to a chief of a far country, saying that Hamlet should be killed. But Hamlet changed the writing on their papers, so that the chief killed his age mates instead." I encountered a reproachful glare from one of the men whom I had told undetectable forgery was not merely immoral but beyond human skill. I looked the other way.

"Before Hamlet could return, Laertes came back for his father's funeral. The great chief told him Hamlet had killed Polonius. Laertes swore to kill Hamlet because of this, and because his sister Ophelia, hearing her father had been killed by the man she loved, went mad and drowned in the river."

"Have you already forgotten what we told you?" The old man was reproachful. "One cannot take vengeance on a madman; Hamlet killed Polonius in his madness. As for the girl, she not only went mad, she was drowned. Only witches can make people drown. Water itself can't hurt anything. It is merely something one drinks and bathes in."

I began to get cross. "If you don't like the story, I'll stop."

The old man made soothing noises and himself poured me some more beer. "You tell the story well, and we are listening. But it is clear the elders of your country have never told you what the story really means. No, don't interrupt! We believe you when you say your marriage customs are different, or your clothes and weapons. But people are the same everywhere; therefore, there are always witches and it is we, the elders, who know how witches work. We told you it was the great chief who wished to kill Hamlet, and now your own words have proved us right. Who were Ophelia's male relatives?"

"There were only her father and her brother." Hamlet was clearly out of my hands.

"There must have been many more; this also you must ask of your elders when you get back to your country. From what you tell us, since Polonius was dead, it must have been Laertes who killed Ophelia, although I do not see the reason for it."

We had emptied one pot of beer, and the old men argued the point with slightly tipsy interest. Finally one of them demanded of me, "What did the servant of Polonius say on his return?"

With difficulty I recollected Reynaldo and his mission. "I don't think he did return before Polonius was killed."

"Listen," said the elder, "and I will tell you how it was and how your story will go, then you may tell me if I am right. Polonius knew his son would get into trouble, and so he did. He had many fines to pay for fighting, and debts from gambling. But he had only two ways of getting money quickly. One was to marry off his sister at once, but it is difficult to find a man who will marry a woman desired by the son of a chief. For if the chief's heir commits adultery with your wife, what can you do? Only a fool calls a case against a man who will someday be his judge. Therefore Laertes had to take the second way: he killed his sister by witchcraft, drowning her so he could secretly sell her body to the witches."

I raised an objection. "They found her body and buried it. Indeed Laertes jumped into the grave to see his sister once more—so, you see, the body was truly there. Hamlet, who had just come back, jumped in after him."

"What did I tell you?" The elder appealed to the others. "Laertes was up to no good with his sister's body. Hamlet prevented him, because the chief's heir, like a chief, does not wish any other man to grow rich and powerful. Laertes would be angry, because he would have killed his sister without benefit to himself. In our country he would try to kill Hamlet for that reason. Is this not what happened?"

"More or less," I admitted. "When the great chief found Hamlet was still alive, he encouraged Laertes to try to kill Hamlet and arranged a fight with machetes between them. In the fight both the young men were wounded to death. Hamlet's mother drank the poisoned beer that the chief meant for Hamlet in case he won the fight. When he saw his mother die of poison, Hamlet, dying, managed to kill his father's brother with his machete."

"You see, I was right!" exclaimed the elder.

"That was a very good story," added the old man, "and you told it with very few mistakes. There was just one more error, at the very end. The poison Hamlet's mother drank was obviously meant for the survivor of the fight, whichever it was. If Laertes had won, the great chief would have poisoned him, for no one would know that he arranged Hamlet's death. Then, too, he need not fear Laertes' witchcraft; it takes a strong heart to kill one's only sister by witchcraft.

"Sometime," concluded the old man, gathering his ragged toga about him, "you must tell us some more stories of your country. We, who are elders, will instruct you in their true meaning, so that when you return to your own land your elders will see that you have not been sitting in the bush, but among those who know things and who have taught you wisdom."

28

Eating Christmas in the Kalahari

Richard Borshay Lee

An *economy* is a social system for the production, exchange, and consumption of goods and services. Using this definition, anthropologists believe that all human societies have economies and that economic systems can work without money and markets.

People in food-foraging societies, like the !Kung San described in this selection, have received much attention by anthropologists. To a large degree, this is because they represent (at least by analogy) the original lifestyle of our ancestors. A major discovery of research on food foragers is that their life is not "nasty, brutish, and short." In fact, the food forager's diet might be an ideal one for people living in industrialized societies.

In the hunter-gatherer economy, anthropologists have discovered that the exchange of goods is based on rules of gift giving or reciprocity. In this selection, Richard Lee tells of his surprise at the !Kung San's lack of appreciation of a Christmas gift. As we have already seen, a group's customs and rules about appropriate social behavior can reflect important cultural values. When people act in unexpected ways, anthropologists see this as an opportunity to better understand their culture and world view. That is the case in this selection.

All people give gifts to each other, but there are rules and obligations about those gifts. In our own society, there are rules about the polite way to receive a present. We are supposed to act appreciative (even if we hate the gift) because the gift is less important than the social relationship at stake. The !Kung break those rules, but in the process, Richard Lee discovers that there are important cultural messages behind their "impoliteness."

As you read this selection, ask yourself the following questions:

- Why did Richard Lee feel obligated to give a valuable gift to the !Kung at Christmas? Why did they think he was a miser?

- Why did the !Kung people's insults about the impending gift bother the anthropologist so much? Were the people treating him in a special way?

- What does Lee mean by saying, "There are no totally generous acts?" Do you agree?

- What are some cultural rules about gift giving in our own society?

The following terms discussed in this selection are included in the Glossary at the back of the book:

cultural values	*hunter-gatherers*
economy	*reciprocal gift*
egalitarian society	

The !Kung Bushmen's knowledge of Christmas is thirdhand. The London Missionary Society brought the holiday to the southern Tswana tribes in the early nineteenth century. Later, native catechists spread the idea far and wide among the Bantu-speaking pastoralists, even in the remotest corners of the Kalahari Desert. The Bushmen's idea of the Christmas story, stripped to its essentials, is "praise the birth of white man's god-chief:" what keeps their interest in the holiday high is the Tswana-Herero custom of slaughtering an ox for his Bushmen neighbors as an annual goodwill gesture. Since the 1930s, part of the Bushmen's annual round of activities has included a December congregation at the cattle posts for trading, marriage brokering, and several days of trance dance feasting at which the local Tswana headman is host.

As a social anthropologist working with !Kung Bushmen, I found that the Christmas ox custom suited my purposes. I had come to the Kalahari to study the hunting and gathering subsistence economy of the !Kung, and to accomplish this it was essential not to provide them with food, share my own food, or interfere in any way with their food-gathering activities. While liberal handouts of tobacco and medical supplies

Lee, Richard Borshay. "Eating Christmas in the Kalahari" from Natural History (Dec. 1969):14–22, 60–64. Copyright © Natural History Magazine, Inc. 2006. Reprinted with permission.

were appreciated, they were scarcely adequate to erase the glaring disparity in wealth between the anthropologist, who maintained a two-month inventory of canned goods, and the Bushmen, who rarely had a day's supply of food on hand. My approach, while paying off in terms of data, left me open to frequent accusations of stinginess and hardheartedness. By their lights, I was a miser.

The Christmas ox was to be my way of saying thank you for the cooperation of the past year; and since it was to be our last Christmas in the field, I determined to slaughter the largest, meatiest ox that money could buy, insuring that the feast and trance dance would be a success.

Through December I kept my eyes open at the wells as the cattle were brought down for watering. Several animals were offered, but none had quite the grossness that I had in mind. Then, ten days before the holiday, a Herero friend led an ox of astonishing size and mass up to our camp. It was solid black, stood five feet high at the shoulder, had a five-foot span of horns, and must have weighed 1,200 pounds on the hoof. Food consumption calculations are my specialty, and I quickly figured that bones and viscera aside, there was enough meat—at least four pounds—for every man, woman, and child of the 150 Bushmen in the vicinity of /ai/ai who were expected at the feast.

Having found the right animal at last, I paid the Herero £20 ($56) and asked him to keep the beast with his herd until Christmas day. The next morning word spread among the people that the big solid black one was the ox chosen by /ontah (my Bushman name; it means, roughly, "whitey") for the Christmas feast. That afternoon I received the first delegation. Ben!a, an outspoken sixty-year-old mother of five, came to the point slowly.

"Where were you planning to eat Christmas?"

"Right here at /ai/ai," I replied.

"Alone or with others?"

"I expect to invite all the people to eat Christmas with me."

"Eat what?"

"I have purchased Yehave's black ox, and I am going to slaughter and cook it."

"That's what we were told at the well but refused to believe it until we heard it from yourself."

"Well, it's the black one," I replied expansively, although wondering what she was driving at.

"Oh, no!" Ben!a groaned, turning to her group. "They were right." Turning back to me she asked, "Do you expect us to eat that bag of bones?"

"Bag of bones! It's the biggest ox at /ai/ai."

"Big, yes, but old. And thin. Everybody knows there's no meat on that old ox. What did you expect to eat off of it, the horns?"

Everybody chuckled at Ben!a's one-liner as they walked away, but all I could manage was a weak grin.

That evening it was the turn of the young men. They came to sit at our evening fire. /gaugo, about my age, spoke to me man-to-man.

"/ontah, you have always been square with us," he lied. "What has happened to change your heart? That sack of guts and bones of Yehave's will hardly feed one camp, let alone all the Bushmen around /ai/ai." And he proceeded to enumerate the seven camps in the /ai/ai vicinity, family by family. "Perhaps you have forgotten that we are not few, but many. Or are you too blind to tell the difference between a proper cow and an old wreck? That ox is thin to the point of death."

"Look, you guys," I retorted, "that is a beautiful animal, and I'm sure you will eat it with pleasure at Christmas."

"Of course we will eat it: it's food. But it won't fill us up to the point where we will have enough strength to dance. We will eat and go home to bed with stomachs rumbling."

That night as we turned in, I asked my wife, Nancy, "What did you think of the black ox?"

"It looked enormous to me. Why?"

"Well, about eight different people have told me I got gypped; that the ox is nothing but bones."

"What's the angle?" Nancy asked. "Did they have a better one to sell?"

"No, they just said that it was going to be a grim Christmas because there won't be enough meat to go around. Maybe I'll get an independent judge to look at the beast in the morning."

Bright and early, Halingisi, a Tswana cattle owner, appeared at our camp. But before I could ask him to give me his opinion on Yehave's black ox, he gave me the eye signal that indicated a confidential chat. We left the camp and sat down.

"/ontah, I'm surprised at you; you've lived here for three years and still haven't learned anything about cattle."

"But what else can a person do but choose the biggest, strongest animal one can find?" I retorted.

"Look, just because an animal is big doesn't mean that it has plenty of meat on it. The black one was a beauty when it was younger, but now it is thin to the point of death."

"Well I've already bought it. What can I do at this stage?"

"Bought it already? I thought you were just considering it. Well, you'll have to kill it and serve it, I suppose. But don't expect much of a dance to follow."

My spirits dropped rapidly. I could believe that Ben!a and /gaugo just might be putting me on about the black ox, but Halingisi seemed to be an impartial critic. I went around that day feeling as though I had bought a lemon of a used car.

In the afternoon it was Tomazo's turn. Tomazo is a fine hunter, a top trance performer . . . and one of my most reliable informants. He approached the subject of the Christmas cow as part of my continuing Bushman education.

"My friend, the way it is with us Bushmen," he began, "is that we love meat. And even more than that, we love fat. When we hunt we always search for the fat ones, the ones dripping with layers of white fat: fat that turns into a clear, thick oil in the cooking pot, fat that slides down your gullet, fills your stomach and gives you a roaring diarrhea," he rhapsodized.

"So, feeling as we do," he continued, "it gives us pain to be served such a scrawny thing as Yehave's black ox. It is big, yes, and no doubt its giant bones are good for soup, but fat is what we really crave and so we will eat Christmas this year with a heavy heart."

The prospect of a gloomy Christmas now had me worried, so I asked Tomazo what I could do about it.

"Look for a fat one, a young one . . . smaller, but fat. Fat enough to make us //gom (evacuate the bowels), then we will be happy."

My suspicions were aroused when Tomazo said that he happened to know a young, fat, barren cow that the owner was willing to part with. Was Tomazo working on commission, I wondered? But I dispelled this unworthy thought when we approached the Herero owner of the cow in question and found that he had decided not to sell.

The scrawny wreck of a Christmas ox now became the talk of the /ai/ai water hole and was the first news told to the outlying groups as they began to come in from the bush for the feast. What finally convinced me that real trouble might be brewing was the visit from u!au, an old conservative with a reputation for fierceness. His nickname meant spear and referred to an incident thirty years ago in which he had speared a man to death. He had an intense manner; fixing me with his eyes, he said in clipped tones:

"I have only just heard about the black ox today, or else I would have come earlier. /ontah, do you honestly think you can serve meat like that to people and avoid a fight?" He paused, letting the implications sink in. "I don't mean fight you, /ontah; you are a white man. I mean a fight between Bushmen. There are many fierce ones here, and with such a small quantity of meat to distribute, how can you give everybody a fair share? Someone is sure to accuse another of taking too much or hogging all the choice pieces. Then you will see what happens when some go hungry while others eat."

The possibility of at least a serious argument struck me as all too real. I had witnessed the tension that surrounds the distribution of meat from a kudu or gemsbok kill, and had documented many arguments that sprang up from a real or imagined slight in meat distribution. The owners of a kill may spend up to two hours arranging and rearranging the piles of meat under the gaze of a circle of recipients before handing them out. And I knew that the Christmas feast at /ai/ai would be bringing together groups that had feuded in the past.

Convinced now of the gravity of the situation, I went in earnest to search for a second cow; but all my inquiries failed to turn one up.

The Christmas feast was evidently going to be a disaster, and the incessant complaints about the meagerness of the ox had already taken the fun out of it for me. Moreover, I was getting bored with the wisecracks, and after losing my temper a few times, I resolved to serve the beast anyway. If the meat fell short, the hell with it. In the Bushmen idiom, I announced to all who would listen:

"I am a poor man and blind. If I have chosen one that is too old and too thin, we will eat it anyway and see if there is enough meat there to quiet the rumbling of our stomachs."

On hearing this speech, Ben!a offered me a rare word of comfort. "It's thin," she said philosophically, "but the bones will make a good soup."

At dawn Christmas morning, instinct told me to turn over the butchering and cooking to a friend and take off with Nancy to spend Christmas alone in the bush. But curiosity kept me from retreating. I wanted to see what such a scrawny ox looked like on butchering, and if there was going to be a fight, I wanted to catch every word of it. Anthropologists are incurable that way.

The great beast was driven up to our dancing ground, and a shot in the forehead dropped it in its tracks. Then, freshly cut branches were heaped around the fallen carcass to receive the meat. Ten men volunteered to help with the cutting. I asked/gaugo to make the breast bone cut. This cut, which begins the butchering process for most large game, offers easy access for removal of the viscera. But it allows the hunter to spot-check the amount of fat on an animal. A fat game animal carries a white layer up to an inch thick on the chest, while in a thin one, the knife will quickly cut to the bone. All eyes fixed on his hand as /gaugo, dwarfed by the great carcass, knelt to the breast. The first cut opened a pool of solid white in the black skin. The second and third cut widened and deepened the creamy white. Still no bone. It was pure fat; it must have been two inches thick.

"Hey /gau," I burst out, "that ox is loaded with fat. What's this about the ox being too thin to bother eating? Are you out of your mind?"

"Fat?" /gau shot back. "You call that fat? This wreck is thin, sick, dead!" And he broke out laughing. So did everyone else. They rolled on the ground, paralyzed with laughter. Everybody laughed except me; I was thinking.

I ran back to the tent and burst in just as Nancy was getting up. "Hey, the black ox. It's fat as hell! They were kidding about it being too thin to eat. It was a joke or something. A put-on. Everyone is really delighted with it."

"Some joke," my wife replied. "It was so funny that you were ready to pack up and leave /ai/ai."

If it had indeed been a joke, it had been an extraordinarily convincing one, and tinged, I thought, with more than a touch of malice as many jokes are. Nevertheless, that it was a joke lifted my spirits considerably, and I returned to the butchering site where the shape of the ox was rapidly disappearing under the axes and knives of the butchers. The atmosphere had become festive. Grinning broadly, their arms covered with blood well past the elbow, men packed chunks of meat into the big cast-iron cooking pots, fifty pounds to the load, and muttered and chuckled all the while about the thinness and worthlessness of the animal and /ontah's poor judgment.

We danced and ate that ox two days and two nights; we cooked and distributed fourteen potfuls of meat and no one went home hungry and no fights broke out.

But the "joke" stayed in my mind. I had a growing feeling that something important had happened in my relationship with the Bushmen and that the clue lay in the meaning of the joke. Several days later, when most of the people had dispersed back to the bush camps, I raised the question with Hakekgose, a Tswana man who had grown up among the !Kung, married a !Kung girl, and who probably knows the culture better than any other non-Bushman.

"With us whites," I began, "Christmas is supposed to be the day of friendship and brotherly love. What I can't figure out is why the Bushmen went to such lengths to criticize and belittle the ox I had bought for the feast. The animal was perfectly good and their jokes and wisecracks practically ruined the holiday for me."

"So it really did bother you," said Hakekgose. "Well, that's the way they always talk. When I take my rifle and go hunting with them, if I miss, they laugh at me for the rest of the day. But even if I hit and bring one down, it's no better. To them, the kill is always too small or too old or too thin; and as we sit down on the kill site to cook and eat the liver, they keep grumbling, even with their mouths full of meat. They say things like, 'Oh, this is awful! What a worthless animal! Whatever made me think that this Tswana rascal could hunt!'"

"Is this the way outsiders are treated?" I asked.

"No, it is their custom; they talk that way to each other too. Go and ask them."

/gaugo had been one of the most enthusiastic in making me feel bad about the merit of the Christmas ox. I sought him out first.

"Why did you tell me the black ox was worthless, when you could see that it was loaded with fat and meat?"

"It is our way," he said smiling. "We always like to fool people about that. Say there is a Bushman who has been hunting. He must not come home and announce like a braggart, 'I have killed a big one in the bush!' He must first sit down in silence until I or someone else comes up to his fire and asks, 'What did you see today?' He replies quietly, 'Ah, I'm no good for hunting. I saw nothing at all (pause) just a little tiny one.' Then I smile to myself," /gaugo continued, "because I know he has killed something big.

"In the morning we make up a party of four or five people to cut up and carry the meat back to the camp. When we arrive at the kill we examine it and cry out, 'You mean to say you have dragged us all the way out here in order to make us cart home your pile of bones? Oh, if I had known it was this thin I wouldn't have come.' Another one pipes up, 'People, to think I gave up a nice day in the shade for this. At home we may be hungry but at least we have nice cool water to drink.' If the horns are big, someone says, 'Did you think that somehow you were going to boil down the horns for soup?'

"To all this you must respond in kind. 'I agree,' you say, 'this one is not worth the effort; let's just cook the liver for strength and leave the rest for the hyenas. It is not too late to hunt today and even a duiker or steenbok would be better than this mess.'

"Then you set to work nevertheless; butcher the animal, carry the meat back to the camp and everyone eats," /gaugo concluded.

Things were beginning to make sense. Next, I went to Tomazo. He corroborated /gaugo's story of the obligatory insults over a kill and added a few details of his own.

"But," I asked, "why insult a man after he has gone to all that trouble to track and kill an animal and when he is going to share the meat with you so that your children will have something to eat?"

"Arrogance," was his cryptic answer.

"Arrogance?"

"Yes, when a young man kills much meat he comes to think of himself as a chief or a big man, and he thinks of the rest of us as his servants or inferiors. We can't accept this. We refuse one who boasts, for someday his pride will make him kill somebody. So we always speak of his meat as worthless. This way we cool his heart and make him gentle."

"But why didn't you tell me this before?" I asked Tomazo with some heat.

"Because you never asked me," said Tomazo, echoing the refrain that has come to haunt every field ethnographer.

The pieces now fell into place. I had known for a long time that in situations of social conflict with Bushmen I held all the cards. I was the only source of tobacco in a thousand square miles, and I was not incapable of cutting an individual off for noncooperation. Though my boycott never lasted longer than a few days, it was an indication of my strength. People resented my presence at the water hole, yet simultaneously dreaded my leaving. In short I was a perfect target for the charge of arrogance and for the Bushman tactic of enforcing humility.

I had been taught an object lesson by the Bushmen; it had come from an unexpected corner and had hurt me in a vulnerable area. For the big black ox was to be the one totally generous, unstinting act of my year at /ai/ai and I was quite unprepared for the reaction I received.

As I read it, their message was this: There are no totally generous acts. All "acts" have an element of calculation. One black ox slaughtered at Christmas does not wipe out a year of careful manipulation of gifts given to serve your own ends. After all, to kill an animal and share the meat with people is really no more than the Bushmen do for each other every day and with far less fanfare.

In the end, I had to admire how the Bushmen had played out the farce—collectively straight-faced to the end. Curiously, the episode reminded me of the *Good Soldier Schweik* and his marvelous encounters with authority. Like Schweik, the Bushmen had retained a thoroughgoing skepticism of good intentions. Was it this independence of spirit, I wondered, that had kept them culturally viable in the face of generations of contact with more powerful societies, both black and white? The thought that the Bushmen were alive and well in the Kalahari was strangely comforting. Perhaps, armed with that independence and with their superb knowledge of their environment, they might yet survive the future.

29

How Many Fathers Are Best for a Child?

Meredith F. Small

Anthropologists study systems of kinship and marriage in many societies for three reasons: first, these issues are very important to the people themselves; second, kinship and marriage are keys for understanding how contemporary cultures work; and finally, because they give us clues as to what patterns of family organization may have existed over the course of human history. As a great deal of anthropological research has revealed, diverse cultures have many different ways of organizing families.

In the United States, we often think of the "traditional" family as a nuclear family: two married parents with their children. Many people ethnocentrically believe that this is the normal or natural family system. Other types of family organization, such as "blended" families, are often described as recent variants. But in fact, the nuclear family model is just one of the many types of kinship organization humans have used at present and in the past—and it is only a relatively recent development in the broader context of human history.

This selection describes a pattern in some South American societies, in which a woman has intercourse with two or more men during her pregnancy and the resulting child is considered as having multiple fathers. This kinship system, like many others across the world, is quite different from the American model of a "traditional" family. However, as this selection argues,

this arrangement helps improve children's likelihood of survival in Barí social communities. In the United States, social scientists have shown that having a father present is beneficial for children's development.

As you read this selection, ask yourself the following questions:

- If one father is good, are two or more better? How many fathers are best for a child?
- Why do the Barí believe a child can have more than one father?
- How do Barí women justify taking lovers during pregnancy?
- From an evolutionary perspective, what is the ideal number of fathers for a child to have in Barí society? Why?
- How is the Barí system similar to and different from the system of frequent divorce and court-enforced "child support" payments in modern American society?

The following terms discussed in this selection are included in the Glossary at the back of the book:

> *multiple paternity*
> *nuclear family*
> *paleoanthropology*

Anthropologist Stephen Beckerman was well into his forties before he finally understood how babies are made. He had thought, as most people do, that a sperm from one man and an egg from one woman joined to make a child. But one summer day, as he and his colleague Roberto Lizarralde lounged around in hammocks, chatting with Rachel, an elderly woman of

the Barí tribe of Venezuela, she pointed out his error. Babies, she explained, can easily have more than one biological father. "My first husband was the father of my first child, my second child, and my third child," Rachel said, recalling her life. "But the fourth child, actually, he has two fathers." It was clear that Rachel didn't mean there was a stepfather hanging around or a friendly uncle who took the kid fishing every weekend. She was simply explaining the Barí version of conception to these ignorant anthropologists: A fetus is built up over time with repeated washes of sperm—which means, of course, that more than one man can contribute to the endeavor.

Small, Meredith F. "How Many Fathers Are Best for a Child?" *Discover Magazine* (March 2003):54–61. Reprinted with permission of the author.

This interview changed not only the way Beckerman and Lizarralde viewed Barí families but also brought into question the very way that anthropologists portray human coupling. If biological fatherhood can be shared—an idea accepted by many indigenous groups across South America and in many other cultures across the globe—then the nuclear family with one mom and one dad might not be the established blueprint for a family that we have been led to expect. If so, the familiar story of traditional human mating behavior, in which man the hunter brings home the bacon to his faithful wife, loses credibility. And if the Barí and other groups work perfectly well with more flexible family styles, the variety of family structures that are increasingly common in Western culture these days—everything from single-parent households to blended families—may not be as dangerous to the social fabric as we are led to believe. People in this culture may simply be exercising the same family options that humans have had for millions of years, options that have been operating in other cultures while the West took a stricter view of what constitutes a family.

Stephen Beckerman folds his 6-foot-4-inch frame into a chair and turns to the mountainous topography of papers on his desk at Pennsylvania State University. Once he manages to locate a map under all the piles, he points to a spot on the border between Venezuela and Colombia where he spent 20 years, off and on, with the indigenous Barí Indians.

The traditional Barí culture, Beckerman explains, has come under attack by outside forces, starting with the conquistadors who arrived in the early sixteenth century. Today Catholic missionaries interact with the Barí, coal and oil companies are trying to seize their land, and drug traffickers and guerrillas are threats. Western influences are apparent: Most families have moved from traditional longhouses to single-family dwellings, and everyone wears modern Western clothes and uses Western goods. However, the Barí continue to practice their traditions of manioc farming, fishing, and hunting, according to Roberto Lizarralde, an anthropologist at the Central University of Venezuela who has been visiting the Barí regularly since 1960. Lizarralde also says that the Barí still have great faith in traditional spirits and ancestral wisdom, including their notion that a child can have multiple biological fathers.

The Barí believe that the first act of sex, which should always be between a husband and wife, plants the seed. Then the fledgling fetus must be nourished by repeated anointings of semen; the woman's body is viewed as a vessel where men do all the work. "One of the reasons women give you for taking lovers is that they don't want to wear out their husbands," Beckerman says. "They claim it's hard work for men to support a pregnancy by having enough sex, and so

lovers can help." Just look, the Barí say. Women grow fat during a pregnancy, while men grow thin from all their work.

Anthropologists study a culture's ideas about conception because those ideas have a profound impact on the way people run their lives. In our culture, for example, conceiving children incurs long-term economic responsibility for both the mother and father. We take this obligation so seriously that when a parent fails to provide for a child, it is usually a violation of law. In the Barí system, when a man is named as a secondary biological father he is also placed under an obligation to the mother and the child. In addition, he is expected to give gifts of fish and game. These gifts are a significant burden because the man must also provide for his own wife and primary children.

Beckerman and his colleagues have discovered that naming secondary fathers has evolutionary consequences. A team of ethnographers led by Beckerman, Roberto Lizarralde, and his son Manuel, an anthropologist at Connecticut College who has been visiting the Barí since he was 5 years old, interviewed 114 Barí women past childbearing years and asked them about their full reproductive histories. "These interviews were a lot of fun," Beckerman says, laughing. "Randy old ladies talking about their lovers." In total, the researchers recorded claims of 916 pregnancies, an average of eight pregnancies for each woman. But child mortality was high—about one-third of the children did not survive to age 15. Naming secondary fathers was a critical factor in predicting which babies made it to adulthood. Secondary fathers were involved in 25 percent of pregnancies, and the team determined that two fathers were the ideal number. Children with one father and one secondary father made it to their teens most often; kids with only one father or those with more than two fathers didn't fare as well. The researchers also found that this decrease in mortality occurred not during the child's life but during fetal development: Women were less likely to have a miscarriage or stillbirth if they had a husband and an additional male contributing food. This result was a surprise because researchers had expected that help during childhood would be more important. "The Barí are not hungry; they are not close to the bone. But it must be the extra fat and protein that they get from secondary fathers during gestation that makes the difference," Beckerman explains as he points to photographs of Barí women who look well nourished, even downright plump.

Barí women seem to use this more flexible system of paternity when they need it. Within families, some children have secondary fathers, while their siblings belong to the husband alone. The team discovered that mothers are more likely to take on a secondary father when a previous child has died in infancy. Manuel Lizarralde claims the strategy makes perfect sense, given the Barí belief that the best way to cure a sick child is for the father to blow tobacco smoke over the child's body. "It is easy to imagine a bereaved mother thinking to herself that if she had only provided a secondary father and so more smoke for her dead child, she might have saved him—and vowing to provide that benefit for her next child."

Beckerman says extra fathers may have always been insurance for uncertain times: "Because the Barí were once hunted as if they were game animals—by other Indians, conquistadors, oilmen, farmers, and ranchers—the odds of a woman being widowed when she still had young children were one in three, according to data we gathered about the years 1930 to 1960. The men as well as the women knew this. None of these guys can go down the street to Mutual of Omaha and buy a life insurance policy. By allowing his wife to take a lover, the husband is doing all he can to ensure the survival of his children."

Barí women are also freer to do as they wish because men need their labor—having a wife is an economic necessity because women do the manioc farming, harvesting, and cooking, while men hunt and fish. "The sexual division of labor is such that you can't make it without a member of the opposite sex," says Beckerman. Initially, the researchers worried that jealousy on the part of husbands would make Barí women reticent about discussing multiple sexual partners. "In our first interviews, we would wait until the husband was out of the house," says Beckerman. "But one day we interviewed an old couple who were enjoying thinking about their lives; they were lying in their hammocks, side by side, and it was obvious he wasn't going anywhere. So we went down the list of her children and asked about other fathers. She said no, no, no for each child, and then the husband interrupted when we got to one and said, 'That's not true, don't you remember, there was that guy . . .' And the husband was grinning."

Not all women take lovers. Manuel Lizarralde has discovered through interviews that one-third of 122 women were faithful to their husbands during their pregnancies. "These women say they don't need it, or no one asked, or they have enough support from family and don't require another father for their child," Lizarralde says. "Some even admit that their husbands were not that happy about the idea." Or it may be a sign of changing times. Based on his most recent visits to the Barí, Lizarralde thinks that under the influence of Western values, the number of people who engage in multiple fatherhood may be decreasing. But his father, who has worked with the Barí for more than 40 years, disagrees. He says the practice is as frequent but that the Barí discuss it less openly than before, knowing that Westerners object to their views. After all, it took the anthropologists 20 years to hear about other fathers, and today the Barí are probably being even more discreet because they know Westerners disapprove of their beliefs.

"What this information adds up to," Beckerman says, "is that the Barí may be doing somewhat less fooling around within marriage these days but that most of them still believe that a child can have multiple fathers."

More important, the Barí idea that biological paternity can be shared is not just the quirky custom of one tribe; anthropologists have found that this idea is common across South America. The same belief is shared by indigenous groups in New Guinea and India, suggesting that multiple paternity has been part of human behavior for a long time, undermining all previous descriptions of how human mating behavior evolved.

Since the 1960s, when anthropologists began to construct scenarios of early human mating, they had always assumed that the model family started with a mom and dad bonded for life to raise the kids, a model that fit well with acceptable Western behavior. In 1981 in an article titled "The Origin of Man," C. Owen Lovejoy, an anthropologist at Kent State University, outlined the standard story of human evolution as it was used in the field—and is still presented in textbooks today: Human infants with their big brains and long periods of growth and learning have always been dependent on adults, a dependence that separates the humans from the apes. Mothers alone couldn't possibly find enough food for these dependent young, so women have always needed to find a mate who would stick close to home and bring in supplies for the family. Unfortunately for women, as evolutionary psychologists suggest, men are compelled by their biology to mate with as many partners as possible to pass along their genes. However, each of these men might be manipulated into staying with one woman who offered him sex and a promise of fidelity. The man, under those conditions, would be assured of paternity, and he might just stay around and make sure his kids survived.

This scenario presents humans as naturally monogamous, forming nuclear families as an evolutionary necessity. The only problem is that around the world families don't always operate this way. In fact, as the Barí and other cultures show, there are all sorts of ways to run a successful household.

The Na of Yunnan Province in China, for example, have a female-centric society in which husbands are not part of the picture. Women grow up and continue to live with their mothers, sisters, and brothers; they never marry or move away from the family compound. As a result, sisters and brothers rather than married pairs are the economic unit that farms and fishes together. Male lovers in this system are simply visitors. They have no place or power in the household, and children are brought up by their mothers and by the mothers' brothers. A father is identified only if there is a resemblance between him and the child, and even so, the father has no responsibilities toward the child. Often women have sex with so many partners that the biological father is unknown. "I have not found any term that would cover the notion of father in the Na language," writes Chinese anthropologist Cai Hua in his book *A Society Without Fathers or Husbands: The Na of China*. In this case, women have complete control over their children, property, and sexuality.

Across lowland South America, family systems vary because cultures put their beliefs into practice in different ways. Among some native people, such as the Canela, Mehinaku, and Araweté, women control their sex lives and their fertility, and most children have several fathers. Barí women are also sexually liberated from an early age. "Once she has completed her puberty ritual, a Barí girl can have sex with anyone she wants as long as she doesn't violate the incest taboo," Beckerman explains. "It's nobody's business, not even Mom's and Dad's business." Women can also turn down prospective husbands.

In other cultures in South America, life is not so free for females, although members of these cultures also believe that babies can have more than one father. The Curripaco of Amazonia, for instance, acknowledge multiple fatherhood as a biological possibility and yet frown on women having affairs. Paul Valentine, a senior lecturer in anthropology at the University of East London who has studied the Curripaco for more than 20 years, says, "Curripaco women are in a difficult situation. The wives come into the village from different areas, and it's a very patrilineal system." If her husband dies, a widow is allowed to turn only to his brothers or to clan members on his side of the family for a new husband.

The relative power of women and men over their sex lives has important consequences. "In certain social and economic systems, women are free to make mate choices," says Valentine. In these cultures women are often the foundation of society, while men have less power in the community. Sisters tend to stay in the same household as their mothers. The women, in other words, have power to make choices. "At the other extreme, somehow, it's the men who try to maximize their evolutionary success at the expense of the women," says Valentine.

Men and women often have a conflict of interest when it comes to mating, marriage, and who should invest most in children, and the winners have sometimes been the men, sometimes the women. As Beckerman wryly puts it, "Anyone who believes that in a human mating relationship the man's reproductive interests always carry the day has obviously never been married."

The Barí and others show that human systems are, in fact, very flexible, ready to accommodate any sort of mating system or type of family. "I think that human beings are capable of making life extremely complicated. That's our way of doing business," says Ian Tattersall, a paleoanthropologist and curator in the division of anthropology at the American Museum of Natural History in New York City. Indeed, such flexibility suggests there's no reason to assume that the nuclear family is the natural, ideal, or even most evolutionarily successful system of human grouping. As Beckerman says, "One of the things this research shows is that human beings are just as clever and creative in assembling their kin relations as they are putting together space shuttles or symphonies."

30

When Brothers Share a Wife

Melvyn C. Goldstein

Marriage is a social institution that formalizes certain aspects of the relationship between males and females. It is an institution that evokes in us deep-seated emotions about questions of right and wrong, good and evil, and traditional versus modern. Within families, arguments may occur about what is appropriate premarital behavior, what is a proper marriage ceremony, and how long a marriage should last. Although these arguments may be traumatic for parents and their offspring, from a cross-cultural perspective, they generally involve minor deviations from the cultural norms. In contrast, anthropology textbooks describe an amazing variety of marriage systems that fulfill both biological and social functions. This selection will show just how different things could be.

Social institutions are geared to operate within and adapt to the larger social and ecological environment. This was the case in the earlier selections on gender roles and family planning; the organization of the family must also be adapted to the ecology. For example, the nuclear family is more adapted to a highly mobile society than is an extended family unit that includes grandparents and others. As society increasingly focuses on technical education, career specialization, and therefore geographic mobility for employment purposes, a system has evolved that emphasizes the nuclear family over the extended family. In a similar way, fraternal polyandry in Tibet, as described in this selection, can meet the social, demographic, and ecological needs of its region.

As you read this selection, ask yourself the following questions:

- What is meant by the term *fraternal polyandry*?
- Is this the only form of marriage allowed in Tibet?
- How do husbands and wives feel about the sexual aspects of sharing a spouse?
- Why would Tibetans choose fraternal polyandry?
- How is the function of fraternal polyandry like that of nineteenth-century primogeniture in England?

The following terms discussed in this selection are included in the Glossary at the back of the book:

arable land	*nuclear family*
corvée	*population pressure*
fraternal polyandry	*primogeniture*
monogamy	

Eager to reach home, Dorje drives his yaks hard over the 17,000-foot mountain pass, stopping only once to rest. He and his two older brothers, Pema and Sonam, are jointly marrying a woman from the next village in a few weeks, and he has to help with the preparations.

Dorje, Pema, and Sonam are Tibetans living in Limi, a 200-square-mile area in the northwest corner of Nepal, across the border from Tibet. The form of marriage they are about to enter—fraternal polyandry in anthropological parlance—is one of the world's rarest forms of marriage but is not uncommon in Tibetan society, where it has been practiced from time immemorial. For many Tibetan social strata, it traditionally represented the ideal form of marriage and family.

The mechanics of fraternal polyandry are simple. Two, three, four, or more brothers jointly take a wife, who leaves her home to come and live with them. Traditionally, marriage was arranged by parents, with children, particularly females, having little or no say. This is changing somewhat nowadays, but it is still unusual for children to marry without their parents' consent. Marriage ceremonies vary by income and region and range from all the brothers sitting together as grooms to only the eldest one formally doing so. The age of the brothers plays an important role in determining this: very young brothers almost never participate in actual marriage ceremonies, although they typically join the marriage when they reach their midteens.

Goldstein, Melvyn C. "When Brothers Share a Wife" from Natural History (March 1987):39–48. Copyright © Natural History Magazine, Inc. 2006. Reprinted with permission.

The eldest brother is normally dominant in terms of authority, that is, in managing the household, but all the brothers share the work and participate as sexual partners. Tibetan males and females do not find the sexual aspect of sharing a spouse the least bit unusual, repulsive, or scandalous, and the norm is for the wife to treat all the brothers the same.

Offspring are treated similarly. There is no attempt to link children biologically to particular brothers, and a brother shows no favoritism toward his child even if he knows he is the real father because, for example, his older brothers were away at the time the wife became pregnant. The children, in turn, consider all of the brothers as their fathers and treat them equally, even if they also know who is their real father. In some regions children use the term "father" for the eldest brother and "father's brother" for the others, while in other areas they call all the brothers by one term, modifying this by the use of "elder" and "younger."

Unlike our own society, where monogamy is the only form of marriage permitted, Tibetan society allows a variety of marriage types, including monogamy, fraternal polyandry, and polygyny. Fraternal polyandry and monogamy are the most common forms of marriage, while polygyny typically occurs in cases where the first wife is barren. The widespread practice of fraternal polyandry, therefore, is not the outcome of a law requiring brothers to marry jointly. There is choice, and in fact, divorce traditionally was relatively simple in Tibetan society. If a brother in a polyandrous marriage became dissatisfied and wanted to separate, he simply left the main house and set up his own household. In such cases, all the children stayed in the main household with the remaining brother(s), even if the departing brother was known to be the real father of one or more of the children.

The Tibetans' own explanation for choosing fraternal polyandry is materialistic. For example, when I asked Dorje why he decided to marry with his two brothers rather than take his own wife, he thought for a moment, then said it prevented the division of his family's farm (and animals) and thus facilitated all of them achieving a higher standard of living. And when I later asked Dorje's bride whether it wasn't difficult for her to cope with three brothers as husbands, she laughed and echoed that rationale of avoiding fragmentation of the family land, adding that she expected to be better off economically, since she would have three husbands working for her and her children.

Exotic as it may seem to Westerners, Tibetan fraternal polyandry is thus in many ways analogous to the way primogeniture functioned in nineteenth-century England. Primogeniture dictated that the eldest son inherited the family estate, while younger sons had to leave home and seek their own employment—for

example, in the military or the clergy. Primogeniture maintained family estates intact over generations by permitting only one heir per generation. Fraternal polyandry also accomplishes this but does so by keeping all the brothers together with just one wife so that there is only one set of heirs per generation.

While Tibetans believe that in this way fraternal polyandry reduces the risk of family fission, monogamous marriages among brothers need not necessarily precipitate the division of the family estate: brothers could continue to live together, and the family land could continue to be worked jointly. When I asked Tibetans about this, however, they invariably responded that such joint families are unstable because each wife is primarily oriented to her own children and interested in their success and well-being over that of the children of other wives. For example, if the youngest brother's wife had three sons while the eldest brother's wife had only one daughter, the wife of the youngest brother might begin to demand more resources for her children since, as males, they represent the future of the family. Thus, the children from different wives in the same generation are competing sets of heirs, and this makes such families inherently unstable. Tibetans perceive that conflict will spread from the wives to their husbands and consider this likely to cause family fission. Consequently, it is almost never done.

Although Tibetans see an economic advantage to fraternal polyandry, they do not value the sharing of a wife as an end in itself. On the contrary, they articulate a number of problems inherent in the practice. For example, because authority is customarily exercised by the eldest brother, his younger male siblings have to subordinate themselves with little hope of changing their status within the family. When these younger brothers are aggressive and individualistic, tensions and difficulties often occur despite there being only one set of heirs.

In addition, tension and conflict may arise in polyandrous families because of sexual favoritism. The bride normally sleeps with the eldest brother, and the two have the responsibility to see to it that the other males have opportunities for sexual access. Since the Tibetan subsistence economy requires males to travel a lot, the temporary absence of one or more brothers facilitates this, but there are also other rotation practices. The cultural ideal unambiguously calls for the wife to show equal affection and sexuality to each of the brothers (and vice versa), but deviations from this ideal occur, especially when there is a sizable difference in age between partners in the marriage.

Dorje's family represents just such a potential situation. He is fifteen years old and his two older brothers are twenty-five and twenty-two years old. The new bride is twenty-three years old, eight years Dorje's

Monogamy

Brothers take wives and divide their inherited land
3 brothers take 3 wives; each bears 3 sons

Polyandry

Brothers share a wife and work their inherited land together
3 brothers take 1 wife; she bears 3 sons

Generation 1

9 sons take 9 wives; each bears 3 sons

3 sons take 1 wife; she bears 3 sons

Generation 2

27 grandsons take 27 wives

3 grandsons take 1 wife

Generation 3

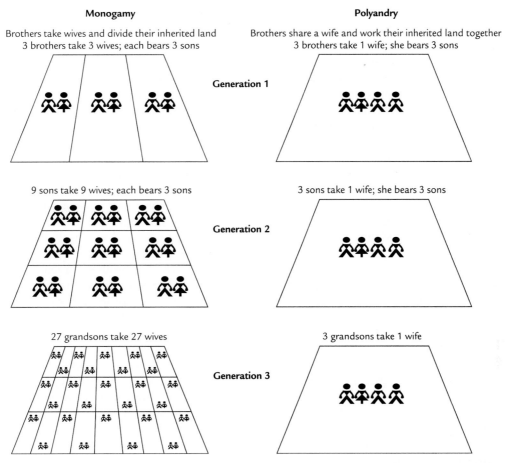

Goldstein, Melvyn C. "When Brothers Share a Wife" from Natural History (March 1987):39–48. Copyright © Natural History Magazine, Inc. 2006. Illustration reprinted with permission of LeMonnier.

senior. Sometimes such a bride finds the youngest husband immature and adolescent and does not treat him with equal affection; alternatively, she may find his youth attractive and lavish special attention on him. Apart from this consideration, when a younger male like Dorje grows up, he may consider his wife "ancient" and prefer the company of a woman his own age or younger. Consequently, although men and women do not find the idea of sharing a bride or a bridegroom repulsive, individual likes and dislikes can cause familial discord.

Two reasons have commonly been offered for the perpetuation of fraternal polyandry in Tibet: that Tibetans practice female infanticide and therefore have to marry polyandrously, owing to a shortage of females; and that Tibet, lying at extremely high altitudes, is so barren and bleak that Tibetans would starve without resort to this mechanism. A Jesuit who lived in Tibet in the eighteenth century articulated this second view: "One reason for this most odious custom is the sterility of the soil, and the small amount of land that can be cultivated owing to the lack of water. The crops may suffice if the brothers all live together, but if

they form separate families they would be reduced to beggary."

Both explanations are wrong, however. Not only has there never been institutionalized female infanticide in Tibet, but Tibetan society gives females considerable rights, including inheriting the family estate in the absence of brothers. In such cases, the woman takes a bridegroom who comes to live in her family and adopts her family's name and identity. Moreover, there is no demographic evidence of a shortage of females. In Limi, for example, there were (in 1974) sixty females and fifty-three males in the fifteen- to thirty-five-year age category, and many adult females were unmarried.

The second reason is also incorrect. The climate in Tibet is extremely harsh, and ecological factors do play a major role perpetuating polyandry, but polyandry is not a means of preventing starvation. It is characteristic, not of the poorest segments of the society, but rather of the peasant landowning families.

In the old society, the landless poor could not realistically aspire to prosperity, but they did not fear starvation. There was a persistent labor shortage throughout Tibet, and very poor families with little or no land and few animals could subsist through agricultural labor, tenant farming, craft occupations such as carpentry, or by working as servants. Although the per person family income could increase somewhat if brothers married polyandrously and pooled their wages, in the absence of inheritable land, the advantage of fraternal polyandry was not generally sufficient to prevent them from setting up their own households. A more skilled or energetic younger brother could do as well or better alone, since he would completely control his income and would not have to share it with his siblings. Consequently, while there was and is some polyandry among the poor, it is much less frequent and more prone to result in divorce and family fission.

An alternative reason for the persistence of fraternal polyandry is that it reduces population growth (and thereby reduces the pressure on resources) by relegating some females to lifetime spinsterhood. Fraternal polyandrous marriages in Limi (in 1974) averaged 2.35 men per woman, and not surprisingly, 31 percent of the females of child-bearing age (twenty to forty-nine) were unmarried. These spinsters either continued to live at home, set up their own households, or worked as servants for other families. They could also become Buddhist nuns. Being unmarried is not synonymous with exclusion from the reproductive pool. Discreet extramarital relationships are tolerated, and actually half of the adult unmarried women in Limi had one or more children. They raised these children as single mothers, working for wages or weaving cloth and blankets for sale. As a group, however, the unmarried women had far fewer offspring than the married women, averaging only 0.7 children per woman, compared with 3.3 for married women, whether polyandrous, monogamous, or polygynous. While polyandry helps regulate population, this function of polyandry is not consciously perceived by Tibetans and is not the reason they consistently choose it.

If neither a shortage of females nor the fear of starvation perpetuates fraternal polyandry, what motivates brothers, particularly younger brothers, to opt for this system of marriage? From the perspective of the younger brother in a landholding family, the main incentive is the attainment or maintenance of the good life. With polyandry, he can expect a more secure and higher standard of living, with access not only to his family's land and animals, but also to its inherited collection of clothes, jewelry, rugs, saddles, and horses. In addition, he will experience less work pressure and much greater security because all responsibility does not fall on one "father." For Tibetan brothers, the question is whether to trade off the greater personal freedom inherent in monogamy for the real or potential economic security, affluence, and social prestige associated with life in a larger, labor-rich polyandrous family.

A brother thinking of separating from his polyandrous marriage and taking his own wife would face various disadvantages. Although in the majority of Tibetan regions all brothers theoretically have rights to their family's estate, in reality Tibetans are reluctant to divide their land into small fragments. Generally, a younger brother who insists on leaving the family will receive only a small plot of land, if that. Because of its power and wealth, the rest of the family usually can block any attempt of the younger brother to increase his share of land through litigation. Moreover, a younger brother may not even get a house and cannot expect to receive much above the minimum in terms of movable possessions, such as furniture, pots, and pans. Thus, a brother contemplating going it on his own must plan on achieving economic security and the good life not through inheritance but through his own work.

The obvious solution for younger brothers—creating new fields from virgin land—is generally not a feasible option. Most Tibetan populations live at high altitudes (above 12,000 feet), where arable land is extremely scarce. For example, in Dorje's village, agriculture ranges only from about 12,900 feet, the lowest point in the area, to 13,300 feet. Above that altitude, early frost and snow destroy the staple barley crop. Furthermore, because of the low rainfall caused by the Himalayan rain shadow, many areas in Tibet and northern Nepal that are within appropriate altitude range for agriculture have no reliable sources of irrigation. In the end, although there is plenty of unused land in such areas, most of it is either too high or too arid.

Even where unused land capable of being farmed exists, clearing the land and building the substantial terraces necessary for irrigation constitute a great undertaking. Each plot has to be completely dug out to a depth of two to two and a half feet so that the large rocks and boulders can be removed. At best, a man might be able to bring a few new fields under cultivation in the first years after separating from his brothers, but he could not expect to acquire substantial amounts of arable land this way.

In addition, because of the limited farmland, the Tibetan subsistence economy characteristically includes a strong emphasis on animal husbandry. Tibetan farmers regularly maintain cattle, yaks, goats, and sheep, grazing them in the areas too high for agriculture. These herds produce wool, milk, cheese, butter, meat, and skins. To obtain these resources, however, shepherds must accompany the animals on a daily basis. When first setting up a monogamous household, a younger brother like Dorje would find it difficult to both farm and manage animals.

In traditional Tibetan society, there was an even more critical factor that operated to perpetuate fraternal polyandry—a form of hereditary servitude somewhat analogous to serfdom in Europe. Peasants were tied to large estates held by aristocrats, monasteries, and the Lhasa government. They were allowed the use of some farmland to produce their own subsistence but were required to provide taxes in kind and corvée (free labor) to their lords. The corvée was a substantial hardship, since a peasant household was in many cases required to furnish the lord with one laborer daily for most of the year and more on specific occasions such as the harvest. This enforced labor, along with the lack of new land and the ecological pressure to pursue both agriculture and animal husbandry, made polyandrous families particularly beneficial. The polyandrous family allowed an internal division of adult labor, maximizing economic advantage. For example, while the wife worked the family fields, one brother could perform the lord's corvée, another could look after the animals, and a third could engage in trade.

Although social scientists often discount other people's explanations of why they do things, in the case of Tibetan fraternal polyandry, such explanations are very close to the truth. The custom, however, is very sensitive to changes in its political and economic milieu and, not surprisingly, is in decline in most Tibetan areas. Made less important by the elimination of the traditional serf-based economy, it is disparaged by the dominant non-Tibetan leaders of India, China, and Nepal. New opportunities for economic and social mobility in these countries, such as the tourist trade and government employment, are also eroding the rationale for polyandry, and so it may vanish within the next generation.

31

Our Babies, Ourselves

Meredith F. Small

Nature or nurture? Genes or environment? A perennial question in anthropology is the relative importance of innate human biology or particular cultural and early-childhood influences in people's social and psychological development. Cross-cultural variation in thought and behavior patterns is the hallmark of human diversity. Most anthropologists believe that there is individual variation within cultural variation. That is, members of a society share ideas of appropriate behavior, including the ways to raise children, and those shared ideas supercede individual variation. The influence of culture on personality development has been a theme in cultural anthropology since the days of Margaret Mead. These questions require us to study child-raising practices in a cross-cultural perspective.

This selection describes how parenting behaviors vary across societies. The way in which we interact with our own babies and children influences the adults they become. Sometimes we use the computer analogy of biology being the hardware (the brain) and culture as the software (the models with which we think and pattern our behavior) to think about nature and nurture. That analogy misses the fact that as babies learn they are physically shaping their neural pathways. With this in mind, the study of parenting and child development is even more important. In this regard, so-called traditional societies might have a lot to teach us.

People may be reticent to learn from others ("If it was good enough for us . . .") or to change behaviors, like extended breast-feeding.

As you read this selection, ask yourself the following questions:

- Why do Americans put babies in their own cribs, or feed them on schedules, or "let them cry it out?" What underlying cultural values might parents be trying to teach?
- How might high infant mortality risk affect parents' behaviors?
- How much stimulation for infants is appropriate? Why did the Dutch mother put her baby down for a nap right after the bath?
- Who is best to take care of a baby? How do people decide that?
- Why do anthropologists report that babies in traditional societies like the !Kung do not cry as much?

The following terms discussed in this selection are included in the Glossary at the back of the book:

adaptation   socialization
ethnopediatrics   weaning

Small, M., R.A. LeVine, S. Harkness, C.M. Super, E.Z. Tronick, R.G. Barr, K.A. Dettwyler, & J.J. McKenna. "Our Babies, Ourselves" from Natural History (Oct. 1997):42–51. Copyright © Natural History Magazine, Inc. 2006. Reprinted with permission.

During one of his many trips to Gusiiland in southwestern Kenya, anthropologist Robert LeVine tried an experiment: he showed a group of Gusii mothers a videotape of middle-class American women tending their babies. The Gusii mothers were appalled. Why does that mother ignore the cries of her unhappy baby during a simple diaper change? And how come that grandmother does nothing to soothe the screaming baby in her lap? These American women, the Gusii concluded, are clearly incompetent mothers. In response, the same charge might be leveled at the Gusii by American mothers. What mother hands over her tiny infant to a six-year-old sister and expects the older child to provide adequate care? And why don't those Gusii women spend more time talking to their babies, so that they will grow up smart?

Both culture—the traditional way of doing things in a particular society—and individual experience guide parents in their tasks. When a father chooses to pick up his newborn and not let it cry, when a mother decides to bottle-feed on a schedule rather than breast-feed on

GUSII SURVIVAL SKILLS
By Robert A. LeVine

Farming peoples of subSaharan Africa have long faced the grim reality that many babies fail to survive, often succumbing to gastrointestinal diseases, malaria, or other infections. In the 1970s, when I lived among the Gusii in a small town in southwestern Kenya, infant mortality in that nation was on the decline but was still high—about eighty deaths per thousand live births during the first year, compared with about ten in the United States at that time and six to eight in Western Europe.

The Gusii grew corn, millet, and cash crops such as coffee and tea. Women handled the more routine tasks of cultivation, food processing, and trading, while men were supervisors or entrepreneurs. Many men worked at jobs outside the village, in urban centers or on plantations. The society was polygamous, with perhaps 10 percent of the men having two or more wives. A woman was expected to give birth every two years, from marriage to menopause, and the average married woman bore about ten live children—one of the highest fertility rates in the world.

Nursing mothers slept alone with a new infant for fifteen months to insure its health. For the first three to six months, the Gusii mothers were especially vigilant for signs of ill health or slow growth, and they were quick to nurture unusually small or sick infants by feeding and holding them more often. Mothers whose newborns were deemed particularly at risk—including twins and those born prematurely—entered a ritual seclusion for several weeks, staying with their infants in a hut with a constant fire.

Mothers kept infants from crying in the early months by holding them constantly and being quick to comfort them. After three to six months—if the baby was growing normally—mothers began to entrust the baby to the care of other children (usually six to twelve years old) in order to pursue tasks that helped support the family. Fathers did not take care of infants, for this was not a traditional male activity.

Because they were so worried about their children's survival, Gusii parents did not explicitly strive to foster cognitive, social, and emotional development. These needs were not neglected, however, because from birth Gusii babies entered an active and responsive interpersonal environment, first with their mothers and young caregivers, and later as part of a group of children.

demand, when a couple bring the newborn into their bed at night, they are prompted by what they believe to be the best methods of caregiving.

For decades, anthropologists have been recording how children are raised in different societies. At first, the major goals were to describe parental roles and understand how child-rearing practices and rituals helped to generate adult personality. In the 1950s, for example, John and Beatrice Whiting, and their colleagues at Harvard, Yale, and Cornell Universities, launched a major comparative study of childhood, looking at six varied communities in different regions: Okinawa, the Philippines, northern India, Kenya, Mexico, and New England. They showed that communal expectations play a major role in setting parenting styles, which in turn play a part in shaping children to become accepted adults.

More recent work by anthropologists and child-development researchers has shown that parents readily accept their society's prevailing ideology on how babies should be treated, usually because it makes sense in their environmental or social circumstances. In the United States, for example, where individualism is valued, parents do not hold babies as much as in other cultures, and they place them in rooms of their own to sleep. Pediatricians and parents alike often say this fosters independence and self-reliance. Japanese parents, in contrast, believe that individuals should be well integrated into society, and so they "indulge" their babies. Japanese infants are held more often, not left to cry, and sleep with their parents. Efe parents in Congo believe even more in a communal life, and their infants are regularly nursed, held, and comforted by any number of group members, not just parents. Whether such practices help form the anticipated adult personality traits remains to be shown, however.

Recently, a group of anthropologists, child-development experts, and pediatricians have taken the cross-cultural approach in a new direction by investigating how differing parenting styles affect infant health and growth. Instead of emphasizing the development of adult personality, these researchers, who call themselves ethnopediatricians, focus on the child as an organism. Ethnopediatricians see the human infant as a product of evolution, geared to enter a particular environment of care. What an infant actually gets is a compromise, as parents are pulled by their offspring's needs and pushed by social and personal expectations.

Compared with offspring of many other mammals, primate infants are dependent and vulnerable. Baby monkeys and apes stay close to the mother's body, clinging to her stomach or riding on her back, and nursing at will. They are protected in this way for many months, until they develop enough motor and cognitive skills to move about. Human infants are at the extreme: virtually helpless as newborns, they need

AN INFANT'S THREE Rs

By Sara Harkness and Charles M. Super

You are an American visitor spending a morning in a pleasant middle-class Dutch home to observe the normal routine of a mother and her six-month-old baby. The mother made sure you got there by 8:30 to witness the morning bath, an opportunity for playful interaction with the baby. The baby was then dressed in cozy warm clothes, her hair brushed and styled with a tiny curlicue atop her head. The mother gave her the midmorning bottle, then sang to her and played patty-cake for a few minutes before placing her in the playpen to entertain herself with a mobile while the mother attended to other things nearby. Now, about half an hour later, the baby is beginning to get fussy.

The mother watches her for a minute, then offers a toy and turns away. The baby again begins to fuss. "Seems bored and in need of attention," you think. But the mother looks at the baby sympathetically and in a soothing voice says, "Oh, are you tired?" Without further ado she picks up the baby, carries her upstairs, tucks her into her crib, and pulls down the shades. To your surprise, the baby fusses for only a few more moments, then is quiet. The mother returns looking serene. "She needs plenty of sleep in order to grow," she explains. "When she doesn't have her nap or go to bed on time, we can always tell the difference—she's not so happy and playful."

Different patterns in infant sleep can be found in Western societies that seem quite similar to those of the United States. We discovered the "three Rs" of Dutch child rearing—*rust* (rest), *regelmaat* (regularity), and *reinheid* (cleanliness)—while doing research on a sample of sixty families with infants or young children in a middle-class community near Leiden and Amsterdam, the sort of community typical of Dutch life styles in all but the big cities nowadays. At six months, the Dutch babies were sleeping more than a comparison group of American babies—a total of fifteen hours per day compared with thirteen hours for the Americans. While awake at home, the Dutch babies were more often left to play quietly in their playpens or infant seats. A daily ride in the baby carriage provided time for the baby to look around at the passing scene or to doze peacefully. If the mother needed to go out for a while without the baby, she could leave it alone in bed for a short period or time her outing with the baby's nap time and ask a neighbor to monitor with a "baby phone."

To understand how Dutch families manage to establish such a restful routine by the time their babies are six months old, we made a second research visit to the same community. We found that by two weeks of age, the Dutch babies were already sleeping more than same-age American babies. In fact, a dilemma for some Dutch parents was whether to wake the baby after eight hours, as instructed by the local health care providers, or let them sleep longer. The main method for establishing and maintaining this pattern was to create a calm, regular, and restful environment for the infant throughout the day.

Far from worrying about "adequate stimulation," these mothers were conscientious about avoiding overstimulation in the form of late family outings, disruptions in the regularity of eating and sleeping, or too many things to look at or listen to. Few parents were troubled by their babies' nighttime sleep routines. Babies's feeding schedules were structured following the guidelines of the local baby clinic (a national service). If a baby continued to wake up at night when feeding was no longer considered necessary, the mother (or father) would most commonly give it a pacifier and a little back rub to help it get back to sleep. Only in rare instances did parents find themselves forced to choose between letting the baby scream and allowing too much night waking.

Many aspects of Dutch society support the three Rs throughout infancy and childhood—for example, shopping is close to home, and families usually have neighbors and relatives nearby who are available to help out with child care. The small scale of neighborhoods and a network of bicycle paths provide local play sites and a safe way for children to get around easily on their own (no "soccer moms" are needed for daily transportation!). Work sites for both fathers and mothers are also generally close to home, and there are many flexible or part-time job arrangements.

National policies for health and other social benefits insure universal coverage regardless of one's employment status, and the principle of the "family wage" has prevailed in labor relations so that mothers of infants and young children rarely work more than part-time, if at all. In many ways, the three Rs of Dutch child rearing are just one aspect of a calm and unhurried life style for the whole family.

twelve months just to learn to walk and years of social learning before they can function on their own.

Dependence during infancy is the price we pay for being hominids, members of the group of upright-walking primates that includes humans and their extinct relatives. Four million years ago, when our ancestors became bipedal, the hominid pelvis underwent a necessary renovation. At first, this new pelvic architecture presented no problem during birth because the early hominids, known as australopithecines, still had rather small brains, one-third the present size. But starting about 1.5 million years ago, human brain size ballooned. Hominid babies now had to twist and bend to pass through the birth canal, and more important, birth had to be triggered before the skull grew too big.

DOCTOR'S ORDERS
By Edward Z. Tronick

In Boston, a pediatric resident is experiencing a vague sense of disquiet as she interviews a Puerto Rican mother who has brought her baby in for a checkup. When she is at work, the mother explains, the two older children, ages six and nine, take care of the two younger ones, a two-year-old and the three-month-old baby. Warning bells go off for the resident: young children cannot possibly be sensitive to the needs of babies and toddlers. And yet the baby is thriving; he is well over the ninetieth percentile in weight and height and is full of smiles.

The resident questions the mother in detail: How is the baby fed? Is the apartment safe for a two-year-old? The responses are all reassuring, but the resident nonetheless launches into a lecture on the importance of the mother to normal infant development. The mother falls silent, and the resident is now convinced that something is seriously wrong. And something is—the resident's model of child care.

The resident subscribes to what I call the "continuous care and contact" model of parenting, which demands a high level of contact, frequent feeding, and constant supervision, with almost all care provided by the mother. According to this model, a mother should also enhance cognitive development with play and verbal engagement. The pediatric resident is comfortable with this formula— she is not even conscious of it—because she was raised this way and treats her own child in the same manner. But at the Child Development Unit of Children's Hospital in Boston, which I direct, I want residents to abandon the idea that there is only one way to raise a child. Not to do so may interfere with patient care.

Many models of parenting are valid. Among Efe foragers of Congo's Ituri Forest, for example, a newborn is routinely cared for by several people. Babies are even nursed by many women. But few individuals ever play with the infant; as far as the Efe are concerned, the baby's job is to sleep.

In Peru, the Quechua swaddle their infants in a pouch of blankets that the mother, or a child caretaker, carries on her back. Inside the pouch, the infant cannot move, and its eyes are covered. Quechua babies are nursed in a perfunctory fashion, with three or four hours between feedings.

As I explain to novice pediatricians, such practices do not fit the continuous care and contact model; yet these babies grow up just fine. But my residents see these cultures as exotic, not relevant to the industrialized world. And so I follow up with examples closer to home: Dutch parents who leave an infant alone in order to go shopping, sometimes pinning the child's shirt to the bed to keep the baby on its back; or Japanese mothers who periodically wake a sleeping infant to teach the child who is in charge. The questions soon follow. "How could a mother leave her infant alone?" "Why would a parent ever want to wake up a sleeping baby?"

The data from cross-cultural studies indicate that childcare practices vary, and that these styles aim to make the child into a culturally appropriate adult. The Efe make future Efe. The resident makes future residents. A doctor who has a vague sense that something is wrong with how someone cares for a baby may first need to explore his or her own assumptions, the hidden "shoulds" that are based solely on tradition. Of course, pediatric residents must make sure children are cared for responsibly. I know I have helped residents broaden their views when their lectures on good mothering are replaced by such comments as "What a gorgeous baby! I can't imagine how you manage both work and three others at home!"

As a result, the human infant is born neurologically unfinished and unable to coordinate muscle movement. Natural selection has compensated for this by favoring a close adult–infant tie that lasts years and goes beyond meeting the needs of food and shelter. In a sense, the human baby is not isolated but is part of a physiologically and emotionally entwined dyad of infant and caregiver. The adult might be male or female, a birth or adoptive parent, as long as at least one person is attuned to the infant's needs.

The signs of this interrelationship are many. Through conditioning, a mother's breast milk often begins to flow at the sound of her own infant's cries, even before the nipple is stimulated. New mothers also easily recognize the cries (and smells) of their infants over those of other babies. For their part, newborns recognize their own mother's voice and prefer it over others. One experiment showed that a baby's heart rate quickly synchronizes with Mom's or Dad's, but not with that of a friendly stranger. Babies are also predisposed to be socially engaged with caregivers. From birth, infants move their bodies in synchrony with adult speech; they are hard-wired to absorb the cadence of speech and the general nature of language. Babies quickly recognize the arrangement of a human face—two eyes, a nose, and a mouth in the right place—over other more Picasso-like rearrangements. And mothers and infants will position themselves face-to-face when they lie down to sleep.

Babies and mothers seem to follow a typical pattern of play, a coordinated waltz that moves from attention to inattention and back again. This innate

THE CRYING GAME
By Ronald G. Barr

All normal human infants cry, although they vary a great deal in how much. A mysterious and still unexplained phenomenon is that crying tends to increase in the first few weeks of life, peaks in the second or third month, and then decreases. Some babies in the United States cry so much during the peak period—often in excess of three hours a day—and seem so difficult to soothe that parents come to doubt their nurturing skills or to begin to fear that their offspring is suffering from a painful disease. Some mothers discontinue nursing and switch to bottle-feeding because they believe their breast milk is insufficiently nutritious and that their infants are always hungry. In extreme cases, the crying may provoke physical abuse, sometimes even precipitating the infant's death.

A look at another culture, the !Kung San hunter-gatherers of southern Africa, provides us with an opportunity to see whether caregiving strategies have any effect on infant crying. Both the !Kung San and Western infants escalate their crying during the early weeks of life, with a similar peak at two or three months. A comparison of Dutch, American, and !Kung San infants shows that the number of individual crying episodes are virtually identical. What differs is their length: !Kung San infants cry about half as long as Western babies. This implies that caregiving can influence only some aspects of crying, such as duration.

What is particularly striking about child-rearing among the !Kung San is that infants are in constant contact with a caregiver; they are carried or held most of the time, are usually in an upright position, and are breast-fed about four times an hour for one to two minutes at a time. Furthermore, the mother almost always responds to the smallest cry or fret within ten seconds.

I believe that crying was adaptive for our ancestors. As seen in the contemporary !Kung San, crying probably elicited a quick response, and thus consisted of frequent but relatively short episodes. This pattern helped keep an adult close by to provide adequate nutrition as well as protection from predators. I have also argued that crying helped an infant forge a strong attachment with the mother and—because new pregnancies are delayed by the prolongation of frequent nursing—secure more of her caregiving resources.

In the United States, where the threat of predation has receded and adequate nutrition is usually available even without breast-feeding, crying may be less adaptive. In any case, caregiving in the United States may be viewed as a cultural experiment in which the infant is relatively more separated—and separable—from the mother, both in terms of frequency of contact and actual distance.

The Western strategy is advantageous when the mother's employment outside of the home and away from the baby is necessary to sustain family resources. But the trade-off seems to be an increase in the length of crying bouts.

---

social connection was tested experimentally by Jeffrey Cohn and Edward Tronick in a series of three-minute laboratory experiments at the University of Massachusetts, in which they asked mothers to act depressed and not respond to baby's cues. When faced with a suddenly unresponsive mother, a baby repeatedly reaches out and flaps around, trying to catch her eye. When this tactic does not work, the baby gives up, turning away and going limp. And when the mother begins to respond again, it takes thirty seconds for the baby to reengage.

Given that human infants arrive in a state of dependency, ethnopediatricians have sought to define the care required to meet their physical, cognitive, and emotional needs. They assume there must be ways to treat babies that have proved adaptive over time and are therefore likely to be most appropriate. Surveys of parenting in different societies reveal broad patterns. In almost all cultures, infants sleep with their parents in the same room and most often in the same bed. At all other times, infants are usually carried. Caregivers also usually respond quickly to infant cries; mothers most often by offering the breast. Since most hunter-gatherer

groups also follow this overall style, this is probably the ancestral pattern. If there is an exception to these generalizations, it is the industrialized West.

Nuances of caretaking, however, do vary with particular social situations. !Kung San mothers of Botswana usually carry their infants on gathering expeditions, while the forest-living Ache of Paraguay, also hunters and gatherers, usually leave infants in camp while they gather. Gusii mothers working in garden plots leave their babies in the care of older children, while working mothers in the West may turn to unrelated adults. Such choices have physiological or behavioral consequences for the infant. As parents navigate between infant needs and the constraints of making a life, they may face a series of trade-offs that set the caregiver–infant dyad at odds. The areas of greatest controversy are breast-feeding, crying, and sleep—the major preoccupations of babies and their parents.

Strapped to their mothers' sides or backs in traditional fashion, human infants have quick access to the breast. Easy access makes sense because of the nature of human milk. Compared with that of other mammals,

WHEN TO WEAN
By Katherine A. Dettwyler

Breast-feeding in humans is a biological process grounded in our mammalian ancestry. It is also an activity modified by social and cultural constraints, including a mother's everyday work schedule and a variety of beliefs about personal autonomy, the proper relationship between mother and child (or between mother and father), and infant health and nutrition. The same may be said of the termination of breast-feeding, or weaning.

In the United States, children are commonly bottle-fed from birth or weaned within a few months. But in some societies, children as old as four or five years may still be nursed. The American Academy of Pediatrics currently advises breast-feeding for a minimum of one year (this may be revised upward), and the World Health Organization recommends two years or more. Amid conflicting advice, many wonder how long breast-feeding should last to provide an infant with optimal nutrition and health.

Nonhuman primates and other mammals give us some clues as to what the "natural" age of weaning would be if humans were less bound by cultural norms. Compared with most other orders of placental mammals, primates (including humans) have longer life spans and spend more time at each life stage, such as gestation, infant dependency, and puberty. Within the primate order itself, the trend in longevity increases from smaller-bodied, smaller-brained, often solitary prosimians through the larger-bodied, larger-brained, and usually social apes and humans. Gestation, for instance, is eighteen weeks in lemurs, twenty-four weeks in macaques, thirty-three weeks in chimpanzees, and thirty-eight weeks in humans.

Studies of nonhuman primates offer a number of different means of estimating the natural time for human weaning. First, large-bodied primates wean their offspring some months after the young have quadrupled their birth weight. In modern humans, this weight milestone is passed at about two and a half to three years of age. Second, like many other mammals, primate offspring tend to be weaned when they have attained about one third of their adult human weight; humans reach this level between four and seven years of age. Third, in all species studied so far, primates also wean their offspring at the time the first permanent molars erupt; this occurs at five and a half to six years in modern humans. Fourth, in chimpanzees and gorillas, breast-feeding usually lasts about six times the duration of gestation. On this basis, a human breast-feeding would be projected to continue for four and a half years.

Taken together, these and other projections suggest that somewhat more than two and a half years is the natural minimum age of weaning for humans and seven years the maximum age, well into childhood. The high end of this range, six to seven years, closely matches both the completion of human brain growth and the maturation of the child's immune system.

In many non-Western cultures, children are routinely nursed for three to five years. Incidentally, this practice inhibits ovulation in the mother, providing a natural mechanism of family planning. Even in the United States, a significant number of children are breast-fed beyond three years of age. While not all women are able or willing to nurse each of their children for many years, those who do should be encouraged and supported. Health care professionals, family, friends, and nosy neighbors should be reassured that "extended" breast-feeding, for as long as seven years, appears physiologically normal and natural.

Substantial evidence is already available to suggest that curtailing the duration of breast-feeding far below two and a half years—when the human child has evolved to expect more—can be deleterious. Every study that includes the duration of breast-feeding as a variable shows that, on average, the longer a baby is nursed, the better its health and cognitive development. For example, breast-fed children have fewer allergies, fewer ear infections, and less diarrhea, and their risk for sudden infant death syndrome (a rare but devastating occurrence) is lower. Breast-fed children also have higher cognitive test scores and lower incidence of attention deficit hyperactivity disorder.

In many cases, specific biochemical constituents of breast milk have been identified that either protect directly against disease or help the child's body develop its own defense system. For example, in the case of many viral diseases, the baby brings the virus to the mother, and her gut-wall cells manufacture specific antibodies against the virus, which then travel to the mammary glands and go back to the baby. The docosahexanoic acid in breast milk may be responsible for improved cognitive and attention functions. And the infant's exposure to the hormones and cholesterol in the milk appears to condition the body, reducing the risk of heart disease and breast cancer in later years. These and other discoveries show that breast-feeding serves functions for which no simple substitute is available.

primate milk is relatively low in fat and protein but high in carbohydrates. Such milk is biologically suitable if the infant can nurse on a frequent basis. Most Western babies are fed in a somewhat different way. At least half are bottle-fed from birth, while others are weaned from breast to bottle after only a few months. And most—whether nursed or bottle-fed—are fed at scheduled times, waiting hours between feedings. Long intervals in nursing disrupt the manufacture of breast milk, making it still lower in fat and thus less

BEDTIME STORY

By James J. McKenna

For as far back as you care to go, mothers have followed the protective and convenient practice of sleeping with their infants. Even now, for the vast majority of people across the globe, "cosleeping" and nighttime breast-feeding remain inseparable practices. Only in the past 200 years, and mostly in Western industrialized societies, have parents considered it normal and biologically appropriate for a mother and infant to sleep apart.

In the sleep laboratory at the University of California's Irvine School of Medicine, my colleagues and I observed mother–infant pairs as they slept both apart and together over three consecutive nights. Using a polygraph, we recorded the mother's and infant's heart rates, brain waves (EEGs), breathing, body temperature, and episodes of nursing. Infrared video photography simultaneously monitored their behavior.

We found that bed-sharing infants face their mothers for most of the night and that both mother and infant are highly responsive to each other's movements, wake more frequently, and spend more time in lighter stages of sleep than they do while sleeping alone. Bed-sharing infants nurse almost twice as often, and three times as long per bout, than they do while sleeping alone. But they rarely cry. Mothers who routinely sleep with their infants get at least as much sleep as mothers who sleep without them.

In addition to providing more nighttime nourishment and greater protection, sleeping with the mother supplies the infant with a steady stream of sensations of the mother's presence, including touch, smell, movement, and warmth. These stimuli can perhaps even compensate for the human infant's extreme neurological immaturity at birth.

Cosleeping might also turn out to give some babies protection from sudden infant death syndrome (SIDS), a heartbreaking and enigmatic killer. Cosleeping infants nurse more often, sleep more lightly, and have practice responding to maternal arousals. Arousal deficiencies are suspected in some SIDS deaths, and long periods in deep sleep may exacerbate this problem. Perhaps the physiological changes induced by cosleeping, especially when combined with nighttime breast-feeding, can benefit some infants by helping them sleep more lightly. At the same time, cosleeping makes it easier for a mother to detect and respond to an infant in crisis. Rethinking another sleeping practice has already shown a dramatic effect: In the United States, SIDS rates fell at least 30 percent after 1992, when the American Academy of Pediatrics recommended placing sleeping babies on their backs, rather than face down.

The effect of cosleeping on SIDS remains to be proved, so it would be premature to recommend it as the best arrangement for all families. The possible hazards of cosleeping must also be assessed. Is the environment otherwise safe, with appropriate bedding materials? Do the parents smoke? Do they use drugs or alcohol? (These appear to be the main factors in those rare cases in which a mother inadvertently smothers her child.) Since cosleeping was the ancestral condition, the future for our infants may well entail a borrowing back from ancient ways.

satisfying the next time the nipple is offered. And so crying over food and even the struggles of weaning result from the infant's unfulfilled expectations.

Sleep is also a major issue for new parents. In the West, babies are encouraged to sleep all through the night as soon as possible. And when infants do not do so, they merit the label "sleep problem" from both parents and pediatricians. But infants seem predisposed to sleep rather lightly, waking many times during the night. And while sleeping close to an adult allows infants to nurse more often and may have other beneficial effects, Westerners usually expect babies to sleep alone. This practice has roots in ecclesiastical laws enacted to protect against the smothering of infants by "lying over"—often a thinly disguised cover for infanticide—which was a concern in Europe beginning in the Middle Ages. Solitary sleep is reinforced by the rather recent notion of parental privacy. Western parents are also often convinced that solitary sleep will mold strong character.

Infant care is shaped by traditions, fads, science, and folk wisdom. Cross-cultural and evolutionary studies provide a useful perspective for parents and pediatricians as they sift through the alternatives. Where these insights fail to guide us, however, important clues are provided by the floppy but interactive babies themselves. Grinning when we talk to them, crying in distress when left alone, sleeping best when close at heart, they teach us that growth is a cooperative venture.

32

"Strange Country This"

An Introduction to North American Gender Diversity

Will Roscoe

Because of the colossal and tragic impact of European conquest in North America, our understanding of the full history of Native America is incomplete. However, the documented history of the tribes we do know about teaches us a significant lesson, namely that these first nations are far more diverse than the singular term Native America suggests. Nevertheless, despite different adaptive strategies, political structures, and cultural lives, alternative gender roles was one of the few widely shared features of Native American societies.

Two-spirit people, or berdaches, are people who fulfill mixed gender roles. Unlike contemporary terms like gay, lesbian, bisexual, and transgender, the term two-spirit represents people whose societies respectfully understand them as both male and female. Two-spirit people have been documented in over 150 North American tribes as people who make critical contributions to their communities. The two-spirit identity was widely understood as the result of divine intervention, and it encompassed much more than sexual preferences. Two-spirit males and females typically specialized in the work of the opposite sex; some berdache women were highly-respected warriors, while some berdache men were known as skilled beadworkers and matchmakers.

In this selection Will Roscoe explains the two-spirit tradition in Native North America including how two-spirit people differed from region to region and tribe to tribe. Understanding different ways people understand gender diversity demonstrates the power of culture over biology in terms of how we construct gender and sexuality.

As you read this selection, ask yourself the following questions:

- What role does sexuality play in berdache identities?
- Is it accurate to define the berdache as homosexual?
- What roles did "two-spirit" people play in Native American societies?
- How has the term berdache evolved and why has it become an accepted anthropological term for third/fourth gender Native Americans? Should anthropologists continue to use this term?
- What is the difference between the third and fourth genders?
- What are some of the differences between Native American alternative genders as found in different geographic regions?

The following terms discussed in this selection are included in the Glossary at the back of the book:

asexual   berdache
Defense of Marriage Act   *third/fourth gender*

In 1833, Edwin T. Denig came up the Missouri River to the country of the Crow Indians in Montana to spend the next twenty-three years of his life as a trader for the American Fur Company. He found himself in an unknown land, surrounded by unfamiliar cultures. Of all the differences he encountered none seemed more alien to him than native practices regarding sexuality and gender. Among the Crow Indians, Denig found that some of the most important and respected individuals were men and women who in American and European societies would be condemned, persecuted, jailed, even executed. Their lifestyles would be called immoral and perverse, their sexuality deemed unnatural.

And yet, among the Crows, men who dressed as women and specialized in women's work were accepted and sometimes honored; a woman who led men into battle and had four wives was a respected chief. As Denig wrote, "Most civilized communities recognize but two genders, the masculine and feminine. But strange to say, these people have a neuter," and with a note of exasperation he added, "Strange country this, where males assume the dress and perform the duties of females, while women turn men and mate with their own sex!"

The social universe of native North America was nowhere more at odds with that of Europe and Anglo-America than in its diverse gender roles. Denig's was not a new discovery. Europeans had been encountering "berdaches"—as third and fourth gender people have come to be called in the anthropological literature—since the days of Spanish conquest, and they reacted much as Denig did: with amazement, dismay, disgust, and occasionally, when they weren't dependent on the natives' goodwill, with violence. As Cabeza de Vaca wrote of his sojourn with the Karankawa Indians of Texas in 1540, "In the time that I continued among them, I saw a most brutish and beastly custom, to wit, a man who was married to another, and these be certaine effeminate and impotent men, who goe clothed and attired like women, and performe the office of a woman." Some years earlier, when Vasco Núñez de Balboa encountered forty *pathicos fœmineo amictu* (male homosexuals dressed as women) in Panama, he had them put to the dogs. The scene is illustrated in sadomasochistic detail in Théodor De Bry's famous *Collectiones peregrinationum.* "A fine action of an honourable and Catholic Spaniard," commented one historian a hundred years later.

In 1986, when the U.S. Supreme Court upheld Georgia's sodomy law, the majority opinion cited "millennia of moral teaching" against homosexuality in support of its decision. Ten years later, when legislation called the Defense of Marriage Act was proposed by a twice divorced congressman and signed into law by an admitted adulterer, it was said that no society that allowed people of the same sex to marry has or could survive, that American values were grounded in Judeo-Christian principles that precluded tolerance of same-sex love and gender difference.

In truth, the ground American society occupies once may have been the queerest continent on the planet. The original peoples of North America, whose principles are just as ancient as those of Judeo-Christian culture, saw no threat in homosexuality or gender variance. Indeed, they believed individuals with these traits made unique contributions to their communities. As a Crow tribal elder said in 1982, "We don't waste people the way white society does. Every person has their gift." In this land, the original America, men who

wore women's clothes and did women's work became artists, innovators, ambassadors, and religious leaders, and women sometimes became warriors, hunters, and chiefs. Same-sex marriages flourished and no tribe was the worse for it—until the Europeans arrived. In this "strange country," people who were different in terms of gender identity or sexuality were respected, integrated, and sometimes revered. How could this be? . . .

The evidence of multiple genders in North America offers support for the theory of social constructionism, which maintains that gender roles, sexualities, and identities are not natural, essential, or universal, but constructed by social processes and discourses. At the same time, it challenges certain assumptions of recent work in postmodern cultural studies, feminism, and queer theory. The only societies many of today's influential cultural theorists have considered have been those of the West (and primarily northwest Europe and North America). Few have ever considered cross-cultural evidence; many show a marked disinclination for empirical evidence of any kind. Consequently, certain elements of Western beliefs and epistemology have been essentialized as universal features of human societies. These include assumptions that "sex" and "gender" are relevant categories in all societies and that sexuality and gender are (always) analytically distinguishable; that sexes and genders are binary and dichotomous and that, by extension, only heterosexuality or the attraction between opposites is natural; that ideology and cultural beliefs regarding gender are always essentialist while gender identities and sexualities are always constructed; and that the fluidity of human desire and the ambiguities of human categories make stable identities and cultural continuity impossible. All of these assumptions are called into question by the example of native multiple genders. As we will see, native beliefs about gender and sexuality were avowedly constructionist, acknowledging the malleability of human desire and identity. At the same time, North American multiple genders emerge as roles with great historical depth and continuity, with parallels in societies worldwide.

THE BERDACHE OR ALTERNATIVE GENDER ROLE

The estimated four hundred tribal groups in North America at the time of European contact represented a diverse array of environmental adaptations, subsistence strategies, social organizations, family structures, languages, and religions. They ranged from the egalitarian, loosely organized bands of Inuit hunter-gatherers in the arctic, to the populous farmers and village dwellers of the southeast, who were organized into castes and ruled by chieftains. Many other North American societies combined hunting and gathering with digging stick horticulture. (True agrarian societies, on the other hand, based on intensive food production with draught animals, were not present.)

Rather than technology, native societies emphasized knowledge, especially familiarity with the environment. Consequently, intuitive forms of knowledge were highly developed. Visions, dreams, and trance states were valued as sources of information, direction, ability, and fortune. Ideals of balance, harmony, and integration between humans and nature were widespread. However, those drawn to native religions because of their apparent resonance with Western environmental and New Age tenets would do well to remember the central role of violence in Plains Indian religions and the concern with wealth among Northwest Coast groups.

Most North American societies were only weakly stratified. In the typical tribal social organization leaders were selected (or confirmed) based on competence, and social control was achieved largely through face-to-face interaction. Work roles were organized on the basis of gender. Within these systems, women made important, sometimes the most important, economic contributions to their families' subsistence. Although the life choices and personal autonomy of women made important, sometimes the most important, economic contributions to their families' subsistence. Although the life choices and personal autonomy of women varied significantly from matrilineal groups like the Hopis, Zunis, and Iroquois to the warrior-dominated Plains tribes, opportunities for women to acquire prestige and take leadership roles existed in every group.

Alternative gender roles were among the most widely shared features of North American societies. Male berdaches have been documented in over 155 tribes. In about a third of these groups, a formal status also existed for females who undertook a man's lifestyle, becoming hunters, warriors, and chiefs. They were sometimes referred to with the same term for male berdaches and sometimes with a distinct term—making them, therefore, a fourth gender. (Thus, "third gender" generally refers to male berdaches and sometimes male and female berdaches, while "fourth gender" always refers to female berdaches. Each tribe, of course, had its own terms for these roles, like *boté* in Crow, *nádleehi* in Navajo, *winkte* in Lakota, and *alyha:* and *hwame:* in Mohave.) Because so many North American cultures were disrupted (or had disappeared) before they were studied by anthropologists, it is not possible to state the absolute frequency of these roles. Those alternative gender roles that have been documented, however, occur in every region of the continent, in every kind of society, and among speakers of every major language group. The number of tribes in which the existence of such roles have been denied (by informants or outsider observers) are quite few. Far greater are those instances in which information regarding the presence of gender diversity has simply not been recorded.

"Berdache" has become the accepted anthropological term for these roles despite a rather unlikely etymology. It can be traced back to the Indo-European root *weld* "to strike, wound," from which the Old Iranian *varta-*, "seized, prisoner," is derived. In Persia, it referred to a young captive or slave (male or female). The word entered western European languages perhaps from Muslim Spain or as a result of contact with Muslims during the Crusades. By the Renaissance it was current in Italian as *bardascia* and *bardasso*, in Spanish as *bardaje* (or *bardaxe*), in French as *berdache*, and in English as "bardash" with the meaning of "catamite"— the younger partner in an age-differentiated homosexual relationship. Over time its meaning began to shift, losing its reference to age and active/passive roles and becoming a general term for male homosexual. In some places, it lost its sexual connotations altogether. By the mid-nineteenth century, its use in Europe lapsed.

In North America, however, "berdache" continued to be used, but for a quite different purpose. Its first written occurrence in reference to third and fourth gender North American natives is in the 1704 memoir of Deliette. Eventually, its use spread to every part of North America the French entered, becoming a pidgin term used by Euro-Americans and natives alike. Its first use in an anthropological publication was by Washington Matthews in 1877. In describing Hidatsa *miáti* he wrote, "Such are called by the French Canadians 'berdaches.'" The next anthropological use was in J. Owen Dorsey's 1890 study of Siouan cults. Like Matthews, he described "berdache" as a French Canadian frontier term. Following Alfred Kroeber's use of the word in his 1902 ethnography of the Arapaho, it became part of standard anthropological terminology.

Although there are important variations in berdache roles, which will be discussed below, they share a core set of traits that justifies comparing them:

- Specialized work roles—Male and female berdaches are typically described in terms of their preference and achievements in the work of the "opposite" sex and/or unique activities specific to their identities.

- Gender difference—In addition to work preferences, berdaches are distinguished from men and women in terms of temperament, dress, lifestyle, and social roles.

- Spiritual sanction—Berdache identity is widely believed to be the result of supernatural intervention in the form of visions or dreams, and/or it is sanctioned by tribal mythology.

- Same-sex relations—Berdaches most often form sexual and emotional relationships with non-berdache members of their own sex.

The most visible marker of berdache gender status was some form of cross-dressing, although this occurred much less consistently than is usually assumed. In some tribes, male berdaches dressed distinctly from both men and women. In other cases, berdaches did not cross-dress at all or only partly. Cross-dressing was even more variable in the case of female berdaches. Often, they wore men's clothing only when hunting or in battle. Similarly, despite the common description of berdaches as "doing the work of the opposite sex," they more often engaged in a combination of men's and women's activities, along with pursuits unique to their status.

Berdaches are also frequently attributed with spiritual powers. This was especially common in tribes, such as those of the Plains, with a vision complex, in which visions or dreams were considered life-defining and believed to convey power. Such beliefs not only justified alternative gender identities, they endowed those identities with special prestige. Even in societies lacking the vision complex, such as the Pueblos of the Southwest, alternative gender roles were sanctioned by tribal myths and portrayed in ceremonies.

The process by which third gender identity was adopted and/or acknowledged varied, but one dominant pattern emerges cross-culturally. Recognition of berdache orientation typically occurred when a boy showed interest and aptitude in women's work or a girl persistently engaged in the activities of boys and men. Significantly, these preferences manifested well before puberty, so that sexual behavior was a less important defining trait. In tribes with a vision complex, supernatural intervention was sometimes credited with determining berdache status, but a close reading of ethnographic and historic reports reveals that in many cases childhood cross-gender interests and skills preceded visions, which merely served to confirm alternative gender identity. Another process has been reported for certain arctic and subarctic groups, in which children were sometimes assigned cross- or mixed-sex identities at birth, which might be modified after puberty. Latitude was still allowed, however, for individual preferences. In those instances when men were required to cross-dress because they were considered cowards or because they were captives, a distinction from true berdache status was recognized.

Unfortunately, there are few accounts of berdache sexuality. This has led some to claim that berdaches were asexual or that the sexual aspects of alternative genders were not important. Harriet Whitehead has argued that "sexual object choice is part of the gender configuration, but its salience is low; so low that by itself it does not provoke the reclassification of the individual to a special status," and Clemmer has concluded, "The berdache was not only—and sometimes not at all—a sexual role." Ironically, in those cases for which detailed evidence about individual berdaches exists (such as Osh-Tisch and Hastíín Klah), almost nothing has been recorded about their sexuality and personal relationships. However, when the sexual preferences of berdaches *have* been reported, a definite pattern emerges. Male and female berdaches were sexually active with members of their own sex and this behavior was part of the cultural expectations for their role.

Indeed, some male berdaches were very active sexually. The Navajo *nádleehí* Kinábahí told Willard Hill that "she" had had sex with over one hundred different men. The Sauk and Fox tribe held an annual dance in which a berdache, or *aya'kwa*, appeared surrounded by all "her" lovers, and Lakota *winkte* bestowed bawdy nicknames as a souvenir of sexual encounters with them. In fact, Lakota warriors sometimes visited *winkte* before going to battle as a means of increasing their own masculinity. In the early eighteenth century, Ojibway men had sex with the berdache Ozaw-wen-dib (Yellowhead), himself an accomplished warrior, "to acquire his fighting ability and courage, by having intimate connection with him". In a similar vein, an Omaha chief once claimed he could change the weather because he had had sex four times with a male berdache.

The active sex life of berdaches led them to be considered fortuitous in all matters relating to sex and romance. Navajo *nádleehí*, Cheyenne *he'eman*, and Omaha *minquga* were matchmakers, while the Mohave believed both male *alyha:* and female *hwame:* were lucky in love. If Mohave berdaches became shamans, they specialized in the treatment of sexual diseases. Pawnee berdaches provided men with love charms for attracting women, while a carved fan from the eastern Sioux depicts male berdaches in a ritual scene associated with the love magic of the elk. (In the Oto origin myth, the figure Elk is described as a berdache.) The autobiography of a Kwakiutl chief provides a rare description of a sexual encounter with a male berdache: "This man, her name was Frances . . ., she caught hold of me, and when I went there she throwed me right into her bed. My, she was strong—awful strong!"

In forming relationships with non-berdache members of their own sex, third and fourth gender natives were "homosexual" in the Western definition of that term. The native view of such relations was more complex, however. Because berdaches were considered members of a distinct gender, native epistemologies classified relationships with them differently than those between individuals who had the same gender identity. Nor were their non-berdache partners labeled in any way; their gender identities and sexualities remained those of men or women. At the same time, knowledge of berdaches' anatomical sex was never denied, and the sexual acts performed with them were recognized (with distinct terms) as different from heterosexual acts. Some male berdaches had relationships with women, although in most cases they were men who were already warriors and husbands who became berdaches on the basis of a vision or dream. Finally, a few berdaches may not have been sexually active at all, although institutionalized celibacy was a foreign concept in native cultures. The only sexual relationships berdaches are not known to have formed are ones involving other berdaches.

The primary characteristic of third gender sexuality in the native view was not its same-sex nature, but the fact that it was nonprocreative. That is, rather than an opposition of heterosexuality to homosexuality, native beliefs opposed reproductive to nonreproductive sex. (This is especially apparent in the case of native terms for berdaches that literally mean "sterile" or "impotent"). Reproductive sex was engaged in to obtain children and fulfill one's kinship role. Nonreproductive sex was engaged in for pleasure and emotional rewards. As such, sexual pleasure was valued in its own right—it forged relationships, it was entertaining, it was necessary for good health. In these belief systems, third and fourth genders represented special instances of nonprocreative sexuality and romantic love. Given the relative absence of restrictions on their sexual availability within a kinship-based social organization, individuals in these roles had more opportunities to engage in sexual activity than did men or women. Although long-term relationships between berdaches and non-berdaches were considered marriages, they do not seem to have been the product of alliance politics between families, to have involved bridewealth or brideservice, or to have been governed by restrictions on the social status of the partners. When such relationships dissolved the disputes involved were usually limited to the couple alone, not their families or clans.

Of all the cultural associations of alternative genders, perhaps the least understood is their relationship to warfare. Many observers have attempted to account for male berdaches by suggesting that the role was a social status imposed on men too weak or cowardly to live up to tribal standards of masculinity. This can be disproved on several grounds. Landes's Dakota informants, for example, clearly distinguished between men who were uninterested in or afraid of warfare and berdaches "who had a dream." In fact, male berdaches regularly participated in many aspects of warfare. This ranged from accompanying war parties to provide support, entertainment, and luck, to joining in the fighting, handling enemy scalps, and directing victory ceremonies. Indeed, some berdaches, such as the Crow Osh-Tisch, the Ojibway Yellowhead, and the Southern Piegan, Piegan Woman, were renowned for their war exploits, while the Sioux remember a berdache who tricked the Sans Arc band into putting down their weapons just as their enemies attacked. Third and fourth gender figures appear as warriors in myths and tales, as well. In fact, most native belief systems ultimately viewed berdaches and successful warriors in similar terms—both were the beneficiaries of supernatural power.

The associations of alternative genders with death, whether through roles as undertakers and mourners in California, or as participants in victory or "scalp" dances, is striking. They point to a nexus of beliefs difficult to grasp from a Western perspective, in which nonprocreative sexuality and fertility, creativity and inspiration, and warfare and death are linked, and these links are represented by third and fourth gender persons.

That berdaches were accepted and integrated members of their communities is underscored throughout the ethnographic literature and confirmed by contemporary natives. In some tribes, alternative genders enjoyed special respect and privileges. In a few cases, berdaches were feared because of their supernatural power. If they were scorned, hated, or ridiculed, it was usually for individual reasons and not because of their gender difference, at least until the twentieth century. In some cases, joking relationships have been mistakenly interpreted as evidence of nonacceptance. In fact, individuals in tribal societies were often subject to teasing precisely because they had high status. In other cases, accounts attributing natives with hostility toward berdaches can be shown to reflect the judgments of Euro-Americans or of informants influenced by Christianity. As Drucker observed, "Most of the informants were inclined to be reticent about sexual matters, apparently feeling that they would be putting themselves in a bad light by discussing such things. This attitude accounts for most of the denials of the existence of berdaches aboriginally. I was told repeatedly that such individuals ('jotes') were to be found 'only among Mexicans.'" What is needed at this point is an analysis of a tribe either definitely lacking such a role or hostile to gender difference based on pre-contact values.

There are no reliable data at present concerning the numbers of berdaches in native populations, although careful work in census records and oral histories may make it possible to make estimates for some tribes in the late nineteenth century. In small groups, with populations of a few hundred, there might have been only one or two berdaches in a given generation. In larger communities, their numbers were sufficient for them to be recognized as a social group (as among the Timucua, Hidatsa, Crow, and Cheyenne). Among the Hidatsa of the upper Missouri River, there was said to be fifteen to twenty-five *miáti* in a village, and among the Yuki of California as many as thirty in the tribe. In any case, the importance of a social role for a given society is not a function of the number of individuals who occupy it—the number of chiefs and medicine people was in most cases no greater than that of berdaches, but no one would dispute their importance to tribal society and history.

Some of the points made so far apply to alternative genders for females as well. As Medicine notes, "warrior women," like male berdaches, occupied "socially sanctioned role alternatives." These were "normative statuses which permitted individuals to strive for self-actualization, excellence, and social recognition in areas outside their customary sex role assignments." Blackwood has argued that alternative female roles were socially and ontologically on par with male roles in the sense of being distinct, lifelong identities. Still, it is clear that female alternative genders were not mirror opposites of those for males, nor were alternative gender roles the only avenue by which women engaged in male pursuits.

Important differences existed between alternative genders in various tribes, as a regional survey reveals:

Southeast. The reports of René Goulaine de Laudonnière and Jacques Le Moyne, who arrived in Florida in 1564 on an expedition to assert French claims to the region, provide a fairly detailed description of male berdaches among the Timucua Indians. Le Moyne painted two pictures of them and engravings based on these paintings were published by Theodore De Bry. One depicts two pairs carrying corpses on stretchers, while two others carry sick or injured persons on their backs. The engraving is captioned "Hermaphrodites as Laborers," and the accompanying text relates that because they are strong, "hermaphrodites" (a term frequently used by Europeans who often assumed without evidence that berdaches were intersexed) accompany warriors to battle to carry provisions and tend to the injured. A second engraving depicts "curly-haired hermaphrodites" bearing baskets of game, fish, and crocodiles to a storehouse.

Alternative gender males among the Karankawa and Coahuiltec Indians of the Texas Gulf Coast also participated in warfare. According to Cabeza de Vaca, "*Hombres amarionadas impotentes,*" while dressing and living like women, carried heavy burdens and were larger than other males. In the eighteenth century, Dumont de Montigny observed a role for males called the "chief of women" among the Natchez of the lower Mississippi. They did women's work, including crafts and gardening, assisted on war parties, and had sex with men. Unfortunately, these early reports are the most detailed available for Southeast tribes, although alternative gender statuses appear to have been present among the the Creek, Chickasaw, Choctaw, Caddo, and Cherokee.

Northeast and woodlands. Although there are no definite reports of alternative gender roles among the Algonkian-speaking and Iroquoian tribes of the Northeast, among the Algonkian Illinois of the Mississippi Valley the status of *ikoueta*, or male berdaches, seems to have been fairly high, judging from the accounts of French explorers and travelers in the late seventeenth century. Males entered the role based on their preference for women's work. They went to war, sang at religious ceremonies, gave advice at councils, and were considered "manitou," or holy. According to Marquette, "Nothing can be decided without their advice." Nearly all the French observers commented on their sexuality—*ikoueta* practiced "sodomy"— typically in the context of a general denunciation of Illinois morality. Similar roles also have been documented among the Winnebago, Sauk and Fox, Miami, and Potawatomi. Among these groups visions or dreams were believed to play a role in determining berdache identity. The Potawatomi considered such individuals "extraordinary." Indeed, the widespread occurrence of this role among Algonkian-speakers of the Plains (the Cheyenne, Arapaho, Blackfoot, and Gros Ventre) and in the subarctic region makes its apparent absence among eastern Algonkians all the more suspect.

Plains. Whereas the traditional cultures of tribes east of the Mississippi were severely disrupted long before the rise of anthropology, the cultures of the Plains have been more systematically studied, and the literature occasionally provides detailed glimpses of alternative gender roles. Table 1 summarizes this evidence for four tribes: the Crow; their relatives, the Hidatsa; the Lakota; and the Cheyenne.

The North American vision complex reached its apex among Plains tribes. Men sought visions that would enable them to kill game and enemies, women sought visions as sources of designs and inspiration for their arts, and male berdaches among the Mandan, Lakota, Assiniboine, Arapaho, Omaha, Kansa, Osage, and Oto had dreams and visions of female deities or

TABLE 1   Cultural Associations of Plains Male Berdaches

	Lakota	Crow	Hidatsa	Cheyenne	Other tribes
Dreams/ visions	had dreams of Double Woman	had dreams that transformed	had dreams of Woman Above or "mysterious women"		Assiniboine, Oto, Osage, Arapaho, Kansa, Mandan, Ojibwa
Moon	were influenced by moon				Omaha, Pawnee, Sauk/Fox, Osage, Kansa, Oto
Power	were holy, foretold future, brought luck	some were medicine people	had special power	were doctors	Arapaho, Sauk/Fox
Religion	led some ceremonies	selected sun dance pole	had role in sun dance and other rites; were members of Holy Women Society	led scalp dance	
Sexuality	had sex with men and gave them obscene names	had sex with men	lived with men	were matchmakers	Omaha (matchmakers), Pawnee (love magic)
Crafts	were skilled in quill- and beadwork	excelled in crafts	were industrious in crafts	were talented	Ponca
Warfare	joined war parties	joined war parties		joined war parties	

the moon that confirmed their identity and gave them distinct abilities. The Osage term for berdache, *mixu'ga* (and its cognates in Omaha, Kansa, and Oto), literally means "moon-instructed" (from *mi*, "moon" and *xu'ga*, "to instruct"). The most frequently cited skills were those of beading, quillwork, and the manufacture and decoration of myriad products made from animal skins. As Benedict related, "The Dakota had a saying, 'fine possessions like a berdache's,' and it was the epitome of praise for any woman's household possessions." These productive skills were a function of supernatural power—both contact with it and possession of it.

Creativity was only one of the forms this power could take. Lakota *winkte* could also predict the future, and they had auspicious powers in relation to childbirth and childrearing that included bestowing names that were considered lucky. The religious dimension of alternative gender roles was perhaps most fully developed among the Hidatsa and Mandan, horticultural village dwellers, and the Cheyenne, who were former village dwellers, Coleman argues that the

reason *he'emane'o* directed the all-important victory dance was because they embodied the central principles of Cheyenne religion, which were balance and synthesis.

Arctic and subarctic. Saladin d'Anglure has described the extremely flexible gender system of the central arctic Inuit, in which arbitrary gender assignments along with individual preferences result in complex and varied "gender histories" for many individuals. Boys and girls are raised in accordance with the gender of one or more names selected for them before their birth. Consequently, some children are raised with cross- or mixed-gender identities. Upon reaching puberty or adulthood they may choose to alter such identities or retain them. Saladin d'Anglure considers such individuals (who are often shamans, as well) to be members of a distinct third gender. In addition, the Inuit believe some infants, called *sipiniq*, change their anatomical sex at birth. (Similar beliefs have been reported for the Bella Coola and the Tlingit.) The Athapaskan-speaking Dene Tha (Slavey or Beaver Indians of Canada) have a related belief in the possibility of cross-sex reincarnation. Among the Ingalik, an Athapaskan group of the Alaskan interior, both male and female berdaches have been reported, and male berdaches often had shamanic powers.

Russian explorers, traders, and missionaries were well aware of gender diversity among Alaskan natives. The explorer Lisiansky reported that a Russian priest almost married an Aleut chief to a berdache before being informed that the "bride" was male. Among the Chugach and Koniag, Pacific Eskimo (Yup'ik) groups, such individuals were believed to be "two persons in one." Despite Russian attempts to suppress the role, third gender individuals were esteemed and encouraged by their families, who considered them lucky. Many were shamans. Early observers reported that some feminine boys were raised as girls from childhood by families lacking a daughter.

In the vast subarctic region, alternative genders have been reported for the Athapaskan-speaking Kaska and among the widely dispersed Cree and Ojibway. The linguistic relationship between terms for male berdaches in Algonkian-speaking groups (including the Fox and Illinois) is evident.

Northwest Coast and Columbia Plateau. Among the Northwest Coast Haisla, berdaches were reportedly "fairly common." A supernatural berdache was portrayed in masked dances by the neighboring Bella Coola. Among the Eyak, however, berdaches did not have supernatural power and their status was low. Alternative male genders have been widely reported for the Columbia Plateau region but with few details. Among the Flathead of western Montana and the Klamath of southern Oregon, berdaches were often shamans. The career of one Klamath *tw!ĩnnă'ĕk*, known as Muksamse'lapli, or White Cindy, has been briefly described by Spier and by McCleod.

West and Southwest. Male and female alternative genders have been documented throughout the Great Basin, California, Colorado River, and Southwest culture areas. They are consistently described as doing the work of the other sex, less consistently as cross-dressing. As elsewhere, they formed relationships with non-berdache members of their own sex. Among some groups (Shoshone, Ute, Kitanemuk, Pima-Papago), families held a kind of initiation rite to confirm male berdache identity. The child was placed in a circle of brush with a bow and a basket (men's and women's objects, respectively). The brush was set on fire, and whichever object the boy picked up as he ran away served to identify his gender preference. The choice of the basket signified male berdache status. Among the Shoshone, who acquired horses and adopted a Plains-oriented lifestyle, male berdaches joined war parties.

In California, third/fourth gender individuals often had ceremonial roles relating to death and burial. Among the Yokuts and Tubatulabal, and possibly the Chumash, male berdaches served as undertakers, handling and burying the deceased and conducting mourning rites. Berdaches also participated in mourning rites among the Monache (Mono), Pomo, Miwok, Achumawi, Atsugewi, and Shasta. Among the Wappo, Mattole, Hupa, Chilula, Tolowa, Maidu, Achumawi, Shasta, and Modoc, male berdaches, and less often female berdaches, were sometimes shamans. One of the last chiefs of the Kawaiisu was a third gender male.

Alternative roles for males (but apparently not females) existed among the Pueblo communities of Isleta, San Felipe, San Juan, Santa Ana, Santo Domingo, Tesuque, Acoma, Laguna, Zuni, and Hopi. Among the western Pueblos, man-woman kachinas, or gods, were portrayed in masked dances and ceremonies. The Zuni *lhamana* We'wha was a religious specialist who regularly participated in ceremonies. Other Pueblo berdaches are described primarily in terms of their specialization in pottery and other pursuits of women.

Alternative gender roles also existed among the Papago and Pima of the Southwest and northern Mexico. Like Plains berdaches, Papago *wiik'ovat* taunted the scalps brought home by warriors, and they were visited for sexual liaisons by men to whom they gave obscene nicknames. A fire test was employed to confirm their identity.

33

Tricking and Tripping

Fieldwork on Prostitution in the Era of AIDS

Claire E. Sterk

Students often think of anthropological fieldwork as requiring travel to exotic tropical locations, but that is not necessarily the case. This reading is based on fieldwork in the United States—on the streets in New York City as well as Atlanta. Claire Sterk is an anthropologist who works in a school of public health and is primarily interested in issues of women's health, particularly as it relates to sexual behavior. In this selection, an introduction to a book by the same title, she describes the basic fieldwork methods she used to study these women and their communities. Like most cultural anthropologists, Sterk's primary goal was to describe "the life" of prostitution from the women's own point of view. To do this, she had to be patient, brave, sympathetic, trustworthy, curious, and nonjudgmental. You will notice these characteristics in this selection; for example, Sterk begins her book with a poem written by one of her informants. Fieldwork is a slow process, because it takes time to win people's confidence and to learn their language and way of seeing the world. In this regard, there are probably few differences between the work of a qualitative sociologist and that of a cultural anthropologist (although anthropologists would not use the term "deviant" to describe another society or a segment of their own society).

Throughout the world, HIV/AIDS is fast becoming a disease found particularly in poor women. Sex workers or prostitutes have often been blamed for AIDS, and they have been further stigmatized because of their profession. In reality, however, entry into prostitution is not a career choice; rather, these women and girls are themselves most often victims of circumstances such as violence and poverty. Public health officials want to know why sex workers do not always protect their health by making men wear condoms. To answer such questions, we must know more about the daily life of these women. The way to do that, the cultural anthropologist would say, is to ask and to listen.

As you read this selection, ask yourself the following questions:

- What happens when Sterk says, "I'm sorry for you" to one of her informants? Why?
- Why do you think fieldwork might be a difficult job?
- Do you think that the fact that Sterk grew up in Amsterdam, where prostitution is legal, affected her research?
- Which of the six themes of this work, described at the end of the article, do you think is most important?

The following terms discussed in this selection are included in the Glossary at the back of the book:

demography	*sample*
fieldwork	*stroll*
key respondent	

Prostitution is a way of life. IT IS THE LIFE.
We make money for pimps who promise us
  love and more,
but if we don't produce, they shove us out the door.
We turn tricks who have sex-for-pay.
They don't care how many times we serve every day.

The Life is rough. The Life is tough.
We are put down, beaten up, and left for dead.
It hurts body and soul and messes with
  a person's head.
Many of us get high. Don't you understand it is
  a way of getting by?

The Life is rough. The Life is tough.
We are easy to blame because we are lame.

—Piper, 1987[1]

Sterk, Claire E. "Tricking and Tripping: Fieldwork on Prostitution in the Era of AIDS." Reprinted with permission of author.

One night in March of 1987 business was slow. I was hanging out on a stroll with a group of street prostitutes. After a few hours in a nearby diner/coffee shop, we were kicked out. The waitress felt bad, but she needed our table for some new customers. Four of us decided to sit in my car until the rain stopped. While three of us chatted about life, Piper wrote this poem. As soon as she read it to us, the conversation shifted to more serious topics—pimps, customers, cops, the many hassles of being a prostitute, to name a few. We decided that if I ever finished a book about prostitution, the book would start with her poem.

This book is about the women who work in the lower echelons of the prostitution world. They worked in the streets and other public settings as well as crack houses. Some of these women viewed themselves primarily as prostitutes, and a number of them used drugs to cope with the pressures of the life. Others identified themselves more as drug users, and their main reason for having sex for money or other goods was to support their own drug use and often the habit of their male partner. A small group of women interviewed for this book had left prostitution, and most of them were still struggling to integrate their past experiences as prostitutes in their current lives.

The stories told by the women who participated in this project revealed how pimps, customers, and others such as police officers and social and health service providers treated them as "fallen" women. However, their accounts also showed their strengths and the many strategies they developed to challenge these others. Circumstances, including their drug use, often forced them to sell sex, but they all resisted the notion that they might be selling themselves. Because they engaged in an illegal profession, these women had little status: their working conditions were poor, and their work was physically and mentally exhausting. Nevertheless, many women described the ways in which they gained a sense of control over their lives. For instance, they learned how to manipulate pimps, how to control the types of services and length of time bought by their customers, and how to select customers. While none of these schemes explicitly enhanced their working conditions, they did make the women feel stronger and better about themselves.

In this book, I present prostitution from the point of view of the women themselves. To understand their current lives, it was necessary to learn how they got started in the life, the various processes involved in their continued prostitution careers, the link between prostitution and drug use, the women's interactions with their pimps and customers, and the impact of the AIDS epidemic and increasing violence on their experiences. I also examined the implications for women.

Although my goal was to present the women's thoughts, feelings, and actions in their own words, the final text is a sociological monograph compiled by me as the researcher. Some women are quoted more than others because I developed a closer relationship with them, because they were more able to verbalize and capture their circumstances, or simply because they were more outspoken.

THE SAMPLE

The data for this book are qualitative. The research was conducted during the last ten years in the New York City and Atlanta metropolitan areas. One main data source was participant observation on streets, in hotels and other settings known for prostitution activity, and in drug-use settings, especially those that allowed sex-for-drug exchanges. Another data source was in-depth, life-history interviews with 180 women ranging in age from 18 to 59 years, with an average age of 34. One in two women was African-American and one in three white; the remaining women were Latina. Three in four had completed high school, and among them almost two-thirds had one or more years of additional educational training. Thirty women had graduated from college.

Forty women worked as street prostitutes and did not use drugs. On average, they had been prostitutes for 11 years. Forty women began using drugs an average of three years after they began working as prostitutes, and the average time they had worked as prostitutes was nine years. Forty women used drugs an average of five years before they became prostitutes, and on the average they had worked as prostitutes for eight years. Another forty women began smoking crack and exchanging sex for crack almost simultaneously, with an average of four years in the life. Twenty women who were interviewed were ex-prostitutes.

COMMENTS ON METHODOLOGY

When I tell people about my research, the most frequent question I am asked is how I gained access to the women rather than what I learned from the research. For many, prostitution is an unusual topic of conversation, and many people have expressed surprise that I, as a woman, conducted the research. During my research some customers indeed thought I was a working woman, a fact that almost always amuses those who hear about my work. However, few people want to hear stories about the women's struggles and sadness. Sometimes they ask questions about the reasons why women become prostitutes. Most of the time, they are surprised when I tell them that the prostitutes as well as their customers represent all layers of society. Before presenting the findings, it seems important to discuss the research process, including gaining access to the women, developing relationships, interviewing, and then leaving the field.[2]

LOCATING PROSTITUTES
AND GAINING ENTREE

One of the first challenges I faced was to identify locations where street prostitution took place. Many of these women worked on strolls, streets where prostitution activity is concentrated, or in hotels known for prostitution activity. Others, such as the crack prostitutes, worked in less public settings such as a crack house that might be someone's apartment.

I often learned of well-known public places from professional experts, such as law enforcement officials and health care providers at emergency rooms and sexually transmitted disease clinics. I gained other insights from lay experts, including taxi drivers, bartenders, and community representatives such as members of neighborhood associations. The contacts universally mentioned some strolls as the places where many women worked, where the local police focused attention, or where residents had organized protests against prostitution in their neighborhoods.

As I began visiting various locales, I continued to learn about new settings. In one sense, I was developing ethnographic maps of street prostitution. After several visits to a specific area, I also was able to expand these maps by adding information about the general atmosphere on the stroll, general characteristics of the various people present, the ways in which the women and customers connected, and the overall flow of action. In addition, my visits allowed the regular actors to notice me.

I soon learned that being an unknown woman in an area known for prostitution may cause many people to notice you, even stare at you, but it fails to yield many verbal interactions. Most of the time when I tried to make eye contact with one of the women, she quickly averted her eyes. Pimps, on the other hand, would stare at me straight on and I ended up being the one to look away. Customers would stop, blow their horn, or wave me over, frequently yelling obscenities when I ignored them. I realized that gaining entrée into the prostitution world was not going to be as easy as I imagined it. Although I lacked such training in any of my qualitative methods classes, I decided to move slowly and not force any interaction. The most I said during the initial weeks in a new area was limited to

"how are you" or "hi." This strategy paid off during my first visits to one of the strolls in Brooklyn, New York. After several appearances, one of the women walked up to me and sarcastically asked if I was looking for something. She caught me off guard, and all the answers I had practiced did not seem to make sense. I mumbled something about just wanting to walk around. She did not like my answer, but she did like my accent. We ended up talking about the latter and she was especially excited when I told her I came from Amsterdam. One of her friends had gone to Europe with her boyfriend, who was in the military. She understood from her that prostitution and drugs were legal in the Netherlands. While explaining to her that some of her friend's impressions were incorrect, I was able to show off some of my knowledge about prostitution. I mentioned that I was interested in prostitution and wanted to write a book about it.

Despite the fascination with my background and intentions, the prostitute immediately put me through a Streetwalker 101 test, and apparently I passed. She told me to make sure to come back. By the time I left, I not only had my first conversation but also my first connection to the scene. Variations of this entry process occurred on the other strolls. The main lesson I learned in these early efforts was the importance of having some knowledge of the lives of the people I wanted to study, while at the same time refraining from presenting myself as an expert.

Qualitative researchers often refer to their initial connections as gatekeepers and key respondents. Throughout my fieldwork I learned that some key respondents are important in providing initial access, but they become less central as the research evolves. For example, one of the women who introduced me to her lover, who was also her pimp, was arrested and disappeared for months. Another entered drug treatment soon after she facilitated my access. Other key respondents provided access to only a segment of the players on a scene. For example, if a woman worked for a pimp, [she] was unlikely . . . to introduce me to women working for another pimp. On one stroll my initial contact was with a pimp whom nobody liked. By associating with him, I almost lost the opportunity to meet other pimps. Some key respondents were less connected than promised—for example, some of the women who worked the street to support their drug habit. Often their connections were more frequently with drug users and less so with prostitutes.

Key respondents tend to be individuals central to the local scene, such as, in this case, pimps and the more senior prostitutes. Their function as gatekeepers often is to protect the scene and to screen outsiders. Many times I had to prove that I was not an undercover police officer or a woman with ambitions to become a streetwalker. While I thought I had gained entrée, I quickly learned that many insiders subsequently wondered about my motives and approached me with suspicion and distrust.

Another lesson involved the need to proceed cautiously with self-nominated key respondents. For example, one of the women presented herself as knowing everyone on the stroll. While she did know everyone, she was not a central figure. On the contrary, the other prostitutes viewed her as a failed streetwalker whose drug use caused her to act unprofessionally. By associating with me, she hoped to regain some of her status. For me, however, it meant limited access to the other women because I affiliated myself with a woman who was marginal to the scene. On another occasion, my main key respondent was a man who claimed to own three crack houses in the neighborhood. However, he had a negative reputation, and people accused him of cheating on others. My initial alliance with him delayed, and almost blocked, my access to others in the neighborhood. He intentionally tried to keep me from others on the scene, not because he would gain something from that transaction but because it made him feel powerful. When I told him I was going to hang out with some of the other people, he threatened me until one of the other dealers stepped in and told him to stay away. The two of them argued back and forth, and finally I was free to go. Fortunately, the dealer who had spoken up for me was much more central and positively associated with the local scene. Finally, I am unsure if I would have had success in gaining entrance to the scene had I not been a woman.

DEVELOPING RELATIONSHIPS AND TRUST

The processes involved in developing relationships in research situations amplify those involved in developing relationships in general. Both parties need to get to know each other, become aware and accepting of each other's roles, and engage in a reciprocal relationship. Being supportive and providing practical assistance were the most visible and direct ways for me as the researcher to develop a relationship. Throughout the years, I have given countless rides, provided child care on numerous occasions, bought groceries, and listened for hours to stories that were unrelated to my initial research questions. Gradually, my role allowed me to become part of these women's lives and to build rapport with many of them.

Over time, many women also realized that I was uninterested in being a prostitute and that I genuinely was interested in learning as much as possible about their lives. Many felt flattered that someone wanted to learn from them and that they had knowledge to offer.

Allowing women to tell their stories and engaging in a dialogue with them probably were the single most important techniques that allowed me to develop relationships with them. Had I only wanted to focus on the questions I had in mind, developing such relationships might have been more difficult.

At times, I was able to get to know a woman only after her pimp endorsed our contact. One of my scariest experiences occurred before I knew to work through the pimps, and one such man had some of his friends follow me on my way home one night. I will never know what plans they had in mind for me because I fortunately was able to escape with only a few bruises. Over a year later, the woman acknowledged that her pimp had gotten upset and told her he was going to teach me a lesson.

On other occasions, I first needed to be screened by owners and managers of crack houses before the research could continue. Interestingly, screenings always were done by a man even if the person who vouched for me was a man himself. While the women also were cautious, the ways in which they checked me out tended to be much more subtle. For example, one of them would tell me a story, indicating that it was a secret about another person on the stroll. Although I failed to realize this at the time, my field notes revealed that frequently after such a conversation, others would ask me questions about related topics. One woman later acknowledged that putting out such stories was a test to see if I would keep information confidential.

Learning more about the women and gaining a better understanding of their lives also raised many ethical questions. No textbook told me how to handle situations in which a pimp abused a woman, a customer forced a woman to engage in unwanted sex acts, a customer requested unprotected sex from a woman who knew she was HIV infected, or a boyfriend had unrealistic expectations regarding a woman's earnings to support his drug habit. I failed to know the proper response when asked to engage in illegal activities such as holding drugs or money a woman had stolen from a customer. In general, my response was to explain that I was there as a researcher. During those occasions when pressures became too severe, I decided to leave a scene. For example, I never returned to certain crack houses because pimps there continued to ask me to consider working for them.

Over time, I was fortunate to develop relationships with people who "watched my back." One pimp in particular intervened if he perceived other pimps, customers, or passersby harassing me. He also was the one who gave me my street name: Whitie (indicating my racial background) or Ms. Whitie for those who disrespected me. While this was my first street name, I subsequently had others. Being given a street name was a symbolic gesture of acceptance. Gradually, I developed an identity that allowed me to be both an insider and an outsider. While hanging out on the strolls and other gathering places, including crack houses, I had to deal with some of the same uncomfortable conditions as the prostitutes, such as cold or warm weather, lack of access to a rest room, refusals from owners for me to patronize a restaurant, and of course, harassment by customers and the police.

I participated in many informal conversations. Unless pushed to do so, I seldom divulged my opinions. I was more open with my feelings about situations and showed empathy. I learned quickly that providing an opinion can backfire. I agreed that one of the women was struggling a lot and stated that I felt sorry for her. While I meant to indicate my genuine concern for her, she heard that I felt sorry for her because she was a failure. When she finally, after several weeks, talked with me again, I was able to explain to her that I was not judging her, but rather felt concerned for her. She remained cynical and many times asked me for favors to make up for my mistake. It took me months before I felt comfortable telling her that I felt I had done enough and that it was time to let go. However, if she was not ready, she needed to know that I would no longer go along. This was one of many occasions when I learned that although I wanted to facilitate my work as a researcher, that I wanted people to like and trust me, I also needed to set boundaries.

Rainy and slow nights often provided good opportunities for me to participate in conversations with groups of women. Popular topics included how to work safely, what to do about condom use, how to make more money. I often served as a health educator and a supplier of condoms, gels, vaginal douches, and other feminine products. Many women were very worried about the AIDS epidemic. However, they also were worried about how to use a condom when a customer refused to do so. They worried particularly about condom use when they needed money badly and, consequently, did not want to propose that the customer use one for fear of rejection. While some women became experts at "making" their customers use a condom—for example, by hiding it in their mouth prior to beginning oral sex—others would carry condoms to please me but never pull one out. If a woman was HIV positive and I knew she failed to use a condom, I faced the ethical dilemma of challenging her or staying out of it.

Developing trusting relationships with crack prostitutes was more difficult. Crack houses were not the right environment for informal conversations. Typically, the atmosphere was tense and everyone was suspicious of each other. The best times to talk with these women were when we bought groceries together,

when I helped them clean their homes, or when we shared a meal. Often the women were very different when they were not high than they were when they were high or craving crack. In my conversations with them, I learned that while I might have observed their actions the night before, they themselves might not remember them. Once I realized this, I would be very careful to omit any detail unless I knew that the woman herself did remember the event.

IN-DEPTH INTERVIEWS

All interviews were conducted in a private setting, including women's residences, my car or my office, a restaurant of the women's choice, or any other setting the women selected. I did not begin conducting official interviews until I developed relationships with the women. Acquiring written informed consent prior to the interview was problematic. It made me feel awkward. Here I was asking the women to sign a form after they had begun to trust me. However, often I felt more upset about this technicality than the women themselves. As soon as they realized that the form was something the university required, they seemed to understand. Often they laughed about the official statements, and some asked if I was sure the form was to protect them and not the school.[3] None of the women refused to sign the consent form, although some refused to sign it right away and asked to be interviewed later.

In some instances the consent procedures caused the women to expect a formal interview. Some of them were disappointed when they saw I only had a few structured questions about demographic characteristics, followed by a long list of open-ended questions. When this disappointment occurred, I reminded the women that I wanted to learn from them and that the best way to do so was by engaging in a dialogue rather than interrogating them. Only by letting the women identify their salient issues and the topics they wanted to address was I able to gain an insider's perspective. By being a careful listener and probing for additional information and explanation, I as the interviewer, together with the women, was able to uncover the complexities of their lives. In addition, the nature of the interview allowed me to ask questions about contradictions in a woman's story. For example, sometimes a woman would say that she always used a condom. However, later on in the conversation she would indicate that if she needed drugs she would never use one. By asking her to elaborate on this, I was able to begin developing insights into condom use by type of partner, type of sex acts, and social context.

CULTURAL ANTHROPOLOGY

The interviewer becomes much more a part of the interview when the conversations are in-depth than when a structured questionnaire is used. Because I was so integral to the process, the way the women viewed me may have biased their answers. On the one hand, this bias might be reduced because of the extent to which both parties already knew each other; on the other, a woman might fail to give her true opinion and reveal her actions if she knew that these went against the interviewer's opinion. I suspected that some women played down the ways in which their pimps manipulated them once they knew that I was not too fond of these men. However, some might have taken more time to explain the relationship with their pimp in order to "correct" my image.

My background, so different from that of these women, most likely affected the nature of the interviews. I occupied a higher socioeconomic status. I had a place to live and a job. In contrast to the nonwhite women, I came from a different racial background. While I don't know to what extent these differences played a role, I acknowledge that they must have had some effect on this research.

LEAVING THE FIELD

Leaving the field was not something that occurred after completion of the fieldwork, but an event that took place daily. Although I sometimes stayed on the strolls all night or hung out for several days, I always had a home to return to. I had a house with electricity, a warm shower, a comfortable bed, and a kitchen. My house sat on a street where I had no fear of being shot on my way there and where I did not find condoms or syringes on my doorstep.

During several stages of the study, I had access to a car, which I used to give the women rides or to run errands together. However, I will never forget the cold night when everyone on the street was freezing, and I left to go home. I turned up the heat in my car, and tears streamed down my cheeks. I appreciated the heat, but I felt more guilty about that luxury than ever before. I truly felt like an outsider, or maybe even more appropriate, a betrayer.

Throughout the years of fieldwork, there were a number of times when I left the scene temporarily. For example, when so many people were dying from AIDS, I was unable to ignore the devastating impact of this disease. I needed an emotional break.

Physically removing myself from the scene was common when I experienced difficulty remaining objective. Once I became too involved in a woman's life and almost adopted her and her family. Another time I felt a true hatred for a crack house owner and was

unable to adhere to the rules of courteous interactions. Still another time, I got angry with a woman whose steady partner was HIV positive when she failed to ask him to use a condom when they had sex.

I also took temporary breaks from a particular scene by shifting settings and neighborhoods. For example, I would invest most of my time in women from a particular crack house for several weeks. Then I would shift to spending more time on one of the strolls, while making shorter and less frequent visits to the crack house. By shifting scenes, I was able to tell people why I was leaving and to remind all of us of my researcher role.

While I focused on leaving the field, I became interested in women who had left the life. It seemed important to have an understanding of their past and current circumstances. I knew some of them from the days when they were working, but identifying others was a challenge. There was no gathering place for ex-prostitutes. Informal networking, advertisements in local newspapers, and local clinics and community settings allowed me to reach twenty of these women. Conducting interviews with them later in the data collection process prepared me to ask specific questions. I realized that I had learned enough about the life to know what to ask. Interviewing ex-prostitutes also prepared me for moving from the fieldwork to writing.

It is hard to determine exactly when I left the field. It seems like a process that never ends. Although I was more physically removed from the scene, I continued to be involved while analyzing the data and writing this book. I also created opportunities to go back, for example, by asking women to give me feedback on parts of the manuscript or at times when I experienced writer's block and my car seemed to automatically steer itself to one of the strolls. I also have developed other research projects in some of the same communities. For example, both a project on intergenerational drug use and a gender-specific intervention project to help women remain HIV negative have brought me back to the same population. Some of the women have become key respondents in these new projects, while others now are members of a research team. For example, Beth, one of the women who has left prostitution, works as an outreach worker on another project.

SIX THEMES IN THE ETHNOGRAPHY OF PROSTITUTION

The main intention of my work is to provide the reader with a perspective on street prostitution from the point of view of the women themselves. There are six fundamental aspects of the women's lives as prostitutes that must be considered. The first concerns the women's own explanations for their involvement in prostitution and their descriptions of the various circumstances that led them to become prostitutes. Their stories include justifications such as traumatic past experiences, especially sexual abuse, the lack of love they experienced as children, pressures by friends and pimps, the need for drugs, and most prominently, the economic forces that pushed them into the life. A number of women describe these justifications as excuses, as reflective explanations they have developed after becoming a prostitute.

The women describe the nature of their initial experiences, which often involved alienation from those outside the life. They also show the differences in the processes between women who work as prostitutes and use drugs and women who do not use drugs.

Although all these women work either on the street or in drug-use settings, their lives do differ. My second theme is a typology that captures these differences, looking at the women's prostitution versus drug-use identities. The typology distinguishes among (a) streetwalkers, women who work strolls and who do not use drugs; (b) hooked prostitutes, women who identify themselves mainly as prostitutes but who upon their entrance into the life also began using drugs; (c) prostituting addicts, women who view themselves mainly as drug users and who became prostitutes to support their drug habit; and (d) crack prostitutes, women who trade sex for crack.

This typology explains the differences in the women's strategies for soliciting customers, their screening of customers, pricing of sex acts, and bargaining for services. For example, the streetwalkers have the most bargaining power, while such power appears to be lacking among the crack prostitutes.

Few prostitutes work in a vacuum. The third theme is the role of pimps, a label that most women dislike and for which they prefer to substitute "old man" or "boyfriend." Among the pimps, one finds entrepreneur lovers, men who mainly employ streetwalkers and hooked prostitutes and sometimes prostituting addicts. Entrepreneur lovers engage in the life for business reasons. They treat the women as their employees or their property and view them primarily as an economic commodity. The more successful a woman is in earning them money, the more difficult it is for that woman to leave her entrepreneur pimp.

Most prostituting addicts and some hooked prostitutes work for a lover pimp, a man who is their steady partner but who also lives off their earnings. Typically, such pimps employ only one woman. The dynamics in the relationship between a prostitute and her lover pimp become more complex when both partners use drugs. Drugs often become the glue of the relationship.

For many crack prostitutes, their crack addiction serves as a pimp. Few plan to exchange sex for crack when they first begin using; often several weeks or months pass before a woman who barters sex for crack realizes that she is a prostitute.

Historically, society has blamed prostitutes for introducing sexually transmitted diseases into the general population. Similarly, it makes them scapegoats for the spread of HIV/AIDS. Yet their pimps and customers are not held accountable. The fourth theme in the anthropological study of prostitution is the impact of the AIDS epidemic on the women's lives. Although most are knowledgeable about HIV risk behaviors and the ways to reduce their risk, many misconceptions exist. The women describe the complexities of condom use, especially with steady partners but also with paying customers. Many women have mixed feelings about HIV testing, wondering how to cope with a positive test result while no cure is available. A few of the women already knew their HIV-infected status, and the discussion touches on their dilemmas as well.

The fifth theme is the violence and abuse that make common appearances in the women's lives. An ethnography of prostitution must allow the women to describe violence in their neighborhoods as well as violence in prostitution and drug-use settings. The most common violence they encounter is from customers. These men often assume that because they pay for sex they buy a woman. Apparently, casual customers pose more of a danger than those who are regulars. The types of abuse the women encounter are emotional, physical, and sexual. In addition to customers, pimps and boyfriends abuse the women. Finally, the women discuss harassment by law enforcement officers.

When I talked with the women, it often seemed that there were no opportunities to escape from the life. Yet the sixth and final theme must be the escape from prostitution. Women who have left prostitution can describe the process of their exit from prostitution. As ex-prostitutes they struggle with the stigma of their past, the challenges of developing a new identity, and the impact of their past on current intimate relationships. Those who were also drug users often view themselves as ex-prostitutes and recovering addicts, a perspective that seems to create a role conflict. Overall, most ex-prostitutes find that their past follows them like a bad hangover.

NOTES

1. The names of the women who were interviewed for this study, as well as those of their pimps and customers, have been replaced by pseudonyms to protect their

privacy. The use of pseudonyms is suggested by guidelines to protect the privacy of study participants (American Anthropological Association; American Sociological Association).

2. For more information about qualitative research methods, see, for example, Patricia Adler and Peter Adler, *Membership Roles in Field Research* (Newbury Park: Sage, 1987); Michael Agar, *The Professional Stranger* (New York: Academic Press, 1980) and *Speaking of Ethnography* (Beverly Hills: Sage, 1986); Howard Becker and Blanche Geer, "Participant Observation and Interviewing: A Comparison," *Human Organization* 16 (1957): 28–32; Norman Denzin, *Sociological Methods: A Sourcebook* (Chicago: Aldine, 1970); Barney Glaser and Anselm Strauss, *The Discovery of Grounded Theory: Strategies for Qualitative Research* (Chicago: Aldine, 1967); Y. Lincoln and E. Guba, *Naturalistic Inquiry* (Beverly Hills: Sage, 1985); John Lofland, "Analytic Ethnography: Features, Failings, and Futures," *Journal of Contemporary Ethnography* 24 (1996): 30–67; and James Spradley, *The Ethnographic Interview* (New York: Holt, Rinehart and Winston, 1979) and *Participant Observation* (New York: Holt, Rinehart and Winston, 1980).

3. For a more extensive discussion of informed consent procedures and related ethical issues, see Bruce L. Berg, *Qualitative Research Methods for the Social Sciences*, 3rd edition, Chapter 3: "Ethical Issues" (Boston: Allyn and Bacon, 1998).

34

Law, Custom, and Crimes against Women

The Problem of Dowry Death in India

John van Willigen and V. C. Channa

Anthropologists find many societies with unusual customs, beliefs, and behaviors. Usually they discover, after careful study and reflection, that these perform some useful function within the society, as discussed in Goldstein's *When Brothers Share a Wife*. But is this always the case? Must we assume that simply because a custom exists it is healthy for the members of society? We think not, and the Christians who were fed to lions and the Aztec slaves who were sacrificed to a blood-thirsty god would most likely agree.

Times change; hunters and gatherers plant crops, tribal people rush headlong into peasantry, and small-scale farmers become urban wage earners. Traditions that helped maintain a healthy society in one context may become dysfunctional in another. For better or worse, traditions and beliefs run deep and are almost impossible to unlearn. It is the nature of culture to resist change.

As you will read, the practice of dousing a bride with kerosene and creating a human torch certainly indicates that the payment of dowry is a traditional practice gone awry. That said, what can be done? Laws, even those that carry serious penalties, are light ammunition against the armor of strongly held cultural beliefs. Governments will solve such problems only through public policy based on in-depth cultural understanding.

As you read this selection, ask yourself the following questions:

- What do you think the authors mean when they suggest that dowry death presents a problem for ethnologists because of ethnological theory's functional cast?

- Why does the institution of dowry make college education problematic for some young women?

- What are the present-day approaches to solving the dowry death problem?

- How can women's access to production roles and property, delocalization of social control, and economic transformation affect the problem of dowry death?

- Dowry-related violence in India is related to the economic value of women. What might be said about the relationship between the economic position and the social status of women in America?

The following terms discussed in this selection are included in the Glossary at the back of the book:

caste	ethnology
cultural materialism	peasants
demography	sex roles
dowry	

A 25-year-old woman was allegedly burnt to death by her husband and mother-in-law at their East Delhi home yesterday. The housewife, Mrs. Sunita, stated before her death at the Jaya Prakash Narayana Hospital that members of her

van Willigen, John and Channa, V.C. "Law, Custom, and Crimes against Women: The Problem of Dowry Deaths in India." Reproduced by permission of the Society for Applied Anthropology (SfAA) from Human Organization 50 (1991) no. 4:369–377.

husband's family had been harassing her for bringing inadequate dowry.

The woman told the Shahdara subdivisional magistrate that during a quarrel over dowry at their Pratap Park house yesterday, her husband gripped her from behind while the mother-in-law poured kerosene over her clothes.

Her clothes were then set ablaze. The police have registered a case against the victim's husband, Suraj Prakash, and his mother.

—*Times of India*, February 19, 1988

This routinely reported news story describes what in India is termed a "bride-burning" or "dowry death." Such incidents are frequently reported in the newspapers of Delhi and other Indian cities. In addition, there are cases in which the evidence may be ambiguous, so that deaths of women by fire may be recorded as kitchen accidents, suicides, or murders. Dowry violence takes a characteristic form. Following marriage and the requisite giving of dowry, the family of the groom makes additional demands for the payment of more cash or the provision of more goods. These demands are expressed in unremitting harassment of the bride, who is living in the household of her husband's parents, culminating in the murder of the woman by members of her husband's family or by her suicide. The woman is typically burned to death with kerosene, a fuel used in pressurized cook stoves, hence the use of the term "bride-burning" in public discourse.

Dowry death statistics appear frequently in the press and parliamentary debates. Parliamentary sources report the following figures for married women 16 to 30 years of age in Delhi: 452 deaths by burning for 1985; 478 for 1986 and 300 for the first six months of 1987 (Bhatia 1988). There were 1,319 cases reported nationally in 1986 (*Times of India,* January 10, 1988). Police records do not match hospital records for third degree burn cases among younger married women; far more violence occurs than the crime reports indicate (Kumari 1988).

There is other violence against women related both directly and indirectly to the institution of dowry. For example, there are unmarried women who commit suicide so as to relieve their families of the burden of providing a dowry. A recent case that received national attention in the Indian press involved the triple suicide of three sisters in the industrial city of Kanpur. A photograph was widely published showing the three young women hanging from ceiling fans by their scarves. Their father, who earned about 4,000 Rs. [rupees] per month, was not able to negotiate marriage for his oldest daughter. The grooms were requesting approximately 100,000 Rs. Also linked to the dowry problem is selective female abortion made possible by amniocentesis. This issue was brought to national attention with a startling statistic reported out of a seminar held in Delhi in 1985. Of 3,000 abortions carried out after sex determination through amniocentesis, only one involved a male fetus. As a result of these developments, the government of the state of Maharashtra banned sex determination tests except those carried out in government hospitals.

The phenomenon of dowry death presents a difficult problem for the ethnologist. Ethnological theory, with its residual functionalist cast, still does not deal effectively with the social costs of institutions of what might be arguably referred to as custom gone bad, resulting in a culturally constituted violence syndrome.

This essay examines dowry and its violent aspects, and some of the public solutions developed to deal with it in India. Our work consists of a meta-analysis of some available literature. We critique the legal mechanisms established to regulate the cultural institution of dowry and the resultant social evils engendered by the institution, and argue that policies directed against these social evils need to be constructed in terms of an underlying cause rather than of the problem itself. We consider cause, an aspect of the problem infrequently discussed in public debate. As Saini asserts, "legal academicians have shown absolutely no interest in the causal roots of dowry as practiced in contemporary India" (1983:143).

THE INSTITUTION

Since ancient times, the marriage of Hindus has required the transfer of property from the family of the bride to the family of the groom. Dowry or *daan dehej* is thought by some to be sanctioned by such religious texts as the *Manusmriti.* Seen in this way, dowry is a religious obligation of the father of a woman and a matter of *dharma* (religious duty) whereby authority over a woman is transferred from her father to her husband. This transfer takes different forms in different communities in modern India (Tambiah 1973). In public discussion, the term "dowry" covers a wide range of traditional payments and expenses, some presented to the groom's family and others to be retained by the bride. Customs have changed through time. The financial burdens of gifts and the dowry payments per se are exacerbated by the many expenses associated with the marriage celebration itself, but dowry payment is especially problematic because of its open-ended nature. As Tambiah notes, "marriage payments in India usually comprise an elaborate series of payments back and forth between the marrying families" and "this series extends over a long period of time and persists after marriage" (1973:92). Contemporary cases such as the death of Mrs. Sunita, often revolve around such continued demands.

A daughter's marriage takes a long time to prepare and involves the development of an adaptive strategy on the part of her family. An important part of the strategy is the preparation for making dowry payments; family consumption may be curtailed so as to allow accumulation of money for dowry. Seeing to marriage arrangements may be an important aspect of retirement planning. The dowries that the family receives on behalf of their sons may be "rolled over" to deal with the daughter's requirements. Families attempt to cultivate in both their sons and daughters attributes that will make them more attractive in marriage negotiations. Many things besides dowry are considered in negotiations: "non-economic" factors have demonstrable effect on the expectations for dowry and the family's strategy concerning the dowry process.

Education is a variable to be considered in the negotiation process. Education of young women is somewhat problematic because suitable husbands for such women must also be college educated. The parents of such young men demand more dowry for their sons. A consideration in sending a young woman to college will therefore be her parents' capacity to dower her adequately so as to obtain an appropriate groom. In any case, education is secondary to a man's earning power and the reputation of a woman's family. Education is, however, important in the early stages of negotiation because of the need to coordinate the level of the education of the men and women. Education qualifications are also less ambiguously defined than other dimensions of family reputation. Physical attractiveness is a consideration, but it is thought somewhat unseemly to emphasize this aspect of the decision.

Advertisements in newspapers are used for establishing marriage proposals (Aluwalia 1969; Niehoff 1959; Weibe and Ramu 1971), but contacts are more typically established through kin and other networks. Some marriages may be best termed "self-arranged," and are usually called "love marriages." In these cases, young men and women may develop a relationship independent of their families and then ask that negotiations be carried out on their behalf by family representatives.

Analysis of matrimonial advertisements shows some of the attributes considered to be important. Listed in such advertisements are education, age, income and occupation, physical attributes, *gotra* (a kind of unilineal descent group) membership, family background, place of residence, personality features, consideration of dowry, time and type of marriage, and language.

Consideration of dowry and other expenditures are brought out early in the negotiations and can serve as a stumbling block. Dowry negotiations can go on for some time. The last stage is the actual "seeing of the groom" and the "seeing of the bride," both rather fleeting encounters whose position at the end of the process indicates their relative lack of importance.

Marriage is a process by which two families mutually evaluate each other. The outcome of the negotiations is an expression of the relative worth of the two persons, a man and a woman, and, by extension, the worth of their respective families. This estimation of worth is expressed in marriage expenditures, of which dowry is but a part. There are three possible types of expenditures: cash gifts, gifts of household goods, and expenditures on the wedding celebration itself. The cash gift component of the dowry goes to the groom's father and comes to be part of his common household fund. The household goods are for use by the groom's household, although they may be used to establish a separate household for the newlyweds. When separate accommodations are not set up, the groom's family may insist that the goods do not duplicate things they already have.

Dates for marriages are set through consideration of horoscopes; horoscopy is done by professional astrologers (*pandits*). This practice leads to a concentration of marriage dates and consequent high demand for marriage goods and services at certain times of the year. During marriage seasons, the cost of jewelry, furniture, clothes, musicians' services, and other marriage related expenditures goes up, presumably because of the concentration of the demand caused by the astrologers.

The expenditures required of the woman's family for the wedding in general and the dowry in particular are frequently massive. Paul reports, for a middle-class Delhi neighborhood, that most dowries were over 50,000 Rs. (1986). Srinivas comments that dowries over 200,000 Rs. are not uncommon (1984).[1]

ETHNOLOGICAL THEORIES ABOUT DOWRY

Dowry had traditionally been discussed by ethnologists in the context of the functionalist paradigm, and much theorizing about dowry appears to be concerned with explaining the "contribution" that the institution makes to social adaptation. The early theoretician Westermarck interpreted dowry as a social marker of the legitimacy of spouse and offspring, and as a mechanism for defining women's social roles and property rights in the new household (Westermarck 1921:428). Murdock suggests that dowry may confirm the contract of marriage (1949). Dowry is interpreted by Friedl as a means to adjust a woman to her affinal home as it rearranges social relationships including the social separation of the man from his parents (1967). Dowry payments are public expressions of the new relationship between the two families, and of the social status of the bride and groom.

Dowry is seen in the social science literature as a kind of antemortem or anticipated inheritance by which a widow is assured of support, and provision for her offspring (Friedl 1967; Goody 1973, 1976). It transfers money to where the women will be and where they will reproduce; as a result, resources are also placed where the children will benefit, given the practice of patrilineal inheritance of immovable, economically valuable property like farm land.

In India, dowry is also seen as an expression of the symbolic order of society. According to Dumont, dowry expresses the hierarchal relations of marriage in India and lower status of the bride (Dumont 1957). The amount of dowry given is an expression of prestige. The capacity to buy prestige through dowry increases the potential for social mobility (Goody 1973). Dowry is a kind of delayed consumption used to demonstrate or improve social rank (Epstein 1960).

There is a significant discontinuity between discussions of dowry in the ethnological theory and in public discourse. Certainly the dowry problem does appear in the writing of contemporary ethnologists, but it is simply lamented and left largely uninterpreted and unexplained.

THE EXTANT SOLUTIONS TO THE PROBLEM

The Dowry Prohibition Act of 1961, as amended in 1984 and 1986, is the primary legal means for regulating the dowry process and controlling its excesses. The laws against dowry are tough. Dowry demand offenses are "cognizable" (require no warrant) and nonbailable, and the burden of proof is on the accused. There are, in fact, convictions under the law.

The act defines dowry as "any property of valuable security given or agreed to be given either directly or indirectly—(a) by one party to a marriage to the other party to a marriage; or (b) by parents of either party to a marriage or by any other person, to either party to the marriage or to any other person" (Government of India 1986:1). The act makes it illegal to give or take dowry, "If any person after the commencement of this act, gives or takes or abets the giving or taking of dowry, he shall be punishable with imprisonment for a term which shall not be less than five years; and with fine which shall not be less than fifteen thousand rupees or the amount of the value of such dowry which ever is more" (Government of India 1986:1). While this section unambiguously prohibits dowry, the third section allows wedding presents to be freely given. Thus the law does not apply to "presents which are given at the time of marriage to the bride (without demand having been made in that behalf)" (Government of India 1986:1). Identical provisions apply to the groom. Furthermore, all such presents must be listed on a document before the consummation of the marriage. The list is to contain a brief description and estimation of the value of the gifts, name of presenting person, and the relationship that person has with the bride and

groom. This regulation also provides "that where such presents are made by or on the behalf of the bride or any other person related to the bride, such presents are of a customary nature and the value thereof is not excessive having regard to the financial status of the person by whom, or on whose behalf, such presents are given" (Government of India 1986:2). Amendments made in 1984 make it illegal for a person to demand dowry with the same penalty as under the earlier "giving and taking" provision. It was also declared illegal to advertise for dowry, such an offense being defined as not bailable, with the burden of proof on the accused person.

This legislation was coupled with some changes in the Indian Penal Code that legally established the concept of "dowry death." That is, "where the death of a woman is caused by any burns or bodily injury or occurs otherwise than under normal circumstances within seven years of her marriage and it is shown that soon before her death she was subjected to cruelty or harassment by her husband or any relative of her husband for, or in connection with, any demand for dowry, such death shall be called 'dowry death,' and such husband or relative shall be deemed to have caused her death" (Government of India 1987:4). The Indian Evidence Act of 1871 was changed so as to allow for the presumption of guilt under the circumstances outlined above. Changes in the code allowed for special investigation and reporting procedures of deaths by apparent suicide of women within seven years of marriage if requested by a relative. There were also newly defined special provisions for autopsies.

To this point, however, these legal mechanisms have proved ineffective. According to Sivaramayya, the "act has signally failed in its operation" (1984:66). Menon refers to the "near total failure" of the law (1988:12). A similar viewpoint is expressed by Srinivas, who wrote, "The Dowry Prohibition Act of 1961 has been unanimously declared to be an utterly ineffective law" (1984:29).

In addition to the legal attack on dowry abuses, numerous public groups engage in public education campaigns. In urban settings, the most noteworthy of these groups are specialized research units such as the Special Cell for Women of the Tata Institute of Social Sciences (Bombay), and the Center for Social Research (New Delhi). Also involved in the effort are private voluntary organizations such as the Crimes Against Women Cell, Karmika, and Sukh Shanti.

These groups issue public education advertising on various feminist issues. The anti-dowry advertisement of the Federation of Indian Chambers of Commerce and Industry Ladies Organization exemplifies the thrust of these campaigns. In the following advertisement, which was frequently run in the winter of 1988 in newspapers such as the *Times of India,* a photograph of a doll dressed in traditional Indian bridal attire was shown in flames.

> Every time a young bride dies because of dowry demands, we are all responsible for her death. Because we allow it to happen. Each year in Delhi hospitals alone, over 300 brides die of third degree burns. And many more deaths go unreported. Most of the guilty get away. And we just shrug helplessly and say, "what can we do?" We can do a lot.
>
> Help create social condemnation of dowry. Refuse to take or give dowry. Protest when you meet people who condone the practice. Reach out and help the girl being harassed for it. Act now.
>
> Let's fight it together.
>
> As parents, bring up educated, self-reliant daughters. Make sure they marry only after 18. Oppose dowry; refuse to even discuss it. If your daughter is harassed after marriage stand by her.
>
> As young men and women, refuse marriage proposals where dowry is being considered. As friends and neighbors, ostracize families who give or take dowry. Reach out to help victims of dowry harassment.
>
> As legislators and jurists, frame stronger laws. Ensure speedy hearings, impose severe punishments. As associations, give help and advice. Take up the challenge of changing laws and attitudes of society. Let us all resolve to fight the evil. If we fight together we can win.
>
> SAY NO TO DOWRY.

Also engaged in anti-dowry work are peasant political action groups such as Bharatiya Kisan Union (BKU). BKU consists of farmers from western Uttar Pradesh whose political program is focused more generally on agricultural issues. The group sponsored a massive 25-day demonstration at Meerut, Uttar Pradesh, in 1988. The leadership used the demonstration to announce a social reform program, most of it dealing with marriage issues. According to news service reports, "The code of social reforms includes fixing the maximum number of persons in a marriage party at 11, no feasts relating to marriage, and no dowry except 10 grams of gold and 30 grams of silver" (*Times of India,* February 11, 1988). Buses plying rural roads in western Uttar Pradesh are reported to have been painted with the slogan "The bride is the dowry." Private campaigns against dowry occur in the countryside as well as among the urban elites, although it is likely that the underlying motivations are quite different.

POLICY ANALYSIS

Our argument is based on the assumption that social problems are best dealt with by policies directed at the correction of causative factors, rather than at the amelioration of symptoms. While current legal remedies directly confront dowry violence, the linkage between cause and the problematic behavior is not made. Here we develop an argument consisting of three components: women's access to production roles and property; delocalization of social control; and economic transformation of society. The pattern of distribution of aspects of the institution of dowry and its attendant problems is important to this analysis. Although dowry practices and the related crimes against women are distributed throughout Indian society, the distribution is patterned in terms of geography, caste rank, socioeconomic rank, urban/rural residence, and employment status of the women. In some places and among some people there are demonstrably more violence, more intensity of dowry practices, and more commitment to dowry itself. Much of the distributional data are problematic in one way or another. The most frequent problem is that the studies are not based on national samples. Furthermore, the interpretation of results is often colored by reformist agendas. There is a tendency to deemphasize differences in frequency from one segment of the population to another so as to build support of dowry death as a general social reform issue. Nevertheless, while the data available for these distributions are of inconsistent quality, they are interpretable in terms of our problem.

Women's Access to Production Roles and Property

Dowry violence is most frequent in north India. Some say that it is an especially severe problem in the Hindi Belt (i.e., Uttar Pradesh, Haryana, Punjab, Delhi, Bihar) (Government of India 1974:75). It is a lesser, albeit increasing problem in the south. There is also a north/south difference in the marriage institution itself. To simplify somewhat, in the north hypergamy is sought after in marriage alliances, in which case brides seek grooms from higher rank descent groups within their caste group (Srinivas 1984). In the south, marriages are more typically isogamous.

The literature comparing north and south India indicates important contrasts at both the ecological and the institutional levels. Based on conceptions developed by Boserup (1970) in a cross-cultural comparative framework on the relationship between the farming system and occupational role of women, Miller (1981) composed a model for explaining the significant north-south differences in the juvenile sex ratio [the ratio of males to females ten years of age and below]. The farming systems of the north are based on "dry-field plow cultivation," whereas in the south the farming systems are dominated by "swidden and wet-rice cultivation" (Miller 1981:28). These two systems make different labor demands. In the wet rice or swidden systems of the south, women are very important sources of labor. In the north, women's involvement in agricultural production is limited. According to Miller, women in the north are excluded from property holding and receive instead a "dowry of movables." In the south, where women are included in the production activities, they may receive "rights to land" (Miller 1981:28). In the north, women are high-cost items of social overhead, while in the south, women contribute labor and are more highly valued. In the north there is a "high cost of raising several daughters" while in the south there is "little liability in raising several daughters." There is thus "discrimination against daughters" and an "intense preference for sons" in the north, and "appreciation for daughters" and "moderate preference for sons" in the south. Miller thus explains the unbalanced-toward-males juvenile sex ratios of the north and the balanced sex ratios of the south (Miller 1981:27–28). The lower economic value of women in the north is expressed in differential treatment of children by sex. Females get less food, less care, and less attention, and therefore they have a higher death rate. In general the Boserup and Miller economic argument is consistent with Engels's thesis about the relationship between the subordination of women and property (Engels 1884; Hirschon 1984:1).

Miller extended her analysis of juvenile sex ratios to include marriage costs (including dowry), female labor participation, and property owning, and found that property owning was associated with high marriage costs and low female labor force participation, both of which were associated with high juvenile sex ratios. That is, the death rate of females is higher when marriage costs are high and women are kept from remunerative employment. Both of these patterns are associated with the "propertied" segment of the population (Miller 1981:156–159). Her data are derived from the secondary analysis of ethnographic accounts. The literature concerning the distribution of dowry practices and dowry death is consistent with these results.

Miller's analysis shows a general pattern of treatment of females in India. Their access to support in various forms is related to their contribution to production (Miller 1981). This analysis does not explain the problem of dowry violence, but it does demonstrate a fundamental pattern within which dowry violence can be interpreted.

The distribution of dowry varies by caste. In her study of dowry violence victims in Delhi, Kumari found that members of the lower ranking castes report less "dowry harassment" than do those in higher ranking castes (Kumari 1988:31). These results are consistent with Miller's argument since the pattern of exclusion of women from economic production roles varies by caste. Women of lower castes are less subject to restrictions concerning employment outside the realm of reproduction within the household. These women are often poor and uneducated, and are subject to other types of restrictions.

In the framework of caste, dowry practices of higher caste groups are emulated by lower caste groups. This process is known as "Sanskritization" and it may relate to the widely held view that dowry harassment is increasing in lower ranking castes. Sanskritization is the process by which lower ranked caste groups attempt to raise their rank through the emulation of higher rank castes. The emulation involves discarding certain behaviors (such as eating meat or paying bride price) and adopting alternatives (Srinivas 1969). Attitudinal research shows that people of the lower socio-economic strata have a greater commitment to dowry than do those of higher strata (Hooja 1969; Khanna and Verghese 1978; Paul 1986). Although the lower and middle classes are committed to dowry, the associated violence, including higher death rates, is more typically a middle class problem (Kumari 1988).

Employment status of women has an effect on dowry. In her survey of dowry problems in a south Delhi neighborhood, Paul (1986) found that the amount of dowry was less for employed middle class women than it was for the unemployed. This pattern is also suggested by Verghese (1980) and van der Veen (1972:40), but disputed by others (Murickan 1975). This link is also manifested among tribal people undergoing urbanization. Tribal people, ranked more toward the low end of the social hierarchy, typically make use of bride price (i.e., a payment to the bride's family) rather than dowry (Karve 1953). As these groups become more integrated into national life, they will shift to dowry practices to emulate high castes while their women participate less in gainful employment (Luthra 1983). Croll finds a similar relationship in her analysis of post-revolutionary China. She says, "it is the increased value attributed to women's labor which is largely responsible for the decline in the dowry" (1984:58).

Both Kumari (1988) and Srinivas (1984) developed arguments based on non-economic factors. Kumari in effect indicated that if dowry could be explained in economic terms, marriage would be simply a calculation of the value of a woman: if the value were high, bride price would be paid, and if the value were low, dowry transactions would occur. This formulation was presented as a refutation of Madan's dowry-as-compensation argument (Kumari 1988). We agree that reducing this practice to purely economic terms is an absurdity. The argument is not purely economic, but it is certainly consistent with a cultural materialist perspective (Harris 1979) in which symbolic values are shaped by an underlying material relationship that is the basis for the construction of cultural reality.

Delocalization of Social Control

Dowry violence is more frequent in cities (Saini 1983). Delhi has the reputation of having a high frequency of problems of dowry (Srinivas 1984:7). The urban-rural distribution pattern may be a manifestation of the effects of the delocalization of dowry. Dowry, when operative in the relationships among local caste groups in related villages, was to an extent self-regulating through caste. *panchayats* (councils) and by the joint families themselves. These groups easily reach into peoples' lives. By contrast, the national level laws have inadequate reach and cannot achieve regulation. While in some areas caste groups continue to function to limit abuses, these groups are less effective in urban settings. Population movements and competition with state level social control mechanisms limit the effectiveness of self-regulation. A government commission study of women's status argues "that because of changed circumstances in which a son generally has a separate establishment and has a job somewhere away from home, the parents cannot expect much help from him, and so they consider his marriage as the major occasion on which their investment in his education can be recovered" (Government of India 1974:74). These views are consistent with the research results reported by Paul, who demonstrates that dowry amounts are higher among people who have migrated to Delhi and those who live in nuclear families, because the families in general and the women in particular are less subject to social constraints (Paul 1986). New brides do not seem to have adequate support networks in urban settings.

Economic Transformation of Society

The custom of dowry has been thrown into disarray by inflationary pressures. The consumer price index for urban non-manual workers has increased from its reference year of 1960 value of 100 to 532 for 1984–85 (Government of India 1987). The media of dowry exchange have changed dramatically because of the increasing availability of consumer goods. It has become increasingly difficult to prepare for giving dowry for a daughter or a sister. Sharma argues that, in part, dowry problems are caused by rapid change in the nature of consumer goods which made it no longer possible to accumulate gift goods over a long period as the latest styles in material goods could not be presented (1984: 70–71).

The current regime of individual dowry seeking and giving is constituted as a kind of rational behavior. That is, it is achieved through choice, is consistent with certain values, and serves to increase someone's utility. There are a number of things sought by the groom's family in these transactions. Wealth and family prestige are especially important. The family prestige "bought" with marriage expenditures, which is relevant to both the bride and groom's side in the transaction, is no doubt very much worth maximizing in the Indian context. From the perspective of the bride's family, dowry payments involve trading present consumption for future earning power for their daughter through acquiring a groom with better qualities and connections. In a two-tier, gender segregated, high unemployment, inflationary economy such as that of India, one can grasp the advantage of investing in husbands with high future earning potential. It is also possible to argue that in societies with symbolic mechanisms of stratification, it is expected that persons will attempt to make public displays of consumption in order to improve their overall performance and so to take advantage of the ambiguities of the status hierarchy system. The demand for both symbolic goods and future earnings is highly elastic. Family connections, education, and wealth seem especially important in India, and they all serve as hedges against inflation and poverty. With women having limited access to jobs and earning lower pay, it is rational to invest in a share of the groom's prospects. If you ask people why they give dowry when their daughters are being married they say, "because we love them." On the other hand, grooms' families will find the decision to forgo dowry very difficult.

SUMMARY

The distributional data indicate that the relationship between the way females are treated in marriage and their participation in economic production is consistent with Miller's development of the Boserup hypothesis. It is assumed that the pattern of maltreatment of females has been subject to various controls operating at the levels of family, caste, and community. Urbanization reduces the effectiveness of these mechanisms, thus increasing the intensity of the problem. This trend is exacerbated by the economic transformations within contemporary Indian society. It is our viewpoint that policies developed to reduce dowry-related violence will fail if they do not increase the economic value of women.

The criminalization of dowry may have been a politically useful symbol, but it has not curtailed the practice. As dowry is attacked, the state has not adequately dealt with the ante-mortem inheritance aspect of the custom. If dowry continues to provide a share of the family wealth to daughters before the death of the parents, then legally curtailing the practice is likely to damage the economic interests of women in the name of protecting them. One might argue that the primary legal remedy for the dowry problem actually makes it worse because it limits the transfer of assets to women. Perhaps this is why research on attitudes toward dowry indicates a continued positive commitment to the institution (Mathew 1987). India is a society in which most people (most particularly the elite) have given and received dowry; most people are even today giving and taking dowries. Declaring dowry a crime creates a condition in which the mass of society are technically criminals. The moral-legal basis of society suffers, and communal, parochial, and other fissiparous forces are encouraged.

To be effective, anti-dowry legislation must make sure that the social utility provided by dowry practices be displaced to practices that are less problematic, and that the apparent causes of the practice be attacked. To do so would mean that attempts to eradicate the social evils produced by the dowry institution need to be based on an examination of women's property rights so as to increase their economic access. Traditional Hindu customs associated with inheritance give sons the right from birth to claim the so-called ancestral properties. This principle is part of the Mitakshara tradition of Hindu law, which prevails throughout India except in Bengal, Kerala, Assam, and northern parts of Orissa. These properties are obtained from father, paternal grandfather, or paternal great-grandfather. According to Sivaramayya (1984:71), "The Hindu Succession Act (the law which controls inheritance) did not abrogate this right by birth which exists in favor of a son, paternal grandson, and paternal great grandson. The availability of the right in favor of these male descendants only is a discrimination against daughters." The right is derived from ancient texts. According to Tambiah (1973:95), the Dharmasastras provide that it is "essentially males who inherit the patrimony while women are entitled to maintenance, marriage expenses and gifts." While the Hindu Succession Act abrogates much traditional law, it specifically accepts the principle of male birthright to the property of the joint family. That is, "When a male Hindu dies after the commencement of the Act, having at the time of death an interest in a Mitakshara coparcenary property, his interest in the property shall devolve by survivorship upon the surviving members of the coparcenary and not in accordance with this Act" (Government of India 1985:3). The Hindu Succession Act in its most recent form provides for the intestate or testamentary inheritance of a female of a share of the family property. Yet the prior

right of males at birth is not abrogated. Hindu males own a share of the family rights at birth; females can inherit it. Testamentary succession overrides the principle of intestate succession, and therefore the interests of females can be usurped simply by writing a will. The other procedures for a female to renounce an interest in family property are very simple. Moreover, according to Sivaramayya (1984:58), "no specific formality is required for the relinquishment of the interest beyond the expression of a clear intention to that effect." Instruments of relinquishment can be and are forged.

The antemortem inheritance function of dowry has been eroded or perhaps supplanted by transfer of goods to the groom's family for their consumption and the expression of the so-called prestige of the family. Indeed social science commentary on dowry in India suggests that this aspect of dowry is relatively unimportant in any case because only a small portion of the total marriage expenditure is under the bride's control. There is evidence that even the clothing and ornaments and other personal property of the bride are being usurped (Verghese 1980). Implementation of a gender-neutral inheritance law as advocated by the Government of India Committee on the Status of Women may serve to increase the economic value of women in general, while it serves as an alternative to the ante-mortem inheritance aspect of dowry. Since dowry constitutes a kind of ante-mortem inheritance, it is logical to change the inheritance laws in conjunction with the restrictions on dowry behavior. Sisters as well as brothers need to have a share in the family wealth from birth, and that right should be associated with legal procedures that increase the difficulty of alienation of property rights. There is no question that such a procedure would serve to erode the stability of the patrilineal family by diluting its economic base.

The Government of India has passed legislation such as the Hindu Succession Act (1956) and the Hindu Adoption and Maintenance Act (1956), both of which inter-alia provide for a woman's right of inheritance from her father. For example, under the Adoption and Maintenance Act, a woman has a claim of rights of maintenance from her husband's father in case she is widowed. Moreover, she has the right to claim inheritance from her deceased husband's estate. In spite of these changes, inheritance provisions are quite different for males and females. The Chief Justice of the Supreme Court of India, Honorable Mr. Justice Y. V. Chandrachud, wrote that in spite of changes, "some inequalities like the right of birth in favor of a son, paternal grandson, and paternal great grandson still persist" (1984:vii). Provision of females with equal rights to inherit ancestral property from birth, or from a bequest, or at the death may reduce dowry problems.

Furthermore, property that is allowed to remain in the name of the deceased for any length of time, as is frequently the case in India, should revert to the state. As it stands, property may remain in the name of a deceased ancestor, while his descendants divide it informally among themselves.

The establishment of a gender-neutral inheritance law represents a significant shift in public policy. We argue that there is a link between pro-male property laws and violence toward women. While we assert this position, we also need to recognize that the property laws give coherence and stability to an essential Indian institution, the joint family. The Mitakshara principle of male inheritance rights is both a reflection and a cause of family solidarity. Modifying this principle in an attempt to reduce violence toward women could have a deleterious effect on family coherence. In addition, the fundamental nature of these institutions makes it inconceivable that there would be substantial resistance to these changes. Yet if one considers this issue in historic terms, it is apparent that during the twentieth century, legal change is in the direction of gender neutrality, a process that started with the Hindu Law of Inheritance (Amendment) Act (1929) and the Hindu Succession Act (1956), and continues through judicial decisions to the present (Diwan 1988:384). As Diwan notes in reference to the changes brought by the Hindu Succession Act of 1956, "the Mitakshara bias towards preference of males over females and of agnates over cognates has been considerably whittled down" (1988:358). Such change is not easy. The changes brought with the Hindu Succession Act in 1956 were achieved only after overcoming "stiff resistance from the traditionalists" (Government of India 1974:135). The same report states, "The hold of tradition, however, was so strong that even while introducing sweeping changes, the legislators compromised and retained in some respects the inferior position of women" (Government of India 1974:135). It must be remembered that the texts that are the foundations of contemporary law include legislation (such as the Hindu Succession Act itself), case law, and religious texts, so that the constitutional question is also a question for religious interpretation, despite the constitutional commitment to secularism.

We are advocating further steps toward gender neutrality of the inheritance laws so that women and men will receive an equal share under intestate succession, and have an equal chance to be testamentary heirs. The law should thus be gender-neutral while still permitting a range of decisions allowing property to stay in a male line if the holder of the property so chooses. The required social adjustment could be largely achieved through the decisions of a family, backed by the power of the state. Families could express their preferences, but the state would not serve to protect the economic interests of males. The process could involve the concept of birthright as well as succession at death. We do not choose to engage those arguments, but do point out that the rapid aging of the Indian population may suggest that a full abrogation of the Mitakshara principle of birthright would be the best social policy because doing so would give older people somewhat greater control over their property in an economy virtually devoid of public investment in social services for older people (Bose and Gangrade 1988, Sharma and Dak 1987).

There are precedents for such policy at the state level. In Andhra Pradesh, the Hindu Succession Act was amended to provide for a female's birthright interest in the Mitakshara property. In Kerala, the Mitakshara property concept was legally abrogated altogether. Other gender asymmetries in the laws of India need to be attacked. The overall goal of policy should be to increase the economic value of women.

Ethnological theory directs our attention to social recognition of marriage and property transfer as functionally important features of the institution. The state can provide a means of socially recognizing marriage through registration and licensure. The law expresses no explicit preference for traditional marriage ritual, and it is possible to have a civil marriage under the provisions of the Special Marriage Act (1954) through registration with a magistrate. Nevertheless, this system co-exists parallel with the traditional system of marriage, which is beyond the reach of state control. Other marriages may be registered under this act if the persons involved so choose, and if a ceremony has been carried out. These special marriages are an alternative to an unregistered marriage.

We conclude that a useful mechanism for state control of dowry problems is the establishment of universal marriage registration, which does not exist at the present time. Marriage registration is also called for by the first Round Table on Social Audit of Implementation of Dowry Legislation (Bhatia 1988), which may serve to provide some monitoring of dowry abuses and perhaps to manifest the state's interest in an effective marriage institution. It would be naive to assume that such a policy would be widely honored, but as it is, low-income persons do not get married because they do not have the resources for marriage under the traditional non-state controlled regime. There are numerous reform groups that organize mass marriage ceremonies of village people so as to help them escape the burden of marriage expenditures. The point is that compliance is a large problem even under current circumstances.

In conclusion, we feel that the causes of the dowry problems are a product of the low economic value of women, loss of effective social control of abuse through delocalization, and pressures caused by economic transformation. The traditional family, caste group, and community controls which have been reduced in effectiveness should be replaced by state functions. The foundation of state control is universal marriage registration and licensure. The impact of the economic value of women on the problem is indicated by the transition from bride price to dowry among tribal people. It is also associated with a reduction in the extent of gainful employment and lower dowry amounts demonstrated for employed women. A broad program to increase the economic value of women would be the most useful means of dealing with the problem of dowry. Further restrictions on dowry without providing for a radically different property right for females is probably not in the interests of Indian women, since dowry represents ante-mortem inheritance. This underlying paradox may explain the commitment to dowry revealed in attitudinal research with Indian women, even though it is also an important feminist issue. The alternatives include the abolishment of the legal basis for the joint family as a corporate unit as has been done in Kerala, or the legal redefinition of the joint family as economically duolineal, as has occurred in Andhra Pradesh.

NOTE

1. For purposes of comparison, a mid-career Indian academic might be paid 60,000 Rs. per year.

REFERENCES

Aluwalia, H. 1969. Matrimonial Advertisements in Panjab. *Indian Journal of Social Work* 30:55–65.

Bhatia, S. C. 1988. Social Audit of Dowry Legislation. Delhi: Legal Literacy Project.

Bose, A. B., and K. D. Gangrade. 1988. *The Aging in India, Problems and Potentialities.* New Delhi: Abhinav.

Boserup, Ester. 1970. *Women's Role in Economic Development.* New York: St. Martin's Press.

Chandrachud, Y. V. 1984. Foreword. In *Inequalities and the Law.* B. Sivaramayya, ed. Pp. iv–vi. Lucknow: Eastern Book Company.

Croll, Elisabeth. 1984. The Exchange of Women and Property: Marriage in Post-revolutionary China. In *Women and Property—Women as Property,* ed. Renee Hirschon, 44–61. London/New York: Croom Helm/St. Martin's Press.

Diwan, Paras. 1988. *Modern Hindu Law, Codified and Uncodified.* Allahabad: Allahabad Law Agency.

Dumont, Louis. 1957. *Hierarchy and Marriage Alliance in South Indian Kinship.* London: Royal Anthropological Institute.

Engels, Fredrich. 1884. *The Origin of Family, Private Property and the State.* New York: International.

Epstein, T. Scarlett. 1960. Peasant Marriage in South India. *Man in India* 40: 192–232.

Friedl, Ernestine. 1967. *Vasilika, A Village in Modern Greece.* New York: Holt, Rinehart and Winston.

Goody, Jack. 1973. Bridewealth and Dowry in Africa and Eurasia. In *Bridewealth and Dowry,* eds. Jack Goody and S. J. Tambiah, 1–58. Cambridge: Cambridge University Press.

_____. 1976. *Production and Reproduction, A Comparative Study of the Domestic Domain.* Cambridge: Cambridge University Press.

Government of India. 1974. *Towards Equality: Report of the Committee on the Status of Women.* New Delhi: Government of India, Ministry of Education and Social Welfare.

_____. 1985. The Hindu Succession Act. New Delhi: Government of India.

_____. 1986. The Dowry Prohibition Act, 1961 (Act No. 28 of 1961) and Connected Legislation (as on 15th January, 1986). New Delhi: Government of India.

_____. 1987. *India 1986, A Reference Manual.* Delhi: Ministry of Information and Broadcasting.

Harris, Marvin. 1979. *Cultural Materialism: The Struggle for a Science of Culture.* New York: Random House.

Hirschon, Renee. 1984. Introduction: Property, Power and Gender Relations. In *Women and Property—Women as Property,* ed. Renee Hirschon, 1–22. London/New York: Croom Helm/St. Martin's Press.

Hooja, S. L. 1969. *Dowry System in India.* New Delhi: Asia Press.

Karve, Irawati. 1953. *Kinship Organization in India.* Bombay: Asia Publishing.

Khanna, G., and M. Verghese. 1978. *Indian Women Today.* New Delhi: Vikas Publishing House.

Kumari, Ranjana. 1988. Practice and Problems of Dowry: A Study of Dowry Victims in Delhi. In *Social Audit of Dowry Legislation,* ed. S. C. Bhatia, 27–37. Delhi: Legal Literacy Project.

Luthra, A. 1983. Dowry Among the Urban Poor, Perception and Practice. *Social Action* 33: 207.

Mathew, Anna. 1987. Attitudes Toward Dowry. *Indian Journal of Social Work* 48: 95–102.

Menon, N. R. Madhava. 1988. The Dowry Prohibition Act: Does the Law Provide the Solution or Itself Constitute the Problem? In *Social Audit of Dowry Legislation,* ed. S. C. Bhatia, 11–26. Delhi: Legal Literacy Project.

Miller, Barbara D. 1981. *The Endangered Sex, Neglect of Female Children in Rural North India.* Ithaca, NY: Cornell University Press.

Murdock, George P. 1949. *Social Structure.* New York: Macmillan.

Murickan, J. 1975. Women in Kerala: Changing Socio-economic Status and Self Image. In *Women in Contemporary India,* ed. A. de Souza, 73–95. Delhi: Manohar.

Niehoff, Arthur H. 1959. A Study of Matrimonial Advertisements in North India. *Eastern Anthropologist* 12: 37–50.

Paul, Madan C. 1986. *Dowry and the Position of Women in India. A Study of Delhi Metropolis.* New Delhi: Inter India Publishers.

Saini, Debi. 1983. Dowry Prohibition Law, Social Change and Challenges in India. *Indian Journal of Social Work* 44(2): 143–147.

Sharma, M. L., and T. Dak. 1987. *Aging in India, Challenge for the Society.* Delhi: Ajanta Publications.

Sharma, Ursula. 1984. Dowry in North India: Its Consequences for Women. In *Women and Property—Women as Property,* ed. Renee Hirschon, 62–74. London/New York: Croom Helm/St. Martin's Press.

Sivaramayya, B. 1984. *Inequalities and the Law.* Lucknow: Eastern Book Company.

Srinivas, M. N. 1969. *Social Change in Modern India.* Berkeley, CA: University of California Press.

_____. 1984. *Some Reflections on Dowry.* Delhi: Oxford University Press.

Tambiah, S. J. 1973. Dowry and Bridewealth and the Property Rights of Women in South Asia. In *Bridewealth and Dowry,* eds. Jack Goody and S. J. Tambiah, 59–169. Cambridge: Cambridge University Press.

van der Veen, Klaus W. 1972. *I Give Thee My Daughter—A Study of Marriage and Hierarchy Among the Anavil Brahmins of South Gujarat.* Assen: Van Gorcum.

Verghese, Jamila. 1980. *Her Gold and Her Body.* New Delhi: Vikas Publishing House.

Weibe, P. O., and G. N. Ramu. 1971. A Content Analysis of Matrimonial Advertisements. *Man in India* 51: 119–120.

Westermarck, Edward. 1921. *The History of Human Marriage.* London: MacMillan and Co.

35

Culture and the Evolution of Obesity

Peter J. Brown

As a people, Americans rank as one of the fattest societies in history. This epidemiological fact remains despite the tremendous amount of money, effort, and worry that Americans put into diet, exercise, and the quest for the perfect body. For some people, particularly young women, the quest to be thin can become such an obsession that they develop life-threatening eating disorders, like anorexia nervosa. But in other cultures, young women may go to great lengths to try to gain weight to look attractive. There are no universal standards of physical beauty; in fact, there is considerable cross-cultural variation. Culture defines normality.

How do conditions like obesity come to be expressed? Biologists usually say that it is a combination of genes and environment. There is good evidence that genes predispose people toward conditions, but there is seldom evidence that the chain of causation is entirely genetic. A complete explanation must be both biological and cultural. In other words, if a condition like obesity is caused by an interaction of genetic and cultural/behavioral predispositions, then both the genes and culture must be the product of evolutionary processes.

In this selection, Peter Brown provides a cross-cultural and evolutionary analysis of how both biological and cultural factors in obesity evolved. This analysis explains the sociological distribution of obesity today. It also emphasizes that peripheral body fat (characteristic of women) is a small health hazard compared to abdominal fat (characteristic of men).

Dietary patterns are obviously shaped by culture. But human tendencies to value meat, fatty foods, and sweets must be understood in the context of our evolutionary past.

As you read this selection, ask yourself the following questions:

- Have you ever noticed that there are gender differences in the locality of fat storage in the body? Why would this be the case?

- Why are fat people ridiculed and discriminated against in the United States? Are these social reactions worse for men or for women?

- What does the author mean when he says that in a rich society, slenderness can be an individual symbol of conspicuous consumption?

- Given the difference in health risk between peripheral body fat and central body fat, why might weight not be the best way to measure one's risk?

- Why do humans like foods that are "bad" for them?

The following terms discussed in this selection are included in the Glossary at the back of the book:

adipose tissue	gender dimorphism
cultural ideals	ideal body images
culture	obesity
epidemiology	sexual dimorphism
food scarcity	

Brown, Peter J. "Culture and the Evolution of Obesity." Reprinted with kind permission of the author & Springer Science+Business Media: Human Nature 2 (1991), no. 1:31–57.

The etiology or cause of obesity can be understood in the context of human cultural and genetic evolution. The cause of human obesity and overweight involves the interaction of genetic traits with culturally patterned behaviors and beliefs. Both these genes and culture traits, remarkably common in human societies, are evolutionary products of similar processes of selection related to past food scarcities. This idea is not new: The notion of "thrifty phenotypes rendered detrimental by progress" was introduced more than a quarter-century ago. In recent years, the evidence for the existence of genes that enable individuals to use food energy efficiently and store energy reserves in the form of fat has been increasingly impressive; those individuals with "fat phenotypes" are likely to develop adult obesity (Stunkard et al. 1986, 1990).

It is important to recognize that these "thrifty" genes are, at least in the human context, necessary but not sufficient factors in the causation of obesity. In actuality, the new discoveries in the genetics of obesity highlight our ignorance about the role of nongenetic or cultural factors, which are usually subsumed in the term *environment* in the medical literature. The purpose of this paper is to examine why and how cultures have evolved behaviors and beliefs that appear to predispose individuals to develop obesity. I believe that an anthropological model of culture has significant advantages over the commonly used undifferentiated concept of "environment" for generating hypotheses about behavioral causes of obesity. This cultural approach is particularly useful for improving our understanding of the social epidemiological distribution of obesity.

It is valuable to raise an obvious question at the outset: Why do people find it very difficult to reduce their intake of dietary fat and sugar even when the medical benefits of this behavioral change are well known to them? The answer is not obvious, since neither the physiological nor the cultural attraction of these foods is well understood. The proximate mechanisms for this attraction are linked to brain physiology and biochemistry (Wurtman and Wurtman 1987). The ultimate answers are linked to our evolutionary heritage. Human predispositions to obesity are found in both genetic and cultural traits that may have been adaptive in the context of past food scarcities but are maladaptive today in the context of affluence and constant food surpluses.

THE PROBLEMS OF OBESITY AND OVERWEIGHT

Throughout most of human history, obesity was neither a common health problem nor even a realistic possibility for most people. Today, particularly in affluent societies like the United States, obesity is very common, affecting about 12 percent of adult men and women; overweight is even more common, affecting an additional 20 to 50 percent of adult Americans depending on the definitions used (Bray 1987). Not only are overweight and obesity relatively common conditions in our society, they are also extremely complex and intractable. Obesity is a serious public health problem because of its causal connection to major causes of morbidity and mortality from chronic diseases, including cardiovascular disease, type 2 diabetes mellitus (NIDDM), and hypertension. On the individual level, obesity and overweight bring with them an enormous amount of personal psychological

pain. The fact that the obese are subjected to significant social and economic discrimination is well documented.

Fat is extraordinarily difficult to shed because the body guards its fat stores. The evidence concerning the effectiveness over a 5-year period of diet therapies indicates that nearly all of the weight that is lost through diets is eventually regained. The remarkable failure of diet therapies has made some researchers rethink their commonsensical theory of obesity as being caused by overeating; the clinical evidence of the past 40 years simply does not support this simplistic notion.

Even in the absence of scientific data about the effectiveness of diet therapy, the diet and weight-loss industry in the United States is remarkably successful in its ability to capture the hope and money of people who perceive themselves to be overweight. This industry thrives because of a complex of cultural beliefs about the ideal body and sexual attractiveness rather than medical advice and the prevention of chronic diseases per se. The American cultural concern about weight loss and the positive valuation of slenderness for women of the middle and upper classes are difficult to overemphasize. Chernin (1981) has referred to this cultural theme as an "obsession" and the "tyranny of slenderness." In this light, it is impossible to claim that obesity is purely a medical issue.

OBESITY AND HUNGER

It is important to remember that for most citizens of the world today, as it has been in the past, the possibility of obesity is remote whereas the possibility of hunger is close to home. There is a palpable irony in the fact of an epidemic of obesity in a world characterized by hunger. For example, in the United States an estimated 20 million people are hungry because they are on a "serious diet;" generally these people are of the middle and upper classes, and most are women. At the same time in the same rich nation, another estimated 20 million Americans are hungry and poorly nourished largely because they lack sufficient money; generally these people are elderly, homeless, or rural inhabitants. This sad symmetry in the estimates of voluntary and involuntary hunger in the United States is a valuable starting point for a discussion of the etiology of obesity. From an evolutionary standpoint, past food shortages have acted as powerful agents of natural selection, shaping both human genetics and behavior.

A theory of the etiology of obesity must not only account for the influences of genes and learned behaviors but also explain its social distribution. Before the problem of causation is addressed, it is worthwhile to examine the nature of human obesity.

CHANGING DEFINITIONS OF OBESITY

The most basic scientific issues regarding obesity are, in fact, controversial. The definitions of obesity and overweight have been the subject of substantial medical debate, in part because they must be based on inferred definitions of normality or "ideal" body proportions. Although obesity refers to excessive adiposity (fat deposits), the most common measurement is not of fat tissue at all but an indirect inference based on measures of stature and total body weight (Bray 1987).

The social history of height and weight standards in the United States is interesting. Until recently, the task of defining both obesity and ideal weights has been the domain of the life-insurance industry. The most well-known table of desirable weights was developed by the Metropolitan Life Insurance Company using correlation statistics between height/weight and mortality among insurance applicants. Ideal weights were based on data from 25-year-old insurance applicants, despite the nonrepresentative nature of the "sample" pool and the fact that in most human populations, individuals increase in weight until around age 50. Obesity was defined as 120 percent of the Ideal Body Weight (IBW), and overweight was defined as 110 percent IBW. Individual life-insurance applicants outside the recommended weight range were required to pay a surcharge on insurance premiums. In 1959, the concept of "frame size" was introduced, although the resulting categories were never given operational definitions using anthropometric measures.

Definitions of obesity have changed throughout history. From 1943 to 1980, definitions of "ideal weights" for women of a particular height were consistently lowered, while those for men remained approximately the same. In 1983, a major debate on the definition of obesity began when Metropolitan Life revised its tables upward, based on new actuarial studies of mortality. Many organizations and experts in the diet industry, including experts in medical fields, rejected these new standards.

In the current medical literature, weight and height tables have been replaced by the Body Mass Index (BMI), defined as body weight (in kilograms) divided by the square of body height (in meters). BMI (W/H^2) is strongly correlated with total body fat, and a value greater than 30 is generally considered obese. Current recommendations include slight increases in BMI with age (Bray 1987). Nevertheless, there continues to be little agreement on precise definitions of either overweight or obesity.

An important added dimension to the questions of definition of obesity involves the distribution of fat around the body trunk or on the limbs. Central or trunk body fat distribution is closely correlated with serious chronic diseases, such as cardiovascular disease, whereas peripheral body fat in the hips and limbs does not carry similar medical risks. Because of this clinically important distinction, measures of fat distribution like waist to hips ratio (WHR), wherein lower WHR values indicate lower risk of chronic disease consequences, will be a valuable addition to future definitions of obesity.

FOUR FACTS ABOUT THE SOCIAL DISTRIBUTION OF OBESITY

Humans are among the fattest of all mammals, and the primary function of our fat is to serve as an energy reserve. The nonrandom social distribution of adiposity within and between human populations may provide a key to understanding obesity. Four facts about this social distribution are particularly cogent for an evolutionary reconstruction: (1) the gender difference in the total percent and site distribution of body fat, as well as the prevalence of obesity; (2) the concentration of obesity in certain ethnic groups; (3) the increase in obesity associated with economic modernization; and (4) the powerful and complex relationship between social class and obesity. Any useful theory concerning the etiology of obesity must account for these social epidemiological patterns.

Sexual Dimorphism

Humans show only mild sexual dimorphism in variables like stature. Males are only 5 to 9 percent taller than females. The sample of adults from Tecumseh, Michigan, seen in Figure 1 are typical. Men are larger than women in height and total body mass, but women have more subcutaneous fat as measured by skinfold thicknesses in 16 of 17 sites (the exception is the suprailiac region—so-called "love handles"). The greatest degree of sexual dimorphism is found in the site of distribution of fat tissue; women have much more peripheral fat in the legs and hips (Kissebah et al. 1989). This difference is epidemiologically important because the greater proportion of peripheral fat in females may be associated with reduced morbidity compared to males with identical BMI values.

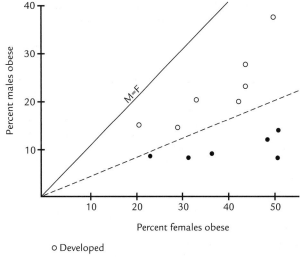

FIGURE 2   Gender differences in prevalences of obesity in 14 populations by general industrial development. Operational definitions of obesity differ between studies. See Brown and Konner (1987) for references. The unbroken line demarcates equal male-female obesity prevalences. The broken line indicates an apparent distinction in gender proportions of obesity in developed and underdeveloped countries. Brown, P. J., & M. Konner. "An Anthropological Perspective on Obesity" from ANNALS OF THE NEW YORK ACADEMY OF SCIENCES 499 (1987), no. 1 29–46. Reprinted by permission of The New York Academy of Sciences & Wiley-Blackwell Publishing.

FIGURE 1   Sexual dimorphism in stature, body mass, and fat measures among white Americans aged 20 to 70 in Techumseh, Michigan. Sexual dimorphism is calculated by comparing male and female means; positive figures refer to greater male measures. Skinfold thicknesses are means of four sites on the trunk or five sites on the arms and legs; the mean dimorphism for all 17 fat measures is –19 percent. Brown, P. J., & M. Konner. "An Anthropological Perspective on Obesity" from ANNALS OF THE NEW YORK ACADEMY OF SCIENCES 499 (1987), no. 1 29–46. Reprinted by permission of The New York Academy of Sciences & Wiley-Blackwell Publishing.

Sex differences are also seen in the prevalence of obesity. Despite methodological differences in the categorization of obesity, data from the 14 population surveys shown in Figure 2 indicate that in all of the studies, females have a higher prevalence of obesity than males. A greater risk of obesity for females appears to be a basic fact of human biology.

Economic Modernization

The social distribution of obesity varies among societies, depending on their degree of economic modernization. Studies of traditional hunting and gathering populations report *no obesity*. In contrast, numerous studies of traditional societies undergoing the process of economic modernization demonstrate rapid increases in the prevalence of obesity. Trowell and Burkitt's (1981) 15 case studies of epidemiological change in modernizing societies conclude that obesity is the first of the "diseases of civilization" to appear. The rapidity with which obesity becomes a common health problem in the context of modernization underscores the critical role of cultural behaviors in the causation of obesity, since there has been insufficient time for changes in gene frequencies.

Figure 2 also suggests that variations in the male-female ratio of obesity prevalence are related to economic modernization. In less industrially developed societies female obesity is much more common than male obesity, but in more affluent societies the ratio is nearly equivalent. Recent World Health Organization data on global obesity also support this observation (Gurney and Gorstein 1988).

Cultural changes with modernization include the seemingly invariable pattern of diet in industrial countries—decreased fiber intake and increased consumption of fat and sugar. Modernization is also associated with decreased energy expenditures related to work, recreation, or daily activities. From the perspective of the populations undergoing economic modernization, increasing average weight might be seen as a good thing rather than a health problem.

Ethnicity

The idea that particular populations have high rates of a genotype that predisposes individuals to obesity and related diseases is not new but is now supported by a convincing body of adoption and twin data (Stunkard et al. 1986, 1990) and by studies of particular obesity-prone populations like the Pima Indians (Ravussin et al. 1988). In the United States, ethnic groups with elevated rates of obesity include African Americans (particularly in the rural South), Mexican Americans, Puerto Ricans, Gypsies, and Pacific Islanders (Centers for Disease Control 1989).

The fact that certain ethnic groups have high rates of obesity is not easy to interpret because of the entanglement of the effects of genetic heredity, social class, and cultural beliefs. The association of obesity with ethnicity is not evidence for the exclusive role of genetic transmission, since social factors like endogamy (marriage within the group) or group isolation are critical for defining the population structure—that is, the social system through which genes are passed from generation to generation.

Social Class

Social class (socioeconomic status) can be a powerful predictor of the prevalence of obesity in both modernizing and affluent societies, although the direction of the association varies with the type of society. In developing countries, there is a strong and consistent *positive association* between social class and obesity for men, women, and children; correspondingly, there is an inverse correlation between social class and protein-calorie malnutrition. In heterogeneous and affluent societies, like the United States, there is a strong *inverse correlation* of social class and obesity for females. The association between obesity and social class among women in affluent societies is not constant through the life cycle. Economically advantaged girls are initially fatter than their low-income counterparts, but the pattern is reversed beginning at puberty. For females, social class remains the strongest social epidemiological predictor of obesity.

OBESITY AND HUMAN EVOLUTION

Human biology and behavior can be understood in the context of two distinct processes of evolution. Biological evolution involves changes through time in the frequency of particular genes, primarily because of the action of natural selection on individuals. Cultural evolution involves historical changes in the configurations of cultural systems, that is, the learned patterns of behavior and belief characteristics of social groups. Cultural evolution includes the striking and rapid transformation of human lifestyles from small food-foraging societies to large and economically complex states in a span of less than 5,000 years.

The Context of Food Scarcities

Food shortages have been very common in human prehistory and history; in fact, they could be considered a virtually inevitable fact of life for most people. As such, they have been a powerful evolutionary force.

A cross-cultural ethnographic survey of 118 nonindustrial societies (with hunting and gathering, pastoral, horticultural, and agricultural economies) found some form of food shortages for *all* of the societies in the sample (Whiting 1958). Shortages occur annually or even more frequently in roughly half of the societies, and every 2 to 3 years in an additional 24 percent. The shortages are "severe" (i.e., including starvation deaths) in 29 percent of the societies sampled. Seasonal availability of food results in a seasonal cycle of weight loss and weight gain in both hunting and gathering and agricultural societies, although the fluctuation is substantially greater among agriculturalists.

Scarcity and Cultural Evolution

A hunting and gathering economy was characteristic of all human societies for more than 95 percent of our history, yet it is represented by only a handful of societies today. In general, food foragers enjoy high-quality diets, maintain high levels of physical fitness, suffer the risk of periodic food shortages, and are generally healthier than many contemporary populations that rely on agriculture. Without romanticizing these societies, the evidence is persuasive enough to suggest a "paleolithic prescription" of diet and exercise for the prevention of chronic diseases (Eaton et al. 1988). This recommendation refers to the quality of preindustrial diets and not to their dependability or quantity.

Approximately 12,000 years ago, some human groups shifted from a food-foraging economy to one of food production. This economic transformation allowed the evolution of urban civilizations. Many archaeologists believe that people were "forced" to adopt the new agricultural economy because of ecological pressures from population growth and food scarcities or because of military coercion. The archaeological record clearly shows that agriculture was associated with nutritional stress, poor health, and diminished stature (Cohen and Armelagos 1984). The beginning of agriculture is also linked to the emergence of social stratification, a system of inequality that improved the Darwinian fitness of the ruling class relative to that of the lower classes. Social inequality, particularly differential access to strategic resources, plays a critical role in the distribution of obesity in most societies.

Certain ecological zones appear to be prone to severe food shortages. For example, archaeological analysis of tree rings from the southwestern United States shows that the prehistoric past was characterized by frequent and severe droughts. The impressive agricultural societies of the prehistoric Southwest had expanded during an extended period of uncharacteristically good weather and could not be maintained when the lower and more characteristic rainfall patterns resumed. Ecological conditions leading to severe scarcity may have acted as strong forces of selection for "thrifty" genotypes.

Scarcity and Genetic Evolution

Since food shortages were ubiquitous for humans under natural conditions, selection favored individuals who could effectively store calories in times of surplus. For most societies, these fat stores would be called on at least every 2 or 3 years. Malnutrition increases infectious disease mortality, as well as decreasing birth weights and rates of child growth. The evolutionary scenario is this: Females with greater energy reserves in fat would have a selective advantage over their lean counterparts in terms of withstanding the stress of food shortages, not only for themselves but also for their fetuses or nursing children. Humans have evolved the ability to "save up" food energy for inevitable food shortages through the synthesis and storage of fat.

Selection has favored the production of peripheral body fat in females, whose reproductive fitness is influenced by the nutritional demands of pregnancy and lactation. This peripheral fat is usually mobilized after being primed with estrogen during the late stages of pregnancy and during lactation. In addition, a minimal level of fatness increases female reproductive success because of its association with regular cycling and early menarche (Frisch 1987).

In this evolutionary context the usual range of human metabolic variation must have produced many individuals with a predisposition to become obese; yet they would, in all likelihood, never have had the opportunity to do so. Furthermore, in this context there could be little or no natural selection against this tendency. Selection could not provide for the eventuality

FIGURE 3 A materialist model of culture. Brown, Peter J. "Culture and the Evolution of Obesity." Reprinted with kind permission of the author & Springer Science+Business Media: Human Nature 2 (1991), no. 1:31–57, Figure 3, "A materialist model of culture."

of continuous surplus simply because it had never existed before.

CULTURE AND ADAPTATIONS TO FOOD SCARCITY

Food scarcities have shaped not only our genes but also, and perhaps more important, human cultures. Because the concept of culture is rarely considered in medical research on obesity, and because I am suggesting that this concept has advantages over the more common and undifferentiated term *environment*, it is necessary to review some basic aspects of this anthropological term. *Culture* refers to the learned patterns of behavior and belief characteristic of a social group. As such, culture encompasses *Homo sapiens'* primary mechanism of evolutionary adaptation, which has distinct advantages of greater speed and flexibility than genetic evolution.

Cultural behaviors and beliefs are usually learned in childhood and they are often deeply held and seldom questioned by adults, who pass this "obvious" knowledge and habits to their offspring. In this regard, cultural beliefs and values are largely unconscious factors in the motivation of individual behaviors. Cultural beliefs define "what is normal" and therefore constrain the choices of behaviors available to an individual.

One useful way of thinking about culture in relation to obesity is a cultural materialist model as seen in Figure 3. This model divides culture into three layers. The material foundation of a cultural system is the economic mode of production, which includes the technology and the population size that the productive economy allows and requires. Population size is maintained by the social system, sometimes called the mode of reproduction. Contingent on the first layer is the system of social organization, which includes kinship patterns, marriage and family practices, politics, and status differentiation. Contingent on the social structure is the ideology or belief system, including ideas, beliefs, and values, both secular and sacred. Most anthropologists believe that the ideology is an extremely important part of culture, in part because it rationalizes and reinforces the economy and social structure. Ideology enables people to make sense of their world and to share their common world view through symbols. As such, ideology includes sacred concepts from religion as well as secular concepts (with symbolic components) like health or sexual attractiveness.

A culture is an integrated system: A change in one part causes changes in the other layers. The materialist model indicates that the direction of causal change is from the bottom layer upward (the solid arrows in Figure 3). An economic change, like the invention of agriculture or the Industrial Revolution, has drastic implications for population size, social organization, and associated beliefs. On the other hand, most people within a society tend to explain things from the top down. Of course, people can hold contradictory beliefs and values that are not necessarily linked to their actual behavior.

CULTURAL PREDISPOSITIONS TO OBESITY

Obesity is related to culture in all three levels of the materialist model.

Productive Economy and Food Scarcity

Humans have evolved a wide variety of cultural mechanisms to avoid or minimize the effects of food scarcities. The most important adaptation to scarcity is the evolution of systems of food production and storage. As noted previously, the primary weakness of preindustrial systems of food production is a vulnerability to food shortages. The universality of food shortages discussed above is largely because of the technological limitations in food production and storage.

On the other hand, the energy-intensive (and energy-inefficient) system of agriculture in industrialized societies produces large surpluses of food. These agricultural surpluses are seldom used to eliminate hunger; rather they are used to transform and process foods in particular ways—often to add calories, fat, or salt. For example, we feed "extra" grain to beef cattle to increase the proportion of fat in their meat; consumers say that this overfeeding makes the meat "juicy." Similarly, potatoes are transformed into french fries and potato chips. From a nutritional standpoint the original vegetable is actually reduced to a vehicle for fat and salt. Endemic hunger exists even in the most affluent societies, where it is caused not by poor production but by inequitable distribution.

Technological changes associated with cultural evolution almost exclusively reduce the energy requirements of human labor. In general, cultural evolution has meant the harnessing of greater amounts of energy through technology (one aspect of the mode of production). To prevent obesity, people in developed societies must burn energy through daily workouts rather than daily work.

Reproduction and Energy Expenditure

The concept of the *mode of reproduction* is also related to predispositions to obesity. Pregnancy and lactation represent serious and continuing energy demands on women in societies that have not undergone the demographic transition. Industrial and nonindustrial societies differ in terms of the historical changes from high to low fertility and the reduction of mortality attributable to infectious disease. Higher numbers of pregnancies and longer periods of breast-feeding place high energy demands on women, especially if they cannot supplement their diet during these critical periods. As a result, women suffer greater risk of protein-energy malnutrition. Conversely, with fewer pregnancies and the reduction of breast-feeding, women in industrial societies have less opportunity to mobilize peripheral fat stores and suffer greater risk of obesity. In contemporary societies like the United States, mothers in lower social classes tend to have more children and to feed their infants with bottled formula rather than breast milk. Use of infant formulas allows women to retain their fat stores. These different social patterns in reproduction may play a role in the inverse association of obesity and social class for females.

Social Structure and Obesity

Characteristics of social organization may function as predispositions to obesity. In highly stratified and culturally heterogeneous societies, the distribution of obesity is associated with ethnicity and social class. Marriage patterns typically illustrate ethnic or social class endogamy, that is, marriage within the group. In the United States, members of ethnic minorities choose marriage partners from the same group at extremely high rates. This social practice may concentrate the genetic predispositions to conditions like obesity in particular subpopulations. Similarly, data suggest a pattern of "assortative mating" by social class as well as body type (particularly stature), which may be related to the genetic etiology of obesity. Genetic admixture with Native American groups of the Southwest has been suggested as a cause of elevated rates of type 2 diabetes mellitus and obesity among Mexican Americans (Gardner et al. 1984).

The pervasive and complex relationship between obesity and social class, or socioeconomic status (SES), is important. SES is related to particular behavior patterns that cause obesity. This statement underemphasizes the fact that these learned behaviors are *characteristic* of particular social groups or classes. In other words, the cultural patterns of social class groups are primary, not the individual behaviors themselves.

From a cross-cultural perspective, the general association between obesity and social position is positive: The groups with greater access to economic resources have higher rates of obesity. This pattern is logical and expected because socially dominant groups with better access to strategic resources should have better nutrition, better health, and consequently greater reproductive success.

As discussed earlier, the remarkable and important exception is women in industrial societies, who exhibit a strong *inverse* correlation between obesity and social class. The challenge for researchers is to explain why and how upper-class women in industrial societies remain thin. For many women the ideal of thinness requires considerable effort, restrained eating, and often resources invested in exercise. The social origins of the ideal of thinness in American women are associated with historical changes in women's economic roles, marriage patterns, and family size.

Low-income people in industrial societies might be considered well off by worldwide standards, and this access to resources is reflected in obesity prevalences. Yet in the context of perceived relative deprivation and economic stability, many people in societies like the United States live in stressful conditions—just one paycheck away from hunger. In terms of life priorities, economic security may be a higher and more immediate objective than more elusive goals like an "ideal body" or even long-term health. Amid the daily stresses of poverty, food may be the most common avenue of pleasure and psychological relief. Ethnographic studies of low-income urban black communities in the United States show a social emphasis on food sharing as a tool for marking family ties and demonstrating community cohesiveness.

Cultural Beliefs as Predispositions to Obesity

The third and possibly most important level of the model of culture shown in Figure 3 encompasses cultural symbols, beliefs, and values. Aspects of ideology relevant to the etiology of obesity include the symbolic meaning of fatness, ideal body types, and perceived risks of food shortages.

Fatness is symbolically linked to psychological dimensions, such as self-worth and sexuality, in many societies of the world, but the nature of that symbolic association is not constant. In mainstream U.S. culture, obesity is socially stigmatized, but for most cultures of the world, fatness is viewed as a welcome sign of health and prosperity. Given the rarity of obesity in preindustrial societies, it is not surprising that they lack ethnomedical terms for obesity. Much more attention is placed on "thinness" as a symptom of starvation, like among the !Kung San (Lee 1979), or in contemporary Africa as a sign of AIDS (sometimes called "the slim disease"). In the context of the AIDS epidemic, plumpness is indeed a marker of health.

Perhaps it is large body size, rather than obesity per se, that is admired as a symbol of health, prestige, prosperity, or maternity in agricultural societies. The Tiv of Nigeria, for example, distinguish between a very positive category, "too big" *(kehe)*, and an unpleasant condition "to grow fat" *(ahon)* (Bohannan and Bohannan 1969). The first is a compliment because it is a sign of prosperity; the second is a rare and undesirable condition.

For women, fatness may also be a symbol of maternity and nurturance. In traditional societies in which women attain status only through motherhood, this symbolic association increases the cultural acceptability of fatness. A fat woman, symbolically, is well taken care of, and in turn she takes good care of her children. Fellahin Arabs in Egypt describe the proper woman as fat because she has more room to bear the child, lactates abundantly, and gives warmth to her children. The cultural ideal of thinness in industrial societies, in contrast, is found where motherhood is not the sole or even primary means of status attainment for woman. The idea that fat babies and children are healthy children is very widespread. Food can be treated as a symbol of love and nurturance; in some cultures it may be impolite for a guest to refuse food that has been offered, but it is taboo to refuse food from one's mother.

In the industrialized United States, ethnic variation in culturally accepted definitions of obesity is significant. Some Mexican Americans have coined a new term, *gordura mala* (bad fatness), because the original term *gordura* continues to have positive cultural connotations (Ritenbaugh 1982). For this group cultural identity has a stronger and independent effect on risk of obesity than socioeconomic status. An ethnographic study of the cultural meanings of weight in a Puerto Rican community in Philadelphia (Massara 1989) documents the positive associations and lack of social stigma of obesity. Additional quantitative evidence suggests significant differences in ideal body preferences between this ethnic community and mainstream American culture. Positive evaluations of fatness may also occur among lower-class African Americans and Mexican Americans. These ethnic groups are heterogeneous, however, and upwardly mobile ethnics tend to resemble mainstream American culture in their attitudes about obesity and ideal body shape.

In a low-income housing project in Atlanta, Georgia, a sociological interviewer was asked by a group of obese black women, "Don't you know how hard it is to keep this weight *on*?" Their views of the advantages of a large body included being given respect and reduced chances of being bothered by young "toughs" in the neighborhood. For these women, fatness was part of their positive self-identity, and if a friend lost weight she was thought to look sickly. Among lower-income groups, the perceived risk of a food shortage—not for the society as a whole but for the immediate family—may be very important, especially if lack of food was personally experienced in the past. The perception of the risk of future "bad times" and insufficient food is the reality upon which people act.

FATNESS AND CROSS-CULTURAL STANDARDS OF BEAUTY IN WOMEN

Culturally defined standards of beauty vary between societies. In a classic example, Malcom (1925) describes the custom of "fattening huts" for elite Efik pubescent girls in traditional Nigeria. A girl spent up to 2 years in seclusion and at the end of this rite of passage possessed symbols of womanhood and marriage-ability—a three-tiered hairstyle, clitoridectomy, and fatness. Fatness was a primary criterion of beauty as it was defined by the elites, who alone had the economic resources to participate in this custom. Similarly, fatter brides demand significantly higher bridewealth payments among the Kipsigis of Kenya (Borgerhoff Mulder 1988).

Among the Havasupai of the American Southwest, if a girl is thin at puberty, a fat woman "stands" (places her foot) on the girl's back so she will become attractively plump. In this society, fat legs and, to a lesser extent, arms are considered essential to beauty. The Tarahumara of northern Mexico consider fat legs a fundamental aspect of the ideal feminine body; an attractive woman is called a "beautiful thigh." Among the Amhara of Ethiopia in northern East Africa, thin hips are called "dog hips" in a typical insult (Messing 1957).

It is difficult to know how widespread among the world's cultures is the association of plumpness and beauty. A preliminary indication can be found through a cross-cultural survey based on data from the Human Relations Area Files (a cross-indexed compilation of ethnographic information on more than 300 of the most thoroughly studied societies). The results of this survey are summarized in Table 1. Although conclusions made from these data are weak because of the small number and possibly nonrepresentative nature

TABLE 1   Cross-Cultural Standards of Female Beauty

	Number of Societies	Percent of Societies
Overall body		
Extreme obesity	0	0
Plump/moderately fat	31	81
Thin/abhorrence of fat	7	19
Breasts		
Large or long	9	50
Small/abhorrence of large	9	50
Hips and Legs		
Large or fat	9	90
Slender	1	10
Stature		
Tall	3	30
Moderate	6	60
Small	1	10

Source: Brown, P. J., & M. Konner. "An Anthropological Perspective on Obesity" from ANNALS OF THE NEW YORK ACADEMY OF SCIENCES 499 (1987), no. 1 29–46. Reprinted by permission of The New York Academy of Sciences & Wiley-Blackwell Publishing.

of the cases, as well as the fact that most ethnographies are difficult to code on this variable, some preliminary generalizations are possible. Cultural standards of beauty do not refer to physical extremes. No society on record has an ideal of extreme obesity. On the other hand, the desirability of "plumpness" or being "filled out" is found in 81 percent of the societies for which this variable can be coded. This standard, which probably includes the clinical categories of overweight and mild obesity, apparently refers to the desirability of fat deposits, particularly on the hips and legs.

Although cross-cultural variation is evident in standards of beauty, this variation falls within a certain range. American ideals of thinness occur in a setting in which it is easy to become fat, and preference for plumpness occurs in settings in which it is easy to remain lean. In context, both standards require the investment of individual effort and economic resources; furthermore, each in its context involves a display of wealth. Cultural beliefs about attractive body shape in mainstream American culture place pressure on females to lose weight and are involved in the etiology of anorexia and bulimia.

IDEAL BODY-TYPE, SIZE, AND SYMBOLIC POWER IN MEN

The ethnographic record concerning body preferences for males is extremely weak, yet preliminary research suggests a universal preference for a muscular physique and for tall or moderately tall stature. In general, members of all human societies appear to admire large body size as an attribute of attractiveness in men, because it symbolizes health, economic success, political power, and social status. "Big men," political leaders in tribal New Guinea, are described by their constituents in terms of their size and physical well-being: He is a man "whose skin swells with 'grease' [fat] underneath" (Strahern 1971). The spiritual power (*mana*) and noble breeding of a Polynesian chief is expected to be seen in his large size. In American society vestiges of a similar idea remain; for example, a "fat cat" is a wealthy and powerful man who can "throw his weight around." The political metaphor of weight and power in American society has been explored by social historians. Most male college students in the U.S., in contrast with women, want to gain weight because it is equivalent to gaining muscle mass and physical power in a process called "bulking up."

CONCLUSIONS

Two sets of conclusions can be drawn from this discussion of culture and its relationship to obesity—one practical and one theoretical. First, recognition of cultural variation in beliefs and behaviors related to obesity needs to be incorporated into health programs aimed at reducing the prevalence of obesity. The second conclusion regards the need for more research on the role of culture, as it interacts with genes, on the etiology of obesity.

The Importance of Culture in Health Interventions

Existing cultural beliefs must be taken into account in the design and implementation of health promotion projects. In an obesity prevention campaign in a Zulu community outside of Durban, one health education poster depicted an obese woman and an overloaded truck with a flat tire, with a caption "Both carry too much weight." Another poster showed a slender woman easily sweeping under a table next to an obese woman who was using the table for support; it had the caption "Who do you prefer to look like?" The intended message of these posters was misinterpreted by the community because of a cultural connection between obesity and social status. The woman in the first poster was perceived to be rich and happy, since she was not only fat but had a truck overflowing with her possessions. The second poster was perceived as a scene of an affluent mistress directing her underfed servant.

Health interventions must be culturally acceptable, and we cannot assume that people place the highest priority on their health. The idea of reducing

risk factors for chronic diseases that may develop later may not be an effective strategy for populations who do not feel empowered or who live in a fundamentally risky world.

Implications for the Etiology of Obesity

The frequency of past food shortages, the social distribution of obesity, and the cultural meanings of fatness, when taken together, suggest a biocultural hypothesis of the evolution of obesity. Both genetic and cultural predispositions to obesity may be products of the same evolutionary pressures, involving two related processes: first, genetic traits that cause fatness were selected because they improved chances of survival in the face of food scarcities, particularly for pregnant and nursing women; second, in the context of unequal access to food, fatness may have been socially selected because it is a cultural symbol of social prestige and an index of general health. Under Western conditions of abundance, our biological tendency to regulate body weight at levels above our ideal cannot be easily controlled even with a reversal of the widespread cultural ideal of plumpness.

This evolutionary model is obviously congruent with the current etiological theory about obesity, which combines genetic predispositions with "environmental" causes. Recent research both in epidemiology and human laboratory research demonstrates without a doubt the central role of genetic heredity in the etiology of obesity. Similar genetic evidence exists for variables like the distribution of fat on the body and basal metabolic rates. To an anthropologist, these important studies are welcome and expected.

The recent advances in understanding the genetic bases of obesity remind us, however, of our ignorance about the precise role of the "environment." One problem is that "environment" has been poorly defined and treated as if it were idiosyncratic for every individual or family. Another problem is that "environment" is essentially treated as a residual category—one that cannot be explained by genetic heredity. This paper has attempted to show how the anthropological concept of culture may be useful in conceptualization of the different components of the "environment" and the generation of hypotheses for future research in behavioral medicine.

The most convincing demonstrations of a strong genetic component for obesity have been in populations with relatively high levels of cultural homogeneity. In social contexts like Denmark, Iowa, or among Pima Indians, the influence of culture—including learned behaviors and beliefs—is minimized by the sample selected for study in order to emphasize the importance of genotypical variation. Essentially, cultural variation has been treated as if it were "noise." An essential goal in future research must be the identification of specific cultural factors—whether economic, social, or ideological—that predispose people to obesity.

From the standpoint of the prevention of obesity, it is critical to stress that genetic predisposition is not destiny. Genetic predispositions to obesity have apparently been maintained in populations throughout most of our species' history, yet it has rarely been expressed phenotypically. Culture is adaptive because it can be changed. Habitual patterns of behavior—of an individual or an entire society—can be changed to reduce morbidity and mortality linked to obesity and overweight. These changes must include social and political efforts to reduce the risk of hunger and food scarcity, even in affluent societies.

REFERENCES

Bohannan, P., and L. Bohannan. 1969. *A Source Notebook on Tiv Religion*. New Haven, CT: Human Relations Area Files.

Borgerhoff Mulder, M. 1988. Kipsigis Bridewealth Payments. In *Human Reproductive Behavior*, eds. L. Betzig, M. Borgerhoff Mulder, and P. Turke, 65–82. Cambridge: Cambridge University Press.

Bray, G. A. 1987. Overweight Is Risking Fate: Definition, Classification, Prevalence and Risks. In *Human Obesity*, eds. R. J. Wurtman and J. J. Wurtman, *Annals of the New York Academy of Sciences* 499: 14–28.

Brown, P. J., and M. Konner. 1987. An Anthropological Perspective on Obesity. In *Human Obesity*, eds. R. J. Wurtman and J. J. Wurtman, *Annals of the New York Academy of Sciences* 499: 29–46.

Centers for Disease Control. 1989. Prevalence of Overweight—Behavioral Risk Factor Surveillance System, 1987. *Morbidity and Mortality Weekly Report* 38: 421–423.

Chernin, K. 1981. *The Obsession: Reflections on the Tyranny of Slenderness*. New York: Harper & Row.

Cohen, M. N., and G. J. Armelagos, eds. 1984. *Paleopathology at the Origins of Agriculture*. New York: Academic Press.

Eaton, S. B., M. Shostak, and M. Konner. 1988. *The Paleolithic Prescription*. New York: Harper & Row.

Frisch, R. E. 1987. Body Fat, Menarche, Fitness and Fertility. *Human Reproduction* 2: 521–533.

Gardner, L. I., M. P. Stern, S. M. Haffner, S. P. Gaskill, H. Hazuda, and J. H. Relethford. 1984. Prevalence of Diabetes in Mexican Americans. *Diabetes* 33: 86–92.

Gurney, M., and J. Gorstein. 1988. The Global Prevalence of Obesity—An Initial Overview of Available Data. *World Health Statistics Quarterly* 41: 251–254.

Kissebah, A. H., D. S. Freedman, and A. N. Peiris. 1989. Health Risks of Obesity. *Medical Clinics of North America* 73: 11–138.

Lee, R. B. 1979. *The !Kung San: Men, Women, and Work in a Foraging Society*. Cambridge, MA: Harvard University Press.

Malcom, L. W. G. 1925. Note on the Seclusion of Girls Among the Efik at Old Calabar. *Man* 25: 113–114.

Massara, E. B. 1989. *Que Gordita! A Study of Weight Among Women in a Puerto Rican Community*. New York: AMS Press.

Messing, S. D. 1957. *The Highland Plateau Amhara of Ethiopia*. Ph.D. dissertation, Department of Anthropology, University of Pennsylvania, Philadelphia.

Ravussin, E., S. Lillioja, and W. C. Knowler, et al. 1988. Reduced Rate of Energy Expenditure as a Risk Factor for Body-Weight Gain. *New England Journal of Medicine* 318: 467–472.

Ritenbaugh, C. 1982. Obesity as a Culture-Bound Syndrome. *Culture, Medicine and Psychiatry* 6: 347–361.

Strahern, A. 1971. *The Rope of Moka*. New York: Cambridge University Press.

Stunkard, A. J., T. I. A. Sorenson, C. Hanis, T. W. Teasdale, R. Chakaborty, W. J. Schull, and F. Schulsinger. 1986. An Adoption Study of Obesity. *New England Journal of Medicine* 314: 193–198.

Stunkard, A. J., J. R. Harris, N. L. Pedersen, and G. McClearn. 1990. The Body-Mass Index of Twins Who Have Been Reared Apart. *New England Journal of Medicine* 322: 1483–1487.

Trowell, H. C., and D. P. Burkitt. 1981. *Western Diseases: Their Emergence and Prevention*. Cambridge, MA: Harvard University Press.

Whiting, M. G. 1958. *A Cross-Cultural Nutrition Survey*. Doctoral Dissertation, Harvard School of Public Health, Cambridge.

Wurtman, R. J., and J. J. Wurtman, eds. 1987. Human Obesity. *Annals of the New York Academy of Sciences* 499.

36

Pocahontas Goes to the Clinic

Popular Culture as Lingua Franca in a Cultural Borderland

Cheryl Mattingly

Technical competence may be a critical component of medical practice, but it alone cannot heal. In U.S. hospitals and clinics, medical technology and practice depend on the ability of patients and physicians to trust, communicate, and understand each other. In urban hospitals, patients, doctors, and other medical personnel may share similar goals, but they may not share the same languages and ethnicities. Linguistic and ethnic diversity have transformed the medical clinic into a cultural borderland, which now more than ever demands anthropological perspectives.

Sickle-cell patients in the U.S. often experience the negative effects of medical treatment undermined by a lack of sociocultural understanding. Sickle-cell anemia is a serious condition in which red blood cells can become stiff, sticky, and sickle-shaped; clumps of sickle cells can block blood flow and lead to chronic pain, infection, and organ failure. This medical condition affects African Americas, Hispanic Americans, as well as populations from Africa, South America, Central America, India, Saudi Arabia, and Caribbean and Mediterranean countries. Because sickle-cell anemia impacts African Americans and Hispanic Americans, the legacies of racial and ethnic divisions in the United States often creep into the treatment of sickle-cell patients. For example, the chronic pain associated with sickle-cell anemia leads some clinicians to inappropriately label African American teenage boys with sickle-cell as "med-seeking" patients.

Establishing effective communication and understanding between patients and caregivers is complicated by ethnic divisions, differences in language, and racial/ethnic stereotyping. Nonetheless, creative clinicians find ways to bridge the cultural borderlands of the medical clinic. In this selection, Cheryl Mattingly examines how global icons like Disney characters and Spider Man help patients and doctors create trust and communicative contexts for healing.

As you read this selection, ask yourself the following questions:

- How is the medical clinic a "border zone?" What is a border zone?

- What is a healing drama and how do they apply to medical practice?

- How do cultural misunderstandings influence medical care?

- How does culture in the hybrid environment of a borderland differ from culture in a more homogeneous context?

- How is the practice of culture a practice of othering?

- In what ways can race and class impact the quality and efficacy of medical treatment?

The following terms discussed in this selection are included in the Glossary at the back of the book:

indigenized	*lingua franca*
othering	*sickle-cell anemia*

The first time I met Pocahontas in a hospital was in the mid-1990s. Of course, as a U.S. citizen, I had known her since childhood. But I had forgotten all about her until she appeared, quite unexpectedly, in hospitals in Chicago and Los Angeles where I was carrying out research. She looked very different than I remembered.

Mattingly, Cheryl. "Pocahontas Goes to the Clinic: Popular Culture as Lingua Franca in a Cultural Borderland" from AMERICAN ANTHROPOLOGIST 108 (2006), no. 3:494–501. Reprinted by permission of Wiley-Blackwell Publishing.

Older, and less, well, historical. She had been dusted off, Disneyfied, transformed into a gorgeous teenage beauty with a head of the most magnificent black hair and a body as enviably proportioned as Barbie. She could sing too. And it was Disney who sent her to the clinic. For not only was she a larger-than-life figure in a popular animated movie, she was packaged into craft sets, costumes, dolls, and an array of other cultural artifacts that began to find their way into all sorts of children's places—including children's hospitals. She traveled internationally as well. I saw her once, resplendently arrayed, hair flowing, on a large poster board in a duty free shop at the Copenhagen airport. Internet chat rooms carried on worldwide conversations about her adventures. Pocahontas had gone global.

This apparently frivolous example of the circulation of global goods has special and, indeed, profound significance in the context of health care, as I have gradually come to realize. Drawing from ethnographic research carried out over the past nine years among African American families who have children with severe illnesses and disabilities, I examine how children's popular culture, exported by such mass media empires as Disney, operates in the fraught borderland that constitutes the urban clinic. Children's films and television programs provide characters and plights that are creatively localized in health care encounters. A child's beloved character can offer a kind of narrative shadow, a cultural resource that children, families, and health care professionals readily turn to in the ongoing task of creating socially shared meaning, especially the sort of meaning that has to do with trying to positively shape a child's future.

Stories, it has long been noted, tend to provoke the imagination. They spur us to consider life in the subjunctive mode (Bruner 1986, 2002), in terms of a "what if" universe of possibilities. Thus, it is not surprising that anthropologists have looked at the way stories created by global media inspire new imaginative constructions of lives and worlds. The study of media has been intimately connected to the reinvention of culture as a contested space, a point of particular relevance to this article. Media is often treated as a force for constructing a distinctive identity—for creating boundaries and marking distinctions—but here I explore it as a vehicle for creating commonalities. Its role as mediator between the worlds of family and clinic takes on special importance in clinical encounters marked by differences in race and social class. Children's popular culture offers resources for building bridges among groups who perceive themselves as Other but who are compelled to collaborate because of the need to tend to a sick or disabled child. A Disneyfied Pocahontas is only one of the mass-marketed figures that plays an important role in the clinic, especially in creating "common ground" between the world of the hospital and home, and among the various key actors who care for severely ill or disabled children. Global icons like these can function as a lingua franca, offering a language of publicly available symbols on which families, health professionals, and children can draw to signal a common heritage or to create shared imaginative space across racial, class, and sufferer–healer divides. Why is a trade language so necessary in the U.S. urban hospital?

WHEN CULTURE IS A BORDERLAND: THE URBAN CLINIC

Urban hospitals constitute an example of what is arguably the most visible site in anthropology these days—the border zone, which James Clifford describes as a place of "hybrid cosmopolitan experiences" (1997:25). Border zones have emerged as part of the refiguration of culture, a shift from the discipline's traditional task of elucidating "the crystalline patterns of a whole culture" to a focus on "the blurred zones in between" (Rosaldo 1989:209). Anthropologists have been moving from the heartlands to the borders for quite some time. This has meant a shift away from studying isolated communities in favor of geographic areas—such as urban centers or national border zones, which are characterized by ethnic pluralism and a fast changing cultural scene. It has also meant paying special attention to sites of heightened commerce among actors who are culturally diverse. A focus on border zones is part of a fertile rethinking of traditional concepts of culture by anthropologists and culture theorists.

In a borderland, culture emerges more vividly as a space of encounter than of enclosure. For many, culture has come to designate a noisy, pluralistic, contested, ever-changing public sphere, rather than a substance, common property, or a shared commitment to a way of life. This perspective emphasizes connections—including media-created connections—that are often political and often unexpected among these diverse communities and commodities.[1] Viewed in this way, culture is not to be found in a group's shared set of beliefs and values so much as in its practices of drawing contrasts and boundaries with other groups as well as challenging those contrasts. This sort of cultural world is characterized by politically charged, difference-making exchanges among actors.

The clinical world has often been recognized as contested terrain. The urban hospital is a place in which misreadings and conflicts routinely arise. The United States is growing rapidly more ethnically diverse, and this means that health care increasingly involves providing treatment for diverse populations. Urban health care in the United States is characterized by a dizzying array of languages, nationalities, racial identifications, social classes, and religions.[2] It has been well documented that ethnic diversity is accompanied by unequal access to health care. Racism also plays a key role in adverse health outcomes. African Americans continue to be one of the least well-served minority groups, a recognition that has provoked examination of the connections between race and health.[3]

A great deal of the work in medical anthropology has explored transactions within biomedical encounters marked by cultural confusions and misunderstandings—border talk, in fact. But the figure of clinic as border zone takes on a decidedly less familiar cast when situated within the recent debates about culture, place, and space that have arisen among scholars far removed from anything clinical—those who have been delivering, or responding to, challenges concerning the location of culture in the face of a globalizing and decolonizing world. This work offers an intriguing vantage point for examining the border activities of health care practices. In this discursive context, the familiar figure of the misunderstood patient emerges as startlingly emblematic, an exemplary citizen of that new nation, the land of the culturally in-between. If the practice of culture is, in part, the practice of Othering, of identifying cultural (and racial) difference in a thousand subtle and unconscious ways, this is of special importance in clinical encounters. Failures of communication are magnified to intense proportions in situations characterized by both perceptions of difference and high stakes. Cultural identities constructed by race, class, gender, and other potentially stigmatizing markers take on profound meaning here. What might, in another context, be a small slight or a confusing conversation, can, under these heightened circumstances, take on enormous importance. To feel neglected by one's doctor when one's child is seriously ill is not the same as being ignored by the grocery clerk.

The primary research that informs this article is a longitudinal ethnography that began in Los Angeles in January 1997 and is still ongoing. It has been carried out by an interdisciplinary team of anthropologists and occupational therapists. We initially recruited 30 African American families from the Los Angeles area whose children (ages from birth to eight) were being treated in several clinical sites. Most, although not all families, were low income. Eighteen of those initially recruited have continued to participate. Others joined subsequently as some families left the study for various reasons (e.g., moving out of state). All families now participating have been part of the project for at least three years.

This continuity of families has allowed us to come to know the ebbs and flows of chronic illness and to witness what that means in the never-ending process of negotiating health care with shifting casts of health professionals and changing bureaucratic processes. The research has involved accompanying families to clinical visits, observing and sometimes videotaping those encounters, and separately interviewing participants about what they perceived happened in the encounters. We have also observed and videotaped children and families at home and in the community, especially at key family events. This kind of longitudinal design has revealed a great deal about clinical encounters as events in family lives and about multiple perspectives between families and clinicians as these develop and change over time.

In this article, I provide examples and quotations from clinicians and family members that exemplify some themes that have arisen repeatedly in our data and are important to the arguments I make here. The data I cite come not only from my own interviews and observations but also from research conducted by other members of the research team.[4]

Not surprisingly, a key issue for families concerns whether or not they can trust their clinicians. The most minute nuances and gestures of health professionals (esp. doctors) are routinely scrutinized, becoming a subject of storytelling and puzzling. What are they trying to tell me? parents wonder. What are they hiding? Do they treat me this way because I'm black? A man without a job? A single mother? Do they think I'm a "ghetto mom?" Do they think I'm abusing my child? Are they experimenting on my child? Are they ignoring me because I'm on Medicaid? Do they think I'm not strong enough, bright enough, educated enough, to hear the truth? These are the sorts of questions asked by families in our research, and they are asked again and again. If cultures are spaces in which cultural differences are constructed and Othering is an everyday occurrence, this is profoundly consequential when a child's health or life is on the line.

THE HAZARDS OF BORDER CROSSING

If health encounters operate in a "border zone," all the key actors—especially minority patients and families—are attempting to cross borders. When children have chronic medical conditions, successful treatment demands cooperation and alliance building among children, family members, and professionals.[5] This can be a daunting task for all involved, especially when clients have had a difficult time receiving decent health care, as is the case with many of the families in this study. When stigmatizing class and racial categorizations arise, or are suspected of arising, tensions intensify. Mistrust on all sides tends to run high. Othering tactics practiced by clinicians are often subtle and largely unconscious, becoming most visible when patients, including parenting kin, are perceived as noncompliant. Explicit racial designations are rarely used, but there is a common taxonomy of "difficult clients" that is often attached to low-income minorities, a language so polite that its stigmatizing influences are largely undetected by clinicians. In our research with children, negative labels are often affixed to the parents rather than the children themselves. In addition to obvious negative markers—such as the "abusive, noncompliant, or neglectful parent"—there is a language of compassion that can also serve to create difference: the "overwhelmed parent," the "too many things going on at home parent," the "doesn't really understand the clinical picture" parent, or the "still in denial" parent.

One of the most insidious features of these categories is that when people have been placed in one of them, their capabilities and strengths are hidden from view. This problem is exacerbated by the fact that health care encounters are based on expert models of service delivery: Clients have problems, professionals have problem-solving expertise. This too, can make it difficult for professionals to see the need to identify their clients' strong points or to learn from them. In addition to the problematic categories that abound in informal health care discourse, professionals also learn narrative strategies that can effectively disguise the abilities of clients. They operate with a common set of narrative scripts or work to construct stories that "make sense" of problematic or difficult clients in a way that leaves little room for the client to emerge as an agent, to influence the framing of the problem or the path of treatment (Mattingly 1998b). Although these problematic features of health care are by no means peculiar to minority populations, they are certainly intensified for minorities in which racial designations are likely to influence the clinical encounter.

One place this has emerged with startling clarity in our study is with children suffering from sickle-cell disease. The sickle-cell clinic has been the place where race is most openly discussed by clinical staff as well as parents. One mother in our study remarked that children with this disease are "not being treated with dignity and respect" in many hospitals, a lack of respect that includes parents as well. Because of some humiliating experiences at the hospital in which her child had been a patient for years, she transferred her daughter to another hospital, even though they lacked the same level of expertise in treating sickle-cell disease. She put it this way: "I'm not a radical. I'm not a feminist. . . . I just think you should be treated a certain way, and I should be treated like the person next to me who maybe is a different skin color."

Several clinicians in our study concurred. One physician who has treated sickle-cell patients for 25 years (and who happens to be white) angrily noted the dismissive way clinical staff tend to view sickle cell, a dismissiveness that also extended to the clinicians who treat such children:

> I'll tell you I don't even listen to them, the attendings. They say, "Ah well, we have a chemotherapy patient coming in so we need to send your sickle patient off the floor because this patient's more important." You know? And I won't tell you what I'd like to say to them. . . . There's very much the attitude that well, this is something that anybody can take care of and it's just like pneumonia. And they don't really believe that there's anything in particular, that special expertise, that's going to help you take care of these kids. And you find out real quick that that's not true.

A vivid illustration of problematic, race-based categorizing is the "med-seeking" label regularly attached to those with sickle-cell disease who go into a pain crisis. Adolescent African American boys, in particular, are often refused crucial pain medication or are seen as crazy, violent, or drug seeking when in a pain crisis. The physician quoted above told the following story in an interview:

> Try being a 17-year-old black male with severe pain going into an emergency room and asking for narcotics and see how far you get. . . . Some of the best advice that I ever heard was from an adult with sickle cell, this is from family day that we had a few years ago. And this adult said, "What you need to do is when you're totally fine, you're not in the middle of a crisis, go to the emergency room and ask to meet the head of the emergency room and sit down for five minutes with him and say, "Hi, my name is blank, remember me? I was an extremist the other night and I'm just on my way to my law firm today, but you know, but on the way to the business I own or the job I have doing X, Y, Z, I wanted to stop in and let you know that I don't always go around in my undershirt and underwear screaming, asking for narcotics."

An African American social worker we also interviewed in this same clinic echoed this: "As soon as the house staff hears there's a sickle-cell patient, something goes up that says, 'I've got a kid here that's drug-seeking, you know, manipulating,' without actually doing any assessment of the child."

The difficulty of not being heard or of being subjected to racially based Othering, although especially articulated with sickle-cell disease, pervades clinical encounters. How do families, children, and clinicians attempt to cross a clinical border zone heightened by racial wariness and mistrust? They cultivate border-crossing skills: They learn to "read the minds" of professional Others, and in light of those readings, to devise strategies to present themselves as worthy of care. Border crossing can be very tricky business because African American clients routinely must be noncompliant to get the care they or their children need. Learning to read the culture of a clinic and of an individual health professional means learning how to execute the right kind of noncompliance that will lead to getting care rather than being turned away or, worse, reported to the social worker as a "problem parent." One mother explained how she has learned to "shuffle through and play this politicking thing"— that is, to appear compliant even in situations in which she knows more about her child's disease than the professional and may privately disregard what the clinician tells her to do. In situations in which she felt she must fight directly, even when she was proved medically correct, she was then faced with yet more "shuffling" and "playing" the "politicking thing" to reestablish good relationships with estranged clinicians. In other words, she had to apologize and act grateful even when she was right to challenge professionals:

> A lot of times you, as parents, you kind of specialize in a disease. You know a lot more than the doctor knows and it's scary when you have doctors that say, "Oh, I'm Dr. So and So" and . . . then they say something off the wall and you know that they are completely wrong. And how do you deal with a doctor and his ego? And so that's part of the game that I've mentioned before. You have to know how to shuffle through and play this politicking thing when you shouldn't have to do that.

CHILDREN'S POPULAR CULTURE AS LINGUA FRANCA

It is within this charged and wary context that the power of children's popular culture needs to be understood. If failed encounters produce and reinforce narratives of the stigmatized Other, successful ones counter these powerful narratives by producing ones in which clinicians and patients come to share, if sometimes fleetingly, a narrative of mutuality and belonging.[6] So, for instance, when an oncologist stops an examination to ask a parent about his or her Thanksgiving and to recount a story about problematic in-laws at the dinner, the oncologist speaks, in an important way, to a shared world of values and practices. The ability of professionals to recognize, acknowledge, and build on commonalities that cross lines of race, class, and culture is as important as recognizing the existence of race-based stereotyping or cultural difference.

Common worlds are routinely created in clinic interactions, drawing on cultural resources that are familiar to all the parties. For clinicians who have sustained relationships with clients, the ability of the actors to call on the small things—a joke remembered, a movie just seen, a disastrous Thanksgiving dinner— can be extremely powerful in forging bonds across formidable social divides. The importance of doing this has been noted repeatedly in the African American community with whom we have been involved. When things go very well in a clinical interaction, as they sometimes do, an important ingredient is that patients, clinicians, and even family caregivers are able to "read" one another well enough to create a shared narrative. That is, they are able to participate as actors in an unfolding story they help construct, one for which they have real commitment and one that embodies or suggests healing possibilities. This is what I have elsewhere called a "healing drama" (Mattingly 1998a, 2000; Mattingly and Lawlor 2001). Healing dramas need not depend on the possibility of curing; in fact, they can embrace death. But they do depend on moments in which shared experiences are created between professionals and clients. Such moments can draw members together even when they come from diverse social positions.

As it turns out, popular culture as offered up by mass media plays a critical role in facilitating the construction of these shared narratives. Global popular culture is often drawn on by families and health professionals to develop a shared story of hope. By *shared*, of course, I do not mean that health professionals and clients come to see or experience things in the same way, but that, at minimum, there is sufficient consensus to agree about treatment options and other practical matters and there is a sense that everyone is working in the best interest of the child. At times, though, there is a kind of collective imagining that goes far beyond this minimal level. Stories from children's popular culture are woven into clinic life and into interactions with home health professionals. They become part of stories acted out or referred to, especially during rehabilitation therapies that try to incorporate treatment into some form of child play. Rehabilitation therapists and aides mention that to treat children, they find that they need to watch the same movies that children are seeing simply to be able to understand them in therapy. Children repeat phrases or initiate actions in therapy that imitate their favorite film stories.

It is no surprise that characters from Disney films turn up with such regularity in pediatric hospitals and find their way into all kinds of clinical sessions. Disney has been the primary exporter of children's popular culture for decades, a matter that has long provoked critiques from, for example, critical social theorists of the well-known Frankfurt School.[7] The power of mass media to shape cultural identities has also been a topic of central concern within contemporary culture theory. Stuart Hall, for example, has argued that mass media is a primary vehicle for ideological production, a means through which groups construct images of their lives (Hall 1997). Mass media might be colonizing but ethnographic studies of the actual practices of cultural production and reception help to complicate the picture of media as ideology machine. Such studies reveal the way that the global is made "local" in specific contexts and show that the meaning of a media text is not given by the text itself but by the processes through which it is taken up and consumed by particular interpretive communities (Abu-Lughod 1991; Metcalf 2001; Rapp and Ginsburg 2001). Reception theories in media studies have been at pains to argue that meaning is a complex and local practice of negotiation between the world of the text and the world of the audience. It is a historically particular and local invention (see Spitulnik 1993 for a review of this literature). In other words, the audience does not merely consume, it "poaches," as Michel de Certeau (1984) puts it, helping to construct meaning through its practices of consumption.

CONSUMING POPULAR CULTURE: CHILDREN AND FAMILIES

Children's popular culture (esp. Disney) is everywhere in the lives of this African American community. Disney and other popular culture products have a fundamental role in the ongoing (playful) practice of these children as they imagine themselves in various scenes, playing various parts. In these playful constructions of possible selves, characters gleaned from Disney (as well as other media) stories provide easily adapted cultural material. Children often try out characters borrowed from scenes in movies or television shows, inviting adults to play their appropriate part in the scenarios they set in motion. The cultural space of Disneyland itself profoundly feeds the imagination of children, shaping a sense of life possibilities even if they are only possibilities that can be played with. For example, one critically ill four-year-old declared, in a fit of wishful thinking, "My daddy's gonna take me to Disneyland with—with Michael Jackson."[8]

When young children identify with certain characters in movies and television programs, it is not simply that they like those characters. Rather, they become those characters, at least for moments at a time, and they do so with particular delight when they can find others who will cooperate. Identifications with a particular character are social achievements, for it takes not only the child but the support

of those around her for this identity to become "real." It requires cooperative efforts if these characters are to be incorporated in the scenes of everyday life. Identity play may be initiated or actively discouraged by parents or other adults. When a three-year-old boy declared that he was one of the "Powerpuff Girls," his mother laughingly told us how she dissuaded him from this identification; he received no social support for seeing himself as a girl. This identity work is far from passive; it is actively carried out through a variety of efforts, often orchestrated by parents, in which the ongoing connection of their child with a popular character is ensured. Parents tell other important adults—including clinicians—about their child's favorite movie characters, thus widening the net of those who participate in the co-construction of a child as fantasy figure. They take their children to Disneyland or even far away Orlando's Walt Disney World to meet "their" special character. They dress children up as these characters for special occasions like birthdays and Halloween. They buy the dolls, coloring books, underwear, lunch boxes, tee shirts, stickers, pillow cases, curtains, and other merchandise that import the character into everyday life. They organize elaborate children's birthday parties to which dozens of people (including many adults) are invited and at which they recreate scenes from the movie in which their child's favorite character stars.

It is striking how consistently a child (or parent) chooses a character similar to the child in gender, racial or ethnic identity, or even disability. Even more intriguing, the kinds of adventures these characters face have their parallels in key events in a child's life. The happy endings that characterize children's movies and television programs offer hopeful visions of a child's future in "real life." Fascinatingly, this match may result from a striking mismatch, where a superhero possesses exactly the qualities that a child conspicuously lacks but longs for. Movie plots and life plots have a curious symmetry, although most often a symmetry by which a character's extraordinary or magical abilities provide a wishful identification for a child.

CONSUMING CHILDREN'S POPULAR CULTURE: THE CLINICAL COMMUNITY

Pediatric clinicians routinely draw on popular culture to connect with children. This is most apparent and most elaborate in rehabilitation therapies in which clinicians struggle to get children to cooperate with what can be painful or difficult exercises. Especially in acute hospital settings, there is a certain desperation in calling on this trade language. Often there is little time to get to know children who must be asked to participate in activities that are likely to frighten or pain them. Over the years, we have interviewed a number of physical and occupational therapists about their use of Disney and other mass media narratives in clinical work. I include some of the comments they have made in our interviews about how and why children's popular culture figures so pervasively in health care encounters. One occupational therapist mentioned that she always looks at children's shoes to see what character or movie they like. Another therapist said,

> It's not like you have a couple of sessions to develop rapport. You're seeing them just that one time and the parents say, "There's this issue and you absolutely have to get this assessment done right now." And the doctor wants to know what you think right then. And you have to develop a rapport very quickly. And that's when you just grab whatever you can that you can just kind of key into them with.

Certain favorite characters are woven into therapy sessions. Many come from Disney films because, as an occupational therapist noted dryly, "They have a pretty big corner on the market." When there is time to listen, a physical therapist pointed out, it is possible to "let them [the children] lead you," which is the very best way to work. A physical and occupational therapist at a pediatric burn unit reflected on the importance of these characters for the children they treated. The therapist noted, mimicking the children, "Different kids, especially at different ages, tend to attach to different things. Like the girls, like we had so many little girl patients that were really into, like, Snow White."

This attachment is used by clinicians as a "motivator" during therapy sessions. A physical therapist offered this example:

> I think we use it as a motivator if they indicate to us that that's something they really like to do. Like my one little girl, Anita, who loves, loves Snow White. I mean it was something. So we would call her Snow White and we would say . . . let's have you walk like a Princess Snow White and we'll go over and see if we can drop little things for the little seven dwarfs.

Children's popular culture can provide a "key" into the world of a child's imagination, a world in which the clinician can become an ally rather than an enemy, and one in which a child can do things impossible in ordinary life. To illustrate, I offer the following example. One occupational therapist told a story about how she came to incorporate "Spiderman" into her sessions with a child suffering severe sensory motor problems. This eight-year-old boy was so afraid of heights he slept with his mattress on the floor and refused to play on swings, slides, or monkey bars on the playground. As a result, he spent many lonely hours at school recess and home while his friends and schoolmates played together. During their first clinic session, she found him extremely shy, remembering that "when Manny first entered the clinic, he had his face buried into his mother's side and he would not turn around or make eye contact with me." After several false starts that yielded only silence, the therapist noticed he was wearing a "Spiderman" shirt and shoes. She decided "it was worth a try" to see if Spiderman could draw him out. When she produced a Spiderman coloring book, "a smile began to creep over his face." Coloring the Spiderman book together began their many Spiderman adventures. As Manny colored, he told her of Spiderman's great feats and enemies, and out of this, as she put it, "a pact had been formed for future therapy sessions" for in all subsequent sessions "Spiderman played a prominent role." Manny donned a special Spiderman vest for therapy time. There was one session the therapist described in some detail because she saw it as a turning point in her work with the boy. For this session, she used a rope hammock swing (a typical piece of therapy equipment for children with sensory motor difficulties), which she announced was a spider's web. (The Spiderman's web, in fact.) After much coaxing, Manny eventually climbed into the web with her, although he was so frightened that his teeth chattered. To distract him, she sang the Spiderman Song, which she also recited for me. This song includes such telling lines as

> Can he swing from a thread?
> Take a look overhead.
> Hey there, there goes the Spiderman!

Manny gradually calmed as he heard the song, which allowed the therapist to begin a game of throwing beanbags at various Spiderman "enemies" (beanie babies she had set up in different spots around the therapy room). She took on the voices of these hapless enemies as Manny bashed them with beanbags. He became so enthusiastic that, in an unprecedented moment, he insisted they swing higher and higher so that even while he was in a "tornado" he could "fight against evil." This therapist was convinced that Manny's capacity to become Spiderman in these therapy episodes was critical to her success with him, as evidenced by his willingness to take on such terrifying challenges as swinging high above ground.

Notably popular icons are extremely versatile cultural resources. The same character can take on different meanings for different children. Whereas for Manny, it is Spiderman's brave capacities to, for example, "swing from a thread" that are salient, for another child facing a different sort of disabling condition, other features become central. For example, Spiderman also became a favorite cultural icon for a boy in our study forced to wear medical masks to treat a severe burn injury to his face. In this case, Spiderman's identity as a "masked hero" is emphasized; in Manny's case, it is his skill at gravity defying leaps through space.

CONCLUSION

Popular culture provides a common language for adults and children, a set of public symbols that they can draw on to try to connect with one another. Even comparative strangers, like health professionals, can readily draw on them to connect to a child they do not know and who is, likely as not, afraid of them.

Globally circulated and mass-produced texts are made meaningful in local ways and offer powerful cultural resources that serve local ends. Popular culture offers characters and plots that are remade, "indigenized" as Arjun Appadurai (1991, 1996) says, to fit specific needs and circumstances. As the Spiderman examples illustrate, the meaning of a popular media text does not reside in the text-in-itself and can never be reduced to mere "consumption;" it always involves situated constructions that do practical work for particular actors.

Popular-culture stories and heroes provide potent vehicles for overcoming the dreary, frightening, or embattled relations between clinicians and patients and do so in a way that supports hope. When clinicians draw on these loved characters in their interactions with children, they may be connecting with children and parenting kin in a far more powerful way than they sometimes realize. When clinicians speak to families only in the medicalized language of statistical probabilities, especially if prognoses are poor, mistrust is easily heightened. It is not that clients want to be lied to or have medical information withheld. But they are also concerned that clinicians support a subjunctive reading of their child's chances and that they make every effort, even for, as parents sometimes say, "a little black kid" (Mattingly 2004). How can families come to trust that professionals have not "given up" on their children, despite the fact that they have severe disabilities and are African American? In the racial climate of the United States, this is not a question that can be asked and answered directly. Clues must be indirect. It is here that, in its own oblique and playful way, the lingua franca of children's popular culture—when exemplified by, for example, a joking exchange between a nurse and mother about how quickly Spiderman recovered from surgery (the very same surgery a child has just undergone)— suggests possibilities that go far beyond the ostensible topic. In a wary place like the

urban clinic, when people are struggling to connect across all kinds of barriers, a Pocahontas or a Spiderman, one might say, travels well.

ACKNOWLEDGMENTS

I would like to thank members (past and present) of the research team: Erica Angert, Nancy Bagatell, Jeanine Blanchard, Jeannie Gaines, Lanita Jacobs-Huey, Teresa Kuan, Stephanie Mielke, Ann Neville-Jan, Melissa Park, Carolyn Rouse, Katy Sanders, and Kim Wilkinson. Particular, heartfelt thanks goes to my long-time research partner, Mary Lawlor. Thanks also to the Narrative Study Group for comments on drafts of this article: Linda Garro, Elinor Ochs, Janet Hoskins, Marjorie Goodwin, Gelya Frank, Nancy Lutkehaus, and again, Mary Lawlor. I gratefully acknowledge support by Maternal and Child Health Bureau (MCJ #060745) and National Center for Medical Rehabilitation Research, National Institute of Child Health and Human Development, National Institutes of Health (1RO1HD38878, 2RO1HD38878).

NOTES

1. A number of scholars have explored how mass media produces connections and even diasporic communities in ways that further complicate any simple use of the term *culture* (Abu-Lughod 1991; Appadurai 1991; Diouf 2000; Erlmann 1996; Mbembe 1992; Metcalf 2001; Pollock et al. 2000; Price 1999; Schein 2002).

2. See Good et al. 2002, Cooper-Patrick et al. 1999, and Doescher et al. 2000.

3. In a careful review of research findings on health disparities, an Institute of Medicine Committee reported that

   minorities are less likely than whites to receive needed services, including clinically necessary procedures. These disparities exist in a number of disease areas, including cancer, cardiovascular disease, HIV/AIDS, diabetes, and mental illness, and are found across a range of procedures, including routine treatments for common health problems. [Institute of Medicine 2002:2; see also Good et al. 2002]

   Although health disparities for all minorities as compared to whites have been consistently documented, African Americans are routinely subjected to the greatest racial stereotyping and to the least access to health services (Bailey 1991; James 1994; Whitehead 1997). Some research indicates this is regardless of social class, education, economic status, or type of health care coverage (Dressler 1993; Good et al. 2002). Other research challenges this in claiming that social class plays a larger role than race, per se, in quality of health care (e.g., Lareau 2002). In any case, it is clear that when race and class are confounded, as they are for most of the families we have been following, receiving good health care services is an ongoing challenge. For further discussion of the connection between race and health, see also Barbee 1993; Jackson 1993; Porter 1994; and Wailoo 2001.

4. For the sake of simplicity and to help protect confidentiality of informants, throughout the article, when quoting participants, I refer to the research team collectively, as in "we interviewed" or "we observed," rather than identifying particular researchers.

5. General concern to improve the capacity of clinicians to communicate with minority clients has spurred a vast, cross-disciplinary literature on "cultural competence" (Brach and Fraser 2000; Guarnaccia and Rodriguez 1996; Lopez 1997; Pierce and Pierce 1996) and on "culturally compatible interventions" (Takeuchi et al. 1995).

6. This point was brought home with force in the way the African American families in our study talked about the meaning of September 11th. They underscored not only the concern to be designated as different from Euro-Americans but also the need to be recognized as sharing a common national culture and heritage (Mattingly et al. 2002).

7. See Henry Giroux's (1999) critique of the Disney empire for a fascinating, and more recent, exposition along these lines.

8. As Giroux states, Disney is hardly a monolithic empire. Rather, he explains,

> The Disney culture offers potentially subversive moments and pleasures in a rage of contradictory and complex experiences. In fact, any approach to studying Disney must address the issue of why so many kids and adults love Disney and experience its theme parks, plays, and travel opportunities as a counterlogic that allows them to venture beyond the present while laying claim to unrealized dreams and hopes. [1999:5]

REFERENCES

Abu-Lughod, Lila. 1991. Writing against Culture. In *Recapturing Anthropology: Working in the Present*, ed. Richard Fox, 137–162. Santa Fe: School of American Research Press.

Appadurai, Arjun. 1991. Global Ethnoscapes: Notes and Queries for a Transnational Anthropology. In *Recapturing Anthropology: Working in the Present*, ed. Richard Fox, 191–210. Santa Fe: School of American Research Press.

_____.1996. *Modernity at Large: Cultural Dimensions of Globalization*. Minneapolis: University of Minnesota Press.

Bailey, Eric. 1991. Hypertension: An Analysis of Detroit African-American Health Care Treatment Patterns. *Human Organization* 50(3): 287–296.

Barbee, Evelyn. 1993. Racism in U.S. Nursing. *Medical Anthropology Quarterly* 7(4): 346–362.

Brach, C., and I. Fraser. 2000. Can Cultural Competency Reduce Racial and Ethnic Health Disparities? A Review and Conceptual Model. *Medical Care Research and Review* 57 (Suppl. 1): 181–217.

Bruner, Jerome. 1986. *Actual Minds, Possible Worlds*. Cambridge, MA: Harvard University Press.

_____.2002 *Making Stories: Law, Literature, Life*. New York: Farrar, Straus, and Giroux.

Clifford, James. 1997. *Routes: Travel and Translation in the Twentieth Century*. Cambridge, MA: Harvard University Press.

Cooper-Patrick, L., J. Gallo, J. Gonzales, H. Vu, N. Powe, C. Nelson, and D. Ford. 1999. Race, Gender, and Partnership in the Patient-Physician Relationship. *Journal of the American Medical Association* 282(6): 583–589.

de Certeau, Michel. 1984. *The Practice of Everyday Life*. S. Rendall, trans. Berkeley: University of California Press.

Diouf, Mamadou. 2000. *The Senegalese Murid Trade Diaspora and the Making of a Vernacular Cosmopolitanism*. S. Rendall, trans. Public Culture 12: 679–702.

Doescher, M., B. Saver, P. Franks, and K. Fiscella. 2000. Racial and Ethnic Disparities in Perceptions of Physician Style and Trust. *Archives of Family Medicine* 9(10): 1156–1163.

Dressler, William. 1993. Health in the African American Community: Accounting for Health Disparities. *Medical Anthropology Quarterly* 7(4): 325–345.

Erlmann, Veit. 1996. The Aesthetics of the Global Imagination: Reflections on World Music in the 1990s. *Public Culture* 8: 467–487.

Giroux, Henry. 1999. *The Mouse That Roared: Disney and the End of Innocence*. Lanham, MD: Rowman and Littlefield.

Good, Mary-Jo DelVecchio, C. James, Byron Good, and A. Becker. 2002. The Culture of Medicine and Racial, Ethnic, and Class Disparities in Healthcare. Pp. 594–625. *Report by the Institute of Medicine on Unequal Treatment*. Washington, DC: National Academy Press.

Guarnaccia, P., and O. Rodriguez. 1996. Concepts of Culture and Their Role in the Development of Culturally Competent Mental Health Services. *Hispanic Journal of Behavioral Sciences* 18: 419–443.

Hall, Stuart. 1997. *Representation: Cultural Representations and Signifying Practices*. London: Sage.

Institute of Medicine. 2002. *Unequal Treatment: What Healthcare Providers Need to Know about Racial and Ethnic Disparities in Healthcare*. Washington, DC: National Academy Press.

Jackson, Eileen. 1993. Whiting-Out Difference: Why U.S. Nursing Research Fails Black Families. *Medical Anthropology Quarterly* 7(4): 363–385.

James, Sherman. 1994. John Henryism and the Health of African-Americans. *Culture, Medicine and Psychiatry* 18: 163–182.

Lareau, Annette. 2002. Invisible Inequality: Social Class and Childrearing in Black Families and White Families. *American Sociological Review* 67: 747–776.

Lopez, Steven. 1997. Cultural Competence in Psychotherapy: A Guide for Clinicians and Their Supervisors. In *Handbook of Psychotherapy Supervision*, ed. C. E. Watkins Jr., 570–588. New York: John Wiley and Sons.

Mattingly, Cheryl. 1998a. *Healing Dramas and Clinical Plots: The Narrative Structure of Experience.* Cambridge: Cambridge University Press.

_____.1998b. In Search of the Good: Narrative Reasoning in Clinical Practice. *Medical Anthropology Quarterly* 12(3): 273–297.

_____.2000. Emergent Narratives. In *Narrative and the Cultural Construction of Illness and Healing,* eds. Cheryl Mattingly, and Linda Garro, 181–211. Berkeley: University of California Press.

_____.2004. Performance Narratives in Clinical Practice. In *Narrative Research in Health and Illness,* eds. B. Hurwitz, T. Greenhalgh, and V. Skultans, 73–94. London: Blackwell Publishing.

Mattingly, Cheryl, and Mary Lawlor. 2001. The Fragility of Healing. *Ethos* 29(1): 30–57.

Mattingly, Cheryl, Mary Lawlor, and Lanita Jacobs-Huey. 2002. Narrating September 11: Race, Gender, and the Play of Cultural Identities. *American Anthropologist* 104(3): 743–753.

Mbembe, Achille. 1992. The Banality of Power and the Aesthetics of Vulgarity in the Postcolony. *Public Culture* 4: 1–30.

Metcalf, Peter. 2001. Global "Disjunctive" and the "Sites" of Anthropology. *Cultural Anthropology* 16(2): 165–182.

Pierce, Robert, and Lois Pierce. 1996. Moving toward Cultural Competence in the Child Welfare System. *Children Youth Services Review* 18(8): 713–731.

Pollock, Sheldon, Homi Bhabha, Carol Breckenridge, and Dipesh Chakrabarty. 2000. Cosmopolitanisms. *Public Culture* 12: 577–589.

Porter, Cornelia. 1994. Stirring the Pot of Differences: Racism and Health. *Medical Anthropology Quarterly* 8(1): 102–106.

Price, Monroe. 1999. Satellite Broadcasting as Trade Routes in the Sky. *Public Culture* 11: 69–85.

Rapp, Rayna, and Faye Ginsburg. 2001. Enabling Disability: Rewriting Kinship, Reimagining Citizenship. *Public Culture* 13(3): 533–556.

Rosaldo, Renato. 1989. *Culture and Truth: The Remaking of Social Analysis.* Boston, MA: Beacon.

Schein, Louisa. 2002. Mapping Hmong Media in Diasporic Space. In *Media Worlds: Anthropology on New Terrain,* eds. Faye Ginsburg, Lila Abu-Lughod, and Brian Larkin, 229–244. Berkeley: University of California Press.

Spitulnik, Debra. 1993. Anthropology and the Mass Media. *Annual Review of Anthropology* 22: 293–315.

Takeuchi, D., S. Sue, and M. Yeh. 1995. Return Rates and Outcomes from Ethnicity-Specific Mental Health Programs in Los Angeles. *American Journal of Public Health* 85: 638–643.

Wailoo, Keith. 2001. *Dying in the City of the Blues: Sickle Cell Anemia and the Politics of Race and Health.* Chapel Hill: North Carolina University Press.

Whitehead, Tony. 1997. Urban Low-Income African American Men, HIV/AIDS, and Gender Identity. *Medical Anthropology Quarterly* 11(4): 411–417.

37

Culture, Poverty, and HIV Transmission
The Case of Rural Haiti

Paul Farmer

AIDS is currently the deadliest infectious disease in the world, killing over 3 million people every year. While antiretroviral drugs have lengthened the lives of many people infected with HIV, these drugs are expensive, and millions of people who need them still cannot afford them. Without medications, counseling, and support, people living with HIV are likely to infect others, and then die.

In the history of this epidemic, anthropologists have played an important role in describing and helping to explain how behavioral practices are related to the transmission of the HIV virus. So, too, have anthropologists helped demonstrate how poverty and other inequalities affect people's likelihood of contracting AIDS in the first place.

In this selection, we learn about the circumstances under which three Haitians developed AIDS, and how circumstances such as poverty and gender inequality put them at dramatically increased risk of infection. Much of the public discourse about AIDS reflects moral judgments about people's lifestyles and places blame for the disease on the sufferers. This selection shows how circumstances beyond individuals' control can place them at risk of infection. Paul Farmer, the author of this selection, is both a physician and an anthropologist, and he has been one of the most prominent and vocal advocates for people whose social and political circumstances place them at increased risk of HIV and other infectious diseases. Students interested in learning more about the work of Paul Farmer might be interested in reading his biography, *Mountains Beyond Mountains*, by Tracy Kidder.

While the biomedical challenge of AIDS is great, the challenge of coping with the human dimensions of AIDS is enormous, requiring resources, compassion, and cross-cultural understanding. Anthropologists have made, and continue to make, important contributions to the efforts of doctors, hospitals, nongovernment organizations, and other people and institutions to cope with the human dimensions of this devastating virus.

As you read this selection, ask yourself the following questions:

- How does poverty affect one's risk of becoming infected with HIV?

- What cultural and political factors influence the distribution of AIDS in Haiti?

- How can HIV infection be seen as *not* the result of bad personal decisions?

- What are some practical suggestions for reducing the human suffering caused by AIDS?

- What does Farmer mean when he says that there is "an AIDS of the North, and and AIDS of the South?"

The following terms discussed in this selection are included in the Glossary at the back of the book:

AIDS	seropositive
epidemic	seroprevalence
HIV	SIDA
medical anthropology	transmission

Haiti, a country of well over seven million inhabitants, is generally considered to be a substantially rural nation,[1] yet few studies of HIV transmission have been conducted in rural parts of the country.

Early reports by Pape and Johnson, based on small studies conducted in 1986–87, noted that the seroprevalence rate for HIV averaged 3 percent "in rural areas."[2] The seroprevalence in 97 mothers of children hospitalized with dehydration was 3 percent; of 245 unscreened rural blood donors, 4 percent had antibodies to HIV. In an area even more distant from urban centers, only 1 percent of 191 adults who came for immunizations were seropositive. Unfortunately, we know little about the individuals bled for these studies. Just how rural were they? What was the nature of their ties to Port-au-Prince and other high-prevalence cities? How did the seropositive individuals come to be at risk for HIV? How did they differ from seronegative controls? How rapidly was HIV making inroads into the rural population? What, in short, are the dynamics of HIV transmission in rural Haiti?

To understand the rural Haitian AIDS epidemic, we must move beyond the concept of "risk groups" to consider the interplay between human agency and the powerful forces that constrain it, focusing especially on those activities that promote or retard the spread of HIV. In Haiti, the most powerful of these forces have been inequality, deepening poverty, and political dislocations, which have together conspired to hasten the spread of HIV. This chapter details research on HIV transmission in a rural area of Haiti—and also recounts some of the ways such large-scale social forces become manifest in the lives of particular individuals.

AIDS IN A HAITIAN VILLAGE

The setting for the research described here is the Péligre basin of Haiti's Central Plateau, home to several hundred thousand mostly rural people. Although all parts of Haiti are poor, the Péligre basin region and its villages may be especially so.

Before 1956, the village of Kay was situated in a deep and fertile valley in this area, near the banks of the Rivière Artibonite. For generations, the villagers farmed the broad and gently sloping banks of the river, selling rice, bananas, millet, corn, and sugarcane in regional markets. Harvests were, by all reports, bountiful; life then is now recalled as idyllic. With the construction of Haiti's largest hydroelectric dam in 1956, however, thousands of families living in this region were flooded out. The displaced persons were largely peasant farmers, and they received little or no compensation for their lost land.

The hilltop village of Do Kay was founded by refugees from the rising water. The flooding of the valley forced most villagers up into the hills on either side of the new reservoir. Kay became divided into "Do" (those who settled on the stony backs of the hills) and "Ba" (those who remained down near the new waterline). By all standard measures, both parts of Kay are now very poor; its older inhabitants often blame their poverty on the massive buttress dam a few miles away and note bitterly that it brought them neither electricity nor water.

Though initially a dusty squatter settlement of fewer than two hundred persons, Do Kay has grown rapidly in the past decade and now counts about two thousand inhabitants. In spite of the hostile conditions, most families continue to rely to some extent on small-scale agriculture. But many villagers are involved in a series of development projects designed to improve the health of the area's inhabitants. Since 1984, for example, a series of outreach initiatives have complemented the work of our growing team of clinicians, based in Do Kay at the Clinique Bon Sauveur. The most significant efforts were undertaken under the aegis of Proje Veye Sante, the "health surveillance project." Proje Veye Sante, conducted in large part by village-based community health workers from about thirty nearby communities, provides preventive and primary care to close to fifty thousand rural people.

Through Proje Veye Sante, AIDS surveillance began well before the epidemic was manifest in the region. It is thus possible to date the index, or first, case of AIDS to 1986, when a young schoolteacher, Manno Surpris, fell ill with recurrent superficial fungal infections, chronic diarrhea, and pulmonary tuberculosis. Seropositive for HIV, he died a year later.

Although Manno Surpris was from another part of the Central Plateau, it was not long before we began to diagnose the syndrome among natives of Do Kay. The sections that follow offer brief case histories of the first three villagers known to have died of AIDS. None had a history of transfusion with blood or blood products; none had a history of homosexual contact or other "risk factors" as designated by the CDC. They did, however, share two important, if poorly understood, risk factors: poverty and inequality.

Anita

Anita Joseph was born in approximately 1966 to a family that had lost its land to the Péligre dam. One of six children, she briefly attended school until her mother, weakened by the malnutrition then rampant in the Kay area, died of tuberculosis. Anita was then thirteen. Her father became depressed and abusive, and she resolved to run away: "I'd had it with his yelling. . . . When I saw how poor I was, and how hungry, and saw that it would never get any better, I had to go to the city. Back then I was so skinny—I was saving my life, I thought, by getting out of here."

Anita left for Port-au-Prince with less than $3 and no clear plan of action. She worked briefly as a *restavèk*, or live-in maid, for $10 a month but lost this position when her employer was herself fired from a factory job.

Cast into the street, Anita eventually found a relative who took her in. The kinswoman, who lived in a notorious slum north of the capital, introduced her to Vincent, a young man who worked unloading luggage at the airport. Anita was not yet fifteen when she entered her first and only sexual union. "What could I do, really?" she sighed as she recounted the story much later. "He had a good job. My aunt thought I should go with him."

Vincent, who had at least one other sexual partner at the time, became ill less than two years after they began sharing a room. The young man, whom Anita cared for throughout his illness, died after repeated infections, including tuberculosis. Not long after his death, Anita herself fell ill with tuberculosis.

Upon returning to Do Kay in 1987, she quickly responded to antituberculous therapy. When she relapsed some months later, we performed an HIV test, which revealed the true cause of her immunosuppression. Following a slow but ineluctable decline, Anita died in February 1988.

Dieudonné

Dieudonné Gracia, born in Do Kay in 1963, was also the child of two "water refugees." One of seven children, he attended primary school in his home village and, briefly, secondary school in a nearby town. It was there, at the age of nineteen, that he had his first sexual contact. Dieudonné remarked that his girlfriend had had "two, maybe three partners" before they met; he was sure that one of her partners had been a truck driver from a city in central Haiti.

When a series of setbacks further immiserated his family, Dieudonné was forced to drop out of secondary school and also to drop his relationship with the young woman. He returned to Do Kay to work with his father, a carpenter. In 1983, however, the young man decided to "try my luck in Port-au-Prince." Through a friend from Do Kay, Dieudonné found a position as a domestic for a well-to-do family in a suburb of the capital.

While in the city, Dieudonné's sexual experience broadened considerably. He had five partners in little more than two years, all of them close to his own age. Asked about the brevity of these liaisons, Dieudonné favored an economic explanation: "A couple of them let go of me because they saw that I couldn't do anything for them. They saw that I couldn't give them anything for any children."

In 1985, Dieudonné became ill and was dismissed from his job in Port-au-Prince. He returned to Do Kay and began seeing his former lover again. She soon became pregnant and moved to Do Kay as the young man's *plase*, a term designating a partner in a more or less stable conjugal union.[3]

During this interlude, Dieudonné was seen at the Do Kay clinic for a number of problems that suggested immunodeficiency: herpes zoster and genital herpes, recurrent diarrhea, and weight loss. In the months following the birth of their baby, the young mother fell ill with a febrile illness, thought by her physician to be malaria, and quickly succumbed. Less than a year later, Dieudonné, much reduced by chronic diarrhea, was diagnosed with tuberculosis. Although he initially responded to antituberculous agents, Dieudonné died of AIDS in October 1988.

Acéphie

Acéphie Joseph was born in 1965 on a small knoll protruding into the reservoir that had drowned her parents' land. Acéphie attended primary school somewhat irregularly; by the age of nineteen, she had not yet graduated and decided that it was time to help generate income for her family, which was sinking deeper and deeper into poverty. Hunger was a near-daily occurrence for the Joseph family; the times were as bad as those right after the flooding of the valley. Acéphie began to help her mother, a market woman, by carrying produce to a local market on Friday mornings.

It was there that she met a soldier, formerly stationed in Port-au-Prince, who began to make overtures to the striking young woman from Do Kay. Although the soldier had a wife and children and was known to have more than one regular partner, Acéphie did not spurn him. "What would you have me do? I could tell that the old people were uncomfortable, worried—but they didn't say no. They didn't tell me to stay away from him. I wish they had, but how could they have known? . . . I looked around and saw how poor we all were, how the old people were finished. . . . It was a way out, that's how I saw it."

Within a short time, the soldier fell ill and was diagnosed in the Do Kay clinic with AIDS. A few months after he and Acéphie parted, he was dead.

Shaken, Acéphie went to a nearby town and began a course in what she euphemistically termed a "cooking school," which prepared poor girls for work as servants. In 1987, twenty-two years old, Acéphie went to Port-au-Prince, where she found a $30-per-month job as a housekeeper for a middle-class Haitian woman who worked for the U.S. embassy. She began to see a man, also from the Kay region, who chauffeured a small bus between the Central Plateau and Port-au-Prince.

Acéphie worked in the city until late in 1989, when she discovered that she was pregnant. This displeased both her partner and her employer. Sans job and sans boyfriend, Acéphie returned to Do Kay in her third trimester.

Following the birth of her daughter, Acéphie was sapped by repeated opportunistic infections, each one caught in time by the staff of the clinic in Do Kay. Throughout 1991, however, she continued to lose weight; by January 1992, she weighed less than ninety pounds, and her intermittent fevers did not respond to broad-spectrum antibiotics.

Acéphie died in April 1992. Her daughter, the first "AIDS orphan" in Do Kay, is now in the care of Acéphie's mother. The child is also infected. A few months after Acéphie's death, her father hanged himself.

Sadly, however, this is not simply the story of Acéphie and her family. The soldier's wife, who is much thinner than last year, has already had a case of herpes zoster. Two of her children are also HIV-positive. This woman, who is well known to the clinic staff, is no longer a widow; once again, she is the partner of a military man. Her late husband had at least two other partners, both of them poor peasant women, in the Central Plateau. One is HIV-positive and has two sickly children. The father of Acéphie's child, apparently in good health, is still plying the roads from Mirebalais to Port-au-Prince. His serostatus is unknown.

Individual Experience in Context

When compared to age-matched North Americans with AIDS, Anita, Dieudonné, and Acéphie have sparse sexual histories: Anita had only one partner; Dieudonné had six; Acéphie had two. Although a case-control study by Pape and Johnson suggested that HIV-infected urban men, at least, had larger numbers of partners than our patients did,[4] research conducted in Anita's neighborhood in Port-au-Prince suggests that her case is not as unique as it would seem:

> The high seropositivity rate (8%) found in pregnant women 14 to 19 years of age suggests that women [in Cité Soleil] appear to acquire HIV infection soon after becoming sexually active. Moreover, this age group is the only one in which a higher seropositivity rate is not associated with a greater number of sexual partners. Women with only one sexual partner in the year prior to pregnancy actually have a slightly higher prevalence rate (although not significantly so) than the others. This suggests that they were infected by their first and only partner.[5]

TABLE 1   Case-Control Study of AIDS in Rural Haitian Women

Patient Characteristics	Patients with AIDS (N = 25)	Control Group (N = 25)
Average number of sexual partners	2.7	2.4
Sexual partner of a truck driver	12	2
Sexual partner of a soldier	9	0
Sexual partner of a peasant only	0	23
Ever lived in Port-au-Prince	20	4
Worked as a servant	18	1
Average number of years of formal schooling	4.5	4.0
Ever received a blood transfusion	0	2
Ever used illicit drugs	0	0
Ever received more than ten intramuscular injections	17	19

The stories of Anita, Dieudonné, and Acéphie are ones that reveal the push-and-pull forces of contemporary Haiti. In all three cases, the declining fortunes of the rural poor pushed young adults to try their chances in the city. Once there, all three became entangled in unions that the women, at least, characterized as attempts to emerge from poverty. Each worked as a domestic, but none managed to fulfill the expectation of saving and sending home desperately needed cash. What they brought home, instead, was AIDS.

How representative are these case histories? Over the past several years, the medical staff of the Clinique Bon Sauveur has diagnosed dozens more cases of AIDS and other forms of HIV infection in women who arrive at the clinic with a broad range of complaints. In fact, the majority of our patients have been women—a pattern rarely described in the AIDS literature. With surprisingly few exceptions, those so diagnosed shared a number of risk factors, as our modest case-control study suggests.

We conducted this study by interviewing the first twenty-five women we diagnosed with symptomatic HIV infection who were residents of Do Kay or its two neighboring villages. Their responses to questions posed during a series of open-ended interviews were compared with those of twenty-five age-matched, seronegative controls. In both groups, ages ranged from 16 to 44, with a mean age of about 27 years. Table 1 presents our findings.

None of these fifty women had a history of prostitution, and none had used illicit drugs. Only two, both members of the control group, had received blood transfusions. None of the women in either group had

had more than five sexual partners in the course of their lives; in fact, seven of the afflicted women had had only one. Although women in the study group had on average more sexual partners than the controls, the difference is not striking. Similarly, we found no clear difference between the two groups in the number of intramuscular injections they had received or their years of education.

The chief risk factors in this small cohort seem to involve not number of partners but rather the professions of these partners. Fully nineteen of the women with HIV disease had histories of sexual contact with soldiers or truck drivers. Three of these women reported having only two sexual partners: one a soldier, one a truck driver. Of the women diagnosed with AIDS, none had a history of sexual contact exclusively with peasants (although one had as sole partner a construction worker from Do Kay). Among the control group, only two women had a regular partner who was a truck driver; none reported contact with soldiers, and most had had sexual relations only with peasants from the region. Histories of extended residence in Port-au-Prince and work as a domestic were also strongly associated with a diagnosis of HIV disease.

How can we make sense of these surprising results? In the sociographically "flat" region around the dam—after all, most area residents share a single socioeconomic status, poverty—conjugal unions with nonpeasants (salaried soldiers and truck drivers who are paid on a daily basis) reflect women's quest for some measure of economic security. In the setting of a worsening economic crisis, the gap between the hungry peasant class and the relatively well-off soldiers and truck drivers became the salient local inequality. In this manner, truck drivers and soldiers have served as a "bridge" from the city to the rural population.

Truck drivers and soldiers will soon no longer be necessary components of the rural epidemic. Once introduced into a sexually active population, HIV will work its way to those with no history of residence in the city, no history of contact with soldiers or truck drivers, no history of work as a domestic. But these risk factors—all of which reflect a desperate attempt to escape rural poverty—are emblematic of the lot of the rural Haitian poor, and perhaps especially of poor women.

HIV in a Haitian Village

Extended residence in Port-au-Prince, work as a servant, and sexual contact with nonpeasants—although these risk factors were far different from those described for North Americans with AIDS, they characterized the majority of our male and female patients afflicted with AIDS. The majority of the residents of the

area served by Proje Veye Sante shared none of these attributes, however. Did this suggest that few would prove to be infected with HIV? Although a good deal of ethnographic research into the nature of AIDS had already been conducted in the region, no research had addressed the question of HIV prevalence among asymptomatic adults.

Troubled by this lacuna, the staff of the clinic and of Proje Veye Sante established the Groupe d'étude du SIDA dans la Classe Paysanne.[6] GESCAP has a mandate to research the mechanisms by which poverty puts young adults, and especially young women, at risk of HIV infection.[7] With community approval, GESCAP is attempting to illuminate case histories with serologic surveys, an expanded case-control study, and cluster studies (such as those that revealed how a single HIV-positive soldier came to infect at least eleven natives of the region, one of whom was Acéphie).

After considerable discussion, the members of GESCAP decided to undertake a study of all asymptomatic adults living in Do Kay. The study was to include all members of the community who might plausibly be sexually active (fifteen years and older) and who were free of any suggestion of immunodeficiency; patients with active tuberculosis were excluded from this study. Anyone who was the regular sexual partner of a person with known HIV infection was also excluded.

Of the first one hundred villagers enrolling in the program, ninety-nine were seronegative for HIV.[8] The one young woman with HIV infection, Alourdes, had a history of extended residence in Port-au-Prince and also in 1985 of regular sexual contact with a salaried employee of the national electric company. This man, who had several sexual partners during his tenure in central Haiti, was rumored to have died of AIDS. In 1986, Alourdes had been the partner of a young man from her home village, a construction worker. He later developed tuberculosis, initially attributed to respiratory contact with his wife, who had pulmonary tuberculosis. Both were later found to be infected with HIV; neither had ever had sexual contact outside the Do Kay area. The discovery of HIV infection in Alourdes, who was known to have risk factors as defined in the case-control study, helped to identify the routes of exposure of the couple who had HIV-related tuberculosis.

Such discrete studies do not, however, fully define the nature of the large-scale social forces at work. The discussion in the following sections summarizes the factors that seem to be most significant in the ultimate rate of progression of HIV in rural Haiti. Perhaps an examination of these forces can serve to inform understandings of the dynamics of HIV transmission in other parts of Latin America and also in areas of Asia and Africa where prevalence rates in rural regions are currently low. It is a cautionary tale that argues for aggressive preventive measures:

> If a disaster is to be prevented in rural Haiti, vigorous and effective prevention campaigns must be initiated at once. And although such efforts must begin, the prospects of stopping the steady march of HIV are slim. AIDS is far more likely to join a host of other sexually transmitted diseases—including gonorrhea, syphilis, genital herpes, chlamydia, hepatitis B, lymphogranuloma venereum, and even cervical cancer—that have already become entrenched among the poor.[9]

Only massive and coordinated efforts may yet avert the ongoing disaster that has befallen urban Haiti, Puerto Rico, inner-city North America, Thailand, Brazil, and many nations in sub-Saharan Africa.

THE DYNAMICS OF HIV TRANSMISSION IN RURAL HAITI

Wherever HIV infection is a sexually transmitted disease, social forces necessarily determine its distribution. Cultural, political, and economic factors, while each inevitably important, cannot be of equal significance in all settings. In rural Haiti, we can identify a number of differentially weighted, synergistic forces that promote HIV transmission.

Population Pressures

Haiti, which covers 27,700 square kilometers, is one of the most crowded societies in the hemisphere. In 1980, only 8,000 square kilometers were under cultivation, giving an effective population density of 626 persons per square kilometer. Unfortunately, Haiti's topsoil is now prey to runaway forces that further compound the overcrowding: "The land suffers from deforestation, soil erosion, and exhaustion; the country is periodically ravaged by hurricanes which cause enormous damage."[10] As the land becomes increasingly exhausted, more and more peasants abandon agriculture for the lure of wage-labor in cities and towns.

Indeed, one of the most striking recent demographic changes has been the rapid growth of Port-au-Prince. More than 20 percent of the Haitian population now lives in the capital, a city of over 1.5 million. Although this concentration is not impressive by Caribbean standards (more than 30 percent of Puerto Ricans live in San Juan), the rate of growth in Port-au-Prince has been striking: "The urban population was 12.2% of the total in 1950, 20.4% in 1971 and an estimated 27.5% in 1980."[11] Haitian demographers estimate that by the year 2000 urban dwellers will constitute 37 percent of the total population.

As is the case with so many Third World countries, internal migration has played the most significant role in the growth of the capital. Locher estimates that "between 1950 and 1971 rural-urban migration accounted for 59% of Haitian urban growth, while natural population increase accounted for only 8%."[12] Neptune-Anglade has observed that the growth of Port-au-Prince is substantially the result of a "feminine rural exodus," leaving the city approximately 60 percent female.[13] Younger women of rural origin—women like Anita and Acéphie—are most commonly employed as servants.[14] Migrants of both sexes maintain strong ties with their regions of origin. In these respects, the three index cases of AIDS from Do Kay are illustrative of the trends documented by demographers and others who speak of Port-au-Prince as "a city of peasants."

Economic Pressures

Rural Haiti, always poor, has become palpably poorer in recent decades. A per capita annual income of $315 in 1983 masked the fact that income hovered around $100 in the countryside; in the late 1990s the average annual per capita income is down to around $175.[15] Accompanying the population growth and a loss of arable land to erosion and alkalinization has been an inevitable growth in landlessness. All of these factors have inevitably had a devastating effect on agricultural production. For example, Girault typifies the decade preceding 1984 as marked chiefly "by the slow-down of agricultural production and by a decrease in productivity."[16]

This decline has been further compounded by striking rural-urban disparities in every imaginable type of goods and service. In 1984, Girault was able to complain that "Port-au-Prince with 17–18% of the national population consumes as much as 30% of all the food produced in the country and a larger share of imported food."[17] Government statistics reveal that the "Port-au-Prince agglomeration" consumed 93 percent of all electricity produced in the country in 1979. As Trouillot notes, the city "houses 20% of the national population, but consumes 80% of all State expenditures."[18]

In short, current economic conditions push people out of the countryside and into the city or, often enough, out of the country altogether. The Haitian people have long since left behind a peasant standard of living (which did not necessarily mean an exceptionally low one). Whereas Haiti was once a nation with an extremely high percentage of landholders, late-twentieth-century Haiti is increasingly a country of unemployed and landless paupers. When the Population Crisis Committee published its "international index of human suffering" in 1992, based on a variety of measures of human welfare, Haiti had the dubious distinction of heading the list of all countries in this hemisphere. Of the 141 countries studied, only three were deemed to have living conditions worse than those in Haiti—and all three of these countries were at the time being consumed by civil war.[19]

Patterns of Sexual Union

In the numerous studies of conjugal unions in rural Haiti, most have underlined the classic division between couples who are *marye* (joined by civil or religious marriage) and those who are *plase* (joined in a conjugal union that incurs significant and enduring obligations to both partners). *Plasaj* (from French, *plaçage*) has generally been the most common form of conjugal union in rural Haiti, outnumbering marriages by two or three to one.

Early studies usually considered *plasaj* to be polygamous, with one man having more than one *plase* partner. This is often no longer the case, as Moral suggested over three decades ago: "It is 'plaçage honnête'—that is, monogamy—that best characterizes matrimonial status in today's rural society."[20] The reason for this shift toward monogamy, he believed, was the same one that leads many rural people to avoid marriage in the first place: formal unions are costly. "If the considerable growth of *plaçage* is to be explained in part by economic factors," continued Moral, "the form that *plaçage* now takes is greatly influenced by the poverty spreading throughout the countryside."

Allman's review suggests that contemporary sexual unions are considerably more complex than the bipolar model just described. In a survey in which women who had sexual relations with the same partner for a minimum of three months were considered to be "in union," interviews revealed an emic typology with five major categories: three of these—*rinmin, fiyanse,* and *viv avèk*—did not usually involve cohabitation and engendered only slight economic support; two others—*plase* and *marye*—were deemed much stronger unions, generally involving cohabitation as well as economic support.[21]

In addition, a number of other sexual practices have often been loosely termed "prostitution," in Haiti a largely urban phenomenon and much understudied.[22] It is clear, however, that unemployed women from rural areas may become involved in occasional and often clandestine sex work (variously described by terms such as *ti degaje, woulman*) when other options are exhausted. There are few avenues of escape for those caught in the web of urban migration, greater than 60 percent unemployment, and extreme poverty.[23]

How are these forms of sexual union related to the dynamics of HIV transmission? To those working in rural clinics, *plasaj* is often implicated in the spread or persistence of sexually transmitted diseases such as gonorrhea and chlamydial disease. Treatment of one or two members of a network is of course inadequate, as even women who have but one sexual partner are indirectly in regular sexual contact with any other *plase* partners of their mate. Regarding HIV, polygamous *plasaj* may be considered a preexisting sociocultural institution that serves to speed the spread of HIV and that constitutes a risk in and of itself, particularly for monogamous women. Women throughout the world bear similar risks—which are compounded wherever gender inequality erodes women's power over condom use.

The unremitting immiseration of Haiti has clearly undermined stable patterns of union such as marriage and *plasaj* by creating economic pressures to which women with dependents are particularly vulnerable. In the wake of these pressures, new patterns have emerged: "serial monogamy" might describe the monogamous but weak unions that lead to one child but last little longer than a year or two. After such unions have dissolved, the woman finds herself with a new dependent and even more in need of a reliable partner.

Equally dangerous, as we have seen, is the quest for a union with a financially "secure" partner. In rural Haiti, men of this description once included a substantial fraction of all peasant landholders. In recent decades, however, financial security has become elusive for all but a handful of truck drivers, representatives of the state (such as soldiers and petty officials), and landholders (*grandòn*). As noted, truck drivers and soldiers are clearly groups with above average rates of HIV infection.

Gender Inequality

"The ability of young women to protect themselves from [HIV] infection becomes a direct function of power relations between men and women."[24] Gender inequality has weakened women's ability to negotiate safe sexual encounters, and this sapping of agency is especially amplified by poverty. The Haitian economy counts a higher proportion of economically active women—most of them traders—than any other developing society, with the exception of Lesotho.[25] It is not surprising, then, that the *machismo* that has so marked other Latin American societies is less pronounced in Haiti.[26] (Even the head of the Duvaliers' dreaded paramilitary force was a woman.) But gender inequality is certainly a force in political, economic, and domestic life. It would be difficult to argue with Neptune-Anglade when she states that, in all regards, rural women "endure a discrimination and a pauperization that is worse than that affecting [rural] men."[27]

Preliminary ethnographic research in the Do Kay area suggests that many rural women do not wield sufficient authority to demand that *plase* partners (or husbands) use condoms. A growing literature documents similar patterns throughout the developing world and in the inner cities of the United States.[28] These considerations lead us to agree with those calling for preventive efforts that are "women-centered." "In societies where the female has a weaker hand," Desvarieux and Pape argue, "effective methods of prevention have a better chance of working if the woman does not have to rely on either the consent or the willingness of her partner."[29]

Other "Cultural" Considerations

Practices such as the widespread and unregulated use of syringes by "folk" practitioners unschooled in aseptic techniques received a fair amount of attention as possible sources of HIV transmission. But far more frequently invoked were "voodoo practices," which played a peculiarly central role in early speculations about the nature of the AIDS epidemic. These speculations, which sparked waves of anti-Haitian sentiment, had the added disadvantage of being incorrect; none of these leads, when investigated, panned out. In urban Haiti, GHESKIO did not even consider these hypotheses worthy of serious investigation.

In our small-scale but in-depth study of AIDS in the Central Plateau, we did not find any strong implication of nonsexual transmission of HIV.[30] Similarly, the Collaborative Study Group of AIDS in Haitian-Americans initiated the first and (so far) only controlled study of risk factors for AIDS among Haitians living in the United States. Compiling data from several North American research centers, the investigators reached the following conclusion: "Folklore rituals have been suggested as potential risk factors for [HIV] transmission in Haiti. Our data do not support this hypothesis."[31] Such hypotheses reflect less an accurate reading of existing data and more a series of North American folk theories about Haitians.[32]

There have been few ethnographic studies of Haitian understandings of AIDS, and most of these have been conducted in Montreal, New York, or Miami. To my knowledge, the only such study conducted in rural Haiti demonstrated that such understandings were in fact changing, at first quite rapidly.

Over time, however, a stable illness representation of *sida*—as AIDS is termed—seemed to evolve.[33]

In the Do Kay region, serial interviews with the same group of villagers permitted us to delineate a complex model of illness causation, one linked fairly closely to understandings of tuberculosis. Villagers often, but not always, cited sorcery in discussions about *sida*, which nonetheless came to be seen as a fatal illness that could be transmitted by sexual contact. Local understandings of *sida* did not seem to affect disease distribution, but certainly they may hamper preventive efforts if not taken into account when designing interventions. Far more disabling, however, has been the nation's political situation.

Political Disruption

It is unfortunate indeed that HIV arrived in Haiti shortly before a period of massive and prolonged social upheaval. Political unrest has clearly undermined preventive efforts and may have helped, through other mechanisms, to spread HIV. Although many commentators observed that political struggles served to divert the public's interest away from AIDS, this was not the case in the Do Kay region. In fact, periods of increased strife were associated with increased public discourse about the new sickness.

But the same political disruptions that may have stimulated commentary about AIDS also served to paralyze coordinated efforts to prevent HIV transmission. For example, although the Haitian Ministry of Health has identified AIDS prevention as one of its top priorities, the office charged with coordinating preventive efforts has been hamstrung by six coups d'état, which have led, inevitably, to personnel changes—and to more significant disruptions. At the time GESCAP was founded, in 1991, *there had been no comprehensive effort to prevent HIV transmission in rural Haiti*. Even in Port-au-Prince, what has been accomplished thus far has often been marred by messages that are either culturally inappropriate or designed for a small fraction of the population (for example, Haitians who are francophone, literate, and television-owning). These messages are especially unsuccessful in rural areas, where even well-funded "social marketing" schemes have had little cultural currency.

A sense of hopefulness, rare in Haiti, returned to the public health community in 1991, when the country's first democratic elections brought to office a social-justice government headed by a progressive priest. A new Ministry of Health promised to make AIDS, tuberculosis, and other infectious pathogens its top priority. But in September of that year, a violent military coup brought a swift end to Haiti's democratic experiment. The impact on the population's health was incalculable.[34]

Political upheaval did not simply hobble coordinated responses to the AIDS epidemic. It has had far more direct effects. One of the most epidemiologically significant events of recent years may prove to be the coup d'état of September 1991. As noted earlier, surveys of asymptomatic adults living in Cité Soleil revealed seroprevalence rates of approximately 10 percent, whereas surveys of asymptomatic rural people were likely to find rates an order of magnitude lower. Following the coup, the army targeted urban slums for brutal repression. A number of journalists and health care professionals estimated that fully half of the adult residents of Cité Soleil fled to rural areas following the army's lethal incursions. It takes little imagination to see that such flux substantially changes the equations describing the dynamics of HIV transmission in rural areas sheltering the refugees.[35] Similar patterns have been noted elsewhere, particularly in sub-Saharan Africa:

> Women living in areas plagued by civil unrest or war may be in a situation of higher risk. In many countries, relatively high percentages of male military and police personnel are infected and their unprotected (voluntary or forced) sexual encounters with local women provide an avenue for transmission. Patterns of female infection have been correlated with the movements of members of the military in parts of Central and Eastern Africa.[36]

Concurrent Disease

The progression of HIV disease depends on host variables such as age, sex, and nutritional status; viral load, CD_4-cell number and function; and concurrent disease. Concurrent illness can alter this progression in at least three ways: first, any serious illness, including opportunistic infections (most notably, tuberculosis), may hasten the progression of HIV disease; second, various diseases can heighten an individual's "net state of immunosuppression," rendering him or her increasingly vulnerable to infection; and, third, certain infections seem to increase the risk of *acquiring* HIV—the point considered here.

Sexually transmitted diseases have been cited as AIDS co-factors in a number of studies, especially those conducted in tropical and subtropical regions.[37] Researchers view STDs as particularly important in the heterosexual spread of HIV, as the virus is less

efficiently transmitted from women to men than vice versa. Thus vaginal and cervical diseases—even those as ostensibly minor as trichomoniasis—may increase the risk of HIV transmission through "microwounds" and even through mere inflammation (as certain lymphocytes are, after all, the target cells of HIV).[38]

Although researchers are now collecting important data about STDs in Port-au-Prince,[39] few studies have focused on rural areas.[40] But there is no evidence to suggest that villagers are more sexually active than their urban counterparts; there is even less evidence to suggest that rural Haitians are more sexually active than age-matched controls from North America. What is evident is that a majority of STDs go untreated—which certainly implies that sores, other lesions, and inflammation will persist far longer in rural Haiti than in most areas of the world.

Other diseases—including leprosy, yaws, endemic syphilis, and various viruses—have been suggested as possible co-factors in "tropical" AIDS, but their roles have not been clarified. It seems safe to add, however, that serious co-infections do enhance the net state of immuno-suppression. Similarly, malnutrition clearly hastens the advent of advanced, symptomatic disease among the HIV-infected, although this dynamic may lessen the risk of transmission: the Haitian variant of "slim disease" is now popularly associated with AIDS, and visible cachexia is likely to drive away potential sexual partners.[41]

Access to Medical Services

Finally, in seeking to understand the Haitian AIDS epidemic, it is necessary to underline the contribution, or lack thereof, of a nonfunctioning public health system. Medical care in Haiti is something of an obstacle course, one that places innumerable barriers before poor people seeking care. Failure to have an STD treated leads to persistence of important co-factors for HIV infection; failure to treat active tuberculosis causes rapid progression of HIV disease and death—to say nothing of its impact on HIV-negative individuals, for HIV-infected patients with tuberculosis have been shown to be efficient transmitters of tuberculosis.[42] Contaminated blood transfusions alternate with no transfusions at all. Condoms are often not available even to those who want them. The cost of pharmaceuticals, always prohibitive, has skyrocketed in recent years. Antivirals are in essence unavailable to most Haitians: in February 1990, "local radio stations announced . . . that for the first time, the drug AZT is available in Haiti. It might as well have been on Mars. A bottle of 100 capsules costs $343—more than most Haitians make in a year."[43] Since that time, it has become possible to find newer, highly active antiretroviral agents in Haiti—but for a prince's ransom.

AIDS, ANALYSIS, ACCOUNTABILITY

Identifying and weighting the various social forces that shape the HIV epidemic is a perennial problem, but one too rarely addressed by medical anthropology, which is often asked to elucidate the "cultural component" of particular subepidemics. By combining social analysis with ethnographically informed epidemiology, however, we can identify the most significant of these forces. The factors listed here are differentially weighted, of course, but each demonstrably plays a role in determining HIV transmission in rural Haiti:

1. Deepening poverty
2. Gender inequality
3. Political upheaval
4. Traditional patterns of sexual union
5. Emerging patterns of sexual union
6. Prevalence of and lack of access to treatment for STDs
7. Lack of timely response by public health authorities
8. Lack of culturally appropriate prevention tools

Many of these factors are a far cry from the ones that anthropologists were exhorted to explore—for example, ritual scarification, animal sacrifice, sexual behavior in "exotic subcultures"—during the first decade of AIDS. But the forces underpinning the spread of HIV to rural Haiti are as economic and political as they are cultural, and poverty and inequality seem to underlie all of them. Although many working elsewhere would agree that poverty and social inequalities are the strongest enhancers of risk for exposure to HIV, international conferences on AIDS have repeatedly neglected this subject. Of the hundreds of epidemiology-track posters presented in 1992 in Amsterdam, for example, only three used "poverty" as a keyword; two of these were socioculturally naïve and did not seem to involve the collaboration of anthropologists.

What were anthropologists doing in the early years of AIDS? The mid to late 1980s saw the formation of task forces and research groups as well as an increasing number of AIDS-related sessions at our professional meetings. The central themes of many of the early

sessions focused on the "special understanding of sexuality" that was, suggested certain speakers, the province of anthropologists. The scenario most commonly evoked was one in which ethnographers, steeped in local lore after years of participant-observation, afforded epidemiologists and public health authorities detailed information about sexual behavior, childbearing, and beliefs about blood and blood contact. This knowledge transfer was deemed indispensable to determining which "behaviors" put individuals and communities at risk for HIV infection.

Fifteen years into the AIDS pandemic, after at least a decade of social science studies of AIDS, we must ask, How substantial were these claims? How many secret, AIDS-related "behaviors" have we unearthed in the course of our ethnography? Anthropologists deeply involved in AIDS prevention now know that many such claims were immodest. Everywhere, it seems, HIV spreads from host to host through a relatively restricted set of mechanisms. We've also learned that preventive efforts, even the most culturally appropriate ones, are least effective in precisely those settings in which they are most urgently needed. Africa, long a favored proving ground for anthropology, offers the most obvious and humbling example. Haiti offers another.

In the interest of enhancing the efficacy of interventions, it's important to pause and take stock of the situation. How might anthropology best contribute to efforts to prevent HIV transmission or to alleviate AIDS-related suffering? One major contribution would be to help show where the pandemic is going, which leads us back to analytic challenges such as these:

> Identifying and differentially weighting the major factors promoting or retarding HIV transmission
>
> Linking the sexual choices made by individual actors to the various shifting conditions that restrict choice, especially among the poor
>
> Understanding the contribution of the culturally specific—not only local sexualities but also kinship structures and shifting representations of disease—without losing sight of the large-scale economic forces shaping the AIDS pandemic
>
> Investigating the precise mechanisms by which such forces as racism, gender inequality, poverty, war, migration, colonial heritage, coups d'état, and even structural-adjustment programs become embodied as increased risk

Anthropology, the most radically contextualizing of the social sciences, is well suited to meeting these analytic challenges, but we will not succeed by merely "filling in the cultural blanks" left by epidemiologists, physicians, scientists, and policy makers. Nor will we succeed without a new vigilance toward the analytic traps that have hobbled our understanding of the AIDS pandemic.[44]

First, we often find widespread, if sectarian, ascription to behaviorist, cognitivist, or culturalist reductionism. Just as many physicians regard social considerations as outside the realm of the central, so too have psychologists tended to reify individual psychology, while economists have reified the economic. Anthropologists writing of AIDS have of course tended to reify culture. We must avoid confusing our own desire for personal efficacy with sound analytic purchase on an ever-growing pandemic: HIV cares little for our theoretical stances or our disciplinary training. AIDS demands broad biosocial approaches. Jean Benoist and Alice Desclaux put it well:

> The conditions limiting or promoting transmission, illness representations, therapeutic itineraries, and health care practices—none of these subjects are captured by disciplinary approaches. They evade even the distinction between biology and social sciences, so tightly are biological realities tied to behaviors and representations, revealing links that have not yet been fully explored.[45]

Second, much anthropologic analysis focuses overmuch (or exclusively) on local factors and local actors, which risks exaggerating the agency of the poor and marginalized. Constraints on the agency of individual actors should be brought into stark relief so that prevention efforts do not come to grief, as they have to date. To explore the relation between personal agency and supraindividual structures—once the central problematic of social theory—we need to link our ethnography to systemic analyses that are informed by history, political economy, and a critical epidemiology. It is not possible to explain the strikingly patterned distribution of HIV by referring exclusively to attitude, cognition, or affect. Fine-grained psychological portraits and rich ethnography are never more than part of the AIDS story.

Third, the myths and mystifications that surround AIDS and slow AIDS research often serve powerful interests. If, in Haiti and in parts of Africa, economic policies (for example, structural-adjustment programs) and political upheaval are somehow related to HIV transmission, who benefits when attention is focused largely or solely on "unruly sexuality" or alleged "promiscuity?" The lasting influence of myths and immodest claims has helped to mask the effects of social inequalities on the distribution of HIV and on AIDS outcomes.

The recent advent of more effective antiviral therapy could have an enormous impact on what it means to have AIDS at the close of the twentieth century—if you don't happen to live in Africa or Haiti or Harlem.

Protease inhibitors and other drugs raise the possibility of transforming AIDS into a chronic condition to be managed over decades, but they also remind us that there are two emerging syndromes: an AIDS of the North, and an AIDS of the South.

Perhaps this does not sound much like an anthropologist speaking. Why talk of latitude (North/South) and class (rich/poor) before speaking of culture? One answer to this question is that, for many of us, the view that AIDS is a culturally constructed phenomenon is not open to debate. AIDS, like sexuality, is inevitably embedded in local social context; representations and responses must necessarily vary along cultural lines. The contribution of cultural factors to the lived experience of AIDS is and will remain enormous. Indeed, the true and vast variation of HIV lies not, as we had been led to believe, in its modes of spread, nor is it found in the mechanisms by which the virus saps the host. The variation of HIV lies, rather, in its highly patterned distribution, in its variable clinical course among the infected, and in the ways in which we respond, socially, to a deadly pathogen.

NOTES

1. In their consideration of unequal exchange and the urban informal sector, Portes and Walton (1982, p. 74) designate Haiti as the most rural of all Latin American nations: in 1950, the nation was described as 88 percent rural; in 1960, 85 percent; in 1970, 81 percent.

2. Pape and Johnson 1988.

3. See Allman 1980 and Vieux 1989 for extended discussions of *plasaj*.

4. See Pape and Johnson 1988.

5. Desvarieux and Pape 1991, p. 275.

6. GESCAP (whose name is translated as "Study Group on AIDS in the Peasant Class") was founded with the generous support of the World AIDS Foundation.

7. Given that the staff of the clinic and of Proje Veye Sante are accountable to the communities served rather than to funding organizations or to research institutions, and given the poverty and non-HIV-related sickness in the region, it is not surprising that research as such is not seen as a high priority. In order to meet our obligations to the community, all serologic studies became part of a *dossier préventif*. This instrument included a series of laboratory examinations (such as hematocrit and RPR), a chest radiograph, and a physical examination. Any abrnormal findings were to be pursued aggressively; free dental care was also offered as part of the program. This proposal was presented to members of the community in four different public meetings, engendering considerable enthusiasm for the undertaking.

8. One additional young woman, the regular sexual partner of a truck driver, was also found to be seropositive. She died suddenly during the course of the study, however, less than a week after a negative physical examination. Although the cause of death is unclear—she had explosive, watery diarrhea and presented in shock—she is not considered in this cohort.

9. Farmer 1992, p. 262.

10. Feilden, Allman, Montague, and Rohde 1981, p. 6.

11. Ibid., p. 4.

12. Locher 1984, p. 329.

13. Neptune-Anglade 1986, p. 150.

14. "Note that, in the cities, the [economically] active 10–14-year-old girls are essentially all domestics.... These 'restaveks' find themselves at the very bottom of the social hierarchy" (ibid., p. 209). My translation.

15. See Farmer 1988b for a review of data concerning the Haitian economy. In a personal communication on 18 September 1998, a desk officer at the US State Department's Haiti desk offered an annual per capita income estimate of $175 (not adjusted for Purchasing Power Parity); she cited internal IMF memos from April 1998 as her source.

16. Girault 1984, p. 177.

17. Ibid., p. 178. For a critical perspective on more recent "food security" issues, see Woodson 1997.

18. Trouillot 1986, p. 201. My translation.

19. Population Crisis Committee 1992.

20. Moral 1961, p. 173. My translation.

21. Allman 1980.

22. But see Laguerre 1982.

23. This is a cursory discussion of a very complex—and changing—subject. For a more complete discussion of sexual unions in Haiti, see Lowenthal 1984, Murray 1976, Neptune-Anglade 1986, Sylvain-Comhaire 1974, and Vieux 1989.

24. United Nations Development Program 1992, p. 6.

25. See Mintz 1964, Neptune-Anglade 1986, and Nicholls 1985.

26. See Murray 1976.

27. Neptune-Anglade 1986, p. 155. My translation.

28. Maria de Bruyn offers a helpful review of these issues as they affect women in developing countries. She writes: "Even if they dare suggest avoiding risky sexual acts or using condoms, they often encounter male refusal, are accused of adultery or promiscuity (the desire to use condoms being interpreted as evidence of extramarital affairs), are suspected of already being infected with HIV or are said to accuse their partners of infidelity" (1992, p. 256). The mechanisms by which gender inequality conspires with poverty to enhance women's risk for HIV are the subject of Farmer, Connors, and Simmons 1996.

29. Desvarieux and Pape 1991, p. 277.

30. Farmer 1992.

31. Collaborative Study Group of AIDS in Haitian-Americans 1987, p. 638.

32. On American "folk models" of Haitians, see Lawless 1992 and, as related to AIDS, Farmer 1992.

33. The word "*sida*" is derived from the French acronym SIDA, for *syndrome immunodéficience acquise*. The French acronym is commonly rendered as S.I.D.A., SIDA, or Sida; *sida* is the Creole orthography. I have adopted the latter here in order to reflect the substantial difference between the terms as used in different national and cultural settings.

34. See Farmer 1996a for a more complete discussion of "Haiti's lost years."

35. Farmer 1996a examines the effects of the 1991 coup d'état on rates of HIV diagnosis in the Kay region.

36. de Bruyn 1992, p. 253.

37. See, for example, Laga, Manoka, Kivuvu, et al. 1993.

38. Poor, young women may be especially at risk of genital trauma: "Non-consensual, hurried or frequent intercourse may inhibit mucus production and the relaxation of vaginal musculature, both of which would increase the likelihood of genital trauma. A lack of control over the circumstances in which the intercourse occurs may increase the frequency of intercourse and lower the age at which sexual activity begins. A lack of access to acceptable health services may leave infections and lesions untreated. Malnutrition not only inhibits the production of mucus but also slows the healing process and depresses the immune system" (United Nations Development Program 1992, pp. 3–4).

39. For example, see Liautaud et al. 1992; Deschamps, Pape, Williams-Russo, Madhavan, Ho, and Johnson, 1993; and Behets, Desormeaux, Joseph, et al. 1995.

40. We do know that in one study of one hundred women presenting to our women's health clinic in 1991 fully 25 percent had trichomoniasis. GESCAP thanks Dr. Anna Contomitros for conducting this study, which included Pap smears. See also Fitzgerald 1996.

41. Data from GHESKIO (e.g., Deschamps et al. 1992) suggest, however, that those ill with HIV disease continue to have sex.

42. DiPerri, Cade, Castelli, et al. 1993.

43. Lief 1990, p. 36.

44. For a review of recent anthropological writings on AIDS, see Farmer 1997b.

45. Benoist and Desclaux 1995, p. 363. My translation.

REFERENCES

Allman, J. 1980. "Sexual Unions in Rural Haiti." *International Journal of Sociology of the Family* 10: 15–39.

Behets, F. M. T., J. Desormeaux, D. Joseph, et al. 1995. "Control of Sexually Transmitted Diseases in Haiti: Results and Implications of a Baseline Study Among

Pregnant Women Living in Cité Soleil Shantytowns." *Journal of Infectious Diseases* 172(3): 764–771.

Benoist, J., and A. Desclaux, eds. 1995. *Sida et Anthropologie: Bilan et Perspectives.* Paris: Karthala.

Collaborative Study Group of AIDS in Haitian-Americans. 1987. "Risk Factors for AIDS Among Haitians Residing in the United States: Evidence of Heterosexual Transmission." *Journal of the American Medical Association* 257(5): 635–639.

de Bruyn, M. 1992. "Women and AIDS in Developing Countries." *Social Science and Medicine* 34(3): 249–262.

Deschamps, M. M., et al. 1992. "HIV Seroconversion Related to Heterosexual Activity in Discordant Haitian Couples." Poster presented at the Eighth International Conference on AIDS/Third STD World Congress, 19–24 July, Amsterdam. Abstract C1087.

Deschamps, M. M., J. W. Pape, P. Williams-Russo, S. Madhavan, J. Ho, and W. Johnson. 1993. "A Prospective Study of HIV-Seropositive Asymptomatic Women of Childbearing Age in a Developing Country." *Journal of Acquired Immune Deficiency Syndromes* 6(5): 446–451.

Desvarieux, M., and J. W. Pape. 1991. "HIV and AIDS in Haiti: Recent Developments." *AIDS Care* 3(3): 271–279.

DiPerri, G., G. P. Cade, F. Castelli, et al. 1993. "Transmission of HIV-Associated Tuberculosis to Health Care Workers." *Infection Control and Hospital Epidemiology* 14: 67–72.

_____. 1988b. "Blood, Sweat, and Baseballs: Haiti in the West Atlantic System." *Dialectical Anthropology* 13: 83–99.

_____. 1992. *AIDS and Accusation: Haiti and the Geography of Blame.* Berkeley: University of California Press.

_____. 1996a. "Haiti's Lost Years: Lessons for the Americas." *Current Issues in Public Health* 2: 143–151.

_____. 1997b. "Ethnography, Social Analysis, and the Prevention of Sexually Transmitted HIV Infections Among Poor Women in Haiti." In *The Anthropology of Infectious Disease*, ed. M. Inhorn and P. Brown, 413–438. New York: Gordon and Breach.

Farmer, Paul, Margaret Connors, Janie Simmons, eds. 1996. *Women, Poverty, and AIDS. Sex, Drugs and Structural Violence.* Monroe, ME: Common Courage Press

Farmer, Paul. 1992. *AIDS and Accusation: Haiti and the Geography of Blame.* Berkeley: University of California Press.

Farmer, Paul. 1996. On Suffering and Structural Violence: A View From Below. *Daedalus*, 125(1): 261-283.

Feilden, R., J. Allman, J. Montague, and J. Rohde. 1981. *Health, Population, and Nutrition in Haiti: A Report Prepared for the World Bank.* Boston: Management Sciences for Health.

Fitzgerald, D. 1996. *Final Report HAS: Project 2005.* Boston: Management Sciences for Health.

Girault, C. 1984. "Commerce in the Haitian Economy." In *Haiti—Today and Tomorrow: An Interdisciplinary Study,* ed. C. Foster and A. Valdman, 173–179. Lanham, Md.: University Press of America.

Laga, M., A. Manoka, M. Kivuvu, et al. 1993. "Non-Ulcerative Sexually Transmitted Diseases as Risk Factors for HIV-1 Transmission in Women: Results from a Cohort Study." *AIDS* 7 (1): 95–102.

Laguerre, M. 1982. *Urban Life in the Caribbean.* Cambridge, Mass.: Schenkman.

Lawless, R. 1992. *Haiti's Bad Press.* Rochester, Vt.: Schenkman Books.

Liautaud, B., et al. 1992. "Preliminary Data on STDs in Haiti." Poster presented at the Eighth *International Conference on AIDS/Third STD World Congress*, 19–24 July, Amsterdam. Abstract C4302.

Lief, L. 1990. "Where Democracy Isn't About to Break Out." *U.S. News and World Report*, 12 February, pp. 34–36.

Locher, U. 1984. "Migration in Haiti." In *Haiti—Today and Tomorrow: An Interdisciplinary Study*, ed. C. Foster and A. Valdman, 325–336. Lanham, Md.: University Press of America.

Lowenthal, I. 1984. "Labor, Sexuality, and the Conjugal Contract in Rural Haiti." In *Haiti—Today and Tomorrow: An Interdisciplinary Study*, ed. C. Foster and A. Valdman, 15–33. Lanham, Md.: University Press of America.

Mintz, S. W. 1964. "The Employment of Capital by Market Women in Haiti." In *Capital, Saving, and Credit in Peasant Societies*, ed. R. Firth and B. Yamey, 56–78. Chicago: Aldine.

Moral, P. 1961. *Le Paysan Haïtien.* Port-au-Prince: Les Éditions Fardins.

Murray, G. 1976. "Women in Perdition: Ritual Fertility Control in Haiti." In *Culture, Natality, and Family Planning*, ed. by J. Marshall and S. Polgar, 59–78. Chapel Hill: Carolina Population Center, University of North Carolina.

Neptune-Anglade, M. 1986. *"L'Autre Moitié du Développement: A Propos du Travail des Femmes en Haïti."* Pétion-Ville, Haïti: Éditions des Alizés.

Nicholls, D. 1985. *Haiti in Caribbean Context: Ethnicity, Economy, and Revolt.* New York.

Pape, J. W., and W. Johnson. 1988. "Epidemiology of AIDS in the Caribbean." *Baillière's Clinical Tropical Medicine and Communicable Diseases* 3(1): 31–42.

Portes, A., and J. Walton. 1982. *Labor, Class, and the International System.* New York: Academic Press.

Sylvain-Comhaire, Suzanne. 1974. "La paysanne de Kenscoff." In *La Femme de Couleur en Amerique Latine*, ed. Roger Bastide. Paris: Anthropus.

Trouillot, M. R. 1986. *Les Racines Historiques de l'État Duvaliérien.* Port-au-Prince: Imprimerie Henri Deschamps.

United Nations Development Program. 1992. *Young Women: Silence, Susceptibility, and the HIV Epidemic.* New York: UNDP.

Vieux, S. 1989. *Le Plaçage: Droit Coutumier et Famille en Haïti.* Paris: Éditions Publisud.

Woodson, D. 1997. "Lamanjay, Food Security, Sécurité Alimentaire." *Culture and Agriculture* 19(3): 108–122.

38

Circumcision, Pluralism, and Dilemmas of Cultural Relativism

Corinne A. Kratz

One of the things about studying anthropology is that we encounter cultural ideas and practices that are very alien to our own. Encountering the "other" can be a challenge in two ways. On an intellectual level, it can be a challenge to understand vastly different cultures and customs—why do people do/believe that? How does it fit within the wider context of their lives? The second of these challenges can be on a personal level, because the beliefs and practices of others might offend our own notions of morality and propriety. Studying and living in other cultures sometimes brings up our own ugly ethnocentrism.

At the same time, it is fair to ask, Are there limits to cultural relativism? Looking cross-culturally, anthropologists can identify some universal (or at least extremely common) elements in cultural codes about proper personal conduct. All societies follow the ethnocentric line of thought that *their own traditions* are correct and right, but at the same time there are gigantic areas of controversy. In a complex society, the laws that are recognized and enforced often reflect the interests of the dominant social group.

The topic of this selection, female circumcision, really bothers some students; they can hardly believe that such cultural practices exist in the twenty-first century. In Africa, female circumcision has been a controversial topic for nearly a century, and there have been repeated international efforts to "eradicate" the custom, as if it were a disease. But this is not simply a medical issue, and to oversimplify the complex issue misses the point.

It is important to recognize that the single term *FGM* (*female genital modification* or *mutilation*) refers to a wide variety of surgeries with different levels of invasiveness. It is also important to remember that the symbolic and ritual meanings of this practice also vary among cultures. Finally, as students of anthropology, we need to recognize that there are at least two different views of what is at stake here, and, as in many other arenas of public controversy, there is real value to a sympathetic understanding of both sides.

This selection has two parts. The first provides a description of female circumcision in Africa—reporting the "facts" almost as it might be reported in a reference book. The second part discusses the author's strategies for *teaching* about the female circumcision controversy in the college classroom context. This controversy is both local and global—it involves traditional cultures, immigrants, and international nongovernmental organizations (NGOs). Understanding the different dimensions of the argument is an important educational goal; hopefully, it will also challenge you to come to your own well-informed opinion.

As you read this selection, ask yourself the following questions:

- For the women in the societies that practice it, FGM is related to beliefs about aesthetics of the body. Can you think of traditions in your own culture that transform or modify the body for purposes of beauty or identity? (Try relating this to Miner's description of body ritual among the Nacirema in Selection 25.)
- What are the potential health complications of female circumcision? What are the possible social complications of not being circumcised?
- What are the human rights issues involved? Is this a question that local societies should debate themselves, or is international intervention necessary?
- Why does this tradition persist even when it is made against the law? Why would loving parents have this done to their daughters?
- Is the analogy to male circumcision in the West appropriate?

The following terms discussed in this selection are included in the Glossary at the back of the book:

clitorectomy	*infibulation*
FGM	*neocolonial*
human rights	*sunna circumcision*

Differences of social and cultural practice have been a source of both puzzlement and edification around the world and throughout human history, interpreted and treated in vastly different ways in different circumstances.[1] They have been perennial resources through which people form their own identities, defining themselves through contrasts with other cultures. Distinctions in dress, cuisine, language, music, and ritual are particularly common as such markers of identity and difference. When ethnic or religious groups and minorities are reviled, differences in cultural practice have been used to help justify derogatory attitudes and discrimination. In other settings, cultural difference and diversity have been celebrated through various forms of multiculturalism.

With such remarkable diversity in the world, however, situations inevitably arise where incompatible social and cultural values, practices, and aesthetics produce conflict or controversy. How should they be dealt with? Cultural relativism would suggest that each set of practices and understandings is valid within its own circumstances and way of life. Yet plural societies combine and blend different beliefs and practices within the same social settings. Further, certain practices seem to challenge the nonjudgmental tolerance that cultural relativism implies (Shweder 2002) and raise serious questions about how to define human rights and who should define them. To many Americans, for instance, religious practices of discipline and self-mortification might seem extreme when they include self-flagellation, or political martyrdom might be taken as a sign of fanaticism. To people in other parts of the world, on the other hand, certain American economic practices might seem exploitative and certain modes of American dress might be seen as indecent or immoral.

Anthropologists seek to understand cultural production, i.e., how cultural meanings and social worlds continually take shape and change through daily interaction, communication, and exchange, through interpretations of personal and community histories and negotiations of political economic differences. They seek to understand the range of experience, meanings, and values produced by the world's diverse societies and cultures, examining how people perceive and make sense of lives and circumstances as different as those of African pastoralists caught in a long civil war, Chinese women working in a silk factory, men in an urban homeless shelter in the United States, contemporary Australians maintaining complex ritual traditions and fighting for land and mining claims, or radical political activists in Europe (Hutchinson 1996; Rofel 1999; Desjarlais 1997; Dussart 2000; Holmes 2000). In doing so, anthropologists may move beyond simple relativism to develop knowledge and judgments based on pluralism. Philosopher and social theorist Isaiah Berlin describes the distinction between relativism and pluralism (1991:10–11):

> "I prefer coffee, you prefer champagne. We have different tastes. There is no more to be said." That is relativism. . . . [Pluralism is] the conception that there are many different ends that men [sic] may seek and still be fully rational, fully men [sic], capable of understanding each other and sympathising and deriving light from each other, as we derive it from reading Plato or the novels of medieval Japan—worlds, outlooks, very remote from our own.
>
> Members of one culture can, by the force of imaginative insight, understand . . . the values, the ideals, the forms of life of another culture or society, even those remote in time or space. They may find these values unacceptable, but if they open their minds sufficiently they can grasp how one might be a full human being, with whom one could communicate, and at the same time live in the light of values widely different from one's own, but which nevertheless one can see to be values, ends of life, by the realisation of which men [sic] could be fulfilled.

Anthropological research may not be able to resolve conflicts and controversies that emerge from social and cultural difference, but the knowledge produced can provide the foundation of understanding needed for engagement and debate grounded in pluralism. It can help to identify the basic value contradictions and issues at stake as well as the different positions and interests in play. It is also important to pay attention to such controversies and debates themselves as cultural phenomena, analyzing their rhetorics, weighing competing arguments, and placing them within their own social and historical contexts. These analytical skills are important in understanding debates concerning issues of social justice, abortion rights, defining human rights, or controversial practices such as *sati* in India, and they are critical to effective political action related to any of these issues.

This essay considers a widespread cultural practice that has many different forms and meanings throughout the world and a long history of sparking debate and controversy at different times and places: forms of genital modification commonly called circumcision. Vehement debates have swirled around male and female circumcision alike, but the essay focuses particularly on practices of female genital modification because they currently receive the greatest attention and are at the center of recent contention. After outlining the varied practices of female genital modification and some of the meanings associated with them, the essay will turn to controversies and debates about these cultural practices.

THE VARIED PRACTICES AND MEANINGS OF FEMALE GENITAL MODIFICATION

Female circumcision is a term commonly used to refer to surgical operations performed in over thirty African, Middle Eastern, and Southeast Asian countries, by immigrants from those communities living elsewhere, and for roughly a century (about 1850 to 1950) by physicians in Europe and the United States. As this geographic and historical span suggests, the operations are embedded in a wide range of cultural and historical contexts and can be quite different in definition, meaning, and effect. All involve surgical modification of female genitals in some way, though this ranges from relatively minor marking for symbolic purposes to the most radical operation, infibulation.[2]

The general term *female circumcision* includes at least three clinically distinct kinds of surgery. Clitoridectomy removes all or part of the clitoris and the hood, or prepuce, covering it.[3] The second type, excision, includes clitoridectomy but also removes some or all of the labia minora; all or part of the labia majora might also be cut. The most extreme form of circumcision, infibulation, goes beyond excision.[4] After removing the labia, the sides of the vulva are joined so that scar tissue forms over the vaginal opening, leaving a small gap for urination and menstruation. Infibulated women often require surgical opening to allow first intercourse and birthing; in many cases women are re-infibulated after each childbirth. In addition to these three well-recognized types of female circumcision, a fourth is sometimes included. The mildest form, this involves a symbolic pricking or slight nicking of the clitoris or prepuce. Excision and infibulation are the most widely practiced types of female genital modification. In Africa, infibulation is common primarily in the Horn of Africa (Somalia, Sudan, Djibouti, Ethiopia).

Whether and how circumcision practices affect women's sexuality is much debated. It is important to distinguish sexual desire, sexual activity, and sexual pleasure when considering this question. Sexual desire and sexual activity may not diminish with female genital operations. Evidence about sexual feeling and pleasure is variable, difficult to define or measure, and hard to come by.[5] Euro-American opponents of the practices assert that circumcised women feel no sexual pleasure, but a number of African women disagree with these assertions. Studies suggest that the effect varies widely with type of operation, with prior sexual experience, and other circumstances as well. Some African activists also suggest that the stress on sexual pleasure in anticircumcision campaigns reflects a recent, primarily Western concept of sexuality.[6]

The operations have also been said to carry a number of health risks. While the range of possible health problems is well known, there has been little epidemiological research to determine how widespread each problem might be in different areas. Immediate risks include infection, shock, excessive bleeding, and urinary retention, risks that are related to hygienic conditions and care during and after the operations. Longer term health problems are most common with infibulation but can be associated with excision as well. Most of these problems are related to heavy scarring and to covering over of vaginal and urinary openings after infibulation: keloid scars, vulvar cysts, retention of urine or menses, painful menstruation, difficulty urinating, and chronic pelvic infections. Clinical studies on the relation between these health problems and genital modification are contradictory, however, and a recent study in Gambia found that many negative consequences commonly cited for the operations were not significantly more common in women who had been cut (Morison et al. 2001).[7]

In many places where female circumcision is practiced, the physical operation is but one moment in an elaborate ceremony that contains many other events. For Okiek people in Kenya, for instance, initiation into adulthood includes circumcision for boys and excision for girls, but the full initiation process continues for several months and includes much more as well: moral teaching, family and community engagement, the negotiation of new social relationships, and important cultural meanings and values. While the operations are a central initiation trial and create a permanent physical mark of adulthood, initiation cannot be reduced to circumcision or excision alone. In many other societies, initiation does not involve circumcision at all.

In every case the purposes and meanings of female genital modification are related to specific cultural understandings of identity, personhood, morality, adulthood, gender, bodily aesthetics, and other important issues. In the Sudan, for instance, it is seen as enhancing a woman's purity, cleanliness, and beauty. For the Kikuyu people of Kenya, circumcision was the foundation of moral self-mastery for women and men alike, performed as part of initiation into adulthood. The age of those circumcised varies widely according to these cultural understandings. In much of Mali and the Sudan, for instance, girls are circumcised at six to eight years, while various communities in Kenya and Sierra Leone perform the operation in the early teens. Yoruba people in Nigeria often circumcise their children at just a few days old, much like male circumcision in the United States and Europe. Circumcision and excision are not connected with initiation for the Yoruba people, but they do relate the operations to moral concepts associated with shame and fertility. Circumcision is not regularly performed after puberty in Africa, where the operation is usually seen as related to a person's social and moral development.[8] The history of female circumcision in Europe and the United States contrasts with most of the world with regard to circumcision age. For roughly a century beginning in the 1850s, clitoridectomy was prescribed for adult women in Europe and the United States as medical treatment for insomnia, sterility, and masturbation (which was defined as an ailment at that time).

Many societies practice male but not female circumcision, but the reverse is rare. Where both are practiced, they can only be understood fully when considered together, in relation to one another. In many societies, cultural meanings and patterns link the two and equate them. A single word refers to both operations in many African languages, and this correspondence is often central to the way their practitioners understand them. The English translation, "female circumcision," maintains this parallel between male and female genital operations, though anticircumcision activists have criticized the term for being misleading (as discussed below).

DEBATES AND CONTROVERSIES ABOUT CIRCUMCISION

Both male and female genital operations have engendered long histories of debate and opposition; these have often involved cross-cultural disagreements about the meaning and worth of the practices. The value of Jewish male circumcision, for instance, was debated in Rome during the first century A.D., and male circumcision has become a topic of heated opposition in the United States again today. The most widespread and vociferous opposition currently centers on female genital modification, but these practices have been the subject of international political controversies and abolition campaigns since at least the 1910s.[9] Contemporary campaigns continue the tradition and rhetoric of colonial and missionary opposition and also build on decades of Africa-based activism. Health consequences have consistently been part of the debate, particularly in relation to infibulation, but the issues have also been defined at times in terms of colonialism, neocolonialism, feminism, sexuality, and human rights.

Controversies can be confusing. Heated arguments based on strong convictions are rarely presented in ways that make clear the different assumptions, perspectives, and interests fueling contention. When controversies cross cultural and national boundaries, they can be very complicated indeed. To begin to understand circumcision debates, it is important to first identify the grounds of controversy: Who is involved, what is it about, and what is at issue. Circumcision controversies concern a wide variety of actors and cross a number of social and legal arenas, from family and household relations to international tribunals. This renders it impossible to characterize the debates in simple terms. It is inaccurate and misleading to describe them merely as contests of women versus men or Africans versus outsiders.

To understand today's debates, it is helpful to think about them in relation to several contexts. Most central are the sociocultural contexts of the varied practices at issue and the history and contexts of the current controversies themselves. An effective way to highlight the issues and perspectives involved is to consider these contexts comparatively, to relate different situations and practices, or to explore similarities and differences between several controversies (e.g., debates about male and female genital operations, debates that occur at different historical periods, or debates that might concern different practices but are presented in similar ways (such as *sati* in India[10]). Examining cultural practices in context also means identifying the different actors, perspectives, and meanings involved (see below). It is important to recognize that trying to understand unfamiliar practices does not necessarily mean supporting them. However, to oppose or help alter practices that some might consider problematic, it is essential to work *with* the people involved, as equal peers. Such understanding is critical to effective engagement.

One of the best-documented historical examples of circumcision controversy took place in central Kenya during the colonial era. Colonial missionaries and administrators there made judgments about which local customs violated Christian behavior and sought to discourage them. Campaigns to abolish female circumcision in central Kenya were among these efforts. When the Church of Scotland Mission and segments of the Church Missionary Society tried to prohibit the practice in the 1910s and 1920s, Kikuyu female circumcision became connected with the anticolonial movement and defense of cultural tradition (Murray 1974, 1976). Jomo Kenyatta, later president of Kenya, was a prominent opponent of colonial attempts to alter Kikuyu custom. These local protests against abolishing female circumcision provided an impetus for starting independent schools and churches in central Kenya.

Arenas encompassed in this debate, then, included British politics (with pressure from feminist parliamentarians and anticolonial activists), rivalries between Christian denominations with missions in Kenya, the colonial administration in Kenya, and local Kenyan communities. In addition to anticolonial movements and defense of cultural tradition, the debate also became connected with relations of authority between men and women and between women of different generations, and even the introduction of maternity clinics.[11] Since 1979, the Kenyan government has conducted several anticircumcision campaigns that were tinged with Christian and colonial overtones, banning female circumcision in 1982, but with little effect. In 1996, a national organization proposed an alternative initiation ceremony as a substitute. Like Kenya, each country has its own such history of circumcision debates and policies.

To place contemporary controversies in context, we should also consider their own history and the different arenas where debates occur. The debates have been related to feminist movements in various times and places, to colonial administration and missionary campaigns, to Islamic religious movements, and a number of other issues. Arenas of debate shift as different parties become involved. Several decades after the Kenyan controversy, in the late 1950s, international efforts to have the World Health Organization (WHO) address female circumcision were not effective. Later, in the 1970s, a number of publicizing efforts and publications converged to galvanize international attention. These included articles in African publications in the mid-1970s, a press conference held in Switzerland before the WHO assembly in 1977, and publications by Fran Hosken (1979) and Mary Daly (1990) in the United States. The Inter-African Committee on Traditional Practices affecting the Health of Women and Children was formed in Geneva in 1977. A 1979 WHO seminar in Khartoum helped to begin regular discussion of female genital operations by international bodies and at regular conferences. The resurgence of anticircumcision activity in the 1970s was also buoyed by the United Nations Decade of Women (1975–1985).

Since the early 1990s, international debates about female genital modification have again become increasingly heated and highly politicized. Greater media coverage in the 1990s and publicity over legal cases concerning African immigrants in France and the United States brought the debates to a wider public than previously.[12] In the United States, involvement by such well-known figures as novelist Alice Walker also helped to publicize and polarize the debate. A number of African scholars and activists based in the United States (such as Seble Dawit, Salem Mekuria, and Micere Mugo) have been highly critical of the way Walker and others have represented female circumcision in Africa.[13] They argue that Walker and others are engaged in neocolonial depictions that demonize African practitioners, distort the social meanings and contexts involved, portray African women only as victims, ignore decades of activism in Africa, and isolate female circumcision from other issues of women's health, economic status, and education.

Both practices of female genital modification and the arenas of debate have shifted over the years as other circumstances changed and different constituencies became involved. Public health education about the potential risks of the operations has increased in most countries where they are practiced. Similarly, an increasing number of female genital modifications are being performed either by specialists who have received some hygienic training or in health clinics and hospitals. As noted above, alternative rituals have also been proposed in some countries, though it is not clear whether they will be widely adopted. Shifts in practice also include adoption of genital modification by noncircumcising communities (Leonard 1999) and modification of long-standing rituals toward what I call "circumcision by pronouncement" or "performative circumcision," i.e., substituting a verbal formula for actual cutting (Abusharaf 1999:7; Hernlund 1999). There are intense debates among African activists about whether a medicalized, minor form of female genital modification should be promoted as an interim substitute for more severe operations (Obiora 1997; Shell-Duncan 2001). African immigrant communities in Europe and the United States often continue traditional practices in new ways in their new homes. Their preservation of the practices has brought all these debates to the fore in those countries as immigrant communities and their children have grown in recent decades. Sweden, Switzerland, the United Kingdom, and several other European countries passed laws restricting the operations in the 1980s and early 1990s. The United States followed suit in 1997.

CONTEXTS FOR UNDERSTANDING THE DEBATES AND ISSUES

These examples illustrate how many different parties and perspectives can become involved in these controversies. In tracing the shape of today's debates, it is useful to distinguish the following three interacting arenas. The social, cultural, and historical contexts of debates about female and male genital operations can be examined for each:

1. *Home countries* are countries in Africa, the Middle East, and Southeast Asia where circumcising practices have traditional standing. There may be a variety of traditions and practices that include genital modification within each home country and a number of different positions within each community, if the practices are debated.

2. The *United States* and *Europe* are the second arena to consider. These countries also have a history of genital operations for both boys and girls. The histories are related to changing understandings of health, class, ethnicity, gender, and sexuality.

In the U.K., for instance, male circumcision had become a middle-class fashion by the 1920s (Lonsdale 1992:388). In Nazi Germany, it was taken as a mark of Jewish identity. In the United States today, white men are more likely to be circumcised than African Americans or Hispanics; higher education levels are also related to higher circumcision rates (Laumann et al. 1997: 1053–1054). Clitoridectomy was a recognized medical treatment for women in these countries for decades, as noted above. Concern about female genital operations within these countries is now related particularly to immigrants from home countries.

3.   The third arena is that of *international campaigns.* Though obviously related to the other two, it is useful to consider how international campaigns differ from debates within the other arenas, how international bodies and action groups establish their legitimacy to intervene in other countries, and how the international arena redefines issues central to particular communities and nations.[14]

In addition to identifying the complex social geographies and range of actors involved, it is equally important to pay attention to the ways that language and rhetoric shape the presentation of issues and convey particular values and judgments. For instance, the growing intensity of the debates became encapsulated in the very terms used for female genital operations between the 1970s and 1990s, illustrating the political divisions and rhetorics involved. *Female circumcision* was the most common term for decades, the English phrase ordinarily used in the debates about British colonial attempts to outlaw female genital operations in Kenya in the 1920s–30s. In the 1970s, anticircumcision activists increasingly criticized the term *female circumcision,* claiming that it condoned a brutal custom by creating what they considered false similarities between male and female circumcision.[15] A more partisan alternative was coined and eventually popularized: *female genital mutilation.*[16] The new term did not attempt impartial description, but condemned the practices through a label that defined them all as intentional mistreatment and disfigurement. Promotion of the new "mutilation" term was part of an escalating anticircumcision campaign that used more sensationalism and gory images.[17] As this term became more common, it was shortened to an acronym, "FGM." Others reject this term as misrepresenting the intentions of African families, criminalizing parents and relatives, and judging them through Euroamerican cultural values.

The increasingly heated and polarized nature of the debate thus became embedded in its very terms.

Attempting to find an appropriate phrase, *New York Times* reporter Celia Duggers used the term *genital cutting* in her late 1996 articles, a term she adopted from demographic and health surveys.[18] A number of other alternative terms also came into use in the mid-1990s, seeking more neutral ground: genital surgery, genital operations, genital modification, and body modification. This last term acknowledges broad similarities among such practices as male and female genital surgeries, genital/body piercing, and other cosmetic surgery. Female circumcision, genital cutting, and FGM remain the most common terms in English, though the acronym FGM has now also been redefined as "female genital *modification*" in efforts to use less polarizing, descriptive language.

Whatever terms are used, the topic at the center of controversy is a generalized category defined and shaped by that very debate. The category is created by extracting and combining fragments from many different cultural practices found in dozens of countries, a variety of practice described above. The fragments all concern genital modification but may share little else. Taken out of their social and cultural contexts, they combine to form a new, abstract category (e.g., "female circumcision"). Scientific, medical language is an important tool in this process. The clinical emphasis makes the general category seem like an objective and universal way to talk about women's bodies, but it also narrows the range of information defined as relevant to the debate. For instance, the physically different operations described above are combined and treated as the same thing, though they vary considerably in extent and effects. The rest of the ceremonies in which the physical operations may be embedded are often ignored.

The terms used in circumcision controversies convey different impressions of the people involved as well. A number of African women and others have objected to the word *mutilation,* for instance, because it misrepresents parents and families. It suggests that they intend harm to their children, likening to child abuse what they themselves might see as a cultural triumph, "carried out for the noblest of reasons, the best of intentions, and in good faith" (Iweriebor 1996). Accounts often demonize women who perform the operations as well. In recent French legal cases, for instance, they were portrayed as avaricious and predatory and received the harshest rulings.

A prominent example concerns the way African or "Third World" women in general are represented as a single, unified group, as seen across a range of sources: news media, informational publicity material produced by action groups, scholarly writing, or novels.[19] This stereotyped concept of "African women" is usually formed by homogenizing divergent circumstances;

it assumes women to be a pre-existent, coherent group with shared interests and desires. This requires removing the concept of "woman" from any specific cultural context and isolating it from related notions that help form understandings of gender. How are differences based on nationality, class, ethnicity, religion, education, or age accommodated in this generalized figure and how might these variations affect the debates? The "average" Third World woman that emerges is set in contrast to elite women, though the contrast is often implicit. Elite women are presented as self-conscious, active, choice-making agents. They are not exclusively Western, but also include women born in the Third World who have joined the campaign against female genital modification. Yet African activists consistently protest that their work is rarely recognized when controversies are described. The rhetoric and structure of these controversies might be examined further by looking at how different kinds of men are portrayed, or by considering parallel cases in contemporary campaigns against male genital operations, abortion, or welfare.[20]

These different portrayals of Third World women and other actors in circumcision controversies are often bound up with notions of "progress" and other values as they have been defined in Euroamerican contexts. But conflicting values are the very crux of controversy. Diverse social and political positions inform the perspectives of those involved, but they are also grounded in different cultural frameworks, competing definitions of the practices at issue, and what seem to be irreconcilable values. In seeking to understand circumcision debates, it can be helpful to identify the various positions on each issue, along with the priorities and cultural values associated with each. Issues at stake would include the following:

Human Rights   Circumcision debates presented in human rights terms often emphasize the integrity and inviolability of the human body, sometimes using analogies with torture and child abuse. As noted above, this falsely attributes evil intent to parents and relatives. "Human rights" as a concept is itself under considerable debate. Should social and economic rights be included? Whose values will be enshrined as universal when there are fundamental disagreements (An-Na`im 1992; An-Na`im and Deng 1990)? How might the language of human rights accommodate the diverse people, practices, and circumstances involved?

Self-Determination   The human rights approach does not fit easily with another common way that circumcision debates are framed, in terms of self-determination.[21] However, self-determination can be defined in relation to individuals, families, or communities, each with rather different implications. Upholding family autonomy, community values, or religious freedom would seem to support continuing traditional practices understood as central to personal and community identity. Does this include male and female initiation ceremonies? How does individual self-determination apply in the intricate contexts of family and community relations? How do questions of self-determination apply to children of different ages?

Health Issues and Sexuality   These were discussed earlier in this essay. Both have been central to debates about female genital modification. Questions of sexuality have also figured in opponents' efforts to explain the operations. They commonly assert that male desire to control female sexuality is the origin and reason for all such practices. This universal conspiracy theory, however, does not correspond to what is known about circumcising practices. There is no evidence or discussion of when or how this might have happened in so many places, how this explanation would account for the variety of circumcising practices, why women also staunchly defend them, or how the theory relates to explanations offered by practitioners.[22]

Yet even when the issues and stances in circumcision controversies are delineated, the fact remains that the debates involve fundamentally different perceptions and lived understandings of aesthetics, morality, society, and personhood that come together with questions of authority, class, power, gender, and history.[23] There are no simple, single answers to the issues they raise. They pinpoint a nexus whose very opaqueness of understanding illustrates recalcitrant problems and issues of cultural translation. In this respect, recent circumcision controversies draw attention to the limits and dilemmas of cultural relativism and moral judgments. How are such judgments, choices, and even laws to be made in plural societies (which ultimately means all societies)? Can incommensurable values be accommodated? As Sir Isaiah Berlin noted, "A certain humility in these matters is very necessary" (1991:18).

CULTURAL AND MORAL VALUES: DILEMMAS OF RELATIVISM

Many people would agree that cultural difference and diversity should be recognized, respected, and accommodated. Cultural relativism has fairly wide currency in the United States as a general way to approach cultural difference, though it coexists with popular notions of cultural evolution and civilizational hierarchy. The relativist view that each society's practices and values are valid and understandable in the particular context of their lives may be easiest to hold, however, when applied to distant people or to practices that seem strange but harmless. What happens when people with incompatible practices and values live closely together, when culturally justified practices seem to be physically harmful, or when an overarching national legal system must deal with radically different values? Does cultural relativism imply moral relativism as well?

The controversies over genital operations present such dilemmas and flashpoints. Usually associated with ceremonial performances, the songs, dances, costumes, and other beliefs that give meaning to the ceremonies are readily accepted as part of "tradition," as markers of particular forms of ethnic or religious identity. Scarification or tattooing might also be recognized and appreciated as part of a different aesthetic or religion, so what is different about genital operations? Why are they seen as an exception that raises this moral dilemma? What other practices pose similar dilemmas?

In the last decade, legal cases dealing with African immigrants in the United States and Europe have raised these issues in particularly clear and urgent ways. Examining these cases—particularly court procedure and sections of testimony—provides a way to again consider the different actors and interests involved, this time in situations even closer to home (Kratz 2002). Among the many questions that these cases raise are the following:

- Legislation is written in general terms, intended as applicable to the broadest range of cases. However, laws are interpreted through individual cases and precedents. Should a case about, for instance, Somali immigrants (who practice infibulation for young girls) serve as precedent for families from Sierra Leone (where initiated individuals are older, the operation is less severe, and family relations are quite different)?

- Whose legal rights should be protected and when? Parents' rights to raise their children in accordance with their beliefs and traditions? What if parents disagree? The rights of the girls affected? What if they *choose* to undergo the operation? What if they are minors legally?

- When female genital operations are outlawed, who is legally responsible and liable for prosecution? At different times and places, the accused have included fathers, mothers, initiates, and surgeons. What constructions of actors, intentions, and meanings are involved in each of these scenarios?

- When court proceedings involve immigrants, how are issues of adequate translation and adequate legal representation handled? These were important problems in the way French cases in the 1990s were handled.

- Are judges, juries, lawyers, and those concerned with civil liberties informed about the communities

and cultural values involved? For instance, a lawyer in one case argued that the girls affected would have psychological problems when they realized they were not like other women, but the "other women" assumed in this statement were not women of the immigrant community. In fact, most women in their own ethnic community had had the operation, making the argument one that would more appropriately support the operation (cf. Matias 1996:4).

- How do gendered differences in immigrant experiences influence knowledge about relevant laws and services and the ways people participate in legal proceedings?

These questions raise some of the difficult practical implications of general issues of cultural translation and the moral dilemmas involved. They provide another way to ground the circumcision debates in specific questions and situations. Such groundings provide useful ways to understand and engage with controversies that are puzzling and sometimes troubling in their passions and complexities.

NOTES

1. This paper includes portions of Kratz (1999a) and (1999b) that have been combined, revised, and updated for inclusion here.

2. Wide variation in female genital modification can be found on the African continent alone, where it is practiced across a band of the continent that includes parts of Mauritania, Senegal, Gambia, Guinea-Bissau, Sierra Leone, Liberia, Mali, Burkina Faso, Côte d'Ivoire, Ghana, Togo, Benin, Niger, Nigeria, Chad, Cameroon, Central African Republic, Democratic Republic of the Congo (formerly Zaire), Sudan, Egypt, Eritrea, Ethiopia, Djibouti, Somalia, Kenya, Tanzania, and Uganda. The percentage of women circumcised in each country varies considerably (e.g., 5–10% in Uganda, 25–30% in Ghana, 80% in the Sudan), as does the kind of operation practiced, its cultural and personal significance, and its history. Female circumcision is not practiced at all in some communities within this broad area, but it is commonplace in others. Regional, ethnic, and religious variation in practice is considerable. Christians, Muslims, and followers of traditional religions all might practice forms of female circumcision. Communities have adopted, abandoned, and modified the practices in various ways over the centuries, in keeping with the complex histories of political and religious influence and interaction among societies on the African continent.

3. This is sometimes called *sunna circumcision*, though *sunna circumcision* might also refer to preputial cutting alone. The name *sunna* relates the practice to Islamic traditions, though most Muslim scholars and theologians deny Koranic justification for female circumcision.

4. Infibulation is also called *pharaonic circumcision,* a name originating in beliefs that the practice was part of ancient Egyptian life.

5. See Apena (1996:8); Kratz (1994:345–346); Lyons (1981:507, 510); Obiora (1997:298). Matias (1996:3) and Ogbu (1997:414–415) cite examples where they are seen as enhancing sexuality. Again, the type of operation is critical. Infibulation is more often discussed as reducing desire (Boddy 1989:54), though Obiora (1997:310) cites another study in the Sudan to opposite effect. As for sexual pleasure, according to Gruenbaum (also writing about the Sudan), some infibulated women do have orgasms, perhaps because "many midwives, fearing hemorrhage, leave much of the clitoral (erectile) tissue intact beneath the infibulation when they perform the surgeries" (1996:462). She notes, though, that other infibulated women report finding sex unsatisfying. See also Parker (1995:514); Obiora (1997:308–310); Koso-Thomas (1987:37–42). Several of these sources note that reports of sexual pleasure are related to sexual experience before circumcision as well as other factors.

6. Even in Europe and the United States, the pleasure-oriented definition of sexuality became prominent in recent decades. In this view, recent international debates about female genital operations have taken a form that resonates particularly with recent Western concerns and anxieties (Parker 1995). The paradoxical nature of questions of sexuality can be brought into relief through comparison. Historically, classical theologians and philosophers made parallel claims about men; they promoted male circumcision because it reduces male sexual passion (Boyarin 1992:486–487; Lyons 1981:503–504). Though circumcised men today might not agree, similar assumptions still inform medical research. A study publicized on National Public Radio in 1997 found that circumcised men are more "sexually adventurous," but explained this as compensation for loss of sexual feeling (Laumann et al. 1997). "Adventurousness" was defined through behavioral range and frequencies, suggesting that sexual interest, desire, and activity were actually greater with circumcision. Considering such gender reversals can raise critical questions about all these claims and show that understandings of sexuality are neither universal nor unchanging.

7. Obiora (1997:292) cites studies that show no obstetric or gynecological complication when infibulation is performed at an early age. Parker (1995:514–516) notes that findings in some studies of health risks from other forms of genital operations are not clear, though it is generally accepted that some complications can occur.

8. See Shell-Duncan and Hernlund (2000) for a collection of case studies on female genital modification in various parts of Africa.

9. Far earlier, in the 1820s, circumcising practices were also at the center of debates in the Sudan (Abusharaf 1999).

10. In the Hindu practice of *sati,* a widow immolates herself on her husband's funeral pyre. *Sati* became the subject of considerable debate in India during British colonial rule, leading to abolition in 1829. The *sati* controversy, like debates about female genital operations, involves a wide range of perspectives and has been framed at various times in terms of women's status, issues of tradition, authority, religious rights, personal autonomy, and humanitarianism. Outlawing *sati* did not make it disappear entirely. "Through the 1970s and 1980s . . . [the same time when circumcision controversies were heating up], either incidents of *sati* increased or greater scrutiny was brought to bear on the issue, primarily by women's organizations" (Courtright 1994:47). In September 1987, the case of Roop Kanwar, a young Hindu woman who burned in Rajasthan, galvanized national debate. Nandy (1988) and Mani (1990b) have noted continuities of language and argument between contemporary Indian positions and earlier colonial debates, parallels similar to those in circumcision controversies. Both debates involve "instabilities of perspective, of meaning, of judgment," and provide avenues for considering the "social history of moral imagination" (Geertz 1983:42). See also Mani (1990a), Nandy (1975), and Teltscher (1995:37–72).

11. Different aspects of this debate are described in Murray (1974; 1976), Pederson (1991), and Lonsdale (1992: 388–397). Descriptions of Kikuyu initiation and contemporary women's attitudes can be found in Davison et al. (1989). Thomas discusses debates in nearby Meru, Kenya, and their connections with many other domains of life (1996; 1997).

12. For instance, several 1990s immigration cases and asylum claims in the United States have been based on arguments about the persecution of women through genital operations. Lydia Oluloro, a Nigerian woman, fought deportation on the grounds that she was protecting her daughters from the procedure. Her case was profiled in newspapers and on television in a segment of *Sixty Minutes* in 1994. A woman from Togo, Fauziya Kassindja, was also granted asylum in 1996, and a woman calling herself "Adelaide Abankwah" received asylum in the United States in 1999. Highly publicized cases in France in the 1990s prosecuted immigrant parents and ritual surgeons who continued the practice in their new country (Verdier 1992; Winter 1994). Kratz (2002) analyzes several asylum cases heard in the United States.

13. See for example Dawit (1997).

14. Actors and institutions involved in each arena might include the following. (1) *In each home country:* National governments and politicians' local NGOs and national action groups; international action groups; churches; religious and ethnic communities whose circumcising practice may differ and whose histories of education and involvement with government also differ. Within each circumcising community, differences of age, gender, education, religion, and wealth also influence positions. For instance, a Christian mother, her non-Christian husband, his educated brother, and their school-child daughter might disagree about whether the girl should participate with her friends in initiation ceremonies during a school holiday. Peters (1997:484–486) discusses the

different positions within the Togolese family and community in the asylum case of Fauziya Kassindja as an actual example. See Gruenbaum (1996:463–470) and the film *Bintou in Paris* for other examples. (2) *In the United States and Europe:* Female genital modification was historically recognized as a viable medical procedure in these countries, "cosmetic" labial surgery on women is currently performed, and male circumcision is also widely practiced. Current female genital operations within their borders are usually debated in relation to immigrant families and communities from various "home countries." Some families and communities have lived outside their home countries for quite a while, with some children born and raised in the United States and Europe. Actors involved in these debates include immigrants themselves (again with differences of gender, religion, ethnicity, education, length of residence, etc.); their community organizations and spokespersons; national, state, and municipal governments, judiciaries, and agencies dealing with immigrants (e.g., Immigration and Naturalization Service, Health and Human Services, child welfare services, etc.); national action groups and organizations concerned with women and children; and international action groups. (3) *In international campaigns:* These actors may also be engaged with those in "home countries" and in the United States or Europe, but they reach beyond national boundaries as well. They include international action groups based in various countries; the United Nations, World Health Organization, and related international agencies and NGOs; journalists; religious officials; national governments and politicians who seek conditionality clauses for foreign policy and provision of aid.

15. In many contexts, however, ritual meanings and patterns unite the two for practitioners, who often use a single word for both operations in local languages.

16. Fran Hosken may have coined the term, though I could not verify this. She certainly played a key role in popularizing it through the Women's International Network (WIN) newsletter she wrote. By the time she wrote the Hosken Report in 1979, *female genital mutilation* had become her standard term. Before 1975, she vacillated between that term and *female circumcision*. Mary Daly also used "genital mutilations" in her 1978 book. In the British parliamentary debates about Kenya, the word *mutilation* was used at times to distinguish between two different types of genital operations (infibulation was not at issue in this controversy), but it did not become the primary term of reference (Pederson 1991:666). The Church of Scotland Mission, however, did begin to use the term *sexual mutilation* (Pederson 1991:671).

17. There are striking parallels between these shifts in rhetoric and tactics and the rhetoric of radical anti-abortion organizations such as Operation Rescue.

18. Duggers eschewed the automatic condemnation of "mutilation," the medical implications of "surgery," and what she considered the "mildness" of "female circumcision" (Moses 1997:4).

19. A number of scholarly papers discuss the problems with these generalized images and show how they are constructed; Mohanty (1988) and Stephens (1989) are a good starting place. Alice Walker's books, *Possessing the Secret of Joy* and *Warrior Marks,* are commonly used as novelistic examples. Walker's representations of African women have also been discussed by a number of scholars; Obiora (1997:323–328) and Mugo (1997) are examples focused on their relation to controversies about female genital modification.

20. Information about campaigns against male genital operations is available from NOCIRC (National Organization of Circumcision Information Resource Centers) or NOHARMM (National Organization to Halt the Abuse and Routine Mutilation of Males). Both can be found through Web searches.

21. Examples of different body modifications illustrate the different kinds and contexts of "choice" involved in self-determination. Operations for breast reduction or enhancement, multiple ear piercings, and body piercings (including genital piercings) are modifications often presented by their American or European practitioners as ways to take control of one's body. These self-definitions are very much like local definitions of female genital operations in initiation, also seen as a sign of self-control, maturity, and both social and personal change. In both cases, the practices are linked to understandings of the body, aesthetics, sexuality, and gender relations, but the understandings are rather different, as are their social and institutional settings.

22. See Gruenbaum (1996:460–463) for further discussion of so-called false consciousness and the costs and benefits of female genital operations for various segments of Sudanese communities.

23. I have talked with many people in the United States who seek a "logical" explanation or rationale for traditions of female genital modification. When I summarize what Okiek in Kenya might say in response—e.g., that initiation is necessary for children to become adults—Americans have a hard time understanding and accepting these as "reasons." What for Okiek are logically satisfying, deeply felt, and natural understandings do not have for Americans the same intuitive sense and resonance. It is equally hard to answer Okiek questions about Americans, whom they sometimes encounter as tourists: Why do the women paint their mouths to look like they drink blood? Why do they walk about without clothing (e.g., in bathing suits)? Don't they feel shame? Why aren't girls initiated—how can they live their entire lives as children?

REFERENCES

Abusharaf, Rogaia Mustafa. 1999. Beyond "The External Messiah Syndrome": What Are Sudanese People Doing to End Ritualized Genital Surgeries? Paper presented at the Annual Meetings of the American Anthropological Association, Chicago. Session on Female Genital Cutting: Local Dynamics of a Global Debate.

An-Na`im, Abdullahi, ed. 1992. *Human Rights in Cross-Cultural Perspectives: A Quest for Consensus.* Philadelphia: University of Pennsylvania Press.

An-Na`im, Abdullahi, and Francis Deng, eds. 1990. *Human Rights in Africa: Cross-Cultural Perspectives.* Washington, DC: The Brookings Institution.

Apena, Adeline. 1996. Female Circumcision in Africa and the Problem of Cross-Cultural Perspectives. *Africa Update* 3(2): 7–8.

Berlin, Isaiah. 1991. *The Crooked Timber of Humanity.* New York: Alfred A. Knopf.

Boddy, Janice. 1989. *Wombs and Alien Spirits.* Madison: University of Wisconsin Press.

Boyarin, Daniel. 1992. "This We Know to Be Carnal Israel": Circumcision and the Erotic Life of God and Israel. *Critical Inquiry* 18(3): 474–505.

Courtright, Paul. 1994. The Iconographies of Sati. In *Sati, the Blessing and the Curse.* Ed. John S. Hawley. New York: Oxford University Press.

Daly, Mary. 1990. African Genital Mutilation: The Unspeakable Atrocities. In *Gyn/ecology.* Boston: Beacon Press (originally 1978).

Davison, Jean, with the women of Mutira. 1989. *Voices from Mutira: Lives of Rural Gikuyu Women.* Boulder: Lynn Rienner.

Dawit, Seble. 1997. Letter from a Female Circumcision Activist. *Colloquium: The On-line Magazine of the Case Western Reserve Law Review.* November 1997.

Desjarlais, Robert. 1997. *Shelter Blues: Sanity and Selfhood Among the Homeless.* Philadelphia: University of Pennsylvania Press.

Dussart, Françoise. 2000. *The Politics of Ritual in an Aboriginal Settlement: Kinship, Gender and the Currency of Knowledge.* Washington, DC: Smithsonian Institution Press.

Geertz, Clifford. 1983. Found in Translation: On the Social History of Moral Imagination. In *Local Knowledge.* New York: Basic Books.

Gruenbaum, Ellen. 1996. The Cultural Debate over Female Circumcision: The Sudanese Are Arguing This One Out for Themselves. *Medical Anthropology Quarterly* 10(4): 455–475.

Hernlund, Ylva. 1999. Ritual Negotiations and Cultural Compromise: An Alternative Initiation in the Gambia. Paper presented at the Annual Meetings of the American Anthropological Association, session on Female Genital Cutting: Local Dynamics of a Global Debate.

Holmes, Douglas R. 2000. *Integral Europe: Fast-Capitalism, Multiculturalism, Neofascism.* Princeton, NJ: Princeton University Press.

Hosken, Fran. 1979. *The Hosken Report.* Lexington, MA: Women's International Network News.

Hutchinson, Sharon. 1996. *Nuer Dilemmas.* Berkeley: University of California Press.

Iweriebor, Ifeyinwa. 1996. Brief Reflections on Clitoridectomy. *Africa Update* 3(2): 2.

Koso-Thomas, Olayinka. 1987. *The Circumcision of Women: A Strategy for Eradication.* London: Zed Books.

Kratz, Corinne. 1994. *Affecting Performance: Meaning, Movement, and Experience in Okiek Women's Initiation.* Washington, DC: Smithsonian Institution Press.

_____. 1999a. Contexts, Controversies, Dilemmas: Teaching Circumcision. In *Great Ideas for Teaching About Africa.* Eds. Misty Bastian and Jane Parpart. Boulder, CO: Lynne Rienner, pp. 103–118.

_____. 1999b. Female Circumcision in Africa. In *Africana: Encyclopedia of the African and African American Experience.* Eds. Kwame Anthony Appiah and Henry Louis Gates, Jr. New York: Perseus Publishing. Co-published with CD-ROM version by Microsoft.

_____. 2002. Circumcision Debates and Asylum Cases: Intersecting Arenas, Contested Values, and Tangled Webs. In *Engaging Cultural Differences: The Multicultural Challenge in Liberal Democracies.* Eds. Richard A. Shweder, Hazel R. Markus, and Martha Minow. New York: Russell Sage Foundation.

Laumann, E. O., C. M. Masi, and E. W. Zuckerman. 1997. Circumcision in the United States: Prevalence, Prophylactic Effects, and Sexual Practice. *Journal of the American Medical Association* 277(13): 1052–1057.

Leonard, Lori. 1999. "We Did It for Pleasure Only": Hearing Alternative Tales of Female Circumcision. Paper presented at the Annual Meetings of the American Anthropological Association, session on Female Genital Cutting: Local Dynamics of a Global Debate.

Lonsdale, John. 1992. Wealth, Poverty, and Civic Virtue in Kikuyu Political Thought. In B. Berman and J. Lonsdale, *Unhappy Valley: Conflict in Kenya and Africa.* London: James Currey.

Lyons, Harriet. 1981. Anthropologists, Moralities, and Relativities: The Problem of Genital Mutilations. *Canadian Review of Sociology and Anthropology* 18(4): 499–518.

Mani, Lata. 1990a. Contentious Traditions: The Debate on *Sati* in Colonial India. In *The Nature and Context of Minority Discourse.* Eds. A. JanMohamed and D. Lloyd. Oxford: Oxford University Press.

_____. 1990b. Multiple Mediations: Feminist Scholarship in the Age of Multinational Reception. *Feminist Review* 35: 24–40.

Matias, Aisha Samad. 1996. Female Circumcision in Africa. *Africa Update* 3(2): 3–6.

Mohanty, Chandra. 1988. Under Western Eyes: Feminist Scholarship and Colonial Discourses. *Feminist Review* 30: 61–88.

Morison, Linda, Caroline Scherf, Gloria Ekpo, et. al. 2001. The Long-term Reproductive Health Consequences of Female Genital Cutting in Rural Gambia: A Community-Based Survey. *Tropical Medicine and International Health* 6(8): 643–653.

Moses, Meredith. 1997. Watching the Watchdog: Female Circumcision in *The New York Times.* Student paper, Emory University.

Mugo, Micere. 1997. Elitist Anti-Circumcision Discourse as Mutilating and Anti-Feminist. *Case Western Reserve Law Review* 47(2): 461–480.

Murray, Jocelyn. 1974. The Kikuyu Female Circumcision Controversy, with Special Reference to the Church Missionary Society's "Sphere of Influence." Ph.D. dissertation, University of California, Los Angeles.

_____. 1976. The Church Missionary Society and the "Female Circumcision" Issue in Kenya, 1929–1932. *Journal of Religion in Africa* 8(2): 92–104.

Nandy, Ashis. 1975. Sati: A Nineteenth Century Tale of Women, Violence, and Protest. In *Rammohun Roy and the Process of Modernization in India.* Ed. V. C. Joshi. Delhi: Vikas Publishing House.

_____. 1988. The Human Factor. *The Illustrated Weekly of India,* 17 January, pp. 20–23.

Obiora, L. Amede. 1997. Bridges and Barricades: Rethinking Polemics and Intransigence in the Campaign Against Female Circumcision. *Case Western Reserve Law Review* 47(2): 275–378.

Ogbu, M. A. 1997. Comment on Obiora's "Bridges and Barricades." *Case Western Reserve Law Review* 47(2): 411–422.

Parker, Melissa. 1995. Rethinking Female Circumcision. *Africa* 65(4): 506–524.

Pederson, Susan. 1991. National Bodies, Unspeakable Acts: The Sexual Politics of Colonial Policymaking. *Journal of Modern History* 63: 647–680.

Peters, Pauline. 1997. Another Bridge to Cross: Between "Outside" and "Inside." *Case Western Reserve Law Review* 47(2): 481–490.

Rofel, Lisa. 1999. *Other Modernities: Gendered Yearnings in China After Socialism.* Berkeley: University of California Press.

Shell-Duncan, Bettina. 2001. The Medicalization of Female "Circumcision": Harm Reduction or Promotion of a Dangerous Practice? *Social Science and Medicine* 52: 1013–1028.

Shell-Duncan, Bettina, and Ylva Hernlund, eds. 2000. *Female "Circumcision" in Africa: Culture, Controversy and Change.* Boulder, CO: Lynne Rienner.

Shweder, Richard. 2002. What About Female Genital Mutilation? And Why Understanding Culture Matters in the First Place. In *Engaging Cultural Differences: The Multicultural Challenge in Liberal Democracies.* Eds. Richard A. Shweder, Hazel R. Markus, and Martha Minow. New York: Russell Sage Foundation.

Stephens, Julie. 1989. Feminist Fictions: A Critique of the Category "Non-Western Woman" in Feminist Writings on India. In *Subaltern Studies VI.* Ed. R. Guha. New York: Oxford University Press.

Teltscher, Kate. 1995. *India Inscribed: European and British Writing on India, 1600–1800.* Oxford: Oxford University Press.

Thomas, Lynn. 1996. "Ngaitana (I will circumcise myself)": The Gender and Generational Politics of the 1956 Ban on Clitoridectomy in Meru, Kenya. *Gender and History* 8(3): 338–363.

_____. 1997. Imperial Concerns and "Women's Affairs": State Efforts to Regulate Clitoridectomy and Eradicate Abortion in Meru, Kenya, c. 1920–1950. *Journal of African History.*

Verdier, Raymond. 1992. The *Exiseuse* in Criminal Court: the Trial of Soko Aramata Keita. *Passages* 3: 1–3 (originally in *Droit et Cultures: Revue semestrielle d'anthropologie et d'histoire,* 1991).

Winter, Bronwyn. 1994. Women, the Law, and Cultural Relativism in France: The Case of Excision. *Signs* 19(4): 939–974.

39

Conflict and Confluence in Advertising Meetings

Robert J. Morais

Not every anthropology student aspires to become a professor, nor do the majority of budding anthropologists dream of a career living and studying with people in remote corners of the world. Over the past twenty-five years, more than half of all new Anthropology PhDs have found employment in non-academic settings such as nonprofit organizations, government agencies, consulting firms, and multinational corporations such as Intel, Microsoft, Motorola, and Kodak.

Corporate anthropology applies methods and theories from cultural anthropology to reveal and decode consumer cultures. The pioneering anthropologist Bronislaw Malinowski encouraged future generations of social scientists to immerse themselves in their study populations to learn how to see culture from within. He advocated meticulous note-taking and participant observation as means to discover the difference between what people say versus what they actually do. Similarly, conventional market research may document what consumers say, but anthropological methods can see beyond that which consumers might tell marketers. As anthropologists have discovered, people often tell researchers what they think the researchers want to hear.

Reaching and understanding consumer cultures have become increasingly difficult for businesses as globalization creates access to new markets, and as technology fragments the mass media into countless specialized television networks, websites, and satellite radio stations. The complexity of modern business drives many executives and entrepreneurs to seek anthropological consultants to study consumer behavior, organizational theory, cross-cultural communication, and management strategies. In this selection, Robert Morais applies anthropological methods to analyze meetings between advertising agencies and their clients. Anthropology can help businesses reach consumers and develop successful new products, but it can also help business executives and account managers understand and improve their relationships with employees, clients, and each other.

As you read this selection, ask yourself the following questions:

- How do advertising meetings fit Van Genep's definition of a rite of passage?

- How does advertising reflect and shape culture?

- How do "creatives" differ from clients and account managers?

- In what ways do seating arrangements in advertising meetings reflect social hierarchies? What other ways are hierarchies performed in advertising meetings?

- Why do clients and account managers sometimes decide not to speak their true feelings? How do account managers read between the lines when clients say one thing but mean another?

The following terms discussed in this selection are included in the Glossary at the back of the book:

cultural validators	*liminal period*
rite of passage	*secret society*

INTRODUCTION

Advertising professionals have written widely on the creative development process (e.g., Della Femina 1970; Steel 1998); scholars have considered how advertising reflects and shapes culture (cf. Henry 1963; Lasch 1979; Schudson 1984; Sherry 1987); and, over the past two decades, there has been a burgeoning interest in the value of anthropology to marketing and advertising (Louis 1985; Miller 1990; Denny 1999; Sanders 2002;

Morais, Robert J. "Conflict and Confluence in Advertising Meetings." Reproduced with permission of the Society for Applied Anthropology (SfAA) from Human Organization 66 (2007), no. 2:151–159.

Wellner 2002; Wasserman 2003; Monari 2005; Murphy 2005; Ante 2006; Inglessis 2006). Ethnographic accounts of advertising agencies are less common. Notable examinations include Malefyt and Moeran's (2003) collection of essays, Moeran's (1996) study of a Japanese advertising agency, Miller's (1997) description of an agency in Trinidad, and Mazzarella's (2003) account of the relationship between the advertising industry and consumerism in India.

This paper focuses on a critical juncture in the creation of advertising: the meeting between the manufacturer (client) and the agency where advertising ideas are presented, discussed, and selected. I shall argue that these meetings contain the defining attitudes, behaviors, and symbols of the client–agency relationship and will offer an analysis that may help advance the understanding of meetings in other cultural contexts.

ADVERTISING IN PERSPECTIVE

Advertising is one component of a marketing mix that includes a wide range of programs designed to increase brand sales. Underhill (2000:32) argues that "while branding and traditional advertising build brand awareness and purchase predisposition, these factors do not always translate into sales." Yet U.S. manufacturers remain committed to advertising, spending $130 billion on it in 2005 alone (TNS Media Intelligence 2006). Given this level of investment, and the fact that consumers tend not even to recall most advertising one day after they are exposed to it (cf. Schudson 1984:3–4; Steel 1998:xi), companies devote considerable time and money to fielding the best advertising they can develop or risk a disappointing return on their investment. For this reason, most U.S. manufacturers that spend heavily on advertising employ agencies that specialize in the creation of ads rather than generate the ads themselves.

Advertising is a highly competitive industry in the United States; agency firings and account reassignments are common. As Malefyt (2003:139, 142–143) points out, a consequence of this volatility is that "the process of ad production . . . is one directed . . . not so much at the brand, consumer or even rival agencies, but towards the client." This behavior reflects Michell and Sander's (1995) finding that advertising development processes and interpersonal relationships have more influence on agency loyalty than the perceived quality of the creative work. Other studies have examined the roles of agency personnel who create advertising (Hirschman 1989; Young 2000)

and interaction across disciplines within agencies and with clients (Kover 1995; Kover and Goldberg 1995). Moeran (1996:79–87) concentrates on events surrounding a presentation in which an agency is competing to win an account (Johnson 2006). Miller's (1997:182–194) ethnography on the development of an advertising campaign in Trinidad could apply to virtually any advertising agency in the United States. This paper focuses sharply on creative meetings and considers the contrasting objectives, strategies, and tactics of the agency and client personnel who attend these meetings.

METHODOLOGY

In 1981, I left academic anthropology and became an advertising executive. For most of my advertising career I served in account management, later moving to strategic planning and research. In mid-2006, I joined a marketing research and consulting firm. After a quarter of a century of work in the field, this is my first report, supporting Reinharz's (1988:168) contention that "there are few published accounts of (going native) since those who have gone native cease to publish." This paper is based upon participation in thousands of creative meetings between 1981 and 2006 while employed at large and mid-sized American advertising agencies and aligns closely to what Sherry (2003:xii) terms "observant participation" and to Kemper's assertion that "advertising executives are ethnographers in the strict sense of the word" (Kemper 2003:35). Formal and informal discussions with numerous account management and creative colleagues and with marketing management clients expanded my perspective and validated my analysis. The formal interviews were conducted over several months; I have had informal conversations about advertising management throughout my advertising career. Most of the meetings my advertising and client colleagues and I observed involved work for food brands, over-the-counter and prescription pharmaceuticals, personal care items, and household cleaning products manufactured by companies ranging in size from multinational corporations to venture capital funded start-ups. The product categories are a limiting factor of this research because these manufacturers are generally creatively conservative. However, these marketers represent a substantial share of the businesses that advertising agencies serve. The names of the companies, informants, and brands have been withheld to preserve confidentiality.

THE MEETING DEFINED

The meeting as a focus of anthropological inquiry does not have a rich tradition; the most extensive attention paid to meetings by an anthropologist is Schwartzman's (1989) study on meetings in a mental health organization. Her definition of a meeting is a useful starting point. For Schwartzman (1989:7) a meeting is:

> A communicative event involving three or more people who agree to assemble for a purpose ostensibly related to the functioning of an organization or group, for example, to exchange ideas or opinions, to solve a problem, to make a decision, or negotiate an agreement, to develop policy and procedures, to formalize recommendations. . .a meeting is characterized by talk that is episodic in nature.

Because advertising creative meetings occur in a designated place, the agency's or client's conference room, for a discrete period of time, normally 60 to 90 minutes, they can be viewed analytically as frames (Goffman 1974; Moeran 2005:43–57). Moeran's (2005: 63–79) discussion of frames in a business context is useful for seeing creative meetings not only as a frame within agency life, but also as the key frame for interpreting and understanding agency/client relationships.

THE MEETING PARTICIPANTS

In creative meetings, agency attendees include account managers and the "creatives," or executives directly responsible for creating the advertising. Larger agencies might also include account planners (Malefyt 2003). Client participants are the marketing management employees of the manufacturing company that has hired the agency.

Advertising agency account managers represent the agency to the client, communicate client needs to the agency, and help ensure that agency departments get the work done on strategy, on time, and on budget. They are relationship managers, problem solvers, and communicators. They are more similar to the client than any other agency staffer. As one client said, they "dress and speak like us; they are more like us (than creative people)." Creatives are organized into copy writer–art director teams that develop the advertising ideas. A creative director, with experience in writing or art direction, supervises creative teams. In creative meetings, the creative director is the selling partner of the account team but argues from a creative rather than a business perspective, which is the function of account managers. Creatives are conceptual, imaginative people who invent, design, and produce "the work." They differ temperamentally and stylistically from their MBA-trained clients. Client marketing managers

conceive and execute the marketing plan for a brand. Their responsibilities include managing product development, quality control, product distribution to retailers, sales tracking, consumer promotions such as coupons, and developing advertising. In advertising creative meetings, clients are the gatekeepers for creative work and they must be convinced that the work merits exposure to consumers.

Advertising creative meetings involve the interaction of client and agency teams as two entities, as well as the interaction of members within teams. Hirschman (1989) speaks to both dimensions when, citing Turow (1984:21), she characterizes clients as patrons of the agency (Hirschman 1989:42–43) and then describes the roles of several participants in the creative development process. Miller, remarking on the tension between account managers and creatives in Trinidad, notes that creatives are "artists" and account managers are responsible for clients' "commercial concern" (Miller 1997:188). Even within creative teams, Young (2000) found that copy writers and art directors have different feelings about creative development. Across agency and client lines, within agencies, and, to a lesser extent, within client teams, contrasting responsibilities and attitudes have a major impact on the conduct and outcome of creative meetings.

GOALS: MUTUAL AND OTHERWISE

Agency and client personnel enter creative meetings to reach agreement on the work and advance the most promising creative ideas to the next step in the development process. Clients hope to manage a smooth process within specified time and production cost parameters. They also strive to showcase their professional skills to management. Clients are acutely aware that their comments during creative meetings are heard not only by the agency but also by their superiors, and clients believe that "looking smart" to both the agency and their superiors is critical. As one client said, "If you say what your boss agrees with and he says he agrees, the agency (as well as your boss) thinks you are smart." Agency personnel share the desire to move the process forward seamlessly. They know that the better the clients appear to their own management, the more loyal these clients will be to the agency. Agency staff enter the meeting with a strong desire to sell specific creative work that makes the agency team, and specific individuals within the agency team, look insightful and inventive.

The agency also has an agency-building agenda; imaginative creative work can help win new business. Additionally, creative work is often "pushed" by individuals who want to build their personal "reel" for future jobs. Most importantly, agencies must leave the

TABLE 1   Hierarchy of Agency and Client Goals

Agency	Client
Preserve the relationship	Look smart and capable
Enhance perception of the agency and one's self	Exhibit leadership and control over the meeting
Sell creative work that the agency will be proud to showcase	Manage the overall development process on a timely basis
Sell creative work in the fewest number of presentation rounds	Help develop creative work with which the entire marketing team is comfortable
Get high copy test scores	Get high copy test scores
Grow brand sales	Grow brand sales

meeting having preserved, and ideally enchanced, their relationship with the client. A smooth development process, high creative test scores, and positive business results are important. Exhibiting leadership and creativity, managing the meeting, accepting the final decision with grace, attaining camaraderie, and just "getting it" (i.e., understanding client personality and culture, listening carefully to client comments, and knowing client preferences) all contribute to the larger objective of a stronger agency–client bond and retention of the account. The hierarchy of goals in creative meetings depicted in Table 1 is based on observations and discussions with agency account managers and creatives and client marketing managers.

BEFORE THE MEETING

The creative development process may be initiated because brand sales are softening, the current advertising is reaching consumer exposure "wear out," a launch of a new product is planned, the agency has won a new account, or a client simply wants new creative work. The client or agency crafts a Creative Brief, the blueprint for creative development. Account managers work out a timetable for development, presentation, testing, and production of the creative work. They review the brief with the creative team, and, before the meeting, provide creatives with intelligence regarding the client's intellectual and temperamental terrain.

Creatives are given two to three weeks to develop ideas. Guided by the Brief, they develop concepts that will challenge their clients' comfort levels and ideas they are fairly sure the client will find acceptable. Conservative ideas carry special risks. As one creative director said, "I always give them something I know will sell, but I have to be careful because everything you put on the table is for sale." Account managers, eager to please the client, request safe work and negotiate with creative directors about which

work to present to a client. If a creative director insists on presenting a storyboard that the account manager believes is marginally related to the strategy, or "edgy," the account manager asks the creative team to present an execution that is "closer in" strategically or more conservative. Often the creative team and account manager strike a deal to offer both approaches. The body of work is reviewed first by the creative director, then with the account management team, and finally with agency management. Several rounds of internal agency meetings occur before creative work is presented to the client.

For this paper, I use a meeting that will culminate in a television commercial as the case in point. There is no standard number of television storyboards that are presented in a creative meeting, but a battery of five to eight ideas is typical. Agencies group storyboards into categories based on executional styles (e.g., realistic "slice of life" situations that are problem or solution oriented, celebrity presenters, demonstrations with competitive comparisons, an image driven idea, or a humorous situation). Sorting is also done according to variations on the strategy that emphasize particular understandings about the target consumer. For example, several advertisements for an over-the-counter wart remover might all be written to a "removes warts in one step" consumer promise while varying thematically. One underscores the time mothers save avoiding a visit to the doctor, another focuses on consumer trust of the brand, and still another connects with the embarrassment that people feel when they have warts. Sorting offers an opportunity for the agency to explain its thinking and demonstrate that no stone has been left unturned in the pursuit of creative ideas. Clients find categorization helpful for organizing and evaluating ideas.

When the work is reviewed in the agency's offices, or even while en route to the client's office, the agency team decides which storyboards to recommend. Many marketers field one or more rounds of advertising testing and usually only three to four storyboards will advance to testing; the remainder of the creative work presented is killed in the meeting. Some clients ask that the agency propose a single storyboard for production, which makes the agency recommendation process more difficult. During the internal agency meeting, an account manager may argue for a storyboard that compares a brand directly with a competitor because he or she believes that a senior client desires this approach. An art director–copy writer team may press for an idea that they want to produce for their own portfolios. The creative director may think his or her idea is the most persuasive or so imaginative that it will help the agency win new business. The decision regarding the agency recommendation is usually made jointly by the creative director and the most senior account manager. There will be a top choice, followed by two to three other options.

Meetings with existing clients rarely involve formal rehearsals. The sequence of the storyboard presentation is discussed before the meeting and account managers prepare their "set ups." Senior account managers may telephone their client counterparts to sell them on the quality of the work beforehand. When clients contemplate an upcoming creative meeting, they hope, as one client said, "that the agency has found the Holy Grail, that these guys will tell you how to sell a brand in a way that you have never seen." Agency professionals enter creative meetings with some trepidation. They understand the strategy, the consumer, and the client, but client response to creative work is unpredictable. Agency anxiety derives not only from the looming assessment of their work but also to the clients' impending judgment of the people who created it.

THE MEETING

The men and women who enter the conference room for a creative meeting exchange cordial remarks about family members or weekend activities to ease tension. Senior clients sit near the center of the table, directly across from the agency presenters, and client subordinates take seats on the same side of the table as their bosses. Agency presenters occupy the center positions, directly across from the clients. More senior advertising agency staff often sit to the extreme right or left of center. The meeting, often referred to as a "copy meeting," begins formally when an account manager delivers the "set up," including the meeting objective, which is to review the advertising. The account manager then outlines the anticipated plan for the new creative work. This could include replacing weak advertising, refreshing a successful campaign,

or exploring advertising that may succeed current advertising after testing among consumers. The outcome of the meeting is expressed: "When we are in agreement about the strongest approaches, we will conduct focus groups, then field quantitative testing, then place the advertising in a test market, and, if the market test is successful, we will air the new creative nationally." After completing the meeting objectives, an account manager or account planner reads the Creative Brief. The Brief commonly includes:

1. the objective of the advertising;
2. a description of the target market segment to whom the advertising must appeal;
3. insights or observations about the target consumer based on research;
4. the positioning or basic selling proposition for the brand that sets it apart from competition;
5. the core promise that the advertising must make to the consumer to compel purchase;
6. support for the promise that provides to the consumer a reason to believe the promise made;
7. a statement on the tonality of the advertising; and
8. mandatories, or items that must be included in the advertising.

The set up for the meeting conveys that the agency understands the business context, reminds attendees of the strategic blueprint on which the creative work is based, and sets up client expectations by framing the creative work. After the set up is completed, the creative director explains how the creative team undertook the assignment and "explored a wide range of approaches." Creative teams responsible for each idea then expose their ideas to the client. Presenters begin with an explanation of the thinking that took the team from the Creative Brief to the creative execution. For example, a commercial for a nutritional brand might be inspired by an insight that people over 50 want to stay healthy to continue to do the things they have always enjoyed. Creatives often use client buzz words. As one associate creative director said, "When you use their language. . . phrases like 'good recall device'. . . it puts them at ease." The art director describes each storyboard frame, then the copy writer reads the copy. Storyboards are presented one by one in this manner until all of them are exposed. As the storyboards are presented, clients jot down notes based on a mental checklist that makes evaluation of creative work more systematic. Client criteria typically include:

1. Their gut reaction—do they like the idea?
2. Is it consistent with objectives?
3. Is it on strategy?

4. Does it connect with the target consumer?

5. Is it clear?

6. Is it distinctive to the brand?

7. Will it cut through the clutter of other advertisements?

8. Is it competitive?

9. Does it reflect the character of the brand?

10. Is it extendable to a long-term campaign?

11. Are the claims and graphics supportable scientifically and/or legally?

After all of the creative work has been presented, the creative director or a senior account manager summarizes the ideas, groups them into categories, and discusses the storyboards the agency feels have the greatest merit. Agencies never disparage any of the work they present—"We love all of our children equally"— but most clients use the agency recommendation as guidance for their own evaluation, although some clients ignore it. In either case, an agency recommendation provides perspective on the relative strength of the ideas and gives clients time to reflect on the work they have been shown. The agency team has lived with the creative work from inception through several rounds of discussion. As one account manager said, "The agency is intimate with the work. The client is not."

After the agency recommendation has been made, clients offer their reactions to the work. Junior client personnel usually speak first followed by coworkers in ascending rank. Junior staff voice thoughts that correspond to their mental checklist. Senior clients provide more expansive remarks on the fit of the advertising with overall brand business objectives, but even company presidents might comment on a turn of phrase or a product demonstration. During this appraisal, at least one client will express appreciation for the range of thinking and the effort that the agency has expended. This statement is intended to set a positive tone for the ensuing critical comments. Agency professionals know it is mere civility. Some clients prefer to reflect on the creative work, listen to a colleague's comments, and speak only if they have something significant to add, but junior and midlevel clients feel pressure to make cogent remarks. As one client noted, "If you have nothing to contribute, you don't belong in the meeting." A client's career development goals are well served by displaying a grasp of creative concepts and an ability to identify the ideas that have the most potential to grow a brand.

When viewing an array of creative ideas, clients will rarely say, "None of this works; go back to the drawing board." Instead, they declare, "This is an interesting range of ideas," which is code for, "I don't like anything you have shown me." Even when clients reject a storyboard, they may select a phrase or graphic that they encourage the agency to include in the next round of creative development. When clients are responding unfavorably, the hearts of creatives sink, but agency professionals know they must respond to the critique. Not every client comment is addressed. Agencies pay most attention to, as one client phrased it, "the biggest paycheck." Another client said, "Pencils are raised when the senior VP talks." Comments by junior clients are heard, but acted upon only if the most senior client present concurs. When all of the clients have responded, the agency expresses its appreciation for their remarks without appearing sycophantic, answers questions that the client has raised, and challenges criticisms tactfully. The agency recommendation is defended with a balance of conviction and conciliation; the agency must convey that it has a well-reasoned point of view while making it clear that it is receptive to the clients' viewpoint. Agencies differ in how resolute they will be in their defense of creative work. An agency that recommends storyboards A, B, and C over D, E, and F may be told by the senior client that only E is acceptable and another round of creative development is required. Some agencies acquiesce immediately or, in agency parlance, "roll over." Other agencies "push back" until they have convinced the client to accept their argument or they have exhausted all hope that the client can be dissuaded from its own position.

Experienced account managers know the difference between what clients say and what they mean. When a client asks, "Why did you choose that particular graphic?" it is code for "I dislike the graphic." The question format avoids direct conflict. The agency must decide to "fight" for the idea or explain why it chose it and offer to consider alternatives. Account managers, generally more conciliatory than creatives, feel that, as one account manager said, "Creatives would be better off listening and ferreting out the real issues," rather than leaping to the defense of their work.

Senior agency executives feel pressure to sell their work to clients. They may believe in the quality of the creative, but they also want to avoid endless rounds of redevelopment. Account managers take the lead in selling an idea; in addition to their persuasive skills and knowledge of the client's temperament and culture, their personal relationship with a client can help win the agency's case (cf. Moeran 1996: 39–68). As they listen to client comments, agency executives consider the source and formulate their response. Does this client want to look smart in front of the boss? Is that client afraid of championing an idea that is outside the threshold of corporate risk? Does he not understand the idea? Does he simply not like it? If a client states that an image campaign is too ethereal and contends that a "slice-of-life" approach would be stronger, and the account manager or creative director knows that this comment is driven by a desire to increase sales quickly with "comfortable" (low risk) creative work, the manager might say, "An image campaign is what our brand needs. If we go this way, we'll be more competitive than ever." Experienced account managers know to stop selling when clients express in tone or intensity that they are closed to further discussion. Moreover, the agency must know how to withdraw gracefully. The client must not be made to feel like a bully; if clients sense that the agency team is beaten down they may request another team within the agency or, worse, consider a new agency. As one creative director phrased it, "A good general knows when to retreat and still retain dignity. You need to be looking to the next meeting, how you will come out in a good position to do better next time." One senior account manager estimated that "You can push clients 10 to 20 percent from where they are, but you will never move them more than 50 percent." When agencies push too hard, frustrated clients may dismiss them because they feel the agency does not understand what they want.

After clients make critical comments, they provide direction to the agency for the next round of creative development. A client will ask that copy be clarified or a product demonstration be simplified. Clear direction is critical. When a client says "I just don't think that tag line works," the agency is not certain what will please the client. When a client says, "I'd like to see a tag line that expresses our brand's superiority over the competition," the agency can craft copy that will be more acceptable in the next round of creative work.

When all of the comments and responses have been voiced, an agency account manager summarizes the agreements reached and the actions that will be taken following the meeting ("Next Steps") along with the timetable for accomplishing them. The happiest outcome for agency and client is to advance the process to focus group assessment or production. A requirement by the client for new creative work or substantial revisions stalls progress. When the former result is achieved, participants congratulate one another and say, "good meeting." Meetings that close without progress are disappointing, but euphemistic phrases such as "Productive meeting" or "We're moving ahead" help mitigate disappointment. Even a "good meeting" may not be good for everyone. Creatives might feel the most conservative work was sold or individual participants may fear they have

performed poorly. A meeting succeeds on all fronts when the agency and client concur that the best work was chosen, clients feel they have been listened to, and the agency feels that it, too, has been heard. Everyone smiles and departs knowing that they did their job well. A good meeting means that the agency–client relationship has been preserved and very likely strengthened. When a meeting fails to achieve its stated objectives, agency account managers know that they must telephone their client and reassure them that the next round of work will be better.

AFTER THE MEETING

Minutes after a creative meeting adjourns and the client and agency teams separate, postmortems begin. Clients usually move on quickly to their next task, although there may be a brief conversation about their delight or disappointment in the agency's work. The agency team engages in a more extensive assessment of the meeting, often replaying specific client comments and agency responses. Many account managers feel that an unsatisfactory creative meeting undermines their credibility with the client who may wonder if, as one account manager said, "I have communicated to the creative team what is in the client's head." Creatives must overcome personal demoralization when clients have requested significant changes in their work. As a creative director said, "The advertising will get worse with changes and changes and rewrites and rewrites." One copy writer noted that sometimes "you come back after a meeting and blow off steam. You can't just sit down and start over again until you have done that." After sufficient discussion, account managers review the actions required for the next step in the creative process with the agency team.

UNDERSTANDING CREATIVE MEETINGS: STRUCTURE, SENTIMENT, AND MEETING MANAGEMENT

Despite options like on-line viewing and conference calls, face-to-face advertising creative meetings occur because they allow direct interaction that connects people emotionally as well as intellectually. For agency professionals, creative meetings are ideal venues to sell creative work and enhance client relationships, enabling agencies to better gauge reactions, negotiate with clients, and showcase themselves personally. For clients, the conference room setting is a superior opportunity for personal performance and professional camaraderie. In face-to-face creative meetings, clients can also demonstrate vividly the power and control they have over their agencies.

STATUS AND ROLE

When senior agency executives select flanker positions to the far left or right of the center of the conference table they do so to stress their separateness from other agency staff and to occupy a perch from which to offer commentary during the creative meeting. Their distance from the fray carries other symbolism; it is a vantage point from which they can make the "big picture" statements that demonstrate a mastery of the full business context of the creative work. Seating is also important for agency managers to assess and respond to client reactions, which is why they place themselves within the direct sight line of senior clients.

The sequence and content of client commentary reflect the status and role of the speaker (see Schwartzman 1989:291–293 on social position and speaking sequences in meetings). The lower the status, the earlier one speaks and the more circumspect the comments. Higher-status clients offer their thoughts after lower level managers, giving them the dual advantage of having heard what their colleagues said and additional time to reflect on the creative work.

RULES OF ENGAGEMENT

The agency team is a kind of secret society (Goffman 1959:104) with unwritten rules of engagement in the presence of those outside the society (Meerwarth, Briody, and Devadatta 2005). Internally, as Hirschman (1989:51) observes, "conflict, mutual distrust and power struggles are inherent in the advertising process, but the agency must show a 'united front' to the client" (Kover and Goldberg 1995:55). One of the more egregious sins occurs when an agency representative deviates from the previously agreed upon agency position during a creative meeting. When this agreement is violated, the consequences can be severe. Reprimands of subordinates who diverge from the agency's recommendation are common; cautionary tales tell of employees who transgressed being fired on the return airplane flight after a client meeting. Clients are under less pressure to express a uniform point of view, but most client cultures encourage consensus, and clients know that moving creative work forward requires agreement on the direction they provide to the agency.

READING THE ROOM

Just before a creative meeting, a well-known advertising executive was asked by one of his agency associates what he recommended. His reply: "Read the room." His meaning: assess client reactions as ideas are presented and adjust the agency recommendation to match the ideas that the client will accept. During creative meetings, agency executives do not watch their colleagues present; they watch their clients. They scan faces for confusion, comprehension, and delight. They study eyes and body language. They pay attention to how many notes clients are taking and they watch for client reactions to specific graphics and copy. When the agency summarizes the body of work, when clients comment, when the agency responds and the client counters, agency executives read the room.

Reading the room helps the agency control creative meetings. When a client is perceived as unreceptive to an agency recommendation, an agency executive formulates a defense that shows cognizance of the client's discomfort: "The idea in this board is totally new in this category. It will startle the consumer and it will cut through the clutter of competitive advertising. This approach may make us a bit uncomfortable but it is precisely the kind of advertising the brand needs right now." If the executive senses that the favored board is being judged extremely poorly and even a strong argument will not persuade the client, the executive will cast a glance at colleagues and soften the agency recommendation: "The idea in this board is totally new in this category. It will startle the consumer and it will cut through the clutter of competitive advertising. But, because it is so cutting edge, we should test it among consumers to see if we have gone too far."

One agency creative director described how he visualizes a conference room swaying as arguments veer side to side. He prepares his arguments and chooses a position based on where the room "lands." He may agree or disagree with the prevailing client point of view, but he will choose his statements carefully to ensure that the meeting does not become contentious. The process of reading the room is like comprehending the difference between a wink and a blink (Geertz 1973:6–7). It requires contextual understanding: knowing the psychology of the participants, the strength of the creative work, the corporate cultures, and the relationships of the meeting attendees. The power and accuracy of an individual manager's intuition, of knowing by seeing and listening, is critical.

DEFENDING THE WORK

Clients may criticize creative work because they believe it is off strategy, it fails their checklist of acceptable advertising, or it is inconsistent with "what we know works." A major issue for creative personnel is how to best protect the integrity of their idea when clients feel, as an associate creative director said, that "challenging their beliefs is like challenging their religion." Kover and Goldberg (1995:56–59) describe several strategies that copy writers use to argue for their work, all of which are also applied by art directors and account managers. These tactics include: 1) selling with passion; 2) a frontal attack, which is effective when clients seek highly creative work; 3) creating work that is likely to sell, a risky proposition, as noted earlier; 4) offering the appearance of acceptance, then doing what they wish, which may be effective with small revisions but is not viable when the issue is whether an idea should even be produced; and 5) the "aleatory game," which entails hoping for the best outcome. Experienced agency account managers lower rising temperatures in creative meetings by intervening with phases such as, "That's a good thought. We'll consider that." Agency colleagues and clients depend upon account managers to control meetings; account managers know that an adroit defense of creative work and the ability to defuse difficult situations is a measure of their value.

Although clients often claim they want breakthrough advertising, most clients are nervous that "edgy" creative work will violate the character of their brand, unless the brand character is, by definition, "edgy." Moreover, many creatives feel that clients often "don't get it" when particularly inventive executions are presented, a reaction that Schudson (1984:81) terms "aesthetic insensitivity." Clients' lack of understanding of a creative idea is demonstrated by the common client practice of expressing a wish that selected copy or graphics used in one storyboard also be used in other storyboards. Similarly, when a client feels that an execution has too much humor, the client may ask the agency to "dial it back." As one creative said, "When they change the board, they pull out the one thread that holds it together." Clients' desire for a recitation of a brand's features, attributes, and benefits can snuff out a creative idea. As a creative director said, "The idea gets whittled away by the client's checklist." Clients believe that they own the creative work. When they want changes, the agency should, after discussion, agree to make them. Creatives feel that they, as the inventors of the idea, own it (Hirschman 1989; Kover and Goldberg 1995; Young

2000), which adds tension to creative meetings. As Kover (1995:604) writes, "Copy writers have a 'reputation' in the folklore of the advertising business. They are charged with defending their work and its integrity against any charge, no matter how small." Kover's explanation for this behavior is that "Copy writers do not merely present advertising, they present *themselves*." (Kover 1995:604, emphasis in original). He notes that copy writers speak about their work as if it is "a piece carved from their private being" (ibid.) and Kover and Goldberg (1995:53) remark on the "resentment" that creatives feel when clients alter their work.

How aggressively creatives and account managers defend creative work is contingent upon agency and client cultures. Many clients see challenges to their criticisms as evidence of agency conviction, and they respond positively, as long as the defense is respectful and cordial. Seeing an agency "roll over" when a storyboard is criticized suggests that the agency has little heart for the work, and the client may wonder why the agency presented it. When the agency fights too long and hard, clients become annoyed. Clients also know when agency executives claim, "I agree with everything you have said," they are about to disagree and prolong a discussion. In such situations, clients anticipate that after the meeting they will have a conversation with a senior account manager who will "fix it." If the account manager cannot deliver what the client wants, then that manager risks replacement by one who will. When the choice is between fighting the good fight for the creative work and protecting the agency–client relationship, the latter is the necessary course. Agency executives understand that advertising may be at the intersection of commerce and art, but commerce is the main drag, and clients control the road.

AGREEMENTS

Agreements are the actions that will be taken to revise, test, or produce creative work after a meeting. The word agreement has an egalitarian and conciliatory connotation; it also implies that the client and agency concur on what needs to be done. However, to *agree* does not always mean to be *in agreement*. The recitation of agreements in creative meetings is, in fact, a recitation of client directives. The word agreement fuels the illusion that the client and agency are peers and it smoothes over disagreements that may have occurred during the meetings, but there is no mistake that the clients are in charge.

IMPRESSION MANAGEMENT AND IMPRESSING MANAGEMENT

Presentations by agencies in creative meetings are performances according to Goffman's definition: "all the activity of a given participant on a given occasion which serves to influence in any way the other participants" (Goffman 1959:15) and are "social dramas" (Turner 1974, 1986). As a creative director said, "The spotlight is on you. You have the chance to convince someone that something you have created is worth the world seeing." A central tenet of Goffman's analysis, impression management, is evident throughout creative meetings. Agencies attempt to impress clients with an understanding of the client's business, their devotion to the brand, and their passion for the creative work. An expression of passion can persuade clients that creative work is worthy of acceptance. As a creative director phrased it, "Passion can be contagious." Meeting participants also aim to impress management. Junior clients want to demonstrate to bosses that they are managing the creative development process effectively and, since they know their judgments are being judged, that they bring their share of insights to the meeting. When creative work is received poorly and no progress is made, a midlevel client can "die inside because it makes my life worse. The process is stalled and I'll get slammed." Junior agency personnel want to impress senior staff as well, and all of the agency presenters must impress their clients.

RITES OF PASSAGE

Creative meetings are a rite of passage as classically defined by Van Gennep (1960; Mocran 1996:94). Creative work is separated from its development while in storyboard form; selected ideas are transformed during the meeting by suggested revisions and then returned to the development process for consumer assessment or airing. Creative meetings are the liminal period (Van Gennep 1960:21), "betwixt and between" (Turner 1964; Malefyt 2003:145; Sherry 2005:72–74), during which the transformation occurs. The successful transition of a storyboard from preclient exposure to initiation as a "client approved board" is hailed with as much jubilation as other rites of passage throughout the world. Meeting participants are transformed as well. It is not only the storyboard that is evaluated in creative meetings, it is also the people who created or contributed to the work. Extending the argument from Geertz (1973) that cocks symbolize men and Kover

(1995) that storyboards represent copy writers, all of the agency and client personnel who display their imagination, intellect, experience, and professionalism in a creative meeting are as exposed and judged as the advertising ideas. In this sense, approval or disapproval of a body of work and the achievement of goals in creative meetings is not just business. It is personal.

CONCLUSION

Creative meetings are, as Schwartzman notes of all meetings, "sense makers" that help participants "define, represent, and also reproduce social entities and relationships" (Schwartzman 1989:39) and they function as "social and cultural validators" that enhance a sense of community and identity within an organization (Schwartzman 1989:41). Moeran observed this phenomenon in a Japanese advertising agency when he noted that meetings are "frames in which participants made sense of their organization and their actions taken therein" (Moeran 2005:14). Sense-making modes in creative meetings include the comprehension of verbal codes that mollify tense situations, the reading of verbal and nonverbal behavior, the understanding of the subtle machinations surrounding the client–agency balance of power, and the craft of negotiation. Miller (1990), writing about an agency in Trinidad, agrees with Moeran, writing about an agency in Japan, that presentations "define and maintain the advertising community as a whole" (Moeran 1993:88). Schwartzman contends that meetings are organization life "writ small" (Schwartzman 1989:39). Similarly, creative meetings contain the essence of client–agency relationships: conflicting objectives, displays of status, opportunities to show supreme insight, to control without appearing controlling, to demonstrate passion without being combative, to persuade without browbeating, and to accept without embracing. Agencies work hard to preserve creative integrity, but preservation of the client–agency relationship is paramount, for without the relationship, there is no creative presentation.

Despite the conflicts in creative meetings, the confluence of professional and personal objectives makes these meetings a powerful mechanism of action in the advertising industry. They function because they provide a venue for commercial ideas to be challenged and often made stronger, and for participants to achieve goals that secure their positions and advance their careers. In creative development, the agency's desire for art shaped by the demands of commerce meets the clients' need for commerce clothed in seductive art.

During creative meetings, the often dazzling fusion of business goals and creativity, and of divergent organizational, attitudinal, and temperamental styles, converge. Some advertising agency executives say, "It's all about the work." Others view their business cynically, as the management of client–agency relationships. Both are correct. The work of the agency is the creative product and the creative meeting itself.

REFERENCES

Ante, Spencer E. 2006. The Science of Desire. *BusinessWeek*, June 6: 99–106.

Della Femina, Jerry. 1970. *From Those Wonderful Folks Who Gave You Pearl Harbor: Front-line Dispatches from the Advertising War*, ed. Charles Sopkin. New York: Simon and Schuster.

Denny, Rita. 1999. Consuming Values: *The Culture of Clients, Researchers and Consumers*. In *The Race for Innovation*, 375–384. Amsterdam: ESOMAR.

Geertz, Clifford. 1973. *The Interpretation of Cultures*. New York: Basic Books.

Goffman, Erving. 1959. *The Presentation of Self in Everyday Life*. New York: Doubleday.

_____. 1974. *Frame Analysis*. Cambridge, Mass.: Harvard University Press.

Henry, Jules. 1963. *Culture Against Man*. New York: Random House.

Hirschman, Elizabeth C. 1989. Role-Based Models of Advertising Creative and Production. *Journal of Advertising* 18(4): 42–53.

Inglessis, Maria Garcia. 2006. For Marketers or Scholars? *Quirk's Marketing Research Review*, December: 58–62.

Johnson, Steve. 2006. The Rational and Emotional "Tells" to Get the Most from Agency Presentations. *Product Management Today*. January: 26–27.

Kemper, Steven. 2003. How Advertising Makes its Object. In *Advertising Cultures*, eds. Timothy Dewaal Malefyt and Brian Moeran, 35–54. Oxford and New York: Berg.

Kover, Arthur J. 1995. Copywriters' Implicit Theories of Communications: An Exploration. *Journal of Consumer Research* 21: 596–611.

Kover, Arthur J. and Stephen M. Goldberg. 1995. The Games Copywriters Play: Conflict, Quasi-Control, a New Proposal. *Journal of Advertising Research*, July/August: 52–62.

Lasch, Christopher. 1979. *The Culture of Narcissism*. New York: W. W. Norton & Company.

Louis J. C. 1985. It's Anthropological: Research Takes a "Cultural" Bent. *Advertising Age*, January 14: 3:31.

Malefyt, Timothy Dewaal. 2003. Models, Metaphors and Client Relations: The Negotiated Meanings of Advertising. In *Advertising Cultures*, eds. Timothy Dewaal Malefyt and Brian Moeran, 139–163. New York: Berg.

Malefyt, Timothy Dewaal, and Brian Moeran, eds. 2003. *Advertising Cultures*. New York: Berg.

Mazzarella, William T.S. 2003. *Shoveling Smoke: Advertising and Globalization in Contemporary India*. Durham, N.C.: Duke University Press.

Meerwarth, Tracy L., Elizabeth K. Briody, and Devadatta M. Kulkarni. 2005. Discovering the Rules: Folk Knowledge for Improving GM Partnerships. *Human Organization*. 64: 286–302.

Michell, Paul C. N., and Nicholas H. Sanders. 1995. Loyalty in Agency–Client Relations: The Impact of the Organizational Context. *Journal of Advertising Research*, March/April: 9–14.

Miller, Annetta. 1990. You Are What You Buy. *Newsweek*, June 4: 59.

Miller, Daniel. 1997. *Capitalism: An Ethnographic Approach*. New York: Berg.

_____. 2003. Advertising, Production and Consumption as Cultural Economy. In *Advertising Cultures*, eds. Timothy Dewaal Malefyt and Brian Moeran, 75–89. Oxford and New York: Berg.

Moeran, Brian. 1993. A Tournament of Value: Strategies of Presentation in Japanese Advertising. *Ethnos* 54: 73–93.

_____. 1996. *A Japanese Advertising Agency*. Honolulu: University of Hawaii Press.

_____. 2005. *The Business of Ethnography: Strategic Exchanges, People and Organizations*. New York: Berg.

Monari, Gina-Louise. 2005. Anthropology: Not Just for Academia. *MedAdNews*, August: 1, 28.

Murphy, Richard McGill. 2005. Getting to Know You. *Fortune Small Business*, June: 41–46.

Reinharz, Shulamit. 1988. *On Becoming a Social Scientist*. Piscataway, N.J: Transaction Books.

Sanders, Elizabeth. 2002. How "Applied Ethnography" Can Improve Your NPD Research Process. *PDMA Visions* 26(2): 8–11.

Schudson, Michael. 1984. Advertising, *The Uneasy Persuasion*. New York: Basic Books.

Schwartzman, Helen. 1989. *The Meeting*. New York: Plenum Press.

Sherry, John. 1987. Advertising as a Cultural System. In *Marketing and Semiotics: New Directions in the Study of Signs for Salc*, ed. Jean Umiker-Sebeok, 441–461. Berlin: Mouton de Gruyter.

_____. 2003. Foreword: A Word from Our Sponsor—Anthropology. In *Advertising Cultures*, eds. Timothy Dewaal Malefyt and Brian Moeran, xi–xiii. New York: Berg.

_____. 2005. We Might Never Be Post-Sacred: A Tribute to Russell Belk on the Occasion of His Acceptance of the Converse Award. In 16th Paul D. Converse Symposium, eds. Abbie Griffin and Cele C. Otnes, 67–77. Chicago: American Marketing Association.

Steel, Jon. 1998. *Truth, Lies, and Advertising.* New York: John Wiley & Sons.

TNS Media Intelligence, February 2006. (Industry Report)

Turner, Victor W. 1964. *Betwixt and Between: The Liminal Period in Rites de Passage.* The Proceedings of the American Ethnological Society, Symposium on New Approaches to the Study of Religion. Pp. 4–20. Washington, D.C.: U.S. Government Printing Office.

_____. 1974. *Dramas, Fields and Metaphors.* Ithaca, N.Y.: Cornell University Press.

_____. 1986. *The Anthropology of Performance.* New York: PAJ Publications.

Turow, Joseph. 1984. *Media Industries: The Production of News and Entertainment.* New York: Longman.

Underhill, Paco. 2000. *Why We Buy.* New York: Touchstone.

Van Gennep, Arnold. 1960. *The Rites of Passage.* Chicago: University of Chicago Press.

Wasserman, Todd. 2003. Watch and Learn. *Adweek,* November 3: 21–22.

Wellner, Alison Stein. 2002. Watch Me Now. *American Demographics,* October: S1–S5.

Young, Charles E. 2000. Creative Differences Between Copy Writers and Art Directors. *Journal of Advertising Research,* May/June: 19–26.

40

Coming of Age in Palo Alto

Katie Hafner

When people imagine anthropologists and anthropological work, they often envision the lone anthropologist living in a grass-roofed hut in the high mountains of New Guinea or in a canvas tent only a stone's throw away from an exciting archaeological dig. These images are not exactly wrong: Anthropologists are still doing such fieldwork in remote places, and such "exotic" work is still necessary for furthering our understanding of humankind. On the other hand, those images are quite incomplete, since many anthropologists work closer to home. Twenty-first-century anthropology encompasses an exceptionally broad range of topics and research settings. Anthropologists are applying the theories and research methods honed in the Australian outback or the Kalahari Desert to modern settings, lending new and innovative insights and creating novel solutions.

When anthropologists describe the continuing processes of culture change, they often begin with an analysis of patterns of technological innovation. So-called traditional societies are sometimes using ancient technologies. In the past two decades, no technological development has been more revolutionary than the Internet; today, it is a technology that we take for granted.

This article profiles several anthropologists who conduct observational research on the social aspects of modern technology and how it is used in people's everyday lives. The title refers both to Margaret Mead's classic anthropological study *Coming of Age in Samoa* and to Palo Alto, California, a part of the famed Silicon Valley and home to numerous successful high-tech companies. The effectiveness of the new technologies from Silicon Valley depends on their acceptability to consumers, so these anthropologists look at consumers in the "natural habitat" of their homes and offices. The anthropologists profiled here work at places like AT&T Labs, Intel, and Media One, using their anthropological training to improve technological products. The concepts and methods of anthropology can be easily applied to both product development and marketing studies for business.

As you read this selection, ask yourself the following questions:

- What does the author mean by "embodied knowledge?"
- How do these observational studies compare with aspects of ethnographic field research?
- How do the anthropologists in this article combine observational studies with ethnographic field research?
- When an anthropologist is employed by a company like Media One, is she or he still doing anthropology?

The following terms discussed in this selection are included in the Glossary at the back of the book:

> *embodied knowledge*
> *ethnography*
> *observational research*

In 1981, while doing postdoctoral field work in cultural anthropology, Bonnie A. Nardi lived with villagers in Western Samoa, trying to understand the cultural reasons that people there have an average of eight children.

Today Dr. Nardi works at AT&T Labs West in Menlo Park, Calif., and has no regrets. She left academia in 1984 and is considered a pioneer among anthropologists who are employed by high-tech companies to examine consumers' behavior in their homes and offices.

"Usually people say, 'What is an anthropologist doing here?'" Dr. Nardi said. "But when I explain that I study how people use technology in order to get new ideas for products and services, it instantly makes sense."

No longer do companies study consumers' psyches only by asking people what they think about technology and how they use it. Now they conduct observational research, dispatching anthropologists to employ their ethnographic skills by interviewing, watching and videotaping consumers in their natural habitats. In the past several years, companies like Apple, Motorola, Xerox, and Intel, as well as telecommunications and cable companies, have brought anthropologists into the corporate fold. The goal is to apply what the anthropologists learn to new product concepts. "It's the extreme form of understanding the customer," Dr. Nardi said.

Half of all anthropologists with doctorates are going to work outside universities, said Susan Squires, president-elect of the National Association for the Practice of Anthropology, which represents anthropologists outside academia. High competitive pressure and short product cycles mean that corporate fieldwork is usually much briefer than academic research and fewer people are studied. While the work might not be considered reliable enough to be published in a traditional anthropology journal, companies can use the results to help them make marketing and product-design decisions.

Observational research isn't new for American industry. It can be traced to the 1930s and 1940s, when social scientists began examining productivity during the Depression and World War II, said Marietta Baba, chairwoman of the anthropology department at Wayne State University in Detroit. "They left industry completely in the 60s and 70s," Dr. Baba said. "They came back in the 80s and there has been a slow, steady increase since then." The rise in corporate employment for anthropologists has roughly paralleled a drop in academic opportunities. Hallmark Cards has an anthropologist. The automotive industry employs at least a dozen, and so does Andersen Consulting.

But it is in the high-tech arena, with intense pressure and high rate of product failures, that studying consumers' habits at very close range is currently most popular, Dr. Squires said.

"We go out into the consumer space, into people's homes—we go to where the people are," said Tony Salvador, an experimental psychologist at Intel, where he is called a design ethnographer. "If we're interested in their homes, we go there. If we're interested in what they do on vacation, we go on vacation with them."

Sometimes an ethnographic inquiry will lead to new ways to use an existing technology or will generate new technologies. It was a 1996 study of pager use in rural China, where there is a scarcity of phones, that prompted Motorola to start thinking seriously about two-way paging outside urban markets, said Jean Canavan, an anthropologist who is the manager of culture and technology initiatives at Motorola.

"The context is really critical," Ms. Canavan said. "If we want to develop technologies that really fit into the way people live their day-to-day lives, then we have to understand how people really live."

Many anthropologists work with a concept called embodied knowledge—tacit, nonscientific knowledge—and look for ways to incorporate such information into product design. Embodied knowledge is "basically the intelligence in your muscles," Dr. Nardi said.

"You aren't born knowing how to ride a bicycle," Dr. Baba said. "You don't learn by reading a book. With experience, your body comes to 'know' how to ride a bike."

Paying attention to embodied knowledge helped Matsushita build a better bread maker in 1987. The company sent a team of engineers to be apprenticed for several months to a master bread chef at the Osaka International Hotel in Japan. The magic ingredient turned out to be a special maneuver the chef executed with his hand while kneading the dough, so the engineers figured out how to mimic the movement with the machine.

"Anthropologists are trained in those patient, detailed ways of watching for hundreds of hours and taking everything down in minute detail, which is where the knowledge is—in the tiny details," Dr. Baba said. An understanding of movement skills has helped in the design of things like the computer mouse, joystick, and touch screen. The mouse, for instance, lets the hand mimic the way the eyes scan a computer screen.

The social aspects of technology particularly interest anthropologists like the ones in Dr. Salvador's group at Intel. Three and a half years ago, the group was set up when the company began considering other consumer products after releasing its Pentium processor. "It was selling really well into homes, and people were saying we have to build more things for the home," he said. "We thought maybe we should understand more about the home."

The group members embarked on a study of 10 families with young children. They visited each family for an evening, eating dinner with the family and analyzing the organization of the home and the family's daily routine.

Dr. Salvador's group found that the kitchen and family room were the most important rooms in the house. "Very rarely are people alone in those spaces," he said. "Social relationships are very important." Dr. Salvador's findings may not seem like much of an epiphany, but his work has helped lead Intel to look beyond the notion of a PC as a device generally used by someone seated at a desk alone in a room and to understand the importance of whole families using and sharing computing devices.

Anne McClard and Ken Anderson, anthropologists who are married to each other, do similar observational research at Media One, a cable provider that AT&T recently agreed to purchase. Ms. McClard and Mr. Anderson are part of Media One's Broadband Innovation Group. Their charge is to find new users and new uses for the company's services and, as Ms. McClard put it, "to make broadband living a reality."

To study Internet usage patterns, companies also install tracking systems on subjects' computers. But those kinds of studies are a poor substitute for the serendipitous twists and turns of actual interviews, anthropologists say.

Dr. Nardi said it was also important to couple interviews with observations to pick up on the knowledge and behavior people exhibit but do not think to mention. In her book *Information Ecologies: Using Technology with Heart* (M.I.T. Press, 1999), Dr. Nardi describes a study she did of a broadcast video and audio system in a hospital. She noticed that the surgical staff told jokes during routine parts of an operation. "This became an issue when the multimedia system began to broadcast audio to remote parts of the hospital," she said in an interview. The jokes and banter, she said, relieved tension during lengthy operations. "But no one would ever have said in an interview, 'We tell jokes during surgery,'" she noted.

Dr. Nardi and her colleagues recommended that the hospital add a feature to the system so the surgeons would know whether the audio component was turned on.

Ms. McClard and Mr. Anderson of Media One have had similar experiences. Last summer, they conducted a study called Always On, in which they observed families with cable modem connections, which allow computers to have a constant connection to the Internet at very high speeds, in an effort to understand what it is like to have such a link to the Internet in one's home.

The two anthropologists found that people with constant connections were often unaware of changes in their behavior. For instance, the people would often walk over to the computer to perform tasks like retrieving E-mail even if they were busy with tasks

somewhere else. But they hardly notice that they are doing it, Mr. Anderson said.

Such observations by anthropologists can be important for sales later on. When Canon first introduced its color printers for the home market in 1995, said Dr. Squires, who works for GVO, a consumer product consulting company in Palo Alto, Calif., consumers did not know what to do with them. So a team of researchers from GVO went into homes to examine refrigerator doors and bedroom walls for the types of printed material families create and exchange. The result was Canon Creative, the greeting card, T-shirt and poster software that comes bundled with the printers. Sales of the printers took off, Dr. Squires said.

But corporate anthropologists operate under constraints that make their jobs harder. Ms. McClard said the year and a half she took for an academic project seemed like "a real luxury" from the standpoint of the corporate world. A project for, say, Media One lasts just a few months.

So many of those anthropologists find it hard to present their findings, often from limited field samples, in a way that interests the people in the company who plan and design products. "Part of the challenge is telling the story in a way that makes it compelling to people who have the power to develop products," Ms. McClard said.

Ms. McClard and Mr. Anderson videotape most of their interviews. "When engineers see the people talking, they are more convinced than if we told them stuff," she said. "We have to bring the experience alive for people. We don't have the numbers. The only thing we have is the experience of the people we go out to see."

Larry Prusak, executive director of I.B.M.'s Institute for Knowledge Management, a research organization, in Cambridge, Mass., said he believed that the number of anthropologists in industry would continue to grow.

"There's going to be a huge flourishing of industrial anthropologists in the next 20 years," he said, adding that this was especially true in the technology sector because companies were continuing to study technology's potential for mimicking human behavior. "We're in the infancy in this area, and I don't think anyone would tell you differently."

41

Just Another Job?

The Commodification of Domestic Labor

Bridget Anderson

For most women, working is a necessity, not an option. There are reasons to celebrate the fact that women have become active participants in the workforce alongside their male counterparts. But this socioeconomic transformation has also created a "double shift" for many women, who work a full day and then return home to the additional unpaid jobs with home, household, and family each night.

Many families try to alleviate this "double shift" by "outsourcing" domestic work to a paid worker. This outsourcing is what the author of this selection means by the "commodification of domestic labor." In other words, domestic labor can be bought and sold like other services or goods. Although domestic labor is an increasingly important commodity in societies throughout western Europe, the United States, and other world regions, it is generally poorly paid. Employers look for potential employees who are willing to work for the lowest wages and, quite frequently, the individuals they hire are migrants from poor, faraway countries.

While the wages middle-income Western families pay their domestic workers may be low by local standards, they are often very high in comparison to wages available in poor countries. As a result, millions of people from countries as diverse as the Philippines, Sri Lanka, Ghana, Nigeria, Columbia, and El Salvador have left their homes and families in order to take their chance of working abroad as a domestic worker. Even educated people with professional experience—among them journalists, teachers, bankers, nurses, and others—are prepared to take on the risks of transnational migration since the benefits are perceived as being so high.

This selection illustrates the difficulties of being a transnational migrant in domestic work. It can be very challenging to work within the intimate space of another person's, or another family's, home—especially within a foreign culture. At the same time is it difficult to live far away from family and friends, including, quite often, one's own children. Relationships between employers and employees are frequently marked by asymmetries of race, nationality, language, class, and citizenship, since many transnational domestic workers have migrated on an undocumented or "illegal" basis. As this selection illustrates, these asymmetries leave transnational domestic workers vulnerable to various forms of discrimination, exploitation, and abuse. Globalization is not just about manufacturing being done in China or call centers in India; globalization hits close to home.

As you read this selection, ask yourself the following questions:

- What is the "commodification of domestic labor?" What factors have contributed to the rise in demand for domestic workers in western Europe?

- Why are so many domestic workers in western Europe transnational migrants from Southeast Asia, West Africa, or eastern Europe?

- From the perspective of the domestic workers the author interviewed, what are the advantages of live-in as opposed to live-out domestic work? What are the disadvantages?

- How do racial stereotypes and other forms of prejudice contribute to the mistreatment of some domestic workers?

- Some employers describe their domestic employees as "one of the family." How might this way of characterizing their employment relationship actually contribute to the exploitation and abuse of the migrant women they employ?

The following terms discussed in this selection are included in the Glossary at the back of the book:

commodification   *maternalism*
domestic labor

description of pub info

Anderson, Bridget. "Just Another Job? The Commodification of Domestic Labor," Reprinted with permission of the author.

Paid domestic work looks in many ways like just another undesirable job. The hours are long, the pay is low, and the tasks are often regarded as demeaning. The same could be said of hamburger flipping or garbage collection. But there is much to distinguish the culture of domestic labor from other kinds of low-wage work. Significantly, domestic work is deeply embedded in status relationships, some of them overt, but others less so. And these relationships are all the more complex because they fall along multiple axes. They are relationships among women, but often women of different races or nationalities—certainly of different classes. They take place in a space that can be intimate, loving, and private but that can also be a form of social plumage, demonstrating to visitors the home owner's comfort and leisure. And the worker, often a migrant without legal protection or proper papers, may depend on the employer for more than her paycheck, just as the employer depends on the worker for more than her elbow grease.

The demand for domestic workers has been steadily rising in Europe, and although one can point to many economic and demographic forces that may have contributed to this trend—the retrenchment of the welfare state, the rise in the ratio of older to younger people, the feminization of the workforce, the rise in divorce, and the decline of the extended family—they leave a good deal unexplained. For instance, many domestic workers are employed by women who do not work outside their homes. Moreover, many paid domestic workers are cleaners rather than carers. While a working couple might need someone to look after their children or elderly relatives, no one *has* to employ a cleaner in the same way. Ironed clothes, dust-gathering ornaments, polished floors, and clean windows are not necessities; but such markers affirm a household's status by displaying its access to financial and human resources.

The migrant domestic workers I interviewed, many of them through a British support organization called Kalayaan, seemed to spend much of their time servicing lifestyles that their employers would have found difficult and even undesirable to sustain had they undertaken their upkeep themselves. Said Aida, a Filipina live-in in Paris:

> Every day I clean for my madam one pair of riding shoes, two pairs of walking shoes, house shoes. That is every day, just for one person. . . . Plus the children: that's one pair of rubbers and one pair of everyday school shoes. . . . Fourteen pairs of shoes every day. My time is already finished. . . . You will be wondering why she has so many bathrobes, one silk and two cotton. I say, Why does madam have so many bathrobes? Every day you have to hang them up. Every day you have to press the back because it is crumpled.

Siryani, a Sri Lankan live-in in Athens, recounted, "They have a very big house, and white carpet everywhere. They have three dogs. I hate those dogs with long, long hair. Even one hair will show on the white carpet."

When a cleaner is not enabling her employers to enjoy an extravagant lifestyle or an impractically appointed home (would Siryani's employers have had both white carpet and dogs if they'd had to clean their own home?), she allows her middle-class, female employer to devote "quality" time to her children and husband. In effect, employing a cleaner enables middle-class women to take on the feminine role of moral and spiritual support to the family, while freeing her of the feminine role of servicer, doer of dirty work. The employment of a paid domestic worker thereby facilitates status reproduction, not only by maintaining status objects but also by allowing the worker to serve as a foil to the lady of the house. Simply by hiring a domestic worker, the employer lowers the status of the work that employee does. After all, the employer has better or more lucrative things to do with her time.

Many middle-class, heterosexual couples in the United Kingdom employ a cleaner once they have children, thereby averting gender and generational conflict over domestic work.[1] But there is no total amount of domestic work that can be divided fairly between equal partners or delegated to someone who is paid to do it. When one does not have to do the work oneself, standards change. Eliska, a Czech au pair in the United Kingdom recounted, "Her teenage daughter changes her clothes five, six times a day and leaves them on the floor. I have to pick them up, wash them, iron them, put them away. I cannot tell her, Tasha, you cannot change your clothes so many times. And my employer does not notice."

Economic explanations, then, fail to fully account for the popularity of domestic workers in middle- to upper-class European households, because they fail to consider the status implications of hiring such workers. Similarly, the prevalence of migrant labor in this sector cannot be attributed only to avoidance of tax and national insurance, for there is a supply of cheap, nonmigrant female laborers willing to work off the books. Despite the relatively high wages of Polish workers in Berlin, they still account for a significant proportion of domestic workers. Filipina workers are the most popular in Athens, and they are also the most expensive.

Significantly, migrant workers are more willing than local ones to live with their employers. Live-in workers may be considerably less expensive than live-out workers, in some cases because their board and lodging are set against their wages, but especially because employers get more labor and greater flexibility for their money. Whatever hours a live-in nanny and housekeeper is supposed to work, there is virtually no time when she can comfortably refuse to "help" her employer with a household task. Domestic workers and au pairs commonly complain of having to be available at both ends of the day, early in the morning for children and late at night for entertaining guests. It is a question not simply of long hours but of permanent availability. Said Teresa, a Filipina domestic in Athens:

> You're working the minute you open your eyes until the minute you close your eyes. You keep your strength and your body going so that you will finish your work. . . . You keep waiting on your employers until they go to sleep because, although you finish your work, for example you finish ironing everything, putting the children or the elder person to bed, even if you put them to bed at ten o'clock, there are still other members of the family. So you keep on observing, "Oh, can I sleep or maybe they will call me to give them food or to give them a yogurt." . . . And even if you are sleeping you sometimes feel that you are still on duty.

A 1998 survey of thirty-nine Kalayaan members found that although the workers were well organized and belonged to a trade union, only 18 percent worked eight hours or less a day. Nearly 30 percent averaged more than twelve hours a day.

Although the long hours, low pay, and lack of privacy render live-in domestic work extremely unpopular among the population in general, migrants, particularly new arrivals, can find it advantageous: problems of accommodations and employment are solved in one, and the worker can both minimize expenses and acclimatize herself to a new language and culture. Moreover, housing is more than a place to live: it is shelter from the police, and many new arrivals are undocumented and terrified of deportation. Employers appreciate live-in migrants because, unlike local domestic workers, migrants cannot leave their employers to go tend to their own sick children or other family obligations. Undocumented workers in particular have extremely limited access to their own families or, really, to any life outside the employing home.

Such women, however, isolated in private households, without papers or legal protection, are strikingly vulnerable to abuse. Their work can be singularly degrading: cleaning cats' anuses, flushing employers' toilets, scrubbing the floor with a toothbrush three times a day, or standing by the door in the same position for hours at a time. One worker told a researcher of a particularly degrading experience: "We were three Filipinas, she brought us into the room where her guests were, she made us kneel down and slapped each one of us across the face."[2] Sadly, these are not isolated instances. Kalayaan keeps annual figures detailing the kinds of difficulties faced by the workers they register. In 1996–1997, 84 percent reported psychological abuse, 34 percent physical abuse, and 10 percent sexual abuse. Additionally, 54 percent were locked in, 55 percent did not have their own beds, and 38 percent were not fed regularly.

Racial stereotypes play a role both in the abuse of domestic workers and in the selection of migrant workers over local citizens in the first place. Certainly, such stereotypes help manufacture a sense of difference between the female employer and her domestic worker: "other" women are presumed suited to such service work, and these others are so alien that some employers actually fear that the migrants' bodies will contaminate their homes. Workers are typically required to wash their clothes separately from those of the family, and they are given their own cutlery and plates. Said Rose, a Ghanaian domestic worker in Athens, of her employer's family, "The daughter wouldn't even accept water from my hand, simply because I am black." Irene, a Filipina I interviewed in Athens, recounted the following story: "I heard children playing house. One child said, 'I am a Daddy.' The other child said, 'I am a Mummy,' and then, 'She is a Filipina.' So what does the child mean? Even the child knows or is already learning that if you are a Filipina, you are a servant inside the house."

Agencies and employers tend to express preferences for specific nationalities of domestic workers, and these preferences often reflect racial hierarchies that rank women by precise shades of skin color. One volunteer from Caritas, the international Catholic social service and relief agency, in Athens told me, "The Ethiopians are very sweet. They are not like the African Africans, who are ugly." Said a worker at an agency in Barcelona, "Moroccans are difficult to place. . . . Their religion is very different, they observe Ramadan. . . . They are very different, though like Peruvians they are brought up to be servile. . . . Filipinas are easiest to place." And according to a community volunteer in Paris, "You know the black people are used to being under the sun, and the people in France think they are very lazy, they are not going very quick, and you know, another breed, but they are very good with children, very maternal."

Some hierarchies are based on particular national or personal prejudices. Greek employers and agencies tend to frown upon Albanians and Ukrainians. In Paris, many employers evince a preference for Haitians, who are generally darker-skinned than the expressly shunned Moroccans and Algerians. Stereotypes differ across European states, but also across households: one household might display an "eccentric" liking for Congolese, for example, on the basis of household myths of an almost folkloric character. A "bad" experience with a domestic worker might lead a family to generalize about her entire nationality. Consider the comments of this Athens employer:

> I have a problem with women from Ethiopia: they are lazy, and they have no sense of duty, though they are good-hearted. . . . I have a lot of experience. I have had ten girls from Ethiopia. They like to be well-dressed—hair, nails; for that they are good. . . . Then the Albanians—that was terrible. They are liars, always telling lies. And telephone maniacs because they have never had telephones. And they had no knowledge of electrical appliances. For seven months I had that girl. . . . Then I had one from Bulgaria. The Bulgarians are more civilized, more sincere, more concerned about work. But they are very unhappy.

Of course, not all employers are racist or abusive. Some women hire migrants in the hope of helping them. Certainly, migrant workers need the money. Why not match the needs of hard-pressed working mothers, on the one hand, with those of desperate migrants on the other?

Many of the domestic workers I met said that traveling abroad had enabled them to make important contributions to their families back home. But most of the more than four thousand workers at Kalayaan had never intended to come to Britain. Some had migrated first to the Middle East, from where they accompanied their employers to London on business trips or holidays; others had taken jobs in their countries of origin and traveled with their employers to the United Kingdom. While domestic workers who had papers felt that their work brought benefits to their families, others, especially those still undocumented, found the price too high. Said Nora, a Filipina working in London, "My life is worse than before. I'm on this dark road with no way out, that's how I feel. . . . All I want to do is go back home, even though we're very poor. But then, what kind of life will my daughter have?"

Hidden costs become apparent to many workers when they return home. They often feel ill at ease in their home countries, where things have changed in their absence, and where they may feel that they no longer belong. When their families meet them at the airport, these women commonly do not recognize their own kin. They talk of the embarrassment of having sex with husbands who have become virtual strangers, and of reuniting with children who doubt their mothers' love. Often a woman's relatives will have died or moved away. It is thus scarcely surprising that such women are very ambivalent when asked whether they would recommend migration to their daughters. Most migrants would prefer that their daughters did not have to make the choice between hunger and moving abroad.

So is employing a migrant domestic worker an act of sisterhood toward a woman in need or of complicity with abusive power structures? Employers often make contact with Kalayaan after they have seen a television program or read an article exposing the situation of migrant domestic workers in London. They want to help, they explain, and to offer board and lodging in return for "help around the house." A place in a British home is proffered as a kind of charity, and the woman's labor power is a little extra on the side. But even under the best of circumstances, the employer has power over the worker, and this power is greatly increased when the worker is an undocumented migrant. How the employer chooses to exercise that power is up to her.

As Judith Rollins has noted, a kind of "maternalism" sometimes marks these relationships, wherein friendliness between the women works to confirm the employer's sense of her own kindness and of the worker's childlike inferiority.[3] Through kindness, pity, and charity, the employer asserts her power. Nina, an employer in Athens, had hired dozens of migrant domestic workers to care for her very disabled mother over the years, because, she said, "This is the Greek way to help foreigners." She claimed to offer exceptional working conditions (though the wages she told me were extremely low) and a loving household. But her employees, she lamented, have turned out to be gold diggers:

> There is no feeling for what I offer. I'll give you an example of the last woman from Bulgaria. . . . I had a bright idea: "She needs to see her friends." Because I was tired of all the turnover, I gave her Sunday off. . . . Now, every morning, including Sundays, the girl wakes, helps grandmother to the toilet and changes her Pamper. . . . Then she goes, but she must be back before seven P.M. . . . Then after all I do for her, the girl says every Sunday she would like to be back at midnight, and not to do any work—that is, not to change the Pamper in the morning.

This worker was being denied twelve consecutive hours off in a week—an arrangement that would still have placed her hours well above the European legal maximum.

Some employers express their maternalism through gifts, giving their domestic workers mostly unwanted, cast-off household goods. Said Maggie, a Zairean working in Athens, "You need the money to feed your children, and in place of pay they give you old clothes. 'I give you this, I give you this.' They give you things, but me, I need the money. Why? I am a human being."

All of these exercises of power, whether through direct abuse, through the insistence that a worker perform degrading tasks, or through acts of maternalism, expose the relationship between worker and employer as something other than a straightforward contractual one. But that is not the only relationship in the domestic workplace that is fraught with ambiguity and complexity. When we hire someone to care for children or the elderly, we cannot pay simply for the physical labor of care, leaving the emotional labor to those who are genetically linked to those cared for. Magnolia, a Dominican nanny in Barcelona, noted, "Sometimes when they say to me that I should give her lots of love, I feel like saying, well, for my family I give love free, and I'm not discriminating, but if it's a job you'll have to pay me."

Indeed many parents hire nannies rather than sending their children to day care precisely because they want their children to develop personal, emotional relationships with the people who care for them. But can the emotional labor of care really be bought? The worker may carry out the physical work of care, entering into a sort of intimacy with the children, but her caring engenders no mutual obligations, no entry into a community, and no real human relationship—just money. A worker may care for a child over many years, spending many more hours with that child than the child's natural mother does, but should the employer decide to terminate the relationship, the worker will have no further right to see the child. As far as the employer is concerned, money expresses the full extent of her obligation to the worker. To the worker, this view is deeply problematic; indeed, it denies the worker's humanity and the very depth of her feelings. Juliette, a nanny from Côte d'Ivoire working in Parma, recalled, "I cared for a baby for his first year. . . . The child loves you as a mother, but the mother was jealous and I was sent away. I was so depressed then, seriously depressed. All I wanted was to go back and see him. . . . I will never care for a baby again. It hurts too much."

The idea that the worker can be considered "part of the family" allows some employers to negotiate these difficulties. Interestingly, this language even appears in U.K. immigration legislation with reference to au pairs. But the analogy does not withstand scrutiny. A relative who contracts a long-term illness is not expelled from the family; domestic workers usually are, even if they are given a nice severance package. And although being a part of the family does not entitle the worker to unconditional love or support, it does entitle the employer to encroach on the worker's off-duty hours for "favors." In fact, many employers will invoke either a contractual or a family relationship under different circumstances, depending on what is most convenient. Writes Miranda Miles:

> The disadvantages of being "one of the family" far outweighed the advantages. Wages tended to be lower and erratically paid on the premise that the maid would "understand" their financial situation. Incorporating a domestic worker into the family circle is usually, although not always, a sure way of depressing wages and possibly hiding even the most discreet forms of exploitation involved in the employer-employee relationship.[4]

These are vexed questions, for while informality clearly leaves workers open to exploitation—excessive hours, for instance, or low pay—workers also value having personal relationships with their employers, particularly because domestic work can be highly isolating. In some cases, a woman will decide to work for low wages precisely because she feels that a particular family is "nice" or an employer "treats me as part of the family." Professionalizing employment relations and rendering them more anonymous may therefore introduce new difficulties. Labor is a social, not simply an economic process.

This is not to say that labor contracts for domestic work are not important. We should welcome the emergence of domestic labor into the realm of recognized and productive work. Professionalization is a means of giving respect to domestic workers as workers, as well as of managing the personal relationships that develop from care work.

Certainly, it is possible to argue for the social significance of care work. Changing an elderly person's incontinence pads is surely as important and as deserving of social respect and status as the work of a stockbroker. But the work of cleaners and housekeepers sometimes occupies a more problematic space. Cleaning can be part and parcel of caring, and tidying up for a disabled person, for instance, can be construed as socially valuable. But many cleaners, like those described at the start of this essay, do work that simply expresses the employer's status, leisure, and power. Can such race-, class-, and gender-based divisions be resolved through contracts? Undocumented migrants, for example, cannot draw boundaries or refuse work they find demeaning. They simply do not have the power. The most effective way to protect them is to make sure that they have basic employment rights, as well as access to the means to implement those rights. For migrants, these rights begin with work permits.

Because both the workers and the employers in this sector tend to be women, it is tempting to draw on notions of sisterhood in order to reform the relationships between employers and employees. But the power relations among these women are very complex, to the point where even acts of kindness work to reproduce an employer's status and self-image, and they do not always, in the end, benefit the worker. This does not mean that employers should not respect their domestic workers but, rather, that they should also be aware that the very act of employing a domestic worker weaves them into a status relationship. Real sisterhood, then, should take concerned women beyond their own homes: it means campaigning and organizing around issues of migration and domestic labor, having as an important first demand that domestic work be treated, in the best sense, like just another job.

NOTES

1. Nicky Gregson and Michelle Lowe, *Servicing the Middle Classes: Class, Gender and Waged Domestic Labour in Contemporary Britain* (London: Routledge, 1994).

2. Margaret Healy, "Exploring the Slavery of Domestic Work in Private Households," unpublished M.A. thesis, University of Westminster, 1994.

3. Judith Rollins, *Between Women: Domestic Workers and Their Employers* (Philadelphia: Temple University Press, 1985).

4. Miranda Miles, Working in the City: The Case of Migrant Women in Swaziland's Domestic Service Sector. In *Gender, Migration and Domestic Service*, ed. Janet Momsen. London: Routledge, 1999.

42

The Kpelle Moot

James L. Gibbs, Jr.

Some scholars argue that law, like marriage, is a major institution found in all societies, although in widely divergent forms. Others argue that law exists only where some individual or group possesses the authority to impose punishments. Debates about what is and what isn't law aside, conflict exists in all societies. Further, all societies have culturally defined mechanisms by which people attempt to settle their differences.

Conflict-management procedures must be geared to meet the needs of particular social systems. In the urban centers of Western society, people live in faceless anonymity. Relations between people can be characterized as single interest. For example, generally a person's landlord is neither kin nor neighbor. The landlord-tenant relationship is not complicated by any other social bonds. A person who has a car accident is unlikely to have run into a friend or a relative. Our legal system, with its narrow focus on the grievance itself, fits our social system of one-dimensional relationships.

In small-scale social systems, people are often involved with one another on multiple levels. A landlord may also be a neighbor and a relative. In such settings, people are born, grow up, grow old, and die in the same community. Because their social relationships are long-term and highly valued, people in such communities need to resolve disputes in a way that maintains good relations.

Today in the United States, government agencies and grassroots organizations are establishing programs—Neighborhood Justice Centers or Dispute Resolution Centers—based on models of consensus and conciliation. According to the *Citizen's Dispute Resolution Handbook,* the potential of local-level conflict resolution was originally recognized in the work of an anthropologist who had described these processes in Africa.

As you read this selection, ask yourself the following questions:

- How are formal courtroom hearings different from moots?
- In what kinds of cases is the formal court effective and in what kinds is it ineffective?
- How is a mediator different from a judge?
- What is the function of the blessing at the beginning of the moot?
- In contrast to the official court, how does the procedure used during the moot facilitate harmony and reconciliation?
- Why does the author consider the moot therapeutic?

The following terms discussed in this selection are included in the Glossary at the back of the book:

clan	multiplex relationship
culture area	palaver
extended family	patrilineal
mediator	single-interest relationship
moot	social control

Africa as a major culture area has been characterized by many writers as being marked by a high development of law and legal procedures.[1] In the past few years research on African law has produced a series of highly competent monographs such as those on law among the Tiv, the Barotse, and the Nuer.[2] These and related shorter studies have focused primarily on formal processes for the settlement of disputes, such as those which take place in a courtroom, or those which are, in some other way, set apart from simpler measures of social control. However, many African societies have informal, quasi-legal, dispute-settlement procedures, supplemental to formal ones, which have not been as well studied, or—in most cases—adequately analysed.

Gibbs, Jr. James. L. "The Kpelle Moot." Africa, 33 (1963), no. 1. Reprinted with permission of the author.

In this paper I present a description and analysis of one such institution for the informal settlement of disputes, as it is found among the Kpelle of Liberia; it is the moot, the *bɛrɛi mu meni saa* or "house palaver." Hearings in the Kpelle moot contrast with those in a court in that they differ in tone and effectiveness. The genius of the moot lies in the fact that it is based on a covert application of the principles of psychoanalytic theory which underlie psychotherapy.

The Kpelle are a Mande-speaking, patrilineal group of some 175,000 rice cultivators who live in Central Liberia and the adjoining regions of Guinea. This paper is based on data gathered in a field study which I carried out in 1957 and 1958 among the Liberian Kpelle of Panta Chiefdom in north-east Central Province.

Strong corporate patrilineages are absent among the Kpelle. The most important kinship group is the virilocal polygynous family which sometimes becomes an extended family, almost always of the patrilineal variety. Several of these families form the core of a residential group, known as a village quarter, more technically, a clan-barrio.[3] This is headed by a quarter elder who is related to most of the household heads by real or putative patrilineal ties.

Kpelle political organization is centralized although there is no single king or paramount chief, but a series of chiefs of the same level of authority, each of whom is superordinate over district chiefs and town chiefs. Some political functions are also vested in the tribal fraternity, the Poro, which still functions vigorously. The form of political organization found in the area can thus best be termed the polycephalous associational state.

The structure of the Kpelle court system parallels that of the political organization. In Liberia the highest court of a tribal authority and the highest tribal court chartered by the Government is that of a paramount chief. A district chief's court is also an official court. Disputes may be settled in these official courts or in unofficial courts, such as those of town chiefs or quarter elders. In addition to this, grievances are settled informally in moots, and sometimes by associational groupings such as church councils or cooperative work groups.

In my field research I studied both the formal and informal methods of dispute settlement. The method used was to collect case material in as complete a form as possible. Accordingly, immediately after a hearing, my interpreter and I would prepare verbatim transcripts of each case that we heard. These transcripts were supplemented with accounts—obtained from respondents—of past cases or cases which I did not hear litigated. Transcripts from each type of hearing were analysed phrase by phrase in terms of a frame of reference derived from jurisprudence and ethno-law.

The results of the analysis indicate two things: first, that courtroom hearings and moots are quite different in their procedures and tone, and secondly, why they show this contrast.

Kpelle courtroom hearings are basically coercive and arbitrary in tone. In another paper[4] I have shown that this is partly the result of the intrusion of the authoritarian values of the Poro into the courtroom. As a result, the court is limited in the manner in which it can handle some types of disputes. The court is particularly effective in settling cases such as assault, possession of illegal charms, or theft where the litigants are not linked in a relationship which must continue after the trial. However, most of the cases brought before a Kpelle court are cases involving disputed rights over women, including matrimonial matters which are usually cast in the form of suits for divorce. The court is particularly inept at settling these numerous matrimonial disputes because its harsh tone tends to drive spouses farther apart rather than to reconcile them. The moot, in contrast, is more effective in handling such cases. The following analysis indicates the reasons for this.[5]

The Kpelle *bɛrɛi mu meni saa*, or "house palaver," is an informal airing of a dispute which takes place before an assembled group which includes kinsmen of the litigants and neighbors from the quarter where the case is being heard. It is a completely ad hoc group, varying greatly in composition from case to case. The matter to be settled is usually a domestic problem: alleged mistreatment or neglect by a spouse, an attempt to collect money paid to a kinsman for a job which was not completed, or a quarrel among brothers over the inheritance of their father's wives.

In the procedural description which follows I shall use illustrative data from the Case of the Ousted Wife:

Wama Nya, the complainant, had one wife, Yua. His older brother died and he inherited the widow, Yokpo, who moved into his house. The two women were classificatory sisters. After Yokpo moved in, there was strife in the household. The husband accused her of staying out late at night, of harvesting rice without his knowledge, and of denying him food. He also accused Yokpo of having lovers and admitted having had a physical struggle with her, after which he took a basin of water and "washed his hands of her."

Yokpo countered by denying the allegations about having lovers, saying that she was accused falsely, although she had in the past confessed the name of one lover. She further complained that Wama Nya had assaulted her and, in the act, had committed the indignity of removing her headtie, and had expelled her from the house after the ritual hand-washing. Finally, she alleged that she had been thus cast out of the house at the instigation of the other wife who, she asserted, had great influence over their husband.

Kɔlɔ Waa, the Town Chief and quarter elder, and the brother of Yokpo, was the mediator of the moot, which decided that the husband was mainly at fault, although Yua and Yokpo's children were also in the wrong. Those at fault had to apologize to Yokpo and bring gifts of apology as well as local rum[6] for the disputants and participants in the moot.

The moot is most often held on a Sunday—a day of rest for Christians and non-Christians alike—at the home of the complainant, the person who calls the moot. The mediator will have been selected by the complainant. He is a kinsman who also holds an office such as town chief or quarter elder, and therefore has some skill in dispute settlement. It is said that he is chosen to preside by virtue of his kin tie, rather than because of his office.

The proceedings begin with the pronouncing of blessings by one of the oldest men of the group. In the Case of the Ousted Wife, Gbenai Zua, the elder who pronounced the blessings, took a rice-stirrer in his hand and, striding back and forth, said:

> This man has called us to fix the matter between him and his wife. May ɣala (the supreme, creator deity) change his heart and let his household be in good condition. May ɣala bless the family and make them fruitful. May He bless them so they can have food this year. May He bless the children and the rest of the family so they may always be healthy. May He bless them to have good luck. When Wama Nya takes a gun and goes in the bush, may he kill big animals. May ɣala bless us to enjoy the meat. May He bless us to enjoy life and always have luck. May ɣala bless all those who come to discuss this matter.

The man who pronounces the blessings always carries a stick or a whisk (*kpung*) which he waves for effect as he paces up and down chanting his injunctions. Participation of spectators is demanded, for the blessings are chanted by the elder (*kpung namu* or "*kpung* owner") as a series of imperatives, some of which he repeats. Each phrase is responded to by the spectators who answer in unison with a formal response, either *e ka ti* (so be it), or a low, drawn-out *eeee*. The *kpung namu* delivers his blessings faster and faster, building up a rhythmic interaction pattern with the other participants. The effect is to unite those attending in common action before the hearing begins. The blessing focuses attention on the concern with maintaining harmony and the well-being of the group as a whole.

Everyone attending the moot wears their next-to-best clothes or, if it is not Sunday, everyday clothes. Elders, litigants, and spectators sit in mixed fashion, pressed closely upon each other, often overflowing onto a veranda. This is in contrast to the vertical spatial separation between litigants and adjudicators in the courtroom. The mediator, even though he is a chief, does not wear his robes. He and the oldest men will be given chairs as they would on any other occasion.

The complainant speaks first and may be interrupted by the mediator or anyone else present. After he has been thoroughly quizzed, the accused will answer and will also be questioned by those present. The two parties will question each other directly and question others in the room also. Both the testimony and the questioning are lively and uninhibited. Where there are witnesses to some of the actions described by the parties, they may also speak and be questioned. Although the proceedings are spirited, they remain orderly. The mediator may fine anyone who speaks out of turn by requiring them to bring some rum for the group to drink.

The mediator and others present will point out the various faults committed by both the parties. After everyone has been heard, the mediator expresses the consensus of the group. For example, in the Case of the Ousted Wife, he said to Yua: "The words you used towards your sister were not good, so come and beg her pardon."

The person held to be mainly at fault will then formally apologize to the other person. This apology takes the form of the giving of token gifts to the wronged person by the guilty party. These may be an item of clothing, a few coins, clean hulled rice, or a combination of all three. It is also customary for the winning party in accepting the gifts of apology to give, in return, a smaller token such as a twenty-five cent piece[7] to show his "white heart" or good will. The losing party is also lightly "fined;" he must present rum or beer to the mediator and the others who heard the case. This is consumed by all in attendance. The old man then pronounces blessings again and offers thanks for the restoration of harmony within the group, and asks that all continue to act with good grace and unity.

An initial analysis of the procedural steps of the moot isolates the descriptive attributes of the moot and shows that they contrast with those of the courtroom hearing. While the airing of grievances is incomplete in courtroom hearings, it is more complete in the moot. This fuller airing of the issues results, in many marital cases, in a more harmonious solution. Several specific features of the house palaver facilitate this wider airing of grievances. First, the hearing takes place soon after a breach has occurred, before the grievances have hardened. There is no delay until the complainant has time to go to the paramount chief's or district chief's headquarters to institute suit. Secondly, the hearing takes place in the familiar surroundings of a home. The robes, writs, messengers, and other symbols of power which subtly intimidate and inhibit the parties in the courtroom, by reminding them of the physical force which underlies the procedures, are absent. Thirdly, in the courtroom the conduct of the hearing is firmly in the hands of the judge but in the moot the investigatory initiative rests much more with the parties themselves. Jurisprudence suggests that, in such a case, more of the grievances lodged between the parties are likely to be aired and adjusted. Finally, the range of relevance applied to matters which are brought out is extremely broad. Hardly anything mentioned is held to be irrelevant. This too leads to a more thorough ventilation of the issues.

There is a second surface difference between court and moot. In a courtroom hearing, the solution is, by and large, one which is imposed by the adjudicator. In the moot the solution is more consensual. It is, therefore, more likely to be accepted by both parties and hence more durable. Several features of the moot contribute to the consensual solution: first, there is no unilateral ascription of blame, but an attribution of fault to both parties. Secondly, the mediator, unlike the chief in the courtroom, is not backed by political authority and the physical force which underlies it. He cannot jail parties, nor can he levy a heavy fine. Thirdly, the sanctions which are imposed are not so burdensome as to cause hardship to the losing party or to give him or her grounds for a new grudge against the other party. The gifts for the winning party and the potables for the spectators are not as expensive as the fines and the court costs in a paramount chief's court. Lastly, the ritualized apology of the moot symbolizes very concretely the consensual nature of the solution.[8] The public offering and acceptance of the tokens of apology indicate that each party has no further grievances and that the settlement is satisfactory and mutually acceptable. The parties and spectators drink together to symbolize the restored solidarity of the group and the rehabilitation of the offending party.

This type of analysis describes the courtroom hearing and the moot, using a frame of reference derived from jurisprudence and ethno-law which is explicitly comparative and evaluative. Only by using this type of comparative approach can the researcher select features of the hearings which are not only unique to each of them, but theoretically significant in that their contribution to the social-control functions of the proceedings can be hypothesized. At the same time, it enables the researcher to pin-point in procedures the cause for what he feels intuitively: that the two hearings contrast in tone, even though they are similar in some ways.

However, one can approach the transcripts of the trouble cases with a second analytical framework and emerge with a deeper understanding of the implications of the contrasting descriptive attributes of the court and the house palaver. Remember that the coercive tone of the courtroom hearing limits the court's effectiveness in dealing with matrimonial disputes,

especially in effecting reconciliations. The moot, on the other hand, is particularly effective in bringing about reconciliations between spouses. This is because the moot is not only conciliatory, but *therapeutic*. Moot procedures are therapeutic in that, like psychotherapy, they re-educate the parties through a type of social learning brought about in a specially structured interpersonal setting.

Talcott Parsons[9] has written that therapy involves four elements: support, permissiveness, denial of reciprocity, and manipulation of rewards. Writers such as Frank,[10] Klapman,[11] and Opler[12] have pointed out that the same elements characterize not only individual psychotherapy, but group psychotherapy as well. All four elements are writ large in the Kpelle moot.

The patient in therapy will not continue treatment very long if he does not feel support from the therapist or from the group. In the moot the parties are encouraged in the expression of their complaints and feelings because they sense group support. The very presence of one's kinsmen and neighbors demonstrates their concern. It indicates to the parties that they have a real problem and that the others are willing to help them to help themselves in solving it. In a parallel vein, Frank, speaking of group psychotherapy, notes that: "Even anger may be supportive if it implies to a patient that others take him seriously enough to get angry at him, especially if the object of the anger feels it to be directed toward his neurotic behavior rather than himself as a person."[13] In the moot the feeling of support also grows out of the pronouncement of the blessings which stress the unity of the group and its harmonious goal, and it is also undoubtedly increased by the absence of the publicity and expressive symbols of political power which are found in the courtroom.

Permissiveness is the second element in therapy. It indicates to the patient that everyday restrictions on making anti-social statements or acting out anti-social impulses are lessened. Thus, in the Case of the Ousted Wife, Yua felt free enough to turn to her ousted co-wife (who had been married leviratically) and say:

> You don't respect me. You don't rely on me any more. When your husband was living, and I was with my husband, we slept on the farm. Did I ever refuse to send you what you asked me for when you sent a message? Didn't I always send you some of the meat my husband killed? Did I refuse to send you anything you wanted? When your husband died and we became co-wives, did I disrespect you? Why do you always make me ashamed? The things you have done to me make me sad.

Permissiveness in the therapeutic setting (and in the moot) results in catharsis, in a high degree of stimulation of feelings in the participants and an equally high tendency to verbalize these feelings.[14] Frank notes that:

"Neurotic responses must be expressed in the thera-peutic situation if they are to be changed by it."[15] In the same way, if the solution to a dispute reached in a house palaver is to be stable, it is important that there should be nothing left to embitter and undermine the decision. In a familiar setting, with familiar people, the parties to the moot feel at ease and free to say *all* that is on their minds. Yokpo, judged to be the wronged party in the Case of the Ousted Wife, in accepting an apology, gave expression to this when she said:

> I agree to everything that my people said, and I accept the things they have given me—I don't have *anything else* about them on my mind. *(My italics.)*

As we shall note below, this thorough airing of complaints also facilitates the gaining of insight into and the unlearning of idiosyncratic behaviour which is socially disruptive. Permissiveness is rooted in the lack of publicity and the lack of symbols of power. But it stems, too, from the immediacy of the hearing, the locus of investigatory initiative with the parties, and the wide range of relevance.

Permissiveness in therapy is impossible without the denial of reciprocity. This refers to the fact that the therapist will not respond in kind when the patient acts in a hostile manner or with inappropriate affec-tion. It is a type of privileged indulgence which comes with being a patient. In the moot, the parties are treated in the same way and are allowed to hurl re-criminations that, in the courtroom, might bring a few hours in jail as punishment for the equivalent of con-tempt of court. Even though inappropriate views are not responded to in kind, neither are they simply ig-nored. There is denial of *congruent* response, not denial of *any* response whatsoever. In the *bεrεi mu meni saa,* as in group psychotherapy, "private ideation and concep-tualization are brought out into the open and all their facets or many of their facets exposed. The individual gets a 'reading' from different bearings on the com-pass, so to speak,[16] and perceptual patterns . . . are jog-gled out of their fixed positions. . . ."[17]

Thus, Yua's outburst against Yokpo quoted above was not responded to with matching hostility, but its inappropriateness was clearly pointed out to her by the group. Some of them called her aside in a huddle and said to her:

> You are not right. If you don't like the woman, or she doesn't like you, don't be the first to say anything. Let her start and then say what you have to say. By speak-ing, if she heeds some of your words, the wives will scatter, and the blame will be on you. Then your husband will cry for your name that you have scattered his property.

In effect, Yua was being told that, in view of the previous testimony, her jealousy of her co-wife was not justified. In reality testing, she discovered that her view of the situation was not shared by the others and, hence, was inappropriate. Noting how the others responded, she could see why her treatment of her co-wife had caused so much dissension. Her interpretation of her new co-wife's actions and resulting premises were not shared by the co-wife, nor by the others hearing a de-scription of what had happened. Like psychotherapy, the moot is gently corrective of behavior rooted in such misunderstandings.

Similarly, Wama Nya, the husband, learned that others did not view as reasonable his accusing his wife of having a lover and urging her to go off and drink with the suspected paramour when he passed their house and wished them all a good evening. Reality testing for him taught him that the group did not view this type of mildly paranoid sarcasm as conducive to stable marital relationships.

The reaction of the moot to Yua's outburst indi-cates that permissiveness in this case was certainly not complete, but only relative, being much greater than in the courtroom. But without this moderated immunity the airing of grievances would be limited, and the chance for social relearning lessened. Permissiveness in the moot is incomplete because, even there, pru-dence is not thrown to the winds. Note that Yua was not told not to express her feelings at all, but to express them only after the co-wife had spoken so that, if the moot failed, she would not be in an untenable position. In court there would be objection to her blunt speaking out. In the moot the objection was, in effect, to her speaking *out of turn.* In other cases the moot sometimes fails, foundering on this very point, because the parties are *too* prudent, all waiting for the others to make the first move in admitting fault.

The manipulation of rewards is the last dimension of therapy treated by Parsons. In this final phase of therapy[18] the patient is coaxed to conformity by the granting of rewards. In the moot one of the most im-portant rewards is the group approval which goes to the wronged person who accepts an apology and to the person who is magnanimous enough to make one.

In the Case of the Ousted Wife, Kɔlɔ Waa, the me-diator, and the others attending decided that the hus-band and the co-wife, Yua, had wronged Yokpo. Kɔlɔ Waa said to the husband:

> From now on, we don't want to hear of your fighting. You should live in peace with these women. If your wife accepts the things which the people have brought you should pay four chickens and ten bottles of rum as your contribution.

The husband's brother and sister also brought gifts of apology, although the moot did not explicitly hold them at fault.

By giving these prestations, the wrong-doer is restored to good grace and is once again acting like an "upright Kpelle" (although, if he wishes, he may refuse to accept the decision of the moot). He is eased into this position by being grouped with others to whom blame is also allocated, for, typically, he is not singled out and isolated in being labelled deviant. Thus, in the Case of the Ousted Wife, the children of Yokpo were held to be at fault in "being mean" to their step-father, so that blame was not only shared by one "side," but ascribed to the other also.

Moreover, the prestations which the losing party is asked to hand over are not expensive. They are significant enough to touch the pocketbook a little; for the Kpelle say that if an apology does not cost something other than words, the wrong-doer is more likely to repeat the offending action. At the same time, as we noted above, the tokens are not so costly as to give the loser additional reason for anger directed at the other party which can undermine the decision.

All in all, the rewards for conformity to group expectations and for following out a new behaviour pattern are kept within the deviant's sight. These rewards are positive, in contrast to the negative sanctions of the courtroom. Besides the institutionalized apology, praise and acts of concern and affection replace fines and jail sentences. The mediator, speaking to Yokpo as the wronged party, said:

> You have found the best of the dispute. Your husband has wronged you. All the people have wronged you. You are the only one who can take care of them because you are the oldest. Accept the things they have given to you.

The moot in its procedural features and procedural sequences is, then, strongly analogous to psychotherapy. It is analogous to therapy in the structuring of the role of the mediator also. Parsons has indicated that, to do his job well, the therapist must be a member of two social systems: one containing himself and his patient; and the other, society at large.[19] He must not be seduced into thinking that he belongs only to the therapeutic dyad, but must gradually pull the deviant back into a relationship with the wider group. It is significant, then, that the mediator of a moot is a kinsman who is also a chief of some sort. He thus represents both the group involved in the dispute and the wider community. His task is to utilize his position as kinsman as a lever to manipulate the parties into living up to the normative requirements of the wider society, which, as chief, he upholds. His major orientation must be to the wider collectivity, not to the particular goals of his kinsmen.

When successful, the moot stops the process of alienation which drives two spouses so far apart that they are immune to ordinary social-control measures such as a smile, a frown, or a pointed aside.[20] A moot is not always successful, however. Both parties must have a genuine willingness to cooperate and a real concern about their discord. Each party must be willing to list his grievances, to admit his guilt, and make an open apology. The moot, like psychotherapy, is impotent without well-motivated clients.

The therapeutic elements found in the Kpelle moot are undoubtedly found in informal procedures for settling disputes in other African societies also; some of these are reported in literature and others are not. One such procedure which seems strikingly parallel to the Kpelle berei mu meni saa has been described by J. H. M. Beattie.[21] This is the court of neighbors or rukurato rw'enzarwa found in the Banyoro kingdom of Uganda. The group also meets as an ad hoc assembly of neighbors to hear disputes involving kinsmen or neighbors.[22]

The intention of the Nyoro moot is to "reintegrate the delinquent into the community and, if possible, to achieve reconciliation without causing bitterness and resentment; in the words of an informant, the institution exists 'to finish off people's quarrels and to abolish bad feeling.'"[23] This therapeutic goal is manifested in the manner in which the dispute is resolved. After a decision is reached the penalty imposed is always the same. The party held to be in the wrong is asked to bring beer (four pots, modified downwards according to the circumstances) and meat, which is shared with the other party and all those attending the rukurato. The losing party is also expected to "humble himself, not only to the man he has injured but to the whole assembly."[24]

Beattie correctly points out that, because the council of neighbors has no power to enforce its decision, the shared feast is not to be viewed primarily as a penalty, for the wrong-doer acts as a host and also shares in the food and drink. "And it is a praiseworthy thing; from a dishonourable status he is promoted to an honourable one . . ."[25] and reintegrated into the community.[26]

Although Beattie does not use a psychoanalytic frame of reference in approaching his material, it is clear that the communal feast involves the manipulation of rewards as the last step in a social-control measure which breaks the progressive alienation of the deviance cycle. The description of procedures in the rukurato indicates that it is highly informal in nature, convening in a room in a house with everyone "sitting around." However, Beattie does not provide enough detail to enable one to determine whether or not the beginning and intermediate steps in the Nyoro moot show the permissiveness, support, and denial of reciprocity which characterize the Kpelle moot. Given the structure and outcome of most Nyoro councils, one would surmise that a close examination of their proceedings[27] would reveal the implicit operation of therapeutic principles.

The fact that the Kpelle court is basically coercive and the moot therapeutic does not imply that one is dysfunctional while the other is eufunctional. Like Beattie, I conclude that the court and informal dispute-settlement procedures have separate but complementary functions. In marital disputes the moot is oriented to a couple as a dyadic social system and serves to reconcile them wherever possible. This is eufunctional from the point of view of the couple, to whom divorce would be dysfunctional. Kpelle courts customarily treat matrimonial matters by granting a divorce. While this may be dysfunctional from the point of view of the couple, because it ends their marriage, it may be eufunctional from the point of view of society. Some marriages, if forced to continue, would result in adultery or physical violence at best, and improper socialization of children at worst. It is clear that the Kpelle moot is to the Kpelle court as the domestic and family relations courts (or commercial and labour arbitration boards) are to ordinary courts in our own society. The essential point is that both formal and informal dispute-settlement procedures serve significant functions in Kpelle society and neither can be fully understood if studied alone.[28]

NOTES

1. The fieldwork on which this paper is based was carried out in Liberia in 1957 and 1958 and was supported by a grant from the Ford Foundation, which is, of course, not responsible for any of the views presented here. The data were analyzed while the writer was the holder of a pre-doctoral National Science Foundation Fellowship. The writer wishes to acknowledge, with gratitude, the support of both foundations. This paper was read at the Annual Meeting of the American Anthropological Association in Philadelphia, Pennsylvania, in November 1961.

    The dissertation, in which this material first appeared, was directed by Philip H. Gulliver, to whom I am indebted for much stimulating and provocative discussion of many of the ideas here. Helpful comments and suggestions have also been made by Robert T. Holt and Robert S. Merrill.

    Portions of the material included here were presented in a seminar on African Law conducted in the Department of Anthropology at the University of Minnesota by E. Adamson Hoebel and the writer. Members of the seminar were generous in their criticisms and comments.

2. Paul J. Bohannan, *Justice and Judgment among the Tiv,* Oxford University Press, London, 1957; Max Gluckman, *The Judicial Process among the Barotse of Northern Rhodesia,* Manchester University Press, 1954; P. P. Howell, *A Handbook of Nuer Law,* Oxford University Press, London, 1954.

3. Cf. George P. Murdock, *Social Structure,* Macmillan, New York, 1949, p. 74.

4. James L. Gibbs, Jr., "Poro Values and Courtroom Procedures in a Kpelle Chiefdom," *Southwestern Journal of Anthropology* (in press) [1963, 18:341–350]. A detailed analysis of Kpelle courtroom procedures and of procedures in the moot together with transcripts appears in: James L. Gibbs, Jr., *Some Judicial Implications of Marital Instability among the Kpelle* (unpublished Ph.D. Dissertation, Harvard University, Cambridge, Mass., 1960).

5. What follows is based on a detailed case study of moots in Panta Chiefdom and their contrast with courtroom hearings before the paramount chief of that chiefdom. Moots, being private, are less susceptible to the surveillance of the anthropologist than courtroom hearings; thus I have fewer transcripts of moots than of court cases. The analysis presented here is valid for Panta Chiefdom and also valid, I feel, for most of the Liberian Kpelle area, particularly the north-east where people are, by and large, traditional.

6. This simple distilled rum, bottled in Monrovia and retailing for twenty-five cents a bottle in 1958, is known in the Liberian Hinterland as "cane juice" and should not be confused with imported varieties.

7. American currency is the official currency of Liberia and is used throughout the country.

8. Cf. J. F. Holleman, "An Anthropological Approach to Bantu Law (with special reference to Shona law)" in the *Journal of the Rhodes-Livingstone Institute,* vol. x, 1950, pp. 27–41. Holleman feels that the use of tokens for effecting apologies—or marriages—shows the proclivity for reducing events of importance to something tangible.

9. Talcott Parsons, *The Social System,* The Free Press, Glencoe, Ill., 1951, pp. 314–319.

10. Jerome D. Frank, "Group Methods in Psychotherapy," in *Mental Health and Mental Disorder: A Sociological Approach,* edited by Arnold Rose, W. W. Norton Co., New York, pp. 524–535.

11. J. W. Klapman, *Group Psychotherapy: Theory and Practice,* Grune & Stratton, New York, 1959.

12. Marvin K. Opler, "Values in Group Psychotherapy," *International Journal of Social Psychiatry,* vol. iv, 1959, pp. 296–298.

13. Frank, op. cit., p. 531.

14. Ibid.

15. Ibid.

16. Klapman, op. cit., p. 39.

17. Ibid., p. 15.

18. For expository purposes the four elements of therapy are described as if they always occur serially. They may, and do, occur simultaneously also. Thus, all four of the factors may be implicit in a single short behavioural sequence. Parsons (op. cit.) holds that these four elements

are common not only to psychotherapy but to all measures of social control.

19. Parsons, op. cit., p. 314. Cf. loc. cit., chap. 10.

20. Cf. Parsons, op. cit., chap. 7. Parsons notes that in any social-control action the aim is to avoid the process of alienation, that "vicious-cycle" phenomenon whereby each step taken to curb the non-conforming activity of the deviant has the effect of driving him further into his pattern of deviance. Rather, the need is to "reach" the deviant and bring him back to the point where he is susceptible to the usual everyday informal sanctions.

21. J. H. M. Beattie, "Informal Judicial Activity in Bunyoro," *Journal of African Administration,* vol. ix, 1957, pp. 188–195.

22. Disputes include matters such as a son seducing his father's wives, a grown son disobeying his father, or a husband or wife failing in his or her duties to a spouse. Disputes between unrelated persons involve matters like quarrelling, abuse, assault, false accusations, petty theft, adultery, and failure to settle debts. (Ibid., p. 190.)

23. Ibid., p. 194.

24. Beattie, op. cit., p. 194.

25. Ibid., p. 193.

26. Ibid., p. 195. Moreover, Beattie also recognizes the functional significance of the Nyoro moots, for he notes that: "It would be a serious error to represent them simply as clumsy, 'amateur' expedients for punishing wrong-doers or settling civil disputes at an informal, sub-official level." (Ibid.)

27. The type of examination of case materials that is required demands that fieldworkers should not simply record cases that meet the "trouble case" criterion (cf. K. N. Llewellyn and E. A. Hoebel, *The Cheyenne Way,* Norman, Okla., University of Oklahoma Press, 1941; and E. A. Hoebel, *The Law of Primitive Man,* Cambridge, Mass., Harvard University Press, 1954), but that cases should be recorded in some transcript-like form.

28. The present study has attempted to add to our understanding of informal dispute-settlement procedures in one African society by using an eclectic but organized collection of concepts from jurisprudence, ethno-law, and psychology. It is based on the detailed and systematic analysis of a few selected cases, rather than a mass of quantitative data. In further research a greater variety of cases handled by Kpelle moots should be subjected to the same analysis to test its merit more fully.

43

Contemporary Warfare in the New Guinea Highlands

Aaron Podolefsky

Within political units—whether tribes or nations—there are well-established mechanisms for handling conflict nonviolently. Anthropologists have described a wide range of conflict resolution mechanisms within societies. Between politically autonomous groups, however, few mechanisms exist. Consequently, uncontained conflict may expand into armed aggression—warfare. In both primitive and modern forms, warfare always causes death, destruction, and human suffering. It is certainly one of the major problems confronting humankind.

New Guinea highlanders can tell you why they go to war—to avenge ghosts or to exact revenge for the killing of one of their own. As we have seen in previous selections, people do not seem to comprehend the complex interrelationship among the various parts of their own social system. Throughout the world, anthropologists find that people do not fathom the causes of their own social behavior. If they did, finding solutions would certainly be a far simpler matter.

The leaders of Papua New Guinea see intertribal fighting as a major social problem with severe economic consequences. Although fighting itself may be age-old, the reemergence of warfare in this area in the 1970s appears to have a new set of causes. In this selection, Aaron Podolefsky shows how the introduction of

Western goods may have inadvertently resulted in changes in economic arrangements, marriage patterns, and, ultimately, warfare.

As you read this selection, ask yourself the following questions:

- What is the theoretical orientation (research strategy) of this paper?
- When did tribal fighting reemerge as a national problem in New Guinea?
- How did intertribal marriage constrain the expansion of minor conflict into warfare?
- How has the rate of intertribal marriage changed? Why did it change?
- How are the introduction of Western goods, trade, marriage, and warfare interrelated?

The following terms discussed in this selection are included in the Glossary at the back of the book:

affinal kin	hypothesis
aggression	lineage
agnates	multiplex relationships
blood relatives	pacification
cross-cutting ties	tribe
cultural materialism	

Podolefsky, Aaron. "Comtemporary Warfare in the New Guinea Highlands." Ethnology: An International Journal of Cultural and Social Anthropology (1984.) Reprinted by permission of Ethnology.

After decades of pacification and relative peace, intergroup warfare reemerged in the Papua New Guinea highlands during the late 1960s and early 1970s, only a few years before national independence in 1975. Death and destruction, martial law, and delay in highlands development schemes have been the outcome.

Most explanations of the resurgence either posit new causes (such as psychological insecurity surrounding political independence from Australian rule or disappointment at the slow speed of development) or attribute the increased fighting to relaxation of government controls which suppressed fighting since the pacification process began. None of the explanations thus far advanced has looked at changes in the structure or infrastructure of highlands societies themselves which could account for behavioral changes in the management of conflict.

This paper employs a cultural materialist strategy in which the efficacy of explanatory models are ranked: infrastructure, structure, and superstructure.[1] From a macrosociological perspective, infrastructural changes unintentionally induced during the colonial era resulted in changes in the structural relations between groups. These changes reduced existing (albeit weak) indigenous mechanisms constraining conflict. Traditionally, groups maintained differential access to resources such as stone used for axes and salt. Axe heads and salt were produced in local areas and traded for valuables available elsewhere. I argue that the introduction and distribution of items such as salt and steel axes reduced the necessity for trade, thereby altering the need for intertribal marriage as well as reducing extratribal contacts of a type which facilitated marriage between persons of different tribes. The reduction of intertribal marriage, over time, resulted in a decay of the web of affinal and nonagnatic kin ties which had provided linkages between otherwise autonomous tribal political units. Thus, the resurgence of tribal fighting is, in part, a result of the reduction of constraints which might otherwise have facilitated the containment of conflict rather than its expansion into warfare. This view sees warfare as one possible end result of a process of conflict management.

An advantage of this strategy is that it suggests a testable hypothesis which runs counter to conventional wisdom and informed opinion that the rate of intertribal marriage would increase after pacification. Some researchers believed that once tribal fighting ended men would be able to wander farther afield and develop relationships with single teenage girls over a wide area. Pacification, then, might reasonably be expected to result in an increase in intertribal marriage. An increase or lack of change in the rate of intergroup marriage since contact would invalidate the explanation. The hypothesis will be tested on data collected in the Gumine District, Simbu (formerly Chimbu) Province, Papua New Guinea.

BACKGROUND

Warfare in traditional highlands societies has been regarded as chronic, incessant, or endemic, and is said to have been accepted as a part of social living in most areas. Indeed, the pattern of warfare was one of the most continuous and violent on record.

However, hostilities were neither random nor did highlanders live in a perpetual state of conflict with all surrounding groups. Some neighboring groups maintained relations of permanent hostility and had little to do with one another. In contrast, most neighboring tribes intermarried and attended one another's ceremonies.

Pacification was an early goal of the colonial administration. By the end of the 1930s fighting was rare in the vicinity of Simbu province government stations. By 1940 Australian authority was accepted and attacks on strangers and tribal fighting had nearly ended, although the entire highlands was not pacified until the 1960s. This period also witnessed the introduction of Western goods such as salt and the steel axe.

Change came quickly to New Guinea. Sterling writes in 1943: "Headhunters and cannibals a generation ago, most of the natives of British New Guinea have now become so accustomed to the ways of the whites that they have been trained as workers and even to assist in administering the white man's law."

From the end of World War II through the 1970s, educational and business opportunities expanded, local government and village courts were introduced, and national self-government was attained in 1975. Highlanders came to expect that development would lead to material gains.[2]

Tribal warfare began to reemerge as a significant national problem in about 1970, five years before independence. By 1973 the government had become concerned that the situation might deteriorate to a point that they could no longer effectively administer parts of the highlands. In 1972, according to government report, 28 incidents involving 50 or more persons were reported in the Western Highlands District. A decade later, Bill Wormsley (1982) reports 60 fights per year in the Enga Province (the figures are of course not directly comparable). Although the level of fighting declined in Enga during 1980 due to the declaration of a state of emergency, it increased again in 1981 and 1982. Martial law has also been declared in the Simbu Province. Deaths lead to payback killing and to demands for compensation payments. Inflated demands for "excess" compensation further compound the problem.

Of the five major theories of warfare outlined by Koch in 1974 (biological evolution, psychological theories, cultural evolution, ecological adaptation, and social-structure analysis), scholars have used only psychological theories and social-structural analysis to explain the recent emergence of tribal warfare.

Some researchers favor explanations which combine the traditional cultural heritage of violence with issues in development. Others seem to argue that the problem lies in the Enga's perception that the government, especially the courts, has become weaker and that this had led to the breakdown in law and order. Rob Gordon notes, however, that the police force in Enga has increased from 72 in 1970 to 300 in 1981, and that the average sentence for riotous behavior has grown from 3 months in 1970 to 9.6 months in 1978–9 with no apparent deterrent effect. Kiaps (field officers), Gordon suggests, have in fact lost power for several reasons. Most interesting from the perspective of the present analysis involves the kiaps' loss of control over access to goods. He (1983:209) states that "The importance that the Enga attach to trade-goods should not be underestimated." An old Engan is quoted as saying "The first Kiaps gave beads, salt, steel axes—everyone wanted it so they all followed the Kiap and stopped fighting. We stopped fighting because we did not want to lose the source of these things." I would add that once they "followed the kiaps" for these goods, previous important trade relations no longer needed to be kept up. In a 1980 study, Gordon also acknowledges problems created by intergroup suspicion, generational conflict exacerbated by education, and decline in men's houses and clan meetings. Similarly, Paula Brown (1982a) believes that pacification was a temporary effect in which fighting was suppressed. The Simbu do not see the government as holding power.

Explanations also combine development problems with psychologically oriented theories. Contemporary violence is sometimes thought to be a protest rising out of psychological strain created by the drastic social change of an imposed economic and political system. In a 1973 paper Bill Standish describes the period leading up to independence as one of stress, tension, and insecurity. He argues that the fighting is an expression of primordial attachments in the face of political insecurity surrounding national independence from Australian colonial rule. Paula Brown (1982a, 1982b) suggests that during the colonial period expectations for the future included security, wealth, and the improvement of life. "Disappointment that these goals have not been realized is expressed in disorder." She suggests that what is needed is a political movement rather than the imposition of Western institutions and suppression of fighting.

The present paper cannot and does not formally refute any of these explanations. Indeed, some make a great deal of sense and fill in part of a very complex picture. However, it is difficult to evaluate the validity of these explanations since very little data are presented. For example, Standish (1973) presents no evidence to assess whether, in fact, the level of stress has changed over time (precontact, postcontact, or independence era), or whether stress is associated with fighting or even with differential levels of awareness about independence, the latter likely expressing itself geographically around centers of population and development.

ETHNOGRAPHIC BACKGROUND— THE MUL COMMUNITY

Mul lies approximately 3 miles east of the Gumine District Headquarters and 32 miles south of Kundiawa, the capital of the Simbu province. The Gumine patrol post was established in 1954. During the early 1960s a dirt road was constructed linking Gumine to the capital and within a few years the road was extended through Mul. Lying at an elevation of about 5,500 feet, Mul is the central portion of a larger tribal territory which extends steeply from the southern edge of the Marigl Gorge to elevations of 8 to 9,000 feet.

The area is densely populated. Land is either cultivated or fallow in grass or scrub regrowth. Individually owned trees are scattered and there are a yearly increasing number of coffee trees. With 295 persons per square mile on cultivatable land, this density is high compared with other highland groups (see Brown and Podolefsky 1976).

The people of Mul are Simbus. Social relations and cultural patterns follow in most important respects those extensively documented by Paula Brown in numerous publications. I will describe here only those dimensions of organization most directly relevant to the resurgence of tribal fighting.

Mul residents trace kinship through males, and their social groupings are patrilineal. Hierarchical segments link themselves as father/son, while parallel segments are seen as brothers. Individuals, however, are less concerned with this overall construct and tend to interact in terms of group composition and alignments. The likelihood of an individual conflict escalating into warfare is directly related to the structural distance between conflicting parties.

The largest political group to unite in warfare is the tribe, a group of several thousand individuals. Tribes are segmented into clans whose members see themselves as a unified group. Generally, individually owned plots of land tend to cluster and people can point out rough boundaries between adjacent clans. Plots of land belonging to members of a particular subclan tend to cluster within the clan area. The subclan section (or one-blood group) is the first to mobilize for warfare. The potential for expansion of such conflicts depends to a large degree on whether the relative position of the groups in the segmentary system lends itself to opposing alignments at the higher levels of segmentation and upon the past relations between the groups.

Unlike subclan sections in most highlands societies there is no restriction upon fighting between sections of the subclan. Within the subclan section, however, there are moral restrictions on internal fighting. If comembers become extremely angry they may attack with fists, clubs, or staffs, but not with axes, arrows, or spears. These restrictions are related to the notion that members of the subclan have "one-blood," and that this common blood should not be shed.

Segmentary principles operate in situations of cooperation as well as conflict. Members of a subclan section may enclose garden plots within a single fence and cooperate in the construction of men's houses.

Brown (1970:99–103) similarly notes that in the central Simbu transactions between clans and tribes are competitive while those within the clan are reciprocal. Generally speaking, in terms of proximity of land holdings and residence, cooperation in gardening and house construction and the willingness to unite in common defense and ceremonial exchange, the solidarity of a social group is inversely related to the position in the segmentary hierarchy.

Cross-cutting these segmentary principles are a variety of interpersonal ties (e.g., affinal and other non-agnatic relations, exchange ties, and personal friendships) which affect behavior in conflict situations. It is these ephemeral or transitory linkages which provide the avenues through which structurally autonomous tribal groups interact.

MARRIAGE AND WARFARE

Marriage and warfare are linked in the minds of New Guinea highlanders. Early writers report indigenous notions that highlanders marry their enemies. The Siane say, "They are our affinal relatives; with them we fight" (Salisbury 1962:25). Enga informants report, "We marry those whom we fight" (Meggitt 1958:278). In an extensive study of Enga warfare, Meggitt (1977:42) supports these assertions by reporting quite strong correlations between rates of intergroup marriage and killing.

While there is little doubt that there is a strong association between marriage and warfare, it is not clear at all that they are causally related in any direct fashion, i.e., warfare causing marriage or marriage causing warfare. It is highly unlikely that warfare causes marriage. Researchers have noted the difficulty in arranging marriages between hostile groups. It is similarly unlikely that marriage causes warfare (although exceptions can certainly be pointed out). While disputes may arise between bride and groom or their families, the relations are generally highly valued and long term. The association between marriage and warfare can be reduced to two separate relationships. First, highlanders most frequently marry their neighbors. Second, highlanders most frequently go to war with their neighbors. This is because in the highlands, where travel is restricted and relations are multiplex, neighbors are the parties most likely to be involved in a dispute. Thus propinquity is causally related to both marriage and warfare; the positive correlation between marriage and warfare is spurious. Indeed, the essence of the argument made here is that if other variables could be "controlled" the association between warfare and marriage would in fact be negative.

The notion that there is no direct (as opposed to inverse) causal relationship between warfare and marriage is critical. Warfare results from precipitating disputes in the absence of sufficiently powerful third party mechanisms and other constraints which control the dispute. One dimension of constraint stems from marriage links.

In her paper "Enemies and Affines," Paula Brown (1964) carefully describes the relevant social relations among the central Simbu. During wedding ceremonies speeches proclaim that the groups of the bride and groom (consisting of subclansmen, some clansmen, kin, and affines) should remain on friendly terms and exchange visits and food. The marriage creates individual ties and obligations outside the clan which, while not institutionalized, are not wholly voluntary. At various stages in the life cycle payments are obligatory. Given the widely documented emphasis on transaction in highlands social relations, it is important to note that whenever a formal food presentation occurs between clans, the donors and recipients are related to one another through marriage. Extratribal relatives play an important role in conflict situations.

> The prevailing hostility between neighboring tribes gives extratribal relatives a special complex role. Men try not to injure their close kin and affines in any conflict between their agnatic group and the group of their relatives, but they may not attempt to prevent or stop hostilities. In any dealings between neighboring tribes, men with connections in both take a leading part; their political sphere of action encompasses both. When intermediaries and peacemakers are required these men are active (Brown 1964:348).

Thus, in Central Simbu, affines played some role in attempting to prevent warfare and were important in restoring peace. No amount of oral history data will tell us how many wars did not occur due to efforts made through these channels. Nor can such data tell us how many wars were shorter or less intense than they would have been had there been fewer cross-cutting ties. The importance of cross-cutting ties is recognized among the densely populated Enga.

> Even while or after two men or groups fight over an issue, others may intervene to urge negotiation and compromise. . . . Whether, however, noncombatants initiate some kind of conciliation or simply stand by and watch the fighting spread depends on a complex set of conditions . . . relevant factors . . . include, for instance, the importance traditionally ascribed to the object in contention (is it a pig or a sweet potato garden?), the number of antagonists, the kinship, affinal, or exchange connections among some or all of them, and between them and interested noncombatants (Meggitt 1977:12).

Moreover, the frequency of intergroup marriage is related to the expansion or containment of a dispute. That is, the more intermarriage the greater the chance

TABLE 1   Marriage Ties by Time Period

	Before Contact		After Contact	
	N	%	N	%
Between tribes	85	75%	30	40%
Within tribes	29	25%	44	60%
Total	114	100%	74	100%

chi squared = 21.86 1 df
p < 0.001 (one tail)
phi = .341

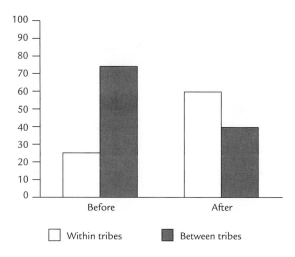

FIGURE 1   Percentage of Marriage Ties. Podolefsky, Aaron. "Contemporary Warfare in the New Guinea Highlands." *Ethnology: An International Journal of Cultural and Social Anthropology* (1984.) Reprinted by permission of Ethnology.

that disputes will be handled without violence or that the violence can be contained.

> Especially within the tribe, the supporters of each party include men with affines on the other side, most of whom are on good terms with their in-laws and have no wish to offend them. In such cases some men stay out of the fight while others, while participating, avoid meeting their affines in combat. This may serve to confine interclan conflict. Between tribes, similar serious disputes can more easily lead to fighting because fewer men have close ties which restrain them from supporting their fellow tribesmen (Brown 1964:352).

In sum, while there is an apparent correlation between marriage and warfare, marriage, in fact, establishes a social relationship which acts primarily as a constraint upon the expansion of a dispute. Second, as Meggitt suggests, it is not merely the marriage ties between the two groups, but also between them and their allies, i.e., the web of affinal relations. Third, the frequency of marriage, or density of the web, is related to efficacy of conflict management processes.

CHANGING PATTERN OF INTERTRIBAL MARRIAGE

A null hypothesis that the proportion of intertribal marriages has gone up or remained the same can be rejected ($p < 0.001$) on the basis of the data shown in Table 1. Thus, we tend to believe, based upon these data, that there has in fact been an overall decline in intertribal marriage.

The data reveal a statistically significant change in the marriage pattern in the anticipated direction. Figure 1 describes the proportion of marriage ties within and between tribes, before and after Western influence. Comparing the intertribal (between) and intratribal (within) marriage rates in the precontact sample (labeled before), we see that intertribal marriage was nearly three times as frequent as intratribal marriage.

Of the 114 marriage ties recorded in the precontact sample, 85 (75 percent) were between members of different tribes while only 29 (25 percent) were within the tribe. This allowed for a dense network of affinal ties between autonomous political groups. In the recent postcontact period (labeled after), in contrast, the number of intertribal marriages drops below the number of intratribal marriages. Of the 74 marriage ties in the postcontact sample, only 30 (40 percent) were between persons of different tribes while 44 (60 percent) were within the tribe. The intertribal marriage rate in the recent period is nearly half that of the precontact period.

The argument presented in this paper is that the dramatic reduction of intertribal marriage rates had significant implications for the structure of relations between politically autonomous tribal groups.

A Secondary Analysis

Sometimes it is possible to replicate one's findings by performing a secondary analysis on data collected by other researchers.

In 1964, Paula Brown published data on the marriage of some men in the Naregu tribe who live in the central Simbu near the capital of Kundiawa. Data for two clans are divided into previous generations (prior to 1930) and present generation. Brown's categories for marriage ties may be collapsed to match those used above.

What should we expect, a priori? Since Brown did not arrange the data to address this particular question, we expect some differences. Her temporal dichotomy is previous and present generation rather than before and after contact. Europeans did not reach this area

TABLE 2   Marriages of Some Men in the Naregu Tribe

	Pre-1930 (Before)		Post-1930 (After)	
	N	%	N	%
Between tribes	154	60%	130	47%
Within tribes	102	40%	144	53%
Total	256	100%	274	100%

chi squared = 8.597 1 df
p < 0.005 (one tail)
phi = .1272

Podolefsky, Aaron. "Contemporary Warfare in the New Guinea Highlands." Ethnology: An International Journal of Cultural and Social Anthropology (1984.) Reprinted by permission of Ethnology.

until the mid-1930s and Brown's data are dichotomized at 1930. This means that precontact marriages are included in the present generation sample. Neither do Brown's data allow for a decade of transition. Based upon these differences in the data sets, we would expect the difference between the previous and present samples to be less extreme than the difference between the before and after sample in the Mul data (i.e., we expect a lower measure of association).

The data in Table 2 reveal a statistically significant change in the marriage pattern, although the association is lower (as we expected it would be) than in Mul. The between-tribe marriage rate (in the sample) dropped from 60 to 47 percent. This change was sufficient to draw Brown's attention. While the analysis fits our predictions, we cannot be certain that the change in marriage pattern observed by Paula Brown in central Simbu represents the same process occurring in Mul nearly twenty years later. Nevertheless, the analysis is intriguing. I think Brown was observing the initial stages of a process of change initiated by a reduction in the necessity for trade.[3]

TRADE AND MARRIAGE

Given the conventional wisdom that pacification would lead to greater intertribal contact and, therefore, an increase in the rate of intertribal marriage, it remains to be explained why the proportion of intertribal marriages decreased. In other words, what forces or situations affected the marriage pattern?

Interviews with young men of marriageable age and some of the oldest men in the community elicited two different perspectives. (Unfortunately, it was not possible for me, being a male, to maintain serious conversation with women on this topic.) Young men

typically explained that they do not find wives from other areas because they are "tired;" they just do not have any desire to travel the long distances to visit women of other areas when there are women close at hand. This emic explanation is not particularly satisfactory from an anthropological perspective.

While the older men could not explain why the distribution of marriages in their younger days differed from that of more recent years, they were able to describe the ways young men and women met prospective spouses from other tribes prior to the coming of Europeans scarcely twenty years earlier. The old men reported that when they were young trade was very important. Salt, stone axes, bird of paradise feathers, shells of different kinds, pandanus oil, carpul fur, and the like were traded between tribes during trading expeditions. Figure 2 maps the trade network as described by the older residents of Mul.

When they were young, the old men reported, they would dress in their finest decorations and travel to the places described in Figure 2. The women at these places, they said, would see them arrayed in all their finery and want to marry them. Of course, the situation may not have been quite this straightforward.

These reports drew my attention to the link between intertribal marriage and trade for scarce necessary and luxury resources. What would be the effect of the introduction of European goods upon trade? And, could this affect marriage patterns?

According to the old men, pigs from Mul were traded south to the lower elevation, less densely populated areas in return for bird of paradise feathers and carpul fur (see Figure 2). Some of the fur and feathers were traded for cowrie shells with people from Sina. Cowries, in turn, were traded to the Gomgales for kina shells. Carpul fur and pandanus oil were traded to the east for salt. Finally, some of the fur and feathers obtained from the south and the salt obtained from the east were traded to the northeast for stone axes and small shells, which had in turn been brought in from even further off.

Enter the ubiquitous steel axe; exit the stone axe. No one in Mul today would use a stone axe. Indeed, it was difficult to find someone who recalled how to attach stone to handle. The effect was that the primary reason for trade between the peoples of Mul and Era (i.e., the need for stone axes) was eliminated and the Muls' need for fur, feathers, and salt was reduced (what may have begun to increase was a need for cash). Similarly, salt increasingly became more readily available. Nowadays it can be purchased at the store on the government station or in small trade stores which stock, for example, three bags of salt, two packs of cigarettes, a bit of rice, and two or three tins

FIGURE 2 Traditional Exchange Network

of mackerel. The availability of salt locally eliminates the need to trade for it and further reduces the need for fur. Thus, two of the five trade routes shown on Figure 2 become totally unnecessary and the usefulness of trade items from a third is reduced.

The elimination of the need to trade for necessary scarce resources allowed some trade relations to atrophy. I use the term *atrophy* since the process was probably one of gradual disuse of trade networks rather than a catastrophic change. The remaining trade relations were reliant upon the need for luxury items such as shells and feathers. Scholars who have done long-term research in New Guinea have described the highlanders' declining interest in these decorative items.

With the introduction of Western goods and the reduction of trade, both the need and the opportunity for intermarriage declined. Intertribal marriage was functional in that it facilitated intergroup economic transactions. While there are a range of rights and obligations as well as affective ties which make marriage into neighboring groups preferable, more distant marriages have recognized importance. This same point was made by Roy Rappaport in his study of the Tsembaga Maring:

While unions between men and women of a single local group are generally preferred, the Tsembaga recognize certain advantages in marriage to members of other local groups . . . unions with groups north of the Sambai River and south of the Bismarks strengthen trading relationships. Bird-of-paradise plumes and shell ornaments are still obtained from these groups and until the 1950s stone axes from the Jimi Valley were traded for salt manufactured in the Simbai Valley (1969:121).

An early paper on the Siani linked trade and marriage directly by focusing on the exchange of nonutilitarian valuables which occurred at marriage and at the rites of passage for children of the marriage (Salisbury 1956). Valuables were traded in from the coast about 70 miles to the northeast. Trading took the form of ceremonial gift exchange between affines. At the same time, Salisbury reports a statistically significant trend for Siane men to obtain wives from the south and west while their sisters marry into groups from the north and east (the direction from which valuables come).

Even more interesting for the present purpose is Salisbury's report on the effect of the introduction of European wealth goods. The European settlements nearest the Siane were in Goroka and Asaroka,

30 miles to the east and north. Groups nearest these (who were already closer than the Siane to coastal wealth) quickly became wealthy in shells, cloth, and other European goods. Salisbury reports that, as a result of this increased wealth, the movement of women in that direction became more pronounced. He also notes that "Neither the wealth difference nor the movement of women is recognized in Siane idealogy."

Thus, Salisbury clearly links marriage patterns to the need to obtain wealth not locally available, although no mention is made of utilitarian goods. While the initial response to "wealthy neighbors" is to increase "wife giving," it is easy to see that once wealth is more evenly (and locally) distributed this reason for marrying out will no longer be of major consequence.

Particularly in the many areas of the highlands where marriages were arranged by families with minimal, if any, consultation with the bride or groom, consideration of trade relations was likely to play a role in the selection of a spouse. Families had an interest in the establishment or maintenance of trade relations.

At the same time that the function of intertribal marriage for maintaining the economic system in terms of access to necessary resources was eliminated, the decline in trade itself reduced the opportunity to make marriage arrangements between non-adjacent groups. Generally speaking, opportunity for marriage is not random but may be structured by factors such as class, caste, religious affiliation, sorority membership, or political borders. Changes in this structure of opportunity may lead to observable changes in marriage patterns. In other words, a change in the visiting (or trading) pattern between autonomous political groups could affect the structure of opportunity. The importance of opportunity remains whether the individuals are free to choose their own mates or whether such choices are made for them.

In central Simbu elders choose a person's spouse for them and, although they can refuse, the bride and groom usually accept even though they may never have met. Brown (1969) reports that some groups do not intermarry because of the lack of opportunity to make arrangements.

Administrative policy and mission influence may have speeded the process. In some areas, such as South Fore or Manga, Australian patrol officers insisted (or at least strongly urged) that brides consent and that women have a right to choose a spouse. Nowadays in central Simbu more marriages are being initiated by the couples themselves. Choice in a mate is likely to further increase the importance of the structure of opportunity.

In sum, the argument here is that the replacement, by Western goods, of resources secured through trade reduced the economic need (function) for intergroup marriage and the opportunity to arrange such marriages. The effects of these changes were not felt immediately because of the extant relations between groups. Over time fewer and fewer intertribal marriages were arranged to replace those of the passing generation. The net effect was a gradual decay of the web of affinal and non-agnatic ties which cut across tribal boundaries.

CONCLUSION

Gordon (1980) has insightfully pointed out that there is very little sense in talking about or planning development if people live in fear of renewed tribal fighting. Moreover, he notes that this is a testing time for anthropologists "who find that their explanatory models are somewhat inadequate." Indeed, few of the explanations begin from a particular theoretical position nor even a unified conceptual model; there is little discussion of the mechanisms by which suggested "causes" result in the behavior being explained; and, little evidence is presented to test the explanations.

In this paper, I have employed a particular theoretic strategy, namely, cultural materialism, in which the efficacy of explanatory models are ranked: infrastructure, structure, and superstructure.

Prior to contact with the outside world, stone axe heads and salt were produced in local areas where these resources were available. Redistribution was accomplished through trade. One of the functions of intertribal marriage was the facilitation of trade between autonomous political groups. With the early introduction of Western goods, particularly steel axes and salt, local production was discontinued and marriage was no longer necessary to maintain these trade relations. As trade was discontinued, so declined the opportunity to make marriage arrangements between non-adjacent groups. Of course, existing marriage ties facilitated continued contact between groups, but probably less frequently, and there was no pragmatic reason for young people to marry others from distant areas. Particularly in the case of women, where such a marriage necessitated a move far from her natal family, there were distinct disadvantages. Thus, as older people died and fewer marriages were arranged between groups, the web of affinal and non-agnatic kin ties decayed. Intertribal marriages provided a linkage through which groups could communicate, and a mechanism and reason for containing conflict. With the decline in intergroup marriage over time, the likelihood of a dispute expanding into full-scale warfare increased.

This explanation began with infrastructural conditions (production) and showed how they were causally related to structural changes (trade relations) which in turn caused further structural changes (the web of kin ties), finally leading to changes in conflict behaviors. I have tried to explain each of the stages in this temporal process, i.e., the relationship between trade and marriage and the relationship between marriage and warfare.

Scientific hypotheses and models can be tested by examining predictions which can be deduced from them. The model which I have outlined predicts the unlikely occurrence that, with pacification and the ability to wander further afield without the threat of life and limb, intertribal marriage actually declined rather than rose as was thought would be the case. The hypothesis was tested on genealogical data collected in this research site as well as on data published earlier from a different area of the Simbu province. This is but a single case study and there is no statistical reason to extend the findings to other areas of the highlands. However, the inability to falsify the hypothesis in this case lends support to the general efficacy of the explanation.

NOTES

1. Financial support from the National Science Foundation (Grant No. BNS76-218 37) is gratefully acknowledged.

2. For a more extensive discussion of this period with special reference to the resurgence of fighting, see Brown 1982a and 1982b.

3. Paula Brown reports (pers. comm.) that recently many Simbu women are marrying outside the Simbu to men they had met in the district or on visits. She notes that there are, now, advantages for older men having a daughter married to a prestigious outsider. Naregu men who migrate probably also marry outsiders.

   Such marriages further the process described here since, although they are extra-tribal, they do not link neighboring potential enemy groups.

REFERENCES

Brown, P. 1964. Enemies and Affines. *Ethnology* 3: 335–356.

_____. 1969. Marriage in Chimbu. In *Pigs, Pearlshells and Women*, eds. R. M. Glasse and M. Meggitt, 77–95. Englewood Cliffs, NJ: Prentice-Hall.

_____. 1970. Chimbu Transactions. *Man* 5: 99–117.

_____. 1982a. Conflict in the New Guinea Highlands. *Journal of Conflict Resolution* 26: 525–546.

_____. 1982b. Chimbu Disorder: Tribal Fighting in Newly Independent Papua New Guinea. *Pacific Viewpoint* 22: 1–21.

Brown, P. and A. M. Podolefsky. 1976. Population Density, Agricultural Intensity, Land Tenure, and Group Size in the New Guinea Highlands. *Ethnology* 15: 211–238.

Gordon, R. 1980. Rituals of Governance and the Breakdown of Law and Order in Papua New Guinea. Paper presented at the annual meeting of the American Anthropological Association. Washington, D.C.

_____. 1983. The Decline of the Kiapdom and the Resurgence of "Tribal Fighting" in Enga. *Oceania* 53: 205–223.

Howlett, D., et al. 1976. *Chimbu: Issues in Development.* Development Studies Centre Monograph No. 4 Canberra.

Koch, K. 1974. *The Anthropology of Warfare.* Addison-Wesley Module in Anthropology No. 52.

Meggitt, M. 1958. The Enga of the New Guinea Highlands. *Oceania* 28: 253–330.

_____. 1977. *Blood Is Their Argument: Warfare Among the Mae Enga Tribesmen of the New Guinea Highlands.* Palo Alto, CA: Mayfield.

Rappaport, R. 1969. Marriage Among the Maring. In R. M. Glasse and M. Meggitt (eds.), *Pigs, Pearlshells and Women,* 117–137. Englewood Cliffs, NJ: Prentice-Hall.

Salisbury, R. F. 1956. Asymmetrical Marriage Systems. *American Anthropologist* 58: 639–655.

_____. 1962. *From Stone to Steel.* London: Cambridge University Press.

Standish, B. 1973. The Highlands. *New Guinea* 8: 4–30.

Wormsley, W. 1982. Tribal Fighting, Law and Order, and Socioeconomic Development in Enga, Papua New Guinea. Paper presented at the meeting of the American Anthropological Association. Washington, D.C.

44

Army Enlists Anthropology in War Zones

David Rohde

In 2007 the U.S. military launched a $41 million project called the Human Terrain System. In hopes of helping U.S. soldiers better understand the cultural landscape in Iraq and Afghanistan, this project places anthropologists in combat zones to advise and help develop counterinsurgency operations.

Each Human Terrain System team consists of a team leader, an area specialist, a social scientist, and a research manager. The only civilian member of the team is the social scientist, typically an anthropologist with specialized knowledge on the region and its people. The team conducts original ground-level research and consults existing documents before presenting their conclusions and counsel to military commanders.

The use of anthropology in war zones is not a novel idea; it has created controversy in previous conflicts including World War II and the Vietnam War. In 1964, for example, a U.S. military project named CAMELOT was ostensibly organized to apply social science research to better understand the conditions which lead to military conflict; critics, however, believed that the military would use the project to destroy populist movements in Latin America, Asia, and elsewhere.

Today, anthropologists from the American Anthropological Association debate the ethics of civilian anthropology in Afghanistan and Iraq. Opponents of the Human Terrain System project argue that collaboration with combat operations violates the association's Code of Ethics which mandates that anthropologists do no harm to the subjects of their research. Advocates, on the other hand, counter that if anthropology can reduce combat casualties and assist civilian victims caught up in the destruction of war, anthropologists should apply their methods and training to reduce human suffering if they can. In this selection, David Rohde portrays both sides of this heated debate.

As you read this selection, ask yourself the following questions:

- What is mercenary anthropology?
- Why do many anthropologists object to using anthropologists in military operations?
- Why do military officials collaborate with anthropologists in combat operations and war zones?
- Is it ethical for professional anthropologists to work in combat operations?

The following terms discussed in this selection are included in the Glossary at the back of the book:

Human Terrain Team	*jirga*
mercenary	*Operation Khyber*

SHABAK VALLEY, AFGHANISTAN

In this isolated Taliban stronghold in eastern Afghanistan, American paratroopers are fielding what they consider a crucial new weapon in counterinsurgency operations here: a soft-spoken civilian anthropologist named Tracy.

Tracy, who asked that her surname not be used for security reasons, is a member of the first Human Terrain Team, an experimental Pentagon program that assigns anthropologists and other social scientists to American combat units in Afghanistan and Iraq. Her team's ability to understand subtle points of tribal relations—in one case spotting a land dispute that allowed the Taliban to bully parts of a major tribe—has won the praise of officers who say they are seeing concrete results.

Col. Martin Schweitzer, commander of the 82nd Airborne Division unit working with the anthropologists here, said that the unit's combat operations had been reduced by 60 percent since the scientists arrived in February, and that the soldiers were now able to focus more on improving security, health care and education for the population.

"We're looking at this from a human perspective, from a social scientist's perspective," he said. "We're not focused on the enemy. We're focused on bringing governance down to the people."

In September, Defense Secretary Robert M. Gates authorized a $40 million expansion of the program, which will assign teams of anthropologists and social scientists to each of the 26 American combat brigades in Iraq and Afghanistan. Since early September, five new teams have been deployed in the Baghdad area, bringing the total to six.

Yet criticism is emerging in academia. Citing the past misuse of social sciences in counterinsurgency campaigns, including in Vietnam and Latin America, some denounce the program as "mercenary anthropology" that exploits social science for political gain. Opponents fear that, whatever their intention, the scholars who work with the military could inadvertently cause all anthropologists to be viewed as intelligence gatherers for the American military.

Hugh Gusterson, an anthropology professor at George Mason University, and 10 other anthropologists are circulating an online pledge calling for anthropologists to boycott the teams, particularly in Iraq.

"While often presented by its proponents as work that builds a more secure world," the pledge says, "at base, it contributes instead to a brutal war of occupation which has entailed massive casualties."

In Afghanistan, the anthropologists arrived along with 6,000 troops, which doubled the American military's strength in the area it patrols, the country's east.

A smaller version of the Bush administration's troop increase in Iraq, the buildup in Afghanistan has allowed American units to carry out the counterinsurgency strategy here, where American forces generally face less resistance and are better able to take risks.

A NEW MANTRA

Since Gen. David H. Petraeus, now the overall American commander in Iraq, oversaw the drafting of the Army's new counterinsurgency manual last year, the strategy has become the new mantra of the military. A recent American military operation here offered a window into how efforts to apply the new approach are playing out on the ground in counterintuitive ways.

In interviews, American officers lavishly praised the anthropology program, saying that the scientists' advice has proved to be "brilliant," helping them see the situation from an Afghan perspective and allowing them to cut back on combat operations.

The aim, they say, is to improve the performance of local government officials, persuade tribesmen to join the police, ease poverty and protect villagers from the Taliban and criminals.

Afghans and Western civilian officials, too, praised the anthropologists and the new American military approach but were cautious about predicting long-term success. Many of the economic and political problems fueling instability can be solved only by large numbers of Afghan and American civilian experts.

"My feeling is that the military are going through an enormous change right now where they recognize they won't succeed militarily," said Tom Gregg, the chief United Nations official in southeastern Afghanistan. "But they don't yet have the skill sets to implement" a coherent nonmilitary strategy, he added.

Deploying small groups of soldiers into remote areas, Colonel Schweitzer's paratroopers organized jirgas, or local councils, to resolve tribal disputes that have simmered for decades. Officers shrugged off questions about whether the military was comfortable with what David Kilcullen, an Australian anthropologist and an architect of the new strategy, calls "armed social work."

"Who else is going to do it?" asked Lt. Col. David Woods, commander of the Fourth Squadron, 73rd Cavalry. "You have to evolve. Otherwise you're useless."

The anthropology team here also played a major role in what the military called Operation Khyber. That was a 15-day drive late this summer in which 500 Afghan and 500 American soldiers tried to clear an estimated 200 to 250 Taliban insurgents out of much of Paktia Province, secure southeastern Afghanistan's most important road and halt a string of suicide attacks on American troops and local governors.

In one of the first districts the team entered, Tracy identified an unusually high concentration of widows in one village, Colonel Woods said. Their lack of income created financial pressure on their sons to provide for their families, she determined, a burden that could drive the young men to join well-paid insurgents. Citing Tracy's advice, American officers developed a job training program for the widows.

In another district, the anthropologist interpreted the beheading of a local tribal elder as more than a random act of intimidation: the Taliban's goal, she said, was to divide and weaken the Zadran, one of southeastern Afghanistan's most powerful tribes. If Afghan and American officials could unite the Zadran, she said, the tribe could block the Taliban from operating in the area.

"Call it what you want, it works," said Colonel Woods, a native of Denbo, Pa. "It works in helping you define the problems, not just the symptoms."

EMBEDDING SCHOLARS

The process that led to the creation of the teams began in late 2003, when American officers in Iraq complained that they had little to no information about the local population. Pentagon officials contacted Montgomery McFate, a Yale-educated cultural anthropologist working for the Navy who advocated using social science to improve military operations and strategy.

Ms. McFate helped develop a database in 2005 that provided officers with detailed information on the local population. The next year, Steve Fondacaro, a retired Special Operations colonel, joined the program and advocated embedding social scientists with American combat units.

Ms. McFate, the program's senior social science adviser and an author of the new counterinsurgency manual, dismissed criticism of scholars working with the military. "I'm frequently accused of militarizing anthropology," she said. "But we're really anthropologizing the military."

Roberto J. González, an anthropology professor at San Jose State University, called participants in the program naïve and unethical. He said that the military and the Central Intelligence Agency had consistently misused anthropology in counterinsurgency and propaganda campaigns and that military contractors were now hiring anthropologists for their local expertise as well.

"Those serving the short-term interests of military and intelligence agencies and contractors," he wrote in the June issue of *Anthropology Today*, an academic journal, "will end up harming the entire discipline in the long run."

Arguing that her critics misunderstand the program and the military, Ms. McFate said other anthropologists were joining the teams. She said their goal was to help the military decrease conflict instead of provoking it, and she vehemently denied that the anthropologists collected intelligence for the military.

In eastern Afghanistan, Tracy wanted to reduce the use of heavy-handed military operations focused solely on killing insurgents, which she said alienated the population and created more insurgents. "I can go back and enhance the military's understanding," she said, "so that we don't make the same mistakes we did in Iraq."

Along with offering advice to commanders, she said, the five-member team creates a database of local leaders and tribes, as well as social problems, economic issues, and political disputes.

CLINICS AND MEDIATION

During the recent operation, as soldiers watched for suicide bombers, Tracy and Army medics held a free medical clinic. They said they hoped that providing medical care would show villagers that the Afghan government was improving their lives.

Civil affairs soldiers then tried to mediate between factions of the Zadran tribe about where to build a school. The Americans said they hoped that the school, which would serve children from both groups, might end a 70-year dispute between the groups over control of a mountain covered with lucrative timber.

Though they praised the new program, Afghan and Western officials said it remained to be seen whether the weak Afghan government could maintain the gains. "That's going to be the challenge, to fill the vacuum," said Mr. Gregg, the United Nations official. "There's a question mark over whether the government has the ability to take advantage of the gains."

Others also question whether the overstretched American military and its NATO allies can keep up the pace of operations.

American officers expressed optimism. Many of those who had served in both Afghanistan and Iraq said they had more hope for Afghanistan. One officer said that the Iraqis had the tools to stabilize their country, like a potentially strong economy, but that they lacked the will. He said Afghans had the will, but lacked the tools.

After six years of American promises, Afghans, too, appear to be waiting to see whether the Americans or the Taliban will win a protracted test of wills here. They said this summer was just one chapter in a potentially lengthy struggle.

At a "super jirga" set up by Afghan and American commanders here, a member of the Afghan Parliament, Nader Khan Katawazai, laid out the challenge ahead to dozens of tribal elders.

"Operation Khyber was just for a few days," he said. "The Taliban will emerge again."

45

Do Muslim Women Really Need Saving?

Anthropological Reflections
on Cultural Relativism and Its Others

Lila Abu-Lughod

Religious differences, including the moral and socio-cultural assumptions subsumed by religion, are extremely important for understanding our globalizing world. After September 11, 2001, the United States went to war in Afghanistan to fight the Taliban, the ruling group in that country, who were believed to be harboring al Qaeda operatives. In addition to the search for Osama bin Laden, a major rationale for going to war was to "liberate" Afghani women from the Taliban. In U.S. political and media discourses, the *burqa*, a black head-to-toe cotton veil mandated by the Taliban for women in public places, became a symbol of women's oppression in Afghanistan.

Prior to invasion by the United States, Afghanistan had a difficult and war-torn history. For years the country was wracked with civil wars, which were made worse by the fact that the United States and the USSR armed rival Afghani factions as pawns in the cold war. (The Taliban became a powerful group during that period in part because of American financial support for the Islamic radicals.) When the Taliban took control of most of Afghanistan in the late 1990s, many Afghans were cautiously optimistic, hoping that the country might finally experience some peace after years of civil war.

In this selection, anthropologist Lila Abu-Lughod argues that the "liberation of women" rationale for going to war was ethnocentric, and that the focus on the *burqa* ignored issues that may be more important to Afghani women, such as living in an area free from war. Important historical and political connections were ignored by U.S. political leaders, she argues, in favor of the simplistic East-West dichotomy that was used to justify invasion. American cultural beliefs about the "other" can be exploited in attempts to sway public opinion.

Although it has largely fallen from the headlines, the United States has continued to maintain a significant military presence in Afghanistan. Poor security and lack of basic infrastructure have remained pressing problems in most of the country. A positive future for Afghani—women and men—is far from assured.

As you read this selection, ask yourself the following questions:

- What was "colonial feminism"? Why was it problematic?
- Why might some women choose to wear a veil?
- In this selection, Abu-Lughod asks, "Can we only free Afghan women to be like us, or might we have to recognize that even after 'liberation' from the Taliban, they might want different things than we would want for them? What do we do about that?" How would you answer this question?
- Why is it problematic to associate feminism with the West?
- How might Americans try to help Afghani women in ways that do not involve "saving" them?

The following terms discussed in this selection are included in the Glossary at the back of the book:

burqa	*ethnocentrism*
colonialism	*Islam*
cultural relativism	*Muslim*

W hat are the ethics of the current "War on Terrorism," a war that justifies itself by purporting to liberate, or save, Afghan women? Does anthropology have anything to offer in our search for a viable position to take regarding this rationale for war?

Abu-Lughod, Lila. "Do Muslim Women Really Need Saving? Anthropological Reflection on Cultural Relativism and Its Others." From *American Anthropologist* 104 (2002), no. 3:783–790. Reprinted by permission of Wiley-Blackwell Publishing.

I want to point out the minefields—a metaphor that is sadly too apt for a country like Afghanistan, with the world's highest number of mines per capita—of this obsession with the plight of Muslim women. I hope to show some way through them using insights from anthropology, the discipline whose charge has been to understand and manage cultural difference.

The question is why knowing about the "culture" of the region, and particularly its religious beliefs and treatment of women, was more urgent than exploring the history of the development of repressive regimes in the region and the U.S. role in this history. Such cultural framing, it seemed to me, prevented the serious exploration of the roots and nature of human suffering in this part of the world. Instead of political and historical explanations, experts were being asked to give religio-cultural ones. Instead of questions that might lead to the exploration of global interconnections, we were offered ones that worked to artificially divide the world into separate spheres—recreating an imaginative geography of West versus East, us versus Muslims, cultures in which First Ladies give speeches versus others where women shuffle around silently in burqas.

Most pressing for me was why the Muslim woman in general, and the Afghan woman in particular, were so crucial to this cultural mode of explanation, which ignored the complex entanglements in which we are all implicated, in sometimes surprising alignments. Why were these female symbols being mobilized in this "War against Terrorism" in a way they were not in other conflicts? Laura Bush's radio address on November 17 reveals the political work such mobilization accomplishes. On the one hand, her address collapsed important distinctions that should have been maintained. There was a constant slippage between the Taliban and the terrorists, so that they became almost one word—a kind of hyphenated monster identity: the Taliban-and-the-terrorists. Then there was the blurring of the very separate causes in Afghanistan of women's continuing malnutrition, poverty, and ill health, and their more recent exclusion under the Taliban from employment, schooling, and the joys of wearing nail polish. On the other hand, her speech reinforced chasmic divides, primarily between the "civilized people throughout the world" whose hearts break for the women and children of Afghanistan and the Taliban-and-the-terrorists, the cultural monsters who want to, as she put it, "impose their world on the rest of us."

Most revealingly, the speech enlisted women to justify American bombing and intervention in Afghanistan and to make a case for the "War on Terrorism" of which it was allegedly a part. As Laura Bush said, "Because of our recent military gains in much of Afghanistan, women are no longer imprisoned in their homes. They can listen to music and teach their daughters without fear of punishment.... The fight against terrorism is also a fight for the rights and dignity of women" (U.S. Government 2002).

These words have haunting resonances for anyone who has studied colonial history. Many who have worked on British colonialism in South Asia have noted the use of the woman question in colonial policies where intervention into sati (the practice of widows immolating themselves on their husbands' funeral pyres), child marriage, and other practices was used to justify rule. As Gayatri Chakravorty Spivak (1988) has cynically put it: white men saving brown women from brown men. The historical record is full of similar cases, including in the Middle East. In turn-of-the-century Egypt, what Leila Ahmed (1992) has called "colonial feminism" was hard at work. This was a selective concern about the plight of Egyptian women that focused on the veil as a sign of oppression but gave no support to women's education and was professed loudly by the same Englishman, Lord Cromer, who opposed women's suffrage back home.

Sociologist Marnia Lazreg (1994) has offered some vivid examples of how French colonialism enlisted women to its cause in Algeria. She describes skits at awards ceremonies at the Muslim Girls' School in Algiers in 1851 and 1852. In the first skit, written by "a French lady from Algiers," two Algerian Arab girls reminisced about their trip to France with words including the following:

> Oh! Protective France: Oh! Hospitable France! . . .
> Noble land, where I felt free
> Under Christian skies to pray to our God: . . .
> God bless you for the happiness you bring us!
> And you, adoptive mother, who taught us
> That we have a share of this world,
> We will cherish you forever! [Lazreg 1994: 68–69]

These girls are made to invoke the gift of a share of this world, a world where freedom reigns under Christian skies. This is not the world the Taliban-and-the-terrorists would "like to impose on the rest of us."

Just as I argued above that we need to be suspicious when neat cultural icons are plastered over messier historical and political narratives, so we need to be wary when Lord Cromer in British-ruled Egypt, French ladies in Algeria, and Laura Bush, all with military troops behind them, claim to be saving or liberating Muslim women.

POLITICS OF THE VEIL

I want now to look more closely at those Afghan women Laura Bush claimed were "rejoicing" at their liberation by the Americans. This necessitates a discussion of the veil, or the burqa, because it is so central to contemporary concerns about Muslim women. This will set the stage for a discussion of how anthropologists, feminist anthropologists in particular, contend with the problem of difference in a global world. In the conclusion, I will return to the rhetoric of saving Muslim women and offer an alternative.

It is common popular knowledge that the ultimate sign of the oppression of Afghan women under the Taliban-and-the-terrorists is that they were forced to wear the burqa. Liberals sometimes confess their surprise that even though Afghanistan has been liberated from the Taliban, women do not seem to be throwing off their burqas. Someone who has worked in Muslim regions must ask why this is so surprising. Did we expect that once "free" from the Taliban they would go "back" to belly shirts and blue jeans, or dust off their Chanel suits? We need to be more sensible about the clothing of "women of cover," and so there is perhaps a need to make some basic points about veiling.

First, it should be recalled that the Taliban did not invent the burqa. It was the local form of covering that Pashtun women in one region wore when they went out. The Pashtun are one of several ethnic groups in Afghanistan and the burqa was one of many forms of covering in the subcontinent and Southwest Asia that has developed as a convention for symbolizing women's modesty or respectability. The burqa, like some other forms of "cover" has, in many settings, marked the symbolic separation of men's and women's spheres, as part of the general association of women with family and home, not with public space where strangers mingled.

Twenty years ago the anthropologist Hanna Papanek (1982), who worked in Pakistan, described the burqa as "portable seclusion." She noted that many saw it as a liberating invention because it enabled women to move out of segregated living spaces while still observing the basic moral requirements of separating and protecting women from unrelated men. Ever since I came across her phrase "portable seclusion," I have thought of these enveloping robes as "mobile homes." Everywhere, such veiling signifies belonging to a particular community and participating in a moral way of life in which families are paramount in the organization of communities and the home is associated with the sanctity of women.

The obvious question that follows is this: If this were the case, why would women suddenly become immodest? Why would they suddenly throw off the markers of their respectability, markers, whether burqas or other forms of cover, which were supposed to assure their protection in the public sphere from the harassment of strange men by symbolically signaling to all that they were still in the inviolable space of their homes, even though moving in the public realm? Especially when these are forms of dress that had become so conventional that most women gave little thought to their meaning.

To draw some analogies, none of them perfect, why are we surprised that Afghan women do not throw off their burqas when we know perfectly well that it would not be appropriate to wear shorts to the opera? At the time these discussions of Afghan women's burqas were raging, a friend of mine was chided by her husband for suggesting she wanted to wear a pantsuit to a fancy wedding: "You know you don't wear pants to a WASP wedding," he reminded her. New Yorkers know that the beautifully coiffed Hasidic women . . . are wearing wigs. This is because religious belief and community standards of propriety require the covering of the hair. They also alter boutique fashions to include high necks and long sleeves. As anthropologists know perfectly well, people wear the appropriate form of dress for their social communities and are guided by socially shared standards, religious beliefs, and moral ideals, unless they deliberately transgress to make a point or are unable to afford proper cover. If we think that U.S. women live in a world of choice regarding clothing, all we need to do is remind ourselves of the expression, "the tyranny of fashion."

What had happened in Afghanistan under the Taliban is that one regional style of covering or veiling, associated with a certain respectable but not elite class, was imposed on everyone as "religiously" appropriate, even though previously there had been many different styles, popular or traditional with different groups and classes—different ways to mark women's propriety, or, in more recent times, religious piety. Although I am not an expert on Afghanistan, I imagine that the majority of women left in Afghanistan by the time the Taliban took control were the rural or less educated, from nonelite families, since they were the only ones who could not emigrate to escape the hardship and violence that has marked Afghanistan's recent history. If liberated from the enforced wearing of burqas, most of these women would choose some other form of modest headcovering, like all those living nearby who were not under the Taliban—their rural Hindu counterparts in the North of India (who cover their heads and veil their faces from affines) or their Muslim sisters in Pakistan.

Even *the New York Times* carried an article about Afghan women refugees in Pakistan that attempted to educate readers about this local variety (Fremson 2001). The article describes and pictures everything from the now-iconic burqa with the embroidered eyeholes, which a Pashtun woman explains is the proper dress for her community, to large scarves they call chadors, to the new Islamic modest dress that wearers refer to as *hijab*. Those in the new Islamic dress are characteristically students heading for professional careers, especially in medicine, just like their counterparts from Egypt to Malaysia. One wearing the large scarf was a school principal; the other was a poor street vendor. The telling quote from the young street vendor is, "If I did [wear the burqa] the refugees would tease me because the burqa is for 'good women' who stay inside the home" (Fremson 2001:14). Here you can see the local status associated with the burqa—it is for good respectable women from strong families who are not forced to make a living selling on the street.

The British newspaper *The Guardian* published an interview in January 2002 with Dr. Suheila Siddiqi, a respected surgeon in Afghanistan who holds the rank of lieutenant general in the Afghan medical corps (Goldenberg 2002). A woman in her sixties, she comes from an elite family and, like her sisters, was educated. Unlike most women of her class, she chose not to go into exile. She is presented in the article as "the woman who stood up to the Taliban" because she refused to wear the burqa. She had made it a condition of returning to her post as head of a major hospital when the Taliban came begging in 1996, just eight months after firing her along with other women. Siddiqi is described as thin, glamorous, and confident. But further into the article it is noted that her graying bouffant hair is covered in a gauzy veil. This is a reminder that though she refused the burqa, she had no question about wearing the chador or scarf.

Finally, I need to make a crucial point about veiling. Not only are there many forms of covering, which themselves have different meanings in the communities in which they are used, but also veiling itself must not be confused with, or made to stand for, lack of agency. As I have argued in my ethnography of a Bedouin community in Egypt in the late 1970s and 1980s (1986), pulling the black head cloth over the face in front of older respected men is considered a voluntary act by women who are deeply committed to being moral and have a sense of honor tied to family. One of the ways they show their standing is by covering their faces in certain contexts. They decide for whom they feel it is appropriate to veil.

To take a very different case, the modern Islamic modest dress that many educated women across the Muslim world have taken on since the mid-1970s now both publicly marks piety and can be read as a sign of educated urban sophistication, a sort of modernity (e.g., Abu-Lughod 1995, 1998; Brenner 1996; El Guindi 1999; MacLeod 1991; Ong 1990). As Saba Mahmood (2001) has so brilliantly shown in her ethnography of women in the mosque movement in Egypt, this new form of dress is also perceived by many of the women

who adopt it as part of a bodily means to cultivate virtue, the outcome of their professed desire to be close to God.

Two points emerge from this fairly basic discussion of the meanings of veiling in the contemporary Muslim world. First, we need to work against the reductive interpretation of veiling as the quintessential sign of women's unfreedom, even if we object to state imposition of this form, as in Iran or with the Taliban. (It must be recalled that the modernizing states of Turkey and Iran had earlier in the century banned veiling and required men, except religious clerics, to adopt Western dress.) What does freedom mean if we accept the fundamental premise that humans are social beings, always raised in certain social and historical contexts and belonging to particular communities that shape their desires and understandings of the world? Is it not a gross violation of women's own understandings of what they are doing to simply denounce the burqa as a medieval imposition? Second, we must take care not to reduce the diverse situations and attitudes of millions of Muslim women to a single item of clothing. Perhaps it is time to give up the Western obsession with the veil and focus on some serious issues with which feminists and others should indeed be concerned.

Ultimately, the significant political–ethical problem the burqa raises is how to deal with cultural "others." How are we to deal with difference without accepting the passivity implied by the cultural relativism for which anthropologists are justly famous—a relativism that says it's their culture and it's not my business to judge or interfere, only to try to understand. Cultural relativism is certainly an improvement on ethnocentrism and the racism, cultural imperialism, and imperiousness that underlie it; the problem is that it is too late not to interfere. The forms of lives we find around the world are already products of long histories of interactions.

We need to look closely at what we are supporting (and what we are not) and to think carefully about why. . . . I do not know how many feminists who felt good about saving Afghan women from the Taliban are also asking for a global redistribution of wealth or contemplating sacrificing their own consumption radically so that African or Afghan women could have some chance of having what I do believe should be a universal human right—the right to freedom from the structural violence of global inequality and from the ravages of war, the everyday rights of having enough to eat, having homes for their families in which to live and thrive, having ways to make decent livings so their children can grow, and having the strength and security to work out, within their communities and with whatever alliances they want, how to live a good life, which might very well include changing the ways those communities are organized.

... For that, we need to confront two more big issues. First is the acceptance of the possibility of difference. Can we only free Afghan women to be like us or might we have to recognize that even after "liberation" from the Taliban, they might want different things than we would want for them? What do we do about that? Second, we need to be vigilant about the rhetoric of saving people because of what it implies about our attitudes.

Again, when I talk about accepting difference, I am not implying that we should resign ourselves to being cultural relativists who respect whatever goes on elsewhere as "just their culture." I have already discussed the dangers of "cultural" explanations; "their" cultures are just as much part of history and an interconnected world as ours are. What I am advocating is the hard work involved in recognizing and respecting differences—precisely as products of different histories, as expressions of different circumstances, and as manifestations of differently structured desires. We may want justice for women, but can we accept that there might be different ideas about justice and that different women might want, or choose, different futures from what we envision as best (see Ong 1988)? We must consider that they might be called to personhood, so to speak, in a different language.

Reports from the Bonn peace conference held in late November to discuss the rebuilding of Afghanistan revealed significant differences among the few Afghan women feminists and activists present. RAWA's position was to reject any conciliatory approach to Islamic governance. According to one report I read, most women activists, especially those based in Afghanistan who are aware of the realities on the ground, agreed that Islam had to be the starting point for reform. Fatima Gailani, a U.S.-based advisor to one of the delegations, is quoted as saying, "If I go to Afghanistan today and ask women for votes on the promise to bring them secularism, they are going to tell me to go to hell."

One of the things we have to be most careful about in thinking about Third World feminisms, and feminism in different parts of the Muslim world, is how not to fall into polarizations that place feminism on the side of the West. I have written about the dilemmas faced by Arab feminists when Western feminists initiate campaigns that make them vulnerable to local denunciations by conservatives of various sorts, whether Islamist or nationalist, of being traitors (Abu-Lughod 2001). As some like Afsaneh Najmabadi are now arguing, not only is it wrong to see history simplistically in terms of a putative opposition between Islam and the West (as is happening in the United States now and has happened in parallel in the Muslim world), but it is also strategically dangerous to accept this cultural opposition between Islam and the West, between

fundamentalism and feminism, because those many people within Muslim countries who are trying to find alternatives to present injustices, those who might want to refuse the divide and take from different histories and cultures, who do not accept that being feminist means being Western, will be under pressure to choose, just as we are: Are you with us or against us?

My point is to remind us to be aware of differences, respectful of other paths toward social change that might give women better lives. Can there be a liberation that is Islamic? And, beyond this, is liberation even a goal for which all women or people strive? Are emancipation, equality, and rights part of a universal language we must use?

Might other desires be more meaningful for different groups of people? Living in close families? Living in a godly way? Living without war? I have done fieldwork in Egypt over more than 20 years and I cannot think of a single woman I know, from the poorest rural to the most educated cosmopolitan, who has ever expressed envy of U.S. women, women they tend to perceive as bereft of community, vulnerable to sexual violence and social anomie, driven by individual success rather than morality, or strangely disrespectful of God.

BEYOND THE RHETORIC OF SALVATION

Let us return, finally, to my title, "Do Muslim Women Need Saving?" The discussion of culture, veiling, and how one can navigate the shoals of cultural difference should put Laura Bush's self-congratulation about the rejoicing of Afghan women liberated by American troops in a different light. It is deeply problematic to construct the Afghan woman as someone in need of saving. When you save someone, you imply that you are saving her from something. You are also saving her *to* something. What violences are entailed in this transformation, and what presumptions are being made about the superiority of that to which you are saving her? Projects of saving other women depend on and reinforce a sense of superiority by Westerners, a form of arrogance that deserves to be challenged. All one needs to do to appreciate the patronizing quality of the rhetoric of saving women is to imagine using it today in the United States about disadvantaged groups such as African American women or working-class women. We now understand them as suffering from structural violence. We have become politicized about race and class, but not culture.

Could we not leave veils and vocations of saving others behind and instead train our sights on ways to make the world a more just place? The reason respect for difference should not be confused with cultural relativism is that it does not preclude asking how we, living in this privileged and powerful part of the world, might examine our own responsibilities for the situations in which others in distant places have found themselves. We do not stand outside the world, looking out over this sea of poor benighted people, living under the shadow—or veil—of oppressive cultures; we are part of that world. Islamic movements themselves have arisen in a world shaped by the intense engagements of Western powers in Middle Eastern lives.

A more productive approach, it seems to me, is to ask how we might contribute to making the world a more just place. A world not organized around strategic military and economic demands; a place where certain kinds of forces and values that we may still consider important could have an appeal and where there is the peace necessary for discussions, debates, and transformations to occur within communities. We need to ask ourselves what kinds of world conditions we could contribute to making such that popular desires will not be overdetermined by an overwhelming sense of helplessness in the face of forms of global injustice. Where we seek to be active in the affairs of distant places, can we do so in the spirit of support for those within those communities whose goals are to make women's (and men's) lives better (as Walley has argued in relation to practices of genital cutting in Africa, [1997])? Can we use a more egalitarian language of alliances, coalitions, and solidarity, instead of salvation?

Even RAWA, the now celebrated Revolutionary Association of the Women of Afghanistan, which was so instrumental in bringing to U.S. women's attention the excesses of the Taliban, has opposed the U.S. bombing from the beginning. They do not see in it Afghan women's salvation but increased hardship and loss. They have long called for disarmament and for peace-keeping forces. Spokespersons point out the dangers of confusing governments with people, the Taliban with innocent Afghans who will be most harmed. They consistently remind audiences to take a close look at the ways policies are being organized around oil interests, the arms industry, and the international drug trade. They are not obsessed with the veil, even though they are the most radical feminists working for a secular democratic Afghanistan. Unfortunately, only their messages about the excesses of the Taliban have been heard, even though their criticisms of those in power in Afghanistan have included previous regimes. A first step in hearing their wider message is to break with the language of alien cultures, whether to understand or eliminate them. Missionary work and colonial feminism belong in the past. Our task is to critically explore what we might do to help create a world in which

those poor Afghan women, for whom "the hearts of those in the civilized world break," can have safety and decent lives.

ACKNOWLEDGMENTS

I want to thank Page Jackson, Fran Mascia-Lees, Tim Mitchell, Rosalind Morris, Anupama Rao, and members of the audience at the symposium "Responding to War," sponsored by Columbia University's Institute for Research on Women and Gender (where I presented an earlier version), for helpful comments, references, clippings, and encouragement.

REFERENCES

Abu-Lughod, Lila. 1986. *Veiled Sentiments: Honor and Poetry in a Bedouin Society*. Berkeley: University of California Press.

———. 1995. Movie Stars and Islamic Moralism in Egypt. *Social Text* 42: 53–67.

———. 1998. *Remaking Women: Feminism and Modernity in the Middle East*. Princeton: Princeton University Press.

———. 2001. Orientalism and Middle East Feminist Studies. *Feminist Studies* 27(1): 101–113.

Ahmed, Leila. 1992. *Women and Gender in Islam*. New Haven, CT: Yale University Press.

Alloula, Malek. 1986. *The Colonial Harem*. Minneapolis: University of Minnesota Press.

Brenner, Suzanne. 1996. Reconstructing Self and Society: Javanese Muslim Women and "the Veil." *American Ethnologist* 23(4): 673–697.

El Guindi, Fadwa. 1999. *Veil: Modesty, Privacy and Resistance*. Oxford: Berg.

Fremson, Ruth. 2001. Allure Must Be Covered. Individuality Peeks Through. *New York Times*, November 4: 14.

Global Exchange. 2002. Courage and Tenacity: A Women's Delegation to Afghanistan. Electronic document, http://www.globalexchange.org/tours/auto/2002-03-05_CourageandTenacityAWomensDele.html. (Accessed February 11).

Goldenberg, Suzanne. 2002. The Woman Who Stood Up to the Taliban. *The Guardian*, January 24. Electronic document, http://222.guardian.co.uk/afghanistan/story/0,1284,63840.

Hirschkind, Charles, and Saba Mahmood. 2002. Feminism, the Taliban, and the Politics of Counter-Insurgency. *Anthropological Quarterly*, Volume 75(2): 107–122.

Lazreg, Marnia. 1994. *The Eloquence of Silence: Algerian Women in Question*. New York: Routledge.

MacLeod, Arlene. 1991. *Accommodating Protest*. New York: Columbia University Press.

Mahmood, Saba. 2001. Feminist Theory, Embodiment, and the Docile Agent: Some Reflections on the Egyptian Islamic Revival. *Cultural Anthropology* 16(2): 202–235.

Mir-Hosseini, Ziba. 1999. *Islam and Gender: The Religious Debate in Contemporary Iran.* Princeton: Princeton University Press.

Moghissi, Haideh. 1999. *Feminism and Islamic Fundamentalism.* London: Zed Books.

Najmabadi, Afsaneh. 1998. Feminism in an Islamic Republic. In *Islam, Gender and Social Change*, eds. Yvonne Haddad and John Esposito, 59–84. New York: Oxford University Press.

———. 2000. (Un)Veiling Feminism. *Social Text* 64: 29–45.

Ong, Aihwa. 1988. *Colonialism and Modernity: Feminist Re-Presentations of Women in Non-Western Societies. Inscriptions* 3–4: 79–93.

———. 1990. State Versus Islam: Malay Families, Women's Bodies, and the Body Politic in Malaysia. *American Ethnologist* 17(2): 258–276.

Papanek, Hanna. 1982. Purdah in Pakistan: Seclusion and Modern Occupations for Women. In *Separate Worlds,* eds. Hanna Papanek and Gail Minault, 190–216. Columbus, MO: South Asia Books.

Safire, William. 2001. "On Language." *New York Times* Magazine, October 28: 22.

Spivak, Gayatri Chakravorty. 1988. Can the Subaltern Speak? In *Marxism and the Interpretation of Culture*, eds. Cary Nelson and Lawrence Grossberg, 271–313. Urbana: University of Illinois Press.

Strathern, Marilyn. 1987. An Awkward Relationship: The Case of Feminism and Anthropology. *Signs* 12: 276–292.

U.S. Government. 1907. *Our Moslem Sisters: A Cry of Need from Lands of Darkness Interpreted by Those Who Heard It.* New York: Fleming H. Revell Co.

———. 2002. Electronic document, http://www.whitehouse .gov/news/releases/2001/11/20011117. (Accessed January 10).

Walley, Christine. 1997. Searching for "Voices": Feminism, Anthropology, and the Global Debate over Female Genital Operations. *Cultural Anthropology* 12(3): 405–438.

46

Cell Phones, Sharing, and Social Status in an African Society

Daniel Jordan Smith

Contemporary processes of globalization have stimulated many anthropologists to begin asking new research questions. One important area of innovative research pertains to the global spread of technology and its influence on local people, practices, values, and behaviors. Globalization involves the worldwide transfer of technology, capital, industry, people, and cultural ideas. It has made the world a smaller place, but it has also increased social inequalities across the "digital divide."

In the twentieth century, radio and television played powerful roles in creating linkages between previously disconnected areas of the world. Without a doubt, new mass media brought the signs, symbols, images, and cultural values of the industrialized "First World" to people and communities in poorer "Third World" regions. The globalization of technology is not a top-down, unidirectional process. New technologies create new ways in which small groups of people can shape the ideas, values, political opinions, and even the actions of large groups of people within a particular town, district, country, or world region.

Recent technological developments are influencing people and communities in new ways, raising new research questions for anthropologists. One such development is the Internet, although on a global scale fewer people have access to that technology than the topic of this selection: cell phones. Like radio and television before them, cell phones create new and unprecedented opportunities for communication across distances. As this selection vividly demonstrates, the ways in which people use cell phones are powerfully influenced by local ideas, values, customs, and practices.

In other words, global processes always take place within local contexts. Both the symbolic meaning and the social rules for using cell phones change in different cultural contexts.

As you read this selection, ask yourself the following questions:

- Why do so many Nigerians who can barely afford life's basic necessities go to such great lengths to acquire a cell phone?

- The author notes that in Nigeria "affluent people are meant to demonstrate and share their prosperity, but in ways that do not humiliate their peers." How is this social ethic expressed in terms of cell phone use?

- What are the basic social rules associated with the "politics of sharing cell phone credit?"

- Why is the author told, "This phone doesn't fit you?" What does this comment tell us about the sociopolitics of cell phones in Nigeria?

- How, and why, has the symbolic significance of cell phone as status symbol changed in the past decade?

The following terms discussed in this selection are included in the Glossary at the back of the book:

consumable commodity
microeconomics
micropolitics of social inequality
reciprocity
social status

INTRODUCTION

On July 19, 2004, the popular BBC Africa Service morning news program, *Network Africa*, carried a curious story from its Nigeria correspondent. He described a

Smith, Daniel Jordan. "Cell Phones, Sharing, and Social Status in African Society." Reprinted with permission of the author.

recent epidemic of rumors circulating in the country, purporting that anyone who answered calls on their cellular telephones originating from several specific numbers risked madness, and even death. I had heard a similar story in the previous few days from dozens of friends and acquaintances in and around the towns of

Owerri and Umuahia in southeastern Nigeria, where I was conducting research. Ironically, cell phone usage around the country surged in the wake of the rumors, as people phoned and sent text messages to friends and relatives, warning them of the "killer numbers."

Once the popular rumors circulated widely, Nigerian newspapers carried stories printing some of the suspected numbers and incorporating quotations from citizens who allegedly witnessed the effects of these sinister calls (Akinsuyi 2004). But the newspapers also published statements from spokespersons for the country's major mobile telephone service providers, denying that such killer numbers existed (Ikhemuemhe 2004). Further, they published interviews with government authorities and university scientists disputing the technological feasibility of transmitting witchcraft through cell phones. Radio call-in programs and television talk shows buzzed with debate about the story, mesmerizing the nation for the better part of two weeks. Eventually, popular attention faded, as it had with regard to a previous rumor suggesting that men who carried cell phones in their pockets or strapped them to their belts risked becoming infertile.

The rumors that mobile phones might be implicated in infertility, madness, and murder are a testament to how dramatically this new technology has affected Nigeria. A few elite Nigerians had access to older cellular telephone technologies beginning in the 1990s, but the number of such phones was minuscule. The introduction of the Global System for Mobile Communications (GSM) technology to Nigeria in 2001 and the liberalization of Nigeria's previously government-controlled telecommunications industry transformed cell phones from an extreme rarity into an everyday technology to which literally millions of ordinary citizens have access. When GSM technology was first introduced in Nigeria, the country had only approximately 500,000 landlines for over 100 million people (Obadare 2004), a number which had not increased significantly in many years. By the end of 2004, less than four years after the first GSM cellular phones and services went on sale to the Nigerian public, the country had over seven million subscribers (Mobile Africa 2005), with some recent estimates putting the number of mobile phones users in Nigeria at over eleven million (PANA 2005).

In addition, millions more people without their own phones were provided easy access to cell phone service, as individual cell phone owners became small-scale entrepreneurs, converting their personal phones into informal businesses. By the time the BBC story was broadcast, thousands of call centers, most with just one or two phones and a single attendant, dotted Nigeria's landscape. Every major city and many small towns are now connected, and countless rural and urban communities that have no running water and little or no electricity service are integrated into the country's vast and expanding mobile telephone network.

Cell phones have produced dramatic changes in communication in Nigeria, with many positive effects. Mobile phones have been integrated into long-standing patterns of social relationship, enabling Nigerians separated by great distances to continue to interact based on expectations of sharing and reciprocity. But just as important, they have become symbols of social status. Nigerians assert and express modern identities by purchasing, using, and publicly displaying the latest consumer commodities. Mastery of the new phone technology is a marker of being middle class, educated, and urban. Yet the reality is that cell phones represent a level of economic achievement that is out of reach to most Nigerians. The majority of new cell phone consumers experience the costs of usage as exorbitant, reinforcing the sense that middle-class status remains elusive. Thus, while the burgeoning popularity of cell phones in Nigeria, and throughout sub-Saharan Africa, represents the aspirations of ordinary people for better lives, this new technology exposes the pronounced and enduring nature of social inequality.

CELL PHONE ECONOMICS

Owning and using a cell phone in Nigeria requires three primary investments: (1) buying a phone; (2) accessing service from one of the country's four major providers through the purchase of a SIM (Subscriber Identity Module) card that is installed in the back of the phone to connect it to the service network; and (3) procuring "recharge cards," through which call time is paid for by loading a unique pin number each time one wants to add credit to an individual account. While the phone and the SIM card are onetime acquisitions, access to service depends on the regular purchase of the recharge cards to load call time as previously purchased amounts are exhausted.

In 2005, new phones are available in Nigeria for as little as 6,000 naira (approximately forty-five U.S. dollars), and as much as 60,000 naira (over U.S. $450), depending on the brand, the model, and the complexity of features offered on the phone. The price of SIM cards declined dramatically in the past several years, to about five to ten dollars, with companies sometimes offering free SIM cards as part of periodic marketing campaigns. The vast majority of customers use the "pay as you go" recharge card system.

Most crucial from the perspective of ordinary Nigerians is the cost of calls themselves. As with every other feature of cell phone service, the cost of calls has declined significantly over the four years since GSM service was introduced. But the price of calls per minute and per second (a choice between these rates is now available to most consumers) is still expensive, relative to both Nigerians' purchasing power and the cost of cell phone service in other countries (Obadare 2004). Importantly, although incoming calls are free, every outgoing call is charged—there are no free minutes per month or at night and on weekends, though lower rates apply in off-peak hours. Further, recharge cards expire. Credit not utilized within a specified period of time is forever lost. For example, ten dollars of credit would typically need to be used within about two weeks.

Initially, when GSM cell phone service was first introduced, domestic calls cost approximately fifty naira (thirty-seven U.S. cents) per minute. Recently, the cost has declined to about twenty-five naira (nineteen cents) per minute, with the precise amount depending upon the volume of calls per month, whether the call is in or out of network, the time of day, and so on. Each of the country's four main service providers (Glomobile, Mtel, MTN, and Vmobile) offers a diverse range of service packages and special deals, but most consumers cannot afford to make enough calls to qualify for the plans that offer the cheapest calling rates. Indeed, an entire discourse of complaint about the high cost of cell phone calls has emerged in Nigeria (Obadare 2004). Popular reaction to the economics of personal cell phone use has generated a new lexicon and a growing repertoire of behaviors designed to mitigate the financial burdens of cell phone ownership.

"THE FIRE THAT CONSUMES MONEY"

In southeastern Nigeria, where I work, and where the predominant language is Igbo, the vernacular name for a cell phone is *oku na iri ego*, which translates literally as "the fire that consumes money." This popular local name reflects ordinary citizens' frustrations with the perceived exorbitant costs of cell phone calls. New linguistic turns of phrase and innovative social practices that have evolved with the proliferation of cell phone technology build on people's aggravation over the strain of cell phone ownership, but they also indicate the degree to which cell phone culture has taken root in everyday life.

Nigerians have adapted their cell phone usage to suit their economic circumstances, and some aspects of the service plans offered by the country's main providers are clearly designed to attract and keep customers who cannot afford to make a high volume of phone calls. For example, the Short Messaging Systems (SMS), through which customers can send "text messages," is extremely popular in Nigeria and typically costs only fifteen naira (about ten U.S. cents) per message. Text messages must be limited in size, usually no more than 160 characters. Text messaging is particularly popular with younger customers and it has generated its own lexicon of abbreviations, an economy of language that has also become part of Nigeria's youth culture, as it has in other settings (for literature on text messaging generally see Fox 2001; Dooring 2002; and Sylvia and Hady 2004).

Text messaging has become a common way for Nigerians who cannot afford regular phone calls to communicate using the new technology. But for older people, and even among young folks, using text messages too frequently without also calling can be interpreted as sign of unwillingness to spend money on a particular relationship—reflecting either stinginess or a lack of deep concern about the relationship or both. As a consequence, although text messaging is extremely popular, people are careful not to rely on it too exclusively, lest they become objects of criticism. In times of economic hardship, the willingness to spend money on a phone call is evidence of interest or commitment to a relationship, whether it is a friendship, a family tie, a business partnership, or a romance. The consequences of the microeconomics of cell phone use reflect the importance and the complexity of how issues of wealth, inequality, and status are negotiated in human relationships.

"FLASH ME, I FLASH YOU"

Other common practices besides text messaging illustrate the economics and micropolitics of cell phone behavior, and the importance of these behaviors in navigating issues of inequality in social relationships. For example, a major consequence of the fact that many cell phone owners cannot afford to maintain credit on a regular basis is the innovation of what Nigerians call "flashing." To "flash" someone means to call the recipient's line and allow the phone to ring just once, so that the incoming number is displayed to the recipient, but the caller hangs up before the recipient answers. This way, the recipient knows the number of the person trying to reach him or her, and hopefully has enough credit to call back. Flashing is possible because one can make a call without paying for it as long as no one picks up. Under the prevailing plans in Nigeria, it is possible to receive incoming calls even when one does not have any credit.

From my experience observing scores of friends and acquaintances receiving flashes, whether or not the recipient of the flash could identify the caller from the incoming number was not necessarily a good predictor of a callback. Sometimes knowledge of the identity of the incoming caller created the incentive to call back immediately, perhaps out of obligation, affection, or some prior awareness about the reason for the call. Conversely, on other occasions, knowledge of the identity of the caller had the opposite effect, the attitude being that anyone who had something important to communicate would find a way to pay for a call, even if only for a minute or two. People often refused to call back after a flash out of suspicion that the caller wanted the recipient to bear the cost of the conversation. Nevertheless, unidentified flashes often sparked curiosity, and people frequently responded to them.

Given that countless Nigerians who own cell phones are often in a position where credit is exhausted or very low, and therefore very precious, flashing can sometimes become a comical exchange in which no one wants to bear the costs of a call. In the Pidgin English that is often the lingua franca in Nigeria, people expressed the phenomenon of reciprocal flashing, in which no one was willing to pay for a call, with the phrase "flash me, I flash you." Mostly in good humor, friends frequently suspected each other of trying to transfer and defray the costs of communication through flashing. As a consequence, people sometimes tried to answer their phones before the end of the first ring, engaging the call before the flasher could hang up. This practice was particularly common when someone flashed more than once, giving the recipient time to prepare for a quick answer. Over the past couple of years I witnessed numerous comic scenes where people plotted to "catch" flashers before they could hang up, making them pay for the connection.

SHARING CREDIT: INEQUALITY AND SOCIALITY

Of course most people who communicate by telephone eventually see each other in person, and past episodes of flashing are often topics of discussion. A typical face-to-face conversation about flashing might include a query by the flasher as to why the recipient did not call back, followed by an admission (or assertion) by the recipient that he or she did not have any credit. The recipient, in turn, may accuse the flasher of having credit and being unwilling to use it. These mostly good-natured conversations reproduce some of the complexity of how people in Nigeria navigate the social representation of wealth more generally. On the one hand, using and sharing one's cell phone liberally are clear signals of wealth, and, like many kinds of conspicuous consumption in Nigeria, seemingly carefree cell phone usage can be rewarded with recognition and prestige. On the other hand, in Nigeria's current economic climate, in

which most people are struggling to make ends meet, a strong ethos prevails in which even the relatively affluent portray themselves as just getting by, particularly among people who are otherwise their peers.

These contradictory dimensions of people's public representations of wealth play out constantly in the arena of cell phone socioeconomics. For those who really are struggling, claiming one has no credit can be a strategy for protecting a precious and dwindling resource. Conversely, using one's cell phone generously even when one cannot actually afford it can be a way of portraying or maintaining social status that is threatened by economic hardship. For those who are better off, claiming not to have credit can be a form of humility, representing oneself as just as much of a victim of Nigeria's unjust political economy as one's peers. But the balance can be precarious. Humility can easily be interpreted as stinginess if a wealthy person persists too long in feigning hardship. However, acting too carefree can be seen as ostentatious or arrogant. Ultimately, affluent people are meant to demonstrate and share their prosperity, but in ways that do not humiliate their peers. The proliferation of cell phones has created a very prominent sphere in which the micropolitics of social inequality in Nigeria are enacted (for other examples see Barber 1995; Cornwall 2002; and Smith 2004).

Although Nigerians' cell phone–related social behaviors illustrate the importance of economics in how people manage their phone usage, including strategizing about the social representation of one's wealth, it would be a mistake to emphasize only the economic dimensions of Nigeria's emerging cell phone culture and its associated behavior. A good deal of cell phone–related behavior requires a social rather than an economic interpretation.

Perhaps the most striking example is the way that Nigerians conceptualize cell phone credit. Clearly, everyone who uses cell phones knows how much phone calls cost, and people are aware of the exact amounts in which recharge cards are sold. Further, as the discussion above regarding the phenomenon of flashing suggests, there is a considerable degree of conscious jockeying with regard to sharing and spending one's credit. However, to a remarkable extent, Nigerians seem to think of cell phone credit in much different terms than they think of money. Once money is transformed into cell phone credit through the purchase and loading of recharge cards, cell phone credit becomes much more like food or drink than money, in the sense that people feel more entitled to share in it without the strict incursion of a debt that would be the case if one asked to borrow money. As with food or drink, there is a strong social expectation that cell phone credit should be shared if one has it.

My awareness of the difference between Nigerian and Western (or at least American) sensibilities in this matter was driven home to me by the experience of an American student who worked as my summer research assistant. She lived with a Nigerian family and found them amazingly hospitable and generous, to the point where they refused to allow her to pay rent or contribute to the household budget for food. She felt guilty about this, knowing the family's limited means, and we devised ways that she could contribute without offending her hosts. But when it came to the student's cell phone, the situation was quite the opposite. She had acquired a cell phone mainly so that her parents could call her at any time from the United States. Over the course of the summer, she found that people in the household had no compunctions about asking if she had credit, and, if she did, they had no hesitation in asking to use her phone to make calls. One young woman in the household asked to use her phone so often that the student finally became exasperated and reported it to me. She could not understand how the same family that was so generous and so unwilling to accept her money could expect to use her cell phone in ways that, from her perspective, seemed so insensitive.

Conceived of as a consumable commodity, cell phone credit was easily incorporated into long-standing traditions of sharing, gift giving, and reciprocity, in which people are expected and often genuinely desire to share without incurring the equivalent of a monetary debt. Of course money too is highly implicated in social relationships, and it can be gifted and shared as well as borrowed, lent, or spent, but it was clear from my student's experience, and from numerous similar interactions that I have since participated in and observed, that cell phone credit is transformed into a medium of social exchange that is much different from money once it is loaded into a phone. Nigerians routinely ask their friends and family, and even acquaintances of less intimacy, whether or not they have credit, in ways they would rarely, if ever, ask so openly about money.

The politics of sharing cell phone credit is nonetheless complicated, both because forms of nonmonetary sharing and reciprocity have their own moral economy, with numerous unspoken rules and expectations, and because cell phone credit is, in fact, in some ways more like money than are consumable commodities like food or drink. Even in the sharing of food and drink, in which Nigerians, like people in many societies, are extremely generous and social, there are expectations of generalized reciprocity (Bearman 1997). Although one does not incur a quantifiable debt by sharing someone's food, if, over time, one only takes and never gives, this will be recognized and admon-

ished in some way. Similarly, with the sharing of cell phone credit, someone asking to make calls on another's phone cannot expect indefinite cooperation if favors are not eventually reciprocated.

However, cell phone credit is still more like money than is a beer or a plate of cooked meat. Although ordinary Nigerians have obviously participated in the conversion of cell phone credit from money into a commodity that carries a more social definition, this transformation is not complete. People routinely lied to their friends about their credit, and I observed countless instances in which people were "caught" misrepresenting their credit. At a club in Nigeria where I play tennis, men would commonly pick up a person's phone while he was on the court to check how much credit was available. Someone caught underreporting his credit would almost certainly have to relent and share his phone. Through such actions people contribute to the demonetization of cell phone credit. But this demonetization did not occur without ambivalence. Indeed, the social expectation that one must share phone credit contributed further to the notion that cell phones are a "fire that consumes money."

As these anecdotes suggest, sociality is at least as important a dynamic in Nigerian social life as inequality, and not just in terms of sharing, but also with regard to the importance of regularly greeting and communicating with people in one's social network. The preeminent value of sociality has greatly influenced cell phone usage, in ways that have significant economic implications, even if economic calculations are not always foremost in the minds of cell phone users. Although much of what I have described above demonstrates that Nigerians are highly conscious of the economics of cell phone use and deeply aware of the social implications of cell phone behavior, it is also true that people's penchant for regular communication for purely social purposes means that people make many calls just to say hello and to be in touch. To have a phone and not use it to reach out to family and friends is similar to the idea of living alone or preferring solitude and privacy to social interaction. For most Nigerians it is not only unconscionable, it is unthinkable (Uchendu 1965). As a consequence, although many Nigerians rightly extol the virtues of the country's new cell phone services for promoting business and facilitating a more effective and productive commercial sector, my observations suggest that the vast majority of ordinary customers use a good deal of their credit making calls that are the cellular telephone version of a friendly visit. All this suggests that while cell phone technology has sparked some changes in social life, in many ways the new technology has also adapted to and been incorporated into longer-standing behavioral customs.

"GLO WITH PRIDE:" CELL PHONES AS STATUS SYMBOLS

As I sat down in the parlor of my friend's house in the southeastern town of Owerri, her twenty-three-year-old son, Uzoma, inquired whether I owned a cell phone. I said I did, and he asked to see it. After a quick inspection of my very simple and obviously low-end Motorola phone, Uzoma declared dismissively: "This phone doesn't fit you." He meant that a person of my status should have a fancier and more expensive phone, preferably the type currently most popular in Nigeria, where the face flips open, the phone has numerous elaborate technical features, and the screen looks like a computer LCD. I defended my simple phone, but I was not surprised at Uzoma's evaluation. I had encountered this reaction to my phone many times before in a society where cell phones have become important markers of social status.[1]

The relatively educated, mostly urban, and at least marginally economically successful Nigerians who own the majority of the country's more than ten million cell phones are acutely aware of the status distinctions conferred by different models. People are constantly noting the quality of their peers' phones, openly conveying approval or disapproval in ways that consciously connect cell phones to social status. Even where people cannot afford to upgrade their phones, the quality of one's cell phone cover and the type and number of accessories owned can be the subject of more fine-grained attempts to assert both status and fashion. Indeed, as status symbols, the cell phones operate at the cusp between economics and fashion, marking both financial position and sense of style. Uzoma assumed I could afford a more expensive phone, so he concluded that I was either too cheap to own a phone fit for a man of my means or too fashion-challenged to know that my phone was a disgrace.

In a huge country like Nigeria, where many people migrate from their villages of origin to cities and towns in search of education, employment, and economic advancement (Geschiere and Gugler 1998; Gugler 2002), the advent of cell phones in a context where landlines served less than 1 percent of the population has revolutionized communication between family and friends separated by long distances. It is little wonder that so many people want cell phones, or that people who can barely afford some of the basic necessities of everyday life make extraordinary

efforts to acquire one. But aside from the practical advantages of cell phone ownership, there is no doubt that cell phones have become an important form of symbolic capital, and that the social status conferred by owning a cell phone is a major motivation for many people (Bourdieu 1984). The cell phone companies cultivate and exploit the symbolic dimensions of cell phone ownership in their advertising, and the pressure of seeing peers enjoy the benefits and social recognition of cell phone ownership induces ever larger numbers of consumers to take the leap.

Whereas just ten years ago, before the advent of GSM technology in Nigeria, cell phones were the exclusive province of the superelite, by 2004 many Nigerians who were not wealthy enough to own their own houses and could not afford to buy a used car were able to acquire the latest marker of modernity. The transition from an elite exoticism to an almost essential accessory for an aspiring middle class happened remarkably fast. Just two years ago, Umuahia, a small city of less than 200,000 that is the capital of Abia State, had not yet been linked to the network of any of the four main service providers. However, for those who really wanted cell phone service, a regional company called Baudex provided a mostly effective but very expensive service.

At the social club where I frequently played tennis, a playground for the town's elite, approximately fifteen to twenty men owned these Baudex phones in the summer of 2003. To call further attention to the status they displayed by owning and sporting these expensive phones, the owners formed a club within the club. They called themselves "*Ofo* United." "*Ofo*" refers to a mystical staff that is the emblem of traditional authority in Igbo society, a symbol that implies supernatural backing. "United" presumably refers to the name of famous football teams, most notably the world-famous Manchester United, but also to teams in Nigeria that use "United" in their names. The members of *Ofo* United sometimes further separated themselves from other members of the larger club, sharing a roasted goat and several cartons of beer, greeting each other saying "*Ofo* United," and brandishing their phones like some sort of secret society symbol. Just a year later, all this changed dramatically, as both MTN and Glomobile had established full service in Umuahia. By the time I left Nigeria in December of 2004, literally every member of the tennis club had a phone, as did the club's receptionists, one of the bar girls, and some of the kitchen staff. *Ofo* United was no more.

As cell phones have come within the reach of more ordinary citizens, their availability has only intensified the status competition associated with the new technology. Just as the poorest Nigerians have for many years worn watches that do not keep time in order to appear better off than they are, one now sees many young people carrying cell phones that are just shells—though being exposed in such a deception is worse than having no phone at all. Because so many people can aspire to having a cell phone, the distinctions noticed with regard to brands, models, and accessories have become even more fine-grained. Many wealthier people now own multiple phones, with one line for each provider, and they carry them wherever they go. Having a cell phone is no longer so distinctive, but having two or three is still notable. Similarly, making calls to friends or relatives in London or New York, seemingly without a care about the higher cost, can still impress one's peers. In late 2004, camera phones were just hitting the Nigerian market, and I have no doubt they will be all the rage in a very short time.

CONCLUSION

Although it is impossible to pinpoint the origin of the "killer numbers" rumors described at the start of this article, I suggest that their currency and appeal were related to popular discontents about the role of cell phones in highlighting and sometimes aggravating social inequality. Some speculated that the rumors were the work of one provider trying to undermine the business of another (the killer numbers were first associated with the phone numbers of one company, though, in time, it spread to them all). Others argued that the rumors were a form of consumer revenge, with the allegations meant to damage the reputation and profits of companies toward which customers felt increasing anger. Still others suggested that the rumors were started by some among the vast majority of Nigerians who still cannot afford to own cell phones, in order to strike fear into those who were intimidating their economic inferiors with their ostentatious use of this flashy new technology. More important than these theories about origin is the speed with which the rumors spread and the extent to which they captured popular imagination. The fascination they generated reflects the fact that, as happy as most Nigerians are for their newfound access to a modern communications technology, ordinary citizens remain extremely discontented over the extent of inequality in their society. The new technology is being interpreted, to a large extent, in relation to these discontents.

NOTE

1. In 2000, the *New York Times* published an article suggesting the importance of cell phones not only for displaying social status generally, but for the attraction of mates. The newspaper account drew on an article in the journal *Human Nature,* entitled "Mobile Phones as Lekking Devices among Human Males" (Lycett and Dunbar 2000). Regardless of whether one finds a sociobiological argument convincing, the association of cell phones with social status seems to strike a chord across many societies.

REFERENCES

Akinsuyi, Yemi. 2004. Anxiety Over 'Satanic' GSM Phone Numbers. *This Day* (Nigeria), July 23.

Barber, Karin. 1995. Money, Self-Realization, and the Person Yoruba Texts. In *Money Matters: Instability, Values and Social Payments in the Modern History of West African Communities,* ed. J. Guyer, 205–224. Portsmouth, NH: Heinemann.

Bearman, Peter. 1997. Generalized Exchange. *American Journal of Sociology* 102(5): 1383–1415.

Bourdieu, Pierre. 1984. *Distinction: A Social Critique of the Judgement of Taste.* Translated by Richard Nice. Cambridge: Harvard University Press.

Cornwall, Andrea. 2002. Spending Power: Love, Money, and the Reconfiguration of Gender Relations in Ado-Odo, Southwestern Nigeria. *American Ethnologist* 29(4): 963–980.

Dooring, Nicolas. 2002. 'Kurzm-wird-gesendet'—Abbreviations and Acronyms in SMS Communication (Short-Message-Service). *Muttersparche.*

Fox, Barry. 2001. No 2MORO for Text Messaging Lingo. *New Scientist* 171(2298): 24.

Geschiere, Peter, and Josef Gugler. 1998. The Urban-Rural Connection: Changing Issues of Belonging and Identification. *Africa* 68(3): 309–319.

Gugler, Josef. 2002. The Son of a Hawk Does Not Remain Abroad: The Urban-Rural Connection in Africa. *African Studies Review* 45(1): 21–41.

Ikhemuemhe, Godfrey. 2004. The Killer Phone Rumour—Operators Cry Foul. *Vanguard* (Nigeria), July 26, 2004.

Lycett, John, and Dunbar, Robin. 2000. Mobile Phones as Lekking Devices among Human Males. *Human Nature* 11(1): 93–104.

Mobile Africa. 2005. Cellular/Mobile Phone Networks in Africa. http://www.mobileafrica.net/mobile-phone-networks-in-africa.php. (Accessed June 7, 2005).

Obadare, Ebenezer. 2004. "The Great GSM (cell phone) Boycott: Civil Society, Big Business and the State in Nigeria." Dark Roast Occasional Paper Series, No. 18. Cape Town: South Africa: Isandla Institute.

PANA (Pan African News Agency). 2005. Nigeria's Phone Subscriber Base Hits 12 Million. *PanAfrican News Agency Daily Newswire,* May 4.

Smith, Daniel Jordan. 2004. Burials and Belonging in Nigeria: Rural-Urban Relations and Social Inequality in a Contemporary African Ritual. *American Anthropologist* 106(3): 569–579.

Sylvia, K. N., and Hady, S. W. 2004. Communication Pattern with SMS: Short Message Service and MMS: Multimedia Message Service as a Trend of Conduct of Modern Teenagers. *International Journal of Psychology* 39 (5–6): 289.

Uchendu, Victor. 1965. *The Igbo of Southeast Nigeria.* Fort Worth, TX: Holt, Reinhart, Winston.

47

The Price of Progress

John H. Bodley

Anthropologists are not against progress: We do not want everyone to return to the "good old days" of our Paleolithic ancestors. On the other hand, the discoveries of cultural anthropologists have made us painfully aware of the human costs of unplanned social and economic change. Anthropologists do not want our society to plunge blindly into the future, unaware and unconcerned about how our present decisions will affect other people or future generations. Cultures are always changing, and the direction of that change is toward a single world system. Cultures change because a society's economy is pulled into the world economy. "Progress" is a label placed on cultural and economic change, but whether something represents "progress" or not depends on one's perspective.

In this selection, John Bodley reviews some of the unexpected consequences of economic development in terms of health, ecological change, quality of life, and relative deprivation. We have seen this same theme in several previous selections—the invention of agriculture, for example. The benefits of economic development are not equally distributed within a developing society. In this selection, we see the relative costs and benefits of economic progress for some of the most marginalized people of the world—the tribal peoples who have been the traditional focus of cultural anthropology research. We believe that the problems detailed here should make our society think about the way cultural change can make people's lives worse; these are issues of social justice.

Anthropologists have been active in seeking solutions to many serious problems. At the same time, most anthropologists believe that tribal peoples have a right to lead their traditional lifestyles and not to be forced into change. In this regard, an organization called Cultural Survival has been active in the international political arena in protecting the land and rights of native peoples.

As you read this selection, ask yourself the following questions:

- What is meant by quality of life? Why might it increase or decrease for a population?

- What are the three ways in which economic development can change the distribution of disease?

- Why do people's diets change? Do people choose diets and behaviors that are harmful to them?

- What is meant by relative deprivation? Can you think of other examples of this process?

- Are tribal peoples more vulnerable to the negative impact of social and economic change than larger industrial societies?

The following terms discussed in this selection are included in the Glossary at the back of the book:

dental anthropology	relative deprivation
ecosystem	self-sufficient
ethnocentrism	swidden cultivation
nomadic band	tribe
population pressure	urbanization

In aiming at progress . . . you must let no one suffer by too drastic a measure, nor pay too high a price in upheaval and devastation, for your innovation.

—Maunier 1949:725

Until recently, government planners have always considered economic development and progress beneficial goals that all societies should want to strive toward. The social advantages of progress—as defined in terms of increased incomes, higher standards of living, greater security, and better health—are thought to be positive, *universal* goods, to be obtained at any price. Although one may argue that tribal peoples must sacrifice their traditional cultures to obtain these benefits, government planners generally feel that this is a small price to pay for such obvious advantages.

In earlier chapters, evidence was presented to demonstrate that autonomous tribal peoples have not *chosen* progress to enjoy its advantages, but that governments have *pushed* progress upon them to obtain tribal resources, not primarily to share with the tribal peoples the benefits of progress. It has also been shown that the price of forcing progress on unwilling recipients has involved the deaths of millions of tribal people, as well as their loss of land, political sovereignty, and the right to follow their own life style. This chapter does not attempt to further summarize that aspect of the cost of progress, but instead analyzes the specific effects of the participation of tribal peoples in the world-market economy. In direct opposition to the usual interpretation, it is argued here that the benefits of progress are often both illusory and detrimental to tribal peoples when they have not been allowed to control their own resources and define their relationship to the market economy.

PROGRESS AND THE QUALITY OF LIFE

One of the primary difficulties in assessing the benefits of progress and economic development for any culture is that of establishing a meaningful measure of both benefit and detriment. It is widely recognized that *standard of living*, which is the most frequently used measure of progress, is an intrinsically ethnocentric concept relying heavily upon indicators that lack universal cultural relevance. Such factors as GNP, per capita income, capital formation, employment rates, literacy, formal education, consumption of manufactured goods, number of doctors and hospital beds per thousand persons, and the amount of money spent on government welfare and health programs may be irrelevant measures of actual *quality* of life for autonomous or even semiautonomous tribal cultures. In its 1954 report, the Trust Territory government indicated that since the Micronesian population was still largely satisfying its own needs within a cashless subsistence economy, "Money income is not a significant measure of living standards, production, or well-being in this area" (TTR 1953:44). Unfortunately, within a short time the government began to rely on an enumeration of certain imported goods as indicators of a higher standard of living in the islands, even though many tradition-oriented islanders felt that these new goods symbolized a lowering of the quality of life.

A more useful measure of the benefits of progress might be based on a formula for evaluating cultures devised by Goldschmidt (1952:135). According to these less ethnocentric criteria, the important question to ask

is: Does progress or economic development increase or decrease a given culture's ability to satisfy the physical and psychological needs of its population, or its stability? This question is a far more direct measure of quality of life than are the standard economic correlates of development, and it is universally relevant. Specific indication of this *standard* of living could be found for any society in the nutritional status and general physical and mental health of its population, the incidence of crime and delinquency, the demographic structure, family stability, and the society's relationship to its natural resource base. A society with high rates of malnutrition and crime, and one degrading its natural environment to the extent of threatening its continued existence, might be described as at a lower standard of living than is another society where these problems did not exist.

Careful examination of the data, which compare, on these specific points, the former condition of self-sufficient tribal peoples with their condition following their incorporation into the world-market economy, leads to the conclusion that their standard of living is *lowered*, not raised, by economic progress—and often to a dramatic degree. This is perhaps the most outstanding and inescapable fact to emerge from the years of research that anthropologists have devoted to the study of culture change and modernization. Despite the best intentions of those who have promoted change and improvement, all too often the results have been poverty, longer working hours, and much greater physical exertion, poor health, social disorder, discontent, discrimination, overpopulation, and environmental deterioration—combined with the destruction of the traditional culture.

DISEASES OF DEVELOPMENT

> Perhaps it would be useful for public health specialists to start talking about a new category of diseases. . . . Such diseases could be called the "diseases of development" and would consist of those pathological conditions which are based on the usually unanticipated consequences of the implementation of development schemes (Hughes and Hunter 1972:93).

Economic development increases the disease rate of affected peoples in at least three ways. First, to the extent that development is successful, it makes developed populations suddenly become vulnerable to all of the diseases suffered almost exclusively by "advanced" peoples. Among these are diabetes, obesity, hypertension, and a variety of circulatory problems. Second, development disturbs traditional environmental balances and may dramatically increase certain bacterial and parasite diseases. Finally, when development goals prove unattainable, an assortment of poverty diseases may appear in association with the crowded conditions of urban slums and the general breakdown in traditional socioeconomic systems.

Outstanding examples of the first situation can be seen in the Pacific, where some of the most successfully developed native peoples are found. In Micronesia, where development has progressed more rapidly than perhaps anywhere else, between 1958 and 1972 the population doubled, but the number of patients treated for heart disease in the local hospitals nearly tripled, mental disorder increased eightfold, and by 1972 hypertension and nutritional deficiencies began to make significant appearances for the first time (TTR 1959, 1973, statistical tables).

Although some critics argue that the Micronesian figures simply represent better health monitoring due to economic progress, rigorously controlled data from Polynesia show a similar trend. The progressive acquisition of modern degenerative diseases was documented by an eight-member team of New Zealand medical specialists, anthropologists, and nutritionists, whose research was funded by the Medical Research Council of New Zealand and the World Health Organization. These researchers investigated the health status of a genetically related population at various points along a continuum of increasing cash income, modernizing diet, and urbanization. The extremes on this acculturation continuum were represented by the relatively traditional Pukapukans of the Cook Islands and the essentially Europeanized New Zealand Maori, while the busily developing Rarotongans, also of the Cook Islands, occupied the intermediate position. In 1971, after eight years of work, the team's preliminary findings were summarized by Dr. Ian Prior, cardiologist and leader of the research, as follows:

> We are beginning to observe that the more an islander takes on the ways of the West, the more prone he is to succumb to our degenerative diseases. In fact, it does not seem too much to say our evidence now shows that the farther the Pacific natives move from the quiet, carefree life of their ancestors, the closer they come to gout, diabetes, atherosclerosis, obesity, and hypertension (Prior 1971:2).

In Pukapuka, where progress was limited by the island's small size and its isolated location some 480 kilometers from the nearest port, the annual per capita income was only about thirty-six dollars and the economy remained essentially at a subsistence level. Resources were limited and the area was visited by trading ships only three or four times a year; thus, there was little opportunity for intensive economic development. Predictably, the population of Pukapuka was characterized by relatively low levels of imported sugar and salt intake, and a presumably related low level of heart disease, high blood pressure, and diabetes. In Rarotonga, where economic success was introducing town life, imported food, and motorcycles, sugar and salt intakes nearly tripled, high blood pressure increased approximately ninefold, diabetes two- to three-fold, and heart disease doubled for men and more than quadrupled for women, while the number of grossly obese women increased more than tenfold. Among the New Zealand Maori, sugar intake was nearly eight times that of the Pukapukans, gout in men was nearly double its rate on Pukapuka, and diabetes in men was more than fivefold higher, while heart disease in women had increased more than sixfold. The Maori were, in fact, dying of "European" diseases at a greater rate than was the average New Zealand European.

Government development policies designed to bring about changes in local hydrology, vegetation, and settlement patterns and to increase population mobility, and even programs aimed at reducing certain diseases, have frequently led to dramatic increases in disease rates because of the unforeseen effects of disturbing the preexisting order. Hughes and Hunter (1972) published an excellent survey of cases in which development led directly to increased disease rates in Africa. They concluded that hasty development intervention in relatively balanced local cultures and environments resulted in "a drastic deterioration in the social and economic conditions of life."

Traditional populations in general have presumably learned to live with the endemic pathogens of their environments, and in some cases they have evolved genetic adaptations to specific diseases, such as the sickle-cell trait, which provided an immunity to malaria. Unfortunately, however, outside intervention has entirely changed this picture. In the late 1960s, sleeping sickness suddenly increased in many areas of Africa and even spread to areas where it did not formerly occur, due to the building of new roads and migratory labor, both of which caused increased population movement. Large-scale relocation schemes, such as the Zande Scheme, had disastrous results when natives were moved from their traditional disease-free refuges into infected areas. Dams and irrigation developments inadvertently created ideal conditions for the rapid proliferation of snails carrying schistosomiasis (a liver fluke disease), and major epidemics suddenly occurred in areas where this disease had never before been a problem. DDT spraying programs have been temporarily successful in controlling malaria, but there is often a rebound effect that increases the problem when spraying is discontinued, and the malarial mosquitoes are continually evolving resistant strains.

Urbanization is one of the prime measures of development, but it is a mixed blessing for most former tribal peoples. Urban health standards are abysmally poor and generally worse than in rural areas for the detribalized individuals who have crowded into the towns and cities throughout Africa, Asia, and Latin America seeking wage employment out of new economic necessity. Infectious diseases related to crowding and poor sanitation are rampant in urban centers, while greatly increased stress and poor nutrition aggravate a variety of other health problems. Malnutrition and other diet-related conditions are, in fact, one of the characteristic hazards of progress faced by tribal peoples and are discussed in the following sections.

The Hazards of Dietary Change

The traditional diets of tribal peoples are admirably adapted to their nutritional needs and available food resources. Even though these diets may seem bizarre, absurd, and unpalatable to outsiders, they are unlikely to be improved by drastic modifications. Given the delicate balances and complexities involved in any subsistence system, change always involves risks, but for tribal people the effects of dietary change have been catastrophic.

Under normal conditions, food habits are remarkably resistant to change, and indeed people are unlikely to abandon their traditional diets voluntarily in favor of dependence on difficult-to-obtain exotic imports. In some cases it is true that imported foods may be identified with powerful outsiders and are therefore sought as symbols of greater prestige. This may lead to such absurdities as Amazonian Indians choosing to consume imported canned tunafish when abundant high-quality fish is available in their own rivers. Another example of this situation occurs in tribes where mothers prefer to feed their infants expensive and nutritionally inadequate canned milk from unsanitary, but *high status,* baby bottles. The high status of these items is often promoted by clever traders and clever advertising campaigns.

Aside from these apparently voluntary changes, it appears that more often dietary changes are forced upon unwilling tribal peoples by circumstances beyond their control. In some areas, new food crops have been introduced by government decree, or as a consequence of forced relocation or other policies designed to end hunting, pastoralism, or shifting cultivation. Food habits have also been modified by massive disruption of the natural environment by outsiders—as when sheepherders transformed the Australian Aborigine's foraging territory or when European invaders destroyed the bison herds that were the primary element in the Plains Indians' subsistence patterns. Perhaps the most frequent cause of diet change occurs when formerly self-sufficient peoples find that wage labor, cash cropping, and other economic development activities that feed tribal resources into the world-market economy must inevitably divert time and energy away from the production of subsistence foods. Many developing peoples suddenly discover that, like it or not, they are unable to secure traditional foods and must spend their newly acquired cash on costly, and often nutritionally inferior, manufactured foods.

Overall, the available data seem to indicate that the dietary changes that are linked to involvement in the world-market economy have tended to *lower* rather than raise the nutritional levels of the affected tribal peoples. Specifically, the vitamin, mineral, and protein components of their diets are often drastically reduced and replaced by enormous increases in starch and carbohydrates, often in the form of white flour and refined sugar.

Any deterioration in the quality of a given population's diet is almost certain to be reflected in an increase in deficiency diseases and a general decline in health status. Indeed, as tribal peoples have shifted to a diet based on imported manufactured or processed foods, there has been a dramatic rise in malnutrition, a massive increase in dental problems, and a variety of other nutrition-related disorders. Nutritional physiology is so complex that even well-meaning dietary changes have had tragic consequences. In many areas of Southeast Asia, government-sponsored protein supplementation programs supplying milk to protein-deficient populations caused unexpected health problems and increased mortality. Officials failed to anticipate that in cultures where adults do not normally drink milk, the enzymes needed to digest it are no longer produced and milk *intolerance* results (Davis and Bolin 1972). In Brazil, a similar milk distribution program caused an epidemic of permanent blindness by aggravating a preexisting vitamin A deficiency (Bunce 1972).

Teeth and Progress

> There is nothing new in the observation that savages, or peoples living under primitive conditions, have, in general excellent teeth. . . . Nor is it news that most civilized populations possess wretched teeth which begin to decay almost before they have erupted completely, and that dental caries is likely to be accompanied by periodontal disease with further reaching complications (Hooton 1945:xviii).

Anthropologists have long recognized that undisturbed tribal peoples are often in excellent physical condition. And it has often been noted specifically that dental caries and the other dental abnormalities that plague industrialized societies are absent or rare among tribal peoples who have retained their traditional diets. The fact that tribal food habits may contribute to the development of sound teeth, whereas modernized diets may do just the opposite, was illustrated as long ago as 1894 in an article in the *Journal of the Royal Anthropological Institute* that described the results of a comparison between the teeth of ten Sioux Indians and a comparable group of Londoners (Smith, 1894:109–116). The Indians were examined when they came to London as members of Buffalo Bill's Wild West Show and were found to be completely free of caries and in possession of all their teeth, even though half of the group were over thirty-nine years of age. Londoners' teeth were conspicuous for both their caries and their steady reduction in number with advancing age. The difference was attributed primarily to the wear and polishing caused by the traditional Indian diet of coarse food and the fact that they chewed their food longer, encouraged by the absence of tableware.

One of the most remarkable studies of the dental conditions of tribal peoples and the impact of dietary change was conducted in the 1930s by Weston Price (1945), an American dentist who was interested in determining what caused normal, healthy teeth. Between 1931 and 1936, Price systematically explored tribal areas throughout the world to locate and examine the most isolated peoples who were still living on traditional foods. His fieldwork covered Alaska, the Canadian Yukon, Hudson Bay, Vancouver Island, Florida, the Andes, the Amazon, Samoa, Tahiti, New Zealand, Australia, New Caledonia, Fiji, the Torres Strait, East Africa, and the Nile. The study demonstrated both the superior quality of aboriginal dentition and the devastation that occurs as modern diets are adopted. In nearly every area where traditional foods were still being eaten, Price found perfect teeth with normal dental arches and virtually no decay, whereas caries and abnormalities increased steadily as new diets were adopted. In many cases the change was sudden and striking. Among Eskimo groups subsisting entirely on traditional food he found caries totally absent, whereas in groups eating a considerable quantity of store-bought food approximately 20 percent of their teeth were decayed. The figure rose to more than 30 percent with Eskimo groups subsisting almost exclusively on purchased or government-supplied food, and reached an incredible 48 percent among the Vancouver Island Indians. Unfortunately for many of these people, modern dental treatment did not accompany the new food, and their suffering was appalling. The loss of teeth was, of course, bad enough in itself, and it certainly undermined the population's resistance to many new diseases, including tuberculosis. But new foods were also accompanied by crowded, misplaced teeth, gum diseases, distortion of the face,

and pinching of the nasal cavity. Abnormalities in the dental arch appeared in the new generation following the change in diet, while caries appeared almost immediately even in adults.

Price reported that in many areas the affected peoples were conscious of their own physical deterioration. At a mission school in Africa, the principal asked him to explain to the native schoolchildren why they were not physically as strong as children who had had no contact with schools. On an island in the Torres Strait the natives knew exactly what was causing their problems and resisted—almost to the point of bloodshed— government efforts to establish a store that would make imported food available. The government prevailed, however, and Price was able to establish a relationship between the length of time the government store had been established and the increasing incidences of caries among a population that showed an almost 100 percent immunity to them before the store had been opened.

In New Zealand, the Maori, who in their aboriginal state are often considered to have been among the healthiest, most perfectly developed of peoples, were found to have "advanced" the furthest. According to Price:

> Their modernization was demonstrated not only by the high incidence of dental caries but also by the fact 90 percent of the adults and 100 percent of the children had abnormalities of the dental arches (Price 1945:206).

Malnutrition

Malnutrition, particularly in the form of protein deficiency, has become a critical problem for tribal peoples who must adopt new economic patterns. Population pressures, cash cropping, and government programs all have tended to encourage the replacement of traditional crops and other food sources that were rich in protein with substitutes high in calories but low in protein. In Africa, for example, protein-rich staples such as millet and sorghum are being replaced systematically by high-yielding manioc and plantains, which have insignificant amounts of protein. The problem is increased for cash croppers and wage laborers whose earnings are too low and unpredictable to allow purchase of adequate amounts of protein. In some rural areas, agricultural laborers have been forced systematically to deprive nonproductive members (principally children) of their households of their minimal nutritional requirements to satisfy the need of the productive members. This process has been documented in northeastern Brazil following the introduction of large-scale sisal plantations (Gross and Underwood 1971). In urban centers the difficulties of obtaining nutritionally adequate diets are even more serious for tribal immigrants, because costs are higher and poor quality foods are more tempting.

One of the most tragic, and largely overlooked, aspects of chronic malnutrition is that it can lead to abnormally undersized brain development and apparently irreversible brain damage; it has been associated with various forms of mental impairment or retardation. Malnutrition has been linked clinically with mental retardation in both Africa and Latin America (see, for example, Mönckeberg, 1968), and this appears to be a worldwide phenomenon with serious implications (Montagu 1972).

Optimistic supporters of progress will surely say that all of these new health problems are being overstressed and that the introduction of hospitals, clinics, and the other modern health institutions will overcome or at least compensate for all of these difficulties. However, it appears that uncontrolled population growth and economic impoverishment probably will keep most of these benefits out of reach for many tribal peoples, and the intervention of modern medicine has at least partly contributed to the problem in the first place.

The generalization that civilization frequently has a broad negative impact on tribal health has found broad empirical support (see especially Kroeger and Barbira-Freedman [1982] on Amazonia; Reinhard [1976] on the Arctic; and Wirsing [1985] globally), but these conclusions have not gone unchallenged. Some critics argue that tribal health was often poor before modernization, and they point specifically to tribals' low life expectancy and high infant mortality rates. Demographic statistics on tribal populations are often problematic because precise data are scarce, but they do show a less favorable profile than that enjoyed by many industrial societies. However, it should be remembered that our present life expectancy is a recent phenomenon that has been very costly in terms of medical research and technological advances. Furthermore, the benefits of our health system are not enjoyed equally by all members of our society. High infant mortality could be viewed as a relatively inexpensive and egalitarian tribal public health program that offered the reasonable expectation of a healthy and productive life for those surviving to age fifteen.

Some critics also suggest that certain tribal populations, such as the New Guinea highlanders, were "stunted" by nutritional deficiencies created by tribal culture and are "improved" by "acculturation" and cash cropping (Dennett and Connell, 1988). Although this argument does suggest that the health question requires careful evaluation, it does not invalidate the empirical generalizations already established. Nutritional deficiencies undoubtedly occurred in densely populated zones in the central New Guinea highlands.

However, the specific case cited above may not be widely representative of other tribal groups even in New Guinea, and it does not address the facts of outside intrusion or the inequities inherent in the contemporary development process.

ECOCIDE

> "How is it," asked a herdsman . . . "how is it that these hills can no longer give pasture to my cattle? In my father's day they were green and cattle thrived there; today there is no grass and my cattle starve." As one looked one saw that what had once been a green hill had become a raw red rock (Jones 1934).

Progress not only brings new threats to the health of tribal peoples, but it also imposes new strains on the ecosystems upon which they must depend for their ultimate survival. The introduction of new technology, increased consumption, lowered mortality, and the eradication of all traditional controls have combined to replace what for most tribal peoples was a relatively stable balance between population and natural resources, with a new system that is imbalanced. Economic development is forcing *ecocide* on peoples who were once careful stewards of their resources. There is already a trend toward widespread environmental deterioration in tribal areas, involving resource depletion, erosion, plant and animal extinction, and a disturbing series of other previously unforeseen changes.

After the initial depopulation suffered by most tribal peoples during their engulfment by frontiers of national expansion, most tribal populations began to experience rapid growth. Authorities generally attribute this growth to the introduction of modern medicine and new health measures and the termination of intertribal warfare, which lowered mortality rates, as well as to new technology, which increased food production. Certainly all of these factors played a part, but merely lowering mortality rates would not have produced the rapid population growth that most tribal areas have experienced if traditional birth-spacing mechanisms had not been eliminated at the same time. Regardless of which factors were most important, it is clear that all of the natural and cultural checks on population growth have suddenly been pushed aside by culture change, while tribal lands have been steadily reduced and consumption levels have risen. In many tribal areas, environmental deterioration due to overuse of resources has set in, and in other areas such deterioration is imminent as resources continue to dwindle relative to the expanding population and increased use. Of course, population expansion by tribal peoples may have positive political consequences, because where tribals can retain or regain their status as local majorities they may be in a more favorable position to defend their resources against intruders.

Swidden systems and pastoralism, both highly successful economic systems under traditional conditions, have proven particularly vulnerable to increased population pressures and outside efforts to raise productivity beyond its natural limits. Research in Amazonia demonstrates that population pressures and related resource depletion can be created indirectly by official policies that restrict swidden peoples to smaller territories. Resource depletion itself can then become a powerful means of forcing tribal people into participating in the world-market economy—thus leading to further resource depletion. For example, Bodley and Benson (1979) showed how the Shipibo Indians in Peru were forced to further deplete their forest resources by cash cropping in the forest area to replace the resources that had been destroyed earlier by the intensive cash cropping necessitated by the narrow confines of their reserve. In this case, a certain species of palm trees that had provided critical housing materials were destroyed by forest clearing and had to be replaced by costly purchased materials. Research by Gross (1979) and others showed similar processes at work among four tribal groups in central Brazil and demonstrated that the degree of market involvement increases directly with increases in resource depletion.

The settling of nomadic herders and the removal of prior controls on herd size have often led to serious overgrazing and erosion problems where these had not previously occurred. There are indications that the desertification problem in the Sahel region of Africa was aggravated by programs designed to settle nomads. The first sign of imbalance in a swidden system appears when the planting cycles are shortened to the point that garden plots are reused before sufficient forest regrowth can occur. If reclearing and planting continue in the same area, the natural pattern of forest succession may be disturbed irreversibly and the soil can be impaired permanently. An extensive tract of tropical rainforest in the lower Amazon of Brazil was reduced to a semiarid desert in just fifty years through such a process (Ackermann 1964). The soils in the Azande area are also now seriously threatened with laterization and other problems as a result of the government-promoted cotton development scheme (McNeil 1972).

The dangers of overdevelopment and the vulnerability of local resource systems have long been recognized by both anthropologists and tribal peoples themselves, but the pressures for change have been overwhelming. In 1948 the Maya villagers of Chan Kom complained to Redfield (1962) about the shortening of their swidden cycles, which they correctly attributed to increasing population pressures. Redfield told them, however, that they had no choice but to go "forward

with technology" (Redfield 1962:178). In Assam, swidden cycles were shortened from an average of twelve years to only two or three within just twenty years, and anthropologists warned that the limits of swiddening would soon be reached (Burling, 1963:311–312). In the Pacific, anthropologists warned of population pressures on limited resources as early as the 1930s (Keesing 1941:64–65). These warnings seemed fully justified, considering the fact that the crowded Tikopians were prompted by population pressures on their tiny island to suggest that infanticide be legalized. The warnings have been dramatically reinforced since then by the doubling of Micronesia's population in just the fourteen years between 1958 and 1972, from 70,600 to 114,645, while consumption levels have soared. By 1985 Micronesia's population had reached 162,321.

The environmental hazards of economic development and rapid population growth have become generally recognized only since worldwide concerns over environmental issues began in the early 1970s. Unfortunately, there is as yet little indication that the leaders of the now developing nations are sufficiently concerned with environmental limitations. On the contrary governments are forcing tribal peoples into a self-reinforcing spiral of population growth and intensified resource exploitation, which may be stopped only by environmental disaster or the total impoverishment of the tribals.

The reality of ecocide certainly focuses attention on the fundamental contrasts between tribal and industrial systems in their use of natural resources. In many respects the entire "victims of progress" issue hinges on natural resources, who controls them, and how they are managed. Tribal peoples are victimized because they control resources that outsiders demand. The resources exist because tribals managed them conservatively. However, as with the issue of the health consequences of detribalization, some anthropologists minimize the adaptive achievements of tribal groups and seem unwilling to concede that ecocide might be a consequence of cultural change. Critics attack an exaggerated "noble savage" image of tribals living in perfect harmony with nature and having no visible impact on their surroundings. They then show that tribals do in fact modify the environment, and they conclude that there is no significant difference between how tribals and industrial societies treat their environments. For example, Charles Wagley declared that Brazilian Indians such as the Tapirape

> are not "natural men." They have human vices just as we do. . . . They do not live "in tune" with nature any more than I do; in fact, they can often be as destructive of their environment, within their limitations, as some civilized men. The Tapirape are not innocent or childlike in any way (Wagley 1977:302).

Anthropologist Terry Rambo demonstrated that the Semang of the Malaysian rain forests have measurable impact on their environment. In his monograph *Primitive Polluters,* Rambo (1985) reported that the Semang live in smoke-filled houses. They sneeze and spread germs, breathe, and thus emit carbon dioxide. They clear small gardens, contributing "particulate matter" to the air and disturbing the local climate because cleared areas proved measurably warmer and drier than the shady forest. Rambo concluded that his research "demonstrated the essential functional similarity of the environmental interactions of primitive and civilized societies" (1985:78) in contrast to a "noble savage" view (Bodley 1983) which, according to Rambo (1985:2), mistakenly "claims that traditional peoples almost always live in essential harmony with their environment."

This is surely a false issue. To stress, as I do, that tribals tend to manage their resources for sustained yield within relatively self-sufficient subsistence economies is not to make them either innocent children or natural men. Nor is it to deny that tribals "disrupt" their environment and may never be in absolute "balance" with nature.

The ecocide issue is perhaps most dramatically illustrated by two sets of satellite photos taken over the Brazilian rain forests of Rôndonia (Allard and McIntyre 1988:780–781). Photos taken in 1973, when Rôndonia was still a tribal domain, show virtually unbroken rain forest. The 1987 satellite photos, taken after just fifteen years of highway construction and "development" by outsiders, show more than 20 percent of the forest destroyed. The surviving Indians were being concentrated by FUNAI (Brazil's national Indian foundation) into what would soon become mere islands of forest in a ravaged landscape. It is irrelevant to quibble about whether tribals are noble, childlike, or innocent, or about the precise meaning of balance with nature, carrying capacity, or adaptation, to recognize that for the past 200 years rapid environmental deterioration on an unprecedented global scale has followed the wresting of control of vast areas of the world from tribal groups by resource-hungry industrial societies.

DEPRIVATION AND DISCRIMINATION

Contact with European culture has given them a knowledge of great wealth, opportunity and privilege, but only very limited avenues by which to acquire these things (Crocombe 1968).

Unwittingly, tribal peoples have had the burden of perpetual relative deprivation thrust upon them by acceptance—either by themselves or by the governments administering them—of the standards of socioeconomic progress set for them by industrial civilizations. By comparison with the material wealth of industrial societies, tribal societies become, by definition, impoverished. They are then forced to transform their cultures and work to achieve what many economists now acknowledge to be unattainable goals. Even though in many cases the modest GNP goals set by development planners for the developing nations during the "development decade" of the 1960s were often met, the results were hardly noticeable for most of the tribal people involved. Population growth, environmental limitations, inequitable distribution of wealth, and the continued rapid growth of the industrialized nations have all meant that both the absolute and the relative gap between the rich and poor in the world is steadily widening. The prospect that tribal peoples will actually be able to attain the levels of resource consumption to which they are being encouraged to aspire is remote indeed except for those few groups who have retained effective control over strategic mineral resources.

Tribal peoples feel deprivation not only when the economic goals they have been encouraged to seek fail to materialize, but also when they discover that they are powerless, second-class citizens who are discriminated against and exploited by the dominant society. At the same time, they are denied the satisfactions of their traditional cultures, because these have been sacrificed in the process of modernization. Under the impact of major economic change family life is disrupted, traditional social controls are often lost, and many indicators of social anomie such as alcoholism, crime, delinquency, suicide, emotional disorders, and despair may increase. The inevitable frustration resulting from this continual deprivation finds expression in the cargo cults, revitalization movements, and a variety of other political and religious movements that have been widespread among tribal peoples following their disruption by industrial civilization.

REFERENCES

Ackermann, F. L. 1964. *Geologia e Fisiografia da Região Bragantina, Estado do Pará.* Manaus, Brazil: Conselho Nacional de Pesquisas, Instituto Nacional de Pesquisas da Amazônia.

Allard, William Albert, and Loren McIntyre. 1988. Rôndonia's settlers invade Brazil's imperiled rain forest. *National Geographic* 174(6): 772–799.

Bodley, John H. 1983. The World Bank tribal policy: Criticisms and recommendations. *Congressional Record,* serial no. 98-37, pp. 515–521. (Reprinted in Bodley, 1988.)

Bodley, John H., and Foley C. Benson. 1979. Cultural ecology of Amazonian palms. *Reports of Investigations*, no. 56. Pullman: Laboratory of Anthropology, Washington State University.

Bunce, George E. 1972. Aggravation of vitamin A deficiency following distribution of non-fortified skim milk: An example of nutrient interaction. In *The Careless Technology: Ecology and International Development*, ed. M. T. Farvar and John P. Milton, 53–60. Garden City, N.Y.: Natural History Press.

Burling, Robbins. 1963. *Rengsanggri: Family and Kinship in a Garo Village*. Philadelphia: University of Pennsylvania Press.

Crocombe, Ron. 1968. Bougainville!: Copper, R. R. A. and secessionism. *New Guinea* 3(3): 39–49.

Davis, A. E., and T. D. Bolin. 1972. Lactose intolerance in Southeast Asia. In *The Careless Technology: Ecology and International Development*, ed. M. T. Farvar and John P. Milton, 61–68. Garden City, N.Y.: Natural History Press.

Dennett, Glenn, and John Connell. 1988. Acculturation and health in the highlands of Papua New Guinea. *Current Anthropology* 29(2): 273–299.

Goldschmidt, Walter R. 1952. The interrelations between cultural factors and acquisition of new technical skills. In *The Progress of Underdeveloped Areas*, ed. Bert F. Hoselitz, 135–151. Chicago: University of Chicago Press.

Gross, Daniel R., and Barbara A. Underwood. 1971. Technological change and caloric costs: Sisal agriculture. *American Anthropologist* 73(3): 725–740.

Gross, Daniel R., et al. 1979. Ecology and acculturation among native peoples of Central Brazil. *Science* 206(4422): 1043–1050.

Hooton, Earnest A. 1945. Introduction. In *Nutrition and Physical Degeneration: A Comparison of Primitive and Modern Diets and Their Effects* by Weston A. Price. Redlands, Calif.: The author.

Hughes, Charles C., and John M. Hunter. 1972. The role of technological development in promoting disease in Africa. In *The Careless Technology: Ecology and International Development*, ed. M. T. Farvar and John P. Milton, 69–101. Garden City, N.Y.: Natural History Press.

Jones, J. D. Rheinallt. 1934. Economic condition of the urban native. In *Western Civilization and the Natives of South Africa*, ed. I. Schapera, 159–192. London: George Routledge and Sons.

Keesing, Felix M. 1941. *The South Seas in the Modern World*. Institute of Pacific Relations International Research Series. New York: John Day.

Kroeger, Axel, and Françoise Barbira-Freedman. 1982. *Culture Change and Health: The Case of South American Rainforest Indians*. Frankfurt am Main: Verlag Peter Lang. (Reprinted in Bodley, 1988: 221–236).

Maunier, René. 1949. *The Sociology of Colonies*. Vol. 2. London: Routledge and Kegan Paul.

McNeil, Mary. 1972. Lateritic soils in distinct tropical environments: Southern Sudan and Brazil. In *The Careless Technology: Ecology and International Development*, ed. M. T. Farvar and John P. Milton, 591–608. Garden City, N.Y.: Natural History Press.

Mönckeberg, F. 1968. Mental retardation from malnutrition. *Journal of the American Medical Association* 206: 30–31.

Montagu, Ashley. 1972. Sociogenic brain damage. *American Anthropologist* 74(5): 1045–1061.

Price, Weston Andrew. 1945. *Nutrition and Physical Degeneration: A Comparison of Primitive and Modern Diets and Their Effects*. Redlands, Calif.: The author.

Prior, Ian A. M. 1971. The price of civilization. *Nutrition Today* 6(4): 2–11.

Rambo, A. Terry. 1985. *Primitive Polluters: Semang Impact on the Malaysian Tropical Rain Forest Ecosystem*. Anthropological Papers no. 76, Museum of Anthropology, University of Michigan.

Redfield, Robert. 1962. *A Village That Chose Progress: Chan Kom Revisited*. Chicago: University of Chicago Press, Phoenix Books.

Reinhard, K. R. 1976. Resource exploitation and the health of western arctic man. In *Circumpolar Health: Proceedings of the Third International Symposium, Yellowknife, Northwest Territories*, ed. Roy J. Shephard and S. Itoh, 617–627. Toronto: University of Toronto Press. (Reprinted in Bodley, 1988.)

Smith, Wilberforce. 1894. The teeth of ten Sioux Indians. *Journal of the Royal Anthropological Institute* 24: 109–116.

TTR: TTR, United States, Department of the Interior, Office of the Territories. 1953. Report on the Administration of the trust territories of the Pacific Islands for the period of July 1, 1951 to June 30, 1952.

United States, Department of State. 1955. *Seventh Annual Report to the United Nations on the Administration of the Trust Territory of the Pacific Islands* (July 1, 1953, to June 30, 1954).

———. 1959. *Eleventh Annual Report to the United Nations on the Administration of the Trust Territory of the Pacific Islands* (July 1, 1957, to June 30, 1958).

———. 1973. *Twenty-Fifth Annual Report to the United Nations on the Administration of the Trust Territory of the Pacific Islands* (July 1, 1971, to June 30, 1972).

Wagley, C. 1977. *Welcome of Tears: The Tapirape Indians of Central Brazil*. New York: Oxford University Press.

Wirsing, R. 1985. The health of traditional societies and the effects of acculturation. *Current Anthropology* 26: 303–322.

48

Moral Fibers of Farmer Cooperatives

Creating Poverty and Wealth with Cotton in Southern Mali

Scott M. Lacy

When the imminent threat of Civil War in the United States threatened to disrupt cotton exports to textile mills in France, French entrepreneurs and government officials sought alternative cotton sources in their African territories and colonies. Counter to the ambitions of the French, cotton production in African territories like the French Soudan was geared toward local consumption not export. To feed the demand of domestic textile mills, the French coerced West African farmers to increase cotton production through taxation and technological inputs. The intensification of cotton production established a cash crop, which to this day, serves as a foundation of the economy of West African nations like Mali and Burkina Faso.

Development officials promote cotton production as a means to combat endemic poverty in rural Malian communities, but cotton farming can create poverty as well. When world cotton prices are high, cotton-producing countries like Mali may reap financial benefits, but when prices fall, small-scale cotton farmers pay the price. Mali ranks as one of the poorest countries in the world, and historically low cotton prices make this country's strength its weakness. In this selection, Scott Lacy examines some of the ways Malian officials have tried to assist family farmers. For decades, communities in Mali organized cotton production through farmer collectives, one per village, but starting in 2003 the government gave farmers a new option allowing the formation of smaller sub-village collectives. The freedom to choose the membership and size of one's local cotton grower association may lift some producers out of poverty, but this freedom may further complicate the economic and social viability of other producers and communities in crisis.

As you read this selection, ask yourself the following questions:

- What is the difference between cotton produced in the United States and cotton produced in Mali?
- How did colonization transform cotton production in rural Malian communities?
- How do decentralized farmer collectives (CPCs) help some farmers but harm others?
- What is the difference between the memberships of Dissan's two cotton collectives (CPCs)?
- How do fluctuations in global cotton prices impact the lives of small-scale family farmers in rural Mali?

The following terms discussed in this selection are included in the Glossary at the back of the book:

brain drain   cash crop
cooperative   subsidy

For several centuries, cotton has been a critical component of the agricultural economy of Mali, West Africa. In fact, presidents, economists, and contemporary development officials have long promoted this cash crop as "white gold" with the potential to lift Mali from its status as one of the poorest countries in the world. After all, Malian farmers grow some of the world's highest quality cotton, and at a fraction of the cost of international competitors; U.S. cotton growers, for example, produce lower-grade cotton and they spend nearly three times as much to produce each harvested kilo. To capitalize on this rare market advantage, in 2002 Malian officials modified national policies

This article was written especially for *Applying Anthropology: An Introductory Reader*, 9/e.

governing rural cotton production based on the idea that decentralizing local farm collectives would encourage farmers to bolster domestic harvests. Initially production statistics confirmed this theory, but the positive effects were short-lived. In the following pages, I describe how farmers from a village in southern Mali adapted to the decentralization of community cotton collectives, and I explore the roles of cotton and cash cropping in rural subsistence economies.

METHODS

This chapter is based on a long-term study in southern Mali starting with fifteen-months of fieldwork in 2001/2 and annual follow-up studies from 2004–2008. While living and working with family farmers in the village of Dissan (11°36N, 7°31W, 344 masl), I conducted two extensive surveys in 2001/2 to learn about household agricultural production, including farmer practices and knowledge of local crops and growing environments, household economies, and community-based farm collectives. In 2001 I surveyed all sixty-six Dissan households and conducted a comprehensive census of the community to acquire baseline data on household farm production and resources. Before the planting season, in March and April 2002, I interviewed a stratified sample of Dissan households (n = 20) to further investigate farmer knowledge and production practices. After completing these first two surveys, I spent a full growing season apprenticing with four households to actively learn about the resources and annual production cycle of Dissan farmers. Since 2004 I have returned to Dissan to conduct annual follow-up studies focused on crop choices, seed systems, and household farm production. Qualitative data used in this chapter come from ethnographic field notes, individual interviews, and a series of informal group interviews recorded between 2001 and 2008.

STUDY COMMUNITY

I was introduced to Dissan when I arrived there in 1994 as a Peace Corps volunteer. Dissan is a rural farming community that traces its origins back to the seventeenth century (Lacy 2004:83–85). In December 2001 there were 881 people living in sixty-six households in Dissan. The household (*du*, in Bamanakan) is an extended family that lives, eats, and works together using common resources. Depending on its size, a household either shares a single compound or a conglomeration of adjacent compounds composed of shaded sitting areas, sleeping quarters, cooking huts, and various storage constructions. According to my 2001 census, the mean number of people per household was thirteen (SD = 8.9). Bamanakan is the primary language spoken in Dissan, however, some community members speak other languages including Arabic, French, Fulani, and Wolof.

Though Dissan is in a relatively wet region of Mali sometimes referred to as the cotton zone, even in good years when many households harvest enough grain to last the year, other households suffer food shortages. Annual rainfall throughout Mali is low and extremely variable, making rain-fed agricultural production a complex and risky enterprise. Nonetheless, every family in Dissan depends on rain-fed agriculture for subsistence, including the teachers of the village primary school who farm to supplement their salaries.

In 2007/8, Dissan households used hand-held hoes, collective labor, and animal-traction plows to cultivate a combined total of 282 hectares of field crops (not including secondary plots of peanuts and rice), including 21.5 hectares of cotton and 161 hectares of sorghum (Table 1). Farmers typically produce sorghum for household consumption and grow cotton as a cash crop or as a means for procuring agricultural inputs and short-term credit (or both). Data from the 2001 survey show that households who acquire credit and inputs through cotton production are the households that plant the most sorghum; they also are more likely to have expensive farm equipment like cultivators, seeders, plows, donkey carts, and sprayers for applying chemical pesticides and herbicides (Table 2). Despite the fact that cotton opens farmer access to

TABLE 1   Dissan agricultural production, 2002 vs. 2007

		2002/3	2007/8
Total hectares planted:			
	Sorghum	155	161
	Millet	20.5	57
	Maize	89.4	42.5
	Cotton	31	21.5
Number of HHs growing:			
	Sorghum	58	57
	Millet	14	30
	Maize	54	34
	Cotton	37	15

TABLE 2 Sorghum cultivation and ownership of farm equipment by household, Dissan, 2001

	Mean sorghum hectares/HH	Percentages of households owning:				
		Plow	Cultivator	Seeder	Donkey cart	Spray pump
Cotton credit HHs, n = 41	2.8	88	71	46	61	49
Other HHs, n = 25	1.7	36	12	4	8	0

small loans and agricultural inputs, cotton production has declined sharply since 2001. In the 2007–8 growing season, only 15 Dissan households grew cotton, in contrast to the 37 households who grew this cash crop in 2002/3.

HISTORICAL OVERVIEW OF COTTON PRODUCTION IN RURAL MALI

Before the French-led intensification of cotton production in colonial West Africa, family farmers in southern Mali grew regional varieties of cotton for a strong domestic market and for self-sufficient household consumption (clothing, blankets, fishing nets, string, etc.). Starting in the 1890s, commercial and colonial interests worked for decades shaping Malian cotton production in an attempt to capture cotton harvests for French textile mills. By 1950 the colonial state was spending approximately 70 percent of its resources on the intensification of cotton production, targeting southern Mali through the introduction of new varieties, agricultural extension, price subventions, and support for rural investment in machinery and fertilizer (Roberts 1996:280). Prior to the introduction of incentives like agricultural extension and credit for purchasing plows and agrochemicals, family farmers in Mali resisted expanding household production beyond local needs.

Dissan elders explained that cotton cash cropping came with plows; widespread extrahousehold cotton production and farmer credits followed the installation of a regional cotton processing facility in the 1960s. Local farmers first acquired plows in the 1960s from the Compagnie Malienne pour le Développement des Fibres Textiles (CMDT), a state agency created by the government of Mali's first president, Modibo Keïta. In the 1970s the CMDT worked with villages to organize cotton producer collectives and began transferring to these village associations production responsibilities such as ordering and distributing inputs, and managing credits and payments (Bingen, Serrano, and Howard 2003:410–411). The efficacy

of the village association strategy developed by the CMDT in the 1970s eventually transformed this once regional program into a national one. Today the CMDT remains the primary agency for agricultural extension services and credit in many southern Malian communities.

CMDT and Collective Cotton Production in Dissan, 1974–2002

In 1974 the CMDT started the process of transferring to villages responsibility for cotton grading, weighing, orders for equipment and inputs, and credit management (Bingen 2000:357). At first, the CMDT appointed existing village social organizations as the body responsible for such tasks, but by the late 1970s it had established an AV ("Village Association") system for southern Mali managed by community officers, including president, treasurer, and secretary. With World Bank financing, the CMDT organized literacy and numeracy programs in Bamanakan to teach farmers skills for effectively managing village cotton production. The AV program proved to be so efficient by CMDT standards that it eventually became national policy.

As the AV system took hold in southern Mali, many Dissan farmers began acquiring more household money through cotton production. The AV merged all Dissan farmers into a single cooperative for organizing local production, spreading individual responsibility and risk among all village cotton farmers. From the CMDT perspective, this system consolidated fiscal accounting and responsibility into manageable units; every year, after receiving one lump sum for the entire village's cotton harvest, the AV distributed crop payments to individual members. When poor harvests or household crop failures led any number of producers to default on their individual loans, the AV absorbed those debts. In 2001, for example, two Dissan households defaulted on their loans and although both households repaid over half their debts, an outstanding balance of roughly US $300 remained. Although $300 accounts for only 2.5 percent of all Dissan loans in

2001, it is substantial debt for a rural farming family in a country like Mali where annual per capita income was a mere $239 for that same year (World Bank 2003). Furthermore, these economic indicators fail to capture the social discord or peripheral economic hardships endured by individuals and communities as a result of loan defaults.

Once established, the AV system provided farmer access to credit, it established de facto community security nets for cotton farmers and gave rural populations a formidable voice in regional and national agricultural policy. Siaka Sangare, long-standing secretary of Dissan's AV, explained that in 1989, when the CMDT attempted to restructure the AV credit system, producers across the country, including Dissan, used their AVs to organize a cotton strike. Through AV leaders, the CMDT brokered a deal that was acceptable to farmers, and the strike was averted (USAID-Mali 2003). However, in 2000 many Dissan farmers joined a national cotton strike in protest of unpaid harvests and low purchase prices. The CMDT typically set purchase prices after the planting season for cotton, forcing farmers to purchase inputs on credit and organize production without any certainty of returns on their investments. Largely due to a saturated global market, not to mention enormous U.S. subsidies for industrial U.S. cotton producers, international prices for cotton fell significantly in 1998 and 1999. Falling prices translated into significant operating deficits for the CMDT, which meant farmers in Dissan and elsewhere had to bear the brunt of these economic losses. In 1998 the CMDT purchase price for cotton was 185 CFA francs (FCFA) per kilogram, and the price dropped to FCFA 150 in 1999 (USAID-Mali 2003). Secretary Sangare noted that unexpectedly lower prices in 1999 put some Dissan farmers in debt, leading many to abandon the crop the following year. However, in 2001, when the CMDT guaranteed a good purchase price before planting (FCFA 200/kg), many farmers returned to cotton production. The national cotton strike certainly influenced the favorable price of cotton in 2001, but rippling effects of the strike extended further; in late 2002 the CMDT announced the AV system would undergo major organizational changes.

The Meeting

In November 2002, shortly after most households had harvested their cotton, the CMDT extension agent who works in Dissan, visited the AV to call an important meeting. The extension agent is an agricultural engineer trained in Katiabougou, Mali, and at the University of Dijon in France. The meeting was one of thousands throughout Mali, organized to familiarize farmers with fundamental changes to the organizational structure of cotton collectives in Mali (Diallo 2004). Though renamed, the AV could still serve as a villagewide cooperative, but under the new system, the AV could be composed of any number of independently organized, subvillage collectives. Using diagrams on the chalkboard of a dilapidated one-room schoolhouse, the extension agent explained in Bamanakan how the new system would empower farmers.

With children peaking in windows and with the sounds of chickens and donkeys in the background, the extension agent sat at a table in front of thirty-five farmers seated on weathered desktops. The CMDT representative began with an announcement: after the 2002 harvest, the CMDT would encourage Malian cotton farmers to establish new collectives that permit members to associate themselves at the subvillage level. According to the agent, villagewide associations reduce incentives for skilled, large-scale producers, because these producers bear financial liability for the catastrophic crop losses and irresponsible credit management of other farmers. The agent occasionally looked down at his notes as he discussed the regulations for forming the new cotton collectives. Farmers listened patiently, a few with modest disinterest, as the agent described eight new rules.

- Each group will be called a CPC (*coopératif pour les producteurs cotonnière*).

- Each CPC must have at least five producers and/or a minimum of ten separate cotton fields.

- Each CPC must produce an annual minimum of 30 metric tons of cotton (slightly less than half of Dissan's combined total of 70.7 metric tons produced in 2002).

- CPC members must be from the same village (associations with people from multiple villages are prohibited).

- Every CPC member must have a certificate of residency (obtainable for a small fee from a regional administrator).

- Each member must sign an official document containing CPC by-laws, organizational structure, and a description of responsibilities for each CPC officer. The document, written in Bamanakan, is made official with the approval and signature of all CPC members and a CMDT officer.

- Each CPC operates for three years, after which it must be renewed as is, modified and renewed, or disbanded.

- All Dissan CPCs collectively constitute the Union des Coopératifs de Dissan.

The extension agent reinforced several CPC policies before taking questions from farmers. First, he explained some of the benefits of the new CPC system. For example, if someone in a CPC turns out to be a poor associate or a bad worker, at the end of the three-year term of the CPC, members can vote to expel the underperforming associate. Meanwhile, CPC members must pay the debts of fellow members in default, but as CPC members they would have recourse. If necessary a CPC can take legal action against members in default using a CMDT legal service available to all CPC members. Some farmers raised their eyebrows when the agent described how the CPC system deals with chronic debtors and rule breakers: in the worse cases, a judge will dispatch gendarmes to claim payment or in-kind restitution. The agent also said that the CPC system will equate to money for community improvements and projects. Under the former system the AV received from the CMDT a sum equal to 2 percent of the gross price of all Dissan cotton delivered to the CMDT scales. These funds were used according to AV by-laws for: operational costs (20 percent), officer stipends (30 percent), and community development projects (50 percent). The extension agent explained that under the CPC system, defaulted loans would no longer drain funds earmarked for community service.

Throughout the meeting, the CMDT representative focused on a central theme, the power of a strong collective voice. Farmers in attendance nodded their heads as the agent recalled how AVs unified farmers during the cotton strike of 2000. Using an intricate diagram of circles within circles, the extension agent demonstrated that the work and efforts of each CPC will have a single, strong voice, while the village collective—the Union des Cooperatives de Dissan—will have an even stronger voice to represent all Dissan CPCs. Although this well-worn selling point may sound trite, there is no doubt that AVs helped farmers organize and amplify their voices en masse in 1989 and 2000 when they successfully convinced CMDT authorities to address farmer concerns regarding AV policy and cotton prices (Lacy 2004:107–108).

From my perspective as an observer, perhaps the most salient yet understated point raised by the extension agent during the meeting was that farmers could use the management skills they develop as members of CPCs to form cooperatives for other crops or animal husbandry. As the meeting drew to a close, some of the biggest cotton producers in Dissan voiced skeptical interest and tacit approval for the new system, but a few producers—one of whom with considerable, old cotton debts—expressed concern about the potential difficulties they may face if they hope to join a CPC to obtain credit.

Farmer Perspectives of the CPC System

The freedom to choose the membership and size of one's local cotton grower association may help some producers prevent monetary losses stemming from the crop failures of other village producers, but this freedom may further complicate the economic and social viability of producers and communities in crisis. Following the meeting I asked several farmers to describe their reactions to the new CPC program. Although most farmers voiced cautious or little interest in the new CPCs, two of them held starkly opposite opinions. The first farmer, an elder named Sidike Sangare said he was suspicious of the new system. During the meeting Sangare remarked that farmers who default on loans eventually pay their debts, and should not be expelled from a group, chased by gendarmes, nor excluded from cotton production, particularly when their households may be in crisis. Under the CPC system the de facto safety net provided by the AV would be transformed into several smaller nets, spreading larger risks among smaller groups of producers. After the meeting Sangare predicted he would not grow cotton the following year. True to his word, elder Sangare abandoned cotton production and focused on grain for future harvests; he eventually repaid his cotton debts, but he passed away a few years later.

On the other side of the spectrum, AV officer Burama Tarawele expressed great optimism about the CPC system. Tarawele was visiting Dissan from Bougoumbala, a neighboring village, and was present at the Dissan meeting. Immediately following the meeting Tarawele said he was pleased the CMDT was finally addressing the problem he termed, "the politics of CMDT." Echoing the extension agent's words, from Tarawele's point of view, the former AV system was counterproductive for large-scale cotton producers like him. Before the formal initiation of the CPC program in the region, Tarawele had already brokered a special arrangement to create a proto-CPC in his village; he and two other farmers decided to create a subvillage collective to independently procure credit and inputs through the CMDT. Though leaving their villagewide cotton association created some quarreling in the village, Tarawele believes people now understand why he and his two partners left the Bougoumbala AV (*decentralization* was the term Tarawele used). He said that the CMDT cooperated with this decentralization because he and his cohorts—all large-scale producers—threatened to abandon cotton. Tarawele said the CPC program will be good for Mali cotton farmers, but admitted that many farmers do not have the skills to apply for, acquire, and effectively manage independent loans. He acquired his banking and management skills in CMDT workshops and as the former secretary of his village AV. Tarawele's ultimate goal is to intensify his cotton production in order to invest in cattle and animal husbandry.

Dissan Creates Two CPCs

Even though Dissan farmers were free to create their first CPCs in 2003, they chose to preserve their villagewide collective. For 2004, however, after several quarrels related to a confidential financial dispute, farmers made a decision that would not have been possible two years earlier. Because the new CPC system encouraged subvillage collectives, farmers resolved their dispute with the dissolution of the villagewide AV. Then the former AV leader formed a CPC with seven other households, while all other cotton-producing households banded together to form a second, much larger CPC. The larger of the two groups built a separate storage shed, and by the

start of the 2004 growing season both CPCs were operational. Though factors like rainfall and pest control have plenty to do with successful cotton farming, they alone do not explain why aggregate Dissan cotton harvests almost doubled in one year under the stewardship of two independent subvillage collectives (Table 3). Following wildly successful harvests, Dissan farmers reported positive initial experiences with both CPCs, but the enthusiasm of the first two years of the new system has waned.

The financial dispute that split Dissan's villagewide collective may have inspired a short-lived competition between the two CPCs which emerged from the conflict. This competition may have bolstered local harvests temporarily, but Dissan cotton production has since declined as most small-scale producers have adopted alternative cash crops such as cereals, peanut, and sesame. Per CPC rules, Dissan cotton growers re-established their CPCs in 2007/8, but many producers chose to abandon cotton. In short, all eight of the former AV leader's CPC members renewed their cooperative and grew cotton, but the second CPC membership decreased from 37 households in 2004 to seven households in 2007. The divergent fates of the two Dissan CPCs are rooted in the unique memberships of both collectives. The former AV leader's CPC attracted large-scale producers with production goals similar to Burama Tarawele, but membership was not directly based on production levels; family alliances and social relationships also played a major role. A cursory look at some of the characteristics of the CPC households indicates that the bifurcation of Dissan's AV consolidated some of the village's more wealthy households, leaving the others to fend for themselves (Table 4). Likewise, in other villages across southern Mali, cotton cultivation has been shown to exacerbate economic disparity among households (Moseley 2005:46–49).

Do Subvillage Collectives and Cotton Increase Poverty, Wealth . . . or Both?

Every year after the CMDT has collected cotton harvests from villages all across the region, farmers listen intently as radio stations announce final production totals for local villages. Cotton is undeniably a major focus of household agricultural production in southern Mali, and transforming the AV system with subvillage cooperatives (CPCs) affects different farmers in different ways. Depending on the resources, skills, and experience of individual producers, the CPC system equates to new opportunities for some farmers, and exclusion from cotton production and farmer credit for others.

TABLE 3   Aggregate Dissan cotton harvests recorded at CMDT facility, Bougouni, 2003–7

	Cotton collective system in use	Number of cotton households	Aggregate harvest (kg)	Households making $0 or debt from cotton harvest
2001/2	1 AV	41	N/A	4 (10%)
2002/3	1 AV	50	70,740	N/A
2003/4	1 AV	23	39,750	2 (9%)
2004/5	2 CPCs	47	98,521	3 (6%)
2005/6	2 CPCs	38	86,989	2 (5%)
2006/7	2 CPCs	26	58,987	6 (23%)
2007/8	2 CPCs	15	14,285	9 (60%)

TABLE 4   Smaller CPC households versus all other households, Dissan, 2001

	Small CPC HHs	Other HHs
Number of:		
Households	8	58
People per HH	23	12
Field hectares cultivated, 2001	10.3	5
Percentage of households owning:		
Plow	100	65
Cattle	100	58
Cultivator	100	46
Donkey cart	100	42
Seeder	83	25

In the short term, successful cotton farmers capable of acquiring and managing credit stand to gain more autonomy over production choices. Furthermore, provided they associate with other stable producers, these farmers may reduce the risk of losses from cotton profits due to crop failures or mismanagement by others. Farmers known to have defaulted on previous loans, whose households may be in crisis (labor shortage, debt, chronic crop loss), face potential difficulties if they seek CPC membership. Just as elder Sidike Sangare abandoned cotton farming because his old cotton debts made him an undesirable associate, Burama Tarawele formed his own CPC to avoid associating with unreliable or crisis-prone farmers. Cotton may not be an equally appealing nor accessible crop choice for farmers of different means.

Elder Sangare was not the only farmer to question whether cotton farming was a worthwhile endeavor. Even before the CMDT announced the changes for cotton collectives, Dissan farmers debated whether or not cotton was "worth it." The Dissan *ton* (a villagewide collective labor organization) decided in 2002 to grow peanuts instead of cotton to raise group funds. This decision was based on the idea that peanuts were a less risky crop and would not require nearly as much labor, in contrast with cotton. Equally important, peanut crops do not require major investment costs for fertilizer, herbicide, and insecticide.

As it evolves, the CPC system will generate new debates and questions about the social, ecological, and financial ramifications of household cotton production in southern Mali, but exactly how these subvillage collectives may or may not transform local production and socioeconomic dynamics has yet to be fully determined. In the long term, three critical issues will determine the success or failure of the CPC system: the

exclusion principle, the efficacy of CPCs in expanding the idea and benefits of cooperatives beyond cotton fields, and the strengthening of individual and collective voices of cotton farmers. In southern Mali, responsibility for household cotton production typically excludes women and poorer households, who, as a result, have limited access to extension services and inputs (Moseley 2001:187).

On the one hand, CPCs may lead farmers to exclude crisis-prone producers like elder Sidike Sangare, but CPCs could have the potential to open new opportunities for formerly excluded farmers. Investing in human capacity in terms of ensuring farmers who want to create a cooperative have the financial and literacy skills necessary to protect their own interests could also, with no small effort, bring women and poorer farmers into their own credit-worthy collectives, particularly if the CPC cotton model is successful in encouraging the formation of new cooperatives for other crops and animal husbandry. After all, if literate farmers with proven track records and strong financial management skills (acquiring and managing credit) break off into subvillage collectives, as they have done in Dissan, they might be less able or less willing to assist those farmers with different skill sets and resources. This new, localized manifestation of brain drain and wealth consolidation has the potential to exacerbate social and financial inequality, rendering cotton as a crop for relatively wealthier households. In the recent past, producer organizations like cotton collectives have been shown to amplify the voices of farmers in southern Mali (Bingen, Serrano, and Howard 2003:407). In the end, what may determine the success or failure of the CPC program is whether or not it bolsters or diminishes the voices and opportunities of all farmers.

REFERENCES

Bingen, James R. 2000. Prospects for Development and Democracy in West Africa: Agrarian Politics in Mali. In *Democracy and Development in Mali*, ed. James R. Bingen, David Robinson, and John M. Staatz, 349–368. East Lansing: Michigan State University Press.

Bingen, Jim, Alex Serrano, and Julie Howard. 2003. Linking Farmers to Markets: Different Approaches to Human Capital Development. *Food Policy* 28: 405–419.

Diallo, Madou. 2004. Situation scolaire: L'heure de vérité à Koulouba. *Le républicain*, December 8. http://www.planeteafrique.com/Web/LeDiplomate/Index.asp?affiche=newsdatabase_show.asp&cmd=articledetail&articleid=252.

Lacy, Scott M. 2004. One Finger Cannot Lift a Stone: Family Farmers and Sorghum Production in Southern Mali. PhD dissertation, University of California, Santa Barbara.

Moseley, William G. 2001. Sahelian 'White Gold' and Rural Poverty-Environment Interactions: The Political Ecology of Cotton Production, Environmental Change, and Household Food Economy in Mali. PhD dissertation, University of Georgia.

_____. 2005. Global Cotton and Local Environment Management: The Political Ecology of Rich and Poor Small-Hold Farmers in Southern Mali. *Geographic Journal* 171 (1): 36–55.

Roberts, Richard. 1996. *Two Worlds of Cotton: Colonialism and the Regional Economy in the French Soudan, 1800–1946.* Stanford, CA: Stanford University Press.

USAID-Mali. 2003. Production and Export Opportunities and Constraints for Coarse Grains. www.usaid.org.ml/ mes_photos/production_and_e.

World Bank. 2003. World Development Indicators 2003. Washington, DC: World Bank. CD-ROM.

Glossary

acculturation   The process of extensive borrowing of aspects of another culture, usually as a result of external pressure, and often resulting in the decline of traditional culture.

action anthropology   Applied anthropological research combined with political advocacy and planned social change in cooperation with the group studied; associated with Sol Tax from the University of Chicago.

adaptation   The process by which an organism or a culture is modified, usually through selection, enhancing the ability of individuals to survive and reproduce in a particular environment.

adaptations   Heritable structures or behaviors of an organism that improve chances of survival and reproduction in a particular environment.

adipose tissue   Fat. A physiological mechanism of energy storage; some adipose tissue, especially when deposited on the central body, is associated with chronic diseases.

adjudication   A process of handling disputes in which the ultimate decision is made by a third party appointed by the legal system.

affinal kin   A kin relationship created by marriage.

affines   Individuals related to one another because of marriage between their families; related through marriage rather than birth.

African Eve   The common maternal ancestor of all anatomically modern human beings.

African survivals   Knowledge, skills, beliefs, and cultural traditions transplanted directly from Africa to other parts of the world through the Atlantic slave trade.

Afrocentric   An explanation based on African origins.

age grade   A social category of people who fall within a particular culturally distinguished age range; age grades often undergo life cycle rituals as a group.

agency   The means, capacity, condition, or state of exerting power.

aggression   A forceful action, sometimes involving physical violence, intended for social domination.

agnates   Individuals sharing a patrilineal kinship tie; people related through the male line.

agnatic   Related through the male kinship line.

agrarian   Relating to agriculture.

agricultural development   Changes in agricultural production intended to improve the system by producing more harvest per unit of land.

AIDS   Acquired immune deficiency syndrome, a fatal disease caused by the human immunodeficiency virus (HIV) and usually transmitted through semen or blood.

altrical   An infantile trait of helplessness, as in infants that require long-term parental attention; opposite of precocious.

Amerindian   Native American populations.

anorexia nervosa   An eating disorder characterized by extreme dieting and a feeling of being fat even though one is underweight.

anthropology   The systematic study of humans, including their biology and culture, both past and present.

anthropometry   Science of the measurement of the human body, including measurement of bones, muscle, fat, and other body tissues.

applied research   Study directed at gaining valid knowledge to help in the solution of human problems.

arable land   Land suitable for cultivation.

arbitration   The hearing and determination of a dispute by a person chosen by the parties or appointed by the legal system with the consent of the parties.

archaeology   The field of anthropology concerned with cultural history; includes the systematic retrieval, identification, and study of the physical and cultural remains deposited in the earth.

argot   A specialized, sometimes secret, vocabulary peculiar to a particular group.

artifact   An object manufactured and used by human beings for a culturally defined goal.

Aryan   Member of a prehistoric people of northern India who spoke an Indo-European language.

asexual   Without sexual desire, or in terms of sexual identity, someone with no apparent sexual drive.

assemblage   In archaeology, a patterned set of artifacts making up one component of a site and usually representing a social activity.

asylum   The process by which immigrants are allowed to remain legally in their host country because of "persecution or a well-founded fear of persecution" in their country of origin.

australopithecine   A member of the genus *Australopithecus*, the hominid ancestors of humans.

Australopithecus   A bipedal primate; an extinct grade in hominid evolution found in the late Pliocene through the mid-Pleistocene in eastern and southern Africa; an ancestor of humans.

Australopithecus afarensis   A bipedal hominid that lived in Africa about 3–4 million years ago, discovered by Johansen and White in the Afar triangle of Ethiopia, and exemplified in the "Lucy" specimen.

Australopithecus anamensis   An early Australopithecine species from sites in northern Kenya that are about 4.2 million years old.

Australopithecus robustus   *See Paranthropus robustus.*

AZT   An antiviral drug used to slow down the replication of HIV, the human immunodeficiency virus that causes AIDS; AZT is very expensive.

Babel   An incoherent collection of speech or noise. In the Bible, Babel was the place where Noah's descendents attempted to build a tower that would reach up to heaven; the project was unsuccessful because God caused the builders to speak different languages, making it impossible for the builders to communicate.

baby boom   Population surge in the immediate post–WWII period; the television generation.

basic research   Study directed toward gaining scientific knowledge primarily for its own sake.

Bedouin   A term used to denote Arabic-speaking desert nomads in the Sahara, Syrian, Arabian, or Nubian deserts. Many Bedouin have adopted sedentary lifestyles, but traditionally the Bedouin were nomads who made a living through animal husbandry.

berdache   An anthropological term which refers to ,"two spirit," Native Americans (Native Americans who fulfill mixed gender roles).

big men   Political leaders in tribal-level societies whose status has been achieved and whose authority is limited.

binocular vision   Overlapping fields of vision, characteristic of primates, which gives depth-perception.

biogenetic   Genetic.

biological anthropology   Subfield of anthropology that studies the biological nature of humans and includes primatology, paleoanthropology, population genetics, anthropometry, and human biology.

biomedicine   Modern medicine as practiced in the United States and Europe; emphasizes the biological causation and remedy for illness.

biophysical diversity   Outward biological appearance resulting from interaction of genes and environment; phenotype.

biotic community   Plants and animals sharing a niche within an ecosystem.

bipedal   Having two feet. In humans, the ability to walk upright on two legs.

blade   A stone tool similar to a knife and having one or more sharp cutting edges.

blood relatives   A folk term referring to consanguineal kin, that is, kin related through birth.

bonobo   Pygmy chimpanzees, more gracile in morphology than common chimpanzees and exhibiting more casual and varied sex than any other non-human primate species.

brain drain   The out-migration of highly skilled and educated people from economically marginalized communities and countries to economically advanced areas and countries.

brideprice   *See* bridewealth.

bridewealth   The presentation of goods or money by the groom's family to the bride's family at the time of marriage; an economic exchange that legitimates the marriage and offspring as members of the father's patrilineage.

burqa   A head-to-toe veil common in Afghanistan, often made of cotton and covering most of the body, including the face.

bush-fallow   A technique used by horticulturalists that allows a garden plot to return to the wild state after a period of cultivation.

cadastral   A government survey and record-keeping system for recording land ownership and property boundaries.

canton   A small territorial division of a country.

capitalism   An economic system characteristic of modern state societies where land, labor, and capital all become commodities exchanged on the market and in which socioeconomic inequality is a constant feature.

carrying capacity   The maximum population size that can be maintained in a given area without causing environmental degradation of the ecology.

cash crop   An agricultural product grown for money instead of food or subsistence.

caste   A ranked group, sometimes linked to a particular occupation, with membership determined at birth and with marriage restricted to others within the group.

ceremony   Public events involving special symbols that signify important cultural values of beliefs.

chief   The political leader of a society that is more complex than a tribal society and is characterized by social ranking, a redistributive economy, and a centralized political authority.

chiefdom   A society more complex than a tribal society, characterized by social ranking, a redistributive economy, and a centralized political authority.

CITES   Convention on International Trade and Endangered Species. An international agreement to limit the capture of endangered animals, including whales, and regulate the market for endangered species; related to the International Commission for the Conservation of Atlantic Tunas (ICCAT) that assigns quotas for tuna fishermen.

civilization   The culture of state-level societies characterized by the following elements: (1) agriculture; (2) urban living; (3) a high degree of occupational specialization and differentiation; (4) social stratification; and (5) literacy.

clan   A kinship group whose members assume, but need not demonstrate, descent from a common ancestor.

class   An economically, socially, and politically similar group of people, e.g., middle class.

clavicle   The collar bone.

clines   A gradient of morphological or physiological change in a group of related organisms, usually along a line of environmental or geographic transition.

clitorectomy (clitoridectomy)   Removal of the clitoris.

Clovis point   A large lancelike projectile fluted at the base and flanked at both sides.

clustering   In epidemiology, the concentration of cases by place of residence and time of diagnosis.

cognates   Words that belong to different languages but have similar sounds and meanings.

cognatic kin   Kinship traced simultaneously through the male and female lines in a nonunilineal pattern of descent.

collective behavior   Patterns of social action.

colonialism   The establishment of government of sovereign rule in a territory through political, social, economic, and cultural domination by a foreign power.

commodification   The transformation of a good or service into something that can be bought and sold with money.

communal   Shared with a group.

comparative framework   An analytical approach in anthropology using the comparison of cultures across time and place.

computational linguistics   A multidisciplinary subfield of linguistics that combines computer science with linguistics to analyze and generate models of the structure of human language.

constructions of femininity   The ways in which a given culture defines appropriate ways of thinking and acting for women. *See* gender roles.

consumable commodity   Something that can be bought or sold and then used up.

consumer society   A characteristic of modern capitalist societies in which the purchase of non-essential material goods and services is an important marker of social status and identity.

contingent truths   Truth based upon the best scientific evidence available at the time and subject to revision as knowledge expands.

contract archaeology   Archaeological survey or excavation, usually before a construction project; cultural resources management.

conversational analysis   A technique in sociolinguistics that focuses on the social and symbolic attributes of verbal interactions.

cooperative   An organization or enterprise assembled for the production and marketing of goods, and for mutual support, benefits, and the distribution of risk.

corporate culture   The cultural characteristics of a workplace.

corporate kin groups   Social groups, like lineages, that share political responsibilities and access to land; characteristic of tribal societies.

correlate   A variable that stands in a consistent observed relationship with another variable.

correlation   A statistical relationship between two variables.

cortical surface   The surface of the cortex, in the brain.

corvée   A system of required labor; characteristic of ancient states.

cranium   The skull, excluding the jaw.

creationism   An ideology, usually based on a literal interpretation of the Bible, that argues against evolution.

creole   A type of language that results from the widespread adoption of a pidgin language as the primary language of a group.

Cro-Magnon   A term broadly referring to the first anatomically modern humans, from roughly 40,000 to 10,000 B.C.; named after a site in southwestern France.

cross-cultural   A standard form of anthropological analysis using the comparison of traditions and practices from different societies.

cross-cultural research   The exploration of cultural variation by using ethnographic data from many societies.

cross-cutting ties   Affinal or trading relationships that serve to counteract the political isolation of social groups in tribal societies.

cross-sectional   Research done across different geographic locales.

cultural anthropology   A field of anthropology emphasizing the study of the cultural diversity of contemporary societies, including their economies, sociopolitical systems, and belief systems.

cultural dissonance   A situation arising from the incompatibility of two or more interacting cultural systems.

cultural evolution   The process of invention, diffusion, and elaboration of the behavior that is learned and taught in groups and is transmitted from generation to generation, often used to refer to the development of social complexity.

cultural ideals   A valued characteristic or belief of a society.

cultural materialism   The idea, often associated with Marvin Harris, that cultural behaviors are best explained in relation to material constraints (including food, producing technology) to which humans are subjected.

cultural pluralism   The simultaneous existence of two or more cultural systems within a single society; multiculturalism.

cultural relativism/cultural relativity   The principle that all cultural systems are inherently equal in value and, therefore, that each cultural item must be understood on its own terms.

cultural reproduction   The process by which cultural behaviors and beliefs are regenerated across generations or spread among people of the same generation; cultural construction creates reality.

cultural resources management   Preservation of the historical and prehistorical heritage; protection of archaeological sites from destruction.

cultural validators   Actions or performances that enhance a sense of identity and belonging within a community or organization.

cultural values   Ideas, beliefs, values, and attitudes learned as a member of a social group.

culture   Learned patterns of thought and behavior characteristic of a particular social group.

culture area   A largely outmoded idea that the world can be divided into a limited number of geographical regions, each defined by a certain set of cultural features that result from common ecological adaptation or history and are shared by all groups in the region.

culture broker   An individual who attempts to negotiate and translate between two cultural groups, particularly in contexts of miscommunication or potential miscommunication.

culture shock   The experience of stress and confusion resulting from moving from one culture to another; the removal or distortion of familiar cues and the substitution of strange cues.

debt peonage   A system of involuntary servitude based on the debt of a laborer to his or her creditor.

decoction   The extraction of flavor by boiling.

Defense of Marriage Act   A federal U.S. law that states that: (a) the federal government may not recognize same-sex or polygamous marriages for any purpose, and (b) no state is obliged to recognize a same-sex marriage conducted or recognized in another state. This law was passed by the U.S. Congress and signed by President Bill Clinton on 21 September 1996.

demography   The statistical study of human populations, including size, growth, migration, density, distribution, and vital statistics.

dental anthropology   A specialization within biological anthropology; the study of the morphology of teeth across time and populations.

dependency   A theory of international economic relations in which an economically powerful nation creates ties with other nations in ways that reduce the possibility of economic independence of the poorer nations.

dependent variable   The resultant phenomenon that is explained by its relationship with an independent variable.

diachronic   The comparative study of social and cultural history in a specific culture area.

dialect   A regional or class-based version of a spoken language, although the difference between dialect and language can be influenced by historical and political considerations.

diffusion   A process of cultural change by which traits of one society are borrowed by another; the spread of cultural traits.

diffusion theory   A theory that cultural change occurs through a process by which traits of one society are borrowed by another.

diseases of civilization   Chronic diseases, such as cardiovascular disease and obesity, that characterize the epidemiological profile of modern capitalist societies and are the result of infrequent exercise and high fat diets.

divergence   The acquisition of dissimilar characteristics by related organisms, generally due to the influence of different environments and resulting in different evolutionary paths.

dividual   As opposed to "individual," someone whose identity or selfhood is tied to his or her relationships with other people.

DNA   Deoxyribonucleic acid; the long-stranded molecule that is the hereditary material of the cell, capable of self-replication and of coding the production of proteins for metabolic functions; most DNA is found on the chromosomes of the cell nucleus, but a small amount is located in the cell mitochondria.

domestic labor   Work performed in the home, such as cooking, cleaning, and taking care of children.

domestication of plants and animals   The invention of farming.

dominance   The principle behind the social ranking hierarchy characteristic of terrestrial primate species.

dowry   Presentation of goods or money by the bride's family to the bride, the groom, or the groom's family.

Ebonics   The rule-based and pattern dialect of English spoken by many working-class urban African Americans; black English vernacular.

economy   The production, distribution, and consumption of resources, labor, and wealth within a society.

ecosystem   A community of plants and animals, including humans, within a physical environment and the relationship of organisms to one another.

edutainment   A marketing technique in consumer-oriented societies in which consumerism and education are simultaneously valued.

egalitarian   A society organized around the principle of social equality; characteristic social formation of food foraging groups.

egalitarian society   A society that emphasizes the social equality of members and makes achieved statuses accessible to all adults.

embodied   Human experience inside an individual body and the expression of culture through the body.

embodied knowledge   Knowledge that seems to reside "in the body" and does not require conscious thought (for example, riding a bike).

engineering anthropology   Collection of anthropometric data for a population to be utilized in technological design for improved efficiency and safety. *See* ergonomics.

epidemic   Higher than normal occurrence of a disease in a particular area.

epidemiological methods   The methods used in epidemiology.

epidemiology   A science that studies the incidence, distribution, and control of disease in a population.

epistemology   The study of the nature of knowledge and its limits.

ergonomics   Human engineering; an applied science concerned with the anthropometric characteristics of people in the design of technology for improved human-machine interaction and safety.

essentialist   A view of reality based on single inherent facts rather than a socially constructed reality.

essentialize   The assumption that all individuals of the same social category (for instance, class, caste, race, gender) have the same beliefs, values, experiences, and other characteristics.

estrus   The phase of the female mammalian cycle during which the female is receptive to males and encourages copulation.

ethnic groups   Groups of people within a larger society with a distinct cultural or historical identity; ethnicity is a common mechanism of social separation in complex, heterogeneous societies.

ethnic markers   Specific artifacts associated with and indicative of certain peoples or ethnicities.

ethnocentrism   The assumption that one's own group's lifestyle, values, and patterns of adaptation are superior to all others.

ethnocide   The attempt to exterminate an entire ethnic group (similar to genocide).

ethnographic methods   The research techniques of cultural anthropology based on long-term participant observations, yielding a description of another culture.

ethnography   An anthropological method that generally involves living in a place for an extended period of time, participating in and observing daily life, and then writing about the culture or the place.

ethnology   The study and explanation of cultural similarities and differences.

ethnomedicine   The medical theories, diagnosis systems, and therapeutic practices of a culture or ethnic group.

ethnopediatrics   The study of how differing parenting styles affect infant health and growth.

ethnoscience   A methodological approach in cultural anthropology that attempts to derive native patterns of thought from the logical analysis of linguistic data.

ethology   The systematic study of animal behavior.

ethos   The world view of a particular society, including its distinctive character, sentiments, and values.

etiology   The theory of causation of a disease or illness.

eugenics   The genetic improvement of the human race through control of breeding.

Eurasia   The continent of Europe and Asia.

Eurocentric   Interpreting the world in terms of Western and especially European values and experiences.

evaluation researcher   A researcher who assesses the impact or outcome of a treatment or program.

Eve   In evolutionary studies of mitochondrial DNA (inherited through the maternal line only), refers to a hypothetical female ancestor of all anatomically modern humans.

evolution   The process of change in the genes or culture of a species or group over time.

evolutionary medicine   An anthropological approach to disease, symptoms, and medical care based upon our evolutionary heritage.

exaptations   A novelty arising from features acquired in one context long before being coopted in another context; for example, hominids had essentially modern vocal systems for hundreds of thousands of years before the probable beginning of language.

excavation   The stage in the process of archaeology in which data are collected.

exchange   A social system for the distribution of goods; reciprocity is a widespread system of exchange between social equals while markets act as a mode of exchange between strangers.

excision   One of three forms of female circumcision; includes clitoridectomy and removal of some or all of the labia minora and labia majora.

exogamous   Relating to a custom that forbids members of a specific group from selecting a spouse from within that group.

extended family   A domestic unit created by the linking together of two or more nuclear families.

extinction   A part of the process of evolution in which a species completely dies out, leaving no direct progeny (in the past 300 years, more than 150 mammal species and several hundred species of plants have become extinct; this is the fastest rate of extinctions in the history of the planet).

fallow   The period during which a unit of agricultural land is not cultivated so that nutrients can be restored to the soil.

family of origin   Nuclear family into which an individual is born and in which he or she is reared.

faunal region   A geographic region with its own distinctive assemblage of animal life.

fecundity   A demographic characteristic of a society referring to its overall capacity for reproduction.

feral   Living in, or pertaining to, the wild; without the benefit of society or culture.

feud   A pattern of reciprocal hostility between families or kin groups, usually involving retribution for past wrongs or deaths; such as blood feud.

FGM   Female genital mutilation or female genital modification. *See* sunna circumcision, excision, infibulation.

fieldwork   The hallmark of research in cultural anthropology, it usually involves long-term residence with the people being studied.

fission   The splitting of a descent group—a residential unit based on shared kinship—into two or more new descent groups or domestic units.

fitness   The ability to reproduce viable offspring.

focus groups   A research strategy in which an investigator leads a small group in discussion on a particular topic; frequently used in market research.

folk taxonomy   A culture's system of classification or grouping of objects, which can reveal the cognitive categories of that group.

food foragers   People living in a society with an economic pattern of harvesting of wild food resources, usually by gathering plants or hunting animals; hunting and gathering.

food loss   Food that is not eaten due to systemic inefficiencies, surpluses, or other types of waste.

food scarcity   The lack of sufficient food to meet the energy requirements of a population; may be the result of failed food production or a socially unequal distribution system.

foraging   Hunting and gathering; the original human economic system relying on the collection of natural plant and animal food sources.

forensic anthropology   A subfield of applied anthropology that uses techniques from biological anthropology and archaeology to help resolve legal matters.

founder effect   A force of evolutionary change resulting from the nonproportional contribution of genes by a founding member of a small population.

FOXP2   A gene that facilitates understanding grammar and speech in humans.

fraternal polyandry   An uncommon form of plural marriage in which a woman is married to two or more brothers at a time.

garbology   The systematic study of current household refuse.

gender   The social classification of masculine or feminine.

gender dimorphism   Physical and physiological differences between males and females; sexual dimorphism.

gender roles   Accepted models of behavior, thoughts, and emotions associated with masculinity and femininity that are culturally defined and learned over the course of one's upbringing and socialization.

genealogy   The systematic study of the consanguineal and affinal kin of a particular person, including his or her ancestors; a common method used in anthropological field studies.

gene pool   The range of variety of genes within a given breeding population.

genetic drift   The evolutionary factor that accounts for random shifts of gene frequencies as a consequence of small population size.

gestation   The carrying of young in the uterus from conception to delivery.

ghetto   A subsection of a city in which members of a minority group live because of social, legal, or economic pressure.

globalization   A contemporary cultural, political, and economic process involving world capitalism by which production and consumption are expanded to be worldwide in scope or application.

Gordian knot   A highly intractable problem or impasse; in Greek legend, a knot tied by King Gordius of Phrygia and cut by Alexander the Great after an oracle said it could be untied only by the next ruler of Asia.

grooming   A typical social interaction between primates involving the search for and removal of debris and ectoparasites from the fur of another animal.

hallucinogen   A substance that induces visions or auditory hallucinations in normal individuals.

hearth   The floor of a fireplace.

heterozygous   Having different genes or alleles in corresponding locations on a pair of chromosomes.

hierarchy   The categorization of a group of people according to status, whether it be ascribed at birth or achieved. A hierarchy refers to group organized in this way.

historical archaeology   A subfield of archaeology that studies the material remains of past societies that had systems of writing. Historical archaeologists are primarily concerned with human societies after 1500 CE.

HIV   The human immunodeficiency virus that causes AIDS.

holistic   Refers to viewing the whole society as an integrated and interdependent system; an important characteristic of the anthropological approach to understanding humans.

homesigns   A system of communicative gestures created by deaf children who are not exposed to established, widespread sign languages such as ASL (American Sign Language).

hominid   An erect-walking bipedal primate that is either human, an extinct ancestor to humans, or a collateral relative to humans.

Homo erectus   An extinct, direct ancestor of modern humans; situated on the evolutionary line between *Homo habilis* and *Homo sapiens;* first appeared about 1.8 million years ago and could be found throughout the Old World until about 200,000 years ago; associated with the first use of fire; similar to modern humans in all body proportions except cranial capacity.

Homo ergaster   A hominid that lived in many of Africa's harshest environments between 600,000 and 1.7 million years ago and had a brain almost two-thirds the size of modern humans.

Homo floresiensis   A species of dwarf human first discovered on Flores, an Indonesian Island. This dwarf human had a small cranial size (417cc), was approximately one meter tall and bipedal. The fossil record dates *H. floresiensis* from 38,000–13,000 years ago. Paleontologists debate whether this dwarf human is in fact a distinct human species or a pathological *H. sapiens.*

Homo habilis   An extinct hominid thought to be the earliest member of the genus *Homo;* situated on the evolutionary line between the australopithecines and *Homo erectus;* associated with the use of stone tools.

Homo neanderthalensis (**Neanderthals**)   A close relative of modern humans that lived from about 200,000 years ago to about 30,000 years ago in Europe and Western Asia. Neanderthals had short, muscular bodies, adapted to cold climates, and had larger brains than modern humans. They were skilled toolmakers and buried their dead.

Homo sapiens   Hominid species including modern humans and immediate archaic ancestors (Neanderthals).

homozygous   Having the same allele (form of a gene) at a certain locus on homologous (matched pair) chromosomes.

horticulture   A plant cultivation system based upon relatively low energy input, like gardening by using only the hoe or digging stick; often involves use of the slash-and-burn technique.

human rights   Related to a post–WW II international movement begun by the United Nations and associated with the 1948 International Declaration of Universal Human Rights. The rights enumerated include: equality before the law; protection against arbitrary arrest; the right to a fair trial; freedom from *ex-post-facto* criminal laws; the right to own property; freedom of thought, conscience, and religion; freedom of opinion and expression; freedom of peaceful assembly and association; also included in the document are economic, social, and cultural rights as the right to work and to choose one's work freely, the right to equal pay for equal work, the right to form and join trade unions, the right to rest and leisure, the right to an adequate standard of living, and the right to education. During the 1990s, human rights efforts often emphasized women's rights.

Human Terrain Team   An experimental and controversial U.S. military program that assigns anthropologists to work with American combat units in Afghanistan and Iraq.

human universal   A trait or behavior found in all human cultures.

hunter-gatherers   Peoples who subsist on the collection of naturally occurring plants and animals; food foragers.

hyperkinetic   Refers to abnormally increased and uncontrollable muscular movement.

hypothesis   A tentative assumption or proposition about the relationship(s) between specific events or phenomena, tentatively set forth as a "target" to be tested.

hypothetico-deductive method   A theory about science, in which a hypothesis is posed from which certain observations are predicted. Observations that agree with those predicted are taken as evidence for the hypothesis, and observations that do not agree with those predicted are taken as evidence against the hypothesis.

ichthyologist A specialist in the study of fish.

ideal body images Culturally defined standards for attractive body shapes.

indigenous The original or native population of a particular region or environment.

indigenized The reconceptualization of a foreign cultural construct or idea to make it fit within a local/indigenous worldview.

infanticide Killing a baby soon after birth.

infibulation One of three forms of female circumcision; includes circumcisions and excision, followed by the sewing up of the sides of the vulva so that scar tissue covers the vaginal opening, except for a small gap for urination and menstruation; requiring some surgical opening for first intercourse and birth; also called pharaonic circumcision.

infidel A nonbeliever with respect to a particular religion.

informant A member of a society who has established a working relationship with an anthropological fieldworker and who provides information about the culture; the subject of intensive interviewing.

institutions Formal organizations within a society.

intelligent design The theory that aspects of the universe, and in particular living things, can best be explained by an intelligent cause rather than an undirected process.

intensive interviewing The ethnographic method of repeated interviews with a single informant.

intercultural communication The exchange of meanings and messages between people from different societies characterized by different underlying ideas, beliefs, and worldviews; may or may not be complicated by the speaking of different languages.

Islam The religious faith of Muslims who profess belief in Allah as the sole deity and in Mohammad as the prophet of Allah.

jirga A meeting of tribal leaders (typically male elders).

key respondent A subject that a researcher finds particularly knowledgeable and amenable to multiple interviews.

kinship A network of culturally recognized relationships among individuals, either through affinial or consanguineal ties.

knapper A person who creates stone blades, as in "flint knapper."

Koran The sacred text of Islam.

kula Traditional long-distance trading network for valuable objects among Trobriand islanders first described by B. Malinowski.

lactose intolerance The inability of adults to digest milk because they no longer produce the enzyme lactase; a biological characteristic of a large proportion of the world's population.

land concentration The degree to which land ownership is concentrated among a small number of people in a society.

land tenure A system of land ownership and inheritance.

language A rule-based and patterned system of communication.

language instinct The innate ability of humans to communicate through the creation of new languages and the learning of pre-existing systems of communication.

late capitalism A form of capitalism emerging in the second half of the twentieth century, characterized by finance capital, globalization, and technological innovation.

Levant The general area of the Middle East.

levirate The practice by which a man is expected to marry the wife or wives of a deceased brother; commonly found in patrilineal descent systems.

lexicon The vocabulary set characteristic of a group; argot.

life history A methodological technique of cultural anthropologists in which a key informant's biography is compiled using multiple interviews.

liminal period An intermediate phase or condition.

lineage Refers to a kin group tracing common descent through one sex from a known ancestor.

lingua franca A language used by populations beyond the region and scope of its native speakers. A single and dominant language used by members of multiple linguistic backgrounds becomes the lingua franca of that multi-ethnic population.

linguistic anthropology A subfield of anthropology entailing the study of language forms across space and time and their relation to culture and social behavior.

linguistic relativity A principle of anthropological linguistics referring to the fact that all languages are equally adequate as systems of communication.

linguistics The study of language, consisting of: (1) historical linguistics, which is concerned with the evolution of languages and language groups through time; (2) descriptive linguistics, which focuses on recording and analysis of the structures of language; (3) sociolinguistics, the way in which speech patterns reflect social phenomena; and (4) ethnosemantics, the study of the connection between reality, thought, and language.

literacy The ability to read; not possible for people who speak unwritten languages.

lithic Referring to stone, especially with regard to artifacts.

longitudinal A research strategy that examines changes in a particular group over time.

Lucy An *Australopithecus afarensis* whose partial skeleton represents one of the earliest hominids found.

luxury A consumer good primarily purchased as a marker of social status.

macrosociological A type of social analysis that emphasizes the influence of large-scale, often global, institutions and forces; opposite of microsociological.

mana A supernatural force inhabiting objects or people.

mandible The lower jaw.

material culture The artifacts and technology of a given society; material culture is the primary data source for archaeological reconstruction.

maternalism Having or demonstrating characteristics associated with mothers and mothering.

matriarchal   A form of social organization or kinship in which women rule a family, clan, or tribe.

matrilineal   Relating to, based on, or tracing decent through the maternal line.

mediator   The role of a disinterested third party in dispute settlement.

medical anthropology   The study of health and medical systems in a cross-cultural perspective; includes the study of biocultural adaptations to disease, ethno-medical systems, and cultural factors in health-seeking behavior.

megalithic   Prehistoric architectural structures made of large stones; typical of societies that were chiefdoms or early states.

mercenary   A person, typically a soldier hired to fight for a foreign army, who works exclusively for financial gain.

meritocracy   A system in which advancement is purportedly based upon ability or achievement of the individual.

metalinguistics   Elements of communication beyond verbal speech; includes the use of gesture, personal space, silence, and nonlinguistic sounds.

microeconomics   Small-scale or individual economic decisions and patterns, such as the ways that individuals budget their cell phone expenditures.

micropolitics of social inequality   Small-scale patterns of power between individuals or small groups, the ways that inequalities between people are played out on a personal level.

microlith   A small stone tool made from small blades or fragments of blades, characteristic of the Mesolithic period, approximately 13,000 to 6,000 B.C.

miscegenation   Marriage or sexual intercourse between a woman and a man of different races, particularly between a white and an African American in the United States.

Mississippian tradition   A prehistoric native American culture in the American Midwest, characterized by mound building, maize horticulture, and a particular set of mortuary customs.

mitochondrial DNA   DNA contained within the mitochondria, or energy suppliers, of cells; inherited only in the maternal line.

moiety system   A social system in which the entire group is divided into two kinship units, which are usually based on unilineal descent and exogamous.

molecular biology   A new branch of biology focusing on molecular structures, most often DNA.

monogamy   Marriage between one man and one woman at a given time.

moot   A public hearing or community assembly to decide local problems and administer justice.

mores   Norms or customs of a society characterized by compelling emotional commitment and rationalized by the culture's belief system.

morphology   The study of form and structure as opposed to function.

mosque   An Islamic place of public religious worship.

mound   An archaeological site feature characteristic of prehistoric Mississippian Indian groups.

multiculturalism   A movement to broaden the range of cultures we study, in reaction to the prevailing opinion that the great accomplishments have been made almost exclusively by males of European descent.

multiple paternity   The concept, occurring in several South American cultures, that every man who has intercourse with a woman during her pregnancy contributes to the formation of the child; therefore, a child may have multiple fathers.

multiplex relationships   Complex social relations characterized by multiple patterns of interaction, for example by kinship, business, political party, ethnicity, and religion.

Muslim   An adherent of or believer in Islam.

mutation   An alteration in genetic material (DNA); the only "creative" factor in evolution.

national character studies   Descriptions of the cultural belief and "typical" personality of people from another culture, an approach used by the culture and personality school of anthropology.

natural selection   The primary force of evolution, first described by Darwin and Wallace, that causes changes in gene frequencies for environmentally adaptive traits due to relative decreases in mortality for certain individuals.

Neanderthals   Taxonomic "lumpers" place these humans in the category of Archaic *Homo sapiens,* while taxonomic "splitters" say these refer to European and western Asian species, called *Homo neanderthalensis,* living from about 200,000 to 30,000 B.C.E. and now extinct; named for the Neander Valley in Germany where this fossil human was first found. A descendant of *Homo erectus.*

negotiation   The use of direct argument and compromise by the parties to a dispute to voluntarily arrive at a mutually satisfactory agreement.

neocolonial   After the age of colonialism, this refers to continued economic and political policies by which a great power indirectly maintains or extends its influence over other areas or people.

Neolithic   A stage in cultural evolution marked by the appearance of ground stone tools and, more importantly, the domestication of plants and animals, starting some 10,000 years ago.

new archaeology   Archaeological analysis, often associated with Lewis Binford, emphasizing the search for the reasons why things happened.

nomadic band   A food-foraging group that moves among a variety of campsites; a society without sedentary villages.

nomenclature   A naming system.

nonreactive measure of behavior   Various methods for collecting social science data that are unobtrusive and unsubjected to bias introduced by the population under study.

norms   Standards of behavior characteristic of a society or social group to which members are expected to conform.

nuclear family   A basic social grouping consisting of a husband and wife and their children, typical of societies with monogamous marriage with the family living at a distance from the parents of the husband and wife.

obesity   A medically defined condition of excessive fat storage.

observational research   Research conducted by documenting what is observed (as opposed to other research techniques such as interviews, questionnaires, or laboratory tests).

occipital   A bone at the base and rear of the cranium.

Operation Khybera   A 15-day U.S. military campaign in Afghanistan in which anthropologists joined 1000 U.S. and Afghan soldiers to clear out more than 200 Taliban insurgents and secure a major road in southeast Afghanistan.

origin myth   A story found in most cultures that explains the creation and population of the world.

orthography   The way in which words in a particular language are written phonetically to include sounds (phonemes) not represented in our alphabet; anthropological linguists usually use the International Phonetic Alphabet (IPA).

osteobiology   The study of skeletal remains.

osteology   The study of the structure and function of bones.

osteoporosis   A pathological decrease in bone mass with age, commonly found in menopausal women and malnourished populations.

othering   A stigmatizing process of defining one's self-identity in opposition to one's perceived characteristics of someone else.

ovulation   The part of the menstrual cycle in which the egg (ovum) is released and fertilization can occur.

pacification   In tribal areas like New Guinea, the establishment by outside authorities of peace from blood-feud warfare.

pair bonding   A pattern of permanent male-female relationships among certain animal species.

palaver   A discussion for purposes of dispute settlement, typically informal and following customary law.

paleoanthropology   The study of human fossil remains.

paleodemography   The study of population patterns among extinct societies through the archaeological analysis of mortuary populations.

Paleolithic   Old stone age; the archaeological period that includes the beginning of culture to the end of the Pleistocene glaciation.

paleontology   The study of the fossils of ancient, usually extinct, animals and plants.

paleopathology   The study of disease patterns in extinct populations, primarily through the examination of skeletal remains.

paradigm   The orthodox doctrine of a science, and the set of beliefs with which new scientists are enculturated; associated with a philosopher of science, Kuhn.

paramount chief   In a ranked society of ascribed statuses, the position at the top of the hierarchy.

Paranthropus robustus   Previously called *Australopithecus robustus*, a large hominid with massive bones and large dentition for grinding found in South Africa; like its East African contemporary *Paranthropus boisei*, it was a descendant of *Australopithecus afarensis* but was also an evolutionary dead-end.

parietal   The bones on the side of the cranium.

participant observation   The primary research method of cultural anthropology, involving long-term observations conducted in natural settings.

parturient   Bringing forth or about to bring forth young.

paternity   The quality of being a father, either a biological father (genetic) or a social father (pater).

patriarchy   A form of social organization in which power and authority are vested in the males and in which descent is usually in the male line.

patrilineal   Descent traced exclusively through the male line for purposes of group membership or inheritance.

patrilocal   A postmarital residence rule by which a newly wed couple takes up permanent residence with or near the groom's father's family.

peasants   Rural, agricultural populations of state-level societies who maintain parts of their traditional culture while they are tied into the wider economic system of the whole society through economic links of rent, taxes, and markets.

pedagogy   The methods and techniques of teaching.

peer review   A scholarly process for the publication of manuscripts and awarding of research funding, in which peers in a discipline review the overall quality of the work to decide if it meets the standards of a discipline.

perimortem   Occurring at or near the time of death, including trauma that caused death.

phylogeny   The tracing of the history of the evolutionary development of a life form.

physical anthropology   Another term for biological anthropology; includes the study of paleoanthropology, population genetics, human adaptation, and primatology.

placenta   Nutrient and waste-exchanging organ in mammals that unites the fetus to the maternal uterus; used in studies of mitochondrial DNA.

plasticity   The ability of many organisms, including humans, to alter themselves behaviorally or biologically in response to changes in the environment.

Pleistocene   The geological period approximately from 600,000 years ago to 12,000 years ago, characterized by recurrent glaciations.

pollen analysis   A technique used by archaeologists for reconstructing the flora and ecology of a site by recovering pollen in the soil and identifying the species that produced them.

pollution   The act of defilement, uncleanness.

polyandry   A relatively rare form of plural marriage in which one woman is married to two or more men.

polygamy   A general term for plural marriage, either polygyny or polyandry.

polygyny   A common form of plural marriage in which one man is married to two or more women; in societies that permit polygyny, the majority of marital unions are monogamous. Extended families may be formed through polygyny.

population   In genetics and biological anthropology, a discrete demographic unit often characterized by in-marriage.

population crash   A sudden and catastrophic decline in the population of an area, usually resulting from massive food shortages or introduced epidemic diseases.

population density   The ratio of the number of people per area of land; closely related to carrying capacity.

population pressure   The situation of population growth in a limited geographical area causing a decline in food production and resources and sometimes triggering technological change.

postmortem   Examination of a body shortly after death (noun); occurring after death, including disturbance of a body by carnivores (adjective).

potassium-argon dating   A method of absolute dating in paleoanthropology using volcanic remains based on the ratio of radioactive potassium to argon, into which the potassium decays.

potlatch   A feast given by a Northwest Coast Native American chief often involving competitive gift-giving, first described by Fraz Boas.

prehistoric   The time before written records.

primate   The order of mammals that includes humans, the apes, Old and New World monkeys, and prosimians.

primatology   A branch of biological anthropology that studies nonhuman primates, in part as models of the evolutionary past.

primogeniture   A rule of inheritance in which the homestead is passed down to the firstborn (male) child.

primordial   Belonging to or characteristic of the earliest stage of development; first in sequence of time.

principal investigator   The lead researcher in a large research project.

privilege   A special advantage, immunity, permission, right, or benefit granted to or enjoyed by an individual, class, caste, or race. Such advantage may be held consciously or unconsciously and exercised to the exclusion or detriment of others.

probability sampling   A data collection sampling technique based on the known proportions of various social groups.

proletariat   The working class in a state-level society, usually residing in urban areas.

psychoactive drugs   Chemicals that affect the mind or behavior and that may cause, among other things, hallucinations.

public archaeology   Cultural resources management.

purdah   The Hindu or Muslim system of sex segregation, which is practiced by keeping women in seclusion.

qualitative methods   Research strategies that emphasize description, in-depth interviewing, and participant observation.

quantitative methods   Research methods that translate behaviors or attitudes into reliable and valid numeric measures suitable for statistical analysis for hypothesis testing.

race   A folk category of the English language that refers to discrete groups of human beings who are uniformly separated from one another on the basis of arbitrarily selected phenotypic traits.

radiocarbon dating   A method of absolute dating in archaeology using organic material and based on the decay rate of the radioactive isotope Carbon-14; useful for objects less than 50,000 years old.

random sample   A data sample selected by a method in which all individuals in a population have equal chance of being selected.

random selection   A complex data sampling method in which all individuals in a population have an equal chance of being selected for participation.

rapid eye movement (REM)   A rapid conjugate movement of the eyes that is associated with paradoxical sleep, a state of sleep also characterized by increased neuronal activity of the forebrain and midbrain, depressed muscle tone, dreaming, and vascular congestion of the sex organs.

reciprocal gift   A mechanism of establishing or reinforcing social ties between equals involving a "present," which is repaid at a later date.

reciprocity   A system of mutual interaction involving the regular exchange of goods or services (for example, inviting someone over for dinner because they previously had you over for dinner).

red queen hypothesis   A description of the process of evolution in which a species must be constantly changing (through natural selection) to keep up with a constantly changing environment.

reforestation   To renew forest cover by seeding or planting.

refugee   According to international law, someone residing outside of his/her country of nationality, or who has no nationality, because of "persecution or a well-founded fear of persecution."

regional economy   As opposed to globalization, this refers to the production, distribution, and consumption of goods and services in a distinct and limited geographical context.

relative deprivation   A concept wherein individuals perceive that they are less well off only in relation to another group or to their own expectations.

religion   Attitudes, beliefs, and practices related to supernatural powers.

repatriate   To restore or return to the country of origin, allegiance, or citizenship.

reproductive success   A variable used in Darwinian analyses referring to an individual's overall achievement in reproduction of their own genes (through direct offspring or kin).

rescue archaeology   Archaeology performed in advance of impending destruction of the site.

rite of passage   Religious rituals that mark important changes in individual status or social position at different points in the life cycle, such as birth, marriage, or death.

ritual   A set of acts, usually involving religion or magic, following a sequence established by tradition.

rockshelter   A cave.

Sahelanthropus tchadensis   A hominid that lived in Sahel region of Africa (contemporary Chad) between 6 and 7 million years ago and which may be humans' oldest hominid relative yet discovered.

salvage archaeology   The attempt to preserve archaeological remains from destruction by large-scale projects of industrial society (such as dam or highway construction).

sample   A subpopulation that is studied in order to make generalizations.

sanctions   Generally negative responses by a social group as a consequence of an individual's behavior; used to maintain social control.

scavenge   To collect and eat carcasses of animals killed by carnivores; thought to be part of the lifestyle of australopithecines.

scientific theory   A testable, correctable explanation of observable phenomena that yields new information about nature in answer to a set of preexisting problems.

séance   A ritual, usually held at night, designed to promote direct contact between people and spirits.

secret society   A social organization or association whose members hide their activities from nonmembers.

segmentary system   A hierarchy of more and more inclusive lineages; functions primarily in contexts of conflict between groups.

self-sufficient   Refers to a characteristic of most pre-state societies; the ability to maintain a viable economy and social system with minimal outside contact.

serial monogamy   The marriage of one woman and one man at a time but in a sequence, usually made possible through divorce.

seropositive   Testing positive for a given disease (such as HIV infection) based on a blood test.

seroprevalence   The prevalence (proportion of people infected in a population) of a given disease based on blood tests.

sex   Determined by biological characteristics, such as external genitalia and having XX or XY chromosomes (contrast with *gender*).

sex roles   Learned social activities and expectations made on the basis of gender.

sexual dimorphism   A condition of having the two sexes dissimilar in appearance.

sexual selection   A type of natural selection resulting from higher reproductive success of males with particular inherited traits that are chosen by females; for example, the male peacock's tail.

shaman   A part-time religious practitioner typical of tribal societies who goes into trance to directly communicate with the spirit world for the benefit of the community.

shifting agriculture   A form of cultivation (horticulture) with recurrent, alternate clearing and burning of vegetation and planting of crops in the burnt fields.

sickle-cell anemia   An often fatal genetic disease caused by a chemical mutation that changes one of the amino acids in normal hemoglobin; the mutant sickle-cell gene occurs with unusually high frequency in parts of Africa where malaria is present.

SIDA   The Spanish, French, Italian, and Haitian Creole acronym for AIDS.

SIDS   Sudden infant death syndrome—the sudden and unexpected death of an infant, also known as crib death.

single-interest relationship   A relationship based solely on one connection, such as landlord-tenant.

site   The location for an actual or potential archaeological excavation; a concentration of the remains of human activities or artifacts.

situated   Formed by a given person's experiences, based on context.

skewed   Biased.

slang   A small set of new and usually short-lived words in the vocabulary or dialect of a language.

slash-and-burn techniques   Shifting form of cultivation (horticulture) with recurrent, alternate clearing and burning of vegetation and planting in the burnt fields; swidden.

social class   In state-level societies, a stratum in a social hierarchy based on differential group access to means of production and control over distribution; often endogamous.

social cohesion   The process by which a social group binds itself together, producing greater cooperation and conformity.

social construction   A reality that is created and agreed on by interpersonal interaction and discourse; opposite of essentialist.

social control   Practices that induce members of a society to conform to the expected behavior patterns of their culture; includes informal mechanisms, like gossip, legal systems, and punishment.

socialization   The development, through the influence of parents and others, of patterns of thought and behavior in children that conform to beliefs and values of a particular culture.

socially validated   Approved or recognized by the culture of a particular social group.

social mobility   The upward or downward movement of individuals or groups in a society characterized by social stratification.

social networks   An informal pattern of organization based on the complex web of social relations linking individuals; includes factors like kinship, friendship, economics, and political ties.

social organization   A culturally inherited system that orders social relations within social groups.

social status   A person's level of prestige in society. Social status is associated with factors like education and employment as well as higher and lower levels of wealth or power. In the United States, for instance, doctors tend to have higher social status than cooks at McDonald's.

social stratification   An arrangement of statuses or groups within a society into a pattern of socially superior and inferior ranks; based on differential access to strategic resources.

society   A socially bounded, spacially contiguous group of people who interact in basic economic and political institutions and share a particular culture; societies retain relative stability across generations.

sociobiology   The study of animal and human social behavior based on the theory that behavior is linked to genetics.

sociocultural   Refers to the complex combination of social and cultural factors.

sociolinguistics   A subfield of anthropological linguistics emphasizing the study of the social correlates to variations in speech patterns.

soil analysis   Detailed description of the chemical characteristics of a sample of soil that can be used as a "fingerprint" to match stolen artifacts with their location of origin.

solidarity   Unity based on community interest, objectives, and culture.

Solutrean   Of or relating to an Upper Paleolithic culture characterized by leaf-shaped finely flaked stone implements.

sorcery   The use of supernatural knowledge or power for purposes of evil, for example causing sickness; used to further the sorcerer's individual social goals.

speciation   The formation of biological species or the process that leads to this end.

species   The largest naturally occurring population that is capable of interbreeding and producing fully fertile offspring.

spurious   Not an actual or causal relationship, as in the correlation between the number of storks and birth rate.

states   A complex society characterized by urban centers, agricultural production, labor specialization, standing armies, permanent boundaries, taxation, centralized authority, public works, and laws designed to maintain the status quo.

stature   Height; can be used as an indirect measure of the health of a population.

status   Position in a social system that is characterized by certain rights, obligations, expected behaviors (roles), and certain social symbols.

stigma   Socially constructed shame or discredit.

stratified societies   A society in which groups experience structured inequality of access not only to power and prestige but also to economically important resources.

stratigraphic level   In an archaeological excavation, a level of occupation at which artifacts may be found; important for relative dating techniques.

stroll   A street where prostitution activity is concentrated.

structure   In anthropology, generally referring to social institutions and patterns of organization.

subculture   The culture of a subgroup of a society that has its own distinctive ideas, beliefs, values, and worldview.

subordinate   Submissive to or falling under the control of higher authority resulting in an inferior position in a social group.

subsidy   financial aid given by a government to a person or group to support an enterprise deemed essential to the public interest. The U.S. government, for example, provides subsidies to farmers and transportation businesses like Amtrak because they provide essential public services which otherwise may not be profitable.

sunna circumcision   One of three forms of female circumcision; this procedure includes clitorectomy (removal of clitoris and hood) and sometimes refers only to the cutting of the hood (prepuce); the name *Sunna* relates the practice to Islamic traditions, although most Muslim scholars and theologians deny any Koranic justification for female circumcision.

superstructure   In the theory of cultural materialism, refers to a society's ideology.

sushi   A traditional Japanese food of rice and thinly sliced raw fish and other ingredients rolled in seaweed and artfully presented to the diner, eaten with a horseradish sauce.

suture line   In osteological studies, the joints between bones, for example in the cranium.

swidden cultivation   A tropical gardening system, also known as slash-and-burn horticulture in which forest is cleared, burned, cultivated, and then left for bush fallow.

symbol   A sign that consistently but arbitrarily represents an object or meaning; the basis of communication within a culture.

synchronic   The analysis of a culture at a single point of time.

syntax   The word order or pattern of word order in a phrase or sentence.

taboo   A supernaturally forbidden act as defined by a culture, violation of which can have severe negative consequences.

technology   The application of science to a practical purpose.

territoriality   Laying claim and defending a territory; tends to be a characteristic of arboreal primate species.

TFR (total fertility rate)   The average number of children born to a woman during her lifetime.

Thalassemia   A hereditary disease that causes a malformation of hemoglobin in the red blood cell, somewhat like sickle-cell anemia; has a high frequency in the Mediterranean region and south Asia, areas with a history of much malaria.

third/fourth gender   Third gender typically refers to male and sometimes female berdaches, while fourth gender only refers to female berdaches.

time-allocation study   A quantitative method that identifies what people do and how much time they spend doing various activities; useful for cross-cultural comparison.

totem   A symbolic plant or animal associated with a social group (clan) used for identification and religious expression.

transmission   Passing of an infectious agent to an uninfected person from an infected group or individual.

transnational culture   A pattern of cultural beliefs and behaviors characteristic of elites throughout the world and often spread through mass media.

tribe   A relatively small, usually horticultural, society organized on principles of kinship, characterized by little social stratification and no centralized political authority, and whose members share a culture and language.

trophic exchanges   Relationships between organisms having to do with food; eating or being eaten.

United Nations World Heritage Site   A historical construction or natural site determined to have outstanding universal value as determined by the United Nations Educational, Scientific, and Cultural Organization (UNESCO). There are 851 World Heritage Sites, 20 of which are in the United States.

universalism   The understanding that certain beliefs, values, rights, or conditions are or should be universal.

urbanization   The worldwide process of the growth of cities at the expense of rural populations.

urban villages   Small (usually segregated) communities of minorities or rural migrants located in cities.

usufruct rights   The legal right of using land (or resources on land) that is not one's private property.

validity   The quality of a measurement tool or variable actually measuring what is intended.

values   The ideas of a culture that are concerned with appropriate goals and behavior.

verb-second structure   A grammar system which dictates a sentence structure in which the verb always follows the subject (also known as SVO structure, i.e. subject-verb-object)

vertebrate   An animal with a spinal column.

virilocal residence   Patrilocal postmarital residence.

walkabout   A custom of Australian aborigines involving a long circular journey to sacred places and a return to home.

war   Violence between political entities, such as nations, using soldiers; to be distinguished from the smaller scale feud.

waste behavior   The behavior and practices of people related to the excess remains of human consumption.

weaning   Acclimating someone (as a child) to take food other than by nursing.

Western culture   A generic term referring to the common beliefs, values, and traditions of Europeans and their descendants.

worldview   The particular way in which a society constructs ideas of space, time, social relationship, and the meaning of life.

woodhenge   A circle of wooden posts arranged to make astronomical observations to chart the passing of the seasons.

Yerkish   An artificial language using a computer that has been taught successfully to great apes at the Yerkes Regional Primate Center.

zeitgeist   The general intellectual, moral, and cultural climate of an era.

Zinjanthropus   The original name given to a 1.75-million-year-old Australopithecine fossil (*Australopithecus boisei*) found in Kenya by Louis and Mary Leakey.

Index